The History and Evolution of Psychology

The History of Psychology course occupies an unusual but critical place in the psychology curriculum at most universities. As the field has become ever more specialized, with the various subdisciplines branching off, The History of Psychology is often the one course where the common roots of all of these areas are explored.

Asking not only "What is psychology?" but also "What is science?" "Why is psychology a science?" and "How did it become one?" this book examines how the paradigm of Psychology was built. Discussing key figures in history in the context of their time, it takes students on a carefully formulated, chronological journey through the build-up of psychology from ancient times to the present, and seeks to draw students into the way science is done, rather than merely presenting them with historical fact. Students will learn not only the "what," but the "why" of the history of psychology and will acquire the necessary background historical material to fully understand those concepts. Organized around a series of moments and cases—such as a shift from scholasticism to rationalism or empiricism, and a shift from idealism to materialism—the book seeks to portray psychology as an on-going, evolving process, rather than a theory.

In a field full of textbooks that focus on dry fact, this book will be a refreshing, novel take on the history of psychology, and will engage students with the methods and philosophy of psychological science.

Brian D. Cox is Associate Professor at Hofstra University, USA. He received his PhD from the University of North Carolina (Chapel Hill) in 1989 and his undergraduate degree from Florida State University in 1982.

The History and Evolution of Psychology

A Philosophical and Biological Perspective

Brian D. Cox

NEW YORK AND LONDON

First published 2019
by Routledge
52 Vanderbilt Avenue, New York, NY 10017

and by Routledge
2 Park Square, Milton Park, Abingdon, Oxon, OX14 4RN

Routledge is an imprint of the Taylor & Francis Group, an informa business

© 2019 Taylor & Francis

The right of Brian D. Cox to be identified as author of this work has been asserted by them in accordance with sections 77 and 78 of the Copyright, Designs and Patents Act 1988.

All rights reserved. No part of this book may be reprinted or reproduced or utilised in any form or by any electronic, mechanical, or other means, now known or hereafter invented, including photocopying and recording, or in any information storage or retrieval system, without permission in writing from the publishers.

Trademark notice: Product or corporate names may be trademarks or registered trademarks, and are used only for identification and explanation without intent to infringe.

Library of Congress Cataloging-in-Publication Data
A catalog record for this book has been requested

ISBN: 978-1-138-20743-1 (hbk)
ISBN: 978-1-138-20744-8 (pbk)
ISBN: 978-1-315-46229-5 (ebk)

Typeset in Bembo
by Apex CoVantage, LLC

To Professors Peter A. Ornstein, Jaan Valsiner, and
the late Robert B. Cairns,
who taught me, by example, that history and theory are the
foundations of any true scholarship.

Contents

Acknowledgements   viii

1. The Study of Science and Psychology from a Historical Perspective   1
2. The Shift From Church Authority to Rationalism: The Times and Philosophy of René Descartes   24
3. Empiricism, Its Legacies and Limitations   47
4. From Argument by Design to Nature Red in Tooth and Claw: The Development of Evolutionist Thought   84
5. Idealism to Materialism and Dualism in Germany   133
6. Seeing Things Whole: The Gestalt Response to Mental Reductionism   179
7. William James and Functionalism   209
8. Behaviorism   264
9. Psychoanalysis: A Theory for Its Time and Place   333
10. The Developmental Approach   394

Bibliography   486
Index   515

Acknowledgements

This book has had a very long gestation. In the time since she was my editorial assistant on the first half of this book, Jennifer Scorey-Vogt has acquired a couple of Masters degrees, done a tour of Iraq with the Army National Guard, been married twice, moved to the other side of the world, started a business, and had a daughter who is now walking. I thank her for her friendship, help and encouragement over all that time. I also thank Eric Leonardis, who helped me at a later time to straighten out many references and other conundrums when we weren't discussing epistemology, history and cognitive science. He has gone on to graduate school in cognitive neuroscience, robotics and much else. His good humor, competence, and openness to new ideas kept my spirits up. Merrideth Miller dealt with the process of counting words to clear the dozens of quotations that I quixotically insisted on having in the book. And I thank Christina Chronister, Julie Toich, Kathryn Smale, and Alex Howard of Routledge and Taylor and Francis, and Kate Fornadel and her copyediting team at Apex CoVantage for their patience and professionalism as I turned this project from an intellectual adventure into an object for sale.

I thank friends, colleagues, reviewers and many students who have commented on chapters in this book. Any errors that remain are my responsibility. Finally, I thank my true friends and family who never doubted that I could finish this book, or who never told me *out loud* that they doubted that I would finish this book. I am forever in your debt.

1 The Study of Science and Psychology from a Historical Perspective

Why Study the History of Psychology? A Preface You Shouldn't Skip

> Science sometimes sees itself as impersonal, as "pure thought," independent of its historical and human origins. It is often taught as if this were the case. But science is a human enterprise through and through, an organic, evolving, human growth, with sudden spurts and arrests and strange deviations, too. It grows out of its past, but never outgrows it, anymore than we outgrow our own childhood.
>
> —Oliver Sacks (2003, p. i)

Although speculations on the human soul and mind go as far back as written history, the made-up word "psychology" is reported to have appeared around 1520 and first appeared in a book title in 1590 (Murray, 1988).

Psychology as a science, however, is less than 150 years old. Depending on which historian you believe, the first psychology laboratory was either a small equipment room at Harvard University in 1875 under the direction of William James or a room in an old building of the University of Leipzig, opened for business by Wilhelm Wundt in 1879. Die-hard experimental behaviorists might say it only became a science in 1913, when John B. Watson put forth the idea that psychology is a purely objective branch of natural science. Statisticians and methodologists might say that psychology only became a science sometime in the 1920s, when Ronald A. Fisher worked out the logic of hypothesis testing, the method that most psychology studies use today. Finally, some physicists and biologists, who have a head start on us, might deny that psychology is a science even yet! This course is the story of what took us so long.

The fact that it took us so long is the first best reason to study the history of psychology. As a science, we are still trying to determine the rules of the game. No self-respecting astronomer will question the Copernican theory of planets, but if someone comes up with a new theory of intelligence tomorrow, some psychologists will listen. Although many of us use statistical inference as our rules of evidence, radical Skinnerians insist upon single subject design and Freudian-influenced therapists swear by the case study methods. In short, the men and women may be dead, but the intellectual battles they fought are still going on.

There are other reasons to study the history of psychology. First, it is nearly a truism that you only find what you are looking for, so it is important to take into account the worldview of our predecessors to understand why they believed the often, to us, strange things they did and not other, to us, more important things. Remember, a future generation might find our obsessions trivial or naive as well; examination of work in the context of its time is important. Second, it is important to study history as a meditation on what science is, why good theories are so practical and why methodology is so hotly debated. Third, as the above quote by the insightful neurologist Oliver Sacks suggests, history shows that a lot of science was and is not very scientific to its practitioners but an emotional, political, artistic, stubborn, lucky task. Fourth, as a student, the study of history helps you to organize a lot of the information you've been getting from other courses into a whole body of knowledge for the first time and to develop a healthy distrust for your textbooks. Fifth, in studying the lives and ideas of psychologists, you may get some inspiration as to how to be a great psychologist yourself. Finally, it is an intrinsically interesting and fun topic, with sex (Which famous psychologist lost his job for fooling around, adulterously, with his graduate student?), violence (How did Pavlov react when there was violence in the streets?), money (Who made a mint in advertising? What psychologist came from the second-richest family in New York?) and heroics (Who stood up to the Nazis?).

As my first step in both gaining your trust as a reader and helping you gain the critical skills to evaluate your textbooks, let me remind you that every author of a text has a point of view and I am no exception. In fact, I have two points of view. The first point of view concerns what I believe a student needs to know to evaluate the historical evidence presented in this book: A student needs to know that, in science, as in scholarship in general, all knowledge is provisional and based on certain principles of selection and organization. In other words, a textbook is not truth, but an argument. This is not the same as saying that all arguments are equally good or that I have not been diligent in tracking down facts in support of my argument. It is to say, however, that you as a reader should do more than simply memorize the contents of this book for the tests your instructor may give you, but think to yourself, "How does the author know that?" Above, for example, you might have noticed that I gave two dates for the founding of the first psychology laboratory. Although the "traditional" date, man and place (i.e. the one celebrated by the American Psychological Association (APA)) was 1879, Wundt and Leipzig, part of the reason that it is traditional is that the man who wrote the first classic history of psychology textbook was a student of a student of Wundt. Wundt also did much more laboratory work than did James, so though he may not have been the first, he did concentrate more on laboratory work. For brevity's sake, I will not always clue you in on my reasoning, but you as a reader must recognize that every historical "fact" carries such judgments.

My second point of view concerns the actual contents of the text. I believe that the existence of psychology in its present form is dependent on two important shifts in the way we see the world. The first of these was a shift from basing our knowledge solely upon texts written by accepted authorities, such as the works of Aristotle or Galen or religious texts, to basing our knowledge on what we can find out for ourselves through observation, experimentation and logical argument. The second shift involves a change around the time of Darwin to explaining the world solely in terms of natural causes instead of such constructs as a spiritual "life force" or an intentionally designed universe. Let me make clear that I am not making a statement here about the existence of God or God's plan for the universe. I am only stating that such claims are beyond the scope of science and that it is a matter of historical fact that we customarily define science in this way today.

So, in view of the preceding paragraphs, it seems natural that before we embark upon the subject matter of the history of psychology as a science, we first need to know what science is (or what philosophers have argued that science is) and what history is (or what philosophers have argued that history is). That is discussed in the next two sections. Some of the examples in the following sections will be taken from other sciences or from areas of history not pertaining to science, to make more general points.

How Science Is Different From Other Human Pursuits: A Primer on the Philosophy of Science

> Objectivity is not the result of disinterested and unprejudiced observation. Objectivity and also unbiased observation are the result of criticism, including the criticism of observational reports. For we cannot avoid or suppress our theories or prevent them from influencing our observations; yet we can try to recognize them as hypotheses and to formulate them explicitly, so that they may be criticised.
> —Sir Karl Popper (1983, p. 48)

Consider for a moment the variety of disciplines that may be studied: The humanities include the plastic and material arts, such as painting and sculpture, the performing arts, such as music, drama and dance, and literature, philosophy and theology. The sciences include the physical sciences such as physics, geology and chemistry, the biological sciences of anatomy, zoology and medicine and the social sciences such as psychology and sociology. This is only a partial list, of course, but the question arises, what makes science different from the humanities? From a philosophical perspective, it is not that science claims to say something about "the truth" or "facts"; religions claim a kind of revealed truth and the arts seek a kind of emotional truth or identification. The methods of arriving at that truth are different. Consider, in regards to art or literature, the old saying, "There's no accounting for taste." This statement actually comes from a quotation in Latin: *De gustibus non disputandum est*, which can be more accurately translated as "there's no *disputing* taste." The grounds of taste are so individual, so based on personal response, that there's no way to say who's right, even though we might argue about it or write critical commentary about it. Of course, an artist hopes that his or her work will appeal to many people, but its worth (aside from its monetary worth) is not open to majority vote.

Similarly, if you say that you have had a revelation from God, there is no way that another person may dispute it—it is an internal experience. In any case, the majority of religion deals with interpretations about internal emotional experiences rather than explanations of the world. Science can tell you how a child died, but not why a child died. The intuition that there is a grand plan in the universe that includes even such tragedies is a comforting thought to many, but the methods of science cannot decide the truth of such things. Science, in this sense, is "a-theistic" in that it follows the **naturalistic hypothesis**, which is concerned with how far we can get in explaining the universe without resorting to supernatural causes. Much of this book will track the modern trajectory that moves from the Universe as a Grand Plan to the Universe as a Mechanism.

None of the above examples is science, for the simple fact that the experiences of truth of art or religion are private and cannot be verified or criticized effectively. Consider some of the terms that have been commonly associated with science, such as *observation*, *test*, *experiment*, *objective* and *fact*. Each of these terms implies experiences that more than one person can have, that are not completely subjective. They concern observations that have been tested through controlled experiment to exclude alternative explanations. Science deals with statements about the natural world that have been evaluated critically. In this sense, objectivity in science is not a synonym for truth but for proof.

Let us say that I have observed something, such as a radio signal from space. I then ask other astronomers to confirm that they have received the signals at other observatories. We then vary the conditions under which the observation is made, by refining our measurements or defining more carefully what an observation would mean. For example, we entertain the hypothesis that this could be a radio transmission from somewhere on earth or a radio emission from natural sources, such as a quasar, or from deliberate transmissions from other beings. Then we describe exactly how those observations are done and invite others to do the same. If the others, having followed our instructions, repeat the instructions and get the same results, then our observation is said to have been replicated. **Replication** is not just that things can be repeated, but that when they are repeated, the same results are obtained. A scientific fact is one that can be replicated, and objectivity is the process of observing, excluding alternative explanations and replicating under conditions that have been precisely set down and described as completely as is practicable. Observations or experiments that have not been replicated are considered to be less trustworthy by the scientific community.

Another interesting difference between science and art is the different role of creativity. In the modern West, originality is a strong and important point in the arts. If you attempt to become an artist by explicitly attempting to "replicate" the paintings of Picasso, to come up with the same results, you would probably be labeled a forger or a copyist, not a "true" artist. If you wish to make new paintings in the style of Picasso under your own name, you may be described as "derivative" unless your artistic statement is itself about style. Suppose (taking an example from psychology this time) you decided to repeat the famous experiment by Solomon Asch, on conformity. In this experiment, seven people in a room claim that the longer of two lines is really the shorter one, in order to induce another subject who is not in on the joke to conform to their judgment. You might repeat the experiment under different conditions: with higher or lower status persons or more or fewer confederates, at a university or a shopping mall, etc. The fact that you repeated the experiment under these conditions—and got similar results—is a plus for science, although it might be a minus if it were considered art. Such copying in this case increases the likelihood that the phenomenon in question is "real" and criticizes the results of the first experiment in a useful way. It is still a creative act, though.

It is not that the insights of science are more valid than the insights of the humanities or religion, only that the insights are discussed and criticized publicly, with a strong set of rules of evidence. Referring to the quote at the top of this section, it is not that scientists are somehow a different species of human, impervious to bias, only that the process of criticism by peers and further experiments protects the results of science from that bias.

The Traditional View of Science

How are discoveries made in science and how are those discoveries placed into the context of a theory of how the world works? Philosophers of science have examined the logic of how evidence is gathered, how theories are proposed and how and why scientists accept new theories to come up with several theories of how scientific progress is made. These theories are accepted by scientists who fall into three different groups: **inductivists**, **falsificationists** and **social revolutionists**.

The first of these, the **inductivists**, believe that science begins with facts (Agassi, 1963). The name of this school comes from these historians' belief in **inductive logic** as the way science is done. In this view, general laws are discovered by collecting many specific facts and then generalizing all those specific facts into general rules or scientific laws. To inductivists, each new instance adds corroborative evidence that a theory is true. In this view, a scientist discovers a particular puzzling fact and sets about to try to explain it by developing a new theory. Examples of these outside of psychology are numerous. For example, Alexander Fleming supposedly discovered penicillin because he was growing some bacteria. In 1928, he was straightening up some Petri dishes in which he had been growing the bacteria, which had been piled in the sink. He opened each one and examined it before tossing it into the cleaning solution. One made him stop in surprise.

Some mold was growing on one of the dishes, which, considering how long the dishes had been lying around, was not unusual. However, all around the mold, the staph bacteria had been killed. The mold proved to be from the Penicillium family. Fleming presented his findings in 1929, but they raised little interest until later.

One similar example from the history of psychology is Max Wertheimer's discovery of apparent movement, which is called the "phi phenomenon" and describes how we can see movement in neon signs or films, even when no movement has actually occurred. Wertheimer was on a train on vacation in Germany when he noticed that two lights on a crossing display were blinking at a rate that made it seem like one light was moving from side to side. He had an insight that caused him to get off the train in Frankfurt, buy a child's toy that capitalized on this phenomenon and consulted some young graduate students at a university there. Thus was Gestalt psychology born (see Chapter 6).

There are many such stories in the history of science. They are distinguished as stories of discovery: A single person or group of superbly objective and unbiased scientists have a singular insight based on a fact or experiment that is observed to have larger consequences. In a larger context, the history of science is simply an accumulation of such events, a marching forward of truth. As Agassi (1963) has suggested, this traditional view reconstructs history to fit the knowledge of the field as discussed in current college textbooks and avoids the false starts and dead ends of the past. Moreover, those who believed, say, the Ptolemaic earth-centered view rather than the Copernican theory of the solar system or the phlogiston theory rather than the oxygen theory are considered to have been lesser scientists than the more recent discoverers. In the inductive view, these events may have actually occurred as described, but this view of how science occurs fails to describe why it is that that particular researcher was so well prepared at that time to make that discovery or why it often took others a long time to accept an observation or theory as true. Moreover, its tendency to focus on the present state of affairs as the inevitable end state misses the point of the creative, risky nature of science—wrong science is often science too! Finally, the focus on facts ignores the way in which theories often condition what facts someone might accept. You only find what you're looking for, and theories prepare you for that surprising fact to be noticed when the time comes.

Popper's Falsificationist View of the History of Science

In 1919, at the age of 17, a young student named Karl Raimund Popper (1902–1994) at the University of Vienna was reveling in the ideas in the air at that vibrant cultural capital. Freud could be heard lecturing there, and the young man was volunteering to work with deprived children under the watchful eye of Alfred Adler, one of the earliest psychoanalysts. Popper had become interested in socialist and, briefly, Marxist ideas. At the same time, he was excited by the theories of Einstein, which were just then undergoing their first important empirical test: A British physicist, Arthur Eddington, had proved that light would be bent by passing near a massive star, just as Einstein had predicted. Popper was particularly impressed by this experiment because he saw it as a risky move: If the light *hadn't* been bent, it would have meant that Einstein's theory was almost certainly wrong. He noted, with some dismay, that the same thing couldn't be said about Freudian, Adlerian or Marxist theories.

Popper later compared psychoanalysis to astrology: You can find confirming evidence of astrology everywhere, but it's very hard to disprove. After you read your horoscope saying, "Romantic interests are in the cards today," your mind casts back to just those events that are related to that area. Because you are always thinking about romantic things and the prediction is vague (or maybe you're reading it in the evening paper, after that day's events, so it's not a prediction), you can always find something that relates to it or even act on your interests following the horoscope.

Freudians also explain behaviors after the fact and can explain opposite types of behavior by the same theoretical construct: for example, fixation in the anal period. One individual might be anally expulsive or exceptionally messy; the anal retentive, by contrast, would like to be messy but has repressed the wish and appears excessively neat. One behavior and its opposite can be just as easily explained by the theory when you are looking for confirmation and you are explaining by looking backwards, knowing the relevant facts, rather than forward, in prediction.

Another example comes from Popper's personal experience working with Alfred Adler, as he mentions in the following quote.

Figure 1.1 Philosopher Sir Karl R. Popper (1902–1994)
Source: Getty Images

> Once, in 1919, I reported to him a case which to me did not seem particularly Adlerian, but which he found no difficulty in analyzing in terms of his theory of inferiority feelings, although he had not even seen the child. Slightly shocked, I asked him how he could be so sure. "Because of my thousandfold experience" he replied; whereupon I could not help saying "And with this new case, I suppose, your experience has become a thousand-and-one-fold."
>
> (Popper, 1962, p. 35)

Popper is illustrating by this example the proverb "To a hammer, everything is a nail." Unlike Einstein, Adler had not put his theory at risk of falsification, in that there is no case that can prove him wrong.

In 1934, Popper published the original German version of *The Logic of Scientific Discovery*, which called into question the view of science as based on inductive observation alone. Following the views of David Hume (see Chapter 3), Popper suggested that you can never really prove a scientific hypothesis or theory inductively, by simply looking for confirming instances of the theory, by looking for more specific instances to convert to a general rule. To use one of Popper's favorite examples, you cannot prove the hypothesis that "All swans are white" simply by finding yet another white swan. There may always be black (or for that matter, blue or yellow) swans that you have yet to meet. It is relatively simple, however, to refute or **falsify** the hypothesis that all swans are white: all you have to do is find a black (or blue or yellow) swan. Of course, people still must agree on the definition of "white" or "swan" and not suddenly change the rules to say that "only white swans are really swans" or "that black swan is really a white swan caught in an oil slick!"

An interesting example of such disproof comes from Jane Goodall's work with chimpanzees. Researchers had suggested that "only humans could make and use tools." Goodall had found and filmed chimpanzees stripping leaves off of branches to use them to get ants and termites out of old logs. Her teacher Richard Leakey was reported to have said after this discovery, "Now we must redefine man, redefine tool or accept chimps as human (Quammen, 2010)." (Some people then redefined man and suggested that only humans make war—Goodall sadly disproved that too.)

Popper has suggested that the best reason for formulating hypotheses in such a way that they can be disproved is so that they can be criticized. The statement "People are motivated to seek pleasure and avoid pain" cannot be effectively disproven because people's views of pleasure and pain differ so much. However, if a person says, "I will perform a task if you feed me Brussels sprouts" and they do not perform the task, their statement about themselves has been disproven. Of course, this statement is disproven for only one person at one time, and ideally, scientific laws are meant to apply to many people at many times, but the idea is the same: A scientific hypothesis which is believed is a conjecture, a possible statement of fact which has yet to be conclusively disproven or falsified.

You will remember above that I said that objectivity is not about truth, but about proof. Contrary to the inductivists, Popper believes that objectivity is not about truth but about disproof. A concise summary of his theory is put in his own words in Table 1.1, but there is one last lesson to be learned from Popper. Because every properly formulated statement in science can be potentially falsified, each statement is only temporarily considered true to the best of our knowledge. If such a formidably well-proven scientist as Newton could be disproved by Einstein, so could anyone else. There is no way in which we can know which statement of possible fact is the *real* one. According to Popper, we may even have hit on the "real" answer, but we'll never actually know it. In practice, a theory may even stand because no one has bothered yet to call it into question, but that doesn't make it true for all time. Popper was highly critical of fields such as psychology, because a high percentage of our hypotheses and theories are constructed in nonfalsifiable terms. They do not put themselves at risk of being disproven. Others have argued that definitive disproof is elusive in a world in which one outcome is simply more probable than another. Finally, some philosophers of science have suggested that disproof, even in such hard sciences as physics, is not enough. When someone does an experiment that calls a theory into question, scientists do not simply smack their heads and say "Of course! How could I have been so foolish?" and change their minds. The process of evaluation of evidence is more conditioned on the beliefs of the community of scientists at a given time, and change proceeds more like a social revolution in that community. We turn to this view next.

Table 1.1 Summary of Popper's Falsificationism

It is easy to obtain confirmations or verifications of nearly every theory—if we look for confirmations.

Confirmations should count only if they are the result of risky predictions; that is to say, if, unenlightened by the theory in question, we should have expected an event which was incompatible with the theory—an event which would have refuted the theory.

Every good scientific theory is a prohibition; it forbids certain things to happen. The more a theory forbids the better it is.

A theory which is not refutable by any conceivable event is nonscientific. Irrefutablity is not a virtue of a theory (as people often think) but a vice.

Every genuine test of a theory is an attempt to falsify it or to refute it. Testablility is falsifiability, but there are degrees of testability: some theories are more testable, more exposed to refutation, than others; they take, as it were, greater risks.

Confirming evidence should not count except when it is the result of a genuine test of the theory; and this means that it can be presented as a serious but unsuccessful attempt to falsify the theory. (I now speak in such cases of "corroborating evidence.")

Adapted from Popper, 1962, pp. 36–37

Kuhn's Conception of Paradigms

Figure 1.2 Physicist, historian and philosopher of science, Thomas S. Kuhn
Source: Getty Images

Thomas S. Kuhn

In 1962, Thomas S. Kuhn (1922–1996), a philosopher initially trained as a physicist, published an extended critique of the traditional view of how science was done and how scientific discoveries came to be accepted over time in *The Structure of Scientific Revolutions*. In this book, Kuhn claimed that science is not a steady forward accumulation of facts and explanations, carried out by unbiased scientists who take facts as their starting point. Rather, he suggested that science is produced by a community of scientists and proceeds by a series of **social revolutions** within that community rather than a stately progress of scientific knowledge. This social community of scientists works within an established, often unspoken system of rules about what constitutes good science rather than bad science or nonscience. This system of rules takes the form of **paradigms** or "universally recognized scientific achievements that for a time provide model problems and solutions for a community of practitioners" (Kuhn, 1962, p. x). Paradigms are theories about how the world works, but as described by Kuhn, they are more than that: they are practically worldviews or the way that scientists see the world (see Table 1.3 for a summary). Paradigms define for a time what problems are important to be solved and the accepted way to solve them. Table 1.2 describes certain former and current paradigms in various sciences.

While scientists are operating under the paradigm, they are engaging in what Kuhn called **normal science**. Normal science is the process of conducting research by the rules of the paradigm, by, for example, replicating studies and extending the generality of what can be discovered by established methods and specific hypothesis testing. Most scientists work their whole life not indulging very much in philosophical pursuits or scientific revolutions, but doing only normal science. For example, the paradigm of molecular biology is centered on the discovery of DNA, and very important normal science tasks under this paradigm are the sequencing and explanation of the human genome, which will take many years.

However, at some points, data that do not fit the paradigm begin to arise. These facts are inconsistent with the current explanation of the world by the paradigm. Scientists become puzzled and focus their attention on these inconsistent facts (called **anomalies** by Kuhn) until a new theory arises to explain them and the old facts. Until this happens, there are arguments and factions within the scientific community affected by the facts. There may even be attempts to ignore them. At some point, a new theory is developed that explains the anomalies as well as the older information and a new paradigm arises through a **paradigm shift**.

Table 1.2 Examples of Paradigms and Paradigm Shifts

	Early paradigm	Displaced by	"Normal" activities
Astronomy	Ptolemaic system	Copernican system	Star charts
Geology	"Terra firma"	Continental drift	Mapping surveys
Physics	Newton's	Relativity system	Ballistics,
Chemistry	Phlogiston combustion	Oxygen combustion	Analysis of compounds
Math	Greek geometry	Non-Euclidian geometry	Accounting Computing Proofs of theorems
Natural Science	Creationism	Darwinism	Description of species, animal behavior
Psychology	?	?	?

The classic example used by Kuhn and discussed in much of his work is that of the paradigm shift from the earth-centered view of the solar system, put forth by the Greek astronomer Ptolemy (c. A.D. 87–150), to the sun-centered (*heliocentric*) view of the solar system put forth by Copernicus (1473–1543), a Polish priest. Astronomy before Copernicus was based on a calculation system of the motion of the planets around a static earth at the center of the solar system. But an earth-centered or terracentric universe causes problems. When viewed from the earth, the motion of the planets is not smooth; for example, from our point of view, the planets move forward at some times of the year and backwards at others (hence their name: "planet" means "wanderer" in Greek). Therefore, Ptolemy's system, in order to predict their motion accurately, had to resort to a system of circles within circles, known as epicycles. This system of some 80 epicycles was rather complex and entailed not only the adding of extra circles throughout the middle ages as observations got more precise, but also the speeding up or slowing down of the rates of each planet throughout the year. Copernicus was offended by the lack of celestial perfection implied by such a system and proposed a system that placed the sun in the center of concentric circular spheres, on which the planets orbited. We know because of the later work of Kepler that the orbits are not circular but elliptical and that Copernicus's heliocentric system was not perfect either, requiring 34 to 38 epicycles and making measurements easier to calculate but not much more accurate. However, in accordance with Kuhn's theory of science, we can see that Ptolemy's paradigm was not working well by the 16th century; it produced many anomalies that required cumbersome ad hoc additions to the theory. Whatever his measurement errors, Copernicus's *idea* proved to be revolutionary. The same data could be explained more simply using a more elegant system, and that system of calculations proved to have greater ramifications for other things. In this case, to believe in Copernicus was to disbelieve in Ptolemy. Even though you could calculate orbits in either system, belief in a stationary sun changes what a scientist thinks Ptolemy's measurements *mean*. One's worldview or paradigm has shifted.

This story is not yet over, however. It is not enough to have a better idea; scientists must come to believe in your idea. If paradigms operate in a social community of scientists, the community must be convinced. Indeed, Copernicus's ideas were not initially seen as revolutionary, particularly in the sense that we see him today of changing humanity's place in the universe. Church astronomers were initially happy about Copernicus's innovations, as they made calculations easier. Almost no other evidence can be seen in astronomy texts of Copernicus's ideas until about 1609. By 1616, however, his work was banned by the Catholic Church and remained so until the mid-19th century, which did not stop the eventual acceptance of his ideas by the scientific community. What happened in the interim was that his ideas were taken up by other scientists (whom we will discuss in the next chapter), notably Galileo (1564–1642), Kepler (1571–1630) and Descartes (1594–1650). Thus, a discovery does not make a revolution; the acceptance of it does. This may take years, even sometimes until older scientists and tenured professors retire or die off, leaving the younger generation in charge. As can be seen in Table 1.2, many sciences have had significant paradigm shifts, such as the shift from creationism to Darwinism or the shift from Newtonian physics to Einstein's revolution.

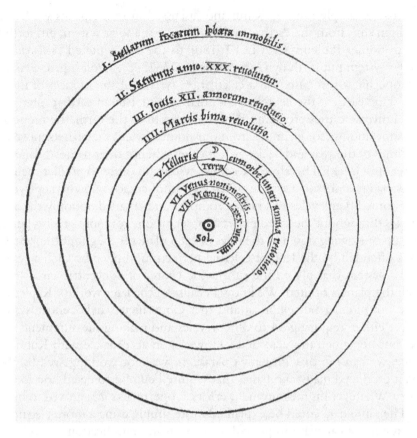

Figure 1.3 Copernicus (1543): Heliocentric model from *De Revolutionibus Orbium Coelestium libri sex* [Six Books on the Revolutions of the Heavenly Spheres]

Table 1.3 The Structure of Scientific Revolutions

—Science is produced by a social community of scientists and proceeds by a series of social revolutions within that community rather than by a stately, cumulative march of discoveries.
—The social community of scientists works within a *paradigm* or "universally recognized scientific achievements that for a time provide model problems and solutions for a community of practitioners."
—The type of science that goes on under the umbrella of a particular paradigm is called by Kuhn "*normal science*" because everybody agrees on the underlying assumptions, they can engage in experiments that are mere "puzzle solving."
—Normal science is threatened by "*anomalies*" findings that cannot be explained by the paradigm.
—A *scientific revolution* occurs when a new theory arises that explains not only the anomalies but also most of the other data previously explained by the preceding theory *and* when scientists accept the new theory.

Adapted from Thomas S. Kuhn (1962)

Critics of Kuhn's Perspective

Kuhn's theory of paradigms in science was one of the most influential philosophies of the last half of the 20th century. You may have even heard the terms "paradigm" or "paradigm shift" used, somewhat inappropriately, in business or the arts. And yet many scientists were not happy with his explanation of how science works. On the one hand, the idea that scientific change happens by a social revolution among a scientific community makes the process seem to some excessively political, as if scientists were merely politicians and their discoveries merely policy statements that they try to convince as many people as possible to believe. Scientists see themselves as striving to uncover truth or at least successive approximations to it. They may have very sophisticated views about how imperfect their theories are, but they are realists: They believe they are finding out something about the real world that will survive the everyday human battles of science. Moreover, as Nobel physicist Steven Weinberg (1998) suggests, scientists do not necessarily experience a worldview change when the paradigm shifts. Physicists still use Newton's system for many everyday calculations and know the difference between his system and Einstein's. And of course, Popperians focus on the logical structure of scientific problems over the social aspects of the process.

Kuhn may have caused some of the confusion himself. Critics have suggested that he used the word paradigm in over 20 different ways. (Horgan, 1996). How big is a paradigm? Does psychology have to have only one paradigm or could, say, behaviorism and psychoanalysis be different paradigms altogether? Kuhn also used the words **puzzle solving** to describe the type of activity that goes on under normal science. This angers many scientists; they consider their task as more noble than solving puzzles. In his defense, Kuhn has called himself adamantly pro-science and suggests that the rigidity and discipline that a science follows during the time that normal science proceeds under a paradigm produces most of its progress. He never meant to imply that science was entirely political. Sure, it is impossible to know whether a theory is true, but not whether it is useful, and as for puzzle-solving, Kuhn apologizes forthrightly: "Maybe I should have said more about the glories that result from puzzle-solving, but I thought I was doing that" (Horgan, 1996, p. 44). He has also said that "paradigm" has become hopelessly overused, by politicians, artists and advertisers as well as scientists. Perhaps this is a sign that Kuhn's theory has struck a chord in the modern imagination.

Kuhn's Theory Applied to Psychology

Most of Kuhn's and Popper's examples of how science develops come from physics, a mathematically precise discipline whose paradigm is well understood and very binding upon the field. What about psychology? What are the accepted problems and methods to solve them in our field, which seems to be increasing rather than decreasing in diversity? Rather than answering this question directly, I shall describe the relevance of Kuhn's theory with an example of how our current paradigm might be threatened by anomalies: the phenomenon of extrasensory perception or ESP.

Let me say at the outset that I do not believe in ESP, nor do most of my colleagues in psychology. What would it take for us to be convinced and how might that lead to a revolution in psychology? According to Kuhn's theory, the first thing that we need are anomalies, observations that are not explained by the current paradigm. Some of you may believe that such anomalies already exist and count anecdotal reports as evidence. Anecdotal reports do not satisfy the criteria mentioned above of replicability and exclusion of alternative hypotheses. They are more like the reports of astrology that Popper criticizes. So, let's say some scientists attempt a study using the standard deck of ESP cards (five repetitions of five shapes in random order). An individual on one side of campus goes through the deck, attempting to send the symbols to a presumed telepath across campus (this is a similar procedure to the experiments by Rhine, 1934). Several trials are done. If, over many trials, a statistically significant result is obtained, in that the telepath guesses more symbols than would be expected by chance, we have a true anomaly. Other scientists attack the anomalous finding based on its procedures. Such a circumstance is common in normal science and is the process of conjecture and refutation or attempts to falsify that Popper discusses. One such experiment, even if not discredited by the process, is likely to be ignored. Many successful experiments constitute replication of the anomaly, and in such a case, many scientists would fall upon the unexplained results with new vigor.

But they are unlikely to be convinced by the simple weight of the evidence, because there is no explanation for it in the related paradigms of biology or physics. Consider that in order to send information telepathically, one would need an organ to do so and the receiver would need a sensory organ. No such organ has been reported in any animal in biology, thereby violating the paradigm of the biological sciences. There would also need to be an energy to transmit it. Neural energy is very weak; even if it could somehow escape the skull, it must travel a long distance. As it travels, it would be weakening to one fourth over two feet and to one ninth of its power over three feet and so on, according to the current paradigms of physics. If one of the known forms of energy were not measured by instruments, a new form would need to be proposed and so forth.

In other words, in order for a revolution to happen in psychology over ESP, several established paradigms would have to be overturned and new plausible explanations found. A revolution depends on anomalies and new explanations. Without both, no change will occur. Is it *possible* under Kuhn's approach that ESP might be true? Of course: no theory is permanent—in fact, no theory is really true in an ultimate sense, only more useful in explaining the current data. But it is highly unlikely to fit under the current paradigm; moreover, many of the studies have not been replicated after all, and so I as a scientist, conclude, for now, that telepathy does not exist.

Thus, we see that the paradigms of psychology are embedded within the other scientific disciplines. One of the goals of this book is to describe how the paradigm shifts in various fields affected the history of psychology. For example, in the next chapter we will discuss how the insights of mathematics and science following Copernicus influenced Descartes to come up with a new method of rational observation of the self and the world, against the position of the medieval Catholic Church, based on an amalgam of religious scriptures and the surviving texts of Aristotle. In Chapter 3, Newton and Boyle's view of physics and chemistry influenced the atomistic empiricist view of the mind championed by Locke, set against the Aristotelian chemistry used by the alchemists. Later chapters describe how the mind became explainable by physiochemical rather than spiritual means and how the Darwinian revolution spread to psychology almost immediately (again, as contrasted with the age-old unchanging "scale of nature," devised by Aristotle and sanctioned by religious authorities). Each of these revolutions made psychology in its current form possible.

I might as well be explicit at this point. I believe that psychology was made possible by two revolutions. First, the philosophical scientific revolution, in which such philosophers as Descartes and Locke made it possible for us to examine the world and ourselves through observation, reflection and logical argument, instead of the appeals to authority that characterized thought in the Middle Ages. Second, perhaps the most momentous revolution in science occurred in the mid-19th century, first with the materialist emphasis on physiochemical explanations for mind and body and then the Darwinian revolution that followed immediately. All of the subsequent changes in psychology, from psychoanalysis to behaviorism, followed from these revolutions.

This is not to say that by these revolutions psychology acquired a stable paradigm immediately or easily. In fact, for much of its history, psychology did not have "universally recognized scientific achievements that for a time provide model problems and solutions for a community of practitioners." Instead, psychology was characterized as what Kuhn calls a **preparadigmatic science**.

In this phase of historical development, the scientific community is fractured. They argue not about results, but about philosophy. During the period of time covered by this book, psychologists argued about what psychology should be about, what methods should be used and what should count as acceptable data. In the preparadigmatic period of a science, books are written that are long on philosophical speculation and short on results. They are trying to state their position and win converts to it. Compare, for example, these two statements, the first by the great 19th-century psychologist and philosopher William James (see Chapter 7) and the second by the behaviorist John B. Watson (see Chapter 8):

> Psychology is the Science of Mental Life, both of its phenomena and of their conditions. The phenomena are such things as we call feelings, desires, cognitions, reasonings, decisions and the like and superficially considered, their variety and complexity is such as to leave a chaotic impression on the observer.
>
> (James, 1890/1983, p. 1)

> Psychology as the behaviorist views it is a purely objective experimental branch of natural science. Its theoretical goal is the prediction and control of behavior. Introspection forms no essential part of its methods, nor is the scientific value of its data dependent upon the readiness with which they lend themselves to interpretation in terms of consciousness.
>
> (Watson, 1913, p. 158)

What's important about these statements is that they are not statements of fact, but statements of definition and by implication, a statement of purpose. The first several chapters of James's book are spent not on data, but in arguing against other people's definitions of the mind-body position. The quote by Watson is the first line of what has come to be called the "behaviorist manifesto" and a manifesto is, of course, a political document.

As the paradigm for a science matures, the practitioners need to spend less time on philosophy, because all of their colleagues believe in the same set of rules of the game. In psychology articles today, the introduction section is often the shortest section of the paper, with most space given to presenting the results. This might suggest that the field has acquired a paradigm. Certainly, all undergraduate psychology majors must take certain courses in methodology and statistics, which suggests that there are some agreed-upon methods. On the other hand, the debate implied by the above quotes is still going on in conflicts between, for example, behaviorists and cognitivists. They typically attend different research conferences and publish in different journals. So, it is not at all clear whether psychology even now has one or many paradigms. Some of this problem turns on the fuzzy definition of paradigm described earlier. Although I believe that virtually all psychologists must follow the modernist philosophical and Darwinian paradigms described earlier in order to be considered full-fledged members of the community of psychologists, under these paradigms, much freedom is allowed.

Our task in this book will be to describe the progress in the development and shifting of the paradigms that made psychology what it is today.

How to Study History

> If we ask ourselves what historians have commanded the most lasting admiration, we shall, I think, find that they are neither the most ingenious, nor the most precise, nor even the discoverers of new facts and causal connections, but those who (like imaginative writers) present men or societies or situations in many dimensions, at many intersecting levels simultaneously, writers in whose accounts human lives and their relations to both each other and to the external world are what (at our most lucid and imaginative) we know that they can be. The gifts that scientists need are not these: they must be ready to call everything into question, to construct bold hypotheses unrelated to empirical procedures and drive their logical implications as far as they can go, free from control by common sense or too great a fear of departing from what is normal or possible in the world. Only in this way will new truths and relations be found—truths which, as in physics or mathematics, do not depend upon the peculiarities of human nature and its activity.
> —Isaiah Berlin (1960, p. 31)

Because this book is also about history as well as science, we now must consider how we know what we know about the history of psychology. What are the methods of history and how are they different from those of science? What sources shall we use and how shall we trust them? Shall we look at history as a history of ideas, of scientists or of the general society? What are the pitfalls of trying to enter into the minds of those who lived long ago?

Only by knowing the answers to these questions can you read a book like this profitably and critically. But even more importantly, you need to know the answers to these questions in case you yourself want to read the original sources from the people we talk about in this book and then place those writings in context. Students often find original historical sources difficult because they are attempting to interpret them from their own framework, ways of speaking and beliefs about the world. A book like this is intended to provide a bridge to that important world, but this section is intended to show you that beneath each paragraph of information on the history of psychology are a number of choices that the historian has made, even if those choices are not made explicit.

Why History Is Not Quite a Science

As the quote above by the famous Oxford philosopher Isaiah Berlin suggests, the qualities of a good historian and a good scientist differ somewhat. As Berlin has noted (1960), the scientist deals in finding lawful *general* rules that apply across individuals, time and place. In order to do so, the scientist constructs variables that examine specific aspects of the world and distances him or her from the individual atom, animal or person. The mathematician cares about individual instances not at all: 2 + 2 = 4 no matter what you are adding. The physicist formulates laws of acceleration, no matter what is falling; the laws of evolution apply to all animals and so forth. The reason the scientist looks for the general rules is to be able to *predict* what will happen next.

The historian deals with *particular* people, times and places. In spite of attempts to develop a science of history by individuals such as Karl Marx, it has been to date quite unsuccessful, for several reasons. First and most obviously, historical happenings are beyond the reach of experimental control. Historical events cannot be isolated, manipulated, repeated and replicated. Under such circumstances, it is impossible to formally separate true from apparent causal factors in history. Second, there are always many causes in history. As Berlin points out, even if one were to prove that the French Revolution were caused by the economics of the peasants, one would not thereby disprove the fact that it was also caused by the weakness of the king or the writings of Rousseau. Third, the data used by historians is incomplete and dependent more on what has been left to survive than what can be gathered systematically under controlled conditions. Some imaginative interpretations are always necessary to fill the gaps. Finally, history is so dependent on many layers of context that it is impossible to construct general laws. One cannot expect today's president to act like President Franklin Roosevelt, because the laws are different, the economics are different, the technology is different, the political systems and the press operate in different ways and so on.

Therefore, the goal of history is to take information from all available sources, any detail that bears on a particular historical moment, in all of its richness. Because this information is so vast and interpretation is so necessary, there is always room for differences of opinion and points of view.

Kinds of History

Because of these many layers of meaning that history deals with, any person writing a history must deal with how he or she will present it. For the purposes of this discussion, let us say that histories can be organized by time (**chronological histories**), persons ("great man" or **biographical histories**), groups (organizational or **sociohistorical histories**) or ideas (**histories of ideas** in the field).

The most obvious of these would be the **chronological histories**. Indeed, it would be somewhat perverse to write a history of psychology backwards, but using time as the only organizing theme would be confusing. First of all, a single timeline does not clearly show how different groups or individuals interact. Look, for example, at the following entry for a psychological timeline (adapted from Street, 1994, pp. 102–104), for 1904:

April 4, 1904
Edward B. Titchener founded The Experimentalists, the club that became the society of Experimental Psychologists in 1929.

April 19, 1904
Carl G. Jung published his first studies on word association.

May 6, 1904
Elisabeth Duffy was born. (Duffy initially formulated the arousal or activation theory of emotion.)

May 10, 1904
G. Stanley Hall's most influential book, *Adolescence*, was published.

December 12, 1904
Ivan P. Pavlov received the Nobel Prize. The prize honored Pavlov's work in the physiology of digestion.

Who are these people and how do they connect together? The timeline describes an international perspective, but it also includes experimentalists and clinicians and works as well as events. This is an extreme example, but is perhaps enough to make the point that chronology tells you little. Every history describes a chronology, but only as a framework, not as content. It tells you what, not how and why.

One of the most popular methods of telling the story of history is through the **biographical** method, otherwise called the "great man" theory of history. This view suggests that the progression of historical events is dependent upon the actions of great leaders and pioneers who made great contributions to society. This method can lead to inspiring reading, because it glorifies the actions of individuals. Everyone is interested in biographies, because a biography has a hero or heroine who takes decisive, innovative action and a narrative with a beginning, middle and end. Biographies even provide instruction to readers about how to live their lives. From the point of view of the history writer, biographical histories provide clear points of focus: one can begin with published works and move on to letters, diaries, review of the work, other biographies, etc. The biographical view is favored by inductivist historians writing from within a science, because it gives credit for particular discoveries, theories and experiments to individuals (just as scientists who write history might wish themselves to be memorialized in the future!).

For these reasons, I will use the biographical method in this book wherever it is appropriate. However, the people featured in history texts are affected by the same economic, political and cultural changes as everyone else. In addition, it is perfectly possible that the most famous proponent of a particular idea may capitalize on and synthesize ideas that were in the air at the time. A famous example is that of Charles Darwin. Although he had formulated his theory of evolution by the early 1840s, he waited until 1859 to publish and did so then only because a colleague, Alfred Russel Wallace, had formulated a very similar theory that he was about to make public. When he did publish, however, the book sold out in a few days. If Darwin's views had been so novel and unanticipated, the work would probably not have sold well, but according to the late paleontologist Stephen Jay Gould (2002), many theories of evolution were discussed at fashionable dinner tables all over England before Darwin published; Darwin himself sent and answered many, many letters in the professional and amateur community of biologists. The first edition of Freud's *Interpretation of Dreams* sold a few hundred copies; the first edition of B.F. Skinner's *Behavior of Organisms* was similarly unheralded and criticized by reviewers. And yet both became very significant in time. Why? They were the same ideas all along, but they needed to wait until the books gathered supporters or a critical mass of ideas developed in the culture. To explain this turn of events, one needs a **sociohistorical** approach. A sociohistorical historian examines not individual great men and women, but social, intellectual and economic trends in the population at large. Indeed, the German term *zeitgeist* ("spirit of the times") is used to describe the view that certain ideas are merely in the air and held by many people, discussed in newspapers and intellectual journals and sermons. A historian studying the development of "the unconscious," for example, would not only study the works of Freud, but the crazes of spiritualism and mesmerism and other popular treatments of hypnotism, dream interpretation and the like. He or she might also comment on the possibility that Freudian therapy gained popularity after World War I, when it had been used to help soldiers with hysterical paralysis or "shell shock." Kuhnians favor the use of at least some sociohistorical evidence, because they are concerned not merely with scientific discoveries but also with how those discoveries are accepted by the community of scientists and the culture at large.

Finally, there are **histories of ideas**. In these histories, certain themes are noticed throughout history. Some examples of these would be a history of how the mechanisms of inheritance works in evolution, the mind-body problem in psychology and philosophy, materialism vs. spiritualism, and cognition and the study of consciousness vs. behaviorism. The investigation of these issues may cross many years in time and involve many people and discoveries, but the idea is the organizing framework of the history. The advantage of this type of history is that similarities in positions across great distances in time can easily be noted. In some ways, for example, psychologists of today still hold some of the mind-body positions of Descartes, Locke or James and may not even know it. Similarly, with a history of ideas, biologists might ask the rather abstract question of how the idea of categorizing species from high to low came about and how this had been shown in the classical world, Christian theology and various theories of evolution.

The disadvantage of histories of ideas is that they can sometimes treat ideas as if they are disembodied, that they weren't thought by particular people at particular times. This approach can therefore oversimplify the thoughts of individuals and the external pressures on them, losing some of the rich detail that separates historical accounts from scientific method.

Presentism vs. Historicism

In 1931, historian Herbert Butterfield published a highly influential book, the *Whig Interpretation of History*. In this book, Butterfield notes that there is a tendency for historians to write on the side of the victors in conflicts, particularly if the historians are themselves descendants of the victors (in this case, the Whigs and the Protestants, who eventually won out in British history). Since we know how history turned out, this tendency is natural, for it seemingly shows how we arrived at this point. But it also distorts history, for it also seemingly justifies the present, implies that the present is the "right" or the "inevitable" way for history to have turned out. This approach to history, the interpretation of the past for the sake of the present, is called **presentism** (Stocking, 1965). Presentism expresses the view that "the winners write the history," thus only those revolutions that are successful end up being praised.

Presentism is a very selective view of history, for it only selects out the straight line of events that lead to the present circumstances. This is the kind of history that is often found in the first chapter of textbooks about a given field of science, and it is the approach that reinforces beliefs about science as a forward-looking, data-driven enterprise (as the inductivist historians claim). Presentism can be easily detected in such chapters by looking for such phrases as "forerunners of behaviorism" or "precursors to the Freudian unconscious." Why bore introductory students with false starts and wrong turns? A moment's reflection will tell you that the most obvious problem with presentism is that it deemphasizes the nervous, emotional, contentious *uncertainty* of history for those who participated in revolutions. They didn't know at the time that they were forerunners of anything. It certainly wasn't clear to the participants in the American Civil War or the Second World War how it would have turned out. Sometimes all it takes to rescue history classes from boredom is to restore that sense of uncertainty.

Presentist histories can lead to serious misconceptions about how new ideas are accepted. In psychology, one of the revolutions that we will talk about is the behaviorist revolution (see Chapter 8). The way it is depicted in some textbooks is that it gained ascendancy very quickly, almost as if it were accepted like the discovery of some new element. Other texts seem to suggest that it raised a furor and a strong negative reaction. In actuality, based on the available published reviews of Watson's remarks that started the revolution and subsequent letters and memoirs, it seems that psychologists accepted some things about it and discounted others (Samelson, 1981). The reaction was actually quite mild, refusing either to take Watson's extremist position or to reject it out of hand.

The myth of its immediate impact developed unconsciously perhaps for reasons of simplicity. Knowing how history has turned out, one looks back for particular moments or writings that clearly express a shift in perspective. The writing that is merely emblematic of a larger trend, one argument among many, then becomes the cause of the shift. Since from our vantage point the effects of the shift are quite large, now the cause must be large and clear as well; hence the discussion of furor against it and conversions to the new position.

Set against presentism is that opposite tendency in history, that of explaining history for the sake of the past or **historicism**. The historian who takes care to show the historicist viewpoint is attempting to get inside the heads of the participants in history to recapture the uncertainty of the times. This means emphasizing at all times that other outcomes in history were possible and that people knew and feared that the outcome was a close call, rather than an inevitable *fait accompli*.

Some examples from the general history of the Civil War might help to make the point. The American Civil War is often presented, in its presentist form, as a war that was inevitably won by the North, because the North had a strong industrial base and the South was, by contrast, feudal, agrarian and relatively poor, as well as more morally reprehensible.

The historian James McPherson (1988), however, reminds us that the Democratic Party in the North, notably in New York, was pro-slavery leaning, and by 1864, many people in the North were tired of the war and in many newspapers, there was a suggestion of suing for peace. Grant, however, made a rather foolhardy charge up Kennesaw Mountain in Georgia and won, bolstering public opinion. As McPherson states, the outcome of the battle, and thus the war, was far from certain even that late in the war.

Another goal of the historicist is to unearth all sides of debates of the time and all the nuances that would have been caught by a participant in those debates. Even something as simple as a single word has significances that we are unaware of. The Gettysburg address begins, "Four score and seven years ago, our fathers brought forth on this continent a new nation, conceived in liberty and dedicated to the proposition that all men are created equal."

This was perhaps the first time Lincoln used the word "nation" instead of Union in a speech, suggesting that the states are subordinate to the federal government. Newspapers picked this up immediately, and there was much discussion about the use of the word. After the war, we began to say, "The United States *is* instead of *are*." Because we now conceive of ourselves as a nation, rather than as a collection of states—a belief that the Civil War itself made inevitable—we are unable to see this subtle difference in meaning (Wills, 1992).

This historicist attention to what people really thought is absolutely crucial for understanding the kind of philosophical and scientific debates in the history of psychology. This is because when people argue for a position, they are simultaneously arguing against a contrary position. As we shall see in subsequent chapters, Descartes was arguing against church orthodoxy, Locke was arguing against Descartes's innate ideas and John B. Watson was arguing against the schools of psychology known as functionalism and structuralism, as well as arguing for behaviorism. You may never have heard of these schools of thought and thus may attempt to understand what

Watson was saying in terms of the present and presentist understanding of behaviorism today. In this you would be wrong, for his criticism of these long-dead or transformed schools form a part of what his words meant in his historical context. To avoid looking at the historical context in which Watson's words are placed would be to ascribe to him words he never wrote and thoughts he never had, even if you think you are speaking the same language and using the same words. The meaning of history is contained in contexts like these.

If you have picked up from the preceding paragraphs that being historicist requires a lot of filling in of gaps with judicious imagination of what people are thinking, you are right. History requires rich interpretation of many sources. But how should these sources be used? How does one make valid conclusions based on historical evidence? A full treatment of this topic would take us beyond the scope of this book, but the next section gives a few pointers.

Care in Establishing Historical Connections

The pioneering memory researcher Hermann Ebbinghaus (1908) once wrote, "Psychology has a long past, yet its real history is short." What he meant is that since the beginning of recorded time, people have been thinking about the causes of their own actions and motivations, but only relatively recently had psychology been a recognized discipline distinct from philosophy, medicine and biology. What this means to the historian of psychology today is that psychologists typically, even now, look to earlier writers in other fields to get ideas for theories within psychology. They also, of course, borrow views from predecessors in psychology as well. And because of that large past, there are many such sources. On the other hand, sometimes a psychologist will come up with a theory that he or she believes to be absolutely new, but which has in fact been stated, in somewhat different terms, by a historical predecessor. This causes a particular problem for the historian of psychology, who is primarily a historian of ideas. The historian must then decide whether the psychologist has been influenced directly by reading and following the work of the predecessor or indirectly by being taught by a follower of the historical figure or by living in a time in which the zeitgeist made it impossible to escape such ideas.

Alternatively, the historian could decide that the psychologist had never been directly or indirectly influenced by the predecessors at all; even though others had said a similar thing before, the psychologist was unaware of the predecessor. According to Sarup (1978), this difference between real historical influences (direct or indirect) and mere resemblances between two ideas with no demonstrable connection between them is the difference between a **foundation** and an **anticipation**.

Examples of foundations are easy to find. Sigmund Freud based his view of the unconscious on several sources. A historian who wishes to claim a connection between Freud and the great French neurologist Jean Martin Charcot is on solid ground: Freud studied with him briefly, translated his works and presented his work in public forums and spoke highly of him in letters (Sulloway, 1979). On the other hand, some writers have noted that Freud's philosophy is similar to that of the philosopher Schopenhauer, but Freud claimed only to have read him late in life (Sarup, 1978). Schopenhauer would then be seen as an anticipation to certain aspects of

Freud's thought. If some enterprising historian uncovers that, for example, any student who attended the University of Vienna in the 1880s read Schopenhauer as a part of their education, then that historian could argue that Freud had been exposed much earlier and had perhaps forgotten (or repressed!) the knowledge. Such a bit of information would help shift what was thought to be only an anticipation to a foundation, but more would be necessary to verify the connection.

It is sometimes difficult to establish historical precedent. Although John B. Watson is associated with behaviorism in general and classical conditioning in particular, it appears that an unknown scholar named Edwin Twitmeyer had described classical conditioning and understood its significance as early as 1902. Pavlov had announced his findings on salivating dogs in 1904. But Watson had not heard of Twitmeyer, nor had he read Pavlov, at the time he gave the speech that led to the behaviorist manifesto in 1913. Thus, his impetus for becoming a behaviorist came from other sources, even though he subsequently praised Pavlov's work.

Historians, then, use all the methods at their disposal to develop a rich picture of past particular events. Some creative judgment is needed in this task, but we must always be careful to try as best as is possible to avoid injecting our present biases into historical circumstances. Furthermore, we can't be sloppy; just because an earlier idea seems to be connected to the ideas of a more current psychologist does not say that the current psychologist was really influenced by that earlier idea. On the other hand, no man is an island; other scientists, other philosophers and the affairs of the day influence the thinking of everyone, including the great psychologists. Teasing out these issues is what history is all about.

The Plan of This Book

This book is divided into three parts, related to some of the paradigm shifts that made psychology in its current form possible. The first paradigm shift concerns the shift from explaining human thought and action from the theological point of view, to explaining thought by the use of logic and no theological philosophical reflection. This is the *philosophical shift*. The second part of this book examines how the embryonic discipline of psychology was affected by the shift towards viewing the natural world, the human body and the mind as mechanistic, materialistic machines without intentional designs or purposes. This is the *materialist-evolutionary shift*. Finally, each of the schools of psychology responded to these paradigms in different ways. We will explore the historical roots of current psychology through each of these separate reactions.

2 The Shift From Church Authority to Rationalism
The Times and Philosophy of René Descartes

The Worldview Before Descartes in the West

> There are seven windows in the head, two nostrils, two ears, two eyes and a mouth; so, in the heavens, there are two favorable stars, two unpropitious, two luminaries and Mercury alone undecided and indifferent. From which and many other similar phenomena of nature, such as the seven metals, etc., which it were tedious to illuminate, we gather that the number of planets is necessarily seven.... Besides, the Jews and other ancient nations, as well as modern Europeans, have adopted the division of the week into seven days and have named them from the seven planets; now, if we increase the number of planets the whole system falls to the ground.... Moreover, the satellites are invisible to the naked eye and therefore can have no influence on the earth and therefore would be useless and therefore do not exist.—an argument against Galileo's discovery of the moons of Jupiter (c. 1610).
>
> —Holton & Roller (1958, p. 160)

In 1600, four years after René Descartes was born, an Italian priest of the Dominican Catholic order named Giordano Bruno was burned at the stake for heresy. In addition to agreeing with Copernicus that the sun, not the earth, was the stationary center of the solar system, Bruno had gone one step further and speculated that the universe was infinite, with an infinite number of suns and worlds with intelligent people on them (Holton & Roller, 1958). Why was such an outlandish piece of science fiction such a threat to the church? The answer to this question sets the stage for the life and times of Descartes and begins our journey into the birth of modern scientific reasoning.

Poor Bruno was caught up in three strands of change that had started in the 1500s: religion, politics and science. First, there was religion: In 1517, Martin Luther had begun his crusade against church corruption and worldly power that ended in his excommunication and the establishment of Protestantism. This threat had led the Catholic Church to become increasingly rigid in its enforcement of orthodoxy in its own domains through the Spanish and Roman Inquisitions, which punished heresy by imprisonment or less frequently, torture or burning for those who refused to recant. In politics, kings saw an advantage to increase their power at the expense of (or in the service of) the church. For example, although it is well known that Henry VIII established the Church of England because the pope would not grant

Figure 2.1 René Descartes, French philosopher and mathematician, 1835. Nineteenth-century engraving of Descartes (1596–1650), who is regarded as one of the great figures in the history of Western thought and is widely considered to be the father of modern philosophy.

Source: Photo by Oxford Science Archive/Print Collector/Getty Images

him a divorce, he had also found it quite convenient to get rich by seizing church landholdings. Thus, by the end of the 1500s, heresy was not only a theological but also quite a worldly concern. And in science, in 1543, two books were published that eventually would help to undermine the medieval view of the world. The first, of course, was Copernicus's *De Revolutionibus Orbium Coelestium* [On the Revolution of the Celestial Spheres], which we discussed in the last chapter. The second book was by Andreas Vesalius (1514–1564), a Belgian professor of anatomy at the University of Padua, in Italy, entitled *De Humani Corporis Fabrica* [On the Construction (or Fabric) of the Human Body]. This was the first anatomy text based greatly on detailed dissection of cadavers. In it, he argues that many of the texts of the Roman anatomist Galen of Pergamon (c. 131–c. 216 C.E.) were wrong. For more than 1000 years,

Galen's work, based on Hippocrates's theory of the four humors (see later) formed the cornerstone of medical knowledge in the Christian West, and medical training was based largely on textual interpretation and apprenticeship (Siraisi, 1990). Galen's comments on the human body were in fact based on the body of a Barbary ape. But as the text was the important thing, not observations, medical professors before Vesalius seldom did their own dissections of cadavers and so this had not been noticed (Cohen, 1985).

The primary problem of both of these books for the church of the time, and medieval scholarship in general, was a simple one. They were suspect because they did not agree with ancient texts from Greek, Roman or church scholars. In fact, Copernicus and Vesalius were loyal sons of the church, who loved the classical authors and did not intend to be revolutionaries. The authors that they had criticized were not even Christian, yet by this time, the works of the ancients had been melded with Christian theology, adapted and winnowed for many centuries. To disagree with them was to disagree with official church position, which became more rigid in the late 16th century in response to the Protestant threat. An *Index of Prohibited Books* was first published in 1559 and by 1616, Copernicus's work was on it. This was the weight of Bruno's heresy. By stating a hypothesis about the universe, he ran afoul of theology, political power and the very way in which knowledge about the world and God was supposed to be obtained.

René Descartes was born into such a world, but it would not be the same when he left it. At his birth, the natural world was thought to be created for humans to rule and to glean lessons from and all things in it had a purpose. At his death, Descartes and his contemporaries had envisioned the world as a machine without a purpose: nature was a little less like a conversation between God and humanity about the purpose of creation and more like a cold object to be observed. Moreover, Descartes had given the human intellect the power to know the truth about anything in the universe that could be observed, even the soul itself.

As it is one of the hallmarks of the historicist approach to history to consider what one is against, as well as what one is for, it is important to look at the nature of medieval scholarship to see why what Descartes said was really important. This discussion will also open the first great, still unsolved, discussion of psychology: the differences among mind, body and soul.

The Influence of Augustine, Aristotle and Aquinas

The three most influential philosophers and theologians of the Middle Ages in the Christian world were Aristotle (384–322 B.C.E.), Augustine (354–430 C.E.) and Thomas Aquinas (1225–1274). Aristotle was an ancient Greek, Augustine was a Christian theologian living in North Africa during the fall of the Roman Empire, and even Aquinas died over 300 years before Descartes's birth. And yet, they still formed the backbone of the curriculum in schools in Descartes's day. These facts tell you something about education in this time: It was not concerned with new knowledge, built upon observation, but old knowledge, based upon unquestioned texts.

The task of scholars in the Middle Ages had been to reconcile the teachings of two kinds of old knowledge: The Bible, as interpreted by the church fathers, of whom St. Augustine was the most influential, and the works of the classical philosophers, of whom Plato and above all, Aristotle, were considered the greatest. The man who struggled to achieve this synthesis was St. Thomas Aquinas, who did not believe that everything that Aristotle said was true (Aristotle had lived, after all, before Christ, so Aquinas could not accept him as the ultimate source of truth) but believed that his writings and particularly his logic could be used as an instrument to prove Christian principles.

Augustine of Hippo

Augustine was the Christian bishop of Hippo, North Africa, in the final, violent days of the Roman Empire, from 396 until his death in 430 C.E. In his work *Confessions*, he describes his torment of leading a sinful life before his conversion in 386. It is a remarkably personal, psychologically insightful work for the time, written in first person. Augustine had a strong sense of sin and among the greatest was that of intellectual pride, the belief that one's own intellect is all that matters. For Augustine, the purpose of investigating things, be they the nature of God or humanity or sin or the natural world, was not to understand how things work, but why they are there and what their purpose is in God's plan (Augustine, n.d./1942). He had been influenced by the Neoplatonists, late Roman followers of the earlier Greek philosopher **Plato** (c. 428–347 B.C.E.). Plato had emphasized that each individual instance of something in the real world was an imperfect representation of the perfect idea of that thing in another realm beyond the natural. He had reasoned that we must have access to these perfect concepts in order to form the notions of better and worse examples of the things that we do see in the world. If we didn't have some idea of the perfect, how would we know what "better" is? And yet we've never seen perfect directly, so it must be in another realm. These perfect **Forms** or **Ideas** are the concepts on which all our thoughts depend, but we never see them; what we see are imperfect copies. Thus when we say that a woman is beautiful, Plato would have said we mean that she partakes in the Beautiful itself—the form Beauty—to some degree. To Plato, the real world is the world of forms; our world is a world of appearances only and true knowledge cannot come from the senses alone. Thus, if we do know something of forms, it is because we had this knowledge before we were born, when our souls were acquainted with forms in the other world (Rowe in Sedley, 2003). If that is true, then our souls are immortal, like the unchanging forms themselves.

This view of a separate spiritual world was perfectly consistent with Augustine's Christian philosophy. To Augustine, the real truth exists in this realm, but fallible, sinful man cannot see it alone, by simply looking at things; we need God to illuminate that world for us. Thus our powers of reasoning are not our own, but always dependent on an outside force. If we try to figure things out by ourselves, we might be distracted by our lustful appetites or vanity into mistaking the purpose of things. The natural world is set before us as a coded message from God, not a set of objects with their own existence, but a set of symbols to be read. All of God's creation, as it comes from God, is good by definition, and our task is to find out why each piece is good, using the gift of rational thought that makes us most like God (Augustine, n.d./1942).

This view had the effect of making people in the early Middle Ages incurious about natural causes and effects in several ways. First, if your only real appeal to causes is God, everything is "explained." Why did it rain? Because God wished it. Why did it stop raining? Because God wished it. Second, Augustine believed that the laws of nature are conditional upon the will of God. Today we are accustomed to think about the world as being governed by predictable laws that run without outside intervention. Thus, when we see something that does not appear to follow a law we know, it is a thing to be explained. Gregor Mendel, in the 19th century, took the appearance of unusual yellow wrinkled peas, instead of smooth green ones, as an opportunity to figure out the laws of inheritance. For Augustine, such an oddity would have been something to marvel at as an act of God. It may even be a miracle. Finally, Augustine believed that natural events have messages for us. If all things are good, even disasters have benefits for us. The trials and tribulations of natural disasters or sicknesses might be seen as punishments or a refiner's fire burning away the impurities of our soul. Everything exists for human use and instruction. For example, Augustine's answer to the question of why there were seven planets (known at that time) was to remind us of the seven cardinal virtues (Augustine, n.d./1942).

Aristotle: "The Philosopher"

Aristotle was born into a wealthy family in Macedonia, the son of the physician to the court of Macedon. He left to study with the great philosopher Plato at his school, the Academy, in Athens, at age 17. There he stayed for 20 years as Plato's star pupil and colleague. He then left, disappointed, when Plato, on his deathbed, designated a nephew as his successor. Aristotle then spent about five years traveling in Asia Minor, researching biology and natural history (see Chapter 4). He was then called to be tutor to the young Alexander of Macedon, later to be called Alexander the Great. When Alexander's father was assassinated in 336 B.C.E., Alexander had no further use for his teacher, so Aristotle returned to Athens to form his own school, the Lyceum. In his 40 years there, he created over 170 works ranging in themes from politics to rhetoric, to ethics, to the nature of the soul (Cooper in Sedley, 2003).

Much of the work of Aristotle had been lost to the West after the fall of the Roman Empire. Following the birth of Islam in the 7th century, however, the Muslims conquered Syria and Asia Minor and found there much of what had been lost. When they conquered Spain in the 11th century, they brought the rest of Aristotle's thought with them. Further contact during the Crusades increased the transfer of information. Thus, while Aristotle preceded Augustine by over a thousand years, his influence on medieval philosophy came afterwards. Once he was rediscovered, however, he became the authority. Aquinas simply called him "The Philosopher."

The Greeks did not have the same reluctance as the early Christians did to rely on their own power of reason alone. They tended, however, to reason about not how things worked, but what they really were and their ultimate purpose. Aristotle asked two very simple questions: What were things in the world? and What caused them to be that way? As to the first question, he was concerned with the definition and the category to which things belong. What is the essential thing we mean when we talk about the definition of "man," "animal," or "rock," and what was nonessential, variable or accidental? Aristotle had said that there were four causes to all things. Formal cause (or essence), material cause, efficient cause and final cause.

An **essence** of something is a collection of attributes that are necessary to its existence or its membership in a particular kind. Thus, for example, the ability to understand language may be essential to the definition of a human being, but the ability to understand Chinese or even the ability to understand spoken language may be an accident, for Chinese needs to be taught and deaf persons can still understand language. One of the most important expressions of the essence of something is its **form** or the pattern or structure that it has, irrespective of an individual instance of it. The form of a statue is not the bronze of which it is made, but the person who it represents; the form of a house is not the bricks and mortar but the ideas represented by the blueprint; the essence of a bird is not the characteristics of a particular bird in your backyard, but those aspects of its structure which make it a bird and not something else (e.g. has feathers, lays eggs, etc.). Thus, the **formal cause** of something is like its definition, its abstract idea. To Aristotle, this definition is not a human one, but one that exists in nature itself. Forms cannot exist alone; they must be made of something. Thus every thing has substance, it has a **material cause**. For Aristotle, there are four base matters or **elements**: earth, fire, water and air, of which all earthly things are ultimately made. (The heavens, earth-centered and fastened to solid heavenly spheres, are made of a pure, indestructible matter known as the quintessence, for "fifth essence.") Of course, all things need to be made by something: the form must be applied to the matter by a maker, which is the **efficient cause** of something, the carpenter for the table, the parent to the child. And as it is the case that everything that is an efficient cause for something else itself has its own efficient cause; thus, there is a cause for everything. Finally, there is the purpose for which a thing is made, its **final cause**. Nature never makes anything that is haphazard or superfluous. It is elegant in its reasons: indeed Aristotle speaks of Reason as the starting point, alike in works of art and nature (Shute, 1964).

Everything in Aristotle's world has an internal goal—as an animal grows, it is pushed by the final cause through the efficient cause to become its ultimate form. Paradoxically, everything strives to be what it already is. An animal is motivated by appetite to eat, to convert that which it is not into itself. It is motivated to reproduce to produce another of its kind, to add another instance of the form to the world. Even falling rocks have goals. They are driven by their internal nature to fall to earth. Aristotle had no concept of gravity, so something with the power of movement needed an impulse inside to give it a shove.

You will notice that we have not yet talked about any mechanisms of how these things happen. There is really no *how* in Aristotle. Although he was marvelously inventive and curious, observant of nature and a wonderful classifier (see Chapter 4), he is mostly concerned with defining those things that exist absolutely and independently from those that depend on other things for their existence or merely appear to exist. Following the methods described in his work, the *Organon* [Tool], he orders and classifies these things using various forms of **deductive logic**. Deductive logic uses the method of **syllogisms**, which involves two premises that lead to conclusions that are necessarily true if the premises are true. Here are two valid conclusions by syllogism:

All mammals are animals	All men are mortal
All men are mammals	Socrates is a man
Therefore, all men are animals.	Therefore, Socrates is mortal.

The first kind of inference concerns classification of sets and the second involves coming to a necessary conclusion about an individual, but both types of conclusion rest on the definition of the words man, mammal and animal rather than on collecting data.

These definitions of man are themselves definitions of what a man is, what is essential. If you need a cause of movement, you simply include it in the definition of what it is. To take another analogy, modern genes can sometimes seem positively Aristotelian: Why do the genes that we have make us human? Because we have human genes that drive us to become human. Aristotle would stop there, but we really want to know the mechanics of the process: how the DNA chemicals instruct the body to make other chemicals and then organs and then a body. If something goes wrong, we do not describe it as simply accidental, something not essential to man and let it go at that. We assume that there is a mechanical explanation.

In Aristotle's *De Anima* [On the Soul], he describes the soul as the power that animates all living beings, but not life itself. The soul is the formal and the final cause of the body. It is like the shape of a brass ball, the cutting power of the axe or the seeing power of the eye. It is also efficient, because it causes change, but it must live in a material, so the body is needed (Hicks, 1965). It doesn't exist like a pilot, separate from and inside the body, but is inseparable from it. Indeed, there are three aspects of soul to Aristotle. First, the nutritive or **vegetative soul** includes the faculties of nutrition, reproduction, growth and decay. Plants only have this kind of soul. Animals, in addition, have the **sensitive soul**, which includes the powers of sensation, appetite, movement and some memory and the ability to form images. Animals, however, have no real power of reflection or choice. Their appetites drive them forward, their senses allow them to find their goals to eat or reproduce and that is all. In this, Aristotle's sensitive soul is very like our concept of instinct. Finally, only humans have the **intellective soul**, which has the power to reflect, to compare and to decide for or against our various appetites. It is the power to think.

What does it think about? Other animals may sense an apple and eat it; only we can conceive of the form of the apple, the concept. We learn of this concept through our senses. Each sense organ has its own particular sensation—indeed, the purpose of the eye, its final cause, is to see. In addition, there are things that we can know by **common sense**, things that one can sense with several senses, such as shape, magnitude, unity and number, motion, rest and time. When we sense an apple, obviously the apple isn't transferred into our body, but according to Aristotle, its form is. There, the material of our body literally takes the form of the apple (because a form can't exist without material cause). Then our intellect contemplates the forms. Thus, our mind is a form that contemplates forms. It is an insubstantial thing that contemplates concepts. The purpose of the intellect is to preserve us and allow us to seek our ultimate good.

Aristotle's contributions to Western thought are so great that they cannot be contained in just one chapter. We shall see in the next section how his thought is virtually woven into the Catholic medieval worldview, but as Greek and Latin were the languages of scholarship all over Europe for several centuries, natural philosophers of the day also had access to his work independently. This means that many areas of modern science and philosophy had to begin by arguing against him. In this book, this means that we will meet him again in Chapter 3, where Francis Bacon sets inductive logic against the deductive logic originated by Aristotle. In the same chapter, Robert Boyle must take on Aristotle to construct the beginnings of modern chemistry. In Chapter 4, Aristotle's taxonomy of animals, the unchanging "scale of nature" must fall to make room for evolution, and even in the 20th century, the work of an Aristotelian scholar, Franz Brentano, becomes the foundation stones of what would become Gestalt psychology (Chapter 6). Thus, Aristotle is not only The Philosopher but The Man to Be Reckoned With.

Thomas Aquinas and Scholasticism

When Aquinas, in the 13th century, tried to understand the world, he had three sources from which he drew: the Scriptures, Augustine and the other church fathers, and Aristotle. In some cases, he could merely graft Christian notions onto Aristotle: The ultimate final cause is our unity with the ultimate good or God. The ultimate efficient cause is God, who made everything. The form of God is perfection, and because from perfection the only way to go is down, God is unchanging. Where Aristotle disagrees with Augustine or the Scriptures, Aristotle loses. For example, Aquinas was adamant that there is only one soul, which is largely the intellective soul. Aristotle was unclear about whether the intellective soul could be separated from the body; Aquinas agrees with him that the soul and body are united in life, but not in death. (Interestingly, though, he uses Aristotle as support for the necessity of a bodily resurrection in the Second Coming—a form is incomplete without material.)

For our purposes, there are two things to remember about Aquinas's way of thinking that later caused Descartes and his contemporaries trouble. First, he argued solely from texts, not from experience or sensation. In *Summa Theologica*, his major work, his reasons for why his fellow contemporary philosophers were wrong were that they had misinterpreted Augustine or Aristotle, neglected a passage or misdefined a word (Aquinas, n.d./1964). In matters of theology, this is not an issue: even medieval philosophers recognized that the existence of God or the soul could not be proven or disproven by sense experience. In matters of the natural world, however, this is a critical problem, for it causes people to ignore their experience. There is a story about two philosophers arguing over how many teeth a horse has based on Aristotle or other ancient authorities. An apprentice philosopher suggests, reasonably enough, that they should simply go out, find a horse and count its teeth. He is roundly chided for his ignorance! The philosophers may have wondered what to do if they had found two horses with different numbers of teeth. They might have to redefine horse or wonder to what degree teeth are essential to the form of Horse or accidental to that particular horse, added on by other forces.

As in law at the appellate courts, much of the discussion was about definitions of words, not facts. Thus, for example, one philosopher argued that nothing must be something, because the Bible said that God created the world "out of nothing." Every noun must correspond to a thing, so "nothing" must simply be undifferentiated "something." This type of philosophy, which focuses entirely on texts out of historical context and without examining whether the texts correspond to the world, was called **scholasticism** and was the primary form of argument until the 1600s.

The second reason Aquinas caused problems for future scientists was that by accepting Aristotle into church reasoning, he made disagreeing with Aristotle about the workings of the natural world the same as disagreeing with the church. When Galileo discovered a new star with his telescope, he called into question Aristotle's claims that the universe was unchanging. When he discovered moons around Jupiter, he called into question Aristotle's idea that planets were affixed to permanent spheres. When he discovered sunspots, he contradicted the idea that the planets were "unblemished orbs." Before these things happened and increased Galileo's fame considerably, astronomers were free to entertain Copernicus's work as a hypothesis. These data, however, made it possible to take the hypothesis seriously. Galileo was called to Rome in 1616 to explain himself; days later, Copernicus's work was banned "until corrected." Galileo struggled mightily to walk the very thin line of being a devout Catholic and scientist and failed. His discussion of Copernicus, ingeniously couched as a simple party conversation by disagreeing friends, was banned, and Galileo, though personal friends with the pope himself, was committed to house arrest (Sobel, 1999).

Before Descartes, then, the natural universe had meaning and purpose. Augustine had conceived of it as a dialogue between God and Humanity. Aristotle confirmed that everything had its purpose in the universe. It was taken for granted that we were subservient to that plan. To say that Descartes himself upset all that would be going too far. He was at a historical moment in which the orthodoxy was breaking down under the rise of humanism in the Renaissance. Vesalius and William Harvey were exploring the body; Copernicus, Brahe, Galileo and Kepler were exploring the heavens. And as we shall see, certain aspects of the older philosophy survived even in Descartes's work.

René Descartes (1596–1650)

Descartes's Quietly Radical Life

> I will say nothing of philosophy except that it has been studied for many centuries by the most outstanding minds without having produced anything which is not in dispute and consequently doubtful and uncertain. I did not have enough presumption to hope to succeed better than the others; and when I noticed how many different opinions learned men may hold on the same subject, despite the fact that no more than one of them can ever be right, I resolved to consider almost as false any opinion which was merely plausible.
>
> —René Descartes (1637/1960, p. 8)

René Descartes was born on March 31, 1596, La Haye, Touraine, France. His family was not of the nobility, but of the wealthy landed middle class. His grandfather had been a doctor and his father was a lawyer and provincial parliamentarian. His mother died when Descartes was a year old, on the birth of a brother. Descartes was not told of the newborn and was somehow led to believe that he was the cause of his mother's death. He was raised largely by his maternal grandmother, tutors and family servants until about the age of 10, when he was sent to the Jesuit school at La Flèche, where he spent the next eight years.

The Jesuit order was founded to be the elite of the Catholic Church, kind of soldiers of the Counter-Reformation, charged with holding the line against Protestant heresy by gaining the hearts and minds of the educated middle and upper classes. But within the boundaries of doctrine, the Jesuits of La Flèche provided an excellent education in the usual subjects of Latin, Greek and French, history and ethics. In addition, there were rigorous courses in logic, physics, metaphysics and philosophy and some of the best training in mathematics to be had in Europe. All of this was taught in an atmosphere that might be described as egalitarian yet stoic discipline, leavened by fierce weekly philosophical debates. The student body was surprisingly diverse for the time, including some boys from the poorer walks of life as well as the gentry, but excessive pride was discouraged. Descartes commented that from this diversity, he learned more about people than he did by traveling. In later life, he showed his gratitude by furthering the mathematics study of a cobbler and a servant (Ariew, 1992).

Every boy, regardless of class, was expected to adhere to a rigid daily schedule. Descartes did benefit from one privilege, however, that the other boys were not accorded. He was allowed, for his health, to stay in bed until late morning, covered in quilts, but with windows wide open as a preventative against tuberculosis. This was a habit he kept up all his life, for it was in this state that he claimed his best ideas came to him in meditation.

But what, exactly, was he taught? We know the curriculum, for when the Jesuits set up their schools in 1586 they said, "In logic, natural philosophy, ethics and metaphysics, Aristotle's doctrine is to be followed" (Ariew, 1992, p. 64) ("natural philosophy" included all of what we would call the sciences). They were in fact very explicit about it:

> Let no one teach or defend anything opposed detracting or unfavorable to the faith, either in philosophy or theology. Let no one defend anything against the axioms received by the philosophers, such as: there are only four kinds of causes; there are only four elements; . . . fire is hot and dry; air is humid and hot.

The Jesuits also specified that God was all-powerful and all-knowing (following Augustine) and (following Aquinas) that the soul was the intellective soul and was immortal, that there were not three souls. Angels do exist as separate beings. The professors were not to teach anything other than "that these texts are established and defined. This is not just an admonition, but a teaching we impose" (Ariew, 1992, p. 65).

Descartes claimed later, in his famous *Discourse on Method*, that he had discarded much that he had learned at La Flèche. As the quote above suggests, he believed that the philosophy of his day was prone to error; he thought that the ethics of the Greeks and Romans were "superb and magnificent palaces built on mud and sand." He believed that history tended to be skewed to give a glorious portrayal of heroes and that the talent for beautiful poetry, fiction and eloquence could not really be taught. He spared only mathematics from his withering criticism. If these criticisms were written as a teenager, we might discount them as the naïve objections of adolescence. But he published these criticisms when he was past 40, after worldly travel and much thought.

In between, he had studied law (which he never practiced) and witnessed, as a less than enthusiastic soldier, several battles of the Thirty Years' War between Catholic and Protestant forces. All the while, he continued studying mathematics. At La Flèche, he had loved mathematics, which for him at the time contained arithmetic, geometry, music, astronomy and mechanics, with some engineering. Math, to Descartes, was the only thing that led to certain truth. He began applying it to everything. In school, he had noticed that in order to understand many of the books he read on the subject, he had only to look at the diagrams and a few sentences to understand the book; he could skip all the tendentious scholastic arguments that so plagued him in other subjects. He noticed that, if one followed a geometric proof closely, by the end of it, one is completely, intuitively, convinced of its findings. The knowledge of this truth is *clear and distinct*. The beauty of Euclid captivated his mind like no other subject.

Even as a young man, he had begun applying the geometrical method to all proofs, to see if he could figure out for himself whether it was true. Most of knowledge consisted of a collection of opinions of others, he later noted, who argued incessantly. Real, elegant knowledge most often was constructed by the labors of one man tackling a problem, not by committee or authority; if one is after real truth, he decided, works by a single hand were more perfect.

While still a soldier, he was stationed in Germany in 1618 when he noticed a placard or poster that contained a certain mathematical problem. (Interestingly, at the time, it was common to print up posters with intellectual problems on them and plaster them up for people to think about; Gaukroger, 1995.) As it was written in Flemish, he asked a Dutchman named Isaac Beekman next to him to translate it into Latin. Descartes struck up an intense friendship with him, because he was excited to find someone else who thought that physics should be explained mathematically, rather than in terms of stones that fall to earth because of their internal motivations. In addition, Beekman was a medical doctor and engineer. Together, they began to solve problems involving the movement and weight of water, the relationship between lengths of strings and music, problems of falling bodies and related abstract problems in geometry. Beekman had taught Descartes that mathematics had not only a pure beauty, but also application in understanding the world (Gaukroger, 1995)!

In 1619, while traveling through Europe on campaigns and billeted with the army in rough weather, Descartes made two electrifying discoveries. First, in March, he wrote to Beekman that in a feverish six days of work, he had discovered a new universal mathematics that unites geometry and arithmetic. It was a powerful new kind of notation that determines the relationship between curves and algebraic equations. Today, we recognize this achievement by teaching algebra through the use of an (x, y) coordinate system that bears his name: the **Cartesian coordinate system** (see Figure 2.2).

Descartes had by now rejected much of Aristotelian philosophy and he had seen the spectacular fruits of doing so. It must have seemed to him, having achieved a wonderful clarity in unifying two branches of mathematics, that he might be on the verge of the answer to knowledge itself. He was at a point of mental exhaustion. He experienced a moment of intense joy. He went to sleep on the dreary night of November 10, 1619, next to a warm stove and had several feverish dreams that contained the words *Quod vitae sectabor iter?* (What road shall I follow?). He awoke and wrote that he had found the "foundations of a marvelous science."

What he had discovered was not a particular science, but a method whereby he claimed one could finally know what was certain. Using the logic of his beloved geometry, pursued with intense reflection, he proposed an epistemology that would discover the very axioms of knowledge. **Epistemology** is the branch of philosophy that deals with the question of how we can know things. How do we know that the world is like it is? How does the external world get into our minds and how does it change in getting there? This discovery told him what he was to do in his life. He sold the title to the family lands so that he could live off the proceeds. He began to work on his philosophy, carefully working out his principles and applying them to other discoveries in mathematics and optics. He moved first to Paris and then, when he found the social and perhaps the religious life there annoying, moved to the Netherlands, where he lived in near seclusion, spending his mornings thinking in bed (Gaukroger, 1995).

DISCOURSE ON METHOD AND MEDITATIONS

It is now time to consider Descartes's most important insights. The most important principle that makes science possible and philosophy possible, for that matter, is the principle that human reason matters. We can, through our own intellectual efforts,

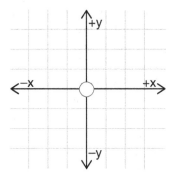

Figure 2.2 By use of the Cartesian coordinate system, algebraic equations can be plotted geometrically, thus uniting geometry and algebra into analytic geometry. This was Descartes's "marvelous science."

without dependence on outside authority, discover the truth. But, says Descartes, much of what we think we know we received from those authorities. We must first set aside all that we think we know and prove to ourselves that we know it. This is Descartes's **method of radical doubt**. Although people had of course doubted before Descartes, seldom had they dared to doubt everything as a matter of principle. Moreover, never had they doubted, so to speak, without a net. Augustine had doubted, but he prayed to God to catch him in his errors. Even Descartes didn't really doubt that the world existed, but he needed to tear down everything so that he could rebuild from the bottom up. He wanted to discover the basic assumptions or axioms, so that he could pose theorems to prove. Nobody proves that "parallel lines never meet." Once you know the definition (and you are in the world of Euclidian geometry, as opposed to other geometries), it is self-evidently obvious. Your **intuition** tells you that it is a **clear and distinct idea**. His method is to doubt his knowledge about the world, himself and even God until he found something that was just as clear as a geometric axiom. How he arrived at this axiom and the consequences of how he arrived at it are important for the future of psychology, so we will now take some time to describe the classic argument. (Be patient; all will be revealed!)

So, starts Descartes, what can I know to exist? Can I trust that the things in the world exist, those things that I experience through the senses? Well, the things that I perceive sure seem vivid, so perhaps they are true. Looking at a triangle seems like more of a rich experience than imagining one in my mind's eye, and looking requires less effort. It is certainly a more clear and distinct experience than trying to imagine a thousand-sided figure, which I can only think about, not imagine as a picture.

But sensation is fallible. It cannot tell me what something really is, because, for example, a piece of beeswax which was gray, solid to the touch and slightly sweet smelling from the honey becomes clear, liquid and not sweet when melted. To use another, classic example that was mentioned by Augustine even 1000 years before Descartes, if you dip an oar in the water it looks bent.

Even more radically, sometimes our dreams are so vivid we think they are actually happening. As a former soldier, he was aware that people who survived amputation sometimes felt the limb, even though it was no longer there. Therefore, it is true that the experience of sensation is not a direct link to the forms in the world, as Aristotle thought, but is at least partly due to ourselves, our nerves and our fallible bodies. Therefore, says Descartes, we cannot be sure that anything in the world exists as we experience it (at least at this point in the argument).

Can I even trust in the reality of myself? Well, I know about my bodily self by sensing it, so I may not be right about that either. In fact, I cannot even be sure that anything I think is true, because, God, if he so chose, could beset me with lying demons so that my inner world corresponded in no way to the real world. Descartes was even prepared to assume (for the moment and only for the sake of argument) that God did not exist and he might be just plain crazy.

But even if that were true, says Descartes, and even if everything I was thinking about were essentially nonsense, *at least I would know I was thinking*. No argument could possibly convince me that it was not true, because even as I considered the argument, I would still be thinking. Furthermore, if thinking is going on, something must be doing it and that something has to be me. *Voila*! I have just proved I exist! "I must finally conclude and maintain that this proposition *I am, I exist*, is necessarily true every time I pronounce it or conceive it in my mind" (Descartes, 1637/1960, p. 82). Although the original Meditations are in French, later Latin summaries, as well as generations of philosophy students, have memorized this conclusion as *Cogito, ergo sum*. I think, therefore I am. This famous proof is therefore called "the *cogito* proof."

Let us stop for a moment and reconsider what Descartes has said here. First, sensation is fallible. Second, sensation is probably in the body. Third, I came to these conclusions with my own powers of reason. And fourth, I have come to an incontrovertible position that that which I call "I" is that which does the reasoning. This philosophy, in which all conclusions are reached by the power of reason, rather than authority and in which reason is always needed as a corrective for sensation, is called **rationalism**.

If you want to justify that reason is superior to sensation, says Descartes, consider that reason is what makes sense make sense. Yes, the oar in the water appears to bend, but we can feel that it is continuous, and if we take it out, it becomes whole again. Our reason can tell us that the melted wax came from the solid wax because it occurred over time and we can reverse the process if we want. We do not know these things just because we sense them, but because we compare the results of our sensations and come to conclusions. We *understand* them. (Remember, Descartes starts by dividing experience into sensation, imagination and understanding—understanding becomes the most real thing!)

Beginning with Descartes, the psychological problem of sensation and perception becomes an interesting problem to be solved. Our sense organs give us certain data (sensation), and something higher than the sense organs helps us to understand that data (perception). To understand how new this was, consider that to Aristotle, it would have made no sense to distinguish between something being really red and something merely being red to someone with excellent eyesight under certain lighting conditions (Gaukroger, 1995). In contrast to Aristotle, Descartes believed that there were several kinds of experiences that can ultimately be trusted and others that could not. Those of the first kind are uncovered (or dis-covered, so to speak) through reason and include size, shape, location, movement, substance, duration and number. These are called **primary qualities** by philosophers and the most important is substance or existence, because all of the others are technically properties of substances and don't exist in the abstract. Other sense experiences that can't really be trusted are artifacts of a particular sense organ: light, color, sound, odor, taste, heat, cold, touch. Philosophers call these **secondary qualities** because of their changeable nature. We might say that an apple is green, but the greenness isn't in the apple alone, but in our ability to perceive it. Is an apple still green at dusk? At midnight? Not really, if our sensation and not our conclusions is all we go by.

The reason Descartes supplied for believing in the truth of the *cogito* proof, as well as the reality of the primary qualities, is that such insights are, to him, **clear and distinct**, as are the results of mathematical proofs. His reason has lifted the fog, and his conclusions seem right and perfect. But how could he, an imperfect being, know of perfection? Exactly. As we've seen above, Plato suggested perfection was in another world; Augustine identified that world as heaven. Aquinas (among others) defined perfection to be the primary attribute of God. From the idea of perfection, Descartes can get himself out of a corner. If all he knows is that he exists, how can he proceed to build a science about the world outside? In this (slightly fishy) way: God could deceive him if He wished, but deception implies that God lacks something in the moral department, which is of course, imperfect, which He cannot be by definition. Thus, God presents Descartes with an ability to reason figure out the world, because he is Perfect and Good. (By the way, Descartes also throws in an old argument from the 11th century that it's imperfect for God not to exist.)

These beautiful, clear and distinct ideas can't come from fallible sense experiences; they can't come from one's fallible parents; they must be taken from the other world and implanted by God when the soul itself is made, before birth, bypassing sensation entirely. They are **innate ideas**. How do we know they are innate, from God? Because they are clear and distinct. How do we know they are clear and distinct? By reason and intuition. Where do these come from? God. You can be forgiven if you are confused by this disappointing piece of scholasticism. Descartes's critics, from his time to this very day, were also not convinced. It will come back in the next chapter.

Now, if you've been paying attention, you will notice that primary qualities are what Aristotle called common sensibles or what were perceived by common sense. Another thing you might have noticed is that in rationalism, the intellective soul—that thing which doubts, understands, conceives, affirms, denies, wills and rejects—is more powerful than the sensitive soul, an idea which you might think would make Aquinas happy. The proofs of God come straight out of earlier scholastic arguments. Such comparisons with Aristotle and commonalities with the church's view of the soul would've been obvious to Descartes's readers at the time, but not perhaps to you until just now, which is why the chapter is constructed this way, to get you to think like an original reader of Descartes, as much as is possible. Indeed, that is part of Descartes's genius. He found a way to appear to have proved, entirely by his own reason, things about the world (and theology) with which his readers would have already been familiar from ancient texts and to add new things as well. He was a man of his time. In spite of his intention to reconstruct from scratch, he ended up reconstructing the world in which he lived.

CARTESIAN DUALISM: THE MIND-BODY SEPARATION

But what is the intellective soul? What is "I"? (Or, what am I?) Or, as Descartes thinks, if I am that which thinks, what is that exactly? It exists, so it has substance, but how big is it? For that matter, where is it?

To see why the answer to this question might be strange, close your eyes, stop up your ears and consider what it would feel like to have no external or internal bodily sensations. If someone moved you, would you then know where you are? Would it really feel like you're in your brain? (People before Descartes's time generally believed that the seat of the soul was in the heart, until the pioneering English physician William Harvey [1578–1657] proved it to be a mere pump.) The philosopher Daniel Dennett, in a more modern twist, considered what it would be like to be a brain in a life-sustaining vat connected in every way to a very sophisticated robot with perfect replication of human sensory and motor capabilities (Dennett, 1981). He concluded that you would believe yourself to be where the robot is, where your senses are. If the connection were broken between body and brain, you wouldn't perceive yourself to be a brain in a vat, but a thinking thing with no discernable boundaries at all.

This is exactly what Descartes decides. The soul/mind is a thing that thinks, but it does not extend in space: it has no size or shape. Although it inhabits the body, it is not the body. The mind/soul is disembodied and separate. But if the mind/soul has no bodily substance, how can it push a heavy body around and where do soul and body meet? The philosophical position that the mind and the body are in some way separate is known as **dualism**, and as we shall see in later chapters, there are many types of dualism. This view that the mind and soul are the same, that they are unextended substance and that they are separate from the body, is called **Cartesian dualism or "substance" dualism**.

Dualism of one sort or another has caused psychology no end of trouble, and it is still causing it. It has also been a concept of enormous creativity. As its name implies, it suggests a separation of some sort between mind and body, but as we are now discussing the 17th century, we must concern ourselves with a third entity, the soul. Descartes did not distinguish between the mind and the soul. The mind/soul consisted of the power to reflect on and choose from our sensations. He also appears to have thought that some individual memory and sense of self, that which makes an individual an individual, were contained in the soul and survived after death. These are the things which are the responsibility of the "I"—the thing which thinks—in the *cogito* proof. In keeping with the theology of his time, he also believed that the soul was indestructible, whereas the body was not. He believed that in spite of their ability to perceive, imagine and remember enough to live in the world, animals did not have souls, because they could not reflect and decide. (Interestingly, one of the functions of humans that Descartes ascribes to the soul is language, which animals also do not have; see the later discussion of Chomsky.) They were, instead, slaves to their passions. The rest of the functions of the mind he ascribed to the body (Gaukroger, 1995). What we know of the world through sensation, perception and imagination are special modes of consciousness that depend on the body and do not survive its death (Cottingham, 1992).

This view is a bit confusing to someone of our time. Fortunately, Descartes left us with a list of the things that could go on without a soul:

> digestion of food, beating of the heart and arteries, the nourishment and growth of the limbs, respiration, waking and sleeping, the reception by the external sense organs of light, sounds, smells, tastes, heat and other such qualities, the imprinting of ideas of these qualities in the organ of "common" sense and the imagination, the retention or stamping of these ideas in the memory, the internal movement of the appetites and passions and finally, the external movements of all limbs which aptly follow both the actions and objects presented to the senses and also the passions and impressions found in the memory.
>
> (Descartes, quoted in Cottingham, 1992, p. 246)

For simplicity's sake, you can note that these are all functions of Aristotle's vegetative and sensitive souls. Descartes placed these things in the brain, which he also considered to be the "principal seat" of the soul, placed there (but taking up no space!) by God.

How does the soul talk to the body? Here, Descartes (and practically everybody else since him) was a bit stumped. He hypothesized that the transmission occurred through the pineal gland, a gland in the center of the brain, the only part of the brain that appeared to him not to be copied in the two hemispheres.

Before going on to consider what Descartes thinks of the body, let's stop a moment to consider how intertwined are our own views are of body, mind and soul. Consider, for the sake of argument, a person operating in a psychotic state of mind, let's say a schizophrenic, who commits a violent act, such as pushing someone onto the tracks in front of an oncoming train. These days, we rule out demonic possession (although if you consider the *cogito* proof, Descartes did not, at first), an entirely external and supernatural cause. We also know that these psychotic states depend on biological underpinnings. We know, for example, that psychotic states can be affected by actions on the body, such as the use of certain medications, and that there are heritable predispositions towards schizophrenia. If we examine the thought processes of a schizophrenic in the throes of the psychosis, we see a number of aspects of disordered thinking. If the schizophrenic imagined the person to be someone else or to be doing something that they manifestly were not, then that is disordered perception or imagination. The impaired decision-making is a fault of the intellect, and the inability to refrain from acting on that decision is a fault of will or volition. Descartes assigned perception and imagination to the body and intellect and volition to the soul. Are we today willing to do this? Perhaps we would like to instead assign all of these qualities (perception, imagination, intellect and volition) to something we call mind, leaving the soul alone. If we do that, what is left for the soul to do? What, for that matter, is left for the body to do? Who is then responsible for the act? If a person commits an immoral act when intellect is impaired, is his or her immortal soul thereby damaged? Can the soul be said to have a disease that originates in the body?

Removing the soul from the equation, as modern psychologists typically do, does not usually help much if the mind is left in, because you are still left with the problem of how much the attributes of the body affect the exercise of the will; if the answer is "a lot," then who or what is responsible?

Legal tests of culpability focus on whether the mind/body knew right from wrong, and since there is usually only one mind to a customer (except on certain episodes of TV legal fiction that consider multiple personality disorder), the judge is at least addressing the question to the right person. If your question, however, is whether it was the mind or the body or in what proportion, you still have a problem of philosophy or science, whatever the legal or moral decision. Finally, you could get rid of mind *and* soul and say that all is body, all is mechanism and chemicals, but then no one is responsible.

You may protest that this sounds a bit like the scholastic arguments described above, that it is philosophy and theology and not science or psychology. It revolves around definitions rather than facts or at least replicable results of experiments. And you would be right. But, if you wish to be a psychologist or to study the history of psychology, you still cannot avoid the questions raised first by Descartes. Debates about whether psychology should be the study of mind, for example, or whether it should instead be the study only of external behavior, are chapters, so to speak, in a book started by Descartes. Questions about whether we would be satisfied with a psychology that examined only the actions of the brain or whether such a thing is even possible are based on the ramifications of dualism.

By separating the soul/mind from the body, however, and localizing it in the brain, Descartes did a useful thing for medicine and psychology. He provided the logic to allow the body to be studied as the rest of the physical world was beginning to be studied by scientists like Galileo. The body is now no longer "ensouled," as Aristotle and Aquinas had said, but merely a dead piece of matter, like a machine. It can therefore be studied like a machine.

In discussing how the body works, Descartes first examines why God would make us in such a way that our senses were fallible. For example, it would seem that for the man to still perceive the foot after it has been amputated, as is common in phantom limbs, it would contradict the view that God does not deceive us. If the body is merely a machine, however, the same processes should be operating when it is broken as when it is well. The following famous passage describes Descartes's reasoning:

> A clock, composed of wheels and counterweights, is no less exactly obeying all of the laws of nature when it is badly made and does not mark the time correctly than when it completely fulfills the intention of its maker; so also, the human body may be considered a machine, so built and composed of bones, nerves, muscles, blood and skin, that even if there were no mind in it, it would not cease to move in all the ways that it does at present when it is not moved under the direction of the will, nor consequently with the aid of the mind, but only by the condition of its organs.
>
> (Descartes, 1637/1960, p. 132)

The nerves in the leg of the wounded man are still doing what they are supposed to do: warning him of pain, sending signals about the world. Although God might tamper with an ensouled body, He doesn't tamper with machines, so he can't change the rules of how the body works, any more than we can make a malfunctioning clock keep good time by magic. We would have to work on its inanimate gears. Under normal conditions, as God made it originally, however, the machine is a very good thing indeed; it helps us to survive and to avoid danger. He is not deceiving us, the machine is. To treat the body like a machine means that it is easier to consider the "how" as well as the "why" and "what" of the body. The body works according to established, discoverable laws. If we did not believe that it did so, if the rules could change at any time, then medical science would be pointless.

THE PASSIONS OF THE SOUL

> For the rest, the true use of our reason in the conduct of life consists only in examining and considering without passion the value of all perfections, those of the body as much as those of the mind, that can be acquired by our conduct.... And since those of the

> body are the lesser [perfections], one can say generally that there is a way to make oneself happy without them. All the same, I am not of the opinion that we need to despise them entirely, nor even that we ought to free ourselves from having the passions. It suffices that we render them subject to reason and when we have thus tamed them they are sometimes the more useful the more they tend to excess.
> —Descartes (1645, in Shapiro, 2007, p. 109)

So, for Descartes the mind/soul is something that thinks, decides and wills, but takes up no space, but the body does extend in space and is separate from and in communication with the lawful, machine-like body. What about emotions? Where are they? Do they reside in the animal body or the heavenly soul?

Descartes took up this question late in life, first in a series of letters to a close friend, an intelligent but melancholic princess, and then in his final work, the *Passions of the Soul*. Princess Elisabeth had read most of Descartes work and turned to the man who had labored to discover how to regulate the mind to lead to truth. Now she wanted advice on how the emotions affected the body and the soul.

The answer to this question emphasizes the problems with the dualism that Descartes set up. Emotions obviously begin in the body, for we see the things that bring us happiness or touch the things that give us pain. Moreover, emotions are experienced in the body as blushing, the racing of the heart and so on. But they are also experienced by the mind/soul. Sadness may be seen by expressions and tears, but the grief or pity that excites it comes from the soul. Furthermore, Descartes believed there are passions of the soul alone, such as intellectual joy or joy in contemplation of God.

He deals with the problem in *The Passions of the Soul* (1649/1988) by first discussing in some detail the way he thinks the body works. He reminds his readers of the insights of William Harvey concerning the heart and the circulatory system. The blood flows in a circular fashion from the body to the heart and is pumped out to the body. It is essentially a pneumatic system, a pressurized system of fluid. Descartes borrows this view for his conceptions of nerves and muscles. A "subtle wind" called animal spirits is sent from the cavities in the brain down the tubes of the nerves. These spirits add to the spirits already in the arm and also open gates that allow the spirits in the arm to flow from one side to the other. Descartes points out the way that the muscles usually oppose one another, for example, as when the arm is bent, one muscle becomes longer and the other shorter. When it relaxes, the system reverses. All of this is excited by the heat of the heart; bodily functions that do not depend on our will, like breathing and digestion, are maintained by the heart alone. And indeed, disturbances from sensations outside the body or inside the body use the same nerves to transmit excitations in the spirits. But the seat of the soul is the pineal gland in the brain, which is bathed in the animal spirits. The excitation brought on by the body is transmitted to the soul because the spirits cause the gland to tilt this way and that. The system can also work the other way: we of course can make our bodies move at will and our soul/mind can remind us how to react to certain sensory stimuli.

In fear, for example, our soul/mind recognizes the object of our fear of, say, a ferocious lion, based on past experience. It immediately sends animal spirits down the nerves to open the pores of the muscles to run. It also sends them to the heart, which pumps blood to the appropriate places, but also produces more spirits that maintain fear. This is why it takes a while for us to calm down after fear or anger, because we cannot just decide to make the surplus go away. This pounding of the heart is what made the ancients feel that the soul was in the heart, but it is not, says Descartes. Our will, which comes from the soul, is therefore often in conflict with the emotions. We may want to strike someone with whom we are angry, but our will prevents us. If we are lucky, we can fortify our will by reminding ourselves of past experience, such as knowledge of the possible consequences of our actions. The animal spirits of the body are pushing the pineal gland one way and the power of the soul and our reminding is pushing it the other. Thus, those with weak souls are "swayed," so to speak, by their passions.

But Descartes believed there is no soul so weak that it cannot obtain mastery over the passions. The key here is habit. A hunting dog, he says, has no soul, but we can still train it to run to the partridge when we shoot and not to eat the partridge until we get there. The passions are generally good and have their purposes and therefore are not themselves to be feared. The natural use of the bodily part of passions is to incite the soul to action. Love, for example, allows us to seek out and associate ourselves with good things. But some passions, such as desire, need to be controlled, for they can overtake us. Descartes sees fear as a desire to flee, for example, and we require the power of will to help us stand our ground. If we give in to desires, we are like animals being taken in by bait. Reason and experience are our defenses against the passions. They help us to know the true good to turn our desires towards, to follow the path of virtue and generosity.

Descartes thus believed in a dichotomy between the will and emotions that corresponded to his dichotomy between the mind/soul and the body. With practice, the mind can have mastery over the emotions.

A Presentist vs. Historicist View of the Cartesian Paradigm Shift

We can now evaluate, in summary, the influence of Descartes's work on the development of modern scientific thought in general and psychology in particular. This is a presentist statement, of course, as it involves weighting certain aspects of Descartes's writing in the context of today's knowledge and perhaps gives him a bit more credit than he deserves. But many of the following developments are traditionally credited to him.

- He made significant advances in the development of mathematics.
- He used these developments to describe the mechanical laws of the physical world.
- He used his own rational thought to question ancient authority and reach his own deductive conclusions.
- He separated sensation from perception and made sensation fallible.
- He encouraged us to think of the mind as separate from the body.
- He was among the first to suggest that the body was a machine, extending the mechanical laws of the physical world to the biological world.
- He emphasized the dichotomy and even the struggle between "cold" cognition and "hot" emotion.

And yet, he was a man of his time. Now that we know of his struggle with both the ideas and the temporal power of the church and Aristotelianism, a historicist analysis can tell us that he felt compelled to offer proofs of God in his work in terms that others could understand. He also tried hard not to deviate from a view of the soul that they could accept. He felt the need to preserve the link between God, the world and humanity through the imposition of innate ideas. Each of these things would be called to question in the following centuries (and in the next chapter), along with the strict separation between the intellect of humans and animals (see Chapter 4).

Did Descartes's innovations constitute a scientific revolution, a paradigm shift? Even before he had published his *Meditations*, some were calling him "the Atlas and Archimedes of this century" (Vrooman, 1970, p. 150). At the Dutch University of Utrecht, there was a pitched battle over Descartes's "mechanical philosophy" that spread to others. Pro- and anti-Cartesian pamphlets were printed. Shortly after his death, the Inquisition put his philosophical works on the Index of Prohibited Books, where they remained until the 20th century, largely because of his view of a soulless body in a Copernican universe. (Descartes had in fact refrained from publishing several works once he learned that Galileo was under house arrest). In the next century, a false story was circulated that Descartes had made a mechanical doll in the form of his illegitimate daughter that he kept with him always and used to prove that we are machines that have no souls (not his position, as we have seen). Textbooks on mathematics were almost immediately influenced by his work on algebra. T.H. Huxley, friend to Darwin, wrote in 1874 that Descartes "did for the physiology of motion and sensation that which Harvey had done for the circulation of the blood and opened up that road to the mechanical theory of these processes." Sir Charles Sherrington, Nobelist researcher in the theory of neurons, wrote in 1946 that

> machines have so multiplied and developed about us that we may miss in part the seventeenth-century force of the word in this connection. By it, Descartes said more than perhaps any other one word he could have said, more that was revolutionary for biology in his time and fraught with change that came to stay.
> (Both quotes cited in Cohen, 1985, p. 158)

The Influence of Descartes Today in Psychology

It is one of the measures of true fame that 350 years after Descartes's death, people are still invoking his name. The ramifications of his thought will permeate the rest of this book in subtle ways, and we'll meet different attempts to deal with dualism, emotion and reason along the way. This section gives just a few provocative examples.

Sometimes, theorists still praise Descartes. As recently as 1966, Noam Chomsky, the linguist most responsible for the innateness hypothesis in language acquisition that led to a revolution in psycholinguistics (the psychology of language), wrote a book called *Cartesian Linguistics*. In it, he praised Descartes for recognizing that one of the prime things that humans can do that no other animals can do is use language in flexible, novel ways to respond to many situations. He recognized, for example, that parrots could make word-like sounds, but that their use of these sounds was more rigid than that of the least intelligent human. Although Chomsky does not invoke God to explain it, some have suggested that his innate "language acquisition device," which allows all humans to learn languages from birth, is the ultimate innate idea. And finally, Chomsky is a true rationalist: Although he did not know how the brain produces language and did not address how the brain might have evolved to produce it, he simply deduced that an innate mechanism must exist by looking at the beautiful, logical structures of many languages.

More often, however, people invoke the name of Descartes only to criticize him, and what they criticize him for most is dualism. Neurophysiologists might be expected to criticize him on this score, because it is their job to study the body side of the equation, and they find the idea of a disembodied mind that controls the body intolerable. Indeed, brain researcher Antonio Damasio, in his book *Descartes's Error* (1994), suggests that keeping the body separate from the mind leads us to underestimate the ways in which illness in the body can cause mental illness and vice versa. More specifically, Damasio takes Descartes to task for separating the bodily emotions from the soulful intellect. He describes a brain-injury patient who lacks most ability to feel emotion. At first glance, the patient, called Elliot, seemed normal. His memory, intellectual functioning, knowledge of social and moral rules and ability to generate the consequences of hypothetical actions were fine, and yet this sophisticated businessman could not complete tasks without getting distracted or decide in his real life what to do next. He had lost all his money in suspect schemes invested in at the urging of others. Descartes was concerned with an excess of emotion interfering with the pure, calm light of reason and indeed constructed his own life to avoid such emotional extremes. Elliot, by contrast, was a man who had too little emotion to place bets on the most pleasant or least painful courses of action and thus either took too long to decide or let events decide for him. Most of us would quickly feel emotion pangs in considering the worst alternatives in our lives and quickly rule them out rather than continuing to consider them with cool equanimity. Damasio concludes from his case that Descartes was wrong: will and rationality, emotion and thought cooperate rather than conflict.

Finally, (for now) we consider the criticisms of philosopher and cognitive scientist Daniel Dennett (cognitive science is a new interdisciplinary field that includes neurophysiology, philosophy of mind, linguistics, cognitive psychology, anthropology and computer science). Dennett, in his book *Consciousness Explained* (1991), calls the standard view of how our mind works the "Cartesian Theatre." In this view, the "I" of "I think, therefore I am" is king. Let's say a person views an apple. The light and dark areas of the apple are transmitted by reflected light to the eye, which converts the light energy to chemical energy (sensation). A bunch of other processes lead to perception of the apple as it travels through the nervous system (recognition, naming) until we find "ourselves" "looking" at the "apple" in our "mind's eye" and saying "That's an apple." In the Cartesian theatre, the idea of "apple" is sitting on a stage, where the spotlight of attention shines on it so that "I" can "look" at it. It's what it means to think about something, to turn our conscious mind to it. Indeed, for Descartes all thought is conscious.

Dennett claims this is all wrong. There is abundant physiological and psychological evidence that a huge amount of work is being done before we are aware of it in consciousness. Take, for example, the "cocktail party" phenomenon. You are at a noisy party, struggling to listen to a conversation and are succeeding. You are conscious of nothing specific outside of the conversation. Someone says your name across the room and you turn your head immediately. How could you hear your name if you weren't listening? "You" weren't listening, but your brain was, so you heard and analyzed it before you were conscious of it.

Dennett further states that your nervous system is taking in rough drafts of what is happening all the time, adding bits on the next half-second pass through time, and there is no time or central place in the brain where each given experience is all done. There is no stage for the Cartesian theatre. The very sense of yourself is an illusion (he calls it the "user illusion."). I am always thinking so therefore I never quite am.

We owe to Descartes ultimately the view of the mind as a disembodied source of cool reason that makes sense of fallible sensation. Passions are apart from it, and the whisper of unconscious thought is silent. The body is dull matter and the soul is immortal. That people are still taking the trouble to argue against this view testifies to its power.

3 Empiricism, Its Legacies and Limitations

Precursors and Definitions

At about the same time as Descartes was working out his rationalist philosophy in France, across the Channel in England reaction against the scholasticism of the Middle Ages was taking a different turn. Whereas Descartes trusted the deductive logic of mathematics over the fallible nature of sensation, Francis Bacon (1561–1626) considered that before we can logically deduce something about a concept, we must know how we came to form it in the first place. As we have seen, Aristotle, and even more so his followers in the Middle Ages, frequently confused the name, the concept or the definition with the particular thing to be studied. Aristotle even believed that the concept was in the world itself, as well as in our minds. But what lies underneath that concept? How do we get from all the individual dogs we know to the concept of dog? The answer is, we take many experiences of similar things (what they look and sound like, how they act, where they are found) and generalize certain things across these individual instances and assign them a common name. The view that all knowledge comes ultimately from experience is called **empiricism**. Experience itself comes first from what is gathered about the world from our senses. Empiricism can be considered an epistemology, because it asks the question, "How does the world out there get into our minds?" and answers, "The basic material of our minds must be from sensations; knowledge comes from our understanding of that sensory experience." When considered beyond the contents of individual minds, empiricism may also be considered a scientific *methodology*. In this sense, the question is rephrased, "What are acceptable data *for science*?" and the empiricist would answer, "The basic data for science should be collected by observation; *scientific* knowledge comes from the judicious analysis of and ultimate replication of those observations." In this chapter, we will largely concern ourselves with the roots of **epistemological empiricism**. Much of the rest of the history of psychology, to be discussed in all of the succeeding chapters, consists of differing points of view on the practice of (and value of) **methodological empiricism**. In this chapter, we will see how Sir Francis Bacon and his successors, the famously named British Empiricists John Locke, George Berkeley and David Hume, addressed the ramifications of basing knowledge on experience.

Francis Bacon and the Inductive Method

> There are and can be only two ways of searching into and discovering truth. The one flies from the senses and particulars to the most general axioms and from these principles, the truth of which it takes for settled and immovable, proceeds to judgment and to the discovery of middle axioms. And this way is now in fashion. The other derives axioms from the senses and particulars, rising by a gradual and unbroken ascent, so that it arrives at the most general axioms last of all. This is the true way, but as yet untried.
>
> —Sir Francis Bacon (1620, Aphorism 19)

Francis Bacon was born into one of the most tumultuous and creative times in English history. He grew up as a member of the royal household under the reign of Elisabeth I, daughter of Henry VIII and the last monarch of the House of Tudor. He served in Parliament and became Lord Chancellor to King James I (who commissioned the famous King James Bible), before being prohibited from serving in government upon receiving a bribe. A tremendous amount of controversy, speculation

Figure 3.1 Francis Bacon (1561–1626)

Source: After an engraving (1738) by Jacobus Houbraken (1698–1780)

and innuendo surrounds historical accounts of his life. Just for fun, here is some of it (everything here is roundly disputed): Not only was he an exact contemporary and admitted fan of Shakespeare's, but many have suspected that Bacon actually wrote his plays. Why did he need an actor and playwright as a "front man?" Because he was supposedly a secret son of Elisabeth's (who was known as the "Virgin Queen") and thus a rightful prince, he is reported to have been a spy and an expert cryptographer and a member of secret societies, who left coded messages all over his (and Shakespeare's) work.

Bacon's great work on philosophy of knowledge and science, the *Novum Organum* (the name means "New Tool" in Latin) (1620), was a repudiation of Aristotle in its very name, as Aristotle's book on logic had been called the *Organum* in Latin (*Organon*, in the original Greek), implying a tool for proper thinking. Aristotle's medieval scholastic followers, as we have seen, were very concerned with definitions and the deductions that could be made from them. Deductive logic is about applying general definitions to particular instances. To take a trivial example, one could reason that (1) all fish have fins; (2) guppies are fish, therefore (3) all guppies have fins. Bacon would have asked the reasonable question, which was not commonly asked at the time: How do we know that all fish have fins and would a fish without fins be a fish? The answer is that it is part of the definition. But how about replacing number 1 with "All dogs are brown" and number 2 with "Fred is a dog," therefore Fred is brown. It may not really be true that all dogs are brown. And yet, said Bacon, many of the philosophers of his day essentially proceeded anyway. They looked at too few examples in the actual world, made a general statement of "fact," then proceeded to build a complex philosophy on it and never looked back. They presumed the truth of the improper generalization as a premise in the next argument and went on to deductively prove the next thing. The proposals got encoded in reference books, and people got in the habit of determining what the authors said before they looked themselves at the actual object (like those who wanted to determine how many teeth a horse has from an authority, discussed in the preceding chapter).

Instead, Bacon proposed that before making a categorical statement, one should collect as many instances as one can of a phenomenon. Before we make a generalization about what is essential to that statement or try to explain the phenomenon, said Bacon, we should explicitly try to get around our bias and look for counterexamples. Bacon describes a man who was looking at a picture commemorating the survivors of a shipping accident. The man noted that all of the survivors had prayed before the trip and suggested that that was why they survived. "What about those who had prayed and went to the bottom anyway?" asked a wise old man in response. This method of reasoning, by collecting many particular examples, looking at what they have in common, comparing them with counterexamples and only then coming up with a general conclusion is called inductive logic. Each conclusion is based on a collection of evidence from the world. Deductive logic means applying a general principle to individual instances, and inductive logic is concerned with collecting and evaluating individual instances to make a generalization.

Bacon thought that inductive logic was better because the world was more marvelous and complicated than humans could imagine. Who would deduce that a marvelous thread could come from a worm, as silk does, if he had not seen it?

Science was, for Bacon, not about idle speculation and argument, but about endowing human life with inventions and riches. The clockmakers knew more about science than the philosophers, because they actually worked with the principles day in and day out. He thought that governments should support the mechanical arts and experimentation. Because the conclusions formed from observation and experiment are tentative, we would make lots of mistakes, but even the mistakes are sometimes useful. He cited the work of the alchemists, who were obsessed with turning other substances into gold. They never found gold, but they discovered chemistry in the process, like the man who lied to his sons about having buried gold in the vineyard. They never found gold, but they sure plowed the field well looking for it!

Finally, Bacon realized that induction, unlike deduction in mathematics, never really reached irrefutable conclusions. If our knowledge comes from observation and we can never see everything, then our knowledge is limited. Helpfully, he made a list of "idols" or false gods that we follow because of our psychological limitations:

Idols of the Tribe: There are limitations common to all humans because of the way we are made. We believe what our senses tell us is true, but our senses are fallible and this is true for everyone.

Idols of the Cave: Each individual person has his or her own experiences that others do not have, through different education, habit or accident. Thus, it is difficult to get beyond our own perspectives.

Idols of the Marketplace: Everyone gets some ideas about the world from others. We are limited in our perspective by language, culture and the assumptions and prejudices of our own social group.

Idols of the Theater: By theater, Bacon is referring to the sort of illusions that philosophers and professors put up for us to believe that are not based in experience, but on received authority. They teach us the wrong way to think.

Mucking about in laboratories (called dabbling in *empirics*), conducting chemical experiments or building clocks was among Bacon's peers considered to be a rather low and common activity compared to the ethereal arguments of theologians (remember that even Descartes did most of his thinking in bed!). But this is what Francis Bacon advocated. Our perceptions and conclusions are so provisional, so limited by our failings, that philosophical reasoning without correction by data is bound to lead to error. And Bacon was so convinced he was right, he even died as the indirect result of an experiment. He was interested in the influence of cold on preserving meat, so he had bought some cleaned chickens and went out in the cold and stuffed their internal cavities with snow. He caught pneumonia and died, but he was pleased, before his death, to know that his experiment had worked. In his life, he had broken new ground that was tilled and planted by later generations of philosophers and, later, psychologists. Some of the basic foundations of epistemological empiricism that he pioneered were the following:

- He believed that sensations provided the raw material for knowledge.
- He believed that people acquired knowledge through induction before deduction.

- He recognized that knowledge based on experience was by its very nature limited and provisional. It is very unlikely that our view of the world is completely accurate in all respects, because of biases in human thought.

In addition, to a modern reader, it appears that he anticipated many aspects of modern science, the basis of methodological empiricism—the reliance on experiment and observation, the faith that scientific investigation leads to practical results, the belief that some results may or may not be replicated and so on. He even foreshadowed the inductivists' philosophy of science, discussed in Chapter 1. He believed that the facts led to the laws, the axioms, the discoveries and the inventions of science:

> Our course and method, however, as we have often said and again repeat, is such as not to deduce effects from effects, nor experiments from experiments..., but in our capacity of legitimate interpreters of nature, to deduce causes and axioms from effects and experiments; and new effects and experiments from those causes and axioms.
>
> (*Novum Organum*, Aphorism 117)

John Locke (1632–1704)

Life and Times, Religion and Politics: A Historicist View

John Locke was born in 1632, at a time of great strife in English society between establishment Anglican and the Calvinist Puritan forces. He was the son of a lawyer in the landed gentry class and a Puritan. Like Francis Bacon, Locke was a man of the world as well as a scholar, who brought his great life experience to the development of his philosophy. He was, at various times in his life, a diplomat, a college professor, a children's tutor, a physician and a political refugee. As a member of the newly founded Royal Society of London for the Advancement of Experimental Knowledge (whose motto is *nullius in verba*: "rely on the mere words of no one"), he was well acquainted with pioneering chemist Robert Boyle. He wrote an influential medical text with the great English physician Thomas Sydenham and wrote one of the first reviews of his friend Isaac Newton's astonishing physics landmark, the *Principia Mathematica*. In spite of the turbulent religious battles of his times from the beginning of the English civil wars in 1642 to the "Glorious Revolution" of 1688, he advocated religious toleration as well as the primary importance of reason. His political philosophies provided a virtual blueprint for Jefferson and Madison in the construction of the American republic. His empiricist epistemology forms the core of Anglo-American philosophy, a core that was solidly in place as the core of psychology for more than 200 years. Even today, the ghost of Locke is present in branches of psychology as diverse as cognitive science and behaviorism. As we did with Descartes, however, before we look forward, we must look briefly back and around the life of Locke to situate his thought in its time.

Even as a young man, Locke was not inclined to take the Aristotelian teachings common in his day at face value. In 1652, he gained a scholarship to Oxford through a combination of intelligence and political connections and remained as a student and professor there for 15 years. But he was not by any means a complacent student. One of his contemporaries described him as "A man of turbulent sprit, clamorous and discontented. While the rest of our club took notes deferentially from the mouth of the master, the said Locke scorned to do, but was ever prating and troublesome." Later in life he was described as a calm and disciplined man, but beneath that exterior was a searching intellect (Axtell, 1968; Cranston, 1957).

Locke's Influences

As a young professor, in 1660 Locke entered into a significant friendship with an aristocratic scientist named Robert Boyle (1626–1691), sometimes called the father of chemistry. Boyle was frustrated by the remnants of both Aristotle and alchemy in chemistry. The old way of chemistry was to suggest that all substances were composed of different proportions of all of the four elements: earth, water, fire and air. The first three of these were represented in the physical world as salt, mercury and sulfur, respectively, and all substances were thought to be composed of all of these and air in different proportions, with no other substances and no fewer than all of them. Sulfur was said, for example, to contribute toughness, odor and flammability to substances. Why? Because, of course, it had an abundance of "sulfurous (i.e. fire) principle." This sounds knowledgeable, but makes no sense at all, because there is no way to measure sulfurous principle. "How do we know a substance has sulfurous principle?" you may ask. "Why because it is flammable, of course," answers the alchemist. "Why is something flammable?" you inquire further. "Because it is full of sulfurous principle." "Can we measure, experience or sense sulfurous principle?" "No, it is an essence, a formal rather than material cause and has no substance per se." "Can you show me how you concluded it was there?" "Well, I have had much experience with it, but perhaps after you apprentice to me awhile, you will become adept in the art of separating out and transforming the sulfurous principle to useful ends, but these are dangerous secrets for the novice."

Boyle ridiculed this kind of logic in his book, *The Sceptical Chymist*. He had read Bacon and Descartes. Like Bacon, he was an ardent experimentalist: He carefully described his chemical and physical experiments and extolled their virtues, frequently taking care to control for extraneous variables. In addition, he wished to take Descartes's mechanical hypothesis to the extreme in chemistry: All things are reducible to matter and motion. There are no mystical "occult" or hidden properties in substances. Boyle proposed instead a **corpuscular philosophy of matter**. All matter, said Boyle, is composed of different arrangements of tiny, microscopic particles called corpuscles, all made of the same stuff. (Boyle's talented lab assistant, Robert Hooke (1635–1703), had made the first English microscope and wrote a best-seller on what he saw with it, so Boyle was well aware of the world of the miniscule.)

No matter how small, all bits of substances consist of the same properties that we can sense when they are larger. These bits have bulk, shape and motion or rest as their only qualities. The differing structures of large collections of these corpuscles would, it was hoped, explain the many different observable properties of substances. Changes in these substances through chemical reactions would involve a simple mechanical rearrangement of these particles and their collision with each other. No

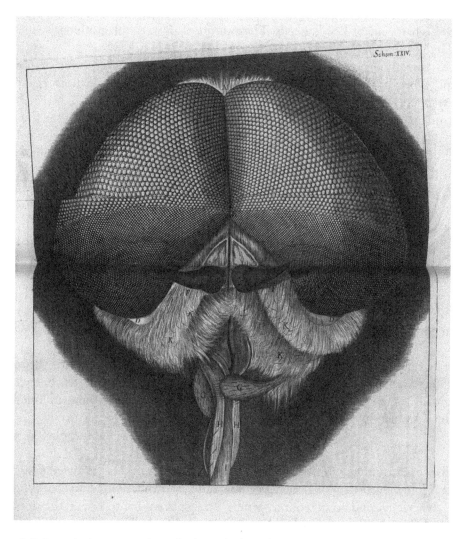

Figure 3.2 A meticulous engraving of a dronefly done from a microscope from Robert Hooke's *Micrographia* (1665)

Source: See more images from this book on the British library website: www.bl.uk/collection-items/micrographia-by-robert-hooke-1665

new matter is formed when glass is made out of sand and ash; the corpuscles have simply been rearranged. We might perceive and classify many substances as containing many properties, but that is simply because of the way the different things act upon our senses, not because we can know they actually contain "sulfurous properties" (Alexander, 1985; Hall, 1966).

Boyle put forth a brilliantly simple example to make his point. A locksmith makes a lock of iron and a key of iron. The locksmith changes the form of the same material, iron, to make each thing. We might later say that a key has "the power to open the lock" or define the key as "something that opens a lock," but all the key and lock differ in is in the size and shape of iron; the "power" is in the definition, not in the object itself. The locksmith who knows the exact dimensions of the lock knows exactly what kind of key it needs. The notion of power adds nothing to the lock and key.

We sense things, said Boyle, not because the color red is a power or form in an apple, but because corpuscles of light bounce off an apple, whose corpuscles are arranged in such a texture as to produce a pattern among the light corpuscles returning to our eye. These excite the physical properties of the eye to see the color red (Alexander, 1985). Isaac Newton (1642–1727), a younger friend to both Boyle and Locke, used the corpuscularian theory of matter as the starting point for his investigations into the nature of light and optics (Westfall, 1980, p. 171). In Locke's review of Newton's masterwork on gravity and the laws of motion, the *Principia Mathematica*, he called Newton one of the "master builders" of the "commonwealth of learning" (Axtell, 1968).

Thus, by the 1670s Locke was steeped in the chemical and physical science of his day. In addition, he was greatly influenced in his medical training by his friend and mentor Thomas Sydenham (1624–1689), the foremost English physician of his day, who was an early devotee of observation in medicine. Sydenham published detailed case histories in the hopes they would lead to more accurate diagnoses and treatment when compared with other patients. He said,

> The function of the physician [is the] industrious investigation of the history of diseases and the effect of remedies, as shown by the only true teacher, experience ... True practice consists in the observation of nature: these are finer than any speculations.
>
> (quoted in Cranston, 1957, p. 92)

All of these influences came together in Locke's theory of knowledge and the mind: He believed that all knowledge was built up from elementary corpuscles of sense experience and arranged into general concepts, so that to Locke, the mind was very like Boyle's conception of the world. In such a view, there is no need for innate ideas, but without them, there is no way of knowing that our knowledge is certainly true; how a group of individuals, with different experiences, come to agree on anything, becomes a more difficult problem. We will discuss these points next.

An Essay Concerning Human Understanding

> Thus the first capacity of human intellect is,—that the mind is fitted to receive the impressions made on it, either through the senses by outward objects or by its own objects when it reflects on them. This is the first step a man makes towards the discovery of anything and the groundwork whereon to build all those notions which ever he shall have in this world. All these sublime thoughts which tower above the clouds and reach as high as heaven itself, take rise and footing here; in all that great extent wherein the mind wanders, in those remote speculations it may seem to be elevated with, it stirs not one jot beyond those ideas which sense or reflection have offered for its contemplation.
>
> —John Locke (1690/1959, Book II, p. 142)

In Locke's time, there were two views of the way the mind related to the world. The Aristotelians thought that we simply perceived the forms that were in the world with our intellective souls. The Cartesians thought that our senses were fallible, but that God saved the connection between us and the world by providing innate ideas that upon reflection are found to be clear and distinct. Locke wanted to have a mind that reflected the scientific world of his friends in the Royal Society. Just as the world is composed of bits of matter and only bits of matter, the mind should be composed of bits of a person's experience and only bits of that individual experience.

It took Locke 20 years to set down this philosophy in print, and he did it by making four points. First, he had to demolish the idea of innate ideas, so that the only thing left to build upon was experience. Second, he had to explain just what kinds of bits of experience we had and how they combined into concepts. Third, he had to explain how because each of us has different experience, our ultimate knowledge is limited. Fourth, he had to explain how we could still talk to each other and believe that anything is true.

Mind Without Innate Ideas

The first part was relatively easy. If we all had innate ideas and the same ones given by God, said Locke, why don't we agree on more things? Why don't children know them immediately? If, as Descartes seemed to imply, you could only know about clear and distinct innate ideas when you were old enough to figure them out, how could we know by then that they were innate and not learned? And anyway, clearness and distinctness or obviousness is no guarantee that something is innate, because aren't some things that we learn, once we learn them, immediately agreed to as obvious? And if we don't know them immediately, but they're still there, how is it possible to know and never to have known something at the same time?

No, said Locke, the view of innate ideas makes no sense, because they cannot be sensed. They sound suspiciously like some mental "sulfurous principle," lurking there unconsciously,[1] unverifiably and conveniently available to seem to "explain" something by giving it a name. Descartes said we need innate ideas because we have ideas that we have not experienced, like infinity, eternity, perfection or God. Locke suggests that, for example, the definition of infinity is based in the easily understandable action of counting, something at bottom experienced by everyone; infinity is simply "counting so high that you can't comprehend the end."

Given all of this confusion about innate ideas, Locke thought it much more honest to simply assume that everyone begins life with a **tabula rasa**—a blank slate or clean sheet of paper with no ideas on it. In this view, one does not need innate ideas to explain what we know. Knowledge comes entirely from our own experience, with no corrective intervention by God. Psychologists have often assumed that Locke meant that humans are therefore born without innate tendencies or differences of any sort, so everything we are comes from the environment and nothing from inheritance. This was *not* Locke's position, as we will see when we look at his ideas on education. Innate ideas are unnecessary and unobservable, but any good empiricist can easily observe temperamental tendencies present early in life.

Qualities vs. Ideas of Sense Experience

So, what makes up our knowledge, if we have no reassurance from innate ideas? Locke says we can get information into our minds in only two ways, first from **sensation**, by looking out at the world, and second, from **reflection**, by looking into the contents of our minds.

Essentially, sensation is the term we give to the process of looking outward with all of our five senses upon the world. What we see, hear, taste, feel or smell out there is not the world itself, but the interaction of the world on those senses—the light bouncing off the corpuscles in the apple to give the experience red, for example. For clarity's sake, Locke offers two definitions to keep the world separate from our minds. He calls the things in an object that *produce* a sensation in us **qualities** and the things that they produce, the actual contents of the mind, **ideas**. Qualities are assumed, but cannot be known; all we know are ideas. Locke assumes that there are two types of qualities that influence our sensation: primary qualities and secondary qualities.

We have met this distinction before, in the last chapter, but Locke puts a particular spin on them. Primary qualities are those qualities that an object has whether we perceive them or not. Taking inspiration from Boyle's theory of chemistry, Locke reasons that even if we divide an object a zillion times into its tiny uniform pieces, it still must logically have four properties: It must have some kind of shape, it must have some kind of solidity (in that two things can't occupy the same space), it must have some kind of size and it must be moving or at rest. It can't exist as a thing in the world without these things, even if a person can't know for sure what they are. All of the other experiences we have are presumably produced by the action, configuration and texture of the conglomeration of the primary qualities of tiny corpuscles (Locke, 1690/1959).

Secondary qualities are the qualities that produce experiences that are partly dependent on our sensory apparatus. Colors, sounds, tastes, etc. are in this category. These do not really exist in the world as such, but only in interaction with us. A good example is the notion of heat from a fire. If we stand a short distance away, we experience heat as warmth. If we really get close, it hurts. In both cases, said Locke, in a surprisingly accurate explanation, these sensations are explained by the vigorous bouncing around of corpuscles, but the experiences themselves of warmth or pain are in us. If I stick you with a pin, is the pain transferred from the pin to us? Of course not—the pin isn't in pain, nor is the pain in the pin, we are in pain and the pain is in us!

Finally, let me include the most famous experiment of this principle attributed to Locke. It is called the "Three Basins Problem." Take three bowls of water: hot, lukewarm and cold. Stick your right hand in the hot water and your left in the cold. When you take out the hand from the hot and put it into the warm, it will seem cool by comparison. If you take the cold hand and put it into the warm, it will feel hot. Therefore, the ideas of cold, warm and hot must be in us, not in the water.

Ideas as Corpuscles

Locke proposed that the primary and secondary qualities in the world produced ideas in us, but since our minds are filled with so many of them, of such varying natures, he didn't assume that every one of them had a quality to go with them. Rather, he thought that ideas entered the mind simple and unmixed, in the sense that they are of "uniform appearance or conception." He called these **simple ideas**. These ideas cannot be distinguished into simpler ideas and the mind cannot make new ones or destroy them. The mind can, however, repeat them, compare them and unite them. Primary qualities produce simple ideas through several senses, and these are the familiar shape, solidity, size and motion. Simple ideas associated with secondary qualities are generally from one sense, such as the ideas of colors, noises, sounds, tones, heat, cold. We do not have names for all of them. In fact, it is a most important point that, although we must talk about these ideas using words, the ideas come before we have general concepts and the words associated with them. These are the elementary bits, or corpuscles, of perception; grouping them and naming them happens with experience over time and according to habit and custom. For example, each experience of any kind of blue we can distinguish one from the other is a separate simple idea. That we decide to call them all "blue" is another matter.

We have been discussing simple ideas of sensation. There are two **simple ideas of reflection**, or what happens when we turn our senses inward on our mind and look at the ideas of sensation. Simple ideas of reflection are acts rather than things. These are the momentary acts of thinking and willing.

Thinking or perception (Locke uses the terms interchangeably), although a single thing, has three purposes. First, it recognizes ideas. Bare naked perception of a sensation is passive, automatic and can't be ignored, but it requires a kind of recognition:

> A sufficient impulse there may be on the organ; but it not reaching the observation of the mind, there follows no perception: and though the motion that uses to produce the idea of the sound be made in the ear, yet no sound is heard.
> (Locke, 1690/1959, p. 142)

Second, when one hears a word, thinking connects it to its underlying ideas, so that you may understand it. Third, it recognizes whether an incoming basic idea belongs with or is different from another idea.

If simple ideas of sensation come together in experience often enough and we take note of them by some kind of recognition, they are grouped together into **complex ideas**. By analogy, simple ideas are to atoms what complex ideas are to compounds. It is habit that makes a complex idea, but it does it so easily that we think that some ideas are simple when they are actually complex. Locke describes a thought experiment of a discovery of Adam.

> One of Adam's children, roving in the mountains, lights on a glittering substance which pleases his eye. Home he carries it to Adam, who, upon consideration of it, finds it to be hard, to have a bright yellow color and an exceeding great weight. These, perhaps, at first, are all the qualities he takes notice in it; and abstracting this complex idea, consisting of a substance having that peculiar bright yellowness and a weight very great in proportion to its bulk, he gives the name *zahab*, to denominate and mark all substances that have these sensible qualities in them.
> Book III, chapter vi, paragraph 46 (Locke, 1690/1959, vol. 2, p. 95)

Locke takes care to say that people of his day would assume that this *zahab*, which we might call "gold," would have a certain inner essence. But that is not so. The word is different from the concept, because the concept, the complex idea, is simply a collection of simple sensory ideas that can be expanded. Further experience with gold could add more ideas to the definition, for example that it is easily pounded down without breaking (pounding, breaking and malleability being complex ideas in themselves) and everyone's experience is a bit different.

Never confuse the word with the idea, because people's ideas can change and become different from one another, hindering understanding. Thus, my "gold" may be different from your "gold." I may have had more experience with it in many different ways than you. (Here, Locke deals with Bacon's "idols of the cave.") The adequacy of our concepts and the ideas we use to talk about them are based upon whether repeated experiences produce constant effects each time I see gold and when you see gold and the common experiences between us allow us to communicate. But our definitions are never finished. In Locke's empiricism, ideas always come before the word, so the word and the ideas may not match.

Some complex ideas are really just convenient groups of simple ideas not connected in nature but in the customs of a culture (here are Bacon's "idols of the marketplace"). Thus, for example, Germans may talk about *schadenfreude* or the French about *esprit*, *élan* or *je ne se quois*. Terms about feelings like these are easily confusable and hard to translate, noted Locke, and their meanings may change over time. We can understand them somewhat if we can unpack them into definitions that contain words that denote ideas more closely related to common experience, *schadenfreude* being "the sweet, yet guilty pleasure we feel when something bad happens to people we do not like." Locke believed that language is meant to quickly convey ideas when my words are converted by you into your ideas. Understanding fails when we use words inconsistently, without agreement among ourselves. Thus, Locke (experienced as he was in the art of diplomacy and political and religious disagreement of his time) was a stickler for definition.

There are complex ideas of reflection, too, called **modes of perception**. Most of these consist of definitions of familiar cognitive abilities. If one applies will to an idea in mind, for example, that is attention. Sometimes we do not apply enough will and the idea fades from the mind. If the idea reappears to us unbidden, from the "storehouse of ideas," that is remembrance; if we have to apply will and effort in voluntary memory, that is recollection. Contemplation (memory held long), study, judging and reasoning are all modes of perception. The process of reflection is applied to ideas of sensation to combine them, abstract generalizations from them, compare them and make relations among them (to judge, for example, whether one idea is greener than another).

In summary, to Locke, knowledge is obtained in the following way. The physical world conveys stimuli to our senses that are converted into ideas, which may or may not match the world itself. The ideas are grouped, based on repeated experiences, into more complex ideas, that may not quite match other people's complex ideas. We utter arbitrary sounds to denote these ideas by words and attempt to communicate. We may then, using these words, attempt to evaluate whether we agree with the statement "All men use tools," or "All dogs are brown." Even if we are persuaded that a statement is true, we might ultimately be wrong, because our experience, everyone's experience, is limited. Locke differs from the rationalists like Descartes not in the value of reason—as we shall see, he valued reason highly. But he insisted that that experience comes *before* reasoning and is checked by it. Our knowledge is ultimately uncertain.

Educational Philosophy

Of all the works of Locke, perhaps the most engaging and useful for a modern psychology student to read is *Some Thoughts Concerning Education* (1693), because it is in this book that Locke practiced what he preached. From the mid-1660s to the 1680s, Locke had served as physician and children's tutor to Exeter House, the home of Lord Anthony Ashley Cooper, later Earl of Shaftesbury. In 1684, another friend, Edward Clarke, asked Locke for childrearing advice for his son, which he gave as long, closely reasoned letters beginning in 1684. After considerable revision, Locke fashioned the letters into a book, but the book still retains the stamp of practical advice written by an experienced teacher to a trusted friend. Locke comes across as a disciplined man, but full of kindness and reason. His advice is never given without explanation and is never doctrinaire. To Locke, a child's good character as well as bad is based firmly on experience, on what a child learns at the hands of his parents, tutors and other members of the household. (Locke wrote his advice about boys, but occasionally mentions that the same principles, with some modifications, would work for girls). Therefore, parents must carefully observe not only the behavior their children, but also of themselves.

Locke squarely states that the nature of children's characters depends on the behaviors of the parents towards them and the habits that they learn from them. If there are no innate ideas of morality, then the parents' responsibilities are great. On the one hand, parents should avoid forgiving the child's faults too readily, not because the parents should have absolute power over their children, but because such faults are far more easily fixed when children are young and have not formed entrenched habits:

> The great mistake I have observed in people's breeding their children has been, that this has not been taken care enough of in its due season; that the mind has not been made obedient to rules and pliant to reason, when at first it was most tender, most easy to be bowed. Parents being wisely ordained by nature to love their children, are very apt, if reason watch not that natural affection very warily; are apt, I say, to let it run into fondness. They love their little ones and 'tis their duty: but they often with them cherish their faults too. They must not be crossed, forsooth; they must be permitted to have their wills in all things; and they being in their infancies not capable of great vices, their parents think they may safely enough indulge their little irregularities and make themselves sport with that pretty perverseness which they think well enough becomes that innocent age.... Thus parents, by humouring and cockering them when little, corrupt the principles of nature in their children and wonder afterwards to taste the bitter waters, when they themselves have poisoned the fountain. For when

their children are grown up and these ill habits with them; when they are now too big to be dandled and their parents can no longer make use of them as play things; then they complain, that the brats are untoward and perverse; then they are offended to see them wilful and are troubled with those ill humours, which they themselves inspired and cherished in them. And then, perhaps too late, would be glad to get out those weeds which their own hands have planted and which now have taken too deep root to be easily extirpated.

(Locke 1693/1968, para. 34–35, pp. 138–139)

On the other hand, Locke was greatly concerned that parents not be too severe on children. Once again, his reasons are based entirely on what such severity would teach the children. Running throughout the book is a very modern recognition that the use of corporal punishment represents a failure of more effective forms of discipline. Moreover, it is a form of discipline that has many undesirable side effects. It encourages the child to use violence when he is older:

Before they can go, they [parents] principle them [children] with violence, revenge and cruelty. Give me a blow, that I may beat him, is a lesson which most children every day hear; and it is thought nothing, because their hands have not strength to do any mischief. But I ask, does not this corrupt their mind? Is not this the way of force and violence, that they are set in? And if they have been taught when little, to strike and hurt others by proxy and encouraged to rejoice in the harm they have brought upon them and see them suffer, are they not prepared to do it when they are strong enough to be felt themselves and can strike to some purpose.

(para. 37, pp. 140–141)

It might make the child sullen and cowardly:

if the mind be curbed and humbled too much in children; if their spirits be abased and broken much, by too strict an hand over them, they lose all their vigour and industry.... For extravagant young fellows, that have liveliness and spirit, come sometimes to be set right and so make able and great men: but dejected minds, timorous and tame and low spirits, are hardly ever to be raised and very seldom attain to any thing.

(para. 46, p. 148)

It might lead to resentment and lying and brutality:

The child submits and dissembles obedience, whilst the fear of the rod hangs over him; but when that is removed and by being out of sight, he can promise himself impunity, he gives the greater scope to his natural inclination, which by this way is not at all altered, but on the contrary heightened and increased in him; and after such restraint, breaks out usually with the more violence.

(para. 50, p. 150)

And if employed by a teacher, the resentment of the beating spreads to the tutor and the subject being learned:

> This sort of correction naturally breeds an aversion to that which it is the tutor's business to create a liking to. How obvious is it to observe, that children come to hate things liked at first, as soon as they come to be whipped or chid and teazed about them? And it is not to be wondered at in them, when grown men would not be able to be reconciled to any thing by such ways. Who is there that would not be disgusted with any innocent recreation in itself indifferent to him, if he I should with blows or ill language, be haled to it, when he had no mind?
> (para. 49, p. 149)

Locke was as wary of specific rewards or bribes for specific behaviors as he was of punishments. The trouble with both of these methods of control is that they are external motivators rather than inducements to develop a conscience. Because the tangible rewards and punishments are external, they are temporary and will not work on a child when he is old enough to have a mind of his own. What Locke wanted instead was to impress upon a child a desire to be in the overall esteem of his parents and friends and to avoid shame and disgrace. Rewards are those things that naturally accompany the esteem of the parents, rather than specific bribes. Withholding a reward is the consequence of disgrace.

> First, children (earlier perhaps than we think) are very sensible of praise and recommendation. They find a pleasure in being esteemed and valued, especially by their parents and those whom they depend on. If therefore the father caress and commend them, when they do well; show a cold and neglectful countenance to them upon doing ill; and this accompanied by a like carriage of the mother; and all others that are about them, it will in a little time make them sensible of the difference: and this, if constantly observed, I doubt not but will of itself work more than threats or blows, which lose their force, when once grown common and are of no use when shame does not attend them; and therefore are to be forborne and never to be used, but in the case hereafter-mentioned, when it is brought to extremity.
> (para. 57, p. 153)

Locke thought even application of displeasure should be judiciously calculated. Decide what faults are severe enough to deserve to show your anger, he tells his friend and seem to be angry for awhile, until the child is behaving well and has shown a small extra measure of remorse before allowing him back into your good graces. Do not give in too early to the child and do not act on your own anger unless you have thought a while and consider it just (para. 60).

Locke's comments on discipline seem so reasonable that it is worth mentioning that such views were not common at the time. When Locke himself had gone to school, children were beaten regularly by adults and by the other boys and he had thought even at the time that it made his classmates often stupid and mean. Locke did think that physical punishment could be used, but only as a last resort—only for obstinacy and rebellion, persistent disobedience maintained in the face of all other punishments and shame.

Perhaps his most extraordinarily forward-looking recommendations, though, focus on what might seem obvious today: A parent should carefully observe both the individual differences among his or her children and the age of the child and make allowances accordingly. Although Locke did not believe in innate *ideas*, he did recognize innate *tendencies*. The following quote demonstrates both allowances for age and temperament. First, Locke extols the virtues of practice over the memorization of rules. He has complained in other passages that some people give young children too many rules of behavior to remember for their age. Then when, inevitably, they forget them, they are beaten. Practice develops habits; those things that are second nature do not need to be remembered. Second, Locke says that if you watch them practice, you learn what their tempers are and can make changes accordingly. Some things cannot be changed, but only influenced. The parent or tutor must teach with careful *observation*, supplemented by *reason*, the hallmarks of the empiricist approach. I quote this paragraph (para. 66) in full, in spite of its length, because it so beautifully summarizes Locke's approach.

> But pray remember, children are not to be taught by rules, which will be always slipping out of their memories. What you think necessary for them to do, settle in them by an indispensable practice, as often as the occasion returns; and if it be possible, make occasions. This will beget habits in them, which, being once established, operate of themselves easily and naturally, without the assistance of the memory. But here let me give two cautions: 1. The one is, that you keep them to the practice of what you would have grow into a habit in them by kind words and gentle admonitions, rather as minding them of what they forget, than by harsh rebukes and chiding, as if they were wilfully guilty. 2ndly [*sic*]. Another thing you are to take care of is, not to endeavour to settle too many habits at once, lest by variety you confound them and so perfect none. When constant custom has made any one thing easy and natural to them and they practise it without reflection, you may then go on to another. This method of teaching children by a repeated practice and the same action done over and over again, under the eye and direction of the tutor, till they have got the habit of doing it well and not by relying on rules trusted to their memories; has so many advantages, which way soever we consider it, that I cannot but wonder (if ill customs could be wondered at in any thing) how it could possibly be so much neglected. I shall name one more that comes now in my way. By this method we shall see, whether what is required of him be adapted to his capacity and any way suited to the child's natural genius and constitution: for that too must be considered in a right education. We must not hope wholly to change their original tempers, nor make the gay pensive and grave; nor the melancholy sportive, without spoiling them. God has stamped certain characters upon men's minds, which, like their shapes, may perhaps be a little mended; but can hardly be totally altered and transformed into the contrary.
>
> He, therefore, that is about children, should well study their natures and aptitudes and see, by often trials, what turn they easily take and what becomes them; observe what their native stock is, how it may be improved and what it is fit

for: he should consider what they want, whether they be capable of having it wrought into them by industry and incorporated there by practice; and whether it be worth while to endeavour it. For, in many cases, all that we can do or should aim at, is, to make the best of what nature has given, to prevent the vices and faults to which such a constitution is most inclined and give it all the advantages it is capable of. Every one's natural genius should be carried as far as it could; but to attempt the putting another upon him will be but labour in vain; and what is so plastered on, will at best sit but untowardly and have always hanging to it the ungracefulness of constraint and affectation.

(pp. 158–160)

These are only some of the recommendations that Locke made that one would be wise to follow today. In other passages, he discusses how important it is for a young child to play and how important it is to gently make allowances for their attention spans and moods in teaching. Faults that are faults of youth alone, that do no one any harm and are not done out of spite or carelessness, should simply be ignored and other behaviors praised instead. He is squarely in favor of fresh air (perhaps too fresh—he wants children to dress thinly, in leaky shoes and without a hat, to get used to the cold), exercise, plain food and eight hours or more of sleep. He takes care to recommend that the child's curiosity be fostered and protected and that he be gradually exposed to the world as it is by means of a worldly but upright man of experience.

Finally, he touchingly describes how to bring a son up, finally as an equal friend. In so doing, he implies to us, the modern reader, what father-son relationships might frequently have been like in the 17th century. There are hints throughout the book that relationships between fathers and sons were often distant, strained and formal in Locke's time. As sons grow older, said Locke, treat them as friends:

And I cannot but often wonder to see fathers, who love their sons very well, yet so order the matter, by a constant stiffness and a mien of authority and distance to them all their lives, as if they were never to enjoy or have any comfort from those they love best in the World, till they had lost them by being removed into another. Nothing cements and establishes friendship and good-will, so much as confident communication of concernments and affairs. Other kindnesses without this, leave still some doubts; but when your son sees you open your mind to him, that you interest him in your affairs, as things you are willing should in their turn come into his hands, he will be concerned for them as for his own; wait his season with patience and love you in the meantime, who keep him not at the distance of a stranger. This will also make him see, that the enjoyment you have is not without care; which the more he is sensible of, the less will he envy you the possession and the more think himself happy under the management of so favourable a friend and so careful a father. There is scarce any young man of so little thought or so void of sense, that would not be glad of a sure friend, that he might have recourse to and freely consult on occasion. The reservedness and distance that fathers keep, often deprives their sons of that refuge, which would be of more advantage to them than an hundred rebukes and chidings.

(para. 96, pp. 202–203)

In his childrearing advice, Locke follows out the implications of an empiricist worldview: If it is true that a child becomes, in large part, what his or her experience is, then the parents' job is to provide that experience. It is also a parent's job to carefully consider what lesson the child would draw from the experience and if that lesson is not what is wanted, then the parent must change his or her own behavior to provide the proper experience. It is also true that the parent's knowledge about his or her child is itself based on experience through careful observation of that particular child, rather than on some abstract maxim or rule. If one considers the *consequences* of child rearing practices at every point, one comes to Locke's point of view: A parent should neither be too strict nor too kind, should consider the age and temper of the child and should teach by example and practice rather than admonition. Sound advice still, three hundred years later.

Berkeley's Idealism

Locke's view of how we come to know the world is essentially a **representational view of perception**: There is a world out there, consisting of qualities that we cannot know directly, that produces the world in our head as ideas, and those ideas are the only way we know the world. The ideas represent, in some way, the world that is assumed to exist. But since all we have to reflect upon are ideas, how do we know exactly what they represent? This limitation to knowledge was distressing to a devout and brilliant young Irishman who was just graduating from Trinity College, Dublin, in the year that Locke died. George Berkeley (1685–1753—pronounced "Barkley") was of comfortable middle-class origins and headed for the Anglican priesthood. He had read Locke's *Essay* cover to cover and was troubled by the notion that we cannot know what the world truly is. Worse, it was not that he disagreed with Locke about that, but he thought he had caught Locke in an error, an error that if he corrected it, would make the limitations to our knowledge even worse. If this situation were left to stand, thought Berkeley, it would lead to outright **skepticism**, the belief that some or all of knowledge is impossible, or even atheism. This, Berkeley felt, he had to stop.

The error was this: Locke, as well as Descartes, had believed in the distinction between primary and secondary qualities, in that the primary qualities, mass, shape and motion, exist independently of an observer, whereas the other, secondary qualities do not. In order to experience color or pain at all, an observer must be there. But Locke assumed that these secondary qualities couldn't be out there alone—color for instance comes from a reflection off a solid object.

Berkeley, not unreasonably, asks why you would assume that there is a solid object out there at all. After all, everything I know depends on my perceptions of it. My visual perception of the boundaries of the table I am sitting at stop at the edge of the brown color of its surface. It feels solid, but (although Berkeley couldn't have known this) the atoms in it are separated by much empty space, if today's physicists are correct. (Physicist Arthur Eddington said, "My scientific table is mostly emptiness. Sparsely scattered in that emptiness are numerous electric charges rushing about with great speed; but their combined bulk amounts to less than a billionth of the bulk of the table itself." Cited in Tipton, 1974, p. 27).

In this way, Berkeley appears to demolish the distinction between primary and secondary qualities; to him, even size, shape, solidity and motion require, like pain or

Figure 3.3 George Berkeley, Bishop of Cloyne (1685–1753)

color, that someone be there to perceive them. For Locke, it was logically necessary that these things exist. Berkeley goes Locke one better. Experience, says Berkeley, offers no real assurance that there is anything but ideas. Rather than speculating how it is that the world of ideas is connected with the outside world, as the representational theory of perception does, let's just simplify things and admit that all we can know to exist are ideas. We have never met an "unexperienced" object—all that we know to exist is that which we have experienced.

Then Berkeley makes a final, rather bizarre leap. He states, in effect, that only ideas can be proved to be real, a philosophy known as **immaterialism** or **subjective idealism**. He believed that existence *is* perception. In other words, he, in effect, would answer the Zen meditation "If a tree falls in the forest and no one is there to hear it, does it make a sound?" with "What tree?" In its most extreme form, if I look to my left and see a painting on the wall, I have no assurance that it still exists when I look to my right and see the telephone on the other wall. If I look back, of course, it's still there, but for all I know that world on the left is not there when I'm looking right and vice versa.

As you might expect, many people found this view absurd. Indeed, at this point, you might wonder what is up. If Berkeley wanted to *reduce* skepticism, suggesting that there is no world independent from our perceptions would seem to be a funny way to do it. Dr. Samuel Johnson, man of letters and coffeehouse wit of 18th-century London, is reported to have contemptuously kicked a stone and said, "I refute Berkeley thus!" More importantly, people pointed out that idealism could not deal with some problems. Let's say, for example, that we start a fire in a hearth and then go away, so that no one is watching it burn. If something must be perceived by someone in order to exist, how can it be that when we come back, the fire has burned down? A serious change has occurred in everyone's absence, so our presence to perceive it cannot be the cause of the change.

Berkeley, bishop of the Irish parish of Cloyne, triumphantly explains that even if none of us is there, someone is always watching: that someone is God. Just as the world as we know it exists because we experience it, the world as a whole exists because God, all-seeing and all-knowing, experiences it. The Universe exists, therefore, in the Mind of God. If we all exist in the same world, rather than in our own isolated ones of our own perceptions, it is because God is watching and essentially places the same ideas into our heads (Tipton, 1974).

Interestingly, Berkeley claimed that all this was common sense. Locke and others had set us on a road where we can't know anything for certain about the world, which could lead to unknowability and atheism. It was a given in his day that God was all-seeing and all-knowing. Berkeley, in effect, deals with the mind-body problem by saying that there is no body or world without God. All existence is ideas; it's just that we and the world are ideas in God's mind.

If the preceding dry discussion makes your head hurt, perhaps it is easier to remember Berkeley's theory by the following famous set of limericks, attributed to philosopher Ronald Knox:

> There was a young man who said, "God
> Must think it exceedingly odd
> If he finds that this tree
> Continues to be
> When there's no one about in the Quad."
> REPLY
> Dear Sir:
> Your astonishment's odd:
> I am always about in the Quad.
> And that's why the tree
> Will continue to be,
> Since observed by
> Yours faithfully,
> GOD.
> (Russell, 1945, pp. 647–648)

Although from a modern standpoint, Berkeley's point of view may seem silly, it was at least a logical method of resolving the mind-body problem. There are two kinds of **monism** that can be put forth against dualism. The first, **materialism** (which we will discuss in more detail in the next chapter), says that all that we think of as mind is merely the effect of the body. There is no mind (or soul), only body. Berkeley's subjective idealism takes the other point of view: All is mind. But without the intervention of God, Berkeley's idealism becomes **solipsism** or the philosophy that nothing can be known beyond the self. It would be left to David Hume to finally remove God and even Descartes's self from the equation, even while accepting Berkeley's notion that the world as we know it is nothing more than secondary qualities. All we can know is what we have experienced by true habit. Paradoxically, perhaps, this rather bleak view leads to interesting ramifications for how cause and effect can be determined in psychology, as we shall see.

Before we move on, however, it is important to note that Berkeley anticipated a point of view used by psychologists throughout much of the 19th century. As we will address in Chapter 5, several schools of psychology, from **functionalism** to **structuralism**, for a time believed that psychology should be only the study of the moment-by-moment workings of the mind. The psychologist's job, in this view, was to **introspect**, to use the mind to look at the mind. In this way, Locke's "reflection" became a method for the field and Berkeley's focus on the inner world became paramount. Among introspectionists, a cardinal error was to commit what was called "the experience error" as it was called by Edward Bradford Titchener or "the psychologist's fallacy" as it was called by William James. The experience error was simply to confuse the thought with the thing thought about. The *thought* of an apple may be an entirely different thing from an actual apple and we can, in fact, know virtually nothing about the actual apple. The psychologist, following Berkeley's insight, had only the workings of the mind to use as data. By the mid-19th century, however, the psychologist did not have God to fall back on, as we shall see in Chapters 4 and 5.

Hume, The Utter Skeptic

David Hume (1711–1776) was born in Edinburgh to a well-off family. His father, a lawyer, died when Hume was young, and he was raised by his devoted mother, who called the boy "uncommon wake-minded" (in the Scottish dialect of the period this meant alert or intelligent). David studied for a time at the University of Edinburgh, supposedly reading law. However, as he states in his autobiography, he was actually reading his favorite Latin authors, Virgil and Cicero. He claimed to have an "insurmountable aversion to everything but the pursuits of philosophy and general learning," and nearly ruined his health with studying, but he was clearly unsuited for business (Hume, 1777, p. 4). So he went to France, near Descartes's old school of La Flèche and set about writing his great work, *A Treatise of Human Nature* (1739). Not that it was immediately recognized as great, you understand: Hume notes that it "fell deadborn from the press, without reaching such distinction, as even to excite a murmur among the zealots" (Hume, 1777, pp. 4–5).

Hume quickly recovered and published some well-received essays and an abbreviated, less technical, rewrite of the *Treatise* called *An Enquiry Concerning Human*

Figure 3.4 David Hume (1711–1776), from a portrait in the Scottish National Gallery (1766) by Allan Ramsay (1713–1784)

Understanding (1748/1777) (Hume, 1739/2000). By the 1750s, he had become one of the more best-selling and controversial authors in Britain. His writings, as we shall see, were often reviled for their atheism and their attitude towards the impossibility of knowledge. People who met Hume in person, however, were often disarmed by his wit and good humor, directed even towards his enemies. They were also surprised at his appearance: Fat and jolly, he did not cut a figure of elegance. One observer said that his appearance reminded him more of a "turtle-eating alderman" than a man of great learning. Perhaps a man who was uncertain about certainty was least likely to be dogmatic in his statements or unaccommodating of contradiction.

Hume's Questioning of God and Miracles

But were this world ever so perfect a production, it must still remain uncertain, whether all the excellences of the work can justly be ascribed to the workman. If we survey a ship, what an exalted idea must we form of the ingenuity of the carpenter who framed so complicated, useful and beautiful a machine? And what surprise must we feel, when we find him a stupid mechanic, who imitated others and copied an art, which, through a long succession of ages, after multiplied trials, mistakes, corrections, deliberations and controversies, had been gradually improving? Many worlds might have been botched and bungled, throughout an eternity, ere this system was struck out; much labour lost, many fruitless trials made; and a slow, but continued improvement carried on during infinite ages in the art of world-making. In such subjects, who can determine, where the truth; nay, who can conjecture where the probability lies, amidst a great number of hypotheses which may be proposed and a still greater which may be imagined?

—David Hume (1779, part 5)

When Berkeley wanted to stem the tide towards outright skepticism, he did it by assuming that all we know are ideas and that we and the world and everything in it are ideas in the Mind of God. Since we now call Hume's brand of philosophy skepticism, you can guess how this battle turned out. But how did Hume prove that nothing that we know about the world or ourselves is certain? He did it by assuming that the first half of Berkeley's plan (that ideas are all we can know for certain) is true and by attacking the second half (that we exist in the Mind of God). Without God, Berkeley's plan is useless.

The first thing that Hume attacked was the existence of miracles in his shortened version of the *Treatise*, called *An Enquiry Concerning Human Understanding* (1748), and he did so in classically empiricist fashion. Bacon had suggested that knowledge came from the inductive method of setting examples against counterexamples and that is what Hume proposed to do with miracles:

A wise man, therefore, proportions his belief to the evidence. In such conclusions as are founded on an infallible experience, he expects the event with the last degree of assurance and regards his past experience as a full *proof* of the future existence of that event. In other cases, he proceeds with more caution: He weighs the opposite experiments: He considers which side is supported by the greater number of experiments: To that side he inclines, with doubt and hesitation; and when at last he fixes his judgement, the evidence exceeds not what we properly call *probability*. All probability, then, supposes an opposition of experiments and observations, where the one side is found to overbalance the other and to produce a degree of evidence, proportioned to the superiority. A hundred instances or experiments on one side and fifty on another, afford a doubtful expectation of any event; though a hundred uniform experiments, with only one that is contradictory, reasonably beget a pretty strong degree of assurance. In all cases, we must balance the opposite experiments, where they are opposite and deduct the smaller number from the greater, in order to know the exact force of the superior evidence.

(Hume, 1748/1977, pp. 73–74)

He then suggests that we are not particularly surprised to see a man die suddenly, for although it may not happen as often as dying slowly, it happens often enough. We see it, we hear reports from credible witnesses, we see the body and see that the person does not reappear following burial and so on. These all count as sources of evidence. If a man were to rise from the dead, however, we would be surprised, because *all* of our evidence to that point suggests that it does not happen—if it happened with any regularity at all, it would not be counted as a miracle. In order to explain the miracle with a counterexample that a good empiricist would come to accept, the explanation for that miracle would have to be sufficient to overcome that huge preponderance of evidence: It would need enough witnesses, in a public place, excluding all known natural causes and all possible natural causes and so forth. In other words, the explanation of the miracle must be more miraculous than the miracle itself. As that is scarcely possible, Hume concludes that miracles do not exist.

In disproving the existence of God, he also contends with the nature of cause and effect. For example, one popular proof of the existence of God is the natural proof, sometimes called the argument from design. The world is so intricate, logical and orderly that it must have an intelligence behind it. So wondrous a machine must have a designer. (See the next chapter for a more detailed discussion of this proposition.) But Hume argues that all we see of God is his effects and from these we must be very careful about describing causes, since we did not see the world being made. Moreover, given the definition of God we have, could we predict in advance that this is just the world that would result? (In this argument, Hume seems to intuitively know the need for scientific hypotheses to be stated *before* experiments! After the experiments, many plausible explanations can be made. (See the discussion of Karl Popper, Chapter 1.) By analogy, we can recall Bacon's example that we would be very unlikely to think that a worm made silk, if all we could see was the silk. At most, when we see a work of painting by an artist, we can conclude that at that time she had certain skills, not that she still does or that she can do sculpture as well or even that she is still alive. Certainly, says Hume, we cannot conclude of God from the effects that he is all-good or all-knowing. These attributes were likely given to God by our admiration for his works we see. Technically, all of these things may be true, but there is no way to argue the point with certainty. Thus, Hume's argument is a subtle plea for tolerance.

Finally, in another work, Hume (1779) attacks the idea that all things must have a cause and that therefore there must be a First Cause or Prime Mover. The argument why a prime mover is needed is based on the assumption that there was a time in which there was nothing and something cannot come from nothing. But why could the universe not have existed forever? We assume, without particular evidence that God exists forever, why not the universe? If the world exists forever, there is no need for God. If we then explain its parts and the causes of those parts, we've explained it all. Anything we can conceive of, says Hume, *may* be true, the question is only how *likely* it is to be true, and that can only be determined by evidence, which, where God is concerned, is hard to come by with any certainty.

Why is this bit of theology important in a psychology textbook? My purpose in introducing it here is not to undermine anyone's faith, but only to set up the beginning of Hume's most important point, perhaps one of the most important points for any scientist, let alone psychologists, to remember. It is this: It is very hard, and perhaps impossible, for us to determine that one thing must necessarily cause another. In the Aristotelian world, the cause is in the definition of the thing itself, its purpose. In the Christian world of Augustine, faith says that the cause is God. In the world of philosophy and science where experience is the only guide, the matter is far more difficult. We now turn to this argument.

Destruction of Necessary Truth

> Let men be once fully persuaded of these two principles, that there is nothing, in any object, considered in itself, which can afford us a reason for drawing a conclusion beyond it; and that even after the observation of the frequent constant conjunction of objects, we have no reason to draw any inference concerning any object beyond that of those which we have experience.
>
> —Hume (1749/2000, Book 1, Section 3.12, para. 20)

How do we come to believe that one thing causes another? Does a key cause a lock to open? If we say that someone did not accept an invitation to a party "because she's shy," what do we mean? If we say that children become violent because they watch a lot of violent television, how do we prove that assertion? How do we determine whether Echinacea helps our cold? This was David Hume's big question, the question of causality. But notice that I did not phrase the question "How do we know what the cause of something is?" but rather "How do we come to believe that one thing causes another?"

Remember, according to the empiricist position, our senses can be fallible and our knowledge inherently uncertain. All we really know are the immediate impressions of our sensations. Following Locke and Berkeley, Hume agreed that our knowledge was wholly dependent upon ideas; following Berkeley, he believed that it was folly for Locke to have speculated on the primary qualities on which these ideas are based. And more than 40 years after Boyle's death, he was still trying to kill the ghost of Aristotle—a key doesn't open a lock because it has the power to do so, and shyness is not an essential power that causes anyone to do anything. What then, is he left with? Only a succession of experiences in our minds and the beliefs we draw from them. There are many possible worlds, as was noted in the quote at the beginning of the last section: "who can conjecture where the probability lies, amidst a great number of hypotheses which may be proposed and a still greater which may be imagined?"

Laws of Association

Hume's answer is perhaps best dealt with in two simple examples. The first example comes from Hume himself and concerns billiard balls. The second is a new example concerning how we might assess causes in human behavior.

Let us assume only a couple of things before we start:

1. Humans receive impressions from the senses; these impressions become available to us as ideas in our minds and memories.
2. Humans make connections or **associations** among immediate impressions and between immediate impressions and past memories.

Imagine that you are standing next to a pool table. There is a billiard ball on a pool table, with a cue ball headed straight for it. What is going to happen next? Well, you say, yawning at the obviousness of your textbook writer (yours truly), of course, it will strike the ball and the second ball will move away. Where it will move depends on the 1739/2000 and the amount of force applied, among other things, but it will move. And (Clack!) the first ball hits the second, moving it away. How did you predict that the cue ball would cause the pool ball to move? Well, you say, I have been at several pool games and this resembles those occurrences. You associate the new impression, first of all, with memories of past occurrences, based on its **resemblance** to them.

Second, you note that the two events, call them "cue ball moving rapidly toward the ball" and "billiard ball moving away from cue ball" happened in close succession. Moreover, the cue ball rapidly moving event came *before* the pool ball moving away event, instead of the other way 'round, so you call the cue ball the cause of the second ball's movement because of its **priority** in the sequence of ideas going through your mind.

Third, the first ball came in contact with the second ball, so that it is highly plausible that it has some causal relationship to moving the billiard ball. If it had not hit the second ball, the cue ball cannot be the cause and it would have rolled right past. Or if there had been another ball in the way, it wouldn't have been the direct cause. Another way of saying this is that there are no intervening mental events between the two. They are next to one another or **contiguous** (Hume, 1738/2000).

Finally, every time you have seen similar events, the same thing happens. You have experienced **constant conjunction** of the two events, "cue ball moving rapidly toward billiard ball" coming first, with no intervening events, and "billiard ball moving away" in all similar situations. Thus, because Hume's four laws of association (resemblance, priority, contiguity and constant conjunction) are seen in this example, you conclude, even before you see the first ball strike the second, that the first ball will strike the second and cause it to move.

But wait a minute. Isn't it just possible that the ball will stop dead, moving nowhere, when it hits the other ball? Or perhaps it will hit the ball and bounce back, leaving the other ball untouched? Or maybe it will disappear or turn into a guinea pig and calmly waddle away before it gets there? (The guinea pig is not in Hume; I made him up.) Not bloody likely, you say. True: not probable, not likely, highly unlikely in fact, but possible. As long as you can conceive of something, create the idea in your mind, it is possible, because all we have to work with is ideas, remember? Thus, it follows that even those things that we're pretty damn sure of could change tomorrow—it is highly probable, based on past experience, that the sun will rise tomorrow, but it is *only* highly probable, not necessarily true. Even if all four laws of association are satisfied, says Hume, you still can't necessarily predict the future from the past. Causality isn't in the essence of the world; it is in us. We decide what is a cause and what is an effect based on experience. The accumulated weight of our experience tells us that it is rather silly to consider several of the options mentioned above.

In psychology, it is good to remember this point, because explanations for the causes of behavior are so numerous. If we take as our event not the clacking of billiard balls, but, say, a fight in a schoolyard when one child punches another in the nose, we might say on one level that he did it because the other child insulted him. An angry remark preceded the punch (priority) very close in time (contiguity). Why would we entertain the notion that an insult could cause a punch? Perhaps we had experienced for ourselves such a sequence, seen it happen to others or heard about it and judged this event, albeit happening with others in a different context, to be essentially similar to those events (resemblance). But does it always happen that this boy, when insulted, lashes out with a punch? Probably not, not even with the same kid (no constant conjunction).

If we wanted to explore further, we could examine whether the puncher generally does this to many different antagonists and whether he does this more often than other children. Then, if we have decided that the tendency to punch is a stable attribute (because, for example, the number of punches in situations that we judge similar is high for this child), we must consider why. It might be because the child has a biological hair trigger to stimulation; it might be that he is modeling behavior seen on television; it might be that his parents either are inattentive to his aggressive behavior or actively promote it; or it might be all of the above or none of the above. If we want to make an even larger statement, such as "Watching violent actions on television makes children more violent," we must widen our focus to look at many children. And even then, if a relationship were found (or better stated, if we concluded that we believed in such a relationship based on our experience), the relationship would likely not be a necessary conjunction, but a statement of probabilities, based on the preponderance of the evidence. And it may be peculiar to a particular time in history or to the sample we selected. In the empiricist worldview, all knowledge is provisional, probabilistic, potentially fallible.

You will note that in this example, I have moved from epistemological empiricism (how a single person comes to know anything through experience) to methodological empiricism (how science makes conclusions based on observation). In so doing, I have fast-forwarded somewhat to the modern day to give a presentist appreciation of what followed from Hume's ideas. Hume, of course, knew nothing of behaviorism or cognitivism or modern philosophy of science or even complex experimentation. He was more concerned with demolishing Descartes's, Aristotle's and Berkeley's arguments. But if we follow his logic, we must give him some of the credit for the notion that we are responsible for the scientific conclusions that we make. We may call them discoveries, but they are decisions about how the world works that we hope will predict what we will see in the future.

Hume's Notion of the Self

> For my part, when I enter most intimately into what I call myself, I always stumble on some particular perception or other, of heat or cold, light or shade, love or hatred, pain or pleasure. I never can catch myself at any time without a perception and never can observe anything but the perception. When my perceptions are remov'd for any time, as by sound sleep; so long am I insensible of myself and may truly be said not to exist. And were all my perceptions remov'd by death and cou'd I neither think, nor feel, nor see, nor love, nor hate after the dissolution of my body, I shou'd be entirely annihilated, nor do I conceive what is further requisite to make me a perfect non-entity. If any one upon serious and unprejudiced reflection, thinks he has a different notion of himself, I must confess I can reason no longer with him. All I can allow him is, that he may be in the right as well as I and that we are essentially different in this particular. He may, perhaps, perceive something simple and continu'd, which he calls himself, tho' I am certain there is no such principle in me.
>
> —Hume (1739/2000, Section 1.4.6, p. 165)

Thus far, Hume has destroyed the reader's certainty in the existence of God, the world and even the necessary connection of causes to effects. Even Descartes, you'll remember, had temporarily doubted these things. What Descartes did not doubt, however, was that there was a unitary "I"—a thing which thinks. Descartes's belief in a soul was based on it. Even Locke, in his separation of the thing that reflects from the senses, seemed to accept the unity of self. Hume was not at all sure that the self, or the soul, existed as a thing independent of our flow of experience:

> The mind is a kind of theatre, where several perceptions successively make their appearance; pass, re-pass, glide away and mingle in an infinite variety. There is properly no simplicity in it at one time, nor identity in different [times]. . . . They are the successive perceptions only, that constitute the mind; nor have we the most distant notion of the place, where these scenes are represented or of the materials, of which it is composed.
> (Hume, 1739/2000, Section 1.4.6, p. 165)

In other words, just as all of our knowledge of the world is from ideas based on sensation, so is knowledge of our selves based on the same thing. From the preceding section, we also know that our preceding thoughts come from the same point of view as our present ones and particularly, if we are looking at the same object, they resemble each other greatly from moment to moment. Furthermore, the change in thought is rather gradual compared to the thinker. Just as we assume a church is the same church if a worker replaces every brick in it, slowly, brick by brick, we assume that we are the same if all of our ideas change slowly and with no break. Our idea of a constant self, therefore, is merely a habit of mind, related to the principles of resemblance and contiguity. Each thought comes next to the other in an unbroken train, and some of the thoughts resemble each other well enough to maintain the connection. The presumed unity goes back years, based on our memory. Even if we forget some things that happened to us, the continuity is so strong that we assume that in some way the self of several years ago is the same self today. Indeed, Hume claims that memory *discovers* the self and aids in its construction over time. Our memory of our self *is* our self.

What about the principle of causality in relation to our self? This leads us into Hume's notion of free will. Can we have an "uncaused" thought? Hume's answer is that we don't really know for sure. His definition of **will** is "nothing but the *internal impression we feel and are conscious of, when we knowingly give rise to any new motion of our body or new perception of our mind*" (Hume, 1739/2000, Section 2.3.1, p. 257, emphasis original). The will, like the self, is not a stable thing but a feeling. When this feeling precedes what we call voluntary action often enough for us to believe it to be a cause—if it comes prior to and in more or less constant conjunction with the action—we will believe it to be the cause of our action. But, of course, this is not the same thing as saying that it *is* the cause of our action. Just as believing from experience that the sun will rise tomorrow is a safe bet but not a guarantee, so too is this conjunction of will and action: we have good reason to believe that our wanting chocolate ice cream caused us to get some, but we cannot be sure. Given that our own thoughts, ideas and behaviors are often more capricious than that, our certainty as to whether we caused something or something caused us to do it varies with the number of times we perceive the conjunction of will-feeling and voluntary action in that situation. In summary, Hume explains well enough why we *believe* in a self that exercises free will, but he declines to bet on whether we have a real self or free will. Hume is nothing if not consistent: just as we know the world through resemblance, contiguity, priority and constant conjunction, so too do we know ourselves the same way.

We will revisit Hume's notions later in Chapter 7 as essential components of the theory of psychologist and philosopher William James (1842–1910). In particular, his notions of the "stream of consciousness" and the slipperiness of self come directly from Hume (even as he was strongly skeptical about the very notion of ideas). James recognized this consistency enough to call himself a "radical empiricist."

The Associationists: David Hartley, James Mill and John Stewart Mill

David Hartley

At approximately the same time as David Hume, David Hartley (1705–1757), a physician who admired Locke and Newton, proposed a dualist theory of visual associations in *Observations on Man* (1749). On the physical side of his dualism, Hartley was impressed by a theory of Newton's concerning sight, explained in questions at the end of his landmark work, *Opticks* [sic]. Newton had suggested that a visual stimulus set up vibrations in the nerves. Dense bodies, said Newton, conserve heat (keeping vibrations going a long time). In such bodies, the waves of vibrations set up by visual or aural stimulation can be propagated a long way. In this way, he explained why visual afterimages occurred after looking at a bright light: just as a vibrating object, such as a tuning fork or glass, takes a while to settle after it is struck, so do the effects of visual stimulation. Moreover, Newton knew that waves of light have certain "bignesses" (what we would call frequencies) associated with certain colors, the most refractable by a prism being the shortest and the least refractable being longer. So the colors of light act directly on the nerves in this way. (Newton, ever the astute experimentalist, experimented on himself to get afterimages by looking into the sun repeatedly one afternoon and had to shut himself in the dark for three days afterward for the afterimages to go away [Westfall, 1980].) Hartley proposed that each stimulus vibrated minute particles in the nerves that in turn set up vibrations in the brain, known as *vibratiuncles*. These vibratiuncles, in turn, excited minute ideas in the mind on the other side of the mind/body dualism. This occurred in a one-to-one correspondence: one stimulus, one vibratiuncle, one idea and by repetition come to be combined with others. Hartley was thus the first psychologist to propose **psychophysical parallelism**. This is the notion that there are nerve impulses (in the body) and ideas (in the mind). Every vibration in the world sets up a vibratiuncle in the brain and every vibratiuncle in the brain is related to every idea in the mind. You can study nerves or you can study ideas, but not both together.

> Any sensations, A, B, C, etc., by being associated with one another a sufficient Number of Times, get such a Power over corresponding Ideas, a, b, c, etc, that

any one of the Sensations A, when impressed alone, shall be able to excite in the Mind b, c, etc. the Ideas of the rest.

(Hartley, 1749/1966, p. 65)

By proposing this mechanism, Hartley brings Locke's empiricism into the body. The vibration mechanism is new, too, because the prevailing theory of the time was similar to Descartes's view of the nerves as hollow tubes animated by pressure. Indeed, the following quote from him looks very much like Locke:

Upon the whole, it may appear to the reader, that simple ideas of sensation must run into clusters and combinations by associations; and that each of these will, at last, coalesce into one complex idea, by the approach and commixture of the several compounding parts. It appears also from observation, that many intellectual ideas, such as those that belong to the heads of beauty, honor, moral qualities, etc., are, in fact, thus composed of parts, which, by degrees, coalesce into one complex idea.

(Hartley, 1749/1966, p. 71)

Hartley stressed that the way that these complex ideas were formed was through repetition of particular experiences happening simultaneously (he called it synchronically) or successively, close together in time, over and over. This importance of frequency of repetition as an important notion in the construction of ideas was merely implied by Locke, but made an explicit central mechanism by Hartley. It is called the property of **mental compounding**.

Scholars believe that Hartley was not influenced by Hume, who did not generally become well known until after Hartley's death. He got his ideas from the Reverend Mr. Gay, who believed that love of happiness was the only innate tendency and that all morals were based on association to pleasant consequences. Hartley had, in fact, a mission to reconcile faith with science. He argues, courageously for his time, that man is a mechanism, in which all actions have a preceding mechanical cause, and he attempts to deny free will at the end of volume 1, but does not deny God. He fervently believed that if someone truly understood the process of how sensations were associated, he or she would avoid lower sensations and choose the higher, more complex and sublime intellectual pleasures. In fact, Hartley goes on to defend Christianity at great length in volume 2, suggesting that the relationships of pleasant and painful associations come from God's hand:

But it appears that from history, that God has so formed the world and perhaps (with Reverence be it spoken) was obliged by his moral perfections to form it, as that virtue must have admirable and pleasing ideas affixed to it, vice odious ones.

(Hartley, 1749/1966, p. 504)

Few people in the 18th and 19th centuries read Hartley directly, however. An abridged edition of Hartley's work by Joseph Priestley (1733–1804), the pioneering chemist and discoverer of oxygen, was far more popular. And it was much more radical, for Priestley lopped off almost all of the theology in volume 2 and included his own essays at the start. Priestley (1790) suggested, for example, that man becomes extinct at death and is not matter and spirit, but only matter. He states explicitly that this means that we are separated from the animals by degree rather than kind and addresses the radical proposition that matter itself might obtain the power to think. Priestly dances on the precipice of materialism—that there is no soul, only matter. He doesn't go over, though. He simply notes that man might be fully *explained* to be only matter, without *reference* to the soul. God's revelations may still exist. Perhaps to cover himself, after the introductory essays, he cuts out all of the sections in which Hartley discusses the nerve side of the equation and focuses only on associations of ideas. We will go over the materialist cliff in the next chapter.

James Mill

Mental compounding was taken to its extreme by an influential book by James Mill (1773–1836). Mill, like Hume, was a Scot and though he was only the son of a tradesman and farmer, he was sent to University of Edinburgh by a scholarship funded by Sir John Stuart. He was trained for the church, but turned out to be a miserably ineffective preacher; indeed, according to his son, John Stuart Mill (1806–1873) he did not really believe in the church and so he supported himself by tutoring and writing for periodicals. After some years of this, he published a highly regarded history of British India and secured a post in London as a functionary for the British East India Company in 1819. His major work on psychology proper was composed during several years' worth of summer vacations as *Analysis of the Phenomena of the Human Mind* (1829) (Mill, 1873).

In this work, James Mill reveals himself to be under the spell of Hartley's view of associationism and mental compounding. The discussion of nerves is entirely missing, suggesting that he's working from Priestley's version. The mind consists of ideas, which come ultimately from experience. The ideas that are most closely associated in the mind are those that are activated together, either synchronically or successively in time. Some of these pairings have been frequently simultaneous or synchronical; the sight and taste of roast beef, the smell and sight and touch of a rose. The sight of lightning and the sound of thunder have been successive, often, rather than synchronical. Some associations are more permanent than others, remembered for longer over time. Some are performed with more certainty, in that we make fewer mistakes with some associations than with others, and some are done with more ease or facility, in that we appear to be putting forth little effort when we speak our own language or perform a well-rehearsed piece on the piano. Some of the associations are so strong as to be without our power to prevent and some are so contradictory as to be difficult to form at all (what is a flat spherical surface, for example?). Simple ideas, through association, become complex ideas and complex ideas become even more complex ideas (called duplex ideas), like adding on boxcars to a train or placing little Russian dolls inside bigger ones.

All this may be well and good, we may say to ourselves when reading Mill's most famous chapter (for psychologists, at any rate) on the association of ideas. Until we come to what is perhaps the most famous paragraph in James Mill for historians of psychology:

> Brick is one complex idea, mortar is another complex idea; these ideas, with ideas of position and quantity, compose my idea of a wall. My idea of a plank is a complex idea, my idea of a rafter is a complex idea, my idea of a nail is a complex idea. These, united with the same ideas of position and quantity compose my duplex idea of a floor. In the same manner my complex idea of glass and wood and others, compose my duplex idea of a window; and these duplex if, united together, compose my idea of a house, which is made up of various duplex ideas. How many complex or duplex, ideas are all united in the idea of furniture? How many in the idea of merchandise? How many more in the idea called Every Thing?
>
> (Mill, 1869, pp. 115–116)

The great historian of psychology E.G. Boring has ridiculed this mental compounding view as the "tinkertoy" conception of the mind—just stick another thing on, until you reach the notion of Every Thing. Mill dumped Hartley's view of the nervous system, but if he hadn't, he would see that if we had to go through all of those ideas to get to "house" (never mind "everything"), it should take an awfully long time for the vibrations to do their vibrating. True, after you practice a piano piece for a long time, it becomes automatic and you can do it faster. It should work in a similar way for "house." But how fast is that and where does all that learning go? James Mill did not address it.

Even James Mill's son, John Stuart Mill, knew there was something wrong with this conception. In the 1869 reissue edition of his father's work that he edited, he appended an 11-page footnote of qualification and complaint after that famous paragraph!

John Stuart Mill

John Stuart Mill (1806–1873) was his father's son in many ways. In fact, he was virtually the product of his father's experiments in education based on the philosophy of **utilitarianism**. Utilitarianism, founded by Jeremy Bentham (1748–1832), is based on the Greatest Happiness Principle: Actions are considered right to the degree that they provide the greatest amount of pleasure for the greatest number of people in society. Actions are wrong to the extent that they cause people pain. Acts themselves are not good; only those acts that lead to good consequences are good. The goal of the utilitarian, therefore, is to increase the sum total of happy consequences not merely for each individual, but for society. Because everyone's view of what is pleasurable is slightly different, no one can be forced to follow the definition of others in what is happiness and therefore everyone, of whatever class, has an equal vote. Punishments may be used, but only when agreed upon by an equal society and only when they prevent a greater pain than the pain administered. The utilitarian believes, optimistically, that such a society can be created. Morality is learned, rather than

Figure 3.5 John Stuart Mill (1806–1873)

innate. Strict moral education is therefore necessary. Indeed, education itself increases the amount of happiness one may conceivably have (otherwise, say the utilitarians, a satisfied pig would be better than a dissatisfied educated human). Therefore, education is good in itself.

James Mill apparently believed that there were no limits to the amount of education that a child could contain. He seems to have wanted John Stuart to become a thinking machine and an apostle to the gospel of utilitarianism. In his posthumously published *Autobiography* (1873), J.S. Mill said that he learned Greek at the age of 3 and read Socrates and *Dialogues* of Plato by the age of 7, and Hume, Aristotle, algebra, calculus, Shakespeare, Milton, Dryden, logic and Plato's *Republic* by the age of 12! He read Hartley last, along with the political economics of Bentham, Adam Smith (1723–1790) and David Ricardo, (1772–1823) the major theorists of capitalism.

To some extent, the father had succeeded in his mission; he had united associationism with utilitarianism in his son. In fact, John Stuart Mill's most-read works are works of political philosophy, namely *Utilitarianism* (1863) and *On Liberty* (1859).

But his father's form of education had its costs. John Stuart later said, in explaining a mental breakdown he experienced at the age of 20,

> My course of study had led me to believe, that all mental and moral feelings and qualities, whether of a good or of a bad kind, were the result of association; that we love one thing and hate another, take pleasure in one sort of action or contemplation and pain in another sort, through the clinging of pleasurable or painful ideas to those things, from the effect of education or experience ...
>
> The doctrine appeared inexpugnable; but now it seemed to me, on retrospect, that my teachers had occupied themselves superficially with the means of forming and keeping up those salutary associations. They seem to have trusted altogether to the old familiar instruments, praise and blame, reward and punishment.... But there must always be something artificial and casual in associations thus practiced.
>
> (J.S. Mill, 1873, pp. 136–138)

He said of this time that he felt

> stranded at the commence of my voyage, with a well-equipped ship and rudder, but no sail; without any real desire for the ends which I had been so carefully fitted out for: no delight in virtue or the general good, but also just as little in anything else.
>
> (J. S. Mill, 1873, p. 139)

John Stuart was not emotionally close to his father, who, like many Victorian Englishmen, was forthright, yet rigid in his moral views, more stingy with praise than with correction and somewhat repressed in his emotions. But John Stuart was devoted to him, and his own associationist theory took the views of Hartley and his father as the starting point. James Mill had often used metaphors that suggested that ideas were put together like building blocks or trains. His son recognized the absurdity of this and simply added to his father's mental compounding another metaphor, known as **mental chemistry**. In the chapter called "Of the Laws of Mind," he states:

> the laws of the phenomena of mind are sometimes analogous to mechanical, but sometimes also to chemical laws. When many impressions or ideas are operating in the mind together, there sometimes takes place a process of similar kind to chemical combination. When impressions have been so often experienced in conjunction, that each of them calls up readily and instantaneously the ideas of the whole group, those ideas sometimes melt and coalesce into one another and appear not as several ideas, but one; in the same manner as, when the seven prismatic colours are presented to the eye in rapid succession, the sensation produced is that of white.
>
> (Mill, 1843/1974, p. 853)

John Stuart differs from his father by saying that the many colors *generate* white, rather than that they *consist* of them. The complex idea is greater than the sum of its parts. The analogy here is the notion that water, while being made of two gases, hydrogen and oxygen, does not itself behave anything like either one. In talking this way about how ideas combine, the younger Mill may have chosen the better metaphor, but there is really no way to test the difference between the two views. How does one isolate and compare ideas with one another?

J. S. Mill tried very hard to set down a way to do this in attempting to develop ways for science to proceed. He wanted to be a true empiricist and find a way for science to be purely inductive, with no innate ideas of any kind, including the innate *a priori* mechanisms of Kant (see Chapter 5). Most scholars think he did not succeed in this (Scarre, 1998). However, in his prolific and dense writings, there are some tantalizing anticipations of modern scientific practice. First, he tried to address Hume's criticisms by saying, in effect, Yes, we can't really prove that the sun will rise tomorrow, but we can't really help in expecting that it will. We can't predict what sensations we may have in the future, but we have lived through a lot of futures that subsequently became pasts, so that for us, objects in the world become **permanent possibilities of sensations**. Second, we can probably never know for sure whether A really causes B, but we expect that there is always some antecedent cause to every effect. This is the **universal law of causation**. This law suggests that there may be many theories that fit the same facts: We can't know *the* cause, but we must propose *a* cause in science. Mill argued that a science of psychology is therefore possible, but its conclusions are always uncertain. Finally, in describing how to determine causes, he describes two interesting laws that describe the basic laws of experimentation:

> *Method of Agreement*: If two or more instances of the phenomenon under investigation have only one circumstance in common, the circumstance in which alone all the instances agree, is the cause (or effect) of the phenomenon.
>
> *Method of Difference*: If an instance in which the phenomenon under investigation occurs and an instance in which it does not occur, have every circumstance in common save one, that one occurring only in the former; the circumstance in which alone the two instances differ, is the effect or the cause or an indispensable part of the cause, of the phenomenon.
>
> (J. S. Mill, cited in Scarre, 1998, pp. 125–126)

In other words, these logical rules essentially state the notion that in order to find anything out in an experiment, one must attempt to vary one variable while keeping all the other relevant variables constant. But Mill said almost nothing about how to apply these rules in psychology (which to him, of course, would mean applying them to associated ideas, rather than behaviors).

Empiricism and Associationism Evaluated

It is appropriate to step back at this point and examine what the key beliefs were of empiricists and associationists and the strengths and weaknesses of these approaches. First, their method is inductive rather than deductive, in that they believed their conclusions were simply generalizations from many examples. From these generalizations would eventually come beautiful laws like those of Newton. In the 18th and

19th centuries, in particular, the inductive method of science was exemplified by the establishment of natural history museums, in which rows of glass cases housed examples of every description. Even though the empiricist psychologists were examining the contents of minds rather than the world, this became their ideal as well. Second, these approaches might be called **atomistic** or **elementaristic**. Theories that are atomistic deconstruct the mind or the world into a limited set of atoms or elements. In the same way that Boyle began the corpuscular philosophy in chemistry, Locke began by saying the basic elements of thought are simple ideas. This notion was carried pretty much intact through at least James Mill; each corpuscle of thought was separate and combined in many ways. If a scientific theory proposes that once scientists have found the elements, they have largely solved the problem, it is also **reductionistic**, in the sense that thoughts can be reduced to ideas and only ideas or that chemistry is elements and only elements. Reductionists like to think that once they have constructed a table of elements, all will become clear.

But at this time and for some time afterwards, psychology was still a branch of philosophy. It was not at all clear to some whether psychology, as a science of observing the mind, could be a science at all. J.S. Mill proposed a science of the mind and behavior of man and called it "ethology," but even he thought its conclusions would be hardly more reliable than conclusions about the weather; in his day, that was not saying much. (Mill's ethology is not to be confused with the current meaning of the word as the subfield of biology dealing with animal behavior; there is no connection between the two meanings.) The empiricists and associationists hardly dealt with the body at all. When Hartley attempted to do so, his views were deemphasized. As we shall see in the next chapter, the body would be brought back, but to resurrect it, the soul had to go.

Associationism adds utilitarianism to classic empiricism. Locke had suggested that simple ideas form complex ideas, and Hume had suggested the principles of resemblance, contiguity, priority and constant conjunction are what make us believe in the reality of causes. But they did not add what motivates us to make some connections and not others. The answer that the associationists give is the pursuit of pleasure and the avoidance of pain. Learning is the accumulation of experience in the service of these pursuits. Such pursuits are natural and selfish. Adam Smith, who was a professor of moral philosophy at Edinburgh near the time of Hartley and Hume, theorized that our natural and selfish pursuit of money can become a system that works, aggregately over all people as an invisible and (ultimately, if not in every case) beneficial mechanism called capitalism. So did the associationists argue that a rational and just society could be produced out of the associations formed by the pursuit of happiness in the individual. In the time of the Mills, this was a relatively radical idea, for the equality of the individual undermined the superiority of the church, the aristocracy and the land-owning class. It is thus a classically liberal doctrine, as the term is used in history. Presently in Britain and America, these ideas would probably be considered conservative or libertarian, however. As an example, take a look at the following quote from John Stuart Mill's *On Liberty*:

> The object of this essay is to assert one very simple principle, as entitled to govern absolutely the dealings of society with the individual in the way of compulsion

and control, whether the means used be physical force in the form of legal penalties or the moral coercion of public opinion. That principle is, that the sole end for which mankind are warranted, individually or collectively in interfering with the liberty of action of any of their number, is self-protection. That the only purpose for which power can be rightfully exercised over any member of a civilised community, against his will, is to prevent harm to others. His own good, either physical or moral, is not a sufficient warrant. He cannot rightfully be compelled to do or forbear because it will be better for him to do so, because it will make him happier, because, in the opinions of others, to do so would be wise or even right. These are good reasons for remonstrating with him or reasoning with him or persuading him or entreating him, but not for compelling him or visiting him with any evil, in case he do otherwise. To justify that, the conduct from which it is desired to deter him must be calculated to produce evil to someone else. The only part of the conduct of any one, for which he is amenable to society, is that which concerns others. In the part which merely concerns himself, his independence is, of right, absolute. Over himself, over his own body and mind, the individual is sovereign.

(J. S. Mill, 1859, p. 13)

As we shall see in the next chapter, the darker implications of this political view would provide one of the cornerstones of Darwinism, an idea that would rock the foundations of the social order, science and psychology.

Note

1. For my sharp-eyed Freudian readers: You will note that Locke did not believe in an "unconscious." Locke thought that people could have once known something that they have forgotten or they might state a conclusion that they came to a long time ago and not be able to know immediately the steps that it took to get to that conclusion. That is different from saying that there are ideas that are actively causing havoc below consciousness while you are thinking something else consciously.

4 From Argument by Design to Nature Red in Tooth and Claw
The Development of Evolutionist Thought

Precursors to Evolution

> Vast chain of being! Which from God began,
> Natures aethereal, human, angel, man,
> Beast, bird, fish, insect, what no eye can see,
> No glass can reach; from Infinite to thee,
> From thee to nothing.—On superior pow'rs
> Were we to press, inferior might on ours;
> Or in the full creation leave a void,
> Where, one step broken, the great scale destroy'd;
> From Nature's chain, whatever link you strike,
> Tenth or ten thousandth, breaks the chain alike.
> —Alexander Pope (1733, cited in Lovejoy, 1936/2001, p. 60)

Humans are great namers and classifiers of the natural world. Even though the Bible reserves to God the creation of the animals and plants, it allows man to name them! (Gen. 2:20). Moreover, to classify something is to consider its relationship to ourselves and where we fit in the great classification scheme. For the first few thousand years of Western culture, that classification scheme was grand, static and complete and we were installed near the top. With the Renaissance and the discovery of Copernicus that we were no longer at the center of the universe, our view of our placement in that system began to change. People began to turn our powers of deduction and observation outward towards the natural world, in the same way that Descartes and Locke had turned them inward. At first, this observation was used to justify rather than to overturn our place in God's hierarchy, the Great Chain of Being, through the field of natural theology, defined as the study of nature in order to prove God's plan. Then this devout practice began to provide the very data to overturn the paradigm and to bring evolution into being as a scientific theory. The theory of evolution did not spring directly from Charles Darwin's mind, but was the product of a long process of change.

Aristotle

Any discussion of classification of the natural world must begin with Aristotle (384–322 B.C.E.), who might be called the first great biologist. We have already discussed some of Aristotle's philosophy in Chapter 2, but what will concern us here are his insights on the natural world of animals. Remember that Aristotle was concerned with what category something belongs to, its essential nature.

Aristotle's teacher, Plato, had thought that the perfect essences, called Ideas, really did exist in a supernatural plane, beyond any individual instance of a thing. A devotee of geometry, Plato had commented that the Idea of the triangle does not depend on the angles or the length of the sides of any particular triangle, but was a concept independent of these details.

Aristotle, however, was less sure that essences were so divine in nature. Aristotle's system of classification in terms of animals' essential characteristics begins with a kind of logical deduction called downward classification, in which more general attributes are higher in a hierarchy than more specific ones. This method is like playing the game "20 questions." One begins by asking yes–no questions based on rather general attributes, such as "Is it alive?" or "Does it move under its own power?" to "Does it have feathers?" and so on (Mayr, 1982). But Aristotle made his classifications only partly through logical deduction; he grouped animals based on what he and others had *observed* of their characteristics as well and tried not to force them into categories. He formed his groups by inspection of their characteristics and by choosing those characteristics that differentiate between them. But given that there are many characteristics of any given animal, which to choose? One could easily differentiate by color or size, but are these essential qualities? Usually, Aristotle thought not. The most important characteristics were some of the ones we use today, such as whether the animals are egg layers or live bearers of young or whether they have warm or cold blood. But unlike Plato, he believed that the differences between species were more continuous and that species could sometimes share attributes. As can be seen in Table 4.1, once he had formed the groups, he began to explain and order them in a hierarchy based on some of the main concepts of his day. For example, Greek and later medieval science was based on a belief that all things were created from four elements—earth, fire, water and air—and have dichotomous properties such as hot vs. cold or wet vs. dry. Thus, what to us are mammals would be hot and fluid beings, with (warm) blood and live birth, made of fire and water, whereas fishes

Table 4.1 Aristotle's Classification of Animals

Blooded Animals	Attributes
Humans	hot and fluid
Live-bearing quadrupeds	hot and fluid
Egg-bearing quadrupeds (reptiles) and snakes	cold and fluid
Birds and scaly animals (laying perfect eggs)	hot and solid
Fishes (laying imperfect eggs)	cold and solid
Bloodless Animals	
Soft shells—crustaceans (lobster)	cold and solid
Softies—cephalopods (octopus, squid)	cold and solid
Insects	cold and dry
Snails and other mollusks	cold and solid

Adapted from Aristotle (1990). *Generation of Animals* (A. L. Peck, Trans.). Cambridge, MA: Harvard University Press.

would be cold and solid beings, made of water and earth with (cold) blood and egg laying. Birds are hot and solid and thus have dry-shelled eggs. Insects have no blood at all (at least as was observed by Aristotle and his informants) and are cold and dry.

To modern eyes, this may seem somewhat fanciful and oversystematized, based on a system of elements that after all can't be investigated, but as we have seen in Chapter 2, those who purported to base their systems on Aristotle's work, from the medieval to the early modern Christian era, did much worse. Aristotle, in many ways, operated like a scientist gathering data to verify or falsify a hypothesis. Concerning how bees procreate, for example, he first states, "The generation of bees is a great puzzle" (Aristotle, n.d./1990, p. 333) and then goes on to enumerate the ways they might procreate (by fetching new bees from some other animal, by union of bee with bee, drone with bee, drone with drone, etc.). He systematically discounts those ways that he has evidence against. He describes the behaviors of all the types of bees reported to him or observed and then concludes,

> This, then, appears to be the state of affairs with regards to the generation of bees, so far as theory can take us, supplemented by what are thought to be the facts about their behavior. But the facts have not been sufficiently ascertained; and if at any future time they are ascertained, then credence must be given to the direct evidence of the senses more than to theories,—and to theories too provided that the results which they show agree with what is observed.
>
> (Aristotle, 1990, pp. 345–347)

This care is seen in all of Aristotle's work on animals. He also describes animals' habitats as well as their essences and describes the known behaviors of many of the 580 animals he mentions in his work. Although he was wrong in many of the particulars by current standards, little in his natural history work appears fanciful; instead, it shows sober attempts to explain the worlds in terms of the information available, in terms available to him and his contemporaries. In addition to being the first biologist, then, he may also be considered a forerunner of the empiricists, anticipating some of their views on the primacy of sense data.

The Great Chain of Being

Aristotle included a ranking system in his classifications. For example, animals that are wet and hot were considered to be higher than those that are cold and dry. In addition, living beings were ranked according to their quality of soul. Soul, to Aristotle, was inseparable from the body but includes all the attributes necessary to it to give the body life (see Chapter 2). These include the ability to receive and utilize nutrition, to have appetites and desires, to sense, to move and to think. All beings have souls, but plants have only the first of this list of abilities, and the various members of the animal kingdom have more of these characteristics until we arrive at humans, who have rational thought.

Thus, the idea of ranking the natural world is a very old one. But after Aristotle, in later Greek and Roman times up to the Middle Ages, this method of ranking began to have a mystical, divine nature. The insights of Plato concerning the perfect world of Ideas were transferred to God in early Christian thought by Augustine, and the rankings of Aristotle became part of church doctrine by Aquinas (see Chapter 2). Not only could the natural world be ranked on logical grounds, but also on theological grounds. If God is good, so the argument goes, then the world is evidence of his goodness and everything in it has its purpose. To remove one species from it, even the "less perfect" ones, would lessen the perfection of the world and perhaps remove something that could provide a lesson to us (Lovejoy, 1936/2001). Remember that, to people in medieval times, everything in the world was a symbol of God's care: A rose is red to symbolize the blood of Christ and the thorns of the rose reminds one of the crown of thorns (Huizinga, 1921/1996). The ranking of the natural world thus forms what was called, in Latin, the *scala naturae*, the scale of nature or the **Great Chain of Being** [Table 4.2]. A preordained, unchanging hierarchy of species in which every being has its necessary place in the universe, including Humanity, which takes its place just below the angels.

This notion of the Great Chain lasted quite a long time, beginning in ancient classical times and continuing for almost 2000 years until doubts about it began in the early 19th century. Even John Locke, in the 17th century, suggested that the theory was "probable":

> In all the visible corporeal world we see no chasms or gaps. All quite down from the descent is by easy steps and a continued series that in each remove differ very little one from the other.... And when we consider the power and wisdom of the Maker, we have reason to think, that it is suitable to the magnificent harmony of the universe and the great design and the infinite goodness of the architect, that the species of creatures should also, by gentle degrees, ascend upwards from us towards his infinite perfection, as we see they gradually descend from us downwards.
>
> (Locke, 1690, cited in Lovejoy, 1936/2001, p. 184)

Table 4.2 The *Scala Naturae*: The living world ranked according to the perfection of essence

Scala naturae
Humans
Whales
Other mammals
Oviparous (egg laying) vertebrates
Birds
Amphibians and reptiles (but see snakes below)
Snakes
Fish
Invertebrates (without red blood)
Cephalopods
Crustacea
Insects, spiders.
Other mollusks, echinoderms.
Sponges, etc.

The poem by Alexander Pope quoted at the beginning of this section is from the 18th century; the chain extends "From Infinite to thee,/From thee to nothing," and to break it at any point, to remove a creature or to try to occupy another place, is to destroy the scale. Another quote from about the same time by the Genevan philosopher Bonnet makes the point even more clear:

> Between the lowest and highest degree of spiritual and corporeal perfection there is an almost infinite number of intermediate degrees. The succession of degrees comprises the *Universal Chain*. It unites all beings, ties together all worlds, embraces all the spheres. One SINGLE BEING is outside this chain and this is HE who made it. This chain extends from the first term, the atom to "the highest of the CHERUBIM".
> (1764, cited in Gould, 1977, p. 23; emphasis in original)

To the 18th-century philosopher, by studying the universal chain, we confirm our own ordained place in it.

Natural Theology

The notion of the Great Chain made the study of the natural world an act of devotion as much as one of knowledge itself. By the 18th century, botany was considered a virtuous pastime for young girls, and many societies sprang up for its study. One studied nature to embellish what came to be called the **argument from design**: How can one explain the great variety and harmony in the world without reference to an intelligent being with a complete plan? God had begun the world with putting forth the great essences of each of the animals and ourselves. It was our job to discover these essences in nature; once they had been discovered, their beauty would be, in a circular fashion, proof of God's existence.

The first great collections of specimens were collected at universities under the auspices of the discipline of natural theology. Expeditions of world exploration and colonization that had begun in the 16th century had brought back many new species of plants and animals, pressed and dried or preserved, as well as many curious bones. This practice had exploded by the 18th century, as the manias for collection and empirical observation were combined with the greater reach of European navies. Some way was needed to bring this deluge of data into the calm order that God's plan seemed to require. It was thought at the time that natural history needed a scientist on the order of Newton to provide the order on earth that Newton himself had provided the heavens.

Several great natural historians took up this task of ordering the world. Carolus Linnaeus (1707–1778) was a devout Swedish botanist with a penchant for logical order. He was most concerned with the problem of how to provide a map of the natural world, first with plants and later with animals, based on characteristics that could distinguish one species from another, using a manageable number of categories. In creating this useful identification manual of God's world, he used external characteristics alone. Taking his cue from the methods of Aristotle, he created the two-word Latin classification system of genus and species that we use, with some modifications, today (e.g. *Homo sapiens* or *Canis familiaris*, for human or domestic dog, respectively). This somewhat artificial system allowed ease of identification, but also highlighted an old problem: Given the enormous variety of individual animals within a species, what are the essential qualities of a species? Linnaeus believed that species were separate, distinct from one another, unchanging. The most important external characteristics were sexual parts, because they dealt with procreation, as that is how the essence of each separate species is passed on. Linnaeus's contemporary, the productive French naturalist George Louis Buffon (1707–1788), disagreed; a follower of Newton, he believed in a continuous range of characteristics among plants and animals and thought Linnaeus's taxonomy of separate essences to be a mere human invention, rather than a mirror of nature. Buffon founded the Paris Natural History Museum, directed the Royal Gardens and wrote a 44-volume natural history rich with descriptions of plants and animals in their natural habitats. Parts of this massive work were read by virtually everyone professing to be educated in Europe in his day. Whereas Linnaeus had focused on the external sexual parts as the most important features for classification, Buffon helpfully brought successful breeding into the definition of species by suggesting that the definition of a species should be their capability to produce fertile offspring. For example, a horse and a donkey may mate, but they will produce an infertile offspring, which we call a mule, confirming their existence as separate species. Buffon also believed that the habits of animals should be used to help determine their species membership (Mayr, 1982).

An opponent of Buffon in Paris, Georges Cuvier (1769–1832), provided the final justification that would later provide evidence for evolution. Cuvier was a careful reader of Aristotle's work; just as Aristotle had said that there was a logic to the ordering of the world, he stated that there was a purpose to every part of animals' bodies:

> Now, as each of the parts of the body, like every other instrument, is for the sake of some purpose, viz., some action, it is evident that the body as a whole must exist for the sake of some complex action. Just as the saw is there for the sake of sawing . . . because sawing is the using of the instrument, so in some way the body exists for the sake of the soul and the parts of the body for the sake of those functions to which they are naturally adapted.
>
> (Aristotle, trans. 1990, 645b)

Cuvier, two thousand years after Aristotle, realized that the study of external characteristics of species was not enough to place them correctly in the Great Chain. One must look at the internal organs and bones of animals as well. In the beauty of how these parts fit, we see the hand of the Designer; in the commonalties of these parts between species, we can help construct the Great Chain. According to his **principle of correlation of parts**, each organ of the body is related to every other, and the survival of the organism depends upon their coordination. Organisms in between species boundaries could not survive, because some of their pieces wouldn't fit. Moreover, each part of the animal is wonderfully adapted to its function and habitat, so much so that Cuvier claimed that he could reconstruct a whole animal from a bone or, in the case of animals who had gone extinct since the flood, from a fossil. In this way, Cuvier founded the field of comparative anatomy (Coleman, 1964). Note in the following quote an emphasis on observation as essential to the formation of laws:

> The most fecund way of obtaining them [empirical laws] is comparison. It consists in successively observing the same body in its different natural positions or in comparing different bodies among themselves as far as we know the constant relations between their structure and the phenomena they manifest. These diverse bodies may be looked upon as a kind of experiment performed by nature, which adds or subtracts from these different parts (just as we try to do the same in our laboratories) and itself shows the results of these additions and subtractions. We are thus able to establish certain laws which rule these relations and are employed like those which are determined by the general [mathematical] sciences.
>
> (Cuvier, 1817, as cited in Coleman, 1964)

Such intricate harmony within the animal and between the animal and its environment was a strong argument from design. Cuvier, too, believed in the static universe and argued vehemently against those who were beginning to believe in changes in species over time. When he saw fossils in different strata of rock, he was forced to conclude that there had not been only one Biblical flood, but many over the course of time. These floods killed off old animals, and the modern animals had always been present but had wandered in from elsewhere or been specially created later by God. He was thus a **catastrophist**: The contradiction between old and new species was resolved by catastrophes or very rare disasters. He also believed in **special creation**: God could and did create new species any time he wanted. There was a problem, however: Cuvier's worldview did not conform with the facts, as was pointed out by the distinguished historian of evolution, Ernst Mayr:

> Cuvier's claim of a complete constancy of organs and their proportions in the higher taxa of animals were completely unsupported by his investigations. If such studies were undertaken by Cuvier, he would have discovered that, contrary to his claims, there are considerable differences in the relative size and configuration of the vital organs in related species, genera and families. But even had he found such differences, as he must have during his dissections, he probably would have merely gone back to the basic principle that each animal had been created to fill its assigned place in nature.
>
> (Mayr, 1982, p. 368)

When Cuvier found data that did fit, they were evidence for the validity of his theories. When he found data that did not, they were evidence that God could make exceptions or that the animal was a variation from a true type. Looking at his work from a presentist perspective, we would say that he did not treat his theory as falsifiable, but as a doctrine. From a historicist perspective, however, we can see that his careful attention to observation was in keeping with the advanced philosophers and scientists of his day.

Thus, building upon the foundation of Aristotle and the early church, a large mass of information was collected and systematized under natural theology. Linnaeus organized the species, Buffon recognized the importance of animal behavior and Cuvier recognized the importance of animal structure and fossils. Buffon and Cuvier recognized that in order to prove the perfect adaptation of animals fitted to their purpose, they must also consider the animal's habitat. Ironically, without all these pieces, Darwin could not have done his work that overturned the paradigm of the Great Chain of Being. He needed the data and methods. But as the above quote points out, the natural theologians could not have made this leap. They were driven, as Kuhn would predict, to ignore anomalies for as long as possible. Yet we cannot say that they were not scientists just because they were wrong; they were engaging in the normal science activities of their day.

Lamarck

Jean-Baptiste Pierre Antoine de Monet de Lamarck (1744–1829), the son of a poor minor nobleman, had been a brave soldier in his teenage years. After being pensioned off after a minor injury, he spent his time eking out a living as a hack writer, and he developed a passionate interest in plants. He wrote an impressive work on French flora in 1779 that brought him to the attention of Buffon, who gave him a job first as tutor to his son and then as assistant at the Museum. When the museum was reorganized in 1793, he finally secured a professorship, but it was in a field that no one else had wanted, the invertebrates. This was a group of animals that few had classified before (most of the invertebrates were simply classified as "worms"). Although Lamarck had been a Linnaean essentialist, he noticed something interesting when he was cataloging the mollusk collection. He noted that many of the recent mollusk species had commonalties with the fossils in the collection. Not only that, but correlating the changes in the mollusk shells with the geological strata in which they were found allowed him to construct, in some cases, an entire lineage of the animal (Burkhart, 1977; Mayr, 1982). From Lamarck's preserved lectures, it seems he underwent a "conversion" experience at age 55, between the time he taught his invertebrate classes in 1799 and 1800. He began to believe that species had changed gradually over very long periods of time, much longer than the 6000 years generally estimated from the Bible. Lamarck had also written on meteorology and geology and recognized, along with a few of his contemporaries, that the process of erosion happens continuously, slowly and gradually. In contrast to Cuvier, Lamarck was a **uniformitarian**. Uniformitarians believed that God created the universe to conform to certain laws; after the creation of the world, God did not intervene. Catastrophes formed a relatively small part of the history of the world. Therefore, scientists could assume that the laws that are observed in the present held uniformly throughout the past history of the world. If weather could gradually wear down mountains or gullies, it could also change animals. He gave examples:

> Variations in the weight of the atmosphere, which impinges upon us from all sides, increase or diminish the tone of our organs and hence speed up or slow down the circulation of body fluids ... fluctuations of temperature open or close

> the routes by which transpiration takes place ... changes in atmospheric humidity either rob us of our natural heat or maintain it.
>
> (Lamarck, 1799, cited in Jordanova, 1984, p. 67)

Lamarck's study of fossils convinced him that these changes in bodies were passed down through inheritance. And if it could happen to clams, how much more could be passed down in humans, who interacted with the world in so many more extensive ways and adapted to their local conditions through behavior as well? Indeed, an animal or man could change over time simply through the use of a certain muscle, building up that muscle for the next generation, or the disuse of an attribute, allowing it to fade away. This principle that physical changes in the body could be inherited and even that things learned by the parent can be passed down to offspring came to be called the **inheritance of acquired characteristics** or the **law of use and disuse**. He stated the principle succinctly:

> in every frequently repeated action, especially those that become habitual, the subtle fluids producing it carve out and progressively enlarge, by the repetition of particular displacements that they undergo, the routes that they have to pass through and render them more and more easy.
>
> (Lamarck, 1815, cited in Richards, 1987, p. 53)

Both bodily changes and learned information that happen to individuals could become part of species inheritance.

Lamarck had created the first truly evolutionary theory. Finally, we come to the point that one species can change its appearance, gradually over generations and even through its own effort. Lamarck was criticized for this view. Cuvier even had the bad taste to ridicule the theory in his eulogy given at Lamarck's funeral. He derided it as "something that might amuse the imagination of the poet" (Cuvier, 1835, cited in Richards, 1987, p. 63). As well he might; now the beautiful correlation of parts was not due to the hand of God, but to the actions of the animals themselves!

But even Lamarck was not as shocking as Darwin, because one could believe, as he did, that the development of the animal world was toward greater and greater perfection. Since intelligence was perfectible too, Lamarck believed that even we would get better and that human society would benefit. Those with most merit (he would pick scientists for the job) would rise to the top of society (Jordanova, 1984). Unfortunately, Lamarck was wrong. Lamarck also believed that species could change in response to environmental circumstances, but not that one species could become another (Mayr, 1982). As we will see, Darwin taught both that one species could transmute into another and, more shockingly, that changes in species happened through massive, capricious and random death, with no beneficial end goal for nature; modern genetics has proven him right.

Before the Paradigm Shift: A Historicist Summary

Let's stop for a moment to consider biology (a word Lamarck invented!) and psychology in the light of Kuhn's theory of scientific change. Natural theology towards the end of its reign was perhaps the first true paradigm in biology. True, it rested on a religious rationale, but the belief in uniform laws for the universe was a concept taken directly from Newton, and the passion for observation and reflection as the way to knowledge was taken directly from Locke. (Lamarck, for example, was well aware of Locke through a French disciple, the philosopher Condillac [1714–1780]). It was only a matter of time until the data collected under the paradigm of argument from design began to contradict the theory: It became impossible to believe that there was only one flood or that the earth was only a few thousand years old or even that species were created only once and not many times through special creation. Inevitably, the idea that species remained stable began to crumble under the weight of anomalies. As Kuhn predicted, there are often bitter battles, as between Lamarck and Cuvier, with each trying to explain away inconsistencies in the other's position. But even Lamarck could not give up the idea that the universe has a general direction and purpose, an idea with a 2000-year history. Darwin's views were both shattering and eagerly read by many, not only because they appeared to conflict with the religion of the time, but also with the science of the time, which were interconnected.

Psychologists were not immune to this. As we will see in later chapters, many psychologists chose Lamarck's way: that humans were perfectible and that human memories could be inherited, even after biology had discarded it. Freud thought that we inherited memories from previous generations, and the founder of developmental psychology G. Stanley Hall used it to explain child behavior. Piaget and Jung were accused of being Lamarckians, with good reason, and many believers in perfecting the intelligence and bodies of the human race through breeding (the eugenicists) believed it as well. Darwin's views were too hard to bear, for some.

Darwin

> With respect to the theological view of the question. This is always painful to me. I am bewildered. I had no intention to write atheistically. But I own that I cannot see as plainly as others do and I should wish to do, evidence of the design and beneficence on all sides of us. There seems to me too much misery in the world. I cannot persuade myself that a beneficent and omnipotent God would have designedly created the Ichneumonidae [a kind of wasp] with the express intention of their feeding within the living bodies of Caterpillars or that a cat should play with mice. Not believing this, I see no necessity in the belief that the eye was completely designed. On the other hand I cannot anyhow be contented to view this wonderful universe and especially the nature of man and to conclude that everything is the result of brute force. I am inclined to look at everything as resulting from designed laws, with the details, whether good or bad, left to the working out of what we may call chance. Not that this notion *at all* satisfies me. I feel most deeply that the whole subject is too profound for the human intellect. A dog might as well speculate on the mind of Newton. Let each man hope and believe what he can. Certainly I agree with you that my views are not at all necessarily atheistical. The lightning kills a man, whether a good or a bad one, owing to the excessively complex action of natural laws. A child (who may turn out to be an idiot) is born by the action of even more complex laws and I can see no reason why a man or other animal, may have been absolutely produced by other laws and that all these laws may have been expressly designed by an omniscient

Figure 4.1 Charles Darwin (1809–1882)
Source: Photo taken in 1854

creator, who foresaw every future event and consequence. But the more I think the more bewildered I become; as indeed I probably have shown by this letter.
—Charles Darwin (in a letter to Harvard botanist Asa Gray, 1860, in Darwin 1892/1958, p. 249)

What was it about Darwin that so distressed people about his particular version of evolution and how did he arrive at that view? As the above quote illustrates, no one was more troubled by the implications of his views than Darwin himself. What Linnaeus, Cuvier and even Lamarck were inclined to see as evidence of, if not the hand of God, then at least the impersonal march of nature towards perfection, Darwin, reluctantly but confidently, ascribed to chance. Even other "transmutationists" who believed in changing species, believed, as Aristotle did, in the final cause or the purpose for something to exist and a direction for its change. Darwin did not share this belief in **teleology**, the view that nature had goals. What nature did have, as Newton and Descartes had pointed out, were natural laws, with an essentially amoral character, disconnected from our human well-being. This view had incalculable effects on biology, psychology and our view of ourselves.

When Charles Robert Darwin was born, on February 12, 1809, it could be said that he had at least one freethinking evolutionist already in his family tree. His grandfather, the wealthy and influential physician Erasmus Darwin (1731–1802), had

Figure 4.2 Erasmus Darwin (1731–1802)
Source: Joseph Wright of Derby (1770)

studied at the best medical school in the British Isles, the University of Edinburgh, Scotland. This was Hume's university, and Erasmus had written a British empiricist view of animal structure and behavior in order to develop a theory of disease. Erasmus's book, *Zoonomia*, followed Hume's and Hartley's associationist principles (see Chapter 3). It stated that all animal motions, which have occurred in succession, become connected together by the repeated efforts of muscles in response to sensations or desires (Richards, 1987). This idea also explains a problem that is inherent in Locke's philosophy. If we grant that there are no innate ideas, then how do we explain instincts? Erasmus Darwin suggested that they were acquired by sensation and experience and passed down to their progeny:

> all warm-blooded animals have arisen from one loving filament, which the GREAT FIRST CAUSE endued with animality, with the power of acquiring new parts, attended with new propensities, directed by irritations, sensations,

volitions and associations; thus possessing the faculty to improve by its own inherent activity and delivering down those improvements by generation to its posterity, *world without end!*

(E. Darwin, 1796, cited in Richards, 1987, p. 36; emphasis in original)

Erasmus was a friend to many of the early industrialists, Unitarian Dissenters, who were not part of the British Anglican establishment, but who were becoming wealthy. As with Erasmus, many in this group were uniformitarians, who believed that God had set the universe running on stable laws that held, in general, for humans as well as animals. The Darwins were Whigs, for the liberalization of land ownership, educational opportunities, laissez-faire capitalism and religious freedom; they were also staunchly anti-slavery. Erasmus designed machines that used the new steam engine in the pottery factory of his friend, Josiah Wedgewood II (founder of the Wedgewood China company). In fact, Josiah's daughter Susannah married Erasmus's son Robert, who had by then studied to become a doctor at his father's alma mater; Charles Darwin was Susannah and Robert's fifth child.

But Charles's mother died when he was eight years old, leaving him in the care of his sisters and his imposing father. Perhaps because of this tragedy, Darwin became a rather reticent child; his schoolmates recalled that he was old before his time. Charles hated reading the classics and learning ancient languages, as was expected of a boy of his class. He spent so much time instead doing sometimes dangerous chemistry experiments (banished to the greenhouse because of the smell!) that his friends nicknamed him "Gas" Darwin. He loved to hunt and ride as well, indulging in an early love of the outdoors.

At age 16, Darwin was sent to Edinburgh to learn medicine, but soon decided he didn't have the stomach for it. As well he might; surgery was done without anesthetic, in bloody, dirty conditions. After a particularly horrible procedure on a child, he never went back to that class. But in his two years at Edinburgh, he learned many things in and out of other classes, which might be seen as goofing off, but which prepared him to be a superb naturalist. He learned to stuff birds and spent much time studying the sea life he could find on the shore. Through his naturalist work, he became acquainted with the then radical ideas of Lamarck. Worse, in 1826, on the day that he presented his first scientific finding about the larvae of sea mats, he was introduced to the dreaded idea of materialism: that the mind and body are not separate entities, but that the mind is simply a result of physical and chemical processes of the brain. The idea provoked such fierce debate that an angry, perhaps fearful member of the society struck lines through the part of the meeting minutes that dealt with the discussion (Desmond & Moore, 1991).

But Darwin was failing as a physician. His father then dreamed up the plan of making him an Anglican priest. The good doctor would buy Charles a parish (this was apparently common; Desmond & Moore, 1991) and in between sermons he could, as many curates did in those days, study nature all he wanted. The next year, Darwin enrolled at a citadel of Anglican orthodoxy, Christ College, Cambridge University. Darwin had to swear allegiance to the faith despite his freethinking background. His natural theology professors were all creationists. Yes, they said, species have become extinct in the past, due to massive upheavals in weather or geology (the catastrophists' position) or through gradual consistent change over time (the uniformitarian position). In either case, God then steps in to perform a special creation to replace the missing species. Darwin devoured the main text in natural theology in preparation for his final exams. The book by William Paley justified the natural world as part of God's beneficent plan. It is actually a theological proof of the goodness and intelligence of God. He originated the famous analogy of God the watchmaker. If you find a stone, perhaps its nature does not require a designer to explain it. A watch however, in its intricate nature, requires a "contriver for the contrivance." How much more likely would it be for animals? Moreover, the design is *good*. God has provided pleasure to his creations, showing his goodness:

> It is a happy world, after all. The air, the earth, the water, teem with delighted existence. In a spring noon or a summer evening, on whichever side I turn my eyes, myriads of happy beings crowd upon my view. "The insect youth are on the wing." Swarms of newborn flies are trying their pinions in the air. Their sportive motions, their wanton mazes, their gratuitous activity, their continuous change of place without use or purpose, testify their joy and the exultation which they feel in their lately discovered faculties. . . . A bee amongst the flowers in spring is one of the most cheerful objects that can be looked upon. Its life appears to be all enjoyment; so busy and so pleased. The whole winged insect tribe, it is probable, are equally intent upon their proper enjoyments and under every variety of constitution, gratified and perhaps equally gratified, by the offices of which the Author of their nature has assigned to them.
>
> (Paley, 1802/1850, p. 465)

Darwin was by all accounts a thoughtful and courteous young man, eager to learn (in natural history at least) and eager to please, so his professors took him under their wings. He learned botany, geology and zoology, while cramming in enough theology to get his degree. He was also madly interested in entomology, collecting species of beetles by the hundreds.

As he neared graduation, one of his professors recommended him as a captain's companion for a survey down and up the South American coasts that would take him eventually around the world. The captain of the *Beagle*, Robert FitzRoy, was a devout and conservative Tory, but Darwin seemed a personable young man, well qualified by training and social station, who would largely pay his own way. Darwin was not on board technically as a naturalist: The ship's surgeon typically did that. Rather, the position of the captain on ship was a lonely one; he was forbidden by custom to socialize with the men on ship and needed someone of his own social station like Darwin to talk to. The previous captain had committed suicide (Desmond & Moore, 1991).

Darwin was more than eager to take the job, despite his tendency to terrible seasickness. Once he got on board in 1831, he became a naturalist with a vengeance, preserving plants, shooting and stuffing birds, pickling fish, tagging bones and specimens from Argentina to Australia, taking side trips inland and packing up and shipping his specimens from various exotic ports of call. (He was so good at this that the ship's surgeon resigned in disgust and envy, taking a ship home from South

America!) He also saw some of his fellow man and wondered how climate and circumstances may have made them different from himself: short South American natives of Tierra del Fuego, thin black Australian aboriginal peoples, brutal European colonial slavemasters. When he was done, he had been away from home five years and had a lifetime of work ahead. He had collected 1529 species and 3907 labeled skins, bones, rocks and corals. His diary ran to 770 pages, his notebooks on geology took up 1383 pages and his notebooks on zoology, 368 pages. He never left England again (Desmond & Moore, 1991).

Darwin donated his specimens to various natural history museums and set down to work. The expert to whom he had given his bird specimens from the Galapagos Islands had noticed something interesting. In that small area of the islands, Darwin had brought back 13 different species of finches and four of mockingbirds. From the tags on the mockingbirds, he noticed that each species had its own island. Darwin had thought these were interbreeding varieties, not species at the time he collected them, but closer inspection found that they were subtly different; each one had a slightly different beak, short and stubby or thin and pointed. Darwin recalled that the governor of the islands had remarked that each island of the Galapagos had its own giant tortoise as well.

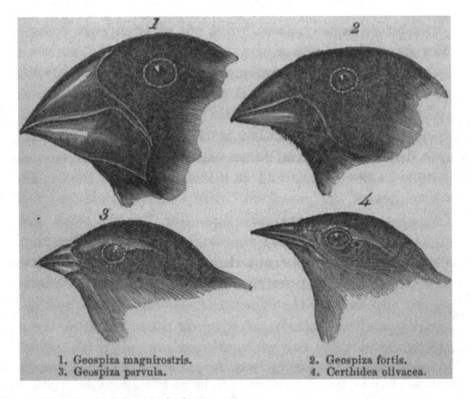

1. Geospiza magnirostris. 2. Geospiza fortis.
3. Geospiza parvula. 4. Certhidea olivacea.

Figure 4.3 Variation in Galapagos finches.

Source: From (1838) *The Zoology of the Voyage of H.M.S. Beagle*, by John Gould. Edited and superintended by Charles Darwin. London: Smith Elder and Co. Public domain.

Furthermore, all of these species were similar to ones he had seen on the South American continent 600 miles away. He had two questions: Why were there so many different species on the islands? And why were all the species so similar to the ones from the mainland even though the Galapagos were based on new volcanic rock and the mainland was not? If animals had been created for their individual place in nature, why these similarities? He came slowly to realize that there had been one or few different species on the mainland that were blown by prevailing winds and currents to individual islands. Once there, he noted, the currents between the islands are deep, turbulent and swift and winds are few, so they become cut off from the others. They breed among themselves, accentuating the differences over time, so that eventually, after many generations, they can no longer mate with the original stock.

The Theory of "Transmutation by Natural Selection"

> It is interesting to contemplate a tangled bank, clothed with many plants of many kinds, with birds singing on the bushes, with various insects flitting about and with worms crawling through the damp earth and to reflect that these elaborately constructed forms, so different from each other and dependent upon each other in so complex a manner, have all been produced by laws acting around us. These laws, taken in the largest sense, being Growth with Reproduction; Inheritance which is almost implied by reproduction; Variability from the direct and indirect action of the conditions of life and from use and disuse: A Ratio of Increase so high as to lead to a Struggle for Life and as a consequence to Natural Selection, entailing Divergence of Character and the Extinction of the less-improved forms. Thus, from the war of nature, from famine and death, the most exalted object which we are capable of conceiving, namely, the production of the higher animals, directly follows. There is grandeur in this view of life, with its several powers, having been originally breathed by the Creator into a few forms or into one; and that, whilst this planet has gone cycling on according to the fixed law of gravity, from so simple a beginning endless forms most beautiful and wonderful have been and are being evolved.
> —Charles Darwin (the final paragraph of *[On] The Origin of Species*, 1859)

Darwin had completed a 250-page summary of his theory by 1844 and thought well enough of it to lock it in a safe with instructions to his wife to publish it if he were to die. But he did not publish it for another 15 years, after he had spent eight years dissecting and studying smelly barnacles in his study, several years gathering data from pigeon breeders and gathering other information. He spent most of his time at Down House, his estate in Kent, with bouts of constant, methodical activity alternating with bouts of serious illness. Some have even suggested that his illness was a psychosomatic result of worrying about how his theory would be received (e.g. Bowlby, 1991).

As often happens, the final impetus to publish came from the fear that he might be beaten to the punch. Another naturalist, Alfred Russel Wallace, had hit upon the same theory and sent Darwin a copy of his paper before publishing it. He had his theory presented by a friend, together with Wallace's, at a scientific meeting. As was usual for Darwin, he was too nervous and ill to present it himself.

But what was so revolutionary in Darwin's work? As Stephen Jay Gould has remarked, the belief in evolution, then called **"transmutation of species,"** was the most common heresy in 19th-century Britain. What was not common was the mechanism that Darwin proposed for it.

Let us examine the theory piece by piece from the quotation above. It is a given that every prosperous species experiences *Growth with Reproduction*, in that species that reproduce well grow in numbers. In doing so, they pass down various characteristics through *Inheritance*. Indeed, between the time he returned from his voyage and the time, over 20 years later, that Darwin published his masterwork, he had studied inheritance principles with farmers who pursue the hobby of pigeon breeding for special characteristics. A particularly colorful or strange bird could be mated with other birds and new characteristics slowly shaped. The breeders called this "picking" or "selection." The characteristics often arrived by accident; indeed, with every species there was a great deal of variety in characteristics, a great deal of *Variability* in production of characteristics for the breeder to choose from. The mating didn't always work in the way intended; nevertheless, when it did, the offspring could be further mated to accentuate the differences. But what, in nature, was the equivalent to the hand of the breeder? To Darwin, this was *the conditions of life*. Variations in local natural disasters, such as flood or drought, affect food supply and kill off organisms. Slow and constant shifts in climate, an increase in predators or competition for mates, cause these changes. At this time, Darwin believed in the possibility of changes in animals by Lamarckian acquired characteristics (variability from *use and disuse*), but he did not share Lamarck's faith in the perfectibility of species. The theory of genetic transmission of characteristics had yet to be proposed, and he therefore did not know that the nature of genetics makes Lamarckian inheritance impossible (Darwin, 1872/1998; Mayr, 1982).

When reproduction is going well, even under benign circumstances, the mathematics of reproduction suggests that there would soon be more animals than food for them; some of them must die. Thus, a *High Ratio of Increase* leads to a *Struggle for Life*. This was based on the theory of the Reverend Thomas Malthus (1766–1834) who had written an essay on human population explosion, in which he stated that population, left unchecked, would double every 25 years or so. As population rises faster than food supply, starvation was inevitable, said Malthus. What's more, Malthus believed that the poor laws that provide charity only increase the probability that the poor will survive and breed, increasing the problem. This political position was held by many in Darwin's social circle in the 1830s when he was first composing the theory of evolution. In this decade, an economic depression was putting one in ten on government relief and forcing thousands to emigrate. Riots and political upheaval were common (Desmond & Moore, 1991). The controversial prevalence of Malthusian rhetoric in British society of the time can be seen in a passage in Dickens's *Christmas Carol*. When Scrooge, a satirical stereotype of a Malthusian, is asked by Bob Cratchit for a contribution to charity, Scrooge mentions grudgingly that his taxes support workhouses. When Cratchit responds that people die there, Scrooge says, "Then let them die and decrease the surplus population!" (Desmond & Moore, 1991). Darwin reports in his autobiography that he specifically transplanted Malthus's political concept to the natural world. It provided the core mechanism for how changes would occur in his theory, but showed a far darker side to the natural world than that of Paley (Darwin, 1892/1958, pp. 42–43).

A consequence to this is that not only would some die, but also some would live. Some of those who would live would live only by chance. Others might survive because a slightly longer beak may have a slightly better chance of getting more food than a shorter beak, increasing the chances of survival. Those that would live would be those that were lucky enough to be better adapted to the circumstances in which they find themselves at that particular time and place. They are hardier in the climate, they could get at more food or they could capture more mates or fend off predators better. Such an animal can be said to have survived **natural selection**. Biologists have noted that "natural selection" is an unfortunate name, because the word "selection" implies an intelligent being deciding what is best (Mayr, 1991). Natural selection is instead a cold, largely random, machine of death; there is no plan to build over time a more perfect animal. If the conditions change later, those who are said to be better adapted now may no longer be better adapted and may die. The animals we see appear well adapted, because we can only see a small time segment, but the adaptiveness is not something contained in the animal as part of its essence. There are no essences, there is only change; what defines adaptiveness are those things that allow survival and reproduction and that can only really be known after the fact.

If the pressures of climate change or competition for food or mates is harsh enough, a slight difference in a physical characteristic confers enough of an advantage to make it more likely that that characteristic is passed down. Then, a bird with a larger beak will have offspring that have slightly larger beaks on average; an increasingly harsh environment providing only food in inaccessible crevices might make it likely that only the offspring with still larger beaks would survive and so on. If the environmental circumstances get progressively more stringent over time, then this leads to *Divergence of Character*, defined as the process of a characteristic becoming more and more pronounced over generations, diverging from the common stock.

Darwin himself never saw this happen in the wild, but his hunch about the Galapagos finches and mockingbirds was a good one. In a 25-year study of Darwin's finches in the Galapagos, Princeton biologists Peter and Rosemary Grant have discovered that not only does divergence of character happen, it can happen quite fast, and living or dying for a finch can turn on a surprisingly small difference (Weiner, 1994). The Grant team has succeeded in identifying and measuring the full-grown beak length of virtually every finch on the island of Daphne Major, a hot, black lava rock in very rough seas. Moreover, through methodically sifting square meters of seeds, they know exactly what the finches eat. They even know how hard it is to eat them; some have very hard shells, requiring a lot of beak force to crack, and some are small and soft. In the Galapagos wet season, many finches can do well, because all kinds of seeds are available. In the dry season, only the birds with deeper, stronger beaks can crack large, dry nutritious nuts. In a drought, such as happened in 1977, only about one in five finches survived, and they had larger beaks and bodies than those who died. Furthermore, since females were smaller, they had died in larger numbers. This left many more males than females. The females then chose the largest males of the remaining lot to breed with when the drought was over, accentuating the difference in the next generation. One variety of finch almost died out, and the remainder tried to mate across species. Most of these parings didn't work, but one pair did reproduce and their offspring flourished in future generations.

Lest you begin to think that the big-beaked finch is simply a "better" finch for all time, you should know that a few years after the drought that favored larger birds, a flood happened that made their food source of hard nuts decline. It was harder for the big birds to survive, because they were big and hungry and they had to waste a lot of energy going after zillions of tiny little seeds with their now clumsy beaks. The distribution of beak sizes in the population shifted back. The shocking thing was that the life and death struggle turned, in some cases, on average beak size differences of less than a millimeter! (Weiner, 1994).

If the species cannot survive, it of course suffers *Extinction of the less-improved forms*. Pandas, for instance, are under threat because of a number of unlucky circumstances: They eat only bamboo, and their digestive systems are so inefficient that they require large quantities of it; the range of bamboo forests are narrowing; they have only one offspring at a time with a long gestation period and they mate infrequently and for life. Theoretically, given the time span of many generations, the panda might "adapt" (although the offspring might not look like pandas!), but if the range of bamboo gets too small too soon, they will go extinct. Individual pandas don't adapt; they either live or die. Species adapt over many generations and if forced to adapt too much, they die out (Gould, 1980).

Darwin's theory has been spectacularly well verified by natural experiments of this sort, as well as by technologies that Darwin never dreamed of. Among living species, we can verify or disprove relationships between organisms by the similarity of their DNA. Among fossils, carbon dating based on a constant rate of radioactive decay of the carbon in organic matter can verify the ages of samples. A scientist can hypothesize a relationship, and others can use these techniques to disprove it. Although the Darwinian paradigm is secure in biology, uniting life from bacteria to humans (see Eldredge, 2000, for an interesting argument of this premise), the "normal science" of proving particular connections or evaluating certain mechanisms goes on still, and fierce battles are still waged over exactly how evolution does its work, as we will see later in this chapter.

Evolution and Humans

The first edition of 1500 copies of *The Origin of Species* sold out in one day on November 24, 1859. The second edition came out less than two months later and sold more than twice as many copies. The book was reviewed by major newspapers and intellectual journals. Darwin was stunned to hear that it was being sold to commuters at train stations. Why was it so in demand?

The general public was interested in natural history, it is true, but it is what the book implied about human nature that made it such a best seller. Darwin had said barely anything about humans, to avoid offending the sensibilities of his readers (and his supportive wife, Emma; as much as she loved him, she thought his views were blasphemous). The reading public was not deterred; some of the establishment reviews discussed the new impermanence of man and the improbabilities of descent from monkeys.

At the British Association for the Advancement of Science meetings in June 1860, a huge public crowd of between 700 and 1000 (among them, very rowdy students) convened to hear a debate on evolution between bishop of Oxford, Samuel Wilberforce, and evolution proponents led by Thomas Henry Huxley (1825–1895). Huxley, who would come to be called "Darwin's bulldog" for his zeal in defending his theory, had worked his way up from hardscrabble beginnings in one of the worst depressions of the century to become a physician, not at conservative Oxford or Cambridge, but at an anatomy college steeped in materialist doctrine. He joined the navy as a ship's surgeon and naturalist and sailed around the world, eventually publishing and widely lecturing on everything from invertebrates to primate anatomy. At the time, he was professor of paleontology at the Government School for Mines, London. He hated the privileges of the established church, for he had reached this success through his own merit (Desmond, 1994).

Wilberforce, by contrast, was everything that Huxley hated: Secure and smug, nicknamed "Soapy Sam" for his slipperiness in debate, he was an archconservative even by church standards on natural history and, unfortunately, he was not well informed in the details.

There were conflicting accounts as to what was actually said at the debate, but the most dramatic account, that became part of legend, was published years later by Huxley's son, relying on his father's recollections:

> In a light, scoffing tone, florid and fluent, [Wilberforce] assured us that there was nothing in the idea of evolution; rock-pigeons were what rock-pigeons had always been. Then, turning to his antagonist with a smiling insolence, he begged to know, was it through his grandfather or his grandmother that he claimed his descent from a monkey?
>
> Huxley slapped his knee and whispered to his companion: "The Lord hath delivered him into mine hands."
>
> On this, Huxley slowly and deliberately arose. A slight tall figure, stern and pale, very quiet and very grave, he stood before us and spoke those tremendous words—words which no one seems too sure of now, nor, I think, could remember just after they were spoken, for their meaning took away our breath, though it left us in no doubt as to what it was. He was not ashamed to have a monkey for his ancestor; but he would be ashamed to be connected with a man who used great gifts to obscure the truth. No one doubted his meaning and the effect was tremendous. One lady fainted and had to be carried out; I for one, jumped out of my seat.
>
> (L. Huxley, 1898, cited in Richards, 1987, pp. 3–4)

This is, of course, history written by the winners. Most of the clergy that day were unmoved, the women were by and large appalled and the students, like students everywhere, just loved a good show. But the gantlet was thrown down. By the time of the sixth edition in 1872, most naturalists had come over to Darwin's position on common descent—the part of the theory that suggests that animals had descended from ancestor species. Even a majority of Anglican clergymen would come around within Darwin's lifetime. Both groups had trouble with the brutal mechanism of natural selection, as opposed to acquired characters, for many years after that (Himmelfarb, 1962; Mayr, 1982). Darwin's theory was nevertheless accepted very quickly, for animals, at least, for a theory of its magnitude. As you may have detected already, part of the reason was politics. Huxley would for years give cheap lectures to the workingmen of London; they were appreciative, because it suggested that position in society, as well as the natural world, might be acquired, rather than divinely given (Desmond, 1994).

When Darwin did begin to talk about the physical and mental and even moral similarities between animals and humans, in *The Descent of Man, and Selection in Relation to Sex* (1871), the response was unshocked, but also unconvinced (Himmelfarb, 1962). Darwin put forth many arguments on the similarities of humans and animals. He began the argument by discussing physical similarities. He noted that man has similar bones to other animals and that man and monkey are susceptible to the same diseases. Monkeys are almost as helpless at birth as humans. If one looks at the embryos of humans and of birds, it becomes clear that the same bones that become wings in birds become hands in man. Man has rudiments of body parts that are common in lower animals. He did not see any other way that so many similarities could occur if at some point we did not have a common ancestor.

On the mental side, Darwin believed strongly that the higher animals have the same basic set of emotional responses that we do and that they are inherited. In *Descent* and several other publications (e.g. Darwin, 1872, 1877) he made the case, using many anecdotes, that their behaviors indicate a whole range of emotions from the simple emotion of anger to the more complex ones of jealousy and magnanimity. He noted that many facial expressions, such as the grin or the sneer, can be commonly seen in apes (Darwin, 1872). He even had studied his own infant son years earlier to determine the basic, inherited emotions; he wished to disprove empiricist beliefs that simple emotions were learned (Darwin, 1877). In *Descent*, he suggested that higher animals shared at least some degree of memory, attention and reason. The following entertaining example is typical:

> Dogs show what might fairly be called a sense of humor as distinct from mere play; if a bit of stick or other such object be thrown to one, he will often carry it away for a short distance; and then squatting down with it on the ground close before him, will wait until his master comes quite close to take it away. The dog will then seize it and rush away in triumph, repeating the same maneuver and evidently enjoying the practical joke.
>
> (Darwin, 1874, p. 69)

Darwin knew that he would be criticized for his position, but he tried even to give evidence of rudimentary behaviors that are related to the highest behaviors of humans. For example, man was considered the only animal to use tools: Darwin noted that monkeys use rocks to crack hard fruits and he had seen an orangutan use a stick as a lever. Language was a large sticking point for doubters of Darwin's thesis: He noted that although language was unique to humans, animals were observed to modify their calls to different prey and with experience. He even attempted to compare the devotion of a dog for his master (with its "love, complete submission to an exalted and mysterious superior, a strong sense of dependence fear, reverence, gratitude, hope for the future" Darwin, 1871, pp. 67–68) with the feelings of "primitive" humans in their religious rites. Obviously this comparison would be insulting to the aboriginal peoples discussed, were they in a position to object. Disturbingly, however, one Anglican reviewer of Darwin's book did not take offense at the comparison of the dog with the aboriginal peoples, but stated, "what is said about savages is beside the mark as to true religion and true belief in God" (Atheneum, 1871, cited in Richards, 1987, p. 200).

Darwin then took pains to explain that humans could be subject to the same consistent laws of natural selection as animals. He noted that in many cases, humans lived in harsh, unforgiving environments. The Fuegians he had met in South America seemed like savages to Darwin (1839, p. 428)—the relativism of modern anthropology was decades away. And yet Nature "by making habit omnipotent" had "fitted the Fuegian to the climate & productions of his country." Because some Fuegians had been brought back to England and turned into near-proper Englishmen, he knew that they could adapt. But he also suspected that the harsh pressures of environment and competition with others for food or mates could change men.

Darwin believed that civilized society had evolved from a more barbarous past, perhaps even to make humans so comfortable as to be beyond the reach of natural selection, which may not have been a good thing:

> We must therefore bear the undoubtedly bad effects of the weak surviving and propagating their kind; but there appears to be but one check in steady action, namely that the weak and inferior members of society do not marry so freely as the sound and this check might be indefinitely increased by the weak in body or mind refraining from marriage, though this is more to be hoped for than expected.
> (Darwin, 1874, p. 131)

But the "reckless, degraded and often vicious members of society, tend to increase at a quicker rate than the provident and generally virtuous members of society" (p. 135), because when they do marry, they marry early and produce many offspring. He did not make the mistake of equating virtue with wealth. Passing down wealth tends to protect inferior members of the family. (This is something that Darwin must have found poignant, as he, a wealthy man who was sick for much of his life, had married his cousin and produced many children, all of them well loved, but not all of them well.)

In the above quotes, we see the first glimmers of what came to be called **Social Darwinism**. Not only do all of the aspects of the struggle for existence determine the physical body of humans, but also their social, religious, moral and rational capabilities. One can believe in evolution without believing in Social Darwinism, simply by accepting that humans are cultural creatures and that not everything we do is determined by biology. As people with values, we may simply decide (or are conditioned by social habits) not to behave in such a way. However, it is surprising how wide a range of political and economic beliefs in the 19th and early 20th centuries claimed to fit under the umbrella of Social Darwinism. On the right, laissez-faire capitalists used evolutionary analogies to support the purifying effects of the marketplace and in some cases (see Herbert Spencer, later) to argue against welfare. On the left, Karl Marx asked Darwin if he could dedicate *Das Kapital* to him (Darwin declined; he was always skittish about all public political announcements and his wife would have been appalled at the atheism! Himmelfarb, 1962).

There are only two bright spots in this grim and morally objectionable philosophy. First, one of the greatest criticisms of Darwin's philosophies of human nature was that he could not explain why humans would sometimes do something for which they or their offspring would not immediately benefit, including lay down one's life for another. He countered that altruism can be explained by the fact that man is a social species and, therefore, what benefits members of his tribe benefits him:

> It must not be forgotten that although a high standard of morality gives but a slight or no advantage to each individual man and his children over the other men of the same tribe, yet that an increase of well endowed men and advancement in the standard of morality will certainly give an immense advantage to a tribe over another. A tribe including many members who from possessing in a high degree the spirit of patriotism, fidelity, obedience, courage and sympathy, were always ready to sacrifice themselves for the common good would be victorious over most other tribes; and this would be natural selection.
>
> (Darwin, 1874, p. 129)

Second, Darwin, coming from a long line of anti-slavery Whigs, did not believe something so trivial as skin color could aid survival to a great degree. Hence, he believed that the great intelligence of humans had been acquired before the differences in skin color arose. Thus, unlike some of his time, he did not agree that races were different species or that one race was inferior to another in intelligence. The race difference could be explained, he thought, by **sexual selection** rather than natural selection. Like the plumage of birds, the skin color doesn't help someone get more food, but it might help someone attract a mate. Sexual selection operates in tandem with natural selection to intensify the effect of certain changes. In the finch example given earlier, even after many of the smaller male finches had been eliminated by natural selection, the largest of the remainder were chosen by female finches to breed with. Darwin spent the last half of the book discussing how this process of selection of stronger or more attractive mates could direct the change in species.

He concluded *Descent* with a chapter on sexual selection in humans that built on this work. He noted that in the animal world, particularly among mammals, the male is generally larger and more aggressive than the female, presumably to have the strength to compete with other males for females. The same appears true for humans, said Darwin. There is a wide variety of different notions of beauty in human culture, and Darwin suggested that what a particular culture likes, it tends to accentuate through makeup or ornamentation. Those cultures or races that do not grow beards tend to remove other unwanted hair on males; those that do grow them tend to accentuate them and compete on that basis. The same is true of broad faces or lighter skin or other characteristics. Those who possess these features are more likely to breed, accentuating the features over generations.

Finally, Darwin believed that there were differences between the sexes in mental strengths and emotional temperaments.

> Woman seems to differ from man in mental disposition, chiefly in her greater tenderness and less selfishness; and this holds good even with savages.... Woman, owing to her maternal instincts, displays these qualities towards infants in an eminent degree; therefore it is likely that she would often extend them towards her fellow-creatures. Man is the rival of other men; he delights in competition and this leads to ambition which passes too easily into selfishness. These latter qualities seem to be his natural and unfortunate birthright. It is generally admitted that with woman the powers of intuition, of rapid perception and perhaps of imitation, are more strongly marked than in man; but some, at least of these faculties are characteristic of the lower races and therefore of a past and lower state of civilization.
> (Darwin, 1874, p. 559)

This quote shows the double-edged sword of Victorian sexism; woman comes off as the "fairer sex" but also the less advanced sex. Darwin suggested that men possessed more "energy, perseverance and courage" but, through the law of acquired characteristics, women might change:

> In order that women should reach the same standard as man, she ought, when nearly adult, to be trained to energy and perseverance and to have her reason and imagination raised to the highest point; and then she would probably transmit these qualities chiefly to her adult daughters.
> (Darwin, 1874, p. 560)

This sounds rather optimistic, until, reading further, one discovers that he expects too few people to take him up on the suggestion to make a difference!

The Cosmic Evolutionism of Mr. Herbert Spencer

One of the first books on human psychology as influenced by evolution was written by the English philosopher, journalist, engineer, social theorist and general polymath Herbert Spencer (1820–1903). Indeed, in the sixth edition of *Origin* (1872), Darwin gave a small plug for Spencer's work: "Psychology will be securely based on the foundation of Mr. Herbert Spencer, that of the necessary acquirement of each mental power and capacity by gradation. Much light will be thrown on man and his history" (p. 647).

Spencer had actually published on some of the basic ideas of evolution before Darwin did. Indeed, the very term "evolution" and the phrase "survival of the fittest" come from Spencer. Like Darwin, he had been influenced by the work of Thomas Malthus, and his first writings invoked the survival of the fittest in nature as an analogy against state-supported charity (the so-called Poor Laws). Speaking of herd animals and carnivores, but referring to humans, he said,

> their carnivorous enemies not only remove from herbivorous herds individuals past their prime, but also weed out the sickly, the malformed and the least fleet

or powerful. By the aid of which purifying processes, as well as by the fighting, so universal in the pairing season, all vitiation of the race through the multiplication of its inferior samples is prevented; and the maintenance of a constitution completely adapted to surrounding conditions and therefore most productive of happiness, is insured.

(Spencer, 1851/1865, p. 353)

He believed that the only role of government was to protect person and property and that it had no responsibility for the poor or the sick. In his job as the editor of the *Economist*, he supported strict laissez-faire capitalism. Individuals, not governments, could support charity, however, and in doing so, they might acquire habits that they could pass down in a Lamarckian way to their offspring, making the world eventually a better place (at least for offspring of those not unfortunate enough to have starved in the process). Thus, Spencer was even more of a social Darwinist than Darwin himself was. Spencer even believed that war had beneficial features for society. In addition to weeding out "weak" tribes, military threat caused societies to band together and form more stable hierarchical organizations (Hawkins, 1997).

In his *Principles of Psychology*, first published in 1855 (revised in 1870), he states boldly that mind can only be understood by understanding how it evolved. This evolution occurred by a continuous increase in adaptation of the inner world to the outer world. Like the other associationists and Hume before them (Chapter 3), Spencer believed that the mind is composed of feelings, gathered originally from sensations, that can combine in many ways, through inductive reasoning and repeated experience to form ideas. But for Spencer, this process continues across individuals and species, saved up by inheritance of acquired characteristics. Unlike Darwin or even Lamarck, however, Spencer was not unduly bothered by how this is done or by collecting data to support his ideas. Evolution was his big idea, and he would apply it everywhere in the universe. The universe begins as an "indefinite, incoherent homogeneity" to a "definite, coherent, heterogeneity" (Spencer, 1870).

In Spencer's system, the universe begins without form, but from a "primordial irritability" matter develops. Nucleated protoplasm eventually develops, which forms itself into organs, which leads to lower animals with primitive sensations, living with a small consciousness of time and space, to more complex animals with more specialized, complex states of consciousness, which leads to ... well, you get the idea. This was quite ambitious for a psychology text; indeed the *Principles* was only one volume of what he called his synthetic philosophy, which included volumes on biology, sociology (of which he is considered one of the founders) and morality. His belief in evolution was utopian. Yes, it began with violence, but he believed that eventually all the bad attributes of humanity would be weeded out and peace would reign.

In part because of his position as a prolific journalist who also wrote on current debates in British national life, Spencer became quite influential for a short time. Darwin, Huxley, John Stewart Mill, Alexander Bain, William James and others read his work (he even had a long affair with the novelist Marian Evans, better known by her pen name George Eliot). And yet, his method was far from scientific. T.H. Huxley, teasing his friend, quipped, "Spencer's idea of a tragedy is a deduction killed by a fact" (Spencer, 1904, p. 467). But in writing one of the first psychology texts of the Darwinian age, he illustrated a tendency to be found in psychology ever since: Psychologists are often so eager to incorporate ideas from other sciences that actual facts take the back seat!

Haeckel's Recapitulation Theory of Evolution

In October 1866, a young, enthusiastic, German biology professor showed up on Darwin's doorstep, heart pounding with anticipation that he would finally meet his hero. The man was Ernst Haeckel (1834–1919), the foremost representative of the Darwinian worldview in Germany. He had read *Origin* in 1860 and was "profoundly moved." Unlike Darwin, he was not shy about promoting the philosophy of Darwinism or, as he called it, *Darwinismus*, in public lectures in Germany attended by hundreds of people. In 1863, well before Darwin had spoken publicly on the nature of man, he had proclaimed that humans had evolved from animals and that man's social

Figure 4.4 Ernst Haeckel (1834–1919)
Source: Photo taken c. 1895

existence was governed by biology. He even suggested that Darwinism provided the justification for the overthrow of "tyrants" and priests (Gasman, 1971).

Haeckel's visits were always exhausting: Aside from his bad English and Darwin's bad German making communication difficult, he insisted upon extending Darwin's vision beyond all limits, just as Spencer did in England. Indeed, the language barrier apparently kept Darwin from realizing that what Haeckel was preaching was not really natural selection, but a more Lamarckian view in which every bit of positive adaptation was saved up through the ages and added on. This view, called the **recapitulation theory** of evolution, is encapsulated by a famous (if now scientifically invalid) phrase: ontogeny recapitulates phylogeny.

This is a handy phrase, because defining the words (invented by Haeckel) defines the theory. **Ontogeny** refers to the life history of a single individual, from the fertilization of the egg to the development of the embryo and fetus, to the development of the child, to adulthood, old age and death. **Phylogeny** refers to the history of the species: in our case this means from lower animals to primates, to *Australopithecus*, to Cro-Magnon man to *Homo sapiens*. To recapitulate simply means to repeat. Thus, Haeckel's theory suggested that the history of the species is repeated in the life of every individual member of that species.

Haeckel had studied the embryos of many different species and noticed how similar they were, particularly at the beginning, and how the later, higher species seemed to "add on" stages to the earlier ones at the end of ontogeny (this is called "terminal addition"). In order to go through many more stages than the lower animals, higher animals also had to condense the stages and go through them faster ("condensation"). Haeckel thought that what had happened is that every animal must go through the adult stages of previous species before adding on new adaptations, probably by Lamarckian means (see Gould, 1977).

In support of his theory, Haeckel collected many interesting facts. In the embryo of the human, he saw similarities to the embryo of birds: The development of wings and the development of arms are similar. He even saw similarities between humans and fishes: Did you know that the human embryo has gills for a time and that a developing human fetus goes through three distinctly different sets of kidneys before birth?

If this is so, then it gives us a reason to study child development, because the child becomes an evolutionary laboratory. Doesn't every child begin first with reflexes, like most animals, then move on to voluntary movement, like mammals, and only then to reason? Indeed, when Darwin published his observations of his infant son discussed earlier, some of the observations noted these similarities (Darwin, 1877).

Unfortunately, Haeckel was wrong. Because evolution works by gene transmission and not Lamarckian inheritance of acquired characteristics, evolution is not a process of a refiner's fire saving up all the good solutions. Yes, evolution is conservative, saving some solutions. But a lot of DNA, we now realize, is random junk. More specifically, it appears that to make a stronger case, Haeckel faked some of his famous pictures of cross-species similarities. We now know that innovations in phylogeny can also be added early in the sequence of embryo development and the sequence can be slowed down or speeded up. Genes are switches, and a mutation might happen anywhere in development to turn things on or off. Why are we talking about a defunct evolutionary theory in a psychology textbook, then? Because many famous

From Argument by Design to Nature 111

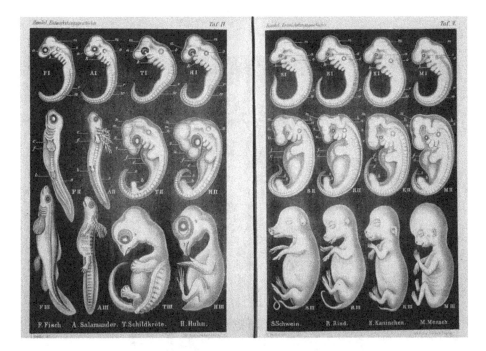

Figure 4.5 Double plate illustration showing embryos of fish (F), salamander (A), turtle (T), chick (H), pig (S), cow (R), rabbit (K), and human (M), at "very early," "somewhat later" and "still later" stages, from Haeckel's *Anthropogenie* published in 1874.

Source: This famous figure is controversial: Some have suggested that Haeckel faked the figures given here. More likely, this was a poster to be used in lectures in large halls. His biographer (Richards, 2008) thinks he may have emphasized similarities and deemphasized differences simply so that they can be seen by everyone attending.

psychologists bet on Haeckel's theory rather than Darwin's and based their own theories on it. At the time, there was little data that could disprove either view, so both were acceptable. We will discuss this next.

Recapitulation in Psychology and Culture

Recaptulationism was common in American as well as European culture until the 1920s, in part because it provided a "scientific" basis for many social prejudices. In the Victorian era, when self-control was prized, it was perhaps useful and even cute to think of young children as "little savages." G. Stanley Hall, the first president of the American Psychological Association and one of the first developmental psychologists, believed that play and nighttime fears of children were ancient holdovers from our evolutionary past:

> I regard play as the motor habits and spirit of the past of the race, persisting in the present, as rudimentary functions sometimes of and always akin to rudimentary organs. The best index and guide to the stated activities of adults in past ages is found in the instinctive, untaught and non-imitative plays of children ... Thus

Figure 4.6 Haeckel was an indefatigable explorer, natural historian, collector and artist, and he knew much about the natural world. He is famous to this day for his art in *Kunstformen der Natur* [*Artforms in Nature,* 1904.] This plate is of Thalamphora (marine plankton).

> we rehearse the activities of our ancestors, back we know not how far and repeat their life work in summative [i.e. additive] and adumbrative [condensed] ways.
>
> (Hall, 1904, p. 202)

Although fears of animals in the night are now irrational, said Hall, it clearly was rational to our ancestors. Thus, our children today are similar to adults of yesterday. When they grow up, they will, quite literally, become civilized.

The great Swiss developmentalist Jean Piaget based his theory, which he called genetic epistemology, on the premises of Haeckel's recapitulation, but this time, children recapitulate the entire history of science![1]

> The fundamental hypothesis of genetic epistemology is that there is a parallelism between the progress made in the logical and rational organization of knowledge and the corresponding formative psychological processes. With this hypothesis, the most fruitful, most obvious field of study would be the reconstituting of human history—the history of human thinking in prehistoric man. Unfortunately, we are not very well informed in the psychology of primitive man, but there are children all around us and it is in studying children that we have the best chance of studying the development of logical knowledge, mathematical knowledge, physical knowledge and so forth.
>
> (Piaget, 1969, p. 4)

Some progressive educators of the time decided to integrate this new "scientific" knowledge into their classroom. A principal of a school in Detroit suggested the following changes in the curriculum:

> The fundamental instincts of first-grade children upon entering school were found to be a restless curiosity, a naive sort of imaginativeness and tendencies toward contrivances of crude order, in short, such instincts as characterize the nomadic period in civilization. Stories about Hiawatha suggested themselves as answering the interest of these children and were successfully used. In the second grade, the Greek myths were found to appeal most strongly to the pupils, as embodying their own instinctive attitude toward life; and after awhile in another grade stories of chivalry were demanded by children in response to the dawnings of chivalric impulse only half dawning in themselves.
>
> (H. M. Scott, principal of the Detroit Normal School, 1897, cited in Gould, 1977, p. 5)

Sigmund Freud's psychosexual stages often baffle contemporary psychology students. Why should every boy, regardless of upbringing, go through an Oedipal stage in the preschool years, in which he fears his father and wants to marry his mother? He is recapitulating a time when young primate males had to fight the alpha male for possession of the females of the troop. Freud insisted that children "are compelled to recapitulate from the history of mankind the repression of an incestuous object choice" (Sulloway, 1978, p. 317).

A careful reader would find references to children reliving the conflicts before their births in all of the psychoanalytic theorists, including Carl Jung and Sándor

Ferenczi and many developmental psychologists of the late 19th and early 20th centuries. But as paleontologist Stephen J. Gould (1977) points out in a wonderful chapter on the pervasiveness of the idea, recapitulation provided support for other prejudices than those about children. It provided a justification for the mistreatment of nonwhite races, who were considered to be in adulthood like the children of the white race, justifying the "Burden of the White Man" to take care of them. Finally, criminals were said to be like children or vice versa: "It is provided by voluminous evidence, easily accessible, that children are born criminals" (Morse, 1892, p. 438, cited in Gould, 1977).

The Darwinian Paradigm Shift Reviewed

Darwin died on April 19, 1882, at 73 years of age. It was a mark of how far he had come in the eyes of his Anglican countrymen that he was buried in Westminster Abbey between Isaac Newton and the great astronomer John Herschel. The erstwhile theology student had become an agnostic, although he had always kept his religious views out of the public eye. In fact, the very term "agnostic" meaning "not knowing" had been coined and popularized by Darwin's friend T.H. Huxley as a polite way to separate science from religion: An atheist knows there is no God, but an agnostic scientist is unsure because he or she has no relevant data with which to make the final decision.

The paradigm of natural theology had proposed special creation; Darwin was a uniformitarian and believed in natural laws. The church was vitalist, in that it believed in the separation of the soul from the body. Darwin, silent on the soul, was a materialist and believed that the mind was a result of the physical properties of the brain. Natural theologians believed that each species had its own divine essence; for Darwin there were no essences, there was only variability in characteristics. Natural theologians were teleological: they believed the universe had a beneficial goal and purpose. Darwin did not believe in a goal or purpose for nature. Many philosophers believed that the addition of reason made humans divine. Darwin argued for continuity between the mind of man and animals. The public was quick to take up this idea, and a shift in the idea of human nature occurred, at least for some. In addition, the average person was reading not only Darwin, but also even more radical proponents of evolution such as Spencer and Haeckel.

Simultaneously, these writers supported new ideas in politics, economics and religion. In some ways, the general public (as well as theorists in psychology and biology!) were not really sure of the positive and negative consequences of evolutionary theory for a long time to come. This, however, is the intellectual climate that surrounded the development of psychology as a science.

Evolution of the Animal Mind: George John Romanes and C. Lloyd Morgan

Darwin's speculations on the mental states of animals laid the groundwork for the field of **comparative psychology** or the study of the development and evolution of animal behavior. Animal behavior had been studied before, of course, by Aristotle and Buffon, among others, but Darwin's theory provided an organizing principle for the data. At first, under Darwin's colleague and protégé George John Romanes (1848–1894), that principle was essentially: How much are animals like us? In his book *Animal Intelligence*, originally published in 1883, Romanes first had to define intelligence as opposed to reflex or instinct. He decided that a reflex is a neuromuscular response to stimuli that was entirely nonconscious and mechanical; an instinct is conscious and adaptive action that is inborn and does not vary across members of a species. Intelligent beings, on the other hand, make new adjustments in reaction to their own individual experiences in life. They intentionally solve problems of life by adapting means to ends. In other words, intelligent beings see goals and take steps to modify the environment to reach those goals.

How, then, do we determine the minds of other animals when we have access only to our own? Romanes suggested that we do this by analogy to our own minds.

> The mental states of an insect may be widely different from those of a man and yet most probably the nearest conception we can form of their true nature is that which we form by assimilating them to the pattern of the only mental states with which we are actually acquainted.
>
> (Romanes, 1883/1906, p. 10)

This sort of method causes problems, however, because Romanes was very liberal with what he called intelligence and how he formed analogies. He wrote about protozoa that sought each other out for "as it sometimes seems, mere sport" (p. 18). Below, one of the respondents quoted approvingly in his book describes the behaviors of ants as if they were wrestling at an ant Olympiad:

> They raised themselves on their hind legs, embraced each other by their forelegs, seized each other by their antennae, feet or mandibles and wrestled, but all in the friendliest fashion. They then let go, ran after each other and played at hide and seek. When one was victorious, it seized all the others in the ring, tumbling them like ninepins.
>
> (pp. 87–88)

Ants even have their own funeral procedures, in which they treat the dead with "some degree of reverence."

An example which sounds patently absurd when talking about ants does not sound so absurd to most dog lovers, but it suffers from exactly the same problem. An anecdote reported in Romanes's book describes a dog named Diver that stole a turkey from the fire and "hid" it in the cleft of a tree concealed by laurels. He quickly returned to the fire before the cook returned, looking "as innocent as a child unborn." The dog had been observed by a man in the yard and when the man came in he found the dog in his old place "pretending" to be asleep. The informant concludes:

> Diver's conduct was all along dictated by a desire to conceal his theft and if he were a man, I should have said that he intended in the case of inquiry, to prove an alibi.
>
> (p. 451)

Some observers of animal behavior, while strongly influenced by Darwin, balked at his and Romanes's overinterpretation of animal minds. C. Lloyd Morgan (1852–1936) had been a student of Darwin's bulldog, T.H. Huxley, and had been influenced by Spencer. He realized that although being generous about animal mental capabilities was a good debating tactic to convince people of the similarities between animals and humans, it was bad science. Essentially, if we project our minds onto animals by analogy, we assume what needs to be proven. A better way would be to try to explain the behavior of animals at the most minimal level of mind possible, allowing the possibility of reason only when the evidence warrants it. The formal statement of this principle is now known as **Morgan's canon**, stated in his book *An Introduction to Comparative Psychology* (1894/1903): "In no case may we interpret an action as the outcome of a higher psychical faculty if it can be interpreted as an outcome of the exercise of one which stands lower in the psychological scale" (p. 53). This principle simply states that some actions, which look at first glance like highly reasoned actions, may instead be the result of instinct or habitual associations of sense impressions.

Morgan's favorite example concerned his fox terrier Tony. If you were to see Tony running ahead of Morgan on his daily walk, he would run right up to the gate and lift the latch with his nose before proceeding. Morgan grants that this is technically intelligent behavior, because the dog has modified his behavior to achieve a goal. But because Morgan was able to examine the development of this behavior over time, he knows that it is not as smart as it seems. Before he learned this trick, Tony would stick his nose between the bars of the fence and look longingly beyond it, pawing at the fence. One day Tony moved his nose to the bars on the gate that happened to be right under the latch. In order to look at something that was not particularly in the direction of the gate, he lifted his head slightly to turn away, accidentally undoing the latch. When he looked back, the gate was open and he went out. It took the dog three weeks to perfect this simple maneuver, which visitors to Morgan's estate would marvel at. It seemed like planful, reasoned behavior, but it was actually the result of associations between sense impressions due to repeated **trial-and-error learning**.

But such seemingly difficult behaviors are highly memorable to dog owners, so that when a writer like Darwin or Romanes sent out their surveys to their correspondents about animal behavior, the extraordinary anecdotes, not the ordinary behaviors, are what they got back.

Morgan had another reason for parsimonious explanation: He wanted to bring the mind closer to the brain, like a good materialist. Reflexes are physiological; instincts are modified by natural and sexual selection; learning habits by association does not require concepts, only senses. Morgan was trying to understand how intelligence could be built from the bottom up, evolutionarily speaking. If we find it incredible that ants would literally hold an Olympics, then we have moved away from Paley's happy bees. We have stopped seeing creation as a mirror of ourselves and see it more as a heartless machine.

Galton's Legacy in Genetics and Psychometrics

> Some people hate the very name of statistics, but I find them full of beauty and interest. Whenever they are not brutalized, but delicately handled by the higher methods and are

Figure 4.7 Sir Francis Galton, 1890s

> warily interpreted, their power of dealing with complicated phenomena is extraordinary. They are the only tools by which an opening can be cut through the formidable thicket of difficulties that bare the path of those who pursue the Science of man.
> —Sir Francis Galton (1889, p. 62)

Perhaps the most direct influence of Darwin's perspective on psychology, aside from that of Darwin himself, comes from his second cousin, Sir Francis Galton (1822–1911). Galton's mother was the daughter of Erasmus Darwin by his second marriage and Francis was her youngest and most precocious child. He could read at 2-1/2 years of age, do math at 4 and read Latin well at 8. His father was a banker from a wealthy industrial family, so Francis had the means to become whatever he wanted. His mother was keen on his becoming a doctor, so his father set up an apprenticeship in medicine at a hospital in his hometown of Birmingham, England. At the age of 16, Galton was thrown into a position with considerable responsibility. He set bones, prepared medicines, changed bandages and helped with surgeries and amputations (then performed without anesthetic). Ever curious, he decided to investigate all of the medicines then available by taking small doses of them, in alphabetical order. He lasted until the letter C, when he took Croton's oil, a powerful emetic and laxative! He later continued his studies at Kings College, Cambridge University. Gradually, he began to realize that he was more interested in mathematics than medicine. He was prone to studying very hard, and after he lost a mathematics competition at Cambridge, he suffered a mental breakdown and did not seriously return to his studies in medicine. After his father's death in 1844, he became restless and like many wealthy young men from the "empire on which the sun never set," he decided to explore exotic areas of the world. He took a boat up the Nile and rode camels to Khartoum. He traveled to Cairo, Beirut, Damascus and Jerusalem. He funded an expedition to South West Africa, during which he negotiated a truce between the warring Damara and Namaqua peoples and reveled in the mathematical calculations of making maps of an area little known among Europeans. This trip exposed him to many cultures and races, but he apparently looked at them with typically English eyes. Later he commented, without a trace of irony, "It is seldom that we hear of a white traveler meeting with a black chief whom he feels to be the better man" (Galton, 1869/1892, p. 329).

Wherever he went, though, he would measure and count. In his own time, it was the fashion among Victorian women to accentuate a certain part of their anatomy (as a decorous Victorian might put it) with a bustle in the back of their dresses. While in Africa, he met Hottentot women who were so well endowed in that area that he had to measure them. He wrote to his brother, "I have seen figures that would drive the females of our native land desperate—figures that could afford to scoff at Crinoline." Reluctant to ask the women if he could measure them directly, he sat at a distance with his surveyor's sextant and "as the ladies turned themselves about, as they always do, to be admired, I surveyed them in every way and subsequently measured the distance of the spot where they stood—worked out and tabulated the results [using trigonometry] at my leisure" (Kevles, 1995, p. 7). He seemed to enjoy relating to the world on a statistical level. When at a boring lecture, he counted the fidgets of the audience members. When traveling in Britain, he secretly rated the beauty of the females he met as a kind of beauty contest among the towns. He measured the height and weight of schoolchildren in the country and the city. Country children were larger, he deduced, due to greater wealth. At the South Kensington International Health Fair, in 1884, Galton set up a booth. For a three-penny admission, he would measure weight, height, arm span, breathing capacity, strength of pull, force of blow, reaction time, sense acuity and judgement. He kept the data of 10,000 people who took the tests (They got a summary of their data, presumably for bragging rights!) (Forrest, 1974).

What is more, he knew how to analyze the data. He was aware of what the mathematician Quetelet called the **law of error**. If several people make a delicate scientific measurement, in astronomical observation, for example, those measurements would not agree perfectly, but would cluster around a mean in a bell-shaped normal curve. Galton's insight was that many natural attributes, such as height and weight, followed such a pattern, not as error, but as a matter of fact. Small samples that follow a normal curve, mixed together, would themselves form a normal curve. It was everywhere in nature. Small wonder that when his cousin Charles Darwin proposed that variability was the engine of evolution, Galton was delighted. He wrote that its publication "made a marked epoch in my own development" and swept away the "dogmatic barriers" of ancient authorities (Galton, 1908, p. 287). Quetelet had focused on the mean (or "norm") of the curve as important, but Galton saw that Darwin's theory gave importance to the tails of the distribution, because those attributes that were a little bit longer or shorter than average were the attributes that would help survival. He thus was the first to attempt to put his cousin's theory to a mathematical test in psychology, which he did in his provocative but flawed work, *Hereditary Genius*.

Hereditary Genius

Galton proposed to do three things in his book *Hereditary Genius* (originally published in 1869). First, he argued that mental abilities, like height, followed a normal distribution. Second, he wanted to prove that the advantages of the parents of superior accomplishment would be passed on to their children at a high rate. Third, he argued that such inheritance could be manipulated to produce a better race of people in the long run.

Proving the normal distribution was the easy part. Using the examination scores from Sandhurst military academy, Galton took pains to show that, as expected, most scores fell about the middle of the distribution, with fewer at the tails on either end. Using an analogy with height in Britain, he mentioned that if the average height was 66 inches, the distribution should predict only about 100 per million individuals taller than 78 inches, and this seemed to be the case. Thus, natural phenomena are normally distributed.

Next Galton discusses a hypothetical distribution of intelligence. If we take a normal distribution and segment it into 16 portions, most people would fall in the middle four groupings. The bottom three ranks would be, in the terminology of the day, "idiots and imbeciles." The third rank above the mean was said to be smarter than the foreman of an average jury; men in the next highest rank achieve "the ordinary prizes of life"; only the highest two ranks would achieve eminence. Galton had as his guide to eminent men and their families a catalog of 2500 men of the time (no women, apparently). He first satisfied himself that 2500 men would represent the proportion of the total men of that age group that should be in the top two ranks. Then he separated them into types of eminence (for example, judges, statesmen, literary men, artists and poets, men of science and in the physical realm, oarsmen and wrestlers). By examining whether sons and nephews of eminent men are also eminent men, by the book, he believed he could determine inheritance. Indeed, he seems to have found (or at least he believed to have found) evidence of a trend: The closer the relationship to the great man, the more likely the sons would be eminent.

How could Galton truly assert that eminence was based on inheritance alone? From our current point of view, of course, it would seem absurd that he did. The criteria for being included in a book on eminence are related as much to fame and social position as intelligence. And eminence in many groups is almost certainly related to wealth and social class, which the fathers would pass down along with their "gemmules" (the theoretical atoms of inheritance before the discovery of genes).

Galton appeared to know about these criticisms and argued against them perhaps a bit too strenuously to be fully believed. First, he claimed, social hindrances are good rather than bad: A man who becomes eminent in spite of them is naturally selected, almost by definition. But wouldn't the strong barriers in British society prevent us from having even more eminent men? No, said Galton:

> Culture is far more widely spread in America and the education of their middle and lower classes far more advanced; but for all that, America most certainly does not beat us in works of first class philosophy and art.... I argue that, if the hindrances to the rise of genius were removed from English society as completely as they have been removed from America, we should not become materially richer in eminent men.
>
> (Galton, 1869/1892, p. 40)

It would take too long to enumerate the logical and factual errors in that quote (although I invite my readers to try). He also suggested that it would be easy to point out average men who had been given all kinds of help but who never became eminent (although he ignored the help given to eminent men). One could also describe men in high places whom nobody cared when they died (as if in order for environmental processes to influence eminence at all, it must do so for all). These arguments suggest that despite his desire to place intelligence on a mathematical footing, his interpretations of the mathematical results were faulty and anecdotal.

Finally, after arguing that ability is normally distributed and that ability is mostly inherited, he wished to argue that by focusing on the upper end of that distribution, we could make a better species of human. Some of this might happen naturally, said Galton, through what he called **assortative mating**: "Able men take pleasure in the society of intelligent women and if they can find such as would in other respects be suitable, they would marry them in preference to mediocracies [sic]" (Galton cited in Forrest, 1974, p. 98). But Galton discovered that, left to their own devices, highly eminent couples would still have many of their children below their own level of intelligence, simply by chance; this purely mathematical consequence of two extreme members of a population marrying is called **regression towards the mean**. If those children married downward through assortative mating, there would be a progressive regression of the mean of the eminent couples towards the mean of the total population. This must be stopped if the race is to be improved.

Galton's answer was to establish a new science of genetics called **eugenics** (from the Greek for "well-born"), in which well-born people could be encouraged, by money or government laws or enlightened zeal of eugenics society members, to consciously marry well in terms of intelligence, morality and physical health. The offspring from such marriages would improve national human breeding stock. As a result, the average intelligence would be raised, but only if those at the bottom of the distribution could be induced not to reproduce. Then the highly intelligent people would earn their own bread through their own (genetic) merits, leading to a kind of utopia:

> The best form of civilization in respect to the improvement of the race would be one in which society was not costly; where incomes were chiefly derived from professional sources and not much through inheritance; where every lad

had a chance of showing his abilities and if highly gifted, was enabled to achieve a first class education and entrance to professional life, by the liberal help of the exhibitions and scholarships which he had gained in early youth; where marriage was held in as high an honour as in ancient Jewish times; where the pride of race was encouraged; where the weak could find a welcome and a refuge in celibate monasteries and sisterhoods and lastly, where the better sort of emigrants and refugees from other lands were invited and welcomed and their descendents naturalized.

(Galton, 1869/1892, p. 362)

We can be forgiven if the events of the 20th century make this optimistic paragraph seem creepy. What was intended by Galton as a way to better humankind now sends chills up our spines, as terms like "better sort of emigrants" and "pride of race" have a double edge (although, to be fair, in Galton's time, the term "race" often meant the human race as a whole).

The Eugenics Movement in England, America and Germany

In 1904, Galton established a research fellowship at University College London to further his new science, and Galton left the bulk of his estate on his death in 1911 to provide an endowment to continually fund a faculty position in his name: the Galton Eugenics Chair. By 1907, a national Eugenics Education Society was founded in Britain, with branches in several cities. Local eugenics groups were founded in America as well. The Galton Society met in New York at the American Museum of Natural History. There was the Race Betterment Society in Battle Creek, Michigan, and societies in Chicago, St. Louis, Wisconsin, Minnesota, Utah and California. Andrew Carnegie, one of the most avid free market social Darwinists, had used Spencer's phrase "survival of the fittest" to justify capitalism; his foundation contributed huge sums to found a eugenics data center at Cold Spring Harbor Laboratory on Long Island. A Eugenics Records office was founded nearby. Graduates of the finer men's and women's universities were trained there to collect data on the families of people confined to homes for the feebleminded or mentally ill. Public lectures and magazine articles were common. There was even a "Fitter Families" association founded in Topeka, Kansas, in 1920. This organization would allow families to compete based on their eugenic fitness; medal winners would tour state fairs in their "human husbandry" sections. At one fair, a board was put up with the following message: "Unfit human traits such as feeblemindedness, epilepsy, criminality, alcoholism, pauperism and many others run in families and are inherited in exactly the same way as color in guinea pigs" (Kevles, 1995, p. 62). At another fair, flashing light counter boards ticked over, claiming that every 15 seconds a hundred dollars of your money is spent supporting a person of bad heredity. A placard asked, "How long are we Americans to be so careful for the pedigree of our pigs and chickens and cattle—and then leave the *ancestry of our children* to blind sentiment?" (Kevles, 1995, pp. 62–63; emphasis in original).

The numbers of official members in these societies were not large in absolute terms, but their impact was great, because many of their members were the best-educated and most-respected members of their communities across the political spectrum, from left to right. These included social radicals such as playwright George Bernard Shaw in Britain and socialist Emma Goldman in New York, as well as free market industrialists and Nobel Prize winners.

Eventually, some of the excesses of the eugenics movement undermined by two advances in evolutionary biology. First, the Lamarckian transmission of acquired characteristics was undermined by an important discovery by biologist August Weissmann (1834–1914). Weismann (1893) believed that the process of development of the germ (reproductive) cells in the body was separate from that of the development of the body cells; thus, whatever happened to the body could not be transferred to the egg or sperm cells to be passed down to offspring. He tested his assumption with a curious experiment. He chopped off the tails of rats and bred the tailless rats together and repeated it through several generations. The tails of the offspring never got shorter, as they would if Lamarck was right. Other experiments preventing the use of body parts during the lives of generations of animals found the same thing. If the mind is the brain and the brain is part of the body, learning (or body building!) cannot, therefore, affect evolution directly. Recombination of hypothetical unchangeable elements of heredity from parents must be the mechanism (Mayr, 1982).

How does this work? The answer came from an industrious Augustinian monk Gregor Mendel, who provided the second advance. Mendel's work was simultaneously rediscovered around 1900 by several different laboratories, having been published in 1866 and then largely forgotten. He had been experimenting with crossing peas by placing the pollen of one on the flowers of another in a monastery garden in what is now Brno, Czech Republic. After breeding some 30,000 plants, Mendel discovered that characteristics, such as wrinkled vs. smooth, yellow vs. green, etc., did not blend together but were passed down intact from generation to generation, sometimes skipping a generation. He had discovered that each plant had two separate individual "elements" of heredity, separated in the sperm and eggs, that recombined in random assortments. Through painstaking mathematical analysis, he discovered the basic principles of dominant and recessive genes (Mendel, 1866/1930; Weiner, 1999).

The theory that incorporates these two advances, removal of Lamarckism and the ideas of Mendelian elements of inheritance, is technically known as **neo-Darwinism**, to distinguish it from Darwin's original theory, which had some elements of Lamarckism and which couldn't specify the genetic mechanism of inheritance. Denial of Lamarck and belief in genetics form pillars that uphold the current paradigm of biology. One might think that these advances would make eugenics more scientifically careful, but in fact, they made things worse for a time, because some theorists of intelligence made the horrible logical mistake to simply say that intelligence was a *single* gene characteristic. (And this, of course, was on top of the horrible mistake of assuming that only genes mattered.) Normal intelligence was a dominant attribute and imbecility a recessive trait (requiring two recessive genes to be expressed). Therefore, said some eugenicists, two intelligent parents would have at least some intelligent children. Two unintelligent parents would clearly have *only* unintelligent children, if the trait were truly recessive.

Perhaps the most prominent eugenicist in America, H.H. Goddard (1866–1957), held this view of intelligence for a time. Goddard, who was a psychologist and director of research of the Vineland Training School for Feeble-Minded Boys and Girls of New Jersey, said,

> If both parents are feebleminded all the children will be feebleminded. It is obvious that such matings should not be allowed. It is perfectly clear that no feeble-minded person should ever be allowed to marry or to become a parent. It is obvious that if this rule is to be carried out the intelligent part of society should enforce it.
>
> (Goddard, 1914, p. 561, quoted in Gould, 1996)

The eugenics movement coincided with the beginning of the technologies of mental testing, particularly the Binet-Simon intelligence tests. Indeed, throughout the first quarter of the 20th century, eugenicists saw mental testing as a scientific boon for the movement. Goddard ran small studies of translated Binet tests on immigrants to Ellis Island and found that around 80% of Eastern Europeans scored below the mental age of 12. Lewis Terman (1877–1956) of Stanford University modified the test so that all children, not just those suspected of retardation, could be tested and conducted extended studies of gifted children. He also repeated the kinds of studies that Galton had done by "estimating" I.Q.s of long-dead geniuses. The test in use today, though much modified and made more sophisticated (see Chapter 10 for more on Binet and his test) is called the Stanford-Binet. Robert Yerkes (1876–1956) even gave types of intelligence tests to over a million men drafted for the army for service in World War I (Gould, 1996). Of course, the test itself is not a bad development if interpreted properly, but almost all of the American adapters initially made strong hereditarian statements, until the difficulty of their task became apparent.[2]

With this hereditarian rationale, programs were begun for sexual sterilization of "mental defectives" in several U.S. states and continued through the 1920s and 30s. One court case against such practices, *Buck vs. Bell*, considered whether the young baby of a woman in a home for the feebleminded, whose grandmother had also been considered mentally deficient, could be sterilized. The only evidence that the baby might herself be retarded came from a social worker's general observations. The case went all the way to the Supreme Court. There, Justice Oliver Wendell Holmes decided that "three generations of imbeciles are enough" and allowed little Vivian Buck to be sterilized. Years later, author Stephen Jay Gould obtained Vivian's elementary school grades. She was a "B" student (Gould, 1981).

In Germany, the eugenics movement was based, of course, on the ideas of Ernst Haeckel, who by the end of his life had become a very popular figure. His book, *The Riddle of the Universe*, had sold a half million copies in Germany alone and had been translated into 25 languages by his death in 1919 (Gasman, 1971). Haeckel was fond of saying that modern Germany should follow the examples of the ancient Spartans, who examined their infants at birth and killed the sickly ones, allowing only the strong to live and reproduce. In this way, Spartans were not only "continually in strength and vigor" but passed that vigor down to subsequent generations. He was pessimistic about the ability of medical science to cure the worst diseases and, if this was so, then treating such possibly hereditary diseases only allows those who have them to live long enough to breed more and pass down more bad genes. He complained that "hundreds of thousands of incurables—lunatics, lepers, people with cancer, etc.—are artificially kept alive ... without slightest profit to themselves or the general body" (Gasman, 1971, p. 95).

He decided that a commission should be set up to decide who should die. After the Nazis came to power, they obliged. A quarter million compulsory sterilizations were done in Germany, dwarfing the number in the U.S. The extermination of people in the insane asylums and hospitals began even before the extermination of Jews and other racial groups, using eugenics as its rationalization.

Embarrassment, and perhaps a resurgence of common sense, is one of the factors that killed the eugenics movement in America. If the Nazis were for it, then we would be against it. For the record, though, the very discovery of Mendelian genetics, properly understood, undermines the most extreme eugenics views. Close relatives who marry increase the possibility that recessive genes (usually deleterious) will be expressed in their offspring; many animal breeders know that excessively inbred strains of animals have a host of genetic problems. Breeders seek **hybrid vigor** or the robustness that comes from breeding outside a small group. Looked at from the Darwinian perspective, the more widely a species interbreeds, the more likely that the gene pool of the species as a whole would have a number of potentially valuable attributes. If a disaster befalls some of the species, perhaps some would survive a change. If all have the same characteristics, as with pandas and some endangered inbreeding populations, such as cheetahs, all may die. If there can be said to be anything that is called "good" for Darwinians, it is wider rather than narrower variability within a species. This view would be repulsive to most eugenicists, but it is the most plausible view to take in light of current biology (which has found little biological validity for the concept of different races of humans, anyway).

The Anti-Eugenicist Backlash

Not everyone believed in the eugenics program. Prominent among its critics was the Catholic Church, which saw eugenics as a way of dictating the methods of sex, conception and childrearing within the sanctity of marriage. Each soul was equal under God, regardless of the state of the body. In England, influential essayist G.K. Chesterton described eugenics as "the principle of the survival of the nastiest" (Chesterton, 1901, p. 488).

Doubts about the hereditary nature of intelligence and its unchangeability were present from the start. Alfred Binet (1857–1911), the French psychologist who created the test (see Chapter 10) that Goddard translated to gather data for the eugenicist program, would have hated the idea that his tests were used for that purpose. He did not mean them to be a measure of innate intelligence but rather current functioning in school; he was extremely careful about prognosis based on his test:

> Our purpose is to be able to measure the intellectual capacity of a child who is brought to us in order to know whether he is normal or retarded. We should therefore study his condition at the time and that only. We have nothing to do

> with either his past history or with his future; consequently, we shall neglect his etiology and shall make no attempt to distinguish between acquired and congenital idiocy.... As to that which concerns his future, we shall exercise the same abstinence; we do not attempt to prepare or establish a prognosis and we leave unanswered the question of whether his retardation is curable or even improvable. We shall limit ourselves to ascertaining the truth with regard to his present mental state.
>
> (Binet, 1905/1916, p. 37)

He chastised teachers for assuming that intelligence could not be changed, that a child would never amount to anything. He also noted an episode in which a teacher had told him that he would never have a true philosophical spirit:

> Never! What a momentous word. Some recent thinkers seem to have given their moral support to these deplorable verdicts by affirming that an individual's intelligence is a fixed quantity, a quantity that cannot be increased. We must protest and react against this brutal pessimism; we must try to demonstrate that it is founded on nothing.
>
> (Binet, 1909, p. 101, cited in Gould, 1996)

American journalist Walter Lippmann was perhaps the most articulate among the anti-eugenicists and the most sophisticated in critiquing their conclusions regarding intelligence. He did not deny that inheritance might be involved in intelligence, nor did he deny that the then new methods of testing could be valuable for identifying children who needed help. He did question in a series of articles in *The New Republic* (1922, reprinted in Block & Dworkin, 1976), however, whether these new technologies could test that heritability accurately:

> The claim that we have learned how to measure hereditary intelligence has no scientific foundation. We cannot measure intelligence when we have never defined it and we cannot speak of its hereditary basis after it has been indistinguishably fused with a thousand educational and environmental influences from the time of conception to the school age.... Gradually, under the impact of criticism, the claim will be abandoned that a device has been invented for measuring innate intelligence. Suddenly, it will dawn upon the testers that this is just another form of examination differing in degree rather than in kind from Mr. Edison's questionnaire or a college entrance examination. It may be a better form of examination than these, but it is the same sort of thing. It tests, as they do, an unanalyzed mixture of native capacity, acquired habits and stored-up knowledge and no tester knows at any moment which factor he is testing.
>
> (Lippmann, 1922, in Block & Dworkin, 1976, pp. 28–29)

Finally, by the end of the 1920s, the eugenicists themselves within psychology were beginning to soften their statements. In part, they began to realize how difficult the accurate measurement of the heredity of intelligence was. The public had a hard time believing that the tests given to servicemen during the First World War had provided an innate mean adult mental age of 12 or 13, and those tests were sloppily administered. With the advent of the Great Depression, it became no longer fashionable to blame poverty on low intelligence, and the privations of socioeconomic environment began to seem like a more viable cause for intellectual deficits. By the 1937 revision of the Stanford-Binet test, Lewis Terman, who had ridiculed Lippman's ideas as coming from his "emotional complexes" and compared him to a bull seeing red, was advising,

> It would require extensive research, carefully planned for the purpose, to determine whether the lowered I.Q. of rural children can be ascribed to the relatively poorer educational facilities in rural communities and whether the gain for children from the lower economic strata can be attributed to an assumed enrichment of intellectual environment that school attendance bestows.
> (Terman, 1937 cited in Gould, 1996, p. 222)

The Unexpected Legacy of Eugenics: Genomes and Statistics

It is one of the ironies of history that scientific discoveries that can be misinterpreted for evil, as we have just seen, can lead to great advantages. One of the greatest ironies is that without the eugenics movement, we might know far less about human genetics than we do now. Although the founders of the Cold Spring Harbor Laboratory, for example, were strong eugenicists, they did collect much of the data that has led to the untangling of hereditary diseases (Kevles, 1995). Indeed, James Watson, who was the director of the laboratory (and co-discoverer, with Francis Crick, of DNA) announced the near-complete sequencing of the human genome on June 26, 2000. This does not mean, however, that scientists are anywhere near knowing what all those genes do, much less know how exactly they contribute to behaviors we can see. But in the future, the discoveries are likely to change the face of psychology.

The second irony, perhaps even more relevant to every student of psychology, is that many, if not most, of the widely used statistical techniques in psychology were devised by Galton and his successors in the Chair of Eugenics that he founded. As Table 4.2 shows, such techniques as the correlation coefficient, the analysis of variance, chi-square analysis, relationship and adoption studies of the heritability of intelligence and others came from the Galton Laboratory. Mathematics knows no politics, of course, and people have used such methods to prove anti-hereditarian points as well as hereditarian ones. Still, the necessity that led to these inventions was the need to understand the mechanisms of evolution—they are techniques for studying differences in variability to be used in a science in which variability is at the core of its theories.

History and Psychology Today: Evolutionary Psychology

As you will see in the rest of this textbook, the theory of evolution affected nearly every psychological theorist working after 1859. But there is one relatively new subfield of psychology that draws explicitly from the ideas of evolution even in its name: evolutionary psychology.

Table 4.3 The Galton Laboratory and Modern Statistics

Statistician	Years at University College	Statistical Technique	Purpose of Technique
Francis Galton (1822–1911)	London Founder of Galton lab (1904)	Developed Correlation Coefficient	measures strength of relationship between two variables
Karl Pearson (1857–1936)	1884–1933	Pearson product moment Correlation	improves calculation of correlation coefficient
		Chi-Square test	tests significance of relationship between "count" variables (e.g. number of votes for two choices)
		Linear regression	constructs best fit line through correlational data
Charles Spearman (1865–1945)	1904–1931	Factor analysis	describes the interrelationships between questions or subtests on mental tests. Derives and names "factors" (e.g. verbal ability). Spearman believed also in an overall "general factor of intelligence" or "g," which is the tendency of a person to score high or low on all tests.
William S. Gossett "Student" (1876–1937)	1906–1907	T-distribution and test test	tests significant differences between two small samples.
Ronald A. Fisher (1890–1962)	1933–1943	Analysis of variance Null hypothesis	tests significant differences among many small samples

Evolutionary psychology is a new area of psychology that draws upon evolutionary biology and anthropology as well as cognitive, neurophysiological and social psychology. This new field is based on several assumptions (Tooby & Cosmides, 1992). First, evolutionary psychologists accept the idea that genes are the driving force in evolution, which is not surprising. But they also believe that organisms that house the genes essentially work not only for their own survival, but that they work proportionally for survival of those genetically similar to them, including their children, their parents and grandchildren, cousins and clan. This view, known as **inclusive fitness**, ascribes a lot of power to genes. In some versions of this theory, as in Richard Dawkins's *The Selfish Gene* (1976), it seems as though genes essentially get organisms to reproduce for them, so that genes can live on. Under an inclusive fitness view of evolution for psychology, we are motivated by nonconscious innate instincts that underlie all learning and make certain kinds of learning possible or impossible. Second, evolutionary psychologists (EPs) are **materialists**: The mind is the brain, and if the brain is as susceptible to evolutionary modifications as the rest of the body, then so are the behaviors that are based on that body. Third, it follows that the mechanism of death and survival in evolution should have fashioned in our brains special "organs" for special adaptive purposes (in quotes here because EPs have largely hypothesized rather than found the mechanisms involved). Instead of having one big thinking and sensing machine (a view of the mind that goes back at least to the empiricists), we have *special separate brain mechanisms* for detecting and learning how to share food, find and keep mates and protect our young and other members of our tribe. Thus, our brain/mind is not a blank slate: Because of the way that our species evolved as hunter-gatherers on the African savannas hundreds of thousands to millions of years ago, we are predisposed to process information about the world in particular ways. We may be exercising conscious or automatic choices in our actions, but those choices and perceptions are subtly conditioned by our evolutionarily derived biology.

It's important to remember that evolution does not do its work on everything: Evolution isn't about creating the most perfect human being, only about creating organisms that survive to reproduce successfully. Thus, a fourth assumption of EPs is that they only want to study the behaviors that aid the survival of ourselves, our offspring and the species in general. EPs study **adaptive traits**, defined as characteristics of organisms that affect reproduction, however distally (Cosmides, Tooby and Barkow, 1992, p. 8.). Everything we do is evolved, of course; music, art, compassion and religion come out of a brain. But not everything we do is necessarily a *product* of evolutionary selection. We were not necessarily naturally selected for our reading and writing ability. Something else that helped us survive (e.g. large brains that can use tools or recognize patterns in sight and sound) also accidentally created our capacity for me to write and you to read this book (Lucky you!). These useful but accidental capabilities that did not help us reproduce thousands of years ago are called **by-products** of evolution. Finally, unlike their predecessors the eugenicists, EPs are relatively *uninterested in individual differences* among people living today. They argue that most of the really important mechanisms for survival in humans are held by all of us, regardless of race or class, and that if any changes are arising at the moment based on current differences among us, they would take hundreds of generations to be evident. Waiting would make it very hard to publish psychology papers in a timely fashion.

A good way to illustrate what EPs do is to make a list of those attributes that are common to all humans that evolution might have selected for. We are a non-monogamous species with frequent periods of fertility throughout the year, in all seasons. We have a small number of highly dependent offspring at once that take a long time to reach sexual maturity. We have a long gestation period, so that both the unborn offspring and its mother are at considerable risk for a long period. We have few natural defenses against our predators, so we band together in social groups. We have relatively sophisticated ways, including language, to maintain order and harmony in those groups and so on.

Evolutionary psychologists have begun to study adaptive behaviors even before the birth of a child. For example, they have helped to explain why mothers have strong food preferences during pregnancy, exhibited as "morning sickness," although it may happen at any time during the day. Margie Profet (1992) theorized that hunter-gatherer societies from which we evolved must have had strong selection pressures for morning sickness in that those who ate the wrong foods at the wrong time would have had fewer viable offspring, leaving the resulting species with built-in protection for fetal development. For example, many bitter and strong plant foods have small but significant amounts of defensive toxins in them; some of these toxins are teratogenic, in that they can cause fetal malformations in large doses at the wrong time in fetal development. The worst time for ingesting them is days 20 to 56 after conception, which is exactly when morning sickness usually occurs. At that time, mothers usually prefer the blandest tasting and least aromatic food possible, which also happens to be often the least toxic food for the developing fetus. Mothers also dislike the taste and smell of meat at this time, which, of course, contains bacteria. (There is even some evidence that their olfactory sensitivity increases at this time, to be better able to smell out the harmful substances.) The hormones that may affect regulation of pregnancy sickness are switched on and off by the developing baby. Finally, there is some evidence that women who have *less* pregnancy sickness have a *higher* rate of miscarriage than those who do not, adding to the argument for its adaptive value.

Because our infants are so helpless at birth, it would be adaptive for them to have evolved some protective abilities. The simplest of these are infant reflexes that allow them to grab and suck at birth. But EPs are mindful of the work over the last 25 years that has emphasized how well adapted babies are at or near birth to recognize the mother's voice, to perceive objects as solid and to recognize meaningful patterns in the world.

So far, these examples seem relatively uncontroversial and reasonably well supported. However, evolutionary psychologists have also generated great controversy with biological hypotheses about aspects of human behavior which we are now accustomed to thinking of as largely determined by social or cultural influence. The following are two representative controversial issues:

Sexual attractiveness: Men make their decisions largely on physical features. They prefer younger, chaste, females, with smooth skin, white teeth, lustrous hair and quick, lively movements. Chastity decreases the chances that the male would be raising someone else's genes, and the other features are indicative of youth, which is correlated with greater fecundity (Buss, 1992; Symons, 1979, 1992). Women are less concerned with a male's age and chastity, as males are fertile much later in life, and are more concerned with the male's ability to protect them and their offspring from threat and hunger. Thus, they seek males who are willing to invest in the rearing of children (Ellis, 1992). Women seek men with obvious attributes of kindness, emotional stability and intelligence, but also status and wealth. Women deny the emphasis on status (Buss, et al. 1990), but one study suggests that men that women choose to marry make 50% more money than men they do not choose to marry (Trivers, 1985).

Jealousy: Male jealousy is common in almost every society, and a high level of violence is seen in competition over females. It is adaptive as a form of "mate guarding," a perhaps unconscious tendency to make sure that offspring from a mate come from the jealous man and not a competitor (Wilson & Daly, 1992). Even more radically, some have suggested that men are more upset by rapes to their mates that do not involve obvious physical harm, because of this supposedly innate tendency to be suspicious of women (Thornhill & Thornhill, 1983; Thornhill & Palmer, 2000).

This is only a partial list; evolutionary psychologists have provided partial explanations to divorce (Fisher, 1992), child abuse (in statistics that show that children are much more likely to be abused by an adoptive than a biologically related parent) (Daly & Wilson, 1988), language (Pinker, 1994, 1997) and childrearing (Mann, 1992; Fernald, 1992).

Criticisms of Evolutionary Psychology

As you might imagine, many people are distressed by the implications of evolutionary psychology. It can, in fact, be maddening. Although you might think that you love a woman for her special intelligence, generosity or charm, as well as her beauty, you are merely reacting to instinct. Culture is largely veneer. Evolutionary psychologists would deal with the first possible criticism, that culture causes mate selection, rather quickly. You might say that mate selection preference might be conditioned by television, magazines or (in cultures without television or magazines) simply longstanding cultural traditions. That may be, say the EPs, but the very form of those cultural traditions might be shaped by the biological commonality of all humans. If we find that in most cultures young women are preferred as mates than older, then we have proven our point. "But what about those who stay monogamous for their lifetimes?" you say, trying a second criticism. In that case their answer would be that in such cases either (a) the male really wants to stray but fears cultural disapproval, or (b) the woman picked the right high-investment male, according to her biologically imperative preferences or (c) this is a low-probability exception to the rule. Suppose, then, you accept that, for example, male jealousy is biologically innate. Then you, the razor sharp critic, might offer as a third criticism, "Yes, it is true I cannot think of a culture in which male jealousy is absent, so you may be right that it has a biological basis, but still, in some cultures violence from such jealousy is seen as justified and the male is judged lightly and the female harshly. In others, penalties against the man for violence ensuing from jealousy are harsh and are becoming harsher with time, as women's independent wealth and power grow. Thus, the way in which cultures sanction the innate behavior modify it so much and in such varying ways that your point, though possibly true, is not very helpful in predicting behavior." Moreover, in many cases, the proposed specialized system (it is likely to be more than a single part) of the brain that acts as a mate selector, for example, has yet to be specified. Finally, Donald Symons (1992) has said to make a claim that a trait or feature is an adaptive one you must make a claim about the past, about the history of an organism during the time that it might reasonably have developed. In other words, you must make a hypothesis about what the **environment of evolutionary adaptiveness** was back in the Pleistocene era, defined as the environmental and reproductive conditions and constraints under which a behavior or "organ" of the mind was supposed to have developed. Such conditions, 15 to 18 million years ago, are hard to know for sure. Critics have noted that it is quite easy to come up with *plausible* evolutionary adaptive reasons for behaviors. Forming testable hypotheses to determine the *right* evolutionary reason is much more difficult. An EP may argue, using fossil bones, archaeological dig sites, similarity to other animals or current hunter-gatherer cultures, that such a trait was adaptive way back then and is unlikely to have changed since then. But you, the critic, have a right to ask to see and critically evaluate the evidence and the logic.

In summary, evolutionary psychology is both a promising and a controversial new field. Where it is successful in determining the physiological underpinning for behavior, as in Profet's research on morning sickness, it can be convincing. It may well turn out that in the exploration of the functions of the genome, more such mechanisms will be found, making this task easier. Some theorists (e.g. Lewontin, 1994), however, imply that even when such mechanisms are discovered, their interactions with the environment will turn out to be so complex that making assumptions about their evolution will become harder, not easier. In such a case, evolutionary psychologists' attempts to tie psychology closer to biology may fail, as did the eugenicists' before them. Years from now, future historians of psychology may be able to tell us which fate occurred.

Evolution's Impact on Psychology: A Presentist Review

In Chapter 1, as you'll recall, we discussed the difference between presentism and historicism. Most of this chapter has been historicist. What did Darwin and his contemporaries think about materialism, evolution and human nature? What social and intellectual forces brought about the paradigm shift at the time and what did the general public think? We even discussed some false starts, such as Lamarckism and recapitulation, that nevertheless made their mark on society in general and psychology in particular. Now, however, it is time to ask a different question, the one asked by a presentist. What does modern psychology take from evolution?

First, it takes the precept of **naturalism**, the idea that scientific laws can explain all phenomena, extending first to living beings and then to the human mind. Second, it takes the view of materialism, that mental phenomena are based on physiochemical processes in the brain. Third, it removes the dividing line between humans and animals. Evolution claims that we are similar historically, in the sense that we all come from the same line of common descent, and physiologically, in that we are all based on DNA that is similar among animals in ways that correspond to that historical lineage. Fourth, we have had to accept that that missing barrier might extend to the mind and intelligence as well. We might be subject to instincts as animals are; on the other hand, animals may have intelligence, just as we do. Finally, it is to be hoped that we have learned the dangers of taking evolutionary explanations too far. Early evolutionists, in the heady days of an intellectual revolution that consumed economics, sociology and social policy, as well as biology and psychology, tended to see evolution as the answer to everything, with tragic results. It is not, but it is a force to be reckoned with.

Notes

1. Piaget's position with respect to recapitulation is actually much more complicated than can be discussed here. See discussions of James Mark Baldwin and Piaget (Chapter 10).
2. This is one reason why I have decided to discuss the details of the construction of Alfred Binet and Theodore Simon's intelligence test in the chapter on the history of developmental psychology. I wish to remove all taint of eugenicism from the creators of the test and show that their test was related to a larger concern for the development of thinking in children, an aspect of Binet's work that is often overlooked.

5 Idealism to Materialism and Dualism in Germany

> Into the whole how all things blend,
> Each in the other working, living!
> How heavenly powers ascend, descend,
> Each unto each the golden vessels giving!
> On pinions fragrant blessings bringing,
> From Heaven through Earth all onward winging,
> Through all the All harmonious ringing!
> —Goethe, *Faust* (translated by George
> Madison Priest [Line 447–454])

At the beginning of the 19th century, psychology was not yet a science. To the extent that it existed at all, it was taught as a subfield of philosophy and used its methods, which included introspection and logical argument. How, when and where did psychology become a separate discipline, one which focused on the collection of data using controlled experimental methods? Most historians of psychology, looking backwards from our current standpoint, have suggested that this movement began in the early to mid-19th century in Germany. Why? There is no one answer. First, German universities had begun, even before Germany was united as a single country, to rise in power and influence due in part to their extraordinary support of intellectual ambition. Nineteenth-century German professors, particularly the leading members of the profession, were expected to study not just a single subject, but all subjects in the sciences and humanities. This all-encompassing knowledge was called *Wissenschaft*. Although today *Wissenschaft* is usually translated as "science," at the time, it connoted a grand view of knowledge. At the beginning of the 19th century, Johann Wolfgang von Goethe exemplified this noble search for *Wissenschaft* in the fictional character of Dr. Faust, who sold his soul to the Devil for all-encompassing knowledge. Through the heroic study of *Wissenschaft*, one was transformed into a highly actualized and respected person or *Kulturträger* (culture-bearer). In this Romantic way, the ideal German professor was expected to come to a distinctive, encyclopedic position that unifies all knowledge (Cahan, 1993). One could call this either a noble task or a delusion of grandeur, but it led to a tendency to cross boundaries that fertilized the growth of psychology. Many of the major figures discussed in this chapter followed this ideal. The philosopher Immanuel Kant was said to throw off "thousands of ideas" in lecture; G.W.F. Hegel spoke mystically of the pursuit of the Absolute. Gustav Fechner contributed to psychology a revolutionary way of measuring the intensity of perception, but what he really wanted to do was prove the unity of body and soul. Hermann Helmholtz painstakingly determined the speed of the nerve impulse, but also did pioneering work on the physiology of muscles and of the eye, as well as to establish the physical notion of conservation of energy. Helmholtz's peers, Emil du Bois-Reymond, Ivan Sechenov, Karl Ludwig and Ernst Brücke, in addition to making groundbreaking discoveries in the field of physiology themselves, influenced or directly taught psychologists as different from one another as Pavlov and Freud. Finally, Helmholtz's student, Wilhelm Wundt, is considered today the father of experimental psychology.

German Idealism

Nineteenth-century German philosophy was at a crossroads. In the first decades of the century, from 1800 to around 1840, philosophers were still concerned with discovering the limitations to our knowledge, as the British empiricists had been. Their methods were intuition and introspection, and the leading philosophers, Kant and Hegel, had come to the conclusion that everything that is known is known through ideas. Essentially, these philosophers practiced a kind of **monism**, in which all that is knowable is mind. For Kant, we can only know the world through concepts or schemata. For Hegel, the universe itself is a vast organism of ideas. This kind of epistemology in which the physical bodily world is ignored in favor of explaining the world in terms of ideas is called **idealism**, and we have seen a form of it earlier, in the philosophy of George Berkeley. Starting in the1840s, a shift occurred, as physiologists developed methods for studying the nervous system. This led to an adoption of the opposite monist position of **materialism**, that the mind could be explained with reference to the nervous system alone, without recourse to the soul or mind. Finally, by 1870, psychology proper had begun and with it, the philosophy of **dualism** became once again the order of the day. The mind or the brain could be studied separately and independently, but the connection between them remained mysterious.

Immanuel Kant

Immanuel Kant was born April 22, 1724, the fourth child of a German saddle maker in Königsberg, East Prussia (Königsberg is now Kaliningrad, Russia). Kant's mother almost immediately recognized that her child had academic gifts and arranged for a theology professor to take charge of young Immanuel's schooling. He was then enrolled in a school that taught mostly Latin grammar: Math and logic were covered briefly, and science, history and geography not at all. One of Kant's classmates described the curriculum as being subjected to the "pedantic and gloomy discipline of fanatics" (cited by Cassirer, 1981/1918, p. 16). Kant later suggested that the rote memorization of religious instruction did not awaken his interest in science and philosophy. In fact, the formulaic and rigid nature of this training led him to mistrust

Figure 5.1 Immanuel Kant (1724–1804)

displays of religion in public life. Even his curriculum, textbooks and syllabi in college at Königsberg were rigidly controlled by the state.

One bright spot in Kant's education was for him the work of Newton. The clear, cool reason of Newton's mathematically based science was a revelation to Kant and one of the influences that directed him towards becoming a professor, not in theology, as was more usual in his time and place, but the new natural philosophy.

Kant's ability to continue in graduate study was hampered by the fact that he was, and would continue to be, quite poor. He spent at least seven generally happy years as a private tutor to the children of a wealthy family. Finally, in 1755, he received his doctorate, which enabled him to teach at Königsberg, but only as a *privatdozent* or a private teacher (similar to an adjunct instructor). As he was paid only a small amount "per head," he was forced to teach over 36 hours of classes a week to make ends meet. In spite of these hardships, Kant seemed indifferent to his physical circumstances and led in these years a lively social life. Kant was a great conversationalist, eater and card player in his younger days. He gained a reputation for an astonishing breadth of knowledge, teaching, often simultaneously, courses in logic, mathematics, metaphysics, physical geography, natural science, ethics, mechanical and theoretical physics (strongly based on Newton and his followers) and anthropology (which for

Kant included certain observations on psychology). It was said that he "threw off ideas by the thousands" and was considered a fine lecturer. He was able to publish only a few works during the period of this crushing workload and though his friends knew he was working on a masterful integration of his knowledge, they despaired of ever seeing it in print (Cassirer, 1981).

In 1770, at the age of 46, he finally received a professorship at Königsberg and his teaching load lightened significantly. From then on, feeling pressed for time in order to accomplish his life's work, he followed a strictly regulated system of self-discipline in writing and rest. It was said in Königsberg that you could set your watch by Kant's afternoon walks. In these later years, he produced several works that revolutionized epistemology (*The Critique of Pure Reason*, 1781), moral philosophy (*The Foundation of the Metaphysics of Morals*, 1785, and *The Critique of Practical Reason*, 1788) and the philosophy of feeling or happiness (*The Critique of Judgement*, 1790). The first of these areas, Kant said, was addressed to the question of "What can I know?" the second area to "What ought I to do?" and the third to "What may I hope?" In addition, he had things to say about how science should be done and by extension how (or even whether) psychology can be done. Nearly his last publication before his death in 1804 was a compilation of his notes on his course on anthropology or what he called "empirical psychology" (*Anthropology From a Pragmatic Point of View*, 1798/1978).

This is an enormous and daunting body of work, both in its substance and its style. As we shall see again later in this chapter, the ideal for a German professor of philosophy in the 18th and 19th centuries was to come up with a theory that handles pretty much everything, and Kant certainly followed this ideal. Fortunately, we needn't discuss Kant's moral philosophy or his thoughts on such topics as happiness and beauty here; we will focus mostly on his theory of knowledge as it relates to psychology. In particular, Kant's question of what a mind must have in order to take in information about the world influenced indirectly the practice of science throughout the 19th century and, in consequence, the practice of psychology then and now.

In order to be precise, Kant constructed a writing style that was exact, yet demanding. He himself said, "it appears scholastic, hence petifogging and arid, indeed crabbed and a far cry from genius" (cited in Cassirer, 1981, p. 140). Later commentators agree with him, except they place him much nearer to genius! My summary of Kant here is greatly simplified, using as little of the special jargon that Kant used as possible.

In *Critique of Pure Reason* (1781/1990), Kant was concerned, as the empiricists were, with the limitations to our knowledge. He agreed with Hume that it was impossible for us to know the outside world of things as they really are. We live instead in a world of sensations or, as he called them, **phenomena**. And yet, if our experience is just a flow of sensations, how do we make sense of it? Associations between individual intuitions or sensations do not simply happen. There must be some mechanism in the mind that allows us to unite moment-by-moment experience into concepts. There must be some sort of *process* that unites the *content* of this or that view of a dog or a house into the concept of a dog or a house. Experience is only the content; if there were not something to unite experience, every single experience would be unique and because there would be no way to give it order, we could not really "know" anything. We do not actually think with experience, says Kant. We think in concepts.

Therefore, Kant concludes that there must be some concepts that are in us before we experience anything. These he called *a priori* **concepts** and they are

1. prior to any experience
2. necessary for the understanding of any experience
3. universal to all experience

Take for example our *a priori* notion of space. When we look out on the sensory world, we see things (or the phenomena of things, at any rate)—let's say, for example, furniture and everything else in the room you're sitting in now. Take away the stuff in the room and you have the room. Take away the room and you have the building. Take away everything and what are you left with? The opposite of everything. Not-things. Kant suggests that you've never really had an experience of nothing, because when you look out, you always see something (even with your eyes closed you can see blackness). Thingness itself requires space. You can divide space, but you can't get rid of it. When we think of things, we must think of space.

Kant's notion of time is even more radical. He declares that it doesn't really exist outside of our experience and yet in a very real sense our consciousness is composed of time. Without it, for example, Hume's notions of priority and contiguity make no sense: When we see that one thing commonly follows another with a constant conjunction, we need a notion of time to make that conclusion. Hence it is necessary that some concept of time exist prior to experience to order that experience for us. Just as space is necessary for us to conceive of the external world, time is considered that which our "internal sense" (i.e. Locke's notion of reflection or looking inward) is made of.

In addition to time and space, Kant came up with a limited set of *a priori* concepts (or categories) of understanding, as seen in Table 5.1. To consider all of these here in turn would take a great deal of space, so a few examples will have to suffice. In the first column, notions of quantity, note that the definition of totality is "many things

Table 5.1 Kant's *A priori* Categories

1 Of Quantity	2 Of Quality
Unity	Reality
Plurality	Negation
Totality	Limitation

3 Of Relation
Of Inherence and Subsistence (*substantia et accidens*)
Of Causality and Dependence (cause and effect)
Of Community (reciprocity between the agent and patient)

4 Of Modality
Possibility—Impossibility
Existence—Non-existence
Necessity—Contingence

considered as a whole," and hence it can be said that Totality = Unity + Plurality. (Similarly, Kant says that Limitation = Reality + Negation and Necessity = Existence + Possibility.) If we want to consider the notion of absolute nothingness (which we have never experienced, but which we can nevertheless conceive of), that would be the negation of totality. Our notion that absolute nothingness does not exist is an *a priori* statement of its modality and so forth.

Perhaps a slightly more contemporary example would help. Computers come with a set of instructions on the chip itself. These instructions are crucial before you ever load programs, because they tell the computer what to do with the stuff in the program: how to move zeros and ones around, storing and retrieving, that sort of thing. The computer is completely inert and useless without them. Unlike random access memory or RAM, you can't normally (and you really shouldn't) erase it. These instructions constitute the absolute minimum that the computer needs to even deal with experience at all. Now, extend our example further to consider the computer as a "thinking machine." What does the computer think when it's first turned on? Nothing (or not about things), because it has not been given any content, any experience to think about. But it's ready to think; it has a set of basic processes to handle experience when it gets it.

When the mind does get experience, say of trees, the "faculty of imagination" unites separate sensations (called intuitions) into concepts called **schemas** (or in the proper Greek plural, **schemata**; both are used frequently in English). The schema of "tree" includes the attributes common to all trees we have met to that date. We cannot help making concepts, because it's only through concepts that we really know anything. When we say to ourselves "That's a tree," our "faculty of understanding," to use Kant's terms, recognizes the tree as an instance of the schema tree. This process of recognition constitutes true consciousness to Kant. Being conscious of the instance and the category or schema, and at the same time identifying an instance as a member of a category, is called **apperception**. The faculty of imagination allows us to put together individual experiences so that we know, but when, through the faculty of understanding, we recognize that we know it, to "know *that* we know," is apperception. Finally, Kant suggests that Hume's flowing, disconnected sense of self couldn't possibly perform this recognition. Instead, for Kant, consciousness must be **unitary**: There must be one focal point that makes judgments, based on all of the sensory information.

Kant said, famously, "Thoughts without content are void; intuitions [sensations] without conceptions, blind" (Kant, 1781/1990, p. 45). Thinking without content is like the computer with only its initial set of instructions; it has nothing to think about, but it is ready to think. Sensations that aren't put into concepts or schemata can't really be recognized *as* anything by our understanding; thus without schemas, we are blind.

All of these *a priori* concepts are said to have **transcendent ideality**, in that they are ideas above experience but necessary to the comprehension of experience. But Kant is also an idealist, because he believed the actual world is unknowable. Kant is a rationalist, like Descartes, because he believes that he has necessarily deduced these that these categories must exist, rather than gathered the knowledge from experience. He is a nativist, because he believes essentially that we are born with these categories. But he differs from Descartes in that the innate components are not ideas like "God" or "infinity" but initial conditions of the mind that allow us to construct these notions.

Kant was eager to rescue philosophy and by extension, science from the extreme skepticism of Hume, but he couldn't simply ignore what Hume had to say. It was true that we would never know exactly how the world was made (or if we happened upon it, we couldn't be sure that we knew it). But we could, as Newton did, describe the lawful rules of our experience. Kant had essentially come up with a cognitive psychology of science. He described how we could take observations (intuitions), come up with categories or schema like "mass," "velocity" or "sulphur," and put them into mathematical forms, like $v = ma$, that work in predictable ways. The theories about science are predictable and understandable by others in part because our minds have these built-in *a priori* structures. If what Kant says is true, then all of our scientific theories are constrained not only by the way we think, but also by the way we *have to* think. The most famous quote attributed to Kant is "The mind is the lawgiver to nature." Although we will never know exactly what causes what in the world, our minds are so constructed as to look for causes. If they weren't, we couldn't understand anything.

Kant's ideal of science was represented by physics and astronomy, the kind of sciences that a person who ranked rationalism above empiricism would love. Science, thought Kant, must lead to universal conclusions about the world. Therefore, it must be amenable to descriptions in mathematics, because mathematical deduction is the only way to reach necessary truths. He considered chemistry, with its emphasis on empirical experiments and inductive reasoning (and then, still incomplete mathematical laws) to be an imperfect science. What did he think, then, of psychology?

He addressed these issues in *Metaphysical Foundations of a Natural Science* (1786) and elsewhere (see Brook, 1994). First of all, for Kant, if psychology were a science, it would be the science of the contents of the "inner sense," conducted by introspection on the mental contents of one's mind. Kant doubted that such a psychology could be made a science. First of all, the content of thought is expressed in time and only time. Physics plots the movement of objects as a function of time, but thought itself is time and no space; how do we measure it? Second, nothing sticks in consciousness. It is always flowing; one thought is separated only by other thoughts; the observer introspecting is the instrument that does the defining and separating. You can't grab a hold of a thought as if it were an object, separate it from others, manipulate it and connect them again according to the dictates of a developing theory. He said,

> Inner experiences are not like external experiences of objects in space, wherein the objects appear side by side and permanently fixed. The inner sense sees the conditions for its definition only in Time and consequently, in a state of flux, which is without that permanence of observation necessary for experience.
> (Kant, 1798/1978, p. 17)

Finally, the only mind an introspector can observe is his or her own, and when he or she does, the observation itself distorts the state of the object observed. All of these aspects made Kant despair of ever seeing a science of the "internal sense," particularly one that reaches universal truths describable by mathematics (Brook, 1994).

Kant even suggested that intense self-observation was hazardous to mental health: "This desire for self-investigation is either already a disease of the mind (hypochondria) or will lead to such a disease and ultimately to the madhouse" (Kant, 1798/1978, p. 17). And yet, Kant was not against a discipline that studies the behaviors, manners, thought processes and customs of human beings, which he called *Anthropology From a Pragmatic Point of View* (1798), subtitled "On the art of knowing the interior as well as the exterior of man." Unlike his more famous technical works, these lectures are both erudite *and* witty, practical and engaging. He discusses the difference between abstract intelligence, useful for the scientist and "horse sense" (*bon sens*), for living in the world. In some ways, his lectures are like a traditional psychology textbook. He discusses the five senses, the efficiency and failures of memory, imagination and distraction and even mental disorders. In these lectures, he follows generally what is called a **faculty psychology**, discussing different functions of the mind as freestanding entities, such as the "faculty of imagination" or the "faculty of desire." But the lectures also offer advice on the right way of living. For example, he notes that politeness is a mere appearance of affability, but one that can create real affection in time:

> Every human virtue in circulation is small change: only a child takes it for real gold. Nevertheless it is better to circulate pocket pieces than nothing at all. In the end, they can be converted into genuine gold coin, though at a considerable discount.
>
> (Kant, 1978/1798, p. 37)

He offers cross-cultural examples, aphorisms, characters from literature, even advice on how to run a dinner party.[1] By current standards, he is outrageously sexist:

> As for scholarly women, they use their books somewhat like a watch, that is, they wear the watch so that it can be noticed that they have one, although it is usually broken or does not show the correct time.
>
> (Kant, 1798/1978, p. 221)

In sum, Kant's evaluation that psychology could not be a science did not mean that observation of human behaviors, manners, customs and thoughts could not be studied at all. He meant only that the study of human life, both inner and outer, was unlikely to result in the kind of beautiful laws that his hero, Newton, created by applying the *a priori* structures of his mind to empirical generalizations about the universe.

Kant's influence on philosophy is great. In the same way that philosophy before him was often consumed with arguments for and against Descartes, philosophy after him was often concerned with positions for or against Kant. Some of the very style of argument in philosophy today—its technical analytic character in particular—owes something to Kant. His influences on psychology are pervasive, but more subtle and often indirect. In the first place, since psychologists were trained at least partially in philosophy until at least the 1920s, they had to address Kant. But more importantly, he provided a kind of foundation for nativism in psychology that melds well with Darwinian notions of nativism. The idea that basic processes (*a priori* categories) can be separated to some extent from content (sense data) underlies many theories of memory and cognition. And the notion of schema is prevalent, for example, in the theories of Sir Frederick Bartlett on memory (Bartlett, 1932/1997) and in the entire work of Piaget (see Chapter 10).

For the purposes of this chapter on 19th-century German psychology, however, it is important to recognize that those who more immediately followed Kant saw his prohibition on an introspective psychology as a challenge. Kant's reservations were clearly stated: (1) He thought that psychology could not be made to yield mathematical formulas and (2) he thought that systematic self-observation could not be made reliable. The first challenge was taken up by Johann Friedrich Herbart (1776–1841) and Gustav Fechner (1801–1887). The second challenge was attempted by Wilhelm Wundt and his followers, after learning the experimental method from Hermann von Helmholtz (1821–1894) and in an entirely different way by the Gestalt psychologists.

G.W.F. Hegel

> The more the ordinary mind takes the opposition between true and false to be fixed, the more is it accustomed to expect either agreement or contradiction with a given philosophical system and only to see reason for the one or the other in any explanatory statement concerning such a system. It does not conceive the diversity of philosophical systems as the progressive evolution of truth; rather, it sees only contradiction in that variety. The bud disappears when the blossom breaks through and we might say that the former is refuted by the latter; in the same way when the fruit comes, the blossom may be explained to be a false form of the plant's existence, for the fruit appears as its true nature in place of the blossom. These stages are not merely differentiated; they supplant one another as being incompatible with one another. But the ceaseless activity of their own inherent nature makes them at the same time moments of an organic unity, where they not merely do not contradict one another, but where one is as necessary as the other; and this equal necessity of all moments constitutes alone and thereby the life of the whole.
> —G.W.F. Hegel (1807/2009, p. 11)

The philosophy professor Georg Wilhelm Friedrich Hegel (1770–1831) was born in the same year as Beethoven and shared many characteristics with him. Although he built his views of human nature on the cool, classical foundations of the Enlightenment philosophers such as Kant (as Beethoven did on the elegance of Mozart), his ambition was much more Romantic. He believed in the inevitable upward evolution of the spirit of humankind, but did not suggest that this upward motion could occur without struggle or tragedy. Both Beethoven and Hegel were, for a time at least, admirers of Napoleon: Beethoven would dedicate (and then furiously undedicate) his *Eroica Symphony* to him. Hegel called Napoleon a great World Soul—an individual who works the will of the great Absolute in history—in spite of Hegel's being virtually evicted from his post at the University of Jena in 1806 by the advancing French Army. And both Beethoven and Hegel were undeniably German: cultured yet autocratic, they attempted to plumb the depths of the soul and occasionally

Figure 5.2 Georg Wilhelm Friedrich Hegel (1770–1831)

ended up being bombastic. In fact, Hegel's belief that culture defines who we are was so all-encompassing that not only did he imply that it was inevitable that he be German, but also that he had a *duty* to be German. And as Beethoven was for a time at the pinnacle of German music, Hegel ended his life as the most influential philosopher at the University of Berlin, the most prestigious university in the country.

In one respect, at least, this somewhat overheated analogy breaks down. Whereas Beethoven's musical ideas were always clearly expressed despite their multi-layered complexity, Hegel's were expressed so badly that some philosophers have written papers suggesting, in frustration, that he was intentionally obscure! And moreover, he was obscure at great length! Finally, his grasp of the science of his day was quite poor and his respect for it was moderate at best. For him it was only one side of the great totality of thought, which he called the Absolute.

And yet, his thought was so much a part of the background of German thought of the 19th century, so deeply in the zeitgeist, that he influenced theorists as diverse as Marx and Freud, as well as Wundt and Fechner (to say nothing of philosophers such as Nietzsche). Those who have a social or sociological bent to their theories, such as the Americans John Dewey, Josiah Royce and James Mark Baldwin (see Chapter 7), owe a debt to him. It is sometimes difficult to trace this influence—in Germany, he was so well known (sometimes by indirect sources) that it was hardly necessary to cite him—but it is there.

Hegel, like Kant, was a rationalist and an idealist. Kant had faith that there was a world out there beyond our capability for perceiving it; thus, the natural world is orderly largely because of the order in our rational minds. Hegel would go further. Our rational minds and the ideas they contain are not just all we *can* know. They are reality itself. Hegel said, famously, that "the real is the rational and the rational is the real." This statement implies that what is real is spirit, not body. This spirit is, moreover, constantly evolving through the use of reason itself. For example, consider the statement that all people are innately good. One could, if one wanted, develop a pretty strong case for this view simply by collecting instances of good actions that people do to one another. Soon, however, you would come to recognize that people are also capable of great evil, and you would have to come up with reasons why this is so. So you might bounce from there to a hypothesis that humans are innately selfish and be able in some way to prove that as well. And from there you might be led to the proposition that different cultures and different individuals might have different views of what constitutes good or evil and so on. The logic that says that opposites can't be true at the same time does not hold. Furthermore, said Hegel, there are many ways of understanding a particular entity. There are moral perspectives, legal perspectives, scientific perspectives and artistic perspectives on human behavior, for example. None of them is completely right and none of them is wrong. They are simply different perspectives on the totality of knowledge, that Hegel called "the Absolute." Kant had set himself the task of finding the irreducible minimum of *a priori* structure that makes reasoning possible, in hopes that he could uncover the basis of thought for all time. Hegel said that, on the contrary, Kant, like all of us, was a creature of his own time and his insights were based on the knowledge developed up to that point. Kant's value was that he had wrestled with two opposites: rationalism, which had claimed that our own reason is sufficient to understand our own minds, and empiricism, which had claimed that all knowledge comes through senses, but had led, finally in Hume, to skepticism that knowledge could be finally known. In Hegel's terms, the first view was the **thesis** and the second, opposing view was the **antithesis** (pronounced An-TITH-e sis) and Kant's view was the **synthesis** of the two views—a new position formed to resolve the contradiction. And of course, Hegel's views were the antithesis to Kant's and so on. This method of reasoning through the clash of thesis and antithesis and their resolution through synthesis is called **dialectic**.

Hegel believed that, in this way, thought was evolving upward toward the Absolute as history progressed. Because he believed that the rational was the real, however, this was not to him just an abstraction for philosophers. History itself was for him a manifestation of the dialectical process. Great "world souls" like Napoleon were instruments of this upward movement toward complete knowledge, but such figures are demanded by the circumstances of the time, ride the waves of history for that moment and are brutally discarded to exile, death or disgrace by the workings of the Absolute in history.

Hegel therefore was not merely a part of the zeitgeist in 19th-century Germany, he made the very concept of zeitgeist a central part of his view of the world, a force that moves us forward in history, even if we are completely unaware of it.

What, then do science and psychology take from Hegel? From today's standpoint I think that several large, but imprecise, ideas that have made it into psychological theory can be attributed, at least in part, to Hegel (below from Levine, 1985).

Organicism. If you read the passage that begins this section again, you will see that Hegel looks at the process of progression of thought as that of an organism going through stages of growth rather than, say, the mathematical proof of Descartes or the chemical model of the empiricist. Organisms are not governed by the same sorts of processes as a clock or a falling body. They grow and change qualitatively as well as quantitatively, as the caterpillar changes into the butterfly. If the outer environment bites them, they attempt to bite back. The notion that development of the mind of a child might be due to the clash between physiological growth and the external stimuli of life is central to the developmental theories of Piaget and Vygotsky (see Chapter 10). Freud's theory is also a stage theory. Moreover, his view of the psyche is the dynamic, dialectical struggle between id and superego mediated by the synthesis of the ego.

Evolution. From the notion that there are early lower stages of spirit or mind and later higher stages, it is an easy step to considering the natural world. Hegel was only one of several philosophers who committed themselves to the view that the world is evolving upward towards perfection. These philosophers, called the *Naturphilosophen*, laid the groundwork for the notions of some theories of transmutation of species. Darwin himself never seems to have read Hegel, although he was at the height of his popularity in Germany when Darwin wrote the first draft of *Origin*. Darwin's German follower Ernst Haeckel was a materialist and a monist, rather than an idealist, but his recapitulation theory, as well as his writings for the general public, seems to be influenced by Hegel, at least through the zeitgeist if by no other route.

Historicism. The notion that beliefs are strongly dependent on their time is a notion that strongly borrows from Hegel. In Chapter 1 of this text, we discussed that a cardinal point of the definition of historicism was to take into account whom the writer was arguing against, because that opposite point of view subtly colors the arguments that are made. This is a clear recognition of the notion of dialectic.

Cultural Determinism and Relativism. Hegel believed that the web of meanings in a particular culture strongly determine what members of that culture may think. Our very self is created through the roles that culture gives to us: father and son, master and slave, member of the state. He believed that we are incomplete without a state and alienated from it if we do not believe in its values. Different states have different values, and individuals in one country are different from those in another land because of this.

Each of the above ideas has in common the notion that an interrelated *system* is the thing worth studying rather than an isolated variable. Culture, for example, is a system of interlocking meanings that guides our lives. History has many causes. An organism works when it is whole, a smoothly functioning system of interlocking parts. Hegel was not the only theorist of the time to think about the importance of systems. In the last chapter, we referred to Adam Smith, one of the founders of capitalist economics. Malthus, certainly, was another systemic theorist who influenced Darwin's thinking. And, of course, after Hegel's death, Karl Marx and Frederick Engels threw out the idealistic tinge of Hegel's thought and took him literally. To them, the dialectic was not between ideas but between classes of people. The synthesis to be made was in people and in social structures. In direct homage to and in contrast with Hegel, who might be called a dialectical idealist, they called their theory **dialectical materialism**, better known as communism. Biological and psychological science would also undergo a shift after Hegel from idealism to materialism, from the soul to the body. It is to this we now turn.

Materialism and Mechanism

What the German idealists left us with were ideas, metaphors and ways of thinking about the human condition. These are things which philosophers are good at. What they did not leave us with is techniques, ways of explicitly measuring what the mind is or the brain and nervous system are. In fact, Kant in particular had strongly doubted whether a science of the mind was even possible. By the 1840s, however, German scientists in physiology were wrestling with the relationship of how the soul related to the body. What made the difference between living and nonliving matter? Were living things merely machines with a physical and chemical basis or was something else needed, a life force or a *vis viva* or *élan vital* as the terms were in Europe of the time? Some scientists believed that the soul's action on the body was instantaneous: No time elapsed between the thought to move the arm and the movement of that arm. Other scientists suspected that there might be a delay, but how to measure it? One would need instruments to do so. The mind itself was problematic, because it would be very difficult if not impossible to get around the paradox that if the mind did in fact suffer a delay, the mind could not itself study the delay in its workings, for then it would have a delay in noticing the delay and so on. Kant himself suggested that thought was how we perceived time, that thought *was* time, for the flow of thought was the stuff of which the perception of the flow of time was made. And finally, could we really hope that thought would be lawful, in Newton's sense? Could we measure the mind precisely enough to develop mathematical laws as to how it did its work? If we could somehow take the study of the mind out of the mind itself, develop ways to collect data about it, to measure and quantify that data and develop mathematical laws as to how it works and then describe how it fits with the senses of the body, then we would have a science of the mind, but not before.

Since this story is a story of the development of technique of measurement, quantification, experiments and instruments, it will be fairly technical. It will deal with electrical pulses, telescopes, chronometers, gears, self-closing switches and smelly organic chemicals. The methods will be borrowed from the hard sciences: astronomy, physiology, chemistry and even physics. By the end of this chapter, the psychology that results, called "the New Psychology" by its proponents (or "brass instrument psychology" by its detractors), will be well on its way to being a laboratory science.

146 Idealism to Materialism and Dualism

And, for all intents and purposes, the soul will have been banished. But the mind will still be there and psychology will still be defined as the study of it. In fact, psychology will be the study of perception; all of the other interesting facets of human mind and behavior will have been banished. As it turns out, they were banished to America, but that is a story for subsequent chapters.

We will take these problems in turn. First, we will have to turn to astronomy to discuss how scientists began to suspect that the mind must take time to do its work and how they dealt with systematic errors in observation that are a result of this problem. Then we will discuss how the great German physiologist and physicist Hermann von Helmholtz and his colleagues began the long process of reducing the nervous system to mere physiochemical processes and determined the speed of the nerve impulse. Next, we will examine how Gustav Fechner put the process of measuring sensation and perception on a mathematical basis. Finally, we will discuss how Wilhelm Wundt, a former student of Helmholtz, attempted to develop a science in which the mind studies itself by experimental self-observation.

The Personal Equation in Astronomy

In 1795 in Britain, at the famous Greenwich Observatory, Astronomer Royal Nevil Maskelyne as having problems with his assistant, David Kinnebrook. One of the key

Figure 5.3 The Octagon Room at the Royal Observatory in Greenwich, England. Note the telescope at the right, the sextant at the left and the three clocks by the door under the paintings. The room is much the same as it was in the 18th century. By convention, the prime meridian, or zero longitude, passes through this room. The Harrison Timekeepers still are headquartered here, measuring time in a much more sophisticated way for modern navigation.

Source: Getty Images

tasks of astronomers was and is to come up with accurate times for the transits of the stars across the night sky. Such accurate measurements were crucial to navigation. To do this, the astronomer would typically set up his telescope to take a bead on a particular star and wait. Inside the eyepiece of the telescope were two very thin parallel wires set closely together. The astronomer was to look at a very accurate clock. He was to note the time to the nearest second and begin counting the seconds aloud with the ticks of the clock as the star moved slowly across his field of view in the telescope. When it was about to cross a wire, he was to note that time in his mind. Then, as it crossed the wire, he was to note the time to the nearest second in his head and estimate to the nearest tenth of a second the time that it crossed to the other side. As you might imagine, this was rather complicated, a task requiring a lot of quick judgments and enormous concentration. At the time, scientists thought that this method should be accurate to about two-tenths of a second. Poor Kinnebrook was coming up with times that differed from his boss Maskelyne by about a half a second. This was bad, but when Maskelyne called his attention to the error, he got even worse. His measurements were coming up consistently almost a second off from the Astronomer Royal. Kinnebrook was regrettably fired (Fancher, 1996).

One can't really assume from this, however, that the more senior person is correct and the assistant is incorrect. Both, after all, are observing the star, and there was not at this time any independent method of observing the star. An astronomer could calculate, however, how much he differed from a colleague, by taking the difference between the measurements of the two. Soon, two things became apparent. First, there were consistent mean differences between any two observers that varied up to a full second. This consistent difference observed between any two observers became known as an astronomer's **personal equation**. The personal equation represents one form of error to be eliminated, but the problem of course is in knowing ultimately who is right. Second, any observer, of course, differs with himself all the time, so that there is variability not only between observers, but also within observers. This kind of error, as the mathematician Quetelet noticed, was distributed in a normal bell curve around a central mean for each observer. This little discovery had rather profound consequences for science in general and psychology in particular. First, the fact that it takes time to make an observation suggests rather strongly that thinking must take time; the action of the soul upon the body is not instantaneous. Second, although philosophers and scientists had known since Descartes that sensation is fallible and that the "real" answer as to the real state of the world is unobtainable, we now have a way to measure the limits of that error. You can't be right, but you can use statistical means to determine how wrong you are.

There are also a number of ways to narrow that error, by removing some aspects of the observer from the equation. What follows is a list of possible ways.

1. Instead of having one observer do all the work of concentration and remembering where and when the stars are, you could have the person at the telescope rap a sharp stick and have a second observer listen to the rap and observe the time. Although this means that the observer is thinking about fewer things, the second observer presumably takes time to hear and respond to the rap.
2. You can have the observer at the telescope squeeze a trigger that stops the hand of the chronometer.

3. You can have a clock so designed that it trips an electromagnet to make a mark on a sheet of paper every second and the observer squeezes the trigger to make another mark on the page when the star crosses the line. Then you can simply get out your ruler to measure the distance between the second marks and the observer's mark.

Each of these methods reduces the amount of time that it takes to make the judgment, but, of course, it doesn't eliminate error entirely. What they do is provide ways to convert time to data without specific introspection. The observer is responding to a stimulus, not himself. Some of these very measures were later used by psychologists for studying consciousness.

Hermann von Helmholtz (1821–1894)

Hermann von Helmholtz was a giant of 19th-century science and medicine. His contributions range from the invention of the ophthalmoscope in medicine to the description of the laws of conservation of energy in physics. His contributions to psychology include most famously his early estimates of the speed of the nerve impulse and an innovative theory of color vision. Perhaps his greatest legacy, however, was his meticulous attention to the logic, methods and equipment of experimental research. It is this contribution that finally helped to introduce the concepts of replication and experimental control into physiology and, from there, into psychology.

Born in 1821 in Potsdam, Germany, Helmholtz was captivated by physics from an early age, after finding some physics texts in his father's library. At this time, however, physical science was still practiced mostly by wealthy gentlemen who had the leisure to pursue it. Helmholtz's father was a high school teacher and thus did not have the funds to send his son to university. The Prussian government had set up scholarships to send poor boys to medical school, in exchange for their agreeing to serve as army doctors for eight years upon graduation. Although Helmholtz's first choice was obviously physics, his decision to go to medical school proved to be a fateful choice. For the first half of his career, he found himself in the useful position of knowing more physics than the physiologists and physicians with whom he spoke and more biology and anatomy than the physicists (Fancher, 1996)!

In medical school, he first encountered Johannes Müller (1801–1858), a groundbreaking anatomist and physiologist at the University of Berlin. Müller's *Principles of Physiology*, written in the late 1830s, was the first widely used textbook that attempted, as far as was then possible, to integrate the principles of physical chemistry with those of physiology to move towards a mechanical view of bodily processes, supported by systematic experimental research. Müller noted, for example, that organic matter decomposes into chemicals, with the addition of water and air. He noted that this process was accompanied by microscopic life and that some people theorized that all life is composed of these "animicules."

Müller, however, had difficulty accepting that organisms could run only by chemical processes. Organic beings are organized into systems that cannot be divided to a certain point without death. He could easily accept the decomposition of organic matter into chemicals, but no one could simply put those chemicals back together and get life. Some force other than heat, light or electricity was necessary. This force or "imponderable matter" drives the generation of new life from the united egg and sperm and provides the extra boost to resist the forces of decay. Remove the force and death occurs:

> Life, therefore, is not simply the result of harmony and reciprocal action of these parts; but is first manifested in a principle or imponderable matter which is in action in the substance of the germ [i.e. egg or sperm] enters into the composition of the matter of this germ and imparts to organic combinations properties which cease at death.
>
> (Müller, 1840, p. 28)

He was uncertain whether sensations were caused because the imponderable nervous fluid passed through the nerve (a tube analogy of nerve action that goes back to Descartes) or were caused by vibrations from the stimuli themselves (Newton's explanation). He thought that the action of the soul upon the body was for all practical purposes instantaneous, but he also was aware of the fact that the part of the brain/mind that dealt with sensation (the "sensorium") took time to work: he cites (Müller, 1840, vol. 1, p. 730) the research on the personal equation described earlier. Contrary to some of his contemporaries, however, he was sure that sensation was dependent on the nerves because of a simple fact. He knew that the auditory nerve received only sound and the optic nerve only sight, no matter how the stimulation is produced. The nervous system of each sense is dedicated to produce only the kind of sensation appropriate to that sense. Müller called this principle the **law of specific nerve energies**. It is easy to demonstrate this. Close your eyes and look to the right as far as you can. Then gently press on the left side of your closed eye. You should see a colored spot, which often remains after you open your eye. The physical stimulus is pressure, but the perception is of colored light. Müller concludes, "sensation, therefore, consists in the communication to the sensorium not the quality or state of the external body [i.e. object] but of the condition of the nerves themselves, excited by the external cause" (Müller, 1840, vol. 1, p. 819).

As a medical student, Helmholtz had helped Müller with experiments on reducing life to its chemical components. He had also learned to do skillful, delicate dissection and work with a microscope. After he received his MD, he continued these experiments in his spare time as an army doctor. His purpose was to determine whether life required a life force to remain alive, as Müller had said, or whether all the energy in life could be simply explained by chemical reactions and the heat given off by those reactions.

The basic outline of Helmholtz's experiments in this area can be easily described: Helmholtz took a detached frog's leg and applied electrical current to it to make the muscles fire. He continued to do this until the muscle was exhausted and would flex no more. He then liquefied the contents of the leg, extracted the fluids, dried and weighed the solids and analyzed everything. He also extracted all the chemicals in a similar way from a fresh leg. When he compared the chemicals from the two legs, he noted that the weight of the total was the same, but that in the exhausted leg, some of the chemicals had been changed by the exertion. Through many repeated experiments, Helmholtz carefully worked out the proportions of chemicals and noted the mathematical relationships in the required chemical reaction. He became almost convinced that there was nothing else left unexplained. He had also accounted for the heat generated and given off by the exhausted muscle, by the use of a thermometer that measured heat to 1/1000th of a degree, which he invented. The care that he took in his experiments shows that Helmholtz was well aware of the need for **control conditions** and replication in experimental design:

- He controlled for blood and moisture by using detached, drained frog's legs.
- He controlled for the possible heat produced by the electricity itself.
- He controlled for possible chemical reactions caused by the electricity.
- He repeated every experiment that he did in his laboratory and every experiment reported in the literature before proceeding. Advanced students in his laboratory repeated experiments he himself had done.

Perhaps his most significant experiments in physiology, however, were those that attempted to measure the speed of conduction of the nerve impulse through the leg. He electrified a frog's leg with a weight on it and thought that he noticed that the time taken to lift the weight depended on the place where the leg was stimulated. But, he said, "our senses are not capable of directly perceiving an individual moment of time with such a small duration" (Olesko & Holmes, 1993, p. 84). So, he set out to prove it by an ingenious experiment. Because he knew the physics of electromagnetism well, he devised a kind of electromagnetic "clock." He knew that when a current passes through an instrument called a galvanometer, a needle on a gauge was deflected from zero to some maximum point. This usually happens quickly, but the distance the needle travels around the gauge is proportional to the amount of time the current has been flowing. He made a gauge that would fix the needle at the maximum point of deflection. He made a circuit in which current flowed through the galvanometer and then down the frog's leg. Then he put a tiny contact on the end of the detached frog's leg. When he started the current, it made the frog's leg lift the contact and break the circuit. Then he could merely read how far the needle had gone around and calculate the amount of time it had taken for the current to make the leg jump from the amount of needle had deflected around the gauge.

Now, as we know today, every experiment, no matter how well controlled, has some variability in its measurements. Helmholtz had discovered this too, so, good scientist that he was, he didn't just give a single number in meters per second in his paper on the speed of the nerve impulse. He gave a range, and he was one of the first scientists to use statistical methods to specify how wrong he might be. In a footnote, he explained that the time between electrical stimulation and action of the muscle was 0.00175 sec plus or minus 0.00014 and that specifically, this meant that you could bet 100 to 1 that the real time difference lies between 0.00228 and 0.00122 sec. (It is worth noting that at the time, some other experts had guessed that the speed of the nerve impulse was well over the speed of light. Elsewhere, Helmholtz noted that his calculations meant that a whale who is injured in his tail might need over a second to know about it [Olesko & Holmes, 1993]!)

Thus, you can see from these examples that almost every aspect of experimental methodology that is today used in psychology was used by Helmholtz. Use of control conditions, replication of experiments, meticulous concern for measurement, careful execution of clearly and publicly described methods and reporting of results with statistical confidence intervals are all present in his reports.

Through these experiments, he became convinced that the action of muscles and nerves could be explained by physiochemical processes alone, without recourse to a life force. He and fellow students of Müller, Emil du Bois-Reymond (1818–1896) and Ernst Brücke (1819–1892), became part of the "1847 group," who followed a materialist hypothesis. They were engaged in developing an "organic physics" in which no life force was necessary to explain the actions of living beings. In fact, Helmholtz, du Bois-Reymond, Brücke, Karl Ludwig (1828–1899) and others of the 1847 group took a solemn oath:

> No other forces than the common physical-chemical ones are active within the organism. In those cases which cannot at the time be explained by these forces one has either to find the specific way or form of their action by means of the physical-mathematical method or to assume new forces equal in dignity to the physical-chemical forces inherent in matter, reducible to the force of attraction and repulsion.
>
> (Cited by Bernfeld, 1949, p. 171)

Müller himself was not dismayed by the wholesale defection of his students to a point of view that excluded the life force. He gave most of his students glowing recommendations for other posts and wished them well.

The view subscribed to by the 1847 group is called the materialist or mechanist hypothesis, in that it invokes only natural causes in explanation, avoiding all spiritual or supernatural causes in living beings. This view also implies the philosophical position of **determinism**, which states that everything must have a knowable cause. Aided by the near-simultaneous rise of evolutionist thought, materialism and determinism soon became core assumptions of the paradigm of biological science. Other students of Müller, Rudolf Virchow and Jacob Henle, instituted reforms in German medicine that were to have far-ranging effects. Their belief that diseases follow strict natural laws was supplemented strongly by advocating experimental procedures. Indeed, the materialist/determinist hypothesis directly influenced psychology in major ways. Helmholtz directly taught both Wilhelm Wundt, the founder of experimental psychology, and Hermann Ebbinghaus, pioneering researcher in memory processes. Ivan Pavlov, pioneer in classical conditioning methods, was taught by Karl Ludwig and influenced by Ivan Sechenov, a roommate of du Bois-Reymond. Even Sigmund Freud was for a time a lab assistant to Ernst Brücke at the University of Vienna (see Figure 5.4).

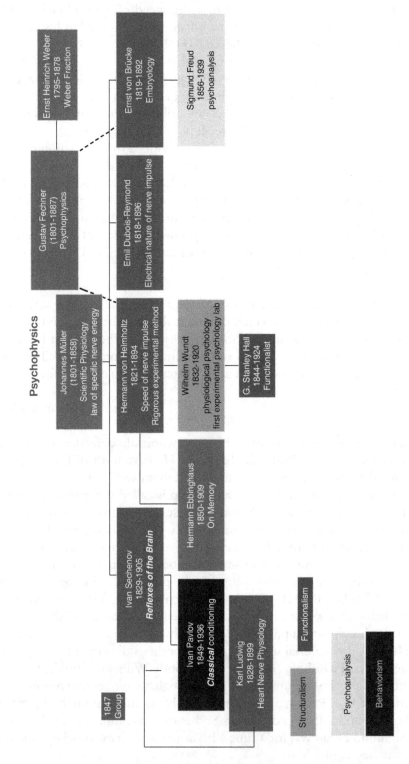

Figure 5.4 Map figure of the influence of Johannes Peter Müller

Gustav Fechner (1801–1887)

Gustav Fechner was born in 1801, the son and grandson of a village pastor in southeastern Germany. He was a precocious student and learned to converse with his father in Latin at a very young age. Unfortunately, his father died in Fechner's childhood, leaving his mother quite poor. He managed, however, to enter medical school at the tender age of 16 (at this time, a medical degree was an undergraduate rather than a graduate course of study). But, like other contributors to psychology (Francis Galton, Hermann Helmholtz, William James and Wilhelm Wundt and even, of course, Charles Darwin), he found medical study not to his liking. He eventually earned a "bachelor's" in medicine, mostly from books, but declined to go for his doctorate, as he had skipped the clinical work. In fact, he despised the lack of scientific rigor that he found in medicine and the kind of quasi-theological arguments found in his classes in the 1820s. Writing under a satirical pen name of "Dr. Mises," he wrote a proof that the moon was made of iodine, to skewer the then current belief of iodine as a cure for all diseases. He wrote other satirical works as well, such as a *The Comparative Anatomy of Angels*, a proof that angels had to be spherical, like round balloons, because, of course, angels, being perfect beings, would have to be the perfect shape (Fancher, 1996)!

To put himself through school at the University of Leipzig, though, he translated several French texts in physics into German and was therefore allowed to teach the subject. In the 1830s, he became a publishing demon, publishing texts on electrodynamics, galvanic current and experimental physics. In his spare time, he edited a pharmaceutical journal and edited and wrote much of an eight-volume encyclopedia of science for the general public. By 1840, he was a highly regarded full professor of physics when his world fell apart. His eyes developed a pathological sensitivity to light, and he was forced to spend his days and nights in almost complete darkness. This sensitivity either caused or was a symptom of a mental breakdown that lasted for most of three years. He had, in fact, abused his eyes by attempting to replicate some of Müller's experiments on eye pressure leading to afterimages, but there was also the extreme overwork that he had subjected himself to. Finally and perhaps most importantly, Fechner was severely troubled by conflicts over materialism vs. the religious worldview and free will vs. determinism. The psychic strain was too much for him. He could not read and spent much of his time in the kind of obsessive rumination common in a severe depression.

By 1845, he had recovered from his illness and on October 22, 1850, he had a vision that an increase in "spiritual intensity" (i.e. the subjective experience of an increase in stimulation) should be linked mathematically with an increase in physical stimuli. In fact, he felt that if he could prove that the relationship between the mind/soul and the body was mathematically predictable, he could prove that the materialist view of the nerves and brain and the idealist view of the mind/soul were essentially two points of view on the same thing (he called these the "night view" and the "day view," respectively). Not incidentally, he would also disprove Kant's assertion that there could not be a science of psychology because the mind could not be described mathematically.

Fechner, the former physics professor, called this new science **psychophysics**, the study of how the subjective experience of perception was related to the world of objective stimuli. In his studies in psychophysics, he was encouraged by the findings of his University of Leipzig colleague Ernst Heinrich Weber (1795–1878). Weber had conducted studies on people's ability to distinguish between two different weights. He had asked the subjects to discriminate the smallest unit they could between the two weights—the so-called **just noticeable difference** (commonly abbreviated jnd). He found that, rather than discriminating the absolute differences between two weights, his subjects were discriminating relative amounts. In other words, a weight of 62 drams could be discriminated from one of 60 drams, but a weight of 120 drams could only be discriminated from a weight of 124. A weight twice as great would have a jnd that was twice as large, but the ratio of the two weights would be constant. This is called today the **Weber fraction** or **Weber constant** (see Table 5.2). Weber found in further investigations that the constant differed depending on the sense being investigated, but the very fact that there *were* constants was encouraging to Fechner. Even though it was clear that our perceptions are not accurate to the external standard, they were predictably related to it. Furthermore, it was clear that there was a minimum to perception in each sense, a weight below which subjects could not detect at all. Weber called this the **absolute threshold**, the minimum stimulus intensity for each sense that a subject could detect at all.

Fechner extended Weber's work and devised several ingenious methods for investigating sensory experience that are still sometimes used today. The **method of limits** was used to determine absolute threshold. A stimulus (the light thrown off by an incandescent filament, for example, or a distance between two points on the skin) is randomly set at a point above the suspected threshold and decreased towards the threshold point in equal steps. At each point, the subject makes a binary choice: they might say "yes, I see it," or no, I don't see it, for the light or "yes, I feel two points,"

Table 5.2 Representative Weber fractions for common continua (From Baird & Noma, 1978)

Continuum	Weber fraction $\Delta S/S$
Finger span	.02
Saturation (red)	.02
Electrical (skin)	.03
Position of point (visual)	.03
Length of lines (visual)	.04
Area (visual)	.06
Heaviness	.07
Brightness (naive observers)	.08
Loudness (1000 Hz, energy units)	.10
Loudness (white noise, energy units)	.10
Taste (salt)	.14
Taste (sweet)	.17
Skin vibration (100–1100 Hz)	.20
Smell (several substances)	.24

or "I feel only one point on my skin." The experimenter keeps going down in equal increments of brightness or narrower spacings of points until all responses are "No." Then the experimenter picks a random point below the suspected threshold and works his or her way up by equal increments until the stimulus is reliably seen. The experiment is repeated a few times and an average computed (Baird & Noma, 1978).

In the **method of adjustment**, there are two lights, a standard and a comparison light. The subject looks at the standard light and adjusts the comparison light to match and then works the knob until the light is exactly felt to be one just noticeable difference above or below it. In the **method of constant stimuli**, random intensities are chosen around a standard and the subject's task is to say "higher" or "lower" than the standard. Each of these methods produce slightly different results, but it has been proven that all are related to each other in mathematical ways by a constant, suggesting that they are measuring the same thing: the predictable relationship between perception and the external world (Baird & Noma, 1978).

Fechner discovered that Weber's constant needed adapting. Yes, it is true that each increase in physical intensity is matched by an increase in perceived intensity, but that increase is not necessarily linear. In fact, Fechner discovered that for every just noticeable difference in perception, there had to be a tenfold increase in the intensity of the physical intensity. The subjective perception and the objective physical stimulus were thus logarithmically related:

$$S = k \log P$$

Where S is the subjective experience of the intensity of the stimulus, P is the measurable intensity of the objective physical stimulus and k is some constant, which differs among the senses.

After his groundbreaking discovery, Fechner, having been given a rather generous pension from his professorial post, devoted the rest of his life to more spiritual pursuits. He had proven to his satisfaction that the day view and the night view were the same thing and linked the outer world systematically with the inner one. He, himself, was more content with studying the inner world. He seems to have resolved his internal conflict between the material and the spiritual world by becoming a kind of pantheistic mystic. He claimed, for example, that plants have souls and that stars have souls. He was dismissive of Darwin and materialism.

Having had his "dark night of the soul," he was eager to offer proofs of the efficacy of belief. He thought there were three such proofs:

The first and weakest was the historical proof—that all cultures believed in some form of higher being. The second proof, the pragmatic proof, was later to become the centerpiece of William James's *Varieties of Religious Experience* (1902), the most influential book on the psychology of religion ever written; it also is seen in James's philosophy of pragmatism. In this view, the truth of a religious belief is seen in the consequences to human happiness of believing it:

> Every erroneous or inadequate assumption shows itself to be such by the fact that when it is accepted as true it entails, through the influence it exercises upon feeling, thought and action, consequences which are injurious to human

> happiness by inducing in us states of mind which are disagreeable and behavior which is obnoxious, producing displeasure and dissatisfaction, either immediately or through its consequences—whereas the truth of an assumption is proved by the contrary consequences.
>
> (Fechner, 1863/1946, p. 113)

James had forgotten having read this particular passage until it was brought to his attention late in life, and then he warmly acknowledged it (Lowrie, 1946). Finally, not surprisingly, the third argument, the theoretical argument, rested upon the empirical process of correcting instances weeded out by the rational process of correcting sensation.

It is somewhat ironic that his psychophysics, that which we consider most important in Fechner's work, occupied very little of his time, in comparison to his theological speculations. Some of these things were not lost on future psychologists. He made the mind measurable. In so doing, his contemporaries saw that he had at once proved Kant's view that mind imposes regular laws on nature, while appearing to disprove Kant's view that psychology could not be a mathematical science. He provided workable, replicable methods for measuring sensation. Some have even claimed that he created the role of an experimental subject in psychology, whose introspections could be measured. By making the subject respond in yes/no dichotomous fashion, he also created "countable" data from inaccessible conscious experience. The subject, in effect, consults his or her own consciousness about a stimulus, makes a decision and reports a datum to be counted (Danziger, 1990). This notion of subject became central to the methods of the man traditionally credited with being the founder of experimental psychology, Wilhelm Wundt.

Wilhelm Wundt

Wilhelm Wundt was born August 16, 1832, at Neckerau, outside Manheim am Rhine, in what was then Prussia, but is now Germany. He was a pastor's son, but his grandfather and great grandfather had been professors. Two of his uncles were medical doctors with university posts. Although his father and mother were both loving, it appears that Wundt's maternal grandfather, who believed in strict discipline, ruled the family. Wundt grew up quite lonely, having been raised essentially as an only child, his elder brother having been sent away to school. Diamond (1980) describes Wundt as the sort of boy who ended up with no Easter eggs from the egg hunt because other boys stole from him. His only friend in childhood was a mentally retarded boy with slurred speech. It is perhaps not surprising that such a boy as young Wilhelm would grow up as a daydreamer who read a lot. His daydreaming, which was accentuated by the death of his father when Wundt was 14, caused him to fail the first year of high school. So he was sent off to live with Uncle Ludwig, a professor at Heidelberg, where he did somewhat better. He was excited by the revolutions going on in Europe in 1848 and made friends, but he was still such a poor student that, despite considerable family connections at Heidelberg, he could not be admitted on scholarship.

Fortunately, young Wilhelm had another professor uncle at the University of Tübingen, with whom he studied cerebral anatomy. When Uncle Friedrich took a post at Heidelberg, Wundt went back and was finally admitted to medical school. He did medical experiments in his mother's kitchen and won a prize for solving an anatomical problem in a competition. (His uncle had written the question.) For his medical dissertation, he experimented on himself by controlling salt in his diet and measuring the salt in his urine. He passed the medical exams first in his class (although he was influenced to steer a course away from medical practice by nearly killing a patient—he gave her iodine instead of a narcotic). He studied with Müller and du Bois-Reymond at Berlin for a short time and began to teach physiology, but fell ill and returned home to Heidelberg.

The overall picture that emerges of Wundt's character is of a man of great ambition and industriousness, but some limitations in intellect, with a prickly, self-protective haughtiness. At this time, in the 1850s, the great Helmholtz was at Heidelberg and Wundt became one of his assistants, in 1858. But all accounts suggest that he did not take much advantage of the position. Ivan Sechenov, who was also working in Helmholtz's lab at the time, said of Wundt, "Wundt sat the whole year unfailingly at some books in his own corner, not paying attention to anyone and not saying a word to anyone. I did not once hear his voice" (Sechenov, 1945/1952, p. 39, cited by Diamond, 1980, p. 30). Lest this be mistaken for mere shyness, it should be noted that Wundt was not shy at all when his interests were threatened. His first book, with the vainglorious title of *The Present State of Knowledge Concerning Muscular Action* (1859), contained experiments that had already been done by others, the conclusions of which he sometimes misreported. One reviewer suggested that in a particular muscle experiment, the result should have been precisely the opposite of what Wundt said it was. The reviewer happened to be right, but Wundt did not apologize, but simply flipped his position and claimed, in the face of obvious evidence, that he had said the right thing all along. Moreover, he lambasted the reviewer, in the most personal terms, for criticizing him in the first place (Diamond, 1980)!

He was also not above taking credit for ideas that were not his. He claimed repeatedly in published accounts to have discovered the notion of **unconscious inference**—the notion that meaningful visual perception requires a large amount of reasoning of which we are not aware. For example, each view of an object impinges upon our retinas as flat, but we integrate those views unconsciously, so that we perceive the object as a single, solid, three-dimensional one (*object constancy*). Or we conclude that an object that is getting smaller in our visual field is moving away from us. This notion of unconscious inference had already been discussed by Helmholtz in a public lecture in 1855, several years before Wundt came on the scene, and yet Wundt repeatedly took credit for it.

Wundt worked for Helmholtz for six years, until 1864. After a short stint as a socialist member for Heidelberg of the local parliament (in which he supported bills for the secularization of the local schools), Wundt returned to research, publishing widely, teaching courses on Anthropology and Medical Psychology and receiving promotions (Bringmann, 1975).

In 1873 and 1874, Wundt published a two-volume textbook that became his claim to fame and marked out his territory of expertise as separate from philosophy. Although the first volume contained much about the nervous system, the text was not physiological in the sense that nerves were its subject. Rather, Wundt wanted to use the methods of physiology, but in the service of the study of consciousness, not nervous impulses. It was physiological in the sense that it applied, for the first time, physiological methods to the study of the mind.

Physiological psychology is, therefore, first of all, *psychology*. It has in view the same principal object upon which all other forms of psychological exposition are directed, the investigation of conscious processes in the modes of connection peculiar to them (Wundt, 1904, p. 2).

The physiological methods of Helmholtz were to be applied to the psychophysics of Fechner; in other words, experimental control of external stimuli and replication were to be applied to the process of a trained observer studying the contents of his or her own mind. Wundt was not blind to the difficulties of this task, sketched out by Kant 75 years before. Observation in Wundt's kind of psychology is not observation of stable external objects, but of fleeting internal perceptions. In Wundt's view, this was precisely why rigorous controls of external stimuli were necessary. The psychological experiment should proceed by creating external conditions aimed at producing coherent determinable processes. By varying the external, so the theory goes, we could vary the internal event in consciousness that the observer or in this case, self-observer, inspects. Wundt therefore called his method **experimental self-observation**.

Experimental self-observation was quite different from philosophical introspection as originated largely by Descartes and as practiced by everyone from Locke and Berkeley to Kant and Hegel. Philosophical introspection was not self-observation per se, but the search for the clear and distinct feeling of the intuition of being right and then constructing arguments to convince the reader of their rightness. Philosophers dealt with metaphysics or questions about what the world is fundamentally made of. In this quest, by the mid-19th century, they had been forced to come to the realization that their own ability to know what the world is made of was hampered by their own sensory and cognitive limitations. Thus, Wundt acknowledged that psychology cannot be concerned with these metaphysical goals but must be concerned with the goal of the study of those sensory and cognitive limitations themselves. What is the conscious mind made of and how does it do its work? To Wundt, this was a task of immense importance, because if the mind is the lawgiver to nature and scientific observations are the basis for natural laws, then the study of how consciousness operates to give us those observations is the foundation of all the sciences. Yet consciousness is entirely an internal, subjective phenomenon, one that in its normal operation is naturally directed outward towards things. The primary problem of experimental self-observation was to devise a way to look at thoughts themselves, not what the thoughts are about, to direct the gaze inward on the contents and processes of consciousness. Because this is an unnatural thing to do, and because he was well aware of Kant's cautions about observing the flowing mind within one's self, Wundt's first task was to devise an instrument for looking into consciousness, an instrument in the form of a person, the rigorously trained self-observationist.

Wundt's Laboratory and Experimental Methods

Wundt arrived at Leipzig University in 1875 as a professor of philosophy but immediately began a free graduate seminar on psychological topics. By 1879, he offered to donate his collection of psychophysical apparatus to the university in exchange for a budget. They turned him down, but he ran the laboratory, in what was initially only a single room, for three years out of his own pocket. He established the first journal for psychological research, entitled *Philosophical Studies* (*Philosophische Studien*) instead of *Psychological Studies* only because there was already a journal by that name that dealt with Spiritism and séances. The university finally gave him a proper lab (with full electrical wiring!), a budget and a raise in salary when he threatened to defect to a rival university in 1883. This is considered, by tradition, the first laboratory for psychological experimentation in the world and is considered, also by tradition, to have been founded in the little room in 1879 (Bringmann, Bringmann, & Ungerer, 1980).[2]

Wundt stocked the laboratory with several things that were common in physiological labs, astronomical observatories and psychophysicists' workrooms. He procured precise chronometers that could be started and stopped with manual or automatic electromagnetic switches; kymographs, which were essentially automatic rotating drums covered with paper or lampblack on which a pen could trace a line; oil lamps that could be increased and decreased in brightness as stimuli for just-noticeable differences in sensation; arc lamps, illuminated by bright electrical sparks, for bright stimulation; split-second, spring-loaded photographic shutters, useful for exposing lighted stimuli for fractions of a section; precise tuning forks and metronomes for auditory stimulation; telegraph keys to close and open circuits for chronometers in a split second to measure how quickly a subject responded to the presentation of stimuli, known as **reaction time**; and motors on which colored cards could be spun around.

Then Wundt stocked his lab with many assistants, graduate students and visitors from abroad (chiefly America: G. Stanley Hall was one of the first students to use the lab and James McKeen Cattell was his first lab assistant—see Chapter 7.) Wundt, trained as both a physiologist and a philosopher, thus found himself in the perfect position at the right time to create the science of psychology as a separate discipline: He had a journal, a lab and a steady flow of graduate students to train in his methods.

The apparatus was necessary to exercise the most stringent and precise control over the stimulation provided in experiments. The role of "experimenter" was thus created to mean the one who prepared and operated such apparatus and took down responses of the subjects; the graduate students were necessary to serve as subjects for experiments, otherwise called "observers," because it was their job to observe their perceptions of their own inner reactions to the strictly controlled stimuli. Before an observer was allowed to contribute his observations of his own inner workings as data of the experiment to be published, he often had to undergo a training period of

Figure 5.5 Hipp Chronoscope (c. 1895). A Swiss timepiece capable of accuracy to about 0.001 seconds. This very expensive clock was essential in Wundtian labs of experimental self-observation.

Source: Getty Images

hundreds of practice self-observations, until his judgments about his own reactions to stimuli became relatively easy and automatic. The observer had thus acquired through practice a trained **inner perception** as natural as perception of the outer world (Danziger, 1980). As a judgment of quality, the name and academic rank of the observer playing the role of subject of the experiment was always cited in the article, in contrast to today's practice (Danziger, 1990). In this way, Wundt thought that he was exercising every bit as much control over the responses as over the stimuli in an experiment. Although experiments were often repeated, the data were rarely averaged across observers; each was reported separately.

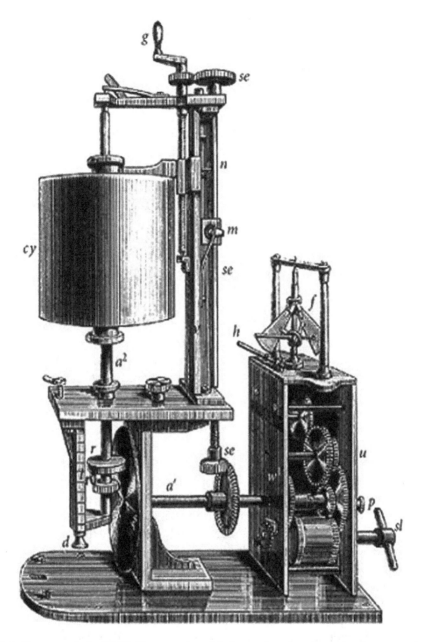

Figure 5.6 Kymograph (c. 1847). Paper or lampblack can be placed on the drum rotating at a constant speed. A pen would automatically inscribe a line and a trigger could mark the line at a specified time.

Now, let us examine Wundt's methods of experimenting. One of Wundt's first and simplest experiments, done in 1864 before even arriving at Leipzig, concerned the inability to experience simultaneously the sight and sound of a stimulus. To do this experiment, Wundt took a dependable German pendulum cuckoo clock and tied a knitting needle to the pendulum crosswise, perpendicular to it. Then he placed bells at the extreme ends of the pendulum's swings so that the knitting needle would ring the bells on either end (i.e. the clock would go "tick, ding! tock, ding!"). He made a scale that was fitted below the pendulum so that it would swing from 0 to 8 and back again. The task of the observer was to report where on the scale the pendulum was when he heard the bell. Invariably, the observer would report hearing the bell not when it rang, but when the pendulum was already on its way back from ringing. The observer could attend to the sight or the sound, but not to both at exactly the same instant. Some time was lost in switching attention between the two events. (The observer was near enough to the clock that the speed of sound was not a significant factor in the difference.)

Once the laboratory was up and running, Wundt attempted more difficult experiments using several different methods. The first method, **paired comparison**, required an observer to render judgements on the relative intensity of a stimulus in comparison with a standard, using the methods of Fechner, Wundt's hero. A second method, reaction time, required a timed judgement to a stimulus, in which an observer would press a telegraph key to close a circuit and stop a clock when a judgement was reached. In these reaction time experiments, Wundt followed an assumption first expressed by Donders (1869) that more complex judgements, requiring more stages of mental activity, took longer to perform in the mind and thus rendered longer reaction times to the key press. A trained observer would sit in a chair at a table with the key in front of him, in a state of expectant heightened awareness. Then the experimenter would start the stimulus and the observer would react quickly as possible to any awareness that a stimulus is on. This would be the stage of mere *sensation*. The experiment could easily be changed so that the observer is asked to press the key only when he can say anything at all about the stimulus; this would be the stage of *perception*, which would take slightly longer to judge. A further experiment asks the observer to press the key only when he recognizes what the stimulus is of, a picture or a word, for example; this stage of recognition is called *apperception* and its judgement takes longer still. Finally, if the observer is asked to make a comparison judgement as to whether a stimulus is larger or smaller, or brighter or dimmer, or higher or lower than another, that is the slow process of *cognition*, in Wundt's terminology. In the nearly 180 experimental studies published between 1880 and 1903 in Wundt's journal *Philosophical Studies*, 176 used relatively quantitative measures of thought such as comparison and reaction time. The other four used qualitative measures of feeling or of qualities of taste or beauty (Danziger, 1980).

Although Wundt directed many studies like these that seemed to be focused on taking apart the conscious experience, he very much recognized that conscious experience in the real world was about putting all of these steps together. He was perhaps most interested in the tendency of consciousness to focus and direct our perceptual experience to the exclusion of other things, what today would be called the property of selective attention, but which Wundt called **volition**, an aspect of the will. Physical phenomena, such as objects falling in space, are passive and as such, obey clear laws, but psychological phenomena happen because of the active thought of a person, who intends or wills to do something. Because of this, Wundt did not think that the mind could be reduced to mere physiochemical forces. Psychic causality required the will of an intentional person. Thus, Wundt called his psychology **volitional psychology** (Blumenthal, 1975).

The Völkerpsychologie

Wundt believed that his experimental studies of individual observers' internal perceptions in the lab were part of natural science, or what was called in German *Naturwissenschaft*. Wundt also maintained, however, that there was a vast amount of human behavior that did not follow natural laws in any Newtonian or Fechnerian sense. This vast area of human experience, which included the study of language and concepts, cultural practices and social interactions, could not, in his view, be studied experimentally. These areas of psychology could not produce the kind of laws that were universal for all people, as Kant had wished; instead, they involved the kind of cultural behaviors that differed across cultures and over history, that Hegel was concerned with (and which Kant had talked about as a separate discipline altogether, as anthropology). It was social-historical science, encompassing the cultural arts of humankind, known as *Geisteswissenschaft*. The 10-volume work that occupied the last 20 years of Wundt's life and was concerned with this non-experimental psychology was called *Völkerpsychologie: An Investigation of the Laws of Development of Language, Myth and Custom*. *Völkerpsychologie* is literally translated as "folk psychology" but is more correctly similar to a word that doesn't exist in English with the senses of cultural psychology, linguistics and social psychology rolled into one. Mid-19th century Germans were also fascinated by ancient myths of their own culture and others as well as those of ancient Greece. Opera composers such as Richard Wagner and Richard Strauss used such themes frequently, and books of folklore became best sellers. Wundt's *Völkerpsychologie* was only one aspect of a larger movement, in which such unifying myths seemed to provide further rationale for the unification of Germany itself (Kerr, 1993).

The *Völkerpsychologie* is no longer read, and only a part of it was translated into English (Wundt, 1912/1916, 1973), but Wundt considered it his "deepest interest," and a work which would surpass his laboratory work in importance. In it, Wundt takes up the notions of Johann Gottfried Herder (1744–1803) and Hegel that all people within a culture or *Volk* have aspects of their thought that makes them similar to one another and dissimilar to those in other cultures. In part, this is due to the way that different languages make us see the world differently and in part this is simply due to the accumulated weight of social and cultural traditions. Wundt theorized that if we looked at similarities and differences among cultures and examined the history of their development, we could then know more about individual minds (Danziger, 1983).

Wundt believed that all humans were born with both strong emotional drives and the ability to mimic others. This led small groups of primitive humans to communicate through gesture, perhaps in different ways for different groups. The need to communicate means that we all become, with gesture, social beings who consider other individuals at all times. We pass down the gestures, which become language, and indeed, in order to communicate, we acquire symbols and ways of communicating that are not created by anyone in particular, but by the group mind or *Volkseele*.

In this way, culture evolves from primitive human societies to the cultured European (Danziger, 1983). It was taken for granted by Wundt, as it was by many in his time, that the cultured European was the pinnacle of development of culture, just as it was taken for granted by many of his countrymen that Germany, newly unified in his day from many small principalities, was the culture of one people. This belief in upward development was a core idea of German thought in the 19th century, beginning with Hegel and moving into the particular variant of evolution espoused by Ernst Haeckel (1838–1914) (see Chapter 4) and the work of Karl Marx (1818–1883) and Friedrich Engels (1820–1895). Some believed it was a spiritual evolution and some believed it was a materialistic evolution, and there are both strains in the *Völkerpsychologie*. Even though this long, repetitive and difficult work has fallen into obscurity, it did not do so without having had some direct and indirect influence on some theorists; both George Herbert Mead (1863–1931) and L.S. Vygotsky (1896–1934) were interested in Wundt's notions of gesture (Valsiner & Van der Veer, 2000). Carl Jung (1875–1961), with his interest in mythology, participated in the same cultural movement that gave *Völkerpsychologie* its name (Kerr, 1993).

Hemann Ebbinghaus

> The method of obtaining exact measurements—i.e. numerically exact ones—of the inner structure of causal relations is, by virtue of its nature, of general validity. This method, indeed, has been so exclusively used and so fully worked out by the natural sciences that, as a rule, it is defined as something peculiar to them, as *the* method of natural science. To repeat, however, its logical nature makes it generally applicable to all spheres of existence and phenomena.
>
> —Hermann Ebbinghaus (1885/1964, p. 7; emphasis in original)

Hermann Ebbinghaus (1850–1909) was one of the men of his generation electrified by "the New Psychology" of Fechner, Helmholtz and Wundt. He studied for his undergraduate degree in Bonn, Halle and Berlin. After he served in the Franco-Prussian War in 1870, he received his doctorate in philosophy from the University of Bonn in 1873. He was making a living as a tutor in England and France when he came upon Fechner's 1860 *Elements of Psychophysics* in a Paris secondhand bookshop. Like many philosophers of his generation, he saw Fechner's proof that psychology could be a mathematical science as revolutionary. Fechner had shown that basic stimulus characteristics, such as brightness of light, were amenable to such mathematical treatment, but he had not investigated higher mental processes of equal importance, such as memory and meaning. Here, saw Ebbinghaus, was a chance to extend Fechner's psychophysics to the workings of memory.

However, had also taken to heart Helmholtz's respect for experimental control, replication and statistical analysis. In 1879 and 1880, he set about the difficult task of proving his insight by an almost herculean set of careful experiments, with himself as subject. After another laborious replication of these experiments, the results were published in what became one of the most influential works on memory and verbal learning, *Über das Gedächtnis* (*On Memory*), in 1885 (Ebbinghaus, 1885/1964).

In this clearly written gem of experimental research, Ebbinghaus carefully addressed how to measure the strength of basic memory processes. Suppose you have once memorized a poem, wrote Ebbinghaus, but cannot recall it a year later. How do you know if it is clearly gone? You could attempt to relearn it; if it took you fewer repetitions of the poem to learn it again (learning being defined nicely as one completely correct, unhesitating performance), then you had some **savings** in memory from the first time. Thus the measure of memory would be number of repetitions required to learn (or relearn) a poem to one perfect recitation.

But Ebbinghaus realized that a poem would not be the ideal stimulus for investigating basic memory, because poems are imbued with meaning and thus the associations produced by the poem would be a confounding factor in the operation of memory. Moreover, different people would have different associations to the poem, adding to the variability of results. Therefore, Ebbinghaus devised a list of 2300 pronounceable consonant-vowel-consonant trigrams (e.g. JOP, DAX, BIF) as a pool of stimuli for his memory work. Some of these turned out to be words, but all were used. These came to be called **nonsense syllables** in English, but Ebbinghaus recognized that no syllable is completely free of associations, only comparatively so, to give a starting point for associations to be formed in the learning process. From this pool of trigrams, always using only himself as subject, he learned and relearned 420 lists of 16 syllables each; with an average of about 34 trials until each of the lists is perfectly recited; this works out to more than 14,000 trials (Slamecka, 1985)! Mindful of the necessity of experimental control, he tried to recite syllables at a rate of 150 beats per minute, to regulate vocal emphasis, to do his experiments at the same time each day, to use all syllables before reusing them for lists, etc. Finally, he borrowed from Helmholtz his pioneering use of statistics, reporting experiments involving many lists averaged together and reported with measurements of "probable error" based on average deviations from the mean and compared to what Quetelet had expected for the normal distribution (standard hypothesis testing had not yet been devised, however).

Using this method, he discovered the following:

- That the number of syllables repeatable without error for one reading of a list is about seven (corresponding well to the modern estimate of short-term memory of seven plus or minus two elements; Miller, 1956).
- As list length increases, the number of repetitions necessary to first correct reproduction increases much faster, particularly in the midrange of list length (12 syllables needed more than 16 repetitions and 36 syllable lists needed 55).
- If the material is a meaningful poem, rather than syllable lists, the time of learning is decreased.
- One half of what was learned was forgotten within eight hours and two-thirds within 24 hours, but only four-fifths a month later; thus most of the forgetting happens quickly.
- He found that if he derived new lists that were like the old, in that large strings were kept together, the new lists were easier to learn compared to a random list of the same syllables.

He reasoned from these findings that syllables learned together set up associations among them proportional to how far they were apart in the list. If they were next to each other, they formed a chain that could be pulled out together, but they set up a "bundle" of associations to all nearby trigrams, not just to the nearest one. One thing he did not mention, however, was the notion of proactive and retroactive interference. The massive number of lists learned would undoubtedly have increased the difficulty of learning new lists or increased the difficulty of recalling old lists. This interference effect was explicitly recognized only after Ebbinghaus, even though it may be found in his data (see Slamecka, 1985).

Wundt, Titchener and the Americans: The Rise and Fall of Structuralism

Wundt was the first philosopher to explicitly call himself a psychologist, and this fact was not lost on the world. Having a laboratory is like having a factory for creating research and for molding researchers in one's image. Many would-be psychologists in training sought training in Wundt's laboratory to learn what came to be called "the New Psychology," based on laboratory work rather than speculation, and almost every one of them went on to found laboratories of their own around the world. Table 5.3 lists a number of Wundt's most important students in North America and the institutions where they founded their laboratories. Some of the individuals on this list studied with Wundt only briefly, but an association with Wundt and indeed any of the "physiological psychologists" of his generation was a ticket to professional advancement in psychology in North America in the last quarter of the 19th century.

Table 5.3 Students of Wilhelm Wundt, With the Name and Location of the University Where They Founded or Maintained a Laboratory

G. Stanley Hall	Johns Hopkins University (Baltimore, MD)
	Clark University (Worcester, MA)
James Mark Baldwin	University of Toronto (Ontario, Canada)
	Princeton University (Princeton, NJ)
James McKeen Cattell	Columbia University (New York, NY)
Hugo Munsterberg	Harvard University (Cambridge, MA)
Frank Angell	Stanford University (Palo Alto, CA)
Edward Wheeler Scripture	Yale University (New Haven, CT)
George Malcolm Stratton	University of California, Berkeley
Edward Aloysius Pace	Catholic University (Washington, DC)
Harry Kirke Wolfe	University of Nebraska (Omaha, NE)
Harlow Gale	University of Minnesota (Minneapolis, MN)
George Patrick	University of Iowa (Ames, IA)
Edward Bradford Titchener	Cornell University (Ithaca, NY)
Lightner Witmer	University of Pennsylvania (Philadelphia, PA)
Charles H. Judd	University of Chicago (Chicago, IL)
Students of Titchener	
Margaret Washburn	Cornell University (Ithaca, NY)
E. G. Boring	Harvard University (Cambridge, MA)

The list of students of Wundt in the German-speaking world, who held academic posts from Zurich to Bonn to Munich, is even longer but difficult to summarize.

The American attitude to Wundt, however, was divided. There were true believers in the new experimental methods of self-observation, but there were also many American students of Wundt who quickly realized the limitation of his methods and began, of necessity and temperament, to create a truly American form of psychology known as functionalism. We will examine the true believers first.

E. B. Titchener

The main proponent of Wundt in North America was actually an Englishman, Edward Bradford Titchener (1867–1927), who had been called to direct a new laboratory at Cornell University. E.B. Titchener had studied philosophy at Oxford as a scholarship student and absorbed there the psychology of the British empiricists and associationists. But he became interested in the new laboratory psychology, which was frowned upon at the time in Oxford, so he went to Leipzig to study for his doctorate with Wundt in 1890. Although he spent barely more than two years with his mentor, those two years were enough to set Titchener on his unalterable mission to carry Wundt's banner in psychology for the rest of his life. He imitated Wundt in many things, even to the extent of borrowing and intensifying his imposing German personality. For example, Titchener would lecture in his doctoral robes (he said they gave him the right to be dogmatic). The lectures would be quite formal, with demonstrations set up by his assistants, who would make a show of filing in after their imposing master and sitting in the front row (Fancher, 1996).

Titchener spent much of his time trying to define and enforce what psychology should and should not be and how experimental self-observation should be done. The following is a listing of his pronouncements on the subject of what psychology is and is not. In contrast to his mentor, Titchener attempted to define psychology only as a laboratory science. In doing so, he focused somewhat less on the aspect of will than Wundt did and ignored all of his sociocultural interests. Titchener's American variant of voluntarism came to be called **structuralism**.

1. Psychology is empirical observation of the world "with man left in."
   Physics, said Titchener, was the study of the external aspects of objects. Physicists inspect the physical world through scientific observation. They analyze that external world into its elements using a strictly logical method. Psychology, said Titchener, was a kind of physics "with man left in." It too should be based on observation and logical analysis, not of the external physical world, but of the vivid immediate internal experiences of which consciousness is composed. Physicists inspect; psychologists introspect.
2. Psychology is the study of mind processes only.
   Although it is important for the psychologist to know about the physical brain and nerves and every thought is the result of a brain act, the study of such physiology is not psychology and cannot be. Titchener was a strict **parallelist** and **dualist**; every mind event has a body event that runs alongside it, but they can't be studied together.

3. Mental processes are not intrinsically meaningful.

   The vivid internal experiences of the man in the street, of the man of common sense, are too tied up with value judgments, too contaminated with meaning acquired from cultural experience. The purpose of a psychological experiment was to carefully strip away this meaning to get down to the elements of conscious processes. Indeed, the basic datum of an introspection is not a thing, like an apple, but the thought of the apple. To confuse the thing with the thought about a thing was called the **experience error** by Titchener and was to be avoided.
4. A psychological experiment is a self-observation that may be repeated, that may be isolated and that may be varied. "Repetition saves hurry and worry; isolation prevents distraction; variation keeps us from jumping at conclusions" (Titchener, 1926, p. 23).
5. Psychological experimentation requires variation of important variables and exclusion of confounding ones. The observed phenomena are slippery and elusive, and the observer is warped and biased by common sense. Therefore, control is necessary.
6. Psychology is done by individuals, not by averaging across individuals. These individual observers must be carefully trained to avoid cultural associations. Titchener was against the use of Galtonian statistics and always, like Wundt, reported the results of his experiments with results of separate individuals. This was Fechner's model and it was strictly observed.
7. Psychology is about what the mind is, not what it is for.

   Titchener gave only lip service to Darwinian evolution and the notion that the mind may have evolved to help us adapt to the world.
8. Culture and practical applications were not a part of the psychological enterprise. Titchener disliked Wundt's *Völkerpsychologie*, social psychology, linguistics and much else and believed that practical application of psychology had to wait until all of the constituents of consciousness were worked out. Psychology was, for him, a pure, basic science.

This was an austere and stern view of psychology. The advantage of this approach was that psychological experiments began for the first time under Titchener, even more so than under Wundt, to look like psychological experiments that we would recognize, particularly ones in verbal learning or cognitive psychology. See how many features of experimentation you can find in Titchener's clear description of an experiment below:

> We may therefore show by an example how psychological experiment is possible. Suppose that we wish to find out how a printed word is perceived—whether we read it letter by letter or take in its form as a whole or take in certain letters clearly and the general form vaguely. We first prepare our material. We print upon cards or photograph upon lantern slides, a large number of words. We employ different printing types; different groups of letters; different lengths of words; single words and groups of words; words properly spelled and words altered by the mutilation or omission of particular letters at different parts of the word. Every one of these classes of stimuli, as the words may be technically

called, is represented by a number of cards or slides. The stimuli are mixed in haphazard order and are thrown upon the screen by a reflectoscope or projection lantern in an otherwise dark room; a pneumatic shutter before the lantern makes it possible to show them for a brief time, say a fifth of a second. All this apparatus is put in charge of the experimenter. When the material is ready and the whole arrangement works properly, an observer is called in. He works for a limited time, at the same hour every day and only after a certain time has been allowed for his eyes to accustom themselves in the dark. The stimuli are presented at regular intervals. The observer reports what he sees at every exposure of a stimulus and the experimenter writes down what he says.

(Titchener, 1926, pp. 23–24)

Titchener also points out that the observations may be made by other observers, in other laboratories, under precisely the same circumstances and concludes, "if many observers, after many observations, give the same account of their perceptive experience, that account may stand as established psychological fact" (p. 25).

Thus, Titchener seems to have the logic of experimentation well worked out, with three very important exceptions. First, he does not seem to have been able

Interior of a Laboratory Room.
([illegible]... of sound.)

Figure 5.7 Interior of laboratory room. Note self-observer in seat at left introspecting on his own conscious experience, and experimenters with metronomes and other equipment (Munsterberg, 1893).

Source: Munsterberg, H (1893). *Psychological laboratory of Harvard University* [equipment catalog]. Classics in the History of Psychology, York University, Canada.

to convert internal qualitative perceptions into countable external dependent variables. Second, self-observation is a very subjective and qualitative experience, so that there is no objective way of knowing when an observer is sufficiently trained. Third, Titchener and his colleagues tended to treat individual differences in responding as error to be stamped out, rather than as real, though perhaps unexplainable, differences among people. Titchener, like Wundt, specifically forbade studies of individual differences as not worthy of psychology. Current methods of statistical hypothesis testing were not yet available to Titchener anyway, had he wanted to use them.

Regarding the first problem, to use a present term, he seemed to have difficulty specifying operational definitions. An **operational definition** is the definition of a construct, such as attention, in terms of how that construct is to be measured. A current cognitive psychologist might present words or nonwords for a fraction of a second. The subject's task would be to press a key when he or she has made a decision as to whether it is a word, and the experimenter would measure the reaction time (in milliseconds) that it would take for the subject to make the decision, in addition to the number of errors. Subjects, usually untrained, can easily do many such decisions in a session (which would be averaged across decisions and across subjects), and all they need keep in mind is "Is it a word or not?" The use of such a method has allowed experimenters to note, for example, that one is faster to recognize something as a word if it is preceded by a related word, e.g. one is faster to recognize "butter" as a word if it is preceded by "bread."

By contrast, when Walter A. Pillsbury, a student of Titchener's at Cornell, did an experiment of word recognition called "A Study in Apperception" in 1897 (Pillsbury, 1897), he allowed "observers" to say anything they wanted after the stimulus (a word, presented for a fraction of a second, with letters missing typed over or substituted). They were to say whether it was a word, what word they thought it was and anything that came to mind. Thus, it would sometimes take up to eight minutes for the experimenter to write down these things, plus emotional reactions to the stimulus, free associations and much else besides. Some of these trials were preceded by an associated word. Indeed, Pillsbury provides the reader of his article with the tables of percent right and wrong in these conditions, but uses only five observers, three of them with doctorates, two who knew the purpose of the experiment and one who did not, and two naïve undergraduates. The results are not averaged, but they do show overall that the experienced observers are more accurate than the naïve ones and that the preceding associations tended to bias observers. Then Pillsbury continues with 20 tables, some with three or four parts each, describing very specific qualitative responses. One of these tables is reproduced as Figure 5.8.

It is easy to see that with such specific uncategorizable responses, it is difficult to tell whether a hypothesis is supported. Indeed, many structuralist experiments, including this one, did not even *have* clear hypotheses, in terms of expected differences in independent variables stated before the methods and results were presented. Results were typically explained after the fact. Results explained after the fact almost always have some explanation, because of the inveterate tendency of humans to come up with some explanation for almost anything. Such procedures, however, hinder the possibility of coming up with the right explanation, should there be one, because every experiment comes up with different results, leading to explanations across studies that rarely match.

TABLE XX.

FALSE RECOGNITIONS.

Subject.	Word Shown.	Word Seen.	Remarks.
C.	caffea	caffea	"Is there such a word?" the subject said, and remarked a moment later, "Yes, I remember it now."
"	fellw	felly (felloe)	A moment later the subject remarked that felloe wasn't spelled with a 'y.'
"	kommonly	kommonly	It seemed all right at first, but later it struck him as queer that it should be spelled with 'k.'
M.	verbati	verbati	"I thought, at first, it was verbatum, then saw it was the plural."
"	kommonly	kommonly	Same phenomenon as with C above.
"	xexter	rexter	"I don't seem to be familiar with that word."
"	window	aiche	"I thought for a moment that *ache* was spelled with an 'i.'" (Read under association of pane. See Table IX.)
"	painxer	paintker (painter)	The first remark was that 't' and 'k' 'seemed a little run together,' and then it was added, "I thought for the moment that *painter* was spelled *paintker*."

Figure 5.8 Data Tables 20 & 21, Pillsbury (1897)

The qualitative nature of the responses led to the problem of what was a proper response, who was allowed to determine what was a proper response and when an observer had been properly trained. In practice, it was up to the head of the lab to determine this. Wundt himself started this tradition. Lightner Witmer (1867–1956) (who was later to open the first applied psychological clinic in the United States) explains what happened to him as a member of Wundt's lab:

> Cattell had put me to work before I left for Europe on a problem of the measurement of reaction times of all classes of persons. Wundt wouldn't hear of this being a psychological problem and banned it immediately, his idea being that experimental psychology was really based on the conscious reaction of subjects and required concurrent introspection... [H]e made Titchener do over again an introspection because the results obtained by Titchener were not such as he, Wundt, had anticipated. Also, he excluded me as subject... because in his opinion my sensory reaction to sound and touch was too short to be a true sensory reaction. He advised me to get a cardboard pendulum and practice so as to increase my reaction time and presumably make it truly sensory. I was disgusted at this suggestion.
> (Witmer, 1948, cited in O'Donnell, 1985, p. 35)

It is obvious that a graduate student working for Wundt, or later Titchener, would endeavor to do what the professor wanted, consciously or unconsciously, to protect his or her professional advancement, if for no other reason. The problem here is that different lab managers or professors might have different ideas about what a good introspection is, so that even if one might try diligently to repeat the experiment done somewhere else, one might not get the same results: One could repeat, but not replicate. Ironically, Wundt and Titchener were committing the error that the Astronomer Royal had made 100 years before by firing his assistant—assuming that the more senior introspector was right!

If we combine all this with the third problem, that Wundt and Titchener absolutely avoided the problem of individual differences, we see that it was very difficult to separate real effects from error: A subjective response was evaluated by a subjective supervising professor who had no way of dealing systematically with the problem that there might be sometimes widely differing kinds of subjectivity among individuals. In spite of the best efforts of the structuralists to control independent variables with precise apparatus and the like, because their dependent variable was controlled by a variable, fallible human self-observer, they could not produce truly replicable studies from their labs.

Understand it was not introspection that was the true problem. Cognitive psychologists have recently conducted many studies that are eerily similar to those of the structuralists, and they deal with subjects' internal perceptions all the time and replicate the results. It was not even ignorance of the scientific method, as the quotes above from Titchener demonstrate. It was the lack of replication of results that led to the failure of Titchener's project.

Apostates and Turncoats From the Structuralist Faith: The Birth of American Functionalism

America in the mid-19th century was a young nation, which looked to Europe as the center of culture. Hence, for a student seeking a post as a university professor in the United States, study in Europe was a feather in his or her cap. For aspiring psychologists, this meant a trip to Germany to study Wundt's "the New Psychology." However, almost as soon as they returned home, many of Wundt's American students found that his psychology was not to their liking. Some of this may have been the result of some disillusionment with Wundt himself. G. Stanley Hall, who visited Wundt in 1879 at virtually the time of the laboratory's founding, described Wundt "as a man who has done more speculation and less valuable observing than any man I know who has had his career" (Hall, 1972, p. 85). Hall also thought Wundt's laboratory methods were sloppy and implied that some of Wundt's amazing lifetime total of 10,000 published pages of work came from simply taking notes incessantly while his graduate students presented on their readings and lab work. Cattell had served as Wundt's lab assistant and had published several studies in Wundt's journal, but upon using such credentials to get a position at the University of Pennsylvania, almost immediately left to study with Galton and later called Galton, not Wundt, his greatest influence.

Others found that the new laboratory psychology was not much use to practically minded Americans. Charles Hubbard Judd (1873–1946), a professor at Yale who received his doctorate from Wundt and remained friendly towards him, relates the following anecdote:

> I recall very well that I had on one occasion been lecturing enthusiastically on Weber's Law to a class of New York City Teachers ... when I was interrupted by one of my gray-haired auditors with this question: "Professor, will you tell us how we can use this principle to improve our teaching of children?" I remember the question better than I do my answer.
>
> (Judd, 1932, cited in O'Donnell, 1985, p. 25)

Judd said in 1907, this time referring to Titchener's structuralism, "I am quite unable to accept the contentions or sympathize with the views of the defenders of a structural or purely analytical psychology" (O'Donnell, 1985, pp. 39–40). Lightner Witmer said that he earned nothing from Wundt but the doctorate and promptly became the first PhD psychologist (as opposed to MD psychiatrists, or as they were sometimes called at this time, "alienists") to open a psychological clinic, in which he often used the Galtonian mental tests devised by his colleague Cattell.

Titchener had removed nearly everything from his definition of psychology that would likely be of interest outside of his own laboratory—one could not study applied subjects, one could not use meaningful stimuli or interpret them simply as any person would and certainly children or animals can't introspect. In a place like America, that simply would not do for long. In the 1890s, well over half of the studies published in Hall's *American Journal of Psychology* followed the experimental self-observation model, which meant that they (1) gave the names of the participants, (2) used the "experimenter-observer" distinction and (3) reported only individual data. But that was the high water mark. As Danziger (1990) reports, over time, psychological studies began to use average people or naïve undergraduates as "subjects" (not "observers"), who were not identified, except by their membership in some category such as age or race. The data were reported as group data using means, and even in basic experimental research journals, the work began to look much more like the work in the *Journal of Applied Psychology* or the *Journal of Educational Psychology*, which had never used Titchener's methods.

Why was Titchener, even more so than his mentor Wundt, so obsessed with paring away meaning from psychology? It would seem, in retrospect, to be a self-defeating task, dooming his work to irrelevancy. His own writings suggest a devotion to the faith in the scientific method, indeed to the idea of what we have come to call **basic science** or **pure science** as opposed to **applied science**. Basic science is science pursued without regard to immediate practical application or profit. The goal of basic science is to simply figure out the abstract laws of the universe, in the belief that the discovery of such general laws would result in wider and sometimes more unexpected benefits than the search for immediate practical applications. There are many examples of the benefits of basic science. For example, researchers on the physiology of the squid found that squids have very large neurons, visible to the naked eye. This allowed us to determine how neurons work in humans, which helped discover neurotransmitters and helped to design medications. Newton's laws were mathematical abstractions that initially ignored real-world confounding factors like friction, but they have had countless applications from construction to space travel.

In Titchener's own day, he was likely aware of the work of Dimitri Mendeleev (1834–1907) on the periodic table of elements. In order for chemistry to succeed, a lump of natural chemical must be subjected to various reagents or heat, to purify the element. Only then, in its pure, abstract form, can its atomic weight be calculated accurately and only after such things have been done could Mendeleev create the periodic table (in 1869) with such precision that he could predict not only where a new element would be found, but also what that new element's properties would be. If only Titchener could come up with a periodic table of the elements of consciousness! But it was not to be. Americans became impatient for applications, and this impatience led first to the functionalist movement (Chapter 7) and behaviorism (Chapter 8), which drew upon the new findings of Darwin to examine thought and behavior as adaptation to the environment.

History and Psychology Today: The Influence of the German Mentalist Tradition in Cognitive Psychology

From the present standpoint, many of the concerns of the early German philosophers and psychologists may seem rather esoteric, suitable only for the interest of historians of psychology. Helmholtz is justly celebrated for bringing a rigorous focus on experimental control, replication of results and statistical interpretation of findings. Wundt, in contrast, is only cited in treatments of the history of psychology, honored in brief as the founder of the first experimental psychology laboratory. Most of his work was never translated into English, which is, for better or worse, the international language of science today. His student Titchener is often the main character in a morality tale about what happens when, first, a psychology uses introspective reports instead of overt behavior as its dependent variable, and second, when psychology retreats too much into areas that do not have a practical application. Not to put too fine a point on it, but it is suggested that such an approach died a deserved death. And besides, Titchener and Wundt committed the unpardonable sin to science of using their authority to sanction right or wrong data. When the definition of psychology became the science of behavior rather than of mental contents, structuralism became an example of what not to do.

And yet, many of the methods used by Fechner never went away; the methods used by Ebbinghaus, Wundt and Titchener resurfaced in the 1950s in a different form after behaviorism (see Chapter 8) began to cede some of its territory to the cognitive revolution that begat information processing and cognitive science. In particular, although his metaphysical interests were jettisoned from the science, Fechner's insights, redefined in modern behavioral terms, still form the bedrock of psychophysics. Ebbinghaus's methodology spawned a minor industry in verbal learning that lasted for more than 30 years, until the 1970s, when the information processing revolution was well positioned to resume work with the kind of reaction time experiments that Wundt and Titchener would recognize as a continuation of their approach.

Weber, Fechner and Psychophysics

Unlike some of the other methods of the structuralists, the insights of Weber and Fechner were never lost for a very good reason: Their equations were basically right! Weber's equation holds for many stimuli at the very middle of the stimulus range and Fechner's equation holds for a much wider range. The subsequent history of psychophysics has addressed itself to the basic question of how the relationship between stimulus intensity of whatever type (light, sound, electrical shock, vibration, etc.) can be mathematically mapped against some response that represents the subject's subjective perception of it. Some questions that may be asked here are: Is it really true that a just noticeable difference is equal at the bottom, near an absolute threshold or as high as one may safely go without hurting someone (That is, does the jnd = 1 everywhere)? How do various senses relate to one another? These two things are dealt with in a more general law called a **power function** or (in honor of the psychophysicist S.S. (Stanley Smith, known as "Smitty") Stevens (1906–1973) **Stevens' Power Law**. This law can be stated as

$$S = kI^a$$

where S = sensation magnitude, k is a constant depending on the scale unit used, I is the stimulus intensity and the exponent a is a power exponent dependent on modality.

In other words, the power law can be used for any kind of stimulus and any kind of sense (sight, sound, smell, taste, touch, shock, cold, etc.); all one need do is figure out what the exponent is[3] (Stevens, 1957, 1960, 1971). For a scientist of the mind, there should be nothing more astonishing that this: How the mind sees the world keeps turning out to be mathematically predictable.

Ebbinghaus and the Verbal Learning Movement of the 1940s–1960s

Hermann Ebbinghaus is considered the father of verbal learning, a subfield of psychology that combined associationism, experimental design and behaviorism. Most verbal learning experiments consisted of serial learning or paired-associate learning tasks, using Ebbinghaus's famous "nonsense syllables." In a serial learning task, a list of syllables would be placed on a **memory drum**, a mechanical device that would reveal items one at a time for a controlled number of seconds each. The subject would go through the list once and then, on the second time through, attempt to recall the list in order one item at a time. The drum would reveal each word to reinforce or correct the attempt. In this way, the number of associations for each item could be carefully controlled. In the paired-associate task (invented by Mary Calkins—see Chapter 7), a drum would present paired syllables (WOF-ZIK) and on the second trial, the window on the drum would open on the first word of the pair and the subject would attempt to recall the paired item (Lachman, Lachman, & Butterfield, 1978).

Many variations on these tasks were tried. One could vary the length of the lists, the speed at which they were presented, the delay for recall, pronounceability, similarity of items and so on. In this way, psychologists showed that they had created dependable independent variables (e.g. list length, time to recall) and dependent variables (number of errors, time or trials to memorize lists, etc.) that were easier to measure than the structuralist's free report. One basic finding from this work is the importance of **interference effects**. If one learns a paired-associate list (A paired with B), it is harder to learn a new set of items paired with the original stimulus (say A-D) than an entirely new paired list, and it is harder to remember the original A-B pairing after the intervening list. Moreover, as Ebbinghaus discovered, even meaningless items suggest meaning to the subjects, and the syllables themselves would differ in the meaning they would suggest. Thus, Deese (1960) came up with a measure of meaningfulness, which was the average number of real words that a subject could free associate to the item in a given time. Syllables, after all, are found in words, and the associations to those words were found to be helpful in recall. Indeed, subjects sometimes mentioned words that they had said to themselves to help them recall the syllables. These **verbal mediators** were a primitive **memory strategy**: a conscious, deliberate manipulation of items in a list to help the subject remember them.

Because meaning was impossible to remove from experiments, researchers accepted reality and abandoned nonsense syllables by the early 1960s and began to use words, but they did not abandon the list learning experiment. The use of free recall (recall in any order) over Ebbinghaus's ordered recall led to the discovery of serial position effects, such that words at the beginning of the list were better remembered than those in the middle of the list when subjects applied a kind of active, elaborated, meaningful rehearsal of the items (the **primacy effect**). Those at the end of the list, being recently heard and subject to little interference, were also remembered well (the **recency effect**). The recency effect evaporated if the subject were asked to do something difficult, such as count backwards by threes (Peterson & Peterson, 1959), leading to the assumption that there is a working memory, a short-term store that can hold the "Magical Number Seven (Plus or Minus Two)" items or meaningful groups of items, as George Miller[4] put it in a landmark 1956 article. The primacy effect represented words that had found their way into a long-term store and were more resistant to forgetting.

In this way, the verbal learning paradigm, based very much on Ebbinghaus's work, set the stage for the birth of cognitive psychology and the information processing paradigm. The **information processing paradigm** is based on the assumption that the mind is a general purpose programmable machine that processes symbolic information. The mind was increasingly seen to be a type of computer, in which there were definite limits to the structure of mind in terms of capacity of information that can be dealt with at one time (hardware), with many strategies or programs to deal with that information (software) and much store data gained by experience with words, objects and their meanings (semantic memory data) (Atkinson & Shiffrin, 1968). Many of the workers in verbal learning saw a way to expand their experiments using the new model and converted to cognitive psychologists by the 1970s, exploring the ramifications of memory strategies and other cognitive programs for both adults (e.g. Murdock, 1962; Rundus, 1971; Craik & Lockhart, 1972) and children (Flavell, 1970; see Schneider & Pressley, 1989, and Ornstein, Baker-Ward, & Naus, 1988, for reviews).

Reaction Time and the Information Processing Paradigm

Reaction time, the measurement of how long it takes to respond to a stimulus sensation, was a common measure in 19th-century psychology. Simple reaction time was used by Galton in his anthropometrics booth at South Kensington International Health Fair (see Chapter 4). The astronomers were trying to get their reaction times as low as possible to respond accurately to celestial bodies crossing the wire in the telescope. But Wundt used Donders's (1869) subtraction method: If Helmholtz was right that thinking took time (and he was), then complex mental activities, as they require more steps in thought, should require more time to complete than simple ones. The logic of the subtraction method is still used today in many experiments, especially in cognitive psychology. We will discuss only two types of these reaction time experiments briefly: the priming experiment and the mental rotation experiment.

The priming experiment is based on an assumption that John Locke or James Mill might have appreciated: Concepts that are often meaningfully associated together are stored in the memory as a network, such that if you have to think of one concept to accomplish a task, you automatically think of closely related concepts. It is said that the meaning of one semantically activates or **associatively primes** the meaning of the other, making it faster to be retrieved. Let's say your task is to say whether a stimulus presented is a word or not: NURSE would be "yes" and PLAME would be "no." Now let's present them together so that you say yes only if you get two real words. If you get NURSE—BUTTER, you take an average of 940 milliseconds to say "yes," but if you get BREAD—BUTTER, it takes you only 855 msec on average to say yes: BREAD primes BUTTER (Meyer & Schvanevelt, 1971). In this task, you don't really have time to introspect, just to give a simple response, and it's easy to train people to do it, so it's not classical Wundtian psychology, but it is the sort of task he might approve of! Similarly, a person is faster to tap a key to say "true" to the sentence "A bird has feathers" than to the sentence "A bird breathes." Even though a bird obviously does both, "feathers" would be stored near "bird" and "breathes" with the higher, farther, more general category "animal," taking longer (Collins & Quillian, 1969). This works (with some exceptions) within a category as well. You are faster to say that a canary is a bird than to say that an ostrich is a bird, because of the number of features shared with the notion of a typical bird (Rips, Shoben, & Smith, 1973).

We know that our powers of visual imagination work in a lawful way because of **mental rotation experiments**. Shepard and Metzler (1971) gave a task to subjects to determine whether two figures are the same, with one simply rotated in space from the other. What the subject would typically do is rotate the second figure to see if it matches the first one. If it did, the subject would press "yes." If the two figures did not match, the subject would say "no." Shepard and Metzler know this because the farther the comparison stimulus is rotated from the original, the longer it takes to say yes when they are the same. The relationship between degrees rotation and reaction time to say yes is even, conveniently, a linear one.

These are merely two classic types of experiments for which reaction time is a useful dependent variable. There are many more, both historically and right up to the present day.

The above examples make me think that old Immanuel Kant, with whom we started this chapter, would be both surprised and pleased by this state of affairs. Contrary to what the great philosopher had predicted, in some areas, at least, the mind can be explained by mathematical relationships and experiments can be done on internal perception, profitably and with scientific rigor. He might be pleased, though, to note that researchers have found that there are built-in limitations and boundaries to our thinking abilities, *a priori* hardware, if you will, that constrains the amount of information that we can take in and process. Wundt would recognize a psychophysicists' laboratory today, once we explained to him that many of his brass instruments, chronometers and the like, are actually squeezed into a laptop computer. And Ebbinghaus would no doubt be astonished to learn that the experiments he did, on himself alone, spawned a minor industry in the workings of memory, all conducted with the methodological and statistical rigor that he would surely have appreciated.

Notes

1. In case you're interested, Kant believed it was important for a philosopher never to eat alone, to avoid the obsessive thoughts that hamper digestion and inhibit rest. A dinner party starts with discussing the latest news, followed by a vigorous exchange in views (drink helps open the heart). When full, the best one can do is to engage in witty banter, flirt with the ladies and leave everyone laughing as they head for home.
2. William James had a demonstration lab of psychophysical equipment at Harvard by 1875, but lacked the organizational skill and inclination to keep it going—see Chapter 7.
3. Things are slightly more complicated than this, but too technical for treatment here. See Baird & Noma, 1978, for details.
4. Miller had studied with S.S. Stevens; Stevens had studied with E.G. Boring at Harvard; Boring himself was a student of Titchener.

6 Seeing Things Whole
The Gestalt Response to Mental Reductionism

> Gestalt theory will not be satisfied with sham solutions suggested by a simple dichotomy of science and life. Instead, Gestalt theory is resolved to penetrate the problem itself by examining the fundamental assumptions of science. It has long seemed obvious—and is, in fact, the characteristic tone of European science—that "science" means breaking up complexes into their component elements. Isolate the elements, discover their laws, then reassemble them and the problem is solved. All wholes are reduced to pieces and piecewise relations between pieces.
>
> The fundamental "formula" of Gestalt theory might be expressed in this way. There are wholes, the behaviour of which is not determined by that of their individual elements, but where the part-processes are themselves determined by the intrinsic nature of the whole. It is the hope of Gestalt theory to determine the nature of such wholes.
>
> —Max Wertheimer (1924/1938, p. 4)

In psychology, as in science in general, progress is often made dialectically, through the battle of two opposing worldviews. Is science best advanced by the analysis of complex ideas into simple ones, compounds into elements, wholes into pieces? Or is it more fruitful to examine wholes, structures, relationships or systems? The first of these positions is called **reductionism** or **elementarism,** and it relies on the faith that once we break a thing apart until we reach irreducible pieces, we can then investigate how they go together. Chemistry from Boyle to the beginning of the 20th century relied on this notion, and psychology, in Locke, the Mills, Wundt and Titchener (and as we shall see, the behaviorism of Thorndike, Watson and Skinner) primarily follow this precept. The second position is called **holism**. In this view, the whole is more than the sum of its parts, an organic or interconnected structure in balanced forces. The holistic worldview stems from (among others) the philosophers Herder and Hegel and has influenced biology through Darwin, economics through both Smith and Marx, sociology through Durkheim and Weber and anthropology through Mead, Whorf and Levi-Strauss. In psychology, its proponents can be found in the functionalism of John Dewey, several psychoanalysts and the developmentalists Piaget and Vygotsky. But this position was perhaps earliest and most eloquently expressed by the founders of Gestalt psychology Max Wertheimer (1880–1943), Kurt Koffka (1886–1941), Wolfgang Köhler (1887–1967) and Kurt Lewin (1890–1947). The German term **Gestalt** has the literal meaning of "form," but it carries much broader connotations of "good form" or a structure that is complete, with natural boundaries, that has the feeling that all of its parts are related to the whole. Unlike the views of Wundt and Titchener, the Gestalt perspective still influences work in perception and cognition, social psychology (through Lewin) education and problem solving (through Wertheimer) and even clinical psychology.

Before we discuss Gestalt psychology itself, it is necessary to examine its roots in the philosophies of three opponents of Wundt in the German-speaking world: Franz Brentano, Christian von Ehrenfels and Carl Stumpf.

Franz Brentano: Indivisible Consciousness

At about the same time that Wundt was beginning his fame in Leipzig, in Catholic Vienna, a former priest and Aristotelian scholar named Franz Brentano (1838–1917) had written *Psychology From an Empirical Standpoint* (1874), which allowed him and his followers to eventually stake out a different position on the mind that indirectly influenced approaches as varied as Gestalt psychology, psychoanalysis and the developmentalists Jean Piaget and L.S. Vygotsky. Brentano believed, along with Wundt and most other philosophers and psychologists of his day, that psychology should be the study of mind and that a kind of introspection should be one of its methods. But he did not believe in Wundt's experimental "physiological" methods of self-observation. Wundt and his followers had always admitted that the laboratory introspection was kind of artificial but thought that this was one of the method's strengths. They had wanted to observe thought processes and not the content, what the thought was about. For Brentano, this reductionistic impulse to reduce thought to its microscopic bits made no sense, because thought was always *about* something, and if you break it up in bits or try to separate what thought is from what it means, you destroy it. If you wanted to study how thought naturally occurred and what it was for, you needed to study this "aboutness" most of all. The tendency of thought to be about things is called **intentionality**, and it is the center of Brentano's **act psychology**.

Furthermore, the tendency for thoughts to be about something, for beliefs to be about something, for wishes, dreams and intentions to be about something, is the key and the irreducible thing that makes things in the mind different from things in the physical world. As philosophers Dennett and Haugeland (1987, p. 139) point out,

> Some things are about other things: a belief can be about icebergs, but an iceberg is not about anything; an idea can be about the number 7, but the number 7 is not about anything; a book or a film can be about Paris, but Paris is not about anything.

If this is true, said Brentano, then Wundt and Titchener's project to observe things of the mind, using internal perception in the same way that they observe things outside the mind, will never work, because thought does not exist as separate things without a goal. Thoughts are not things to be observed at all but acts by an intentional person. If you turn back to Chapter 2 and ponder this for a moment, you will see that Brentano brings back Aristotle here and his notion of everything and every act having a purpose.

Brentano (1874/1973) believed that when, for example, we heard a tone, the mental experience includes the object (the tone) and the recognition that we have heard it, the "act of hearing." These always occur together, thus it makes no real sense to try to separate the content from the thinking, as Wundt and Titchener tried to do. Brentano also asserted that *all thought is conscious* (in contrast from his erstwhile student Freud, who took five courses from him at the University of Vienna—see Chapter 9) and that *consciousness is unitary*, rather than a collection of bits of consciousness or even, as Leibnitz had said, separate consciousnesses. (It would take a lot of space to list Brentano's arguments here, but one point at least is fun to ponder: When we experience two things as simultaneous, where is the experience of simultaneity, in thing 1 or thing 2? That's right—it's in neither; the perception of "two things happening at the same time" is one thing.) In summary, Brentano believed that in thought there were qualitatively different acts that were not present in the world of things; therefore observing thought was not like observing things. He asserted that thought itself was goal directed, unitary and holistic, rather than a static collection of things that could be teased apart by ever more precise analysis into mental elements. In all of these ways, he set out a view of psychology that was diametrically opposed to the voluntarism of Wundt or the structuralism of Titchener.

Stumpf and von Ehrenfels: The Philosophy Behind Gestalt

Franz Brentano had two famous students who would carry on his ideas and provide a bridge to an entirely new school of psychology based on the natural tendency of humans and other higher animals to perceive and to act in goal-directed, holistic ways: Carl Stumpf (1848–1936) and Christian von Ehrenfels (1859–1932). Both of these men were philosophy professors (Stumpf at the University of Berlin and Ehrenfels in the German University of Prague) in the broad older German sense, but they understood the importance of laboratory psychology. But for our purposes, interestingly enough, perhaps the most important thing about them was that they were both musicians.

In 1890, von Ehrenfels asked a penetrating question: What is a melody? Is it a collection of notes? Well yes, but it can't be just a collection of notes, because different notes can make the same melody. "Twinkle, Twinkle, Little Star" can be played in the key of C or F or any key. Indeed, if you twist a couple of notes to make it in a minor key, it doesn't really sound like a new melody, it sounds more like "Sadly Twinkle Little Star," a variation on a theme of the original melody. One can accompany the melody with different chords or speed it up or slow it down or flip it over or take fragments of it and turn it into jazz and it is still recognizable. If this were true, then if Wundt laboriously were to analyze music in a note-by-note fashion, he would not get very far. It's not the sum of the notes that make up a melody, but certain invariant relationships among the notes, the patterns that remain the same even when all of these things have changed. Von Ehrenfels called these holistic properties that melodies have *Gestaltqualitäten* or "Gestalt qualities," and was the first to use Gestalt in this sense (Ehrenfels, 1890/1988).

Carl Stumpf had a conception of psychology as "the study of daily life raised to a science" (Ash, 1995, p. 108). He believed that the human mind was innately constructed to directly perceive the structures in the world. No summing up of tiny bits of consciousness by Helmholtz's "unconscious inference" is necessary.

He was an avid chamber musician and combined his interest in music with his philosophical approach in an important pioneering work on the psychology of musical perception, the *Tonpsychologie* (1883), in which he argued that Helmholtz's task of reducing perception to physics and physiology was only half the battle. Subjective psychological interpretation of sound is also important. In this work and elsewhere, he criticized the Wundtian perspective, particularly its blind inductivist empiricism and reductionistic elementarism: He thought that a single observation of sound from a musically trained individual was more valid than a thousand from a nonmusical trained observer. In this case, more data was not necessarily better. When Wundt protested that a student had made 110,000 introspective observations, Stumpf contemptuously suggested that one might as well decide the issue by vote (Ash, 1995).

Stumpf taught at one time or another all four of the founders of Gestalt psychology and, as director of the psychology institute at Berlin, Germany's most prestigious university, influenced many more. He imbued them all with the importance of the concept that scientists sometimes call **elegance**—it is not only important that a scientific theory be right, it must also be beautiful and enticing and compelling enough to suggest other research and demonstrations. Such a lofty goal is difficult to achieve, and Stumpf avoided cranking out work for its own sake. In the time that Wundt supervised 59 dissertations, Stumpf supervised four. In a speech on Stumpf's 70th birthday, Max Wertheimer, student and friend, said of his mentor: "so round, so complete in itself is everything for you.... We always feel: This is not just any individual fact, but everywhere principles are at work" (Wertheimer, 1918, cited in Ash, 1995, p. 41).

The Phi Phenomenon: The Founding of Gestalt Psychology in a Flash of Insight

The founding of Gestalt psychology is a lesson of chance favoring the prepared mind. Max Wertheimer was brought up in a financially comfortable and cultured German Jewish family residing in Prague. He was enticed as a boy into philosophy by the works of Baruch Spinoza, the great Renaissance philosopher, an interest that was reinforced when he heard the charismatic von Ehrenfels lecture at Charles University in Prague. After receiving his undergraduate degree there in 1902, he went to study with Stumpf at Berlin for a few years and then to Würzburg to finish his doctorate. He spent the next few years immersed in psychology, neurology and ethnomusicology. In 1910, after finishing a paper on the music of a culture in Ceylon, he was on his way to a vacation in Germany's Rhineland when, as the story goes, all his thinking on the brain, the mind, musical relationships and von Ehrenfels's *Gestaltqualitäten* came together in a flash of insight. He noticed, looking out the window of his train, that the lights of the train crossing were flashing repeatedly in a peculiar way. Rather than appearing as two separate lights flashing on and off, as they actually were, it appeared that one light was moving back and forth from one side to the other of the crossing display. Wertheimer was so excited by this phenomenon that he got off the train prematurely in Frankfurt and bought a children's stroboscopic toy and some cardboard cutouts so that he could experiment with flashing lights and figures in his hotel room. In the morning, he went to a new university in Frankfurt, where Wertheimer knew that Stumpf's former student Wolfgang Köhler was working as a laboratory assistant (Ash, 1995).

Köhler immediately provided Wertheimer with some lab space and served as the first subject for his moving light experiments. Köhler was prepared to know their value as well. Like Wundt, he had been brought up in a family of ministers, teachers and college professors. A mathematician and physicist had taken him under his wing when he was only 16 and convinced him that philosophy could only proceed with a thorough grounding in mathematics and natural science. Köhler received that grounding and then proceeded to Berlin to study with Stumpf, as well as with the great physicist and theoretician of electromagnetism, Max Planck. His days were split between listening to exciting discussions of quantum physics and doing work on the psychophysics of sound with Stumpf. Like Wertheimer and Stumpf, Köhler was a skilled musician; he was well aware that musical perception was a perception of meaning as well as sound. The ink was barely dry on his dissertation when the young assistant (he was only 23) welcomed Wertheimer to Frankfurt.

Kurt Koffka had recently completed a dissertation on the visual perception of rhythm with Stumpf. He was only 24 when he arrived in Frankfurt with his wife shortly thereafter, on what would prove to be only a temporary appointment, but he later called his meeting with Max Wertheimer "one of the crucial moments of my life" (Koffka, cited in Ash, p. 111). The three men saw each other nearly every day for a year, working closely to examine Wertheimer's phenomenon of the lights that moved but didn't really move, which they called the phenomenon of **apparent movement** or the **phi phenomenon**.

What was it that so excited these men that they essentially dropped everything for the next year to study this little phenomenon? I believe they recognized the phi phenomenon as what philosopher of science Thomas Kuhn calls an **exemplar**. It is a simple but telling experiment that serves as a prototype for many further experiments and also serves to help overturn a preceding paradigm. The Gestaltists asked the question, "Where is the movement?" Is the movement something that happens in the eye itself, a sensation? Is it on the other hand a judgment, in that we see one light and then concentrate on a second light and erroneously decide that it is the same light? They completed a careful set of experiments with lights in a darkened room that varied the time interval between the lights, as well as other variables such as color, form and intensity, and found that the answer to the two questions above is "Neither." When the two lights were flashed about 30 msec apart, they are perceived as simultaneous. Above 200 msec apart, they are perceived as separate lights going on and off. At about 60 msec, subjects always reported that it appears as though the light moved from one side to another. The fictitious movements produced negative afterimages like ordinary objects, a phenomenon which happens in the central nervous system, not the eye. The movement occurs at far too fast a rate to allow for comparative judgements between the lights. Indeed, some theorists thought that putting a lighted line between the two lights would destroy the illusion if the conscious judgement of "one light + another light = movement" were involved. This did not happen; observers saw the light as going behind the line. Therefore, wrote Wertheimer, people were not taking perceptual elements and adding them together, but directly perceiving the relationship between them holistically. The ability to perceive relationships among stimuli directly, without adding up pieces of consciousness, was innate.

What's more, everybody could see the apparent movement. Not only did you not need laborious training in introspection to see it, laborious attention to the phenomenon does not make it go away, as it would if one could decompose it into its constituent parts with practice—if anything, the phenomenon becomes more vivid. When one light is, say, red and the other is green, the perception is, weirdly, that the light changes to green *between* the two lights, even before the green light really goes on! The results of these experiments with lights, lines, colors, forms, etc., suggested to the Gestaltists that what they were observing was a natural, innately given response to stimuli. They had succeeded in "raising daily life to a science." They had also found in the motion of the lights a visual analogue of the motion of a melody that von Ehrenfels had discussed over a decade before. Kurt Koffka remembered clearly the moment, sitting in Wertheimer's apartment, that this analogy came to him and remembered the "thrill of the experience" many years later (Ash, 1995, p. 131).

The founding and growth of Gestalt psychology follows Thomas Kuhn's view of how a new school arises and attempts to overthrow a prevailing paradigm. First, following Wertheimer's publication of the phi phenomenon experiments in 1912, the new school began attracting converts, not of the old guard, but of new researchers who had little stake in the old system. (Indeed, many of their students were women.) Second, in a preparadigmatic period of a science, Kuhn notes that competing schools spend a lot of their time arguing what psychology *should* be about. At the beginning of Gestaltism, that prevailing paradigm was the Wundtian introspective method, but as Gestaltism grew, it had to contend with functionalism and (following about 1913) behaviorism in America as well. To set themselves apart from these schools, the Gestaltists said that psychology should not focus on elements, regardless of whether those elements are elements of consciousness or behavior. Psychology should be about how people really experience the world, they said; heavily trained self-observers cannot tell us this and neither can purely external analyses of behavior.

Philosophical Principles of Gestalt Psychology

It may be helpful at this point to list some of the philosophical principles of Gestalt psychology. The clearest statements of these principles came late, in texts in English by Köhler (*Gestalt Psychology*, 1929 and 1947) and Koffka (*Principles of Gestalt Psychology*, 1935).

First, psychology, being a young science, should concern itself with **qualitative relationships** among phenomena at the **molar level** rather than quantitative investigations relying on molecular bits of behavior or consciousness. Köhler (1947) cautioned that we should not affix quantities to psychological entities until we understand how they fit together functionally. Physics, chemistry and biology all observed their phenomena in the natural world before extracting quantitative variables:

> One can hardly exaggerate the value of qualitative information as a necessary supplement to quantitative work. In the absence of such information, behavior psychology will easily become as sterile as supposedly it is exact. Too great an interest in available quantitative methods is not a promising state of mind at a

time when the development of psychology depends upon the discovery of new questions than upon the monotonous repetition of standardized methods.

(Köhler, 1947, p. 49)

Second, the proper data for human psychology should be the **direct experience of naïve observers**. For Gestaltists, the meaning of an experience to the person experiencing it matters. It makes no sense to train self-observers until all meaning is drained away. For a diner looking at a plate, its "plateness" is what matters to the diner's intentional goal of a place to rest food, not whether it appears as a circle or an ellipse when she looks down at it. Similarly, although one might measure anger by the amount of adrenaline in the blood, that is not a person's direct experience of it; Gestaltists believed that it would be easier to replicate results about people's inner experiences if their inner logic about those experiences were preserved. Therefore, a science of psychology must consist of the natural beliefs and thoughts of untrained subjects.

Third, organisms act on "**concrete experienced order**" in the environment. This means that although behavior is *regulated* by the external physical or "geographical" environment, it is *experienced* as a psychological environment.

Kurt Koffka was fond of telling an old German legend to illustrate this point: On a cold winter's night, a traveler arrives exhausted on horseback at an inn after traveling a long distance. He was relieved to have found the inn, because the snow was so deep that he couldn't find any landmarks. Speaking with the innkeeper, he pointed the way he had come. The innkeeper, amazed, said, "Why, you've just ridden across the Lake of Constance!" The rider, shocked by the realization that he had ridden across treacherous ice rather than solid ground, dropped dead at the innkeeper's feet (Koffka, 1935).

Physical stimuli in the environment do not determine behavior; beliefs about the environment determine behavior.

Gestaltists were also fond of emphasizing that perception is more important than sensation. Sensation essentially involves the conversion of physical stimuli (e.g. light and dark patterns impinging on the retina) into neural impulses, but perception (e.g. the recognition of a triangle) involved interpretation of those impulses at higher levels of the brain into something that would be meaningful for the organism. Helmholtz had realized and in fact largely discovered this difference and implied that a lot of thinking was going on unconsciously between one and the other by unconscious inference.

Gestaltists thought that much of this inference was unnecessary, because animals had evolved in environments where such meaningful perception was so crucial that it had to be hard-wired into the brain. Specifically, Gestaltists believed in **psychophysical isomorphism** or a one-to-one correspondence between sensation and perception of wholes. When one sees a triangle, a triangle is literally mapped onto the brain itself as a form. If this is true, structuralism was dead, because separating sensation and perception in consciousness in introspection is an illusory and pointless task—perception is done in one seamless process unavailable to consciousness until after it is done.

This is not to say that Gestaltists were medieval Aristotelians or Cartesians: The visual meanings of "chair" or "cow" are obviously not innate and in the brain at birth. But we are set up to give a kind of wordless meaning to almost any pattern we see, through what came to be known as the **Gestalt laws of perception**. Take a look at Figure 6.1. All of the minifigures in this figure are made up only of dots, and yet a certain grouping of dots is immediately evident.

Figure 6.1a demonstrates the notion of *proximity*. This figure is seen as a set of columns and not as rows even though, logically, there is nothing to prevent us from "adding up" the dots either way. Some dots, however, are closer to others in the rows, making the configuration look like columns. Figure 6.1b demonstrates the principle of *similarity*, the notion that even if some dots aren't closer to others, when they are different colors, the colors are grouped together. (This figure is from a clinical test for color blindness called the Ishihara test. When the dots are red and green rather than black and white shown here, you would see the number 42 in red, if you have normal color vision; the black and white version mimics what a red/green color blind person would see.) Other laws of perception are *continuity* (Figure 6.1c), which states that we are much more likely to follow lines through perceptually than to

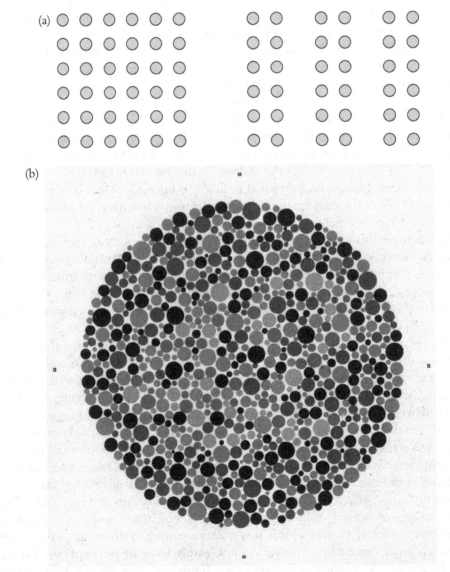

Figure 6.1

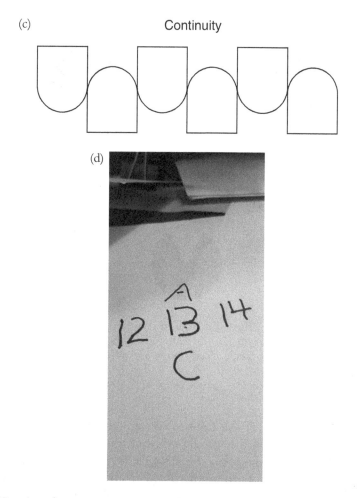

Figure 6.1 (Continued)

break them up, and *closure* or *prägnanz* (6.1d), which implies that we supply missing bits of information to make a form consistent with the surrounding context. This little diagram suggests that learning also contributes to how the brain sees wholes. The central figure is interpreted as B in the vertical and as 13 in the horizontal. Both of these are learned symbol systems and yet we still use innate perception of wholes to figure them out. Finally, the law of *simplicity* suggests that when we decompose figures, we prefer to do it in the simplest, most regular way possible, even though other ways are also possible. In other words, we look for "good Gestalts."

We can easily perceive figures that are not even really there, as in the so-called Kanizsa triangles of Figure 6.2. We can easily perceive figures in more than one way as well. Figure 6.3 shows some **reversible** or **ambiguous figures**. In Figure 6.3a, if you look long enough, you can see both a rabbit and a duck; in Figure 6.3b, an old woman with a wart on her nose or a young woman looking demurely away from the viewer. Typically, the experience of this is that there is no in-between. You see one and then you see the other; your attention to the meaning of the figure shifts back and forth. These famous figures bring everything about Gestalt together. When

Figure 6.2 This famous figure is called the 'Kanizsa triangle illusion' after its inventor, Italian Gestaltist Gaetano Kanizsa (1913-1993). When the Pac-Man-like circles are properly aligned, a white triangle clearly pops out. When they are moved, the triangle disappears.

you reflect on the meaning of the figures, you are reflecting on your own inner experience, but you are doing it naturally, without training. Almost everybody can see the shifts, so that the introspection, if that's what it is, is easily and unambiguously replicable. In this case, sensation does not equal perception, because the same sensation of light/dark area leads to two different perceptual meanings. Those meanings are holistic, in that the relationships among the parts of the figures are perceived all at once, rather than piecemeal. And of course, the perception of order is in the psychological rather than the geographical realm; it is a kind of addition of meaning by the organism between stimulus and response, and that meaning is subservient to the intention or goal of perception.

Insightful Apes: Wolfgang Köhler and Animal Psychology

> American animal psychology makes animals (or people) seek the way out of mazes, over the whole of which there is no general survey from any point inside; the first time they get out is, therefore, necessarily by chance and so, for these scientists, the chief question is how the experience gained can be applied in further tests. In intelligence tests of the nature of our roundabout-way experiments, everything depends upon the situation being surveyable by the subject from the outside.
>
> —Wolfgang Köhler (1925/1948, p. 18)

After the groundbreaking work with Wertheimer and Koffka on the phi phenomenon was launched, Wolfgang Köhler was appointed by Stumpf and Max Planck

Figure 6.3 (a) Duck-rabbit illusion (Joseph Jastrow, 1889); (b) Old-woman, young-woman illusion (My Wife and My Mother-In-Law, by the cartoonist W.E. Hill, 1915)

Source: Adapted from a picture going back at least to an 1888 German postcard

to direct an "anthropoid" research station on Tenerife, in the Spanish territory of the Canary Islands, off the northwest coast of Africa. It was the first such station in the world, established in 1912 with apes imported from the then German colony of Cameroon. Köhler arrived in December 1913, at the age of 26. Köhler claimed that he was stranded at the station during World War I because neutral Spanish ship captains refused to transport German citizens, for fear of becoming a target of war in the straits of Gibraltar. His account of the research conducted there between 1914 and 1917 was published first privately and later in English as *The Mentality of Apes* (1925).

Here was Köhler's chance to put some of the Gestaltists' ideas to the test with lower animals and to refute associationistic or behavioristic views of animal learning. In particular, the prevailing associationistic theory of animal learning was that of "trial-and-error learning" originated by C. Lloyd Morgan (see Chapter 4) and refined by E.L. Thorndike (see Chapters 7 and 8). This was a reductionistic, elementaristic approach to learning: Behaviors were added to an animal's repertoire through random successes in the environment being reinforced as simple habits. Complex activity was explained simply as a gradual additive process of consolidating together these simple habits. Following Morgan's canon, researchers were reluctant to ascribe true thought processes and problem-solving abilities to nonhuman animals.

Köhler believed that, frequently, those who espoused the trial-and-error philosophy made problems that animals could only solve by random methods by hiding the means to the goal. For example, frequently, an animal would have to press a lever or a latch to get to a food goal, but the mechanism of the latch was not in plain sight, so that there would be no way for an animal to figure out exactly how it worked, even if it had been intelligent enough to do so. Thus, trial-and-error methods were the only methods open to the animal.

Köhler believed, however, that if all of the aspects to the solution of how to retrieve the food were visible, apes could assess the situation and devise surprisingly complex methods for reaching their goal. The simplest set of experiments that Köhler set up were **roundabout-way (*umweg* in German) experiments**, also known as **detour problems**. Typically, a situation would be set up for an animal in which some barrier was interposed between the animal and its goal of food or freedom. Köhler set up situations in which an animal could, for example, see a piece of fruit through a fence or bars, but the most direct way to the food would be through the bars. The animal could, however, get at the fruit if it turned *away* from its goal for a moment to go backwards and around a barrier wall. Chickens appeared to accomplish this task by bouncing back and forth randomly behind the bars and would seemingly find their way around only short barrier walls by accident. Dogs could find their way smoothly around walls, but only, interestingly, if the food was relatively far from the bars. Otherwise, the tantalizing smell of the meat close to the bars would act like a magnet and the dog would press its nose up against the bars, "forgetting" to find another way around. Köhler's 15-month-old daughter, just beginning to walk, would look for a moment at an attractive object and then seemingly intentionally look for a way around. When she found the way, she would laugh with recognition and waste no time in getting to the object. Apes were much more like the human than the chicken, looking back for a long moment and going around the wall in one smooth movement.

Although it might take an ape some time to devise the solution, once discovered, the solution is implemented suddenly and is not forgotten, and the task is performed virtually without error. This aspect of sudden solution (defined as reaching the goal without error), followed by repeated error-free performance, is called **insight** and is a crucial concept for Gestaltists. The experience of insight, for humans or animals, is a feeling that all relevant parts of the problem are seen to "fit"—it is a holistic "aha" experience of the Gestalt of the situation.

Köhler demonstrated that the apes of his station could solve relatively complicated roundabout problems. For example, a basket that the apes knew usually contained food was filled with bananas and rocks and hoisted high above them on a rope hung over a tree. The basket was then set to swinging as a pendulum that brought it close to a scaffold high enough to reach the basket.

> Chica, Grande and Tercera are let in upon the scene. Grande leaps for the basket from the ground and misses it. Chica, who, in the meantime, has quietly surveyed the situation, suddenly runs toward the scaffolding, waits with outstretched arms for the basket and catches it. The experiment lasted about a minute.
>
> (Köhler, 1925, p. 195)

The apes could use implements to solve the problems. They were observed to stand upon boxes to reach bananas or use a four-meter stick like a pole vaulter to get at a hanging banana. (Chica, the ape who discovered this method, loved using the stick for its own sake as well; she was observed to interrupt her dinner just to jump with the stick!) In one case, the chimp Grande was able to construct a four-box tower to reach the banana. None of these were done with great speed or smooth deliberation, but there was a lot of what looked like "pondering" (Köhler reported humorously that the chimp Sultan seemed to be thinking, "There's something about that box.") Sometimes it took several days to reach complex solutions, and occasionally solutions appeared to be forgotten. The chimps could imitate other chimps better than they could imitate humans. But they did not teach others. They could also not collaborate fully and intentionally. Although they sometimes seemed to help another with a box tower, they never shared the spoils; the ape who gets to the top first won and ran off with the fruit for himself!

They could also make implements. One experiment involved placing a couple of sticks that fit together to make a longer stick in a cage. A banana was placed beyond the bars of the cage. After Sultan tried his hand and a single stick, he became enraged and frustrated. A couple of hours later, while playing with the sticks, he noted that they fit together and immediately went to try to retrieve the banana and was successful. Thereafter, he did not hesitate to put the sticks together and even accomplished a triple-stick maneuver.

It is clear that in most cases, some trial and error was involved and that really complicated behaviors were seldom devised all at once (for example, to make a three-box tower or a two-stick implement, the apes needed some experience with one box or one stick first). But the speed with which they took up a new innovation was impressive, and errors dropped right away. From these experiments, Köhler concluded that apes had minds: They could hold a goal in mind without looking at it and they could discover, keep and use novel behaviors.

Köhler closed down the station in 1920; the massive inflation in the Deutschmark following World War I (million-mark postage stamps were not uncommon and people needed wheelbarrows full of cash to buy bread) made it very expensive to run and Köhler's and his family's health had suffered. Ronald Ley (1990), however, has put forth another tantalizing hypothesis for the existence of the ape station altogether. He has suggested that Köhler was a spy for the Germans during the First World War. The location of the station, high on a hill, could look out over the sea lanes leading towards the Straits of Gibraltar, a very strategic location. The British were also concerned that German U-boats were being supplied, illegally, by the neutral Spanish on the island. There was evidence in German military files of radio transmissions from that area. On a visit to the island of Tenerife in 1975, Ley managed to interview Köhler's ape handler, then quite old. Manuel Gonzales de Garcia told Ley in whispered tones that Köhler had a wireless in his house, a very uncommon device at the time, as electricity was also uncommon; the frontispiece of the German edition of the book had a picture of the house with electrical connections, evidently installed by Köhler. Ley determined that there was a German weather station on the island with a generator. The British believed there were spies on the island, the Spanish believed that the Germans were spies, and so on. One of Köhler's sons recalls a conversation with a likely German spy on Tenerife years after the fact that said that Köhler had been in "constant communication" with Germany (see Ley, 1990, p. 212). Ley found no "smoking gun" documentary evidence for his hypothesis, however, and some scholars are unconvinced by what is essentially circumstantial evidence (see Ash, 1995, p. 461, note 40). Such disputes, however, are what make history fun. (Did I mention that upon return from Tenerife, Köhler, who had never had a full-time professorial position, was selected to succeed Stumpf as director of the Psychological Institute at Berlin, the most prestigious post in the profession, housed after the First World War in the Kaiser's former Imperial Palace, to boot? A deal perhaps? Forget I mentioned it.)

Gestalts in Human Problem Solving and Education

The interest in problem solving in apes was soon followed by the study of problem solving in humans. The Gestaltists were uncommonly well versed in the most cutting-edge mathematics and physics of their day. Köhler had studied with Max Planck (1858–1947), a pioneer in the area of entropy and heat transfer and one of the fathers of quantum theory. (To provide another connection to psychology, Planck had studied with and been hired by Helmholtz, after Helmholtz left physiology for theoretical physics.) Köhler himself had written a book on field theory physics while on Tenerife. Max Wertheimer was close friends from 1916 onward with Albert Einstein (1879–1955) and in fact studied the processes of his thought in extensive interviews about his discovery of the theory of relativity, described in his final book, *Productive Thinking*. Kurt Lewin and Kurt Koffka were very interested in the abstract area of mathematics of surfaces, known as **topology**, that is crucial in understanding fields.

This interest in physics had two important ramifications for the way Gestaltists approached human thought. First, the notion of a **field** was developed when physicists realized that they would never truly explain the world in terms of the motion of individual particles in space. Thus, reductionism was losing its appeal in physics and being replaced by the notion of **lines of force** in the **constraints** of space. The best physical example is perhaps the magnetic fields seen at the poles of a magnet. The lines of force are easily seen in iron filings, and it is the shape of the field that matters, not the individual filings. Koffka (1935) gave a nice example of forces in psychology. A novice soccer player who looks directly at a goalie while kicking usually follows a "psychological line of force" and the ball is kicked directly to the goalie, which of course is not what the player wants. To succeed he must learn to look away from the goalie and "reconfigure the psychological space." In American football, the runner must exchange figure for ground, so that the holes in the line are seen as more vivid, more real than are the hulking linebackers in the runner's way. In problem solving, as we shall see below, this means that we must first see the underlying *structure* of the problem, the relation of part to whole, rather than the pieces that make up the problem, the individual behaviors, what the problem seems on the surface to be about.

Second, the Gestaltists' experience with mathematics and physics gave them an even stronger appreciation of the importance of insight. Typically, a mathematician's insight comes all at once, though it may take him or her years to figure out the proof. Einstein had had an insight at the age of 16 that if one were to ride on a beam of light, time would be different than it would be standing still. It took him seven years to figure out the implications of his vision; when he finally did so, it took him a mere five weeks to write his paper on relativity in his spare time as an obscure patent clerk in Bern, Switzerland. This notion of idea, followed by hard work, followed by insight forms the core of the notion of the Gestaltists' way of solving problems.

The Gestaltist perspective on problem solving led to a small industry of devising problems that lead to an "aha" experience when solved. Look, for example, at Table 6.1. Try to solve the first problem, a classic devised by one of Köhler's graduate students, Dunker, in 1935. (1) Try to determine the real rules, the constraints that you must follow. (2) Make sure they are real constraints. (3) If you get stuck, try **brainstorming**: Produce as many solutions, no matter how far-fetched, quickly and without evaluation. You can go back and throw out the bad ones later, by checking them against the constraints of the problem to see if they satisfy them. The object of brainstorming is to allow one to free one's thinking from ingrained habits, so that more original solutions will come up.

If you still haven't solved the problem, try to solve problem 2 first and then go back to it. It has been shown that people who solve the second problem first, find the first problem easier, than if it is attempted the other way around (Gick & Holyoak, 1980). My final hint is that the two problems are actually the same, even though they look very different (a barrier prevents the passage of a large amount of rays or soldiers). One is analogous to the other, so this is called analogical problem solving. The abstract underlying structure is the same, but what the problems seem to be about is wildly different. When solved, most people feel a feeling of aha, or a shift in perception, that is similar to that in the reversible figures above. All parts of the problem are seen to relate to each other in a good Gestalt, a pleasing whole.

Table 6.1 Analogical Problem Solving

Duncker's Operation Problem
1. Suppose you are a doctor faced with a patient who has a malignant tumor in his brain. It is impossible to operate on the patient, but unless the tumor is destroyed, the patient will die. There is a kind of ray that can be used to destroy the tumor. If the rays reach the tumor all at once at a sufficient intensity, the tumor will be destroyed. Unfortunately, at this intensity, the healthy tissue that the rays pass through on the way to the tumor will also be destroyed. At lower intensities, the rays are harmless to the healthy tissue, but they will not harm the tumor either. What type of procedure might be used to destroy the tumor with the rays and at the same time avoid destroying the healthy tissue?
Source: Adapted from Duncker, 1935/1945, p. 2, by Gick & Holyoak, 1980, pp. 307–308

Gick & Holyoak's (1980) Analog
2. A small country fell under the rule of an iron dictator 150 years ago. The dictator ruled the country from a strong fortress. The fortress was situated in the middle of the country, surrounded by farms and villages. Many roads radiated outward from the fortress like spokes from a wheel. A great general arose who raised a large army at the border and vowed to capture the fortress and free the country of the dictator. The general knew that if his entire army could attack the fortress at once it would be captured. His troops were poised at the head of one of the roads leading to the fortress ready to attack. However, a spy brought the general a disturbing report. The ruthless dictator had planted mines on each of the roads. The mines were set so that small bodies of men could pass over them safely, since the dictator needed to be able to move troops and workers to and from the fortress. However, any large force would detonate the mines. Not only would this blow up the road and render it impassable, but the dictator would then destroy many villages in retaliation. A full-scale attack on the fortress therefore appeared impossible. How could the general's army defeat the dictator under these daunting conditions?
Source: Adapted from Gick & Holyoak, 1980, p. 351

Table 6.2 Principles of Problem Solving: Adapted from Wertheimer (1959)

Solving the problem
  I. Define the goal: *Convergent*
  II. Get the facts
    —implied as well as explicit
    —do not assume constraints
  III. What facts absolutely constrain solution?
  IV. Generate many solutions without evaluation: *Divergent*
    —Brainstorm
  V. Evaluate solutions in regard to facts and goal: *Convergent*
If this doesn't work:
  VI. Incubate: *Divergent*
  VII. Return to III or IV

Let's get back down to earth with a more practical problem in teaching children to solve problems in area of figures described at length by Wertheimer in his posthumously published work *Productive Thinking* (1945/1959; see also Cox, 1997). To Wertheimer, the object of teaching was to guide children toward the *discovery* of relations that are constrained both by the perceptual structure of a situation and by the goal of the problem-solving task in that situation. Thus, for example, in teaching how to calculate area, the teacher may show a large and a small rectangle and ask,

"How can we find which is bigger?" If there is no answer, Wertheimer suggests that the instructor move on to examples in which the child can find the relevant structure relating to his or her life, such as a story about finding the differences in the sizes of farms or neighborhoods. One might also cut a piece of cardboard the size of the difference or measure with blocks, showing how the cardboard fits or how many blocks are needed. The rectangle can then be divided up into equal portions for measurement, by dividing the area into an x by y grid and the formula, through counting, can be derived. Wertheimer does not teach the actual operations involved in area calculation. Rather, he guides the child's attention to the relationships among the figures, so that these procedures for calculation can be discovered and constructed.

Once the child can calculate the area of a rectangle, it is possible to examine transfer to problems involving a parallelogram, using a cardboard figure. Instead of giving only verbal instructions involving measurement, one might cut off the triangle part at one end of the parallelogram and then place it where it "fits" into the rectangle. Again, if the child does not understand, Wertheimer suggests that the teacher connect the abstract geometric example to one in "real life." Following this step, other examples are given that are more general abstractions of the "missing piece principle." These would be irregular figures, that appear quite different from the parallelogram, but for which, like the parallelogram, a cut-out area on one part of the figure would be exactly compensated by a protuberance on another part. An important feature of such training is to allow the child to examine figures for which the principle will definitely not work, but which look somewhat similar to those for which the principle does work, so that he or she may determine the limits of the application of the strategy. Finally, repetition and practice are added, but the practice must be with several types of figures mixed together, so as to insure that individual response patterns are not fixed as isolated habits to a particular stimulus but are established as responses relating to the entire structural configuration.

Again, throughout the entire teaching process, which is essentially as much a construction of a Gestalt as a discovery of one there already, Wertheimer deliberately avoids giving instructions and permits the child to keep open the choices for solution of the problem. The child is encouraged to avoid applying a particular operation until a broad sample of appropriate and inappropriate exemplars has been given, avoiding the strengthening of particular habits over ones useful in the whole situation. In fact, Wertheimer says that the explicit teaching of the application of specific rules, in a step-by-step (he would say "piecemeal") fashion forces children to look only at the parts at the expense of the whole. Such children, thought Wertheimer, are bound by rote to the rules already given them. They complain that the teacher "hasn't given them a problem like that yet" and refuse to solve it. One can see in this small example the battle in education between whole language vs. phonics or a preference to teach addition and subtraction together, rather than one after the other.

Kurt Lewin: Gestalt in Developmental, Industrial and Social Psychology

> Psychology needs concepts which can be applied not merely to the facts of a field like child psychology, animal psychology or psychopathology, but which are equally applicable to all of them. One should be able to use the same concepts for problems of emotional

> life as for problems of behavior; or for problems concerning the infant, the adolescent and the aged; the healthy and the sick; animals and human beings, the personality and the environment.... The unification of the different fields of psychology seems quite hopeless until we have an adequate psychology of will and needs and personality.
>
> —Kurt Lewin (1936, p. 5)

Of the founding Gestaltists, Kurt Lewin[1] was most interested in taking Gestalt theory beyond perception and cognition into social, organizational and developmental psychology. He recognized that, from the time of Fechner to Wundt to the Gestaltists, the most researched area of psychology was that of perception. But by the 1920s, there was still no adequate experimental theory of will, of needs and of personality. (There was, of course, the work of Freud, but Lewin suggested that the method of basing laws on case studies "seemed methodologically unsound to most scientists" [Lewin, 1936, p. 3]). Instead, Lewin was after a simple but flexible way of representing the way that persons feel as though there are forces and constraints acting on them, from within and without. For Lewin, as for Koffka, it is not the geographical environment that is important, but the organism's experience of it. Thus, different animals with different capabilities, goals and needs would experience the environment in different ways. So would a preschooler, an adolescent or an adult. Lewin expressed this subjective notion of behavior-environment interaction as a **life space**, which was defined as the totality of possible events which determine the behavior (B) of an individual (P) in an environment (E). Behavior is a function of a life space, which in turn is a function of both person and environment: $B = f(L) = f(P, E)$.

The Life Space and Developmental Psychology

A simple example of this approach was presented at the International Congress of Psychologists, at Yale University, in 1929 (Marrow, 1969). Lewin had made a film of his wife's 18-month-old niece, Hannah, trying to sit on a rock, which she had never done before (Thiel & Kreppner, 2002). In order to sit on the stone, of course, Hannah would have to turn her back to it, but she was not sure that if she took her eyes off it, she would be able to do it. So, she circled the stone several times while looking at it, trying to find a way to sit down, while looking. Then, finally, she put her head between her legs and backed over to the stone. It was as if the stone exerted a force on the child that she could not break. Like Köhler's dog, who could not find a way around a barrier to meat when its tempting aroma was too present, the child needed to go away from the goal (turn around and back up) in order to solve the problem, but couldn't. The stone's pull was too strong. Another way of looking at it is as an 18 month old's ability to create a complete representation in her mind of the rock and turn it around in her head and use it to guide her behavior, going backward. Then, the rock serves as a motivation, but the lack of ability serves as a temporary constraint in the child's life space, a limitation on the range and quality of her movement.

When an organism looks at the environment, it always sees it in terms of its usefulness towards reaching a goal. Hannah doesn't see the rock as just a rock; she sees it as "a place to sit." The rock had, as Lewin would say, an *afforderungscharakter*.

"Huh?" you might ask, "what the heck is that?" Lewin's translators had the same problem. At first they called it "invitational character," in the sense that the rock invites sitting. Then, a translator hit upon the use of the word **valence**; in chemistry, an atom or compound with a positive charge, a charge that attracts, has a positive valence, and one with a negative charge, that repels, a negative valence. In this sense, the rock had a **positive valence** in the field of Hannah's behavior at that moment concerned with the goal of sitting. Goals set up the way that an organism will perceive a space: Goals set up **fields of force** that charge the objects within them with meaning in relation to the goal. If Hannah were not intent on sitting, the rock might not have that valence. Technically, it has a positive valence within the field of force concerned with sitting. Some things have **negative valence**: For example, spinach has a negative valence for a child who hates it; in order for parents to get him to eat it, they must appeal to other, stronger positive valences, "Eat your spinach and then you can have your dessert," or "It will make you big and strong, like daddy." They might also make the negative valences of other things within the life space of the child at that moment more obvious: "Eat your spinach or no T.V. for you tonight!" Some of the barriers to completing a goal are **quasi-physical**, in Lewin's terminology: For a two-year-old, eating sloppy spinach with a fork is a sloppy proposition, because her fine motor coordination has yet to develop or the fork is too large in relation to the tiny child to be operated efficiently. Thus, you would predict that the quasi-physical barriers to eating spinach "properly" would dictate that many two-year-olds would take an easier course—using their fingers. A barrier is called a **quasi-physical fact** because it is not just in the physical environment, but in the function between the person and the environment. Eating spinach with a fork is a quasi-physical barrier in the life space of most two-year-olds, but not in the life space of most 10-year-olds.

There are **quasi-social facts** as well. "Eat your spinach or no dessert for you" has strong valence for a two-year-old, propelling her to eat, to get around the strong social barrier in place between her and her dessert. If a waiter said the same thing to you, you would look at him incredulously. You have the greater force in relation to him in that social situation, the field of force operating in the goal structure of having a restaurant meal.

Quasi-social facts represent barriers or attractions in the social world in the same way that quasi-physical facts affect navigation through the physical world. They are dependent upon the skills and perceptions of the individual, as much as they are on the other people themselves. Puberty can be said to be (among other things) a time when the valence of the opposite sex switches for most children from negative to positive! When it is negative, there are a whole host of unarticulated but strongly followed rules about the very limited times and conditions under which one is allowed to interact with the opposite sex. The quasi-social facts enforce social boundaries. When the valence becomes positive, there are exciting new possibilities and formidable barriers in the life space of the adolescent that were not there at all when he or she was only eight years old!

Lewin also categorized the kinds of conflicts in valences that are present in the life space of children. One of the easiest of these would be the **approach-approach conflict**, such as the conflict between going to a picnic and playing at home. There is, as one might say these days, no "downside risk" to this decision, so it is made rather quickly, though if one becomes disenchanted with the original choice, some "oscillation" back to the other choice might occur. Alternatively, some tasks have both positive and negative valences in the same object. This is an **approach-avoidance conflict**, in the sense that climbing a tree has a positive valence of fun, thrill or challenge that is counterbalanced by the fear of falling from a precarious height. One would in this case have to weigh the relative strengths of the valences to predict the outcome of the choice.

But the most interesting and difficult conflict is the choice of the lesser of two evils, the **avoidance-avoidance conflict**. How would a child deal with, for example, the threat of punishment vs. cleaning his or her room, an aversive task. The child is pushed away from both and would attempt, as Lewin said, to "leave the field," to do anything to avoid both punishment and completing the task, such as bargain or procrastinate. Under such conditions, the parent may react by restricting the child's freedom by constructing quasi-physical barriers (locking the child in his or her room) or social barriers by escalating negative valence of punishment ("Do it now or else you can't go to the movies!") or providing positive valence to the task ("Clean your room and then we'll go for ice cream!"). Some parents restrict a child's freedom of action so much, so often, in so many situations, that the child becomes inhibited, internalizing the quasi-social barriers within him- or herself.

Lewin's genius was in transforming psychological conflicts and tensions in situations into spatial representations. Figure 6.4 shows how he would represent the entire psychological situation of forces within constraints within boundary circles that represent the extent of fields of force. Outside the circle is the nonpsychological space, but within it are all the forces that aid or impede reaching a goal in an individual's perception. (Technically, these bloblike circles are called Jordan curves, but his students and colleagues usually called them, affectionately, "Lewin's eggs.") Lewin therefore called his system **topological psychology**, because topology is the area of mathematics that deals with boundaries, barriers and forces in space. He also used the term **vector psychology** as an analogy to the process, in physics, of calculating a vector between forces: Equal forces at right angles to one another propel a body in a 45-degree angle direction or vector, for instance. The same might be said to be true in psychological forces. Lewin's highest goal for his topological psychology was to map out all of the forces and constraints determining a person's behavior at any given moment; the resultant vector of the person's most probable next move could then be calculated.

The topological approach was useful as well for mapping out developmental changes or cultural differences. Lewin, as a new immigrant, noted with appreciation the differences between children in Germany and the United States. American children treated adults more like equals than would have ever been allowed in Germany up to that time. In other words, the **zone of permitted action** of a child was either physically or in matters of personal choice wider than in Germany (Lewin, 1948/1997). Middle-class American mothers spoke softly to their children and explained the reasons for their punishments, whereas German parents were more likely to issue orders at a louder volume. Both cultures seemed to value good behavior and obedience in their children, but the obedience was gained in a different way. Lewin noted that American parents were likely to say thank you to their children

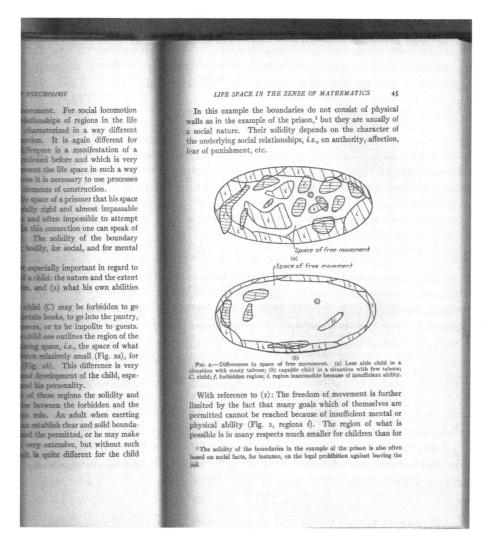

Figure 6.4 An example of the use of Lewin's "eggs" (Jordan curves) in topological psychology: In the first figure, a young child © is highly constrained by forbidden zones (f) and things she cannot yet do (i), and thus her zone of free movement is small; this would also mean that in the presence of her constraining parent, her behavior may be more predictable, as she has few choices. In the second figure, the child's space of free movement has expanded as she has matured.

Source: Lewin, 1936, p. 45

for performing a household chore or demand even if the parent had needed to apply considerable pressure on the child to ensure compliance with the request. German parents were more likely to insist that the child "do it faster next time."

Lewin believed that this mode of child rearing had far-reaching social consequences. At the narrowest level, when a parent said thank you after appropriately disciplining a child to comply, it meant that parents in America were more eager to reestablish quickly a certain equality in relations between them and their children, whereas German parents preferred to maintain their distance. Lewin believed that this distance was internalized in the adult personality of Germans, in that Germans would not let new acquaintances into close relationships with them very readily. In Lewin's terms, the life space that refers to our personality has many layers and in Germans, only the outermost layers are permeable to new individuals. Americans, by contrast, will be friendly more readily with many more individuals; there remained an intimate, secret inner core, but that core of secrecy was much smaller for Americans than for Germans.

This in turn had political consequences. If more layers of a person are permeable in American society, this leaves more room for compromise and reconciliation. For example, in America, there are two very broad political parties with large intra-party differences; when one party wins, it is the tradition of the loser to make a generous concession speech. Senators across party lines often have cordial personal relations in spite of their strong political differences. In Germany, by contrast, there were, in Lewin's time, many hard-edged parties in often bitter irreconcilable conflict. A scientific conflict was also likely to become personal. (Although his biographer points out that Lewin was often quite generous in hearing others' views, they would not often change his own perspective; Köhler and Wertheimer, by contrast, were capable of shouting down others with whom they disagreed [Marrow, 1969].) Thus, culture and personality fed on each other and formed a kind of equilibrium.

For Lewin, this was both ominous and encouraging. He noted with some bitterness that one of the first things the Nazis had done was to gain control of nursery schools in Germany and demand that kindergarten teachers never explain their orders to their little charges (Lewin, 1948/1997, p. 18). They had evidently read their Hegel and thought that they understood clearly Hegel's notions of the dependence of the person on the *Volk* or people and the people as subservient to the interests of the state. But Lewin loved America as soon as he arrived there and set about understanding what it was that made democracy so resilient in the United States—in its children, its adults and its institutions. This was not merely an academic interest to him, but an urgent practical one; he was astute enough to know that if and when World War II was won and the Nazi machine was destroyed, it would have to be replaced by something. Democracy had failed there after the First World War, with unimaginably horrible consequences. He was determined that it not fail again.

The contributions of Lewin and his students Ronald Lippitt and Ralph K. White at the Iowa Child Research Station to this effort were deceptively simple (Lewin, Lippitt, & White, 1939; White & Lippitt, 1960). In 1938, they hit upon the idea of setting up boys' and girls' clubs, after-school groups of 10- and 11-year-olds led by adults with different leadership styles. An example task would be to complete a paper-mache mask. One group, the autocratic group, was led by an adult who dictated all task procedures one at a time. No choice was given as to how the mask would be completed, and children were assigned their different roles and work partner by the leader alone. The leader praised and criticized each member's work without objective reasons and remained kind but aloof.

By contrast, in the democratic group, all policies were a matter of group agreement under the general guidance of the leader. The leader would take a role in instructing how to work with the materials, but always tried to give two or three choices as to how to complete the task. Group members were free to choose how and with whom they would work. Criticism, when given, was objective and patiently explained.

Analysis of the films of the group interaction showed that although the leaders of both groups did provide leadership in terms of more assertions by the leaders than an average group leader, the autocratic leaders made more than twice as many such attempts to control than did the democratic leaders. More importantly, there were 30 times more hostile domination attempts among the group members in the autocratic groups and even the selection of a scapegoat on whom to blame errors. They ganged up on one child so mercilessly that he ceased coming to the club. In the child-to-child talk of the democratic groups, there were many more "we" statements than "I" statements; in the autocratic groups the reverse was true. Children in the autocratic group were very submissive to the leader, but not submissive to their peers.

When, in subsequent experiments, a virtually leaderless laissez-faire group was added, it was made abundantly clear that democracy does not just happen in the absence of control. A high level of aggression and apathy was found in this group as well. Indeed, Lewin believed that the most important lesson to be learned in democracy was not how to be a leader, but how to be an engaged and tolerant follower. In one experiment, children were shifted from autocracy to democracy and vice versa. Lewin stated,

> There have been few experiences for me as impressive as seeing the expression in children's faces change during the first day of autocracy. The friendly, open and co-operative group, full of life, became within a short half-hour a rather apathetic-looking gathering without initiative. The change from autocracy to democracy seemed to take somewhat more time than from autocracy to democracy. Autocracy is imposed upon the individual. Democracy he has to learn.
> (Lewin, 1939/1948, p. 66)

Lewin and Industrial Psychology: Total Culture of the Workplace

Lewin almost immediately took the results of this work with children and applied it to the business world (Marrow, 1969). In 1939, he was called in by managers to address a problem at a manufacturing plant in Virginia that was not measuring up to the levels of productivity of the company's other plants. The workers were paid by the piece for their work, so the lack of productivity hurt themselves as well, and yet there seemed to be nothing that the managers could do. Punishments applied to individual workers only made them angry, and despite the relatively high wages offered at the plant compared to the surrounding rural community during the Great Depression, many of the workers quit. Apparently, the workers found that the quota was unrealistic and so they felt no personal responsibility when they failed to meet it. Lewin and his colleagues initiated a number of studies that eventually verified the following points:

- If a number of workers were transferred from a more efficient plant, the local workers could benefit by modeling these workers and learning their techniques, to learn that the goal could be made without strain.

- When production goals were instituted in small groups of workers by vote (and management agreed to implement workers' suggestions on improvements), production would steadily rise.
- This improvement would occur most strongly only if discussions led to a democratically obtained decision. A group that was only asked to discuss the problem and not to vote on it did not improve as much.
- At the plant there were frequent retooling procedures that decreased production and produced frustration. Groups of workers who had these changes imposed from above in an autocratic fashion did not recover from the loss of production; those who were allowed to participate in decision-making process accepted and met management's higher goals of production much more quickly. Thus, it appeared that the democratic leadership style, as long as it led to a clear decision, led to higher productivity with less frustration than an autocratic style.

Indeed, Lewin's biographer reports that he and his colleagues were generally liked by the workers (who might usually be expected to dislike suggestions of a foreign Jewish professor with a German accent in the middle of World War II). But Lewin's philosophy was a great improvement at the time over the autocratic efficiency methods of "**Taylorism**," or **scientific management**. Taylorism was a top-down management style invented by a mechanical engineer, Fredrick W. Taylor (1856–1915), before the First World War that used time-and-motion studies, sometimes timing production tasks to a hundredth of a second, to increase efficiency of workers. Taylor believed that the natural tendency of workers was to take it easy ("to do as little as he safely can"; Taylor, 1911, p. 13) or, worse in his view, to create a social system among themselves to swindle management out of the fruits of workers' best efforts. Taylor advocated total control of work and central planning by management; individuality was the enemy of efficiency. He encouraged payment by the piece, contingent on following elaborate efficiency rules. Bonuses would be given for exceeding quotas, but then the bonus level would become the new floor for setting quotas and so on.

In such a climate, Lewin's alternative views were no doubt seen as relatively humane by the workers. As early as 1920, in an article called "The Socializing of the Taylor System" (Lewin, 1920/1999), Lewin noted that demands for productivity should be carefully balanced by the "inner value" of work to the worker. Lewin disagreed with Taylor's belief that the factory should be seen as a machine and the workers in it, cogs. Instead, he believed that the more appropriate metaphor was to see a company and the workers in it as a "total culture." Democratic leadership styles were both empowering and efficient, allowing a measure of self-control of one's own work within a larger organizational structure, while still meeting the goals of the corporation. Indeed, the intrinsic mechanism for obtaining feedback built into a democratic leadership system also allowed the social structure of the workplace to seek its own equilibrium over time and to remain flexible to changes.

Lewin's work concerning industry was also a good illustration of his vector psychology in action: By looking at all the forces increasing and decreasing production and the goals of both workers and management, Lewin always attempted to "vector" a solution to the social forces within social and physical constraints. Lewin and his colleagues were interested in doing what he came to call **action research**: As much as possible, Lewin believed research should be done in the setting in which the results would eventually be used, with as many of the realistic constraints that that setting offered as possible. And then, when the research was completed, the improvements, once proven, could be immediately put into action. The practical emphasis of action research does not mean that Lewin forsook basic research for applied research. Every proposed new change in method was evaluated against one or more control groups within the factory. Lewin's desire for elegant experimental research grounded in theory was not replaced by practical considerations but enhanced by them. He believed that experimental evidence, especially when gained in the context of the factory itself, is more convincing than just opinion.

In at least one case, Lewin and his colleagues were forced to take some strong measures to overcome skepticism to their experimental evidence. Plant managers would not hire older women, because they were seen to be less productive. Lewin, after some initial studies, proved that this was not the case; older women were just as efficient, if not more so, than their younger coworkers. When their foremen refused to believe the data, Lewin's colleagues guided the foremen towards constructing their own study and *collecting the data themselves*! Only then was the negative stereotype of older women given up in the face of the foremen's own evidence.

Lewin and the Foundations of Social Psychology

Lewin and his colleagues also were committed to resolving issues of racism, anti-Semitism and stereotyping in business and society. He worked tirelessly to get his colleagues, friends and family members out of Nazi Germany and thus knew intimately of the horrors of Hitler's Third Reich. He was not always successful; his own mother died in the Holocaust. After he gained American citizenship, in 1940, he joined in secret work with the Office of Strategic Services, the precursor of the Central Intelligence Agency. In 1944, realizing that his interests had changed from child development to the social aspects of group dynamics, he moved from Iowa to Cambridge, Massachusetts, to found the Research Center for Group Dynamics at the Massachusetts Institute of Technology. This center (moved to the University of Michigan after Lewin's death) would be concerned with areas such as group productivity, social influence, social perception of others, relationships between racial and religious groups, the way individuals come to identify with groups and, last, the training and development of leadership skills. Astoundingly, Lewin's inexhaustible energy and self-confidence drove him to found simultaneously the Commission on Community Interrelations of the American Jewish Congress. Although the purposes of the C.C.I. overlapped somewhat with that of the M.I.T. Center, its main goal was to deal with issues of prejudice. These included topics such as how to minimize the tensions of integrating neighborhoods and workplaces and how best to educate children, adults and community leaders to be tolerant and accepting of outgroup members in their midst (Marrow, 1969). In short, the two centers together mapped out what became almost the entire program of social psychology for the next 50 years and trained or consulted with an entire generation of pioneers in social psychology!

Conclusion: Gestalt Theory in Historical Context

Textbooks in the history of psychology, including this one, tend to focus strongly on the history of ideas. For the Gestaltists, for example, the main ideas are how the notion of intentionality, borrowed from Brentano's philosophy, led to the notion that all human perception, thinking and actions are infused with goals. We tend to organize our thinking and perception in terms of goals and obstacles to those goals, by means of psychological fields of force. This notion was borrowed from physics and mathematics at the turn of the 20th century. The Gestaltists said that we are built to see relationships among elements rather than the elements themselves. We are holistic rather than reductionistic or elementaristic in our thinking. A "proper" psychology is a psychology of lawful relationships among psychological forces perceived by the individual rather than a catalog of how ideas or states of consciousness aggregate into clumps. It all sounds quite abstract, clean and theoretical.

And yet Gestalt psychology was born in the most turbulent period of German history, and the Gestaltists themselves were not immune to its effects. Political history affects science as much as the history of ideas. All four of the founders eventually ended up in America due to the horrors of Nazi Germany. Koffka, who had studied briefly in Edinburgh and spoke excellent English, took a post first, in 1928, at Smith College; Wertheimer and Lewin were forced out by a Nazi law in 1933 that excluded Jews from the civil service, of which professors were a part. Wertheimer accepted a position at the New School for Social Research in New York City. Lewin ended up at the University of Iowa and then M.I.T. Köhler, the only non-Jewish founder, stayed on in Germany as long as he could, but he was one of the few German professors who was a public critic of the Nazi regime. He protested the firing of his Jewish colleagues, not only within the university, but also in a widely read newspaper editorial (Ash, 1995). He had hoped the high prestige accorded to professors in Germany would protect him and allow him to continue, but at times he feared arrest. In spite of this, he publicly provoked the Nazis at the start of his lectures; he gave the Nazi salute, as required by law, but then pointedly disagreed with the ideas it signified (Henle, 1978). His students attempted to have a torchlight procession in his honor, but the Nazi-dominated student government of the University of Berlin denied it. Köhler's Institute in Berlin was subjected twice to raids of Nazi students (with the quiet approval of some in the university administration; Ash, 1995). When he was in America to lecture at Harvard in 1935, he was "allowed" to resign his post at Berlin. He took an offer at Swarthmore College in Pennsylvania. The Berlin Institute never recovered its prewar glory. The influence of Gestalt in America was truncated somewhat by the early deaths of three of its founders: Koffka died in 1941, Wertheimer died in 1943 and Lewin in 1947. In addition, the Gestaltists had arrived in America during the heyday of behaviorism (Sokal, 1984). It is good to remember this historicist fact, because almost everything that Wertheimer, Köhler and Koffka wrote for American audiences takes aim at behaviorism, as much as stating their own positions. Lewin, who once stated, "There is nothing so practical as a good theory," was more pragmatic, but even he hated the tendency of Americans to rely too much on statistics (Lewin, 1931/1999). Köhler remained at Swarthmore until his death in 1967, but his later work was largely philosophical (see Köhler, 1971). He did, however, become the president of the APA, and he received a lifetime achievement award.

History and Psychology Today: Gestaltism and Experimental Social Psychology

It is perhaps only a slight exaggeration to say that Gestaltism is the foundation for the modern discipline of social psychology. Barone, Maddux, and Snyder (1997) even claim that Lewin "single-handedly created applied social psychology" (p. 35), but many of the areas of concern of contemporary social psychology were outlined by students or colleagues of Wertheimer and Köhler as well. A complete discussion of these connections would take up more space than we can give it here (see e.g. Ash, 1995; Mandler & Mandler, 1964, and the biography of Lewin by Marrow, 1969, for more details), so we will focus on only three of the most famous colleagues and students of the Gestaltists and the areas that they helped pioneer: Fritz Heider, Leon Festinger and Solomon Asch.

Fritz Heider: Balance Theory and Attribution

> In everyday life we form ideas about other people and about social situations. We interpret other people's actions and we predict what they will do under other circumstances. Though these ideas are usually not formulated, they often function adequately. They achieve in some measure what a science is supposed to achieve: an adequate description of the subject matter which makes prediction possible. In the same way one talks about a naïve physics which consists of the unformulated ways we take account of the mechanical laws in our adapted actions, one can talk about a "naïve psychology" which gives us the principles we use to build up our picture of the social environment and which guides our reactions to it.
>
> —Fritz Heider (1958, p. 5)

Fritz Heider (1896–1988) was born in Vienna but spent much of his youth in Graz, Austria. He came from an intellectually curious family, who gave Fritz an extraordinary amount of freedom in his education and choice of career for that time and place. Influenced by his father, he disliked dry academic arguments but loved the life of the mind. (Whenever he got too theoretical, his father would say, "You won't get a dog from behind a warm stove with that argument!" [Heider, 1983]). Like his parents, he enjoyed painting and music as hobbies, so he combined this interest with that of philosophy to complete a dissertation on the issue of how we perceive objects as distinct from background based on light and dark areas, called *Thing and Medium*. This dissertation, completed with Alexis Meinong (1853–1920; a teacher of von Ehrenfels and admirer of Brentano), gradually came to the attention of Kurt Lewin and then of the other Gestaltists in Berlin. Heider attended classes there but also did practical work, such as teaching in an experimental school for orphan boys and constructing job aptitude tests. Eventually, this led Kurt Koffka to invite him to follow him to Smith College in Northampton, Massachusetts, to do research in a local school for the deaf. There he met and immediately fell in love with a bright and beautiful student, Grace Moore, who became his wife and close colleague for life. They both taught at Northampton and later at the University of Kansas with fellow Gestaltists Roger Barker and Teresa Wright.

Heider became strongly interested, along with Lewin, with applying the perceptual insights of Gestalt to the social world. In particular, Heider's unpretentious nature combined with the elegance of Gestalt theory to give us what he called his **commonsense psychology**. Rather than attempting to explain human motivation by dark unconscious impulses, as Freud did (see Chapter 9) or to remove the inner cognitive world and focus on external reinforcement, as the behaviorists did (see Chapter 8), he proposed to take people more or less at their word. Gestaltists claimed that their data should be the direct experience of naïve observers and that people act on concrete experienced order. Why couldn't the same things be true of social interactions among people? Just as we can't help but perceive the physical world in meaningful ways, we make these social interpretations almost automatically. Heider even produced a film that was nothing more than a small triangle and a larger triangle moving about. People reported that it looked as if the larger triangle was "chasing" the small one (Heider & Simmel, 1944).

One of the first things that Heider noticed about the social world that is different from the physical world is that we assume other people have intentions of their own and explain causality on this basis. In other words, we **attribute** to people certain things based on their behavior and our knowledge of the constraints on their behavior. For example, Heider noticed that when a bad thing happened to him, he was angriest when he thought it was another person's deliberate fault; when he determined that there were reasonable external causes for the person's behavior, he immediately became less angry.

Consider the following example: An impatient driver is following another car that is moving rather slowly up to a fork in the road. The car in front pauses a moment before the fork and the driver behind interprets that as a signal to pass. Just as the impatient driver attempts to pass on the left, the car in front takes the left fork, cutting him off and forcing him to slam on his brakes. Now the impatient driver is angry, speeds up, passes the car and deliberately slams on his brakes unexpectedly several times to "teach him a lesson." The impatient driver has made an **internal attribution** about the other driver, assuming that there is something stable, internal and bad about him ("He's a jerk, doesn't know how to drive, deliberately cut me off, etc."). Perhaps if the driver had noted that the street sign marking the fork was hidden by the tree and that the driver in front, in trying to decide which fork to take, had seen it at the last minute, he might be less angry. Indeed, the person in the other car does not think himself a jerk; he perceives that he acted that way because of external circumstances. In this case, the navigation task was made difficult by the hidden sign, so the driver makes an **external attribution** about the cause of his own behavior (although he no doubt thinks that the guy who just passed him is a jerk, doesn't know how to drive and deliberately cut him off!). There is an imbalance to our knowledge in watching ourselves or other people. We can more easily see the external causes to our own behavior than of someone else, so we make external attributions as to the causes of our behavior, but internal attributions as to the causes of the behavior of others. This later came to be called the **fundamental**

attribution error (see e.g. Jones & Harris, 1967) and formed the basis of a whole field of endeavor in social psychology called **attribution theory**, which has thus far spawned more than 40 years of subtle and interesting experiments.

What's more, said Heider, we value consistency in our own behaviors. Let's suppose that a really good buddy of yours loved the latest Star Wars movie and you hated it. To be consistent, you would need to (a) dislike your friend (unlikely, one hopes), (b) come to like the movie, (c) convince your friend to dislike the movie or (d) decide that you can "differentiate" your opinion of your friend: dislike his taste in movies, but like him for other reasons. This is Heider's (1958) **balance theory of sentiments**, which suggests that we like our likes to be balanced with respect to one another. In any triad of things (person, person and movie, in the last case), we like the "product of the affective valences" to come out positive. (Liking your friend × his liking the movie × your disliking the movie works out to "positive times positive times negative = negative"; liking your friend × your being convinced to dislike the movie after all × his disliking the movie is a positive times a negative times a negative, which comes out positive. Balance theory also explains the commonsense adage that an enemy of my enemy is my friend (negative times negative = positive).

Leon Festinger: Cognitive Dissonance Theory

The cognitive dissonance theory of Leon Festinger (1919–1989) is also based on the notion of the desire for humans to have consistent beliefs. Festinger received his doctorate from Kurt Lewin at Iowa, moved with him to the Research Center for Group Dynamics and moved with the center to the University of Michigan after Lewin's death.

Festinger's insight concerns what happens when we agree of our own free will to do something we do not want to do. The classic study (Festinger & Carlsmith, 1959) first asks experimental subjects to do a long series of very boring tasks (such as moving spools of thread around or giving a quarter turn to hundreds of screws) in the interest of a study on "motivation." After this is completed, the subjects are told that they were in the control condition and then asked to convince someone else that the task was interesting. In other words, they are asked to lie, to set up a dissonance between what they know to be true and what they would be saying. To be sure, said the experimenter, we will pay you for your trouble. One group of subjects was paid only a dollar to convince the other person (well, O.K., that would be worth about seven dollars in 2014, but it was still a small amount). Another group was paid $20 (about $140 today) to lie and a third group (the *real* control group) was paid nothing and not asked to lie. The control group, not asked to lie, rated the original excruciatingly boring task as about 6 on a 25-point scale of enjoyment, and the people paid $20 rated it about a 9 after they had lied. The payment was sufficient justification for their actions. Those who were paid only one dollar said they had really enjoyed the original boring task (about 23 out of 25)! Only the last group experienced severe **cognitive dissonance** and changed their mind. They evidently thought, "I convinced someone I liked it for only a dollar; I must have liked it."

Many others in social psychology can trace their lineage to the Gestaltists. The classic **conformity experiments** of Solomon Asch (1907–1996) (e.g. Asch, 1955) proved that when seven people have already publicly stated that an obviously short line is really long, the eighth person, the real subject of the experiment, will go along between 30% and 50% of the time, depending on the prestige of the confederates who are in on the game. Asch's mentor was Max Wertheimer, and his colleague, for almost 20 years at Swarthmore, was Wolfgang Köhler. One of Asch's students, in a postdoctoral year, was Stanley Milgram, whose classic **obedience studies** showed that 65% of people would give a man apparent shocks of 450 volts, even under protests, after several innocuous suggestions from a man in a lab coat (At least they were led to believe that they were administering shocks).

What all of these studies in social psychology have in common is the notion that people under tension and conflict seek resolution of those conflicts. Koffka's notion that we operate according to perceived *forces* and *constraints* in the environment is true for the social as well as the physical landscape. They also explore the world of *intention* and *goals* that was noted by Brentano, the great-grandfather of Gestalt. People act on belief rather than real constraints. And finally, these studies elegantly take into account, as much as possible, the whole of forces acting on people's thought and behavior as they really act. They have achieved the goal that Carl Stumpf set out for his Gestaltist students: that psychology be "the study of daily life raised to a science."

Note

1. "Lewin" has been pronounced both in the German pronunciation ("LaVEEN") and the American ("LOOwin"). Lewin himself changed the pronunciation when he came to the U.S. to ease his children's adjustment to the new society. Either pronunciation is correct.

7 William James and Functionalism

In the preceding two chapters, we have been discussing the roots of psychology in the German revolutions in philosophy and physiology. In 1875, at roughly the same time that Brentano and Wundt were becoming famous, a newly minted MD, who had been teaching anatomy and physiology as a way of keeping busy while recuperating from a nervous breakdown, was assigned to teach his first course at Harvard in "the New Psychology," without ever having taken such a course himself. That man was William James. Up until then, in spite of being a member of the second-richest family in the state of New York, William, in his own mind, had not amounted to much. He had not begun an illustrious writing career, like his younger brother Henry; he had not distinguished himself in the Civil War, like his even younger brothers Robertson and Wilkerson. He even suspected that his Harvard medical degree was a bit of a fake: Some of the examining board were friends of the family and he had had an easy time of the exam. He never intended to practice medicine anyway.

And yet William James would soon begin the long process of writing one of the indisputable gems of the history of psychology. *The Principles of Psychology*, said the distinguished historian of ideas Jacques Barzun, was an American masterpiece:

> It is a masterpiece in the classic and total sense—no need of a descriptive or limiting word before or after: not "of observation" or "of prose writing," not more "scientific" than "humanistic." One can point to these and other merits if one is so inclined, but the fused substance defies reduction to a list of epithets. No matter how many unexpected qualities are found in it—wit, pathos, imaginative understanding, polemical skill, moral passion, cosmic vision and sheer learning—the work remains always greater than their sum.
>
> (Barzun, 1983, p. 34)

It is also a masterpiece that, more than any other single work, is responsible for leading American psychology away from the psychology of Wundt and imbuing it with the characteristics of its author. If American psychology is today remarkably intellectually diverse, open-minded, inclusive of many ideas and pragmatic in the best sense of the word, then it owes those characteristics in large part to William James and the school he inadvertently founded, American functionalism. And then he went on to make his mark on American philosophy with his philosophy of pragmatism and the psychology of religion with *The Varieties of Religious Experience*. Before we discuss his ideas, however, we will spend some time on his life and that of his remarkable family, perhaps America's most famous intellectual family of the 19th century.

William James

Figure 7.1 William James (January 11, 1842—August 26, 1910)
Source: Courtesy of MS Am 1092 (1185), Houghton Library, Harvard University

The James Family

William James the psychologist (1842–1910) was the grandson of William James of Albany (1771–1832), who emigrated from Ireland around the time of the Revolutionary War with little money. Through hard work and shrewd business sense, he became rich off the new Erie Canal, amassing a fortune worth the equivalent of perhaps 1.7 billion in today's dollars (Lewis, 1991; amount converted to 2018 dollars). The James family came to own half of Albany and all of Syracuse in New York. By the time William the psychologist came along, it would be said that the fortune allowed three generations of the family to get along without "being guilty of a stroke of business." But William of Albany was a stern man, a rock-ribbed Calvinist Presbyterian, who used his money as a means of control over his unruly children. The psychologist's father, Henry Sr. (1811–1882), William's fourth son, rebelled against the strictures and was determined to raise his own children in a more liberal fashion.[1] In fact, as a man of leisure, he saw the education of his children, particularly his boys, as almost his primary occupation, and he was always somewhat dissatisfied with their schooling. In New York or Newport, Rhode Island, he would get disgusted by American provincialism and impulsively take the whole family off to Europe. When there, the father would typically meet with Thomas Carlyle, Alfred Lord Tennyson, John Stuart Mill and others. There, after a season or two, he would get disgusted by European snobbery and long for good old American values and come back. Thus, the James children were educated in irregular fashion by tutors, governesses and private schools in London, Paris, Geneva, Bonn, Boulogne, New York and Newport. Young William was so brilliant that he could be interested anywhere on almost any subject. He was fluent in French at 14, in German at 18 and a talented artist and budding scientist, to boot. Young Henry, the future novelist, was so brilliant and introverted that he was bored by almost any schooling at all. Robertson and Wilkerson, the youngest boys, were gregarious and indifferent to school in any form. Alice, the baby of the family, was quiet, but sharply observant of the ways of the traveling circus that was her family. The family reacted to all the movement by becoming remarkably close; Henry James once described the James family as being like a country all its own, wherever the family may have traveled.

If you think that being with that family was both exhilarating and exhausting, you would be right. Picture the following scene at the James home in Newport, Rhode Island, around 1860. Henry Senior, a man with boundless energy, barges in, full of enthusiasm about a public lecture he has just given, yet again, on the mysteries of Swedenborg, a mystic who believed that God is not a personality but "Infinite Divine love and wisdom in union with the soul of man" (Allen, 1967, p. 19). Henry Sr. seems like a character out of Dickens—short, paunchy, balding, with a peg leg and round spectacles. Ralph Waldo Emerson, a family friend, described Henry Sr. as "the most childlike, unconscious and unblushing egoist it has ever been my fortune to encounter in the ranks of manhood" (Allen, 1967, p. 13). His children were embarrassed when other children asked what their father did, so he told them, "Say I'm a philosopher, say I'm a seeker for truth, say I'm a lover of my kind, say I'm an author of books, if you like, but best of all, just say I'm a student." In this scenario, around the dinner table are the father and the stable, sensible mother Mary James and their five children: William, 18 years old; Henry, 16; Wilkerson, 15; Robertson, 14; and Alice, 11. The poet's son, Edward Emerson, is a witness:

> "The adipose and affectionate Wilkie," as his father called him would say something and instantly be corrected by the little cock-sparrow Bob, the youngest, but good naturedly defend his statement and then Henry (Junior) would emerge from his silence in defence of Wilkie. Then Bob would be more impertinently insistant [sic] and Mr. James would advance as Moderator and William, the eldest, join in. The voice of the Moderator presently would be drowned by the combatants and he soon came down vigorously in the arena and when, in excited

argument, the dinner knives might not be absent from eagerly gesticulating hands, dear Mrs. James, more conventional, but bright as well as motherly, would look at me, laughingly reassuring, saying, "Don't be disturbed Edward, they won't stab each other. This is usual when the boys come home." And the quiet little sister ate her dinner, smiling, close to the combatants. Mr. James considered this debate, within bounds, excellent for the boys. In their speech, singularly mature and picturesque, as well as vehement, the Gaelic (Irish) element in their descent always showed. Even if they blundered, they saved themselves by wit.

(Allen, 1967, p. 67)

Thus, William James had an extraordinary education by a freethinking and indulgent father. But such a generous father was even more difficult to deal with than a stern one. He let them know that they could do whatever they wanted, as long as they became great. He forbade his elder boys from entering the Civil War (he

Figure 7.2 Henry James Sr. (1811–1882), William's father, shown here in 1854 with William's brother, the future novelist, at age 11, Henry James Jr. (1843–1916)

considered them, probably correctly, as not tough enough for the experience), but allowed Wilkie and Bob to enlist as white officers in Union regiments of free blacks, the Massachusetts 54th and 55th. In the attack on Fort Wagner in South Carolina (depicted in Edward Zwick's movie *Glory*), Wilkie's regiment, lost three-quarters of its men. Wilkie and Bob came home wounded and broken by the experience. Surely as much was expected from William and Henry in their respective fields.

Evolution and Physiology

William was admitted to Harvard's then new Lawrence Scientific School in 1861, where he was to study chemistry, but switched to anatomy. In 1864, he entered Harvard Medical School. Like his teacher, Dr. Oliver Wendell Holmes (father of William's friend, the future distinguished Supreme Court justice), he was skeptical of medicine at the time. James wrote to his parents that, excepting surgery, much of medicine was "humbug." "[A] doctor does more by the moral effect of his presence on the patient and family, than by anything else. He also extracts money from them" (cited in Allen, 1967, p. 98). As it happens, though, in these years, James was exposed to what was then cutting-edge experimental physiology, from teachers and peers who had studied with the best scientist-practitioners in the French clinical tradition (some of whom taught Freud; see Chapter 9), as well as with Helmholtz's peers in Germany (Taylor, 1996). Much of this found its way into his psychology. Indeed, James is by now so famous for his work in psychology and philosophy that it is sometimes overlooked that some of his earliest work involved electrical stimulation of the cortex in animals (Taylor, 1996).

Barely three years after the publication of *The Origin of Species*, James was influenced by his professors of comparative anatomy, Jeffries Wyman, who was open to Darwin's theory, and Louis Agassiz, a formidable Swiss naturalist, who believed in special creation. William even went on an expedition to South America with Agassiz, in 1865, where he caught smallpox instead of zoological specimens. Although he admired Agassiz's excellent command of zoological details, he found his creationist thinking somewhat rigid. Indeed, among William's earliest publications are capable, informed reviews of books by Darwin's bulldog, T. H. Huxley (1864), his fellow evolutionist, Alfred Russel Wallace (1864) and Darwin's *The Variation of Animals and Plants Under Domestication*. In the latter, James expresses dismay that in Darwin's theory, the only law appears to be caprice: "caprice in inheriting, caprice in transmitting, caprice everywhere in turn" (James, 1868/1987, p. 234).

In this, he had caught Darwin's message exactly right: Caprice, or chance, is the central engine of evolution. Almost alone among the major psychologists of his day (see Chapter 4), he would continue to emphasize the lack of direction in Darwinism. Although he used Herbert Spencer's evolutionist *Principles of Psychology* (1870) as the textbook in his first psychology course, he came to believe his theory of upward evolution to be vague and overblown. He was profoundly distrustful, in fact, of anyone who would claim to make cosmically grandiose theories: He called Haeckel's work a "schoolboy performance" (James, 1875, p. 297) and woe to anyone who employed any of the theories of G.W.F. Hegel in their arguments (James, 1882/1912). In any case, in casting his lot with Darwin, he had bet on the right horse; in his own *Principles of Psychology* (1890), as we will soon see, natural selection would become a metaphor for consciousness itself.

The Power to Choose

One more episode in James's life is crucial in understanding his subsequent psychology and philosophy, and that is the matter of his nervous breakdown. After returning from Brazil, he went to Germany, where he took a course with du Bois-Reymond in Berlin and intended to study with Wundt and Helmholtz, but never got around to it. His nerves and back were failing, so he went to the therapeutic "baths" in Dresden. This did not help, so he returned to Harvard and Cambridge, where he completed his medical thesis and the then easy 10-minute oral examination for the MD. And then, in early 1870, at the age of 28, he collapsed.

He wrote of the experience of depression years later, disguised as that of a "Frenchman," but that James admitted was about himself:

> Whilst in this state of philosophic pessimism and general depression of spirits about my prospects, I went one evening in a dressing room in the twilight to procure some article that was there; when suddenly there fell upon me without warning, just as if it came out of darkness, a horrible fear of my own existence. Simultaneously there arose in my mind the image of an epileptic patient whom I had seen in the asylum, a black haired youth with greenish skin, entirely idiotic, who used to sit all day on one of the benches or rather shelves against the wall, with his knees drawn up against his chin and the course grey undershirt, which was his only garment, drawn over them, inclosing his entire figure ... That shape am I, I felt, potentially. Nothing I possess can defend me against that fate, if the hour should strike for me as it struck for him. There was such a horror of him and such a perception of my own momentary discrepancy from him, that it was as if something hitherto solid within my breast had given way entirely and I became a mass of quivering fear. After this, the universe changed for me altogether. I awoke morning after morning with a horrible dread in the pit of my stomach and with a sense of the insecurity of life that I never knew before and that I have never felt since. It was like a revelation; and although the immediate feelings passed away, the experience has made me sympathetic with the morbid feelings of others ever since. It gradually faded, but for months, I was unable to go into the dark alone.
>
> (James, 1902/1982, pp. 160–161)

Some of James's biographers have interpreted this passage literally to mean that sometime in 1870, William James was committed to the McLean Asylum, a private mental hospital long affiliated with Harvard, where he may have witnessed the scene (e.g. Anderson, 1980; Feinstein, 1981; Richards, 1987). Others conclude that the story is not relating a single episode, but is true of James only in the metaphorical sense, as William James was plagued with depressions on and off throughout his life, sometimes it seems at the end of each school year (e.g. Simon, 1998. See especially Menand, 1998, for some expert historical sleuthing).[2] In addition to a possible biological predisposition for depression, one cause (or symptom) of his malady was an obsession with the mind-body problem. He had clearly gotten the materialistic bug in Germany, and the possibility that life was therefore meaningless weighed on his mind. If the materialistic hypothesis that all things have a natural cause were true, then there would also be no free will:

> I'm swamped in the empirical philosophy. I feel that we are Nature through and through, that we are wholly conditioned, that not a wiggle of our will happens save as the result of physical laws; and yet, notwithstanding, we are *en rapport* with reason.
> (James letter in 1869, cited in Allen, 1967, p. 164)

He began the road back by borrowing an inspiration from the French philosopher Renouvier on April 29, 1870:

> I think that yesterday was a crisis in my life. I finished the first part of Renouvier's second *Essais* and see no reason why his definition of Free Will—the sustaining of a thought *because I choose to* when I might have other thoughts—need be the definition of an illusion. At any rate, I will assume at present—until next year—that it is no illusion. My first act of free will shall be to believe in free will.... I will go a step further with my will and not only act with it, but believe as well; believe in my individual reality and creative power. My belief, to be sure, *can't* be optimistic—but I will posit life (the real, the good) in the self-governing resistance of the ego to the world. Life shall be built in doing and suffering and creating.
> (cited in H. James [Wm.'s son], 1920, vol. 1, p. 147; emphasis in original)

His breakdown and recovery, the first of many in his life, shows the core of William James's philosophy, which influenced his psychology greatly. On the one hand, he was fully aware of the materialist basis for modern physiology and was well acquainted with Darwin's ideas. On the other hand, he refused to accept these mechanisms as fate. Surely a person's belief could change his own outlook. His own father, after all, had suffered a breakdown and had pulled himself out of it by belief in a generous God. William was unable to accept the literal religious solution, but recognized that the act of believing itself, whether or not the belief in God could be proved true, would be beneficial. As we shall see, in his psychology, he would try to reconcile with the mind's ability to choose with the body's purely mechanical workings. In his psychology of religion, he would avoid attempting to prove whether a God exists, while focusing on how belief in God is useful. And in his philosophy, called pragmatism, he would propose that the ultimate value of a particular philosophy is whether believing it makes any real difference in the world.

The Principles of Psychology

In 1878, after teaching psychology, as well as anatomy and physiology for several years and setting up a very small laboratory for Wundtian "physiological psychology" experiments, James felt himself ready to make a major statement in psychology. He signed a contract with a publisher for a book, which was supposed to take two years to complete. It took 12. It is not merely a compendium of facts and experimental results, although it has such things in it. It is a thoroughgoing revision of what psychology should be about, a demanding and far-ranging exploration of the mind and how it might be related to the brain. Indeed, it is an explanation of why we need a mind at all, what it might be composed of and how it is meant to be used. In a time when everybody who was anybody in psychology looked to Germany for the state of the art, it is not German. In spite of the fact that William James was one of the most traveled and cosmopolitan men in America, and in spite of the fact that it alludes to work in several different languages, it seems paradoxically American.

The experience of reading it, which I suggest to every psychologist, is both daunting and inspiring. It is difficult because it was not written in our own time, because it demands some philosophical sophistication and because its views of the mind are still radical even today. It is inspiring, because just as you're about to give up, there will be a brilliantly clear, even funny example of what James is talking about that gives you something to think about. As in reading Shakespeare, it takes a while to get into the mindset, but when you do, you begin to hear the particular Jamesian voice: erudite, curious about everything, compassionate, serious but not sober. My job will be to guide you through the difficult parts and provide you with the inspiring parts, so that you can hear James's voice.

The first chapters of the *Principles* are concerned with the same philosophical problems that had troubled James in 1870 and that had troubled the philosopher-psychologists of his day. Remember, in Chapter 1, how Thomas Kuhn suggested that before a science has a paradigm, writers must argue in great detail their philosophical assumptions. James's first task was therefore to convince his readers what psychology is and should be. How do we reconcile the materialistic physiological world with the mental world? James was well aware of the problem of having mental events cause physical ones and vice versa, which had been around since Descartes. If we look at only the physical side and claim that we are nothing but the physical, we are a mechanical robot, an automaton; if we claim we are nothing but thought, we are only spirit. Neither of these solutions is acceptable, as it either reduces thought to physiology or simply ignores the work of scientists like Helmholtz. Dualism is the only answer, but he describes this answer in a particularly vivid way:

> To comprehend completely the consequences of the [automaton] dogma so confidently enunciated, one should unflinchingly apply it to the most complicated examples. The movements of our tongues and pens, the flashings of our eyes in conversation, are of course events of a material order and as such their causal antecedents must be exclusively material. If we knew thoroughly the nervous system of Shakespeare and as thoroughly all his environing conditions, we should be able to show why at a certain period of his life his hand came to trace on certain sheets of paper those crabbed little black marks which we for shortness' sake call *Hamlet*. We should understand the rationale of every erasure and alteration therein and we should understand all this without in the slightest degree acknowledging the existence of the thoughts in Shakespeare's mind. The

words and sentences would be taken, not as signs of anything beyond themselves, but as little outward facts, pure and simple. In like manner we might exhaustively write the biography of those two hundred pounds, more or less, of warmish albuminoid matter called Martin Luther, without ever implying that it felt.

But, on the other hand nothing in all this could prevent us from giving an equally complete account of either Luther's or Shakespeare's spiritual history, an account in which every gleam or thought or emotion should find its place. The mind-history would run alongside the body-history of each man and each point in the one would correspond to, but not react upon, a point in the other. So the melody floats from the harp-string, but neither checks nor quickens its vibrations; so the shadow runs alongside the pedestrian, but in no way influences his steps.

(*Principles*, pp. 136–137)

This sort of dualism is called **parallelism** or **double-aspect dualism**. It's not Cartesian dualism: by this time, there is no soul in psychology. Every mind event must have a brain and nerve event—they are in fact the same—but it is impossible to study them at the same time. To James, psychology was the study of the mind events, but that doesn't mean we should ignore the brain.

So, for James, psychology is the study of the mind side of the equation, first and foremost. It is the "Science of Mental Life, both of its phenomena and of its conditions. The phenomena are such things as we call feelings, desires, cognitions, reasonings, decisions and the like" (James, 1890/1983, p. 15). So, far so good. But are we therefore restricted only to ourselves in psychology, since these seem to be interior things, depending on consciousness, or can we study minds of children and animals? How do we know if something has a mind? James's answer, for both us and other organisms, is that we know something has a mind when it appears to have a choice in doing this or that. Consciousness is a "selecting agency," a "fighter for ends." In his own words, "*The pursuance of future ends and the choice of means for their attainment are thus the mark and criterion of the presence of mentality in a phenomenon*" (*Principles*, p. 21, emphasis original). To paraphrase some of his examples, we don't think iron filings or champagne bubbles have minds, even though they move, because they will not make detours around obstacles; if they meet a barrier, they stay there. If Romeo and Juliet are separated by a wall, however, they don't run to the wall and stick to it; Romeo scales the wall.

Moreover, it is no accident that those organisms that are higher on the evolutionary scale seem to make more choices, because consciousness has evolved. Reflexes and instincts are more likely to be body things and not mind things, precisely because they operate in a rigid fashion. We could have a brain that is made only of rigid reflexes, and they would always fire off when they meet the right stimulus. They would be reliable, but narrow in response, not adaptable to many different situations. We could instead have a very flexible brain that fires off in many different situations, but it would make lots of mistakes; it would be an unstable equilibrium. Some of those mistakes would be, no doubt, deadly. If there were no preference in the organism, it would not evolve, as the bad accidents and the good ones would balance; if it preferred something that was bad for it, it would be even worse off ("An animal that should take pleasure in a feeling of suffocation would, if that pleasure were efficacious enough to make him immerse his head in water, enjoy a longevity of four or five minutes" [*Principles*, p. 146]). So, the fact that we prefer things, on the whole (not always), that are good for us is due to the fact that they would be the ones to survive evolution in the largest number. "Good" and "bad" here are determined after the fact, where good means "helps survival."

So, animals are evolved to select things that help them survive because only those who did select such things would have survived! Lower animals can survive only in narrow environments, because of their rigid responses. Animals that survive in many environments must be equipped to make choices among many different things. They must, therefore, have a mechanism to evaluate those things in terms of the survival goal, of dealing with uncertainty. We are never more conscious than when we are confused, says James; if we know what to do, we rely on habit. Thus, those animals that have evolved to make choices are more likely to have survived novel threats, and the mechanism that allows them to choose is consciousness. Consciousness is most valuable in dealing with new uncertain situations. It may have evolved by Darwinian accident, by natural selection, but now that we've got it, boy is it useful!

Now the last two paragraphs, a summary of Chapter 5 in *The Principles*, are about the brain side of the equation. What would the mind look like, the melody that floats from the harp strings of that brain? The answer is:

1. It would exhibit great instability in its moment-to-moment action, always on, always changing.
2. It would choose ideas and responses that would help the organism survive and adapt to current conditions, which are "good" in those terms.
3. It would not always be right, because there is no ultimate good that it knows about, only good for that moment and the state of knowledge of that organism.
4. Those selections that it makes would be more likely to occur again if the selection does accomplish a goal, does help survival, either directly or indirectly.

In other words, James first made the argument of how consciousness could have evolved bodily or materially and then claimed that the mind would also operate in a Darwinian manner. Consciousness is about the survival of the fittest idea.

Except for one thing. To James, there was no such thing as ideas. He was not an associationist, like James Mill or John Stuart Mill. He said,

> This multitude of ideas existing absolutely, yet clinging together, weaving an endless carpet of themselves, like dominoes in ceaseless change or the bits of glass in the kaleidoscope—whence to they get their fantastic laws of clinging and why do they cling in just the shapes they do?
>
> (p. 17)

For James, the brain is made up only of firings or nervous impulses, electrical energy, and it is not necessarily the case that each impulse leads to one idea; the impulses may sum up, leading to a discharge that makes us have a mental idea, but the ideas are not things in themselves. He did not believe in Locke's metaphor of the "storehouse of ideas," and he certainly didn't agree with James Mill's or John Stuart Mill's notions of a compound idea that is made up of many subideas. Nor does he wish to assume that there are "things" stored unconsciously in the mind. You may think of your "mother" as a complex idea, but every time you think of her, the concept of mother has been subtly changed by all the other times that you have thought about her. You call the mother that you think about now as the same idea as the mother that you thought about when you were 12, but it is not. That thought is not stable, and therefore ideas are not stable entities contained in the mind like gold nuggets.

James claimed that he was a *naturalist of the mind* or even a *radical empiricist*. (As a radical empiricist, he follows Hume's preference for ruthless observation of the mind's processes, without his reliance on ideas or impressions [James, 1912]). He believed that introspection, the observer reflecting on his own inner experience, was the most important method for psychology (Remember, he defined psychology as the study of *mental* life; he would have us study the thoughts of Martin Luther, not his "warmish albuminoid matter."). And the objects of study for psychology are *thoughts about things*, not things. We have seen this before, of course; the structuralists called it the experience error and James called the same phenomenon the **psychologist's fallacy**—assuming that the thing and the thought of the thing are the same. He wanted his psychology to be *only* about what he could observe about the mind directly, with no other assumptions.

Hadn't Wundt already done that, you may ask? Well, no, said James, because his experimental self-observation distorts the process of thinking, artificially chops it up into bits. True, the elements obtained by Wundt's method are not ideas, but elements of consciousness. But in the *Principles*, James states about the experimental method of Weber, Fechner and Wundt that

> This method taxes patience to the utmost and could hardly have arisen in country whose natives can be *bored*. [. . .] The simple and open method of attack having done what it can, the method of patience, starving out and harassing to death is tried; the mind must submit to a regular *siege*, in which minute advantages gained day and night by the forces that hem her in must sum themselves up at last into her overthrow. There is little of the grand style in these new prism, pendulum and chronograph-philosophers. They mean business, not chivalry.
>
> (p. 192; emphasis in original)[3]

In part, his dislike for Wundt was simply a difference in temperament. (And some of it was envy for Wundt's phenomenal productivity: An American student gave Wundt a typewriter, which James called an "evil gift" because it would allow Wundt to churn out even more work.) Although James set up a laboratory in 1875, he didn't have the patience for using it for much more than class demonstrations. But he also thought that there was a danger that the structuralists might be amassing a lot of so-called facts that either could not be replicated or, if reliable, would not be linked to a useful theory.

So, in sum, what James was after was a mind that reconciled Darwinian principles with the power of choice. He clearly thought that associationism and structuralism were not the answer. What was his answer? We turn to this most famous idea of William James next.

The Stream of Consciousness

> Consciousness, then, does not appear to itself chopped up in bits. Such words as chain or train does not describe it fitly as it presents itself in the first instance. It is nothing jointed; it flows. A river or a stream are the metaphors by which it is most naturally described. In talking of it hereafter, let us call it the stream of thought, of consciousness or of subjective life.
>
> (*Principles*, p. 233)

Jacques Barzun (1983) relates the following story about William James that points up a critical aspect of his thought and will get us started on understanding his major idea. He is walking across Harvard Yard with a boy from Harvard and a girl from Radcliffe. The students are talking with James about the lecture he has just given, and he responds to them excitedly as if they were his equals. Barreling down on them is a distracted old man with a flowing beard. He is muttering to himself, walking fast, not looking where he is going. The group has to step aside to avoid being run over. When he is a safe distance away, the girl says to James, "Whoever he is, he's the epitome of the absent-minded professor."

"What you really mean," says James, "is that he is present-minded somewhere else" (Barzun, 1983, p. 6). Then he turns away from the students to go visit a student in the dorm who is sick and who might need a doctor but is too stubborn to send for one.

James's goal for his psychology was to provide a description of the mind in process without any assumptions. It is an extreme present-mindedness. The notion that we have experiences stored up is an assumption. The notion of stable ideas is an assumption. The notion of elements of consciousness is an assumption. There is, in the mind, only a continuous flow of experience. It is always now in the mind, even when one is thinking of the past. Thought just goes on. James said that in order to be truly accurate about the description of the mind as process, always flowing, it is best not to say "I think," but "it thinks," in the sense of "it rains."

In other words, one can talk of the **stream of consciousness**. There are five characteristics of this stream:

1. Every thought tends to be a part of a personal consciousness.
2. Within each personal consciousness, thought is always changing.
3. Within each personal consciousness, thought is perceived as continuous.
4. It always appears to deal with objects independent of itself.
5. It is interested in some parts of these objects to the exclusion of others and welcomes or rejects—*chooses* from among them, in a word—all the while.

(*Principles*, p. 220, emphasis original)

The first notion, that *every thought is personal*, means simply that my thoughts are mine and your thoughts are yours. This is one of those statements that seems trivial but turns out to have profound consequences. We experience consciousness as an "I," not a "we" and not as "this thought" or "that thought" but as "my thought." Every thought is *owned*. James discusses an exception to this rule to show how critical it is. Some patients of the French psychologist Pierre Janet (see Chapter 9) developed split selves under hypnotic states. Moreover, I cannot know directly what you know and because of that, our experiences are different (recall Bacon's "Idols of the Cave," Chapter 3).

The second characteristic of consciousness, the notion that *thought is always changing*, has two aspects. First, it always flows along. To get some idea of how this might work, close your eyes and attempt to think of absolutely nothing. Chances are, you cannot easily do it. Thoughts are always popping into your head.

The notion of a constantly changing stream also means that you can't think the same thought twice or have the same experience twice:

> The grass out the window now looks to me of the same green in the sun as in the shade and yet a painter would have to paint one part of it dark brown, another part bright yellow to give its real sensational effect ... The eye's sensibility to light is at its maximum when the eye is first exposed and blunts itself with surprising rapidity. A long night's sleep will make us see things as twice as brightly on wakening.... We feel things differently according as we are sleepy or awake, differently at night and in the morning, differently in summer and winter; and above all differently in childhood, manhood and old age.
>
> (*Principles*, pp. 225–226)

If you think about an event in your life or a person in your life, as for example, your mother now as opposed to say, five years ago, your view has changed. You may say you remember something about your mother years ago, but what James is saying is that memory is not retrieved in a neat little wrapped package but is retrieved through the lens of and colored by all of your previous experience with your mother, and that experience is changed every time you think of her. Just as you can't step in the same river twice, you can never have the same thought twice.

The third characteristic of the stream is that it is *continuous*. There are no breaks in it. Even when we lose track of time, when we notice it again, the stream is perceived as ours. When we sleep, the stream goes on in dreams, but even if we are technically unconscious and do not remember parts of the stream, when we wake up, the stream is still ours. It may seem as though there are breaks in it, but the breaks, says James, are like the joints in bamboo, bumps in a continuous process:

> A silence may be broken by a thunder-clap and we may be so stunned and confused for a moment by the thought as to give no instant account of what happened. But that very confusion is a mental state and a state that passes us straight over from the silence to the sound. The transition between the thought of one object and the thought of another is no more a break in the thought than a joint in a bamboo is a break in the wood. It is a part of consciousness as much as the joint is a part of the bamboo.
>
> (*Principles*, pp. 233–234)

The fourth characteristic of consciousness is *that it always appears to deal with objects independent of itself*. Of course, this is merely appearance, because all the mind has to deal with are the results of perceptual processes, as should be obvious by now (see Chapters 2 and 3). But consciousness must have something to grab hold of to do its work. We must be careful not to misinterpret, however, what the object is that it grabs ahold of. The object is not a thing, but a momentary pulse of consciousness. It is not the apple, but a particular moment of thought about an apple:

> If, for example, the thought be "the pack of cards is on the table" we say, "Well, isn't it a thought of the pack of cards? Isn't it of the cards as included in the pack? Isn't it of the table? And of the legs of the table as well? The table has legs—how can you think the table without virtually thinking its legs? Hasn't our thought, then, all these parts—one part for the pack and another for the table? and within the pack-part a part for each card? As within the table-part a part for each leg? And isn't each of these parts an idea? And can our thought, then, be anything but an assemblage or pack of ideas, each answering to some element of what it knows?"
>
> <u>Now not one of these assumptions is true</u>. The thought taken as an example is, in the first place, not of "a pack of cards" it is of "the-pack-of-cards-is-on-the-table" an entirely different subjective phenomenon, whose Object implies the pack and every one of the cards in it, but whose constitution bears very little resemblance to that of the thought of the pack *per se*. What a thought *is* and what it may be developed into or explained to stand for and be equivalent to, are two things.
>
> (*Principles*, p. 269, underline added; italics in original)

The above argument is obviously a blow against the idea theory of mind, but it is also a blow in favor of the notion of present-mindedness. If we consider when we might utter "the-pack-of-cards-is-on-the-table," it is probably in some situation like answering the question, "Where is the pack of cards?" In such a situation, it is the "where-ness" that we wish to emphasize, not what tables or packs are made of. If we answer "the-pack-of-cards-is-on-the-table" to the question, "What is that on the table?" it would be the "what-ness," not the pack-ness or the table-ness and so on. *At that moment*, a thought has a particular function in ever-changing, ongoing thought and every time we utter the same phrase, it might mean something slightly different.

And finally, the fifth and most crucial aspect of the mind is *that it chooses, it selects, it is interested in some things to the exclusion of others*. There are therefore two aspects of thought; the flow of the stream, a moment-by-moment procession of thoughts, feelings, images, perceptions, bits of memory. This is the stream of consciousness, but if that were all consciousness was, we could never do anything. There must also be some faculty of attention that picks certain aspects of the stream and holds them for a moment to connect it with another bit, to isolate it and put it to use for a current purpose. There is the stream, which just is always there, and attention, which snatches thought bubbles like a fishing pole snatches up fish.

In your mind at this moment there may be, at least available to your consciousness, a feeling of irritation and confusion as you read this. You may be angry at the "author" for putting it so obtusely (that is, unclearly). You may be momentarily conscious that your seat is uncomfortable, that the room is warm or cold, of an embarrassing memory of a stupid remark made on a date last night (Your mind is now "wandering"; focus, please!). The essence of reasoning is that you ignore some thoughts and feelings and select others and attempt to connect some of the contents of the ever-changing stream into a "train of thought." This is not done automatically; it takes effort. We must actually construct our train out of near-random variability in the flow of thought.

In this way, James has constructed a model of consciousness that is a consequence of Darwinian brain evolution and works almost like evolution itself. Our everyday conscious experience is a highly variable stream of thought bubbles; the human organism, in adapting to the environment that it finds itself in, selects from that stream what appears at the moment to be the most adaptive thought to act upon at that time. If it turns out to be useful, the organism attempts to repeat the sequence and turn it into habit, leaving consciousness to deal with new threats. It is a balance between scientific mechanism and free will.

I have gone on at some length about the Jamesian view of consciousness, because it is somewhat difficult for those new to his ideas to absorb them. To cement the concepts in the reader's mind, it's necessary to put them all together in a contemporary working example, before we go on to examine the implications of the Jamesian consciousness for the rest of his psychology and for psychology in general.

Suppose you are ready to go for a drive, but you cannot find your keys. What this means in Jamesian terms is that you are desperate for the thought bubble about the location of your keys to reach your conscious mind. So you try a number of habits that have been successful in the past in bringing this about. You go down a list of likely locations; you retrace your steps mentally or literally. You are not really in control of the stream—you can't just go to the address of that memory and lift it off the shelf. Instead, you must wait for the memory to reappear and try to increase the probability of its reappearance by trying certain methods.

The discovery of those keys is the first step in firing off a long string of habits in getting the car started. Although you are certainly conscious while doing these things, each individual step requires little notice now. Habits are "the enormous flywheel of society, its most precious conservative agent" that allow us to save up the useful discoveries (*Principles*, p. 125). When you were first driving, you now remember, it was very tiring to keep track of all the things you needed to do; it was a novel activity and required a lot of expenditure of conscious thought. In fact, now you realize being fully conscious of every move you make while you drive is actually likely to increase your possibility of a car accident, as the well-practiced pianist cannot consider every note before playing it. As you are driving along, your consciousness is occupied with new things. If it is a place you have not been to, you must focus on how to get there. If you reach a difficult entrance ramp to the freeway, you may turn the radio down to concentrate.

On the freeway, going 60 miles an hour, many perceptions, thoughts and feelings flow through your mind. Your attention is always switching, like a flashlight in a dark room, to different stimuli that you assume to be external to you on the road and some, such as hunger, that are internal. A thought that has no doubt occurred to many of us one time or another (although as my consciousness is different than yours, there is no way for me to know for sure) is that if you suddenly veered a couple of feet to one direction, you could collide with a car or truck and possibly *die*. Most of us let that thought bubble pass and do not pick it (as we say, we don't "dwell" on it), but it is there. If you are the sort of person for whom such thoughts do come to the top of your stream frequently, you may develop a phobia of driving. Those who are seized with fear when going over a bridge are not much different from the rest of us, but the thought that it is perfectly possible to go off the edge keeps coming up for them, uncontrollably. The rest of us don't attend to the thought. Our ability to keep away from such thoughts takes energy; we put our energy into other feedback loops to keep other, more pleasant thoughts occurring in the stream, but our control of the stream is really a matter of hope that we can, over time, harness the wonderful, ever-changing flow of the stream to help us adapt to and survive in our world.

The Self

In spite of the stream of consciousness, says James, we still have a strong sense of self. We believe that "I am the same self that I was yesterday" (*Principles*, p. 316). Our consciousness is personal and we own our thought. We also feel we own our bodies and much else. As a starting point, James defines a man's self as

> *the sum total of all that he* CAN *call his*, not only his body and his psychic powers, but his clothes and his house, his wife and children, his ancestors and friends, his reputation and works, his lands and horses and yacht and bank-account. All these things give him the same emotions. If they wax and prosper, he feels triumphant; if they dwindle and die away, he feels cast down—not necessarily in the same degree for each thing, but in much the same way for all.
> (*Principles*, pp. 279–280; emphasis in original)

The people and things of this list, outside the person, plus the person's body, are part of what James calls the **empirical self** or me. He includes them in the self, because if you wound them you wound a person's self. We've all known people who seem to live the adage: "love me, love my car." Alternatively, I have known several academics who, before they got the PhD (in pre-word-processor days) kept the text of their dissertation in the freezer in case the house burned down, so important was the work and the distinction on which it depended, to them (I actually had a dissertation student whose house *did* burn down, so it's not a bad idea).

In addition, one has **social selves**. Properly speaking, you have as many social selves as there are persons in your life whose opinion you care about.

> Many a youth who is demure enough before his parents and teachers swaggers and swears like a pirate among his tough young friends. We do not show ourselves to our children as to our club companions to our customers as to the laborers we employ, to our own masters as to our intimate friends. From this there results what practically is a division of the man into several selves; and this

may be a discordant splitting, as where one is afraid to let one set of his acquaintances know him as he is elsewhere; or it may be a perfectly harmonious division of labor, as where one tender to his children is stern to the soldiers or prisoners under his command.

(*Principles*, p. 282)

It is worth noting that although it is possible to create selves in a self-conscious manipulative way, for most of us, shifting among many of our selves is as natural and automatic as anything we do; the context we are in calls forth the proper self.

Above all these is what James calls the **spiritual self**. This is our catalog of inner abilities or faculties that we perceive ourselves to own. Our pride in our intelligence, good memory, morality, ability to speak and write and make ethical decisions is the spiritual self. So are the acts of attending, assenting, negating and making an effort. The spiritual self is the inner, subjective self, the self-conscious self that selects, evaluates and rejects. It is the spiritual self that puts the things in the ongoing stream to use, that picks the things that are useful at that moment. It is that which reflects. Many of us would call it our "true" self, but by this point in our discussion, you may begin, properly, to wonder whether a true self exists. (You might have occasion to say, "I'm not myself today." If not, then who are you?)

Among the things the spiritual self reflects on are the other selves, the possible selves, the selves-to-be. The self of all the other selves, the lynchpin self that "pulls yourself together" evaluates your actions and passes judgment. Do we feel satisfied or dissatisfied in ourselves? James calls this *self-feeling* or self-love, but we might call it self-esteem. We also *aspire* to increases in our material self (someday we'll own that mansion) or increases in our social selves, so that important others might feel good about us. We compare our perception of our current self with our ideal self and are gratified or defeated.

By now, it's getting crowded in there. There's bound to be conflict:

Not that I would not, if I could, be both handsome and fat and well dressed and a great athlete and make a million a year, be a wit, a bon-vivant and a lady-killer, as well as a philosopher: a philanthropist, statesman, warrior and African explorer, as well as a "tone-poet" and saint. But the thing is simply impossible. The millionaire's work would run counter to the saint's; the bon-vivant and the philanthropist would trip each other up; the philosopher and the lady-killer could not well keep house in the same tenement of clay. Such different characters may conceivably at the outset of life be possible to a man. But to make any one of them actual, the rest must more or less be suppressed.

(*Principles*, p. 295)

Each of us, says James, must choose where to place our bets. There are many possible arenas, not all of which we care about. If you disparage my knowledge of psychology, them's fightin' words: If I think you're wrong, I'll fight; if I think your criticisms have merit, I'll be deeply wounded. But if Tiger Woods came up to me and said, "What good are you—you can't hit a golf ball even 100 feet!" I would look at him as if he were crazy, laugh and say, "So what?" I have, as James would say, decided, like a merchant, "not to carry that line of goods at all," so insults about my golf ability wound me not at all.

James even has a little equation concerning self-esteem: self-esteem = accomplishments divided by pretensions. For each of the sub-areas of the self that we have decided to care about, we evaluate what we've done in comparison with what we aspire to do. On the one hand, an individual of modest accomplishment is fine if he has few ambitions. On the other hand, a perfectionist might have many accomplishments to her credit, but not feel good about herself, because the denominator of the ratio is very large; her standards are very high. And the number of these little ratios depends on how many areas each person has decided to care about.

The self, then, to James, is multifaceted. We all have many roles: parent, sibling, lover, boss, employee. We are adequate in some and have disappointed ourselves in others. We switch, moment by moment, back and forth among them as required, sometimes changing ourselves nearly automatically right down to our body posture and tone of voice and back within minutes. Our duties or aspirations for one conflict with the duties and aspirations for the others. And yet, for most normal people, each of us owns a whole set of these and we are not in the least put out by it. There is one more self, even above the inner-reflecting spiritual self. It is called **pure ego**. The pure ego is defined as the *perception of the unity of the self*, the sense of personal identity that all sane people have, the feeling of warmth of my personal consciousness that pervades all the selves.

All philosophers and theologians have struggled with this. Religious thinkers often put the soul here. (Indeed, in several places in the *Principles*, James thought it necessary to argue that the soul adds nothing to psychology that the mind does not have, which is not the same thing as arguing that it does not exist.) Kant thought it was the thing that apperceives. James essentially adds one more possibility. We *need* the unitary self, even if it is an illusion, because our ability to adapt in the world requires that we *own* what we know to make use of it. This unitary self is functional for us. We organize our experience through our self in order to help us survive.

William James on Altered Mental States

What about those who have lost themselves, who are delusional? Doctors who worked in mental asylums were called alienists in James's day, because the people with whom they worked were said to be "alienated from themselves." The Jamesian sense of self allows for this. He describes in the final pages of the chapter on the consciousness of self what happens in the disordered self. Sometimes, he said, people remember who they were, but perceive who they are now as a totally different person: People report that their voices no longer appear to be theirs. People occasionally talk about their past selves in the third person, as in "Do you think that the good woman would ever come back?" In such cases, one self looks at another and notices something wrong with it. Sometimes, selves alternate, particularly under hypnosis, so that not only are there several selves, but also some do not remember the others. James is particularly interested in the work of Pierre Janet, a French investigator of hysterical neuroses and multiple personalities before Freud (see Chapter 9). Janet reports that "absences" occur in some patients, in which profound personality changes occur, disowned by the other personalities. Memory lapses and anesthetic paralyses were common in these states. It is as if each self is a separate entity and the pure ego has fallen down on its job to own them both and arbitrate. Sometimes this separation was purposely accomplished, as in cases in which a person is hypnotized or leads a séance.

All of these insights of James (and Janet) preceded Freud's first publication on these notions; Freud was still undergoing his medical training and postdoctoral work at this time. Since Freud's view of an active unconscious is still very popular, it is worth noting that James did not really believe in layers of consciousness, in which some things are actively "buried" below a preconscious and a conscious state. Everything is just a part of the ongoing conscious stream. Instead, he preferred a simpler, more benign explanation for what others called unconscious thoughts:

> When I decide that I have, without knowing it, been for several weeks in love, I am simply giving a name to a state which previously *I have not named*, but which was fully conscious; and which, though it was a feeling towards the same person for whom I now have a much more inflamed feeling and though it continuously led into the latter and is similar enough to be called by the same name, is yet, in no sense identical with the latter, least of all in an "unconscious" way. . . . A faint feeling may be looked back upon and classified and understood in its relations to what went before or after it in the stream of thought. But it, on the one hand and the later state of mind which knows all these things about it, on the other, are surely not two conditions, one conscious and the other "unconscious," of the same identical psychic fact. It is the destiny of thought that, on the whole, our early ideas are superseded by later ones, giving fuller accounts of the same realities. But none the less do the earlier and the later ideas preserve their own substantive identities as so many successive states of mind. To believe the contrary would make any definite science of psychology impossible.
> (*Principles*, p. 175; emphasis in original)

James preferred to often refer to the altered states of hypnosis or multiple personalities as a "splitting" of consciousness. At other times, he spoke of **subliminal** consciousness, meaning a possible state of consciousness just offstage, on the margins of consciousness (Taylor, 1996). (The term subliminal was used by Weber and Fechner, among others, to imply sensations below threshold). He was well aware of the notion of false memories (vol. 1, p. 373) in both normal and abnormal individuals and often noted that such false states of mind could be easily produced by hypnotists, therapists, doctors, spiritualists and charlatans. He was well versed in the work of Janet, Binet (who before his work on intelligence, did some work on hysterical patients) and Charcot, all of whom influenced Freud, and James reviewed Freud's first major publication on psychoanalysis (i.e. Breuer & Freud, 1893–1895/1978). James, however, was ever careful about maintaining his independence from these theorists. To believe in the Freudian notion of the unconscious, he would have to believe in stored, active ideas, which would violate his own conception of the mind. He apparently recognized the danger in interpreting the flow of consciousness as being an outgrowth of certain things repressed, but *really* there in the unconscious.

In 1909, he actually met Freud and Jung, and he heard Freud lecture and reported to a French colleague,

> I hope that Freud and his pupils will push their ideas to their utmost limits, so that we may learn what they are. They can't fail to throw light on human nature; but I confess that he made on me personally the impression of a man obsessed with fixed ideas.[4] I can make nothing in my own case with his dream theories and obviously "symbolism" is a most dangerous method.
>
> (H. James, 1920, pp. 327–328)

James was fascinated by all types of altered states of consciousness. He continued to study hypnosis throughout the 1890s (Taylor, 1996). He tried ether and nitrous oxide, both of which, at times in 19th-century America, were used as party drugs. He even tried peyote (Taylor, 1996)! When James was under the influence of these drugs, he felt a great euphoria and a connection to the meaning of life and, ever the scientist, he would write down what he thought it was. When he came to, he recognized that what he had written was always meaningless, though often hilarious, drivel. (One poem began: "What is Nonsense but a kind of Onsense?") In 1896, in a series of unpublished lectures on exceptional mental states, he addressed the following topics: dreams and hypnotism, automatism (automatic subconscious writing), hysteria, multiple personality, demoniacal possession, witchcraft, degeneration and genius. He took, as always, a critical but open-minded view of these areas; in the first four topics, he was interested in proving that such states were the extreme end of a normal continuum of our multifarious selves, that the insane are not that different from us; in the next four, he suggested that social conditions explained the beliefs in the occult and that genius and degeneration were not invariably caused by physiological disorders (see Taylor, 1996).

Much of this work got James into considerable trouble with the rising establishment of American psychology, which was at that time composed largely of students of Wundt. James had been a founder, member and officer of the American Society for Psychical Research since the mid-1880s. His reason for founding the society was to subject the claims of mediums, clairvoyants and other so-called spiritualists to scientific investigation. Spiritualism, the belief in speaking to the dead through mediums, had captured the popular imagination following a religious revival in early 19th-century America and Britain and continued through James's life—so much so that it had become a minor industry. People who sincerely believed that they had such powers (whether they had them or not) were mixed with deliberate frauds and charlatans. There was a popular fascination with hypnotism (or mesmerism, as it was called, after Franz Anton Mesmer—see Chapter 9) and scientific interest in hysteria and multiple personalities and a love of ghost stories (including a few written by William's novelist brother Henry).

Many scientists, with their materialistic hypothesis, were understandably concerned that they *not* give credence to such supernatural phenomena. James wrote to friends that he believed he was risking his scientific credentials by studying them at all, but he was determined to go in with an open mind. Most of the time, he was forced to admit (but, to his credit, usually did publicly admit) that the mediums were either frauds or delusional. In one case, however, of a certain Mrs. Piper, James believed that the medium had knowledge that she could not have obtained by natural means (although she failed a standard clairvoyance card test administered by James himself), and James wished to keep the hypothesis open. After all, in his methods of introspection, James could not tell *where* insights came to the stream of thought, particularly in altered states—they *might* have been from a supernatural realm. His beloved father had believed in a great beyond, even though he could never quite bring himself to agree. In his last letter to his dying father in 1882, he said,

> as for the other side and Mother [who had herself recently died] and our all possibly meeting, I *can't* say anything. More than ever at this moment, I do feel that if that *were* true, all would be solved and justified.
> (H. James, 1920, vol. 1, p. 220, emphasis original)

This was all too much for his colleagues, who in spite of their respect for him were sometimes savage in their disagreement. Historian Eugene Taylor (1996) is convinced that these investigations of the paranormal resulted in attempts to write James out of psychology. In 1898, James Cattell, erstwhile student of Wundt and Galton and by then editor of *Science*, engaged in a public dispute with James over reports of Mrs. Piper's clairvoyance. Cattell not only disagreed, but also felt he had to because James was so eminent in the field that others would follow James: "We acknowledge his [James's] leadership, but we cannot follow him into the quagmires" (cited in Taylor, 1996, p. 103). In 1899, Hugo Münsterberg, student of Wundt and a colleague at Harvard that James himself had hired to run the psychological laboratory, agreed. About spiritualism, Münsterberg stated by fiat, "the psychologist rejects everything without exception" (cited in Taylor, 1996, p. 106). G. Stanley Hall, one of James's former students (see later), wrote a history of psychology in 1912, two years after James's death, that did not even mention James. E.B. Titchener stated flatly in 1898, "No scientific-minded psychologist believes in telepathy" (cited in Taylor, 1996, p. 109). Moreover, he said that not believing in such things furthers the cause of science.

In other words, James's peers had decided that psychology should not be about psychic phenomena. A paradigm was forming, whether they knew it or not. In 1898, James became a professor of philosophy, not psychology.

The Varieties of Religious Experience

> I have no living sense of commerce with a God. I envy those who have, for I know the addition of such a sense would help me immensely. The Divine, for my active life, is limited to abstract concepts which, as ideals, interest and determine me, but do so but faintly, in comparison with what a feeling of God might effect, if I had one. It is largely a difference in intensity, but differences in intensity may make one's whole centre of energy shift.... yet there *is something in me* which *makes response* when I hear utterances made from that lead by others. I recognize the deeper voice. Something tells me, "*thither lies truth*"—and I am *sure* it is not old theistic habits and prejudices of infancy ... Call this, if you like, my mystical germ.
> —William James (in a letter to J.H. Leuba, 1904, excerpted in H. James, 1920, vol. 2, p. 211, emphasis original)

Since his recovery from depression through his belief in free will, James was interested in the power of belief to heal one's self. Many, if not most, people turn to religion for solace. In 1898, James, a popular public lecturer, was invited to give a series of lectures on natural religion at Edinburgh University, Hume's alma mater in Scotland. The lecture series was quite well attended, and a revised version of the lectures was published in 1902 as *The Varieties of Religious Experience*. The work is one of the most influential books on the psychology of religion ever published and has never been out of print. In 2000, the New York Public Library cited it as #2 on a list of the hundred most influential works of American nonfiction in the 20th century.

There are many ways to look at this text. It is not commonly read in psychology courses, except in divinity schools, but it is of interest to us here nonetheless. First, the book is a veritable encyclopedia of how people coped before "psychotherapy" was invented as a discipline. Second, it has wide ramifications for popular psychology movements. The founders of Alcoholic Anonymous, for example, have explicitly said that the conception of God and belief used by them and by other 12-step movements is taken directly from *Varieties* (Walle, 1992). Finally, it is part of the ongoing discussion of mind, brain and soul that bedevils (no pun intended) psychology to this day. If American psychology is much wider than what Wundt had in mind, William James's willingness to address the general public on topics like this is part of the reason.

In *The Varieties*, James was concerned first to describe the subjective nature of religious experiences and then to argue for the usefulness of such experiences, *even if* we would never be able to conclusively prove that God or a supernatural realm existed. He pointedly did not discuss religions, their theologies, their organization or their rituals. Such things, he said, were added on historically as a result of or as ways to aid in recreating the primary religious state of mind, the psychological experience of religion, which was the true subject of James's lectures. He also largely avoided addressing rational systems of ethics or philosophy, as not pure enough examples of religion. If you want to study a thing, said James, you want to study the full-strength versions, the religious experiences that could not be mistaken for something else: mysticism, conversion experiences, epiphanies, saintliness. Only then will you know what the essential difference is between religious experiences and other kinds of thought. Finally, James recognizes that the subjective nature of the experience makes it unlikely that one person could define a religious experience for someone else. Therefore, he defines religion as "*the feelings, acts and experiences of individual men in their solitude, so far as they apprehend themselves to stand in relation to whatever they may consider the divine*" (James, 1902/1982, p. 31, emphasis original). Each person gets to define the divine in his or her own way.

James recognized that the way in which an individuals "stand in relation to whatever they may consider the divine" is influenced greatly by their temperament and experience. He describes three major religious personalities: the **healthy-minded,** the **sick soul** and the **divided soul**.

The *religion of healthy-mindedness* is an approach taken by many people who refuse to dwell on the reality of evil and pain. Some persons with this view either are merely fortunate to be sunny in temperament and therefore never need to be "reborn." James puts Emerson, Walt Whitman and other Unitarians and transcendentalists in this camp.

The following is a quote from the Unitarian minister, Edward Everett Hale, quoted by James.

> I observe, with profound regret, the religious struggles which come into many biographies, as if almost essential to the formation of the hero. I ought to speak of these, to say that any man has an advantage, not to be estimated, who is born, as I was, into a family where the religion is simple and rational; who is trained in the theory of such a religion, so that he never knows, for an hour, what these religious or irreligious struggles are. I always knew God loved me and I was always grateful to him for the world he placed me in.... I can remember perfectly that when I was coming to manhood, the half-philosophical novels of the time had a deal to say about the young men and maidens who were facing the "problem of life." I had no idea what the problem of life was. To live with all my might seemed to me easy; to learn when there was so much to learn seemed pleasant and almost of course; to lend a hand if one had a chance, natural and if one did this, why, he enjoyed life because he could not help it, without proving to himself that he ought to enjoy it.
>
> (James, 1902, pp. 82–83)

Other followers of the religion of healthy-mindedness were followers of the "mind-cure" movement—essentially a "power of positive thinking" approach. These individuals pull themselves up from physical or mental illness simply by refusing to recognize the power of their pain. They give up worrying or "fearthought"; avoid the "misery habit" or the martyr-habit and their lives are thereby redeemed.

Yet even though some aspects of this approach were used by James himself and gently urged upon others, he did not think it necessarily superior to other ways. Some people have simply had too much pain in their lives for such an approach to be credible, said James. For some, sin is a real force, either in its merely numerous individual instances or, more seriously, as an existential state of humanity. These are the sick souls among us.

> There are some men who seem to have started in life with a bottle or two of champagne to their credit; whilst others seem to have been born close to the pain-threshold, which the slightest irritants fatally send them over.... Even if we suppose a man so packed with healthy-mindedness as never to have experienced in his own person any of [the] sobering intervals [of life], still, if he is a reflecting being, he must generalize and class his lot with that of others; and in doing so, he must see that his escape is just a lucky chance and no essential difference. He might just as well have been born to an entirely different fortune. And then the hollow security! What kind of frame of things is it of which the best you can say is "Thank God, it has let me off clear this time."
>
> (James, 1902/1982, pp. 135–137)

In discussing the sick soul, he describes many instances of what he recognizes are undoubtedly clinical depression. But unlike Freud, he recognizes them as being more than that; they become part of the story of people's lives. He says that the meaning of our world is a pure gift of the individual spectator's mind. Each person's unique view and emotions transform all she sees. Love is the most extreme of this—if it comes, it comes, if it does not, no process of reasoning can force it. So it is, even with depression. If they are there, one's outlook on life changes greatly and whether they be there or not depends on non-logical conditions. Is it any wonder then that some ascribe these things to external forces? Is it also easier to understand then why healthy-mindedness is not adequate to some and why in many religious stories of the 19th century, which were like the self-help books of today, a conversion can be seen as a triumph, a part of their story.

James's third category, the divided soul, can be exemplified by Paul's words in Romans 7:19: "For I do not do what I want, but I do the very thing that I hate ... I can will what is right, but I cannot do it." These are individuals who are tortured by self-loathing, divided within themselves, paralyzed by guilt. Again, characteristically, James does not describe this as mere neurosis or even something to be cured by right thinking. He merely describes it and then, following it, describes the feeling of relief that the subsequent unity, however arrived at, gives. He says that the unity may come suddenly or abruptly, through changed feelings or action, through intellectual insights or mystical experience. It need not be religious, but for many, the religious feeling of letting go, whether it is the letting go to a Christian God or Zen experience, is a profound one. And when he talks about conversion, a critical belief of many Protestant sects and certainly familiar to James's readers, he neither condescends to the believer nor takes it literally as a supernatural experience. He describes it as the shifting of one's *"habitual center of his personal energy"* (James, 1902, p. 391; emphasis in original). The things that are *allowed to matter* have changed. But he was also aware that whether you are once-born or twice-born, these ways are *effective* for different individuals, and he had the compassion to be really tolerant—that is, not just to live and let live, but to study these approaches to achieve true respect for each of these ways.

As a psychologist and philosopher who was wrestling with the materialist hypothesis, as well as altered states of mind, James took pains not to reduce religious experiences *only* to physiological processes and disorders, although they might be associated with such biological things. Many people with religious insights might be certifiably crazy. Moses, after all, saw a burning bush, and George Fox, the founder of Quakerism, wandered about barefoot in what he thought were the burning streets of Lichfield, England, seeing rivers of blood. But there is much more to the psychology of religion than the neurology of it. It has positive effects much larger than its supposed causes. He wrote, disapprovingly,

> Medical materialism finishes up Saint Paul by calling his vision on the road to Damascus a discharging lesion of his occipital cortex, he being an epileptic. It snuffs out Saint Teresa as a hysteric, Saint Francis of Assisi as an hereditary degenerate.
> (James, 1902/1982, p. 13)

James even objects to the view that religion equals sex:

> It seems to me that few conceptions are less instructive than this reinterpretation of religion as perverted sexuality. It reminds one ... of the famous Catholic taunt

that the Reformation [had its beginnings] in Luther's wish to marry a nun:—its effects are infinitely wider than the alleged causes and for the most part opposite in nature.

(James 1902/1982, pp. 10–11)

How then and in what sense can religion be said to be true, in James's eyes? Many people have religious insights; they are purely subjective, witnessed by only one person. Some of them may be crazy. Even in James's day, scientists were starting to criticize religion as only the way that primitive man understood the world. Can we therefore not evaluate or criticize religious belief? Although it is pointless to criticize pure traditional religious stories and rituals, said James, yes, we may evaluate religious behavior by a simple criterion: What are the consequences of maintaining that belief? First of all, does it help someone cope with the anxieties of the world? Second of all, does it produce, in the person's outward behavior, positive results for other people and the world at large? In other words, to use a religious verse: "By their fruits ye shall know them."[5]

As the quote at the start of this section notes, James himself could not fully believe in a God, much as he might have wished to. He could only say that the religious impulse comes from the subliminal part of a person's consciousness, and whether there was a supernatural component to that he could not say, and many of his colleagues and correspondents argued that he should not say. But he refused to throw the baby out with the bathwater. To William James, to believe is a very active verb; a belief is not a thing held, it is an action done. He would not belittle anyone who has used religion as a spur to action or as personal solace.

Pragmatism

Finally, we turn briefly to William James's most important accomplishment after he abandoned psychology (or psychology abandoned him). He helped to found and popularize a particularly American form of philosophy, which goes by the name of pragmatism. The term was first used by James's friend, Charles Sanders Peirce (1839–1914). Peirce was a member of the "Metaphysical Club" in Cambridge in the 1870s, an informal group that gathered to discuss the future of philosophy in the wake of Darwinism (Menand, 2001). (Other members included James and Oliver Wendell Holmes Jr.) Stated succinctly, **pragmatism** is the philosophy that the worth of an idea is judged by the consequences that believing that idea could conceivably have. If believing in a theory can make no conceivable difference in the world of action, then the theory is worthless (Peirce, 1878).

But Peirce, though a genius, was irascible, arrogant and unable to teach effectively or complete things he started. Twenty years after Peirce coined the term, he was also destitute. William James, having arrived at similar conclusions himself in the late1890s, thought that by taking Peirce's name for his own philosophy, the fame that the name William James would bring to it would save his friend from abject poverty. He was wrong, but the name stuck, even though almost every pragmatist, including Peirce and James himself, came to hate the name.

In a series of lectures late in life, James took Peirce's notion, blew the dust off it and made a vivid case for it, one that made it important for the conduct of science. "Pragmatism . . . asks its usual question. Grant an idea or belief to be true," says James,

> [W]hat concrete difference will its being true make in anyone's life? How will the truth be realized? What experiences will be different from those which would obtain if the belief were false? What, in short, is the truth's cash value in experiential terms? . . . *True ideas are those that we can assimilate, validate, corroborate and verify. False ideas are those that we cannot* . . . that therefore is the meaning of truth, for it is all that truth is known-as.

He goes on,

> The truth of an idea is not a stagnant property inherent in it. Truth *happens* to an idea. It *becomes* true, is made true by events. Its verity *is* in fact an event, a process: the process, namely of its verifying itself, its veri-*fication*. Its validity is a process of valid-*ation*.
> (James, 1907/1974, p. 133, emphasis original)

This definition is important in two ways. First, James points out that what we know about something extends only as far as the method we use for investigating it. Knowing the truth about something depends intimately on what we *do* to it. In a famous example, he suggests that if you have never taken apart a clock, you obviously do not "know" it in the mechanical sense, but only in the functional sense of how it measures time and relates to your life in that way. In this sense, James anticipated the scientific notion of **operationalism**, the scientific notion that variables are defined by the procedures used to measure them.[6] You accept, of course, "on credit" as it were, that it is a machine and that someone has made it and so on and indeed, nothing has contradicted thus far those notions. You may go on relying on the clock to tell time, without bothering about the rest, as long as your belief is not contradicted (let's say you investigated it and found no gears; this might call into question your received notion that a clock is a machine. People in James's day might have had trouble with a quartz digital watch). If you attempt to verify something and you fail, then your beliefs must change.

The second major aspect of James's pragmatism that concerns us here is that notion of contradiction. We prefer to maintain our beliefs until something upsets them, specifically until they come in conflict with other beliefs. My analysis in Chapter 1 concerning why a scientist might not believe in ESP is essentially based on this notion. If you believe in ESP, the way it must work contradicts several other beliefs about how physics, biology and anatomy must work. If it is truly important to you that your beliefs about these areas are in agreement (as James would say, if the ESP hypothesis is a "live" hypothesis for you—see James, *The Will to Believe*, 1896), it is crucial to resolve such contradictions before it is accepted.

Also, in Chapter 1, we discussed Thomas Kuhn's notion of paradigm, which is a set of assumptions and procedures accepted by practitioners in a field. We also discussed Karl Popper's falsificationist philosophy. To both of these philosophers of science, in different ways, a good theory is a theory which is *useful*, rather than true for all time, in that it explains most of the facts then in evidence. Generally, these explanations are couched in accepted modes of measurement. A good experiment is one that has "cash value," to use James's term. The way the experiment turns out either affirms (leaves unchallenged) or disproves (contradicts) something about the theory in question. A good experiment is one that has *consequences* for the theory. When an anomaly occurs, it essentially is a contradiction to the set of beliefs specified by the paradigm. The first line of attack against an anomaly is to challenge a scientist's measurement procedures, his or her ways of verifying the statements in the study; for no truth is independent of the way we try to measure it. These are essentially pragmatic tests of truth. Pragmatism has become, whether we know it or not, the day-to-day method of science.

The Contributions of William James

> Sow an action, reap a habit; sow a habit, reap a character; sow a character, reap a destiny.
> —William James (note in the margin of his copy of
> *Psychology: The Briefer Course*, 1892)[7]

This long discussion of the life and ideas of William James is meant to emphasize his large role as a transitional figure and the first creator of a distinctively American psychology. As a psychologist, he was a philosopher and as a philosopher, a psychologist. His psychology was constructed to incorporate three strains of thought of his time: First, he rejected the notion of a self-contained idea in the empiricist-associationist approach beginning with Locke and running through John Stuart Mill, while keeping Hume's notions of the self as nothing but the flow of experience. Second, he recognized the importance of materialism, determinism and mechanism in the work of Helmholtz and Fechner, while remaining skeptical of their acolyte Wundt. And third, he reluctantly accepted the notions of Darwin and placed the notions of adaptation to local conditions, the survival of the fittest thought, at the center of his notion of consciousness. And yet, in his heart, he was always rooting not for the person as a machine, an automaton, but for the person as someone who acts, who decides, who selects, who believes and in believing, changes his or her own life. This is perhaps a bald-faced contradiction, an attempt to believe simultaneously in determinism and free will, to believe simultaneously that every thought in the mind is based on a nerve impulse, but that we are not merely a sum of those impulses. But psychology today reflects that contradiction. Everything from sound insights about neurobiology to the wooliest sort of pop psychology can be found in the work of William James, and that is why many psychologists continue to read him.

Mary Whiton Calkins

As his new *Principles of Psychology* was warm from the press, in 1890 William James accepted as his graduate student a remarkable woman, Mary Whiton Calkins (1863–1930). Calkins was the daughter of a self-made evangelical minister and his Boston

Figure 7.3 Mary Whiton Calkins (1863–1930)

Brahmin wife, and she was brought up to revere learning and to share her parents' abiding love for the classics and German culture (she had been taught German at 3). In 1884, after she graduated with a degree in classics from Smith College she was offered a post teaching Greek at Wellesley at the age of 25. But in her last year at Smith, she had become interested in psychology. The president of Wellesley offered Calkins a deal: If she would take up "the New Psychology," he would pay for a year of graduate work (Scarborough & Furumoto, 1987).

But Calkins did not know where she could study psychology. German universities did not admit women; the best she could do there would be to pay a professor or two to give her lessons in his home. And in America, there were as yet only a handful of universities that (1) offered graduate education, (2) admitted women and (3) had any psychology laboratories. Harvard seemed ideal; it was only 10 miles east of her home in Newton, MA, where she would have to take care of her ailing mother. However, not only did it not admit women, but members of its board of trustees and the administration were adamant against it, even if many of its faculty were not.[8] Her father went to plead with the president of the college. William James went to argue personally for her admittance and wrote warmly to Calkins, "It is flagitious that you should be kept out.—Enough to make dynamiters of all you women. I hope and trust that your application will break the barrier" (James, 1890, cited in Scarborough & Furumoto, 1987, p. 33). The Harvard Corporation did not relent: She could come to Harvard as a *guest*, not as a student. She also arranged for private tutoring in laboratory methods that fall with G. Stanley Hall's student and colleague Edmund Sanford at Clark University, 40 miles west of Newton.

Her course with James that year took place in his home, at first with three male students, but they all dropped out, leaving Calkins to immerse herself in the *Principles* with its author as guide, next to the fire in James's library (Calkins, 1930/1961). Her paper for that course, on association, was her first published work. She extended her work on association with Hugo Münsterberg, who had just arrived to supervise Harvard's laboratory. In her dissertation on the association of numbers with colors, she created a new method that would be used in memory studies for decades to come, the **paired-associate method**. In this method, items are learned in pairs, and one of the items of each pair would serve as a retrieval cue for the other. She found that frequency of pairings in a list was more important than the vividness or recency of pairing in making the items more memorable.

So, in 1896, she submitted the dissertation for review and passed, having fulfilled all of the requirements for the PhD. Despite the unanimous support of the psychology/philosophy faculty for Calkins against the administration, Harvard refused to grant her degree. She was later offered a Radcliffe degree, but Calkins refused on principle—she had studied at Harvard, not Radcliffe, and if she relented, she felt that Harvard would never admit women (Radcliffe women graduate students continued for decades to study on the physical premises of Harvard but to receive Radcliffe degrees—they were finally allowed Harvard diplomas in 1963 [Scarborough & Furumoto, 1987]).

Mary Calkins's most important, if controversial, contribution to psychological theory was what she called **self psychology**, a theory that she proposed as a third way of interpreting consciousness, inclusive of and alongside the structural and functional views. Calkins was elected the first woman president of the APA in 1905. In her presidential address (published as Calkins, 1906) and a series of articles thereafter (Calkins, 1908a, 1908b, 1908c, 1915), she argued for the self as a "basal fact" of psychology. Siding with James, she believed that all perceptions were the perceptions of *someone*: All introspections came with a feeling of ownership. Structuralists such as Titchener believed that, ultimately, looking in should be as unbiased as looking out and so, said Calkins, they had not encouraged their introspectors to comment on their subjective experiences of self. Functionalists, on the other hand, knew that each conscious thought was imbued with a goal, but Calkins believed that they overemphasized how much of those goals were related to biological, as opposed to social or simply personal, adaptations. The self, present in everyday life in such statements as "I approve of myself," is a crossroads, a uniter of all experience and as such is central to it. Because the self is in all of our thoughts, Calkins thought it is perhaps impossible to experiment on it; because we have many selves, it may even be difficult to define. Psychology, to her, takes place in *persons*, not in self-observers.

Mary Calkins wrote some 50 papers and four books in her career, but her theory failed to catch on in her own time, for several reasons. Most obviously, she spent her career at a then all-women's undergraduate college and lacked a platform and graduate students to promulgate her views more effectively. Although she was well regarded among her male colleagues within psychology,[9] she could not form a "school." Second, although she founded the psychological lab at Wellesley, she did not use it much after 1900, turning her interest to philosophical and theoretical subjects. She thus did not come up with any methods to study the self (Furumoto, 1991). And finally, although when she began her work on the self, there were some with similar views, by mid-career, the movement towards behaviorism had begun, forestalling further acceptance of her views.

G. Stanley Hall

> Hall was wordy, superficially acquainted with several scientific fields, domineering and almost hypnotic in his ability to persuade others, at least so long as they were in his dynamic presence. He was an extraordinarily stimulating if controversial classroom teacher and lecturer, though not a particularly skilled practitioner of the new "scientific" experimental psychology he originally advocated in this country. Perhaps his greatest skill was in recognizing scientific talent early and either nurturing or championing it, as in his most famous enterprise, the presentation of Sigmund Freud to American psychologists and psychiatrists in 1909. Dorothy Ross's [in Hall's biography] characterization of him as "the psychologist as prophet" is precisely on target.
> —Koelsch (1987, p. 16, cited in Sokal, 1990, p. 116)

Granville Stanley Hall (1844–1924) was another transitional figure for psychology, born in the generation that had its philosophical and theological underpinnings undermined by the Darwinian revolution. Through a combination of luck and persistent ambition, he contrived to be at the right place at the right time for almost every movement in biological science or psychology. He was the only man among the founders of psychology to have studied with both James and Wundt; he founded several journals still being published today and was the first president of the American Psychological Association, in 1892. He was a pioneer in the use of questionnaires and the first American developmental psychologist. When he got carried away, he even claimed to have founded the first psychological laboratory in America, forcing William James to remind him sternly in print that he had earned his doctorate, the first in America, in James's lab! (Taylor, 1996). A man of considerable contradictions, he was a religious Darwinist and a man of decidedly old-fashioned racist and sexist views who nevertheless gave some of the first women in psychology their start and supervised the first psychology PhD given to a black man in America. As much as any single man, he left psychology in America on a solid professional footing.

G. Stanley Hall was born to stern Victorian religious parents in the farming town of Ashfield, MA. The serious and studious young man was slated for the ministry when he went to Williams College in 1862 and the Union Theological Seminary in 1867. But he caught the enthusiasm for the philosophical currents then coming out of Germany and the Darwinian movement. In particular, he was enthralled by the all-encompassing grandeur of Hegel's philosophy and sailed to Germany in 1869. At first, he saw in Hegel's concept of the Absolute as a way to unify Christianity with reason. To Hall, the Divine was a system of reason that underlay and shaped all things, and he interpreted Hegel's view of the evolution of history as "God coming to consciousness in man" (Ross, 1972). Like the young biologist Ernst Haeckel (who was giving fiery lectures on the topic that he called "Darwinismus" all over Germany when Hall was there—see Chapter 4), he believed Hegel's philosophy of evolution in history to be compatible with Darwin's evolution of species. He was to become a lifelong recapitulationist. In fact, this view of the child as a window into the history of the species was to form the basis of his developmental psychology (see later and Chapter 10).

When he returned from Germany, financial considerations required him to spend what he considered a miserable year as a minister and a three-year stint as a jack-of-all-trades professor, teaching almost every subject at a struggling college in Ohio. By this time, his enthusiasm for the ministry was dead, but his enthusiasm for psychology had grown, so, while teaching English at Harvard to support himself, he took an opportunity to study with William James, a man only two years his senior and just beginning in psychology himself. He earned under James the first PhD in America specifically conferred in psychology (as opposed to philosophy) in 1878, for a laboratory dissertation on "The Muscular Perception of Space."

He then departed for Germany again, hoping that real German scientific experience would endear him to the president of newly founded Johns Hopkins University in Baltimore. So, like many psychologists who came after him, G. Stanley Hall went back to Leipzig in 1878 more for professional advancement than true belief. When he enrolled, he found that he was unimpressed with Wundt. Hall described him "as a man who has done more speculation and less observing than any man I know who has had his career. His experiments, which I attend I think utterly unreliable and defective in method" (letter from Hall to James, Dec. 1878; cited in Ross, 1972, p. 85). He also had thought that Wundt's phenomenal publishing productivity was largely due to his ability to simply publish the notes of graduate seminars in which the students did all the work. And yet, like a Zelig or Forrest Gump of psychology, he found himself in Leipzig at the right place in the right time again, exactly when Wundt opened his lab and gave his first physiological psychology course.

This experience (and a nice letter from William James, who wouldn't leave Cambridge for Baltimore himself) secured him his coveted position at Johns Hopkins, first part time and then full time in 1884. While there, he taught Joseph Jastrow (1863–1944) and John Dewey (1859–1952), but by 1888, he had been hired away to be the founding president of Clark University in Worchester, MA, where he spent the rest of a stormy career. Almost immediately, two disasters befell him. In 1890, both his wife and child died in an accident and, by 1892, the president of then new University of Chicago had hired away two-thirds of his faculty and 70% of his students (White, 1992). Money troubles with the rich founder of Clark, coming so soon after personal tragedy, had accentuated the defensive aspects of Hall's personality; his secretive and domineering actions had alienated the faculty (Ross, 1972).

Hall created enemies and strained friendships at this time as well, with consequences for psychology. He was very much in favor of laboratory research in these years and severely criticized those who were not. His review of James's *Principles of Psychology* was harsh: He called it "worse than waste . . . philosophic and scientific precocity and lack of self control" (Hall, 1891, p. 590). In an editorial in his *Journal*, he lambasted psychologists like James as "arm-chair professors who lack patience for the tedious details of laboratory research" (Hall, 1895, cited in Ross, 1972). Hall so favored "Clark men" in his *American Journal of Psychology* that it led to the founding of *Psychological Review*. His claim to have founded the first American psychological laboratory was received with near universal refutation and condemnation (which didn't prevent his assertion from being repeated in some history of psychology textbooks; Taylor, 1996).

Undaunted, Hall began to carve a niche for Clark University in the area of psychology and education, known as pedagogy. He started yet another journal, *Pedagogical Seminary* (still published as *The Journal of Genetic Psychology*). He embarked on a vast study of childhood and young adulthood through the use of questionnaires sent out to parents, 194 of them between 1894 and 1915, answered in essay form. In February 1895, for example, he sent out *Some Common Traits and Habits* and asked parents to describe the behaviors of "showing off":

> Describe mincing, acting a part, putting on airs, acts or words thought to show superfine manners or breeding, playing the role of another self. How far is this due to vivid imagination, how long kept up, is it sustained or practiced when alone or only before others and are the traits assumed systematized or incoherent.
> (Hall, 1895, cited in White, 1992, p. 29)

Hall's questionnaires investigated many other areas: vocal expression, pantomime, children's thoughts, feelings for animals, crying, laughing, pity, unselfishness and sense of honor. He investigated school processes and subjects and included questions on examination techniques on teaching of reading, writing and arithmetic. He even had questionnaires that dealt with religious experiences, moral education and confession. The fruits of many of these questionnaires were distilled into Hall's sprawling two-volume work *Adolescence* (Hall, 1904), considered one of the earliest works in American developmental psychology (and which covers more than just adolescence as defined today).

The overall impression of Hall's questionnaires are that they are scattershot and wide ranging, intended to collect information for information's sake, a criticism lodged against them from the start. But Hall did have a theory of child development, and it was one based on evolution or, to be more specific, Ernst Haeckel's recapitulation theory (see Chapter 4). The idea that the developing child could be seen as a reenactment of the history of the human race. In this scheme, preschool children are like "primitive" humans: unable to reason and instead indulging in fantasies, fascinated with animism and magic:

> The growing mind repeats the racial myth-making in many ways. Thoughts are constantly being made from feelings and the sense world and the fancy world are often inextricably mixed, in the child, as in the savage and indeed, in the most highly trained and intellectual adult. . . . The child, especially, lives in two worlds at the same time; the world or sense and the world of fancy; the world of his own outer experience and the world of racial experiences, which well up within him. . . .
>
> Truth, for the child, is thus only in part a matter of sense experience. He is constantly at work creating for himself, out of his own instincts, a body of

truth to use in his own self development, in ways but little controlled by his environment.

(Partridge, 1912, pp. 61–62)

(This is from Partridge's condensation of Hall's thought, explicitly authorized by him in the Foreword.)

"He thinks in rhythm or rhyme, uses analogy, holds inconsistent thoughts, in the same conception, is fragmentary, imaginative, suggestible—in all these ways repeating the traits of racial development" (Partridge, 1912, p. 67).

As the child grows, however, his or her memory becomes much better for instruction: indeed, to Hall, their basic rote memory was the best it would ever be in ontogeny; this was the time for instruction of things that do not require the use of higher reasoning.

> Insight, understanding, interest, sentiment, are for the most part, only nascent and most that pertains to the true kingdom of mature manhood is embryonic.... But the senses are keen and alert, reactions immediate and vigorous and the memory is quick, sure and lasting and many a moral and social [concept?] licit and non-licit are rapidly unfolding. Never again will there be such susceptibility to drill and discipline, such plasticity to habituation or such ready adjustment to new conditions. It is the age of external and mechanical training. Reading writing, drawing, manual training, musical technic, foreign tongues and their pronunciation, the manipulation of numbers and of geometrical elements and many kinds of skill now have their golden hour and if it passes unimproved, all these can never be acquired later without a heavy handicap and loss
>
> (Hall, 1904, pp. 1, vii–xix)

The last part of this quote puts forth the **critical period hypothesis**—the notion that if something is not learned at the proper time, it might be difficult to learn it later. His view is biological and **maturational**, in the sense that development is largely a case of nurturing unfolding biological development, rather than learning. Hall's view of development is also a **stage theory of development**: Growth in a stage theory is not just continuous, but composed of discontinuous qualitative shifts. Older children are not different from younger children just because they know more, but also because they experience the world in qualitatively different ways. In this, he strongly influenced his student, Arnold Gesell (1880–1961), a strong advocate of the maturational view of development.

In part because Hall thought that development was so much a process of maturation, he thought that pushing children to be too smart too early, especially girls and those of nonwhite races, would be damaging, as seen in this quote arguing against academic kindergarten for girls:

> Oversophistication here may actually enfeeble or pervert the maternal instinct; and there is a type of scholastic old-maidishness that is positively dangerous for young maidenhood in the glory of its first maturity, the touch of which tends to whither and breed distrust of the best things in the soul, because it generates

> repression, prim proprieties and self-consciousness rather than all-sided expansion and expression.
>
> (Hall, 1911, vol. 1, p. 6)

This could lead girls to have hysterical neuroses later in life, which develop from a needy thirst for attention:

> Without knowing it, these hysterical girls feel robbed of their birthright. Their burgeoning women's instinct to be the center of interest and admiration bursts all bonds and they speak and act out what with others would be only secret reverie.
>
> (Hall, 1911, vol. 1, p. 363)

Hall's belief in the recapitulation hypothesis extended to cultures and races. He believed, for example, that African races and cultures were similar to children or perhaps adolescents of the white race.[10] This belief led him to what we would today consider a strange mix of left and right political views. He claimed to be against white imperialism:

> The time has now, in our judgment, fully come when not merely philanthropy but science and even broadly-based economy should teach us that primitives have certain inalienable rights to life, liberty and the pursuit of happiness and that ruthless interference with their customs should cease.
>
> (Hall, 1910, cited in Muschinske, 1977, p. 331)

But this is because the Africans have a long way to go, in Hall's opinion and should "have the same right to linger in the paradise of childhood." Missionaries were wrong to try to put Christian ideas in "small souls" and "rusty brains." Like many white men of his generation, he believed that both blacks and Native Americans had a poor work ethic, but his solution was not to make them work harder or to improve their working conditions and freedom, but to leave them alone until their culture grew up! He called the white colonizers the "Great Exterminators" and suggested finally that it would have been better for the Africans had whites never explored the continent at all (Muschinske, 1977).

America's Introduction to Psychoanalysis: The 1909 Clark Conference

In 1909, Clark University was celebrating its 20th anniversary and President Hall wanted to celebrate with a grand international conference. He invited 29 lecturers from all the sciences, among them Sigmund Freud. He had also invited Wundt, but he cordially declined due to ill health and other engagements. So Hall filled the hole in his roster with a young associate of Freud, Carl Jung. Freud's faithful acolyte, the Hungarian analyst Sándor Ferenczi, joined them for the trip. At the conference, they met up with British psychoanalyst (and Freud's authorized biographer) Ernest Jones and American psychoanalyst A.A. Brill. All in all, quite a coup for the

Figure 7.4 In this famous photo of the 1909 Psychology Conference at Clark University, G. Stanley Hall is dead center in the front. The back row includes from left to right: American psychoanalyst A. A. Brill, English psychoanalyst and Freud's authorized biographer, Ernest Jones, loyal Hungarian analyst Sàndor Ferenczi. Sigmund Freud is in the bottom left of the photo; Carl Jung is at the bottom right.

Source: Getty Images

new psychoanalytic movement and a feather in Freud's cap, who generally loathed America and Americans, but who was willing to overlook this for an expense-paid trip and the promise of an honorary doctorate.

Freud was not yet as well known in America as he would become after the First World War and was hungry for the recognition it would bring. Hall, for his part, found that he had much in common with Freud. Both, of course, had a deep appreciation of German culture. In addition, Hall had thought that American prudery regarding sex was unhealthy. His own sexual awakening had taken place in the then more liberal climate of Germany many years before, and he had studied and taught the psychology of sex as an academic subject frequently (Rosenzweig, 1994). He had come to agree with Freud that sex was a basic instinctual drive. Yet, Freud and Hall were still Victorian men; they both considered the sexual drive so strong that it must be controlled by cultural prohibitions and **sublimation**, defined as the redirection of sexual energy into culturally valued pursuits. Sublimation was in fact a major preoccupation voiced in the pages of Hall's *Adolescence* (1904). The strength of the sex drive explained the sublime emotional experience of religious ecstasy in the theories of both men, but Hall considered this a good thing, while Freud abhorred religion in all its forms (Hall, 1904, particularly volume 2; Freud, 1933). Finally, both Freud and Hall had constructed stage theories of development based on the evolutionary notion of recapitulation (for Freud, this formed the rationale for the Oedipus complex; see Chapter 9).

Hall's Students

> Dr. Hall usually started the discussion off with a few deviously generous comments on the importance of the material that had been presented, then hesitantly expressed just a shade of doubt about some of the conclusions drawn and finally called for "reactions." When the discussion had ranged from thirty minutes to an hour and was beginning to slacken, Hall would sum things up with an erudition and fertility of imagination that always amazed us and made us feel that his offhand insight into the problem went immeasurably beyond that of the student who had devoted months of slavish drudgery to it. I always went home dazed and intoxicated, took a hot bath to quiet my nerves, then lay awake for hours rehearsing the drama and formulating the clever things I should have said and did not.
> —Lewis M. Terman (cited by Sokal, 1990, p. 119)

Hall's biological, sexist and racist views evidently were shared by some of his students, most notably, intelligence testing pioneers Henry H. Goddard, who brought the Binet test to America, translated it and misused it, and Lewis M. Terman, who at Stanford converted the instrument to a test of the whole range of intelligence that became the Stanford-Binet test (see Chapter 4).

Hall and Women in Psychology

And yet, in spite of these beliefs, Hall and his policies as the president at Clark University furthered the education of many women. True, he was against coeducation (and feminism) and forbade female undergraduates at Clark, but during his time as president there, 150 women received graduate degrees in all its departments. One feminist scholar suggests that only Cornell was as open to women graduate students in America at the time (Rosenberg, 1982). Among Hall's own students in psychology, for example, were Phyllis Blanchard, who had interests in Hall's research areas of adolescence and who subsequently had a long career at the Child Guidance Clinic in Philadelphia, and Amy Tanner, who after receiving her PhD from working with Dewey at Chicago and postdoctoral work with Hall spent 11 years on the faculty at Clark, before her disappointment in professional advancement at Clark sent her into social work. Diehl (1986) suggests that the contradiction in Hall's views of women can be explained in the facts that he could stand women only in a subservient position (this was true of his relations with male students and faculty as well; Sokal, 1990). In addition, Hall considered that women's role in the child study movement of the time would be the professionalization of women's traditional roles: Blanchard worked with children, for example, and Tanner was in social work; the majority of graduate work of women at Clark was in education. And of course, one reason for

Hall's acceptance of women was money: From 1892 to 1919, enrollment of women in graduate programs ballooned from 484 to 5775 (Diehl, 1986).

Francis Cecil Sumner

In spite of holding views that we would today consider racist, Hall also facilitated the education of Francis Sumner (1895–1954), the first African-American to receive a PhD in psychology. Sumner began in extremely humble and difficult circumstances. When he entered Lincoln University in Pennsylvania in 1911, at the age of 15, he did not even have a high school diploma, as there had been no academic high school for blacks in Virginia, where he grew up; his self-educated father had tutored him as best as he could and cultivated young Francis's voracious reading habits. Lincoln University was the first black college in America founded in 1853, among many founded by white Abolitionist missionaries around the time of the American Civil War. Within the next 25 years, many more black colleges and universities would spring up, gradually providing roles for African-American scholars and professors, as well as students. As soon as Sumner graduated magna cum laude from Lincoln in 1915, he wrote to G. Stanley Hall, who admitted him to the graduate program.[11] Once at Clark, Sumner's respect for Hall had led him to switch from English (in which he received a second BA) to psychology, even though he was warned that there might be little demand in black colleges for the subject. Although his studies were interrupted by his service in World War I, Sumner was able to submit his dissertation *Psychoanalysis of Freud and Adler* for acceptance by the faculty and received his PhD on June 14, 1920.

Like many educated African-American men of his day, Sumner simultaneously fulfilled his professional goals and worked as a leader in his community for civil rights, occasionally causing friction with college administrations by publicly promoting aspects of the philosophies of W.E.B. DuBois and Booker T. Washington. After teaching in black colleges in Louisiana, Ohio and West Virginia, he finally secured a position as full professor and founding chairperson of the Department of Psychology at Howard University in Washington, DC, in 1930. Howard was then, as it is now, one of the premier historically African-American institutions in America, and Sumner set about making the psychology department one of the best and most productive of new black psychologists.

Probably the most famous of Sumner's students (as undergraduates) were Kenneth Bancroft Clark (1914–2005) and his wife, Mamie Phipps Clark (1914–1983). After receiving his PhD from Columbia in 1940, Kenneth Clark had a distinguished career at City College in New York City. The Clarks' research on 200 young black children in segregated schools suggested that they identified white dolls as possessing more positive attributes than brown dolls and preferred to play with white dolls as early as three years of age. These findings suggested that segregation in itself was psychologically harmful to children and formed a key piece of evidence in the landmark desegregation case, *Brown vs. [Kansas] Board of Education*, argued before the Supreme Court in 1953 by NAACP lawyer (later Supreme Court Justice) Thurgood Marshall.

The Board of Education had contended that racially segregated schools were justified as long as they were "separate but equal." Psychological evidence was critical in the case, as noted in the opinion by Chief Justice Earl Warren:

> Segregation of white and colored children in public schools has a detrimental effect upon the colored children. The impact is greater when it has the sanction of the law, for the policy of separating the races is usually interpreted as denoting the inferiority of the negro group. A sense of inferiority affects the motivation of a child to learn. Segregation with the sanction of law, therefore, has a tendency to [retard] the educational and mental development of negro children and to deprive them of some of the benefits they would receive in a racial[ly] integrated school system.
>
> ... We conclude that, in the field of public education, the doctrine of "separate but equal" has no place. Separate educational facilities are inherently unequal.
> (Brown v. Board of Education, 347 U.S. 483, 1954)

Functionalism

William James did not precisely father functionalism, but he is, intellectually, its grandfather. In order (based on the years that they studied with him), the following functionalists studied with him: G. Stanley Hall, Mary Whiton Calkins, James Rowland Angell, Robert W. Woodworth and E.L. Thorndike. (For the record, he also taught other famous folks in American life, such as President Theodore Roosevelt, activist W.E.B. Du Bois and writer Gertrude Stein. Roosevelt remained a friend to James, in spite of political differences, all their lives. DuBois, the first African-American PhD at Harvard [in sociology, in 1895], was encouraged by James [among others] in his intention to abandon philosophy for social activism and founded the NAACP. And Gertrude Stein's literary work has been called "stream of consciousness" writing.)

Many others were attracted to James through reading *The Principles of Psychology* (known simply as "The James") or its abridged version, *Psychology: The Briefer Course*, (known affectionately as "The little James" or "The Jimmy"), which were together the dominant psychology texts from 1890 to 1910 in America.

Functionalism, unlike Titchener's structuralism, was a broad, diffuse and inclusive psychology. It also was a practical and pragmatic psychology. Although there is no specific school of functionalism today, that is perhaps because the principles of functionalism have been so absorbed into psychology that everybody is now a functionalist. To learn what it is, we need to first discuss a seminal article by psychologist, activist and philosopher of education and democracy John Dewey.

John Dewey (1859–1952)

Even though the roots of functionalism go back to Darwin, the birth of functionalism as a specific movement in psychology is usually dated from an article by John Dewey (1859–1956), in 1896. This article, entitled "The Reflex Arc Concept in Psychology," was initially prompted by a routine conflict between two sets of experimental results.

Figure 7.5 John Dewey (1859-1952)

Titchener had postulated, based on studies of Wundt, that in the reflex arc there are two processes: the sensory reaction and the muscular reaction or response. He claimed that the processes involved in sensation had more steps than in the response. Therefore, he proposed that subjects would be faster to throw a switch in reaction to an auditory stimulus if they concentrated their conscious attention before the stimulus on the simple muscular response to be made rather than the sensation. James Mark Baldwin (1861–1935) of Johns Hopkins University presented data that instead suggested that there were two types of people, those for whom the motor response was faster and those for whom the sensory response was faster. Finally, James Rowland Angell (1869–1949) and Addison Moore (1866–1930), colleagues of Dewey's at the then new University of Chicago, had showed that, yes, at the beginning of a series of experiments, before any practice at the task, some people indeed had faster motor times and some had faster sensation times. After practice with both types of reactions, however, the response times had converged, so that subjects' reaction times became similar. Angell and Moore argued, following James's view, that consciousness was for novel reactions, that what had happened was that each subject had focused his attention on the part of the perception-idea-response arc that was weakest for him. Over time, however, all parts of the arc had become automatic and habitual and thus the reaction times of the two types of individuals converged. Angell and Moore therefore stated that it was not that the sound was associated with the ear and the response with the hand but that a progressive feedback loop was set up between the ear and hand so that eye-hand coordination became increasingly automatized (Backe, 2001).

In his reflex arc article, Dewey (1896) makes two points with these findings:

1. Many of his colleagues had suggested that the reflex arc sequence ran as follows: The stimulus produces a sensation, which produces a mental idea, which sets off a response. The physiological stimulation somehow becomes an insubstantial idea and this ghostly idea produces a bodily response. Part of this separation of the stimulus and response is due to a separation between the central nervous system, the realm of ideas and the peripheral nervous system, a physical system mediated by the spinal cord. Dewey saw this central/peripheral split as similar to the mind/body split and wanted to get rid of it. Instead, it is better to conceive the stimulus-response sequence as a complete and ongoing sensory-motor *circuit*, rather than an arc: the hand is constantly shifting its movement in response to stimulation and when the task is repeated, all parts of the circuit become increasingly coordinated.
2. The formation of this circuit depends on its function in the ongoing activity of the organism. A loud sound, said Dewey by way of example, means something different when one is reading a book or when one is hunting, watching in a dark place on a lonely night or performing a chemical experiment. The completion of the task depends on the goal of the organism. The process of reacting to a sound is not a chain of separate bits of consciousness; it is a function, the *act* of hearing.

Let's use Dewey's example of the child reaching towards a candle flame[12] to explain his reasoning. Instead of the flame being a stimulus for the child's automatic response, Dewey suggests the action is somewhat more complicated. The child has first to be attracted by the flame and turns her head and eyes toward it. She is attracted by it and initiates a goal-directed response, an attempt to bring about a stimulus. The eyes and hand form a guided feedback loop, with the eyes and hand issuing midcourse corrections toward the goal. As the hand gets near the candle, the child's perceptions of the flame change. If the child is burned, the perceptions of the original flame change to pain. The pain is then, at least partially, substituted for the attraction and thus the stimulus has changed. The response, says Dewey, is not "merely to the stimulus, it is into it" (Dewey, 1896, p. 359). Response affects a stimulus as much as a stimulus prompts a response (Bredo, 1998).

In other words, a stimulus is not just out there, as some behaviorists would later claim; neither is it a stable piece of consciousness that we can inspect, as Titchener would claim. Some interpretation of a stimulus, a decision of whether the sound is relevant to the ongoing process of reading or hunting or whether it is attractive or not, must happen before it becomes a stimulus at all. As in the candle example, the character of the stimulus may change, depending on the result of the response. It all depends on its purpose in the ongoing process of an organism adapting to the world.

Dewey's perspective in this article was influenced by a goal of his own. He was deeply concerned with the problems of dualisms—mind/body, central/peripheral, subject/object, stimulus/response—and wanted psychologists to avoid breaking up processes artificially into dichotomies. He had started his education, at the University of Vermont, as a Hegelian (see Hegel in Chapter 5). Like Hall, with whom he subsequently studied at Johns Hopkins, Dewey was first enthralled by the notion that religion and philosophy might be unified and then gave it up (Menand, 2001). Indeed, he wrote a *Psychology* (1884; one of the first such textbooks in America) that, following the idealist Hegel, discussed the mind in terms only of the conflict of ideas within it, with no emphasis on the nervous system. (Predictably, William James disliked it.) At the end of his life, Dewey reflected back on this time: "Hegel's synthesis of subject and object, matter and spirit, the divine and the human ... [was] no mere intellectual formula, it operated as an immense release" (Dewey, 1960, p. 10, cited by Bredo, 1998). Another aspect of Dewey's thought, the tendency to see organic interrelationships of part to whole, was influenced by taking a college course that used a physiology textbook written by Darwin's friend, T.H. Huxley:

> I have an impression that was derived from that study [i.e. of the physiology course] a sense of interdependence and interrelated unity.... Subconsciously, at least, I was led to desire a world that would have the same properties as had the human organism in the picture of it derived from study of Huxley's treatment.
> (Dewey, 1930/2008, p. 147)

With the publication of James's *Principles of Psychology*, Dewey gave up Hegel's views that the ideal was the real and that there was an Absolute in favor of James's twin hypotheses that underneath every act was a physiological basis and that because our consciousness is personal, we are essentially isolated in our pursuit of knowledge. Dewey said of James's book that the biological conception of the psyche was its most influential factor and that "it worked its way more and more into all my ideas and acted as a ferment to transform old beliefs" (Dewey, 1930/2008, p. 157).

As a philosopher, Dewey also conceived of the notion of **instrumentalism**, which was almost synonymous with James's definition of pragmatism. In this view, knowledge does not exist out there on a separate plane (as Plato would have it) but is created in the action of individuals in attempts to adapt to their environment, on the fly. Thought is an instrument, a tool, and if use of that tool helps us succeed, we call the result of that success knowledge. If we have solved a problem, we have knowledge; if we have not, we attempt to fashion a new tool, a new argument, concept or set of procedures to solve the problem. It is knowledge as know-how: practical, jury-rigged, provisional. It doesn't touch the Absolute, but as long as it's useful, who cares? It would be hard to imagine a philosophical statement that was more American and less German than instrumentalism!

Dewey's reflex arc paper was a dramatic statement against structuralism. But in order to win the battle for supremacy in psychology, it would be helpful to (1) write a textbook, (2) rise to positions of professional power and (3) commandeer a journal. That was left to James Rowland Angell (1869–1949) and James Mark Baldwin (1861–1935).

James Rowland Angell had studied with James for a year at Harvard and with Dewey at University of Michigan; Dewey brought Angell to Chicago. Angell stated that James's book was "extraordinarily stimulating" and the strongest influence on his thought in 20 years (Angell, 1961). He became a convert to the functionalist faith. In 1904, he published an introductory psychology textbook in which he wrote,

> adoption of the biological point of view ... will mean not only that we shall study consciousness in connection with physiological processes wherever possible, but it will also mean that we shall regard all of the operations of consciousness—all our sensations, all our emotions, all our acts of will—as so many expressions of organic adaptations to our environment.
> (Angell, 1904; cited in Backe, 2001, p. 328)

The combination of Dewey's reflex arc paper with Dewey's shift from Hegelism to instrumentalism/pragmatism and Angell's text allowed William James to trumpet the rise of a new "Chicago School" of psychology in 1904.

By 1906, Angell was elected president of the American Psychological Association (following the term of James's former student Mary Whiton Calkins, in 1905) and used the opportunity of his presidential address, entitled "The Province of Functional Psychology," to evangelize, gently, for the new approach. Angell set forth three basic tenets for functionalism in this talk (Angell, 1907):

1. Functionalism studies mental operations rather than mental contents; it is the study of the how and why of consciousness rather than the what of consciousness.
2. Functionalism is the study of how the mind mediates between the environment and the needs of the organism.
3. Functionalism is concerned with both sides of the mind-body problem. It relies on dualism, in that consciousness as a control mechanism and in its power for reflective thought is a powerful concept, rather than a mere outgrowth of body. On the other hand, the powers of consciousness are rooted in and limited by the physiology of the nervous system and our evolutionary makeup.

But beyond these minimal principles, Angell conceived functionalism as a much bigger tent than Titchener's structuralism, allowing for many points of view, and as such, it grew. Titchener was so disgruntled by the ascendancy of functionalists within the APA that he split off to form an "experimentalists" group to house the Wundtian loyalists in 1904. Titchener resolutely prohibited all applied work from his society, as well as work concerning children or animals, a prohibition that lasted until his death in 1927.

Founding a journal as a way to promote a point of view within psychology was a time-honored practice. The German journal *Philosophische Studien* published almost exclusively the work from Wundt's lab (forcing Ebbinghaus, Stumpf and Helmholtz, among others, to support *Zeitschrift für Psychologie* in opposition [Ash, 1995]). When G. Stanley Hall wanted to promote "the New Psychology" in America, he founded the first psychology journal in the United States, *The American Journal of Psychology*, in 1888.

Psychological Review was founded by James McKeen Cattell (also an editor of *Science* magazine) and James Mark Baldwin in 1894. Both had studied with Wundt;

Cattell was Wundt's first lab assistant and Baldwin had spent a semester in Leipzig. But by now, they were functionalists.

James McKeen Cattell (1860–1944)

Cattell had studied briefly with Hall before obtaining his doctorate from Wundt, but he later met and corresponded with Galton, whom he considered "the greatest man he had ever known." He thereafter took up Galton's method of anthropometric testing of reaction time to sight and sound and naming colors, as well as such tasks as basic memory span and the speed with which one could mark off all of the "a's" on a printed page. He coined the term **mental tests** for these sorts of activities. He abandoned experimental self-observation. He much preferred using regular people rather than psychologists as subjects ("It is usually no more necessary for the subject to be a psychologist than for the vivisected frog to be a physiologist," he said [Cattell, 1906, p. 597]). He conducted a 12-year program of this work, beginning with Hall, through his doctoral work with Wundt and then at the University of Pennsylvania in the 1880s and Columbia in the 1890s. Most of the time, he appeared to be collecting data for data's sake, with little advance hypotheses for the collection of the data. He would figure out what they meant later. Cattell claimed to be following the inductive empiricism of Francis Bacon when he said, "The best way to obtain the data we need is to make the tests and determine from the results what value they have" (Cattell, 1893, cited by Sokal, 1987). Beginning in 1894, one of his graduate students began to evaluate whether the scores on these simple tests significantly correlated with course grades of the college student subjects. He found that they did not; correlations hovered around .05. It was not even clear whether simple reaction time to sound or sight was correlated with speed to find letters on a page (Sokal, 1987). After this failure, Cattell withdrew largely from his own research, but continued his editing duties for *Psychological Review*, *Science* and a compilation of biographies still produced today: *American Men of Science*. In addition, he founded The Psychological Corporation, which today publishes many tests, such as the Weschler Adult Intelligence Scale, the Weschler Intelligence Scale for Children and the Beck Depression Inventory.

Lightner Witmer (1867–1956)

> I believe that there is no valid distinction between a pure science and an applied science. The practical needs of the astronomer to eliminate the personal equation from his observations led to the invention of the chronograph and the chronoscope. Without these two instruments, modern psychology and physiology could not possibly have achieved the results of the past fifty years. If Helmholtz had not made the chronograph an instrument of precision in psychology and physiology; if Fechner had not lifted a weight to determine the threshold of sensory discrimination, the field of scientific work represented today by clinical psychology could never have been developed. What retards the progress of one retards the progress of the other; what fosters one, fosters the other. But in the final analysis, the progress of psychology, as of every other science, will be determined by the value and amount of its contributions to the advancement of the human race
>
> —Lightner Witmer, (from the article "Clinical Psychology" in the first issue of *The Psychological Clinic*, 1907/1996, p. 249)

Lightner Witmer was the founder of clinical psychology as a helping profession distinct from psychiatry or education. Though he was originally guided into psychology by Cattell and received his doctorate from Wundt, he entered into applied work in the same way that many clinical psychologists do to this day: by his involvement with an interesting case. After receiving his undergraduate degree from the University of Pennsylvania, Witmer was a teacher at a private high school assigned to tutor a boy in English, in hopes of helping him to pass Penn's entrance exam. Witmer knew that the boy's spelling was atrocious and that his essay skills were marginal at best. Although the boy seemed to be of normal intelligence, he could not dissect a sentence into parts of speech. Although he was able to hear even soft sounds, he was quite incapable of even hearing the difference between words like *grasp* and *grasped*. Witmer called this difficulty "verbal deafness," and realized that the boy's problems with spelling and parsing were actually a problem with hearing. He spelled the way he heard (and spoke), but what he heard was wrong. Simply by teaching the boy to articulate better and to note the corresponding spelling differences, Witmer helped him to improve to such a degree that he entered and graduated from the University of Pennsylvania, though not without considerable difficulty (Witmer, 1907/1996).

Witmer kept this case in mind throughout his graduate work with Wundt and after he continued in psychology, in the position that his mentor Cattell had resigned at Columbia University in New York. In 1896, one of Witmer's psychology graduate students, also a teacher, mentioned a 14-year-old student with severe spelling difficulties. Witmer's careful observation determined that the boy had what we would probably call the learning disability dyslexia. This boy, whose pseudonym was recorded as "Charles Gilman," became the first recorded case in "clinical psychology"; later that year, after seeing perhaps 20 clients and ascertaining from school superintendents a need for such services, Witmer was to found the first psychological clinic in America, at the University of Pennsylvania.

The clinic served not only as a place for treatment but also for education and hands-on training. Although the clinic also treated adult clients and later offered vocational consultation, its central focus was on children with academic or behavioral problems. Witmer emphasized that students should know about the normal development of children before taking courses offered by the institute in abnormal and exceptional child psychology or diagnostic teaching or intervention in schools (Fagan, 1996). His hands-on weekly clinics often demonstrated diagnostic techniques: with the help of graduate student testers; he would bring a child onto the stage of a large amphitheater, seat him or her in child furniture on stage and begin testing and questioning in a relaxed manner (dropping for these tasks the stern, authoritative persona he used in lecture courses) (McReynolds, 1996). The work of his clinic was reported, usually as case studies, in his journal, *The Psychological Clinic*. Finally, Witmer's graduate students often went on to found clinical psychology programs from New Jersey to Washington State. One student, David Mitchell, a 1913 Witmer PhD, is considered the first PhD psychologist to open a private practice, which he did in New York City in the 1920s. (Psychotherapy in private practice, however, was an uncommon choice for psychologists until after the Second World War; the money that the Veterans' Administration provided then for psychotherapy for returning servicemen allowed more psychologists to venture out from clinics or hospitals, where they had often been under the supervision of psychiatrists; see Humphreys, 1996.)

Witmer himself could be called more of an "interventionist" than a psychotherapist. He said that he borrowed the term "clinical" from medicine, but the word referred in his case to the comprehensive method of evaluation practiced by the best doctors, rather than to medical diagnosis per se. In addition to referring patients to the requisite medical practitioners, the clinical psychologist was to interview a child's parents and teachers, visiting his or her school and home, to devise a treatment plan. Although many of the treatments devised by Witmer included special types of careful teaching, he was not concerned with devising new pedagogy but with suggesting to the child's parents ways to cope with their difficulties. The focus was always on the individual child. Witmer used the new psychological tests, including the Binet test and some of Cattell's tests, but he was highly critical of those who would overinterpret the scores of such tests. He emphasized more the acquisition of specific skills than "cures." He was reluctant to issue long-term prognoses. Witmer was well aware that some of his techniques were as yet untested and so maintained a pragmatic approach to his profession. His theoretical pronouncements were few and speculative, and he produced no experimental outcome studies of treatments. As the quote at the start of this section shows, however, he would likely approve of the melding of treatment with science that has become the norm over the last 50 years.

E.L. Thorndike

Edward Lee (E.L.) Thorndike (1874–1949) was born in Williamsburg, Massachusetts, in 1874. Because his father was a Methodist minister, the family was obliged to stay in any one town only a few years at a time, so the children were encouraged to become self-reliant. E.L.'s parents valued a kind of plainspoken honesty, modesty, general public-spiritedness and above all industriousness in their children. Indeed, these are exactly the characteristics that are often ascribed to Thorndike in adulthood—to himself, he was a hard taskmaster: driven, hardworking, a prolific writer, teacher and researcher. To others, in spite of being almost painfully shy and lacking in social polish, he was a kind and loyal friend and family man. He was also incisively intelligent: He racked up academic prizes in both high school and at Wesleyan College in Connecticut (his GPA there was said to be the highest in nearly 50 years; Joncich, 1968, p. 76). The combination of all of these traits and abilities leads to a full-rounded portrait of a man who is at once impatient and sarcastic with received opinions, pomposity and impractical philosophical positions that could not be backed up with evidence and yet generous both to the people around him and to society at large, in the sense that he had a deep desire that his work would be *useful* (Joncich, 1968). All in all, these were fitting characteristics for a founder of both educational psychology and operant behaviorism, fields that, at their best, marry theory with practice and focus, above all, on results.

E.L. Thorndike began his journey in psychology in 1893, his junior year at Wesleyan, when he read James's *Principles of Psychology*. As it did for Calkins, Angell, Dewey and many others of his generation, this book sparked his interest like no

Figure 7.6 E.L. Thorndike (1874–1949)
Source: Getty Images

other. In an autobiographical statement more than 40 years later (see Thorndike & Murchison, 1936), he describes it as probably the most stimulating book he had ever read and the only book outside of literature that he had bought as an undergraduate without having been assigned it.

He went to study with James in 1894 and stayed two years, taking practically every course that James taught, soaking up James's adaptationist functional philosophy while learning about psychological experimentation from other faculty members and taking courses in zoology and Galtonian statistical methods. But James himself had moved beyond laboratory work and allowed Thorndike free rein to follow his own course. In 1896, the Welsh comparative psychologist C. Lloyd Morgan (see Chapter 4) lectured at Harvard on a tour of America on his notion of "trial-and-error" learning. Morgan had suggested that one should be very cautious about explaining the actions of animals with regard to ideas and conceptual thought. Instead, two years earlier, he had coined a law that became known as Morgan's canon: "In no case may we interpret an action as the outcome of a higher psychical faculty if it can be interpreted as an outcome of the exercise of one which stands lower in the psychological scale" (Morgan, 1894/1903, p. 53). Thorndike was in the audience when he demonstrated that chickens, through near random trial and error, would learn quickly to peck only at a pile of sweet corn kernels rather than bitter ones.

Thorndike immediately tried to test this hypothesis on schoolchildren, setting up a simple learning task in which they were rewarded with a bit of candy for choosing the right alternative in answer to a question. Then, as well as now, there was some tension between psychology and education, and the principal of the school in which he was working refused to allow Thorndike to continue. So Thorndike immediately set about using chickens for his trial-and-error learning experiments. At first, he attempted to do the experiments in his apartment, but not unreasonably, perhaps, his landlady objected strenuously: either Thorndike or his chickens would have to go. (The experiments initially involved more than just learning. After the chickens learned, they were bred and the eggs incubated—Thorndike was attempting to test Lamarck's notion that the learning could be passed down to offspring, but his landlady didn't care. Apart from the noise and the mess of the chickens, she thought that the incubator might burn down the house [Joncich, 1968].) William James generously offered the use of his own basement, in which Thorndike set up perhaps the first animal mazes in psychology, with the routes constructed by stacking up books in patterns. The James children got lots of amusement from the deal as well!

Just when his work was going well, however, shy and serious Thorndike was dealt a severe personal blow. The love of his life, Bess Moulton, rejected his offer of marriage, and he decided to apply for a fellowship at Columbia University in faraway New York with James McKeen Cattell so as not to be reminded of her. He took his two "most educated" chickens with him in a basket on the train to New York. He completed his doctoral dissertation there, cobbling together "puzzle boxes" in an attic on campus with cats and monkeys as well as chickens. The dissertation, published in 1898 as "Animal Intelligence: An Experimental Study of the Associative Processes in Animals," would become a classic in psychology, which would lay the foundation of operant behaviorism. (We will discuss this story in greater detail in the next chapter; for now we will focus on Thorndike's functionalist educational psychology.)

Soon, with glowing recommendations from James and Cattell, Thorndike received a post in Teachers College, Columbia University. From that post, he would essentially create educational psychology as a scientific discipline. (By the way, he would also get the girl and prosper; he married Bess Moulton in 1900 and by 1904 he was one of the highest paid education professors in the country—$3500 a year!)

Thorndike and Educational Psychology

At the end of the 19th century, America's educational system was ripe for change. As late as 1890, the vast majority of Americans never progressed beyond the eighth grade, which was typically the end of state education; only 1% of the population were enrolled in high schools (Joncich, 1968). The teachers were by and large poorly trained and transient. Anyone who themselves had finished high school could be a teacher; it was a popular half-way stop for young men and women who wanted to save for college or for women to support themselves before marriage. Even those who were trained to see teaching as a profession were subjected to an amalgam of moralistic statements, emphasis on teaching by rote and preparation to teach a curriculum that still focused on reading, writing and arithmetic in the lower grades, ancient history, literature and languages in high schools. More practical strains of education, such as the methods of accounting or farming or law, were typically acquired through adult learning classes or apprenticeships outside of school itself.

Yet, late 19th-century America placed great hope in its children. A so-called **child study movement** was flourishing, which consisted of groups of mothers who gathered to discuss the latest writings on how to raise children, and professors such as G. Stanley Hall were eager to provide this information (Borstelman, 1983). Hall recommended that school curriculums take into account the epoch in human history that children of given ages were recapitulating, moving from the fantasy years of preschool to the emphasis on raw memory in the middle grades up to reasoning at age 12 or 13. Another view of school curriculum was exemplified by the **mental discipline** or **formal discipline** approach: In this view, the mind was like a muscle that needed to be exercised on difficult tasks, so that a Latin or geometry class became more than a way to acquire a particular skill; it became a way to increase the capacity of the mind itself.

Such a point of view had a long history, going back at least to Kant's faculty psychology. The purpose of education then was to increase one of the several innate "powers" of mind. At the end of the 18th century and remaining until the early 19th century, Kant's idealism was united to the brain and body by Franz Joseph Gall (1758–1828), promoter of the infamous fad of phrenology. Gall had claimed that the exercise of a particular faculty would increase the amount of brain tissue in the area ostensibly devoted to it. The areas of increased activity would be seen in raised areas on the skull. The list of faculties numbered more than 30 and included such dubious abilities as approbativeness—the organ of the brain that purportedly dealt with our wish to be liked by others—or reverence—the organ that contains love of God. Part of the fad, which persisted as late as 1850 in America, was then to have the bumps on one's head "read" by Gall and his followers, to find what one excelled in. There was, of course, no scientific validity in any of these methods, as they had never been satisfactorily tested. But these old ideas were simply grafted on to the new biological Lamarckism by the 1890s to become the educational theory of formal discipline—no longer crude faculty theory or phrenology, but the same ideas with a new evolutionary twist. One of the most famous adherents of the formal discipline approach was none other than then future U.S. president Woodrow Wilson, who in his capacity as president of Princeton University said, "The mind takes fiber, facility, strength, adaptability, [and] certainty of touch.... The college should give elasticity of faculty and breadth of vision so that [students] shall have a surplus of mind to expend" (Wilson, 1902; in Thorndike, 1913, p. 363).

Thorndike strongly disagreed with both Hall and the formal disciplinarians. He called Hall "essentially a literary man rather than a man of science and artistic rather than matter of fact." His questionnaire work on children lacked "detailed experimentation, intricate quantitative treatment of results or rigor and subtlety of analysis" (Thorndike, cited in Joncich, 1968, p. 168). And he strongly disagreed with formal discipline's emphasis on the increase of mental capacity through mental exercise, calling it a theory which likens to the "ability to amounts of something which can be stored in a bank, to be drawn on at leisure" (Thorndike, 1903, p. 85).

Instead, Thorndike believed that people learned as a direct consequence of having solved particular problems of adapting to their environments. Like his mentor James, he believed that someone's knowledge was limited to the methods he or she had used to acquire it. People acquire particular habits of mind, rather than generalized increases in capacity. Like his colleague Dewey (who was to move to Columbia from Chicago in 1905), he believed that successful problem solving—satisfying a goal through particular responses—*was* knowledge. Unlike either of these men, he was more of an experimenter than a philosopher and was thus the ideal man to put American pragmatism to its test in the psychology lab and classroom.

Thorndike and his colleague and friend Robert S. Woodworth (1869–1962) devised a series of ingeniously simple experiments to prove their point, based on the rather basic idea that education really was all about transfer of training. After all, what one ideally wants out of school is not just to learn a skill or principle in school, but to also be able to apply it where it is effective outside of school. Even more fundamentally, education is about being able to transfer what one learns in situation A to its use in situation B. If the mind is like a muscle that increases its general capacity to lift with exercise, then transfer should be easy, in the same sense that if one can lift a 50 lb. barbell, one can lift a 50 lb. television set. Transfer between situations A and B should be nearly 100%, assuming one has reached perfection on task A. If, however, learning things consists largely in learning specific habits to solve specific adaptive problems, transfer might be more difficult. Under this theory, only those habits of mind that are useful in situation A that also prove useful in situation B would transfer. Transfer would be considerably less than 100%.

To test this hypothesis, Thorndike and Woodworth (1901a, 1901b, 1901c,) trained people to estimate the area, in square inches, on a particular set of stimuli, say, paper squares between one and three square inches in size. When someone becomes nearly perfect in estimating the area of stimuli this size, including ones in this range on which they had not been trained (so they're making judgements, not just remembering the answers), the task is changed. Now the subject is given triangles of the same one- to three-inch range or squares that are larger or rectangles, etc., and asked to perform the same estimation task. Subjects are, at least temporarily, less than half as well on the new task, in spite of the fact that only one factor is changed at a time. And the further the new stimuli were from the old ones, the worse the subjects got. Similar percentages of improvement were found in judgments of weight and length and picking out verbs as compared with other parts of speech, as well as a host of other comparisons (Thorndike & Woodworth, 1901a, 1901b, 1901c; Thorndike, 1913). Therefore, education on specific tasks does not have benefits for a wider set of tasks.

Thorndike and Woodworth called the habits of mind that were similar in situations A and B the **identical elements** of the two situations. These elements were not identical stimuli in the two situations per se, but instead similar *mental actions* or habits related to stimuli. They give the following example and definition:

> We may say "I tend to judge this with a minus error" and the habit of saying this may be beneficial in all cases. The habit of bearing this judgement in mind

or of unconsciously making an addition to our first impulse is thus an identical element of both functions.

(Thorndike & Woodworth, 1901a, p. 256)

The identical elements theory is part of a larger approach that came to be called **connectionism**. Thorndike defined it this way:

> Any fact of intellect, character or skill means a tendency to respond in a certain way to a certain situation—involves a situation or state of affairs influencing the man, a response or state of affairs in the man and a connection or bond whereby the latter is the result of the former.
>
> (Thorndike, 1922, p. 1)

He has used the vague terms "situation" and "state of affairs" intentionally; never, for Thorndike, are the stimulus and response taken for granted. He felt that human behavior was *selective* in that the first step in forming an association was to select the stimulus out of the stimulus field and then to choose the response to connect with it:

> All man's behavior is selective. Man does not, in any useful sense of the words, ever absorb or re-present or mirror or copy the situation uniformly. Even when he seems most subservient to the external situation . . . it appears that his sense organs have shut off important features of the situation from him.
>
> (Thorndike, 1906, p. 22)

The stimulus was never a "given" to Thorndike; his view of transfer was based on extracting "essential elements" of many separate stimuli from what he called the "gross total stimulus situation": "The mind's most frequent act is to connect one thing with another, but its highest performance is to think a thing apart from its elements" (Thorndike, 1906, p. 133).

If this seems very Jamesian, it is no accident; Thorndike dedicated more than one book to William James and sent him copies of his work. At one point, he even sent him $100 (real money in 1904), because he was afraid that sales of his book would cut into sales for James's *Principles of Psychology*. James hardly needed the money; he sent the check back with hearty congratulations!

Thorndike's connectionist educational philosophy advocated breaking down each task to be learned into their component mental habits, so that competence could be built from the ground up. Again echoing James, he claimed that once these habits are practiced and integrated, they would become automatic, allowing for greater range of adaptation to new circumstances. Indeed, Thorndike was in a sense a forerunner of what would later come to be called **mastery learning**: In mastery learning, one practices the operation of a particular rule, in the learning the steps of how to calculate area of polygons, for example, until he or she is near-perfect and then adds one slight twist to new problems, moving from square to rectangle to parallelogram to more challenging figures, always practicing to habit the skills being learned (see Cox, 1997, for more on the controversies between Thorndike and the Gestaltists in education).

The connectionist approach slowly won over practical American school systems, encouraging them to drop subjects like Latin and to put in their place an emphasis on skills for life and the workplace. This did not happen by accident. Thorndike himself preached for the change (Joncich, 1968).

Some charged that Thorndike was only promoting rote memorization: The Gestaltist Wertheimer derided Thorndike's methods as "piecemeal" approaches (Wertheimer, 1945/1959).

Thorndike defended himself in several ways. First, he said, he had always been careful, well before the Gestaltists (e.g. in *The Principles of Teaching*, 1906) to make sure that the habits children were learning made sense. He encouraged teachers to always use some unit of measurement in their problems, such as inches or pounds, and never to use problems that would not occur in the real world, simply for theoretical reasons (e.g. to avoid problems such as "Suzy has seventeen-eighteenths of a dollar"). Second, he cautioned to be careful to promote habits that would not later have to be broken. Although he acknowledged the logical impulse behind teaching multiplication as multiple addition, he warned that such an approach might confuse children when they come to multiplying fractions. He answered the critics, teachers and psychologists, who accused him of rote learning this way:

> The psychologists of to-day do not wish to make the learning of arithmetic a mere matter of acquiring thousands of disconnected habits, nor to decrease by one jot the pupil's genuine comprehension of its general truths. They wish him to reason not less than he has in the past, but more. They find, however, that you do not secure reasoning in a pupil by demanding it and that his learning of a general truth without the proper development of organized habits back of it is likely to be not a rational learning of that general truth, but only a mechanical memorizing of a verbal statement of it.
>
> (Thorndike, 1913, p. 7)

A final contribution of Thorndike to educational psychology, indeed to educational testing and psychology in general, must be mentioned here. He was a great proponent of measurement in psychology. He is reported to have said, "All that exists can be measured and measured in some amount." By now, you should be familiar with the desire for using mathematics to explain the world as one of the defining characteristics of the scientific enterprise: Descartes, Newton, Kant, Galton, Fechner, Helmholtz, Wundt, Ebbinghaus and others were enchanted by numbers. Even the Gestaltists, who detested counting for counting's sake, made use of the specialized mathematics of topology. Thorndike had the same mathematical faith. He wrote,

> Physics could not have progressed to its present knowledge about the movement of bodies in space if its only scales for length and weight and time had been *short, long, very long* and *light, heavy, too heavy to lift, too heavy for two men to lift*. Replacing the scale *of freezing, cold, tepid, warm, hot, hot as boiling*, by the thermometer, helped largely to create knowledge of heat. So scales to measure such educational forces as the teacher's interest in his work or the ingenuity of his questions and such educational products as knowledge of arithmetic, enjoyment of music, ability

to write English, ability to manage wood-working tools and the like, are much needed.

(Thorndike, 1910, p. 212, cited in Joncich, 1968, p. 286, emphasis original)

And he practiced what he preached. He required his graduate students in education to take the first course in educational statistics offered (in 1902) in America and wrote the first textbook on the subject for the purpose. In the optimistic days before the First World War, teachers, school principals and administrators taught by Thorndike believed that better record keeping, measurement and statistical analysis would assist in educational reform. One of Thorndike's students, Frederick J. Kelley (1880–1959), completed a dissertation on how unreliably teachers graded essay examinations and, in part because of that work, created what is recognized as the first multiple choice test, for a reading exam in Kansas in 1915! (Samelson, 1987).

In part following in the footsteps of his second mentor, Cattell, and certainly outstripping his influence, Thorndike was involved at least to some degree in almost every advance in mental testing until his death in 1949. He collaborated with Robert Means Yerkes in the construction of the Army Alpha and Beta Tests, primitive and somewhat inaccurate measures of the intelligence of recruits in World War I. He and his colleagues created tests to select aviators for that war, as well. He created tests for reading, mathematics, history and other school subjects. His tests in the world of work ranged from assessments for factory work to an instrument to select Foreign Service officers. Indeed, with his colleagues Cattell and Woodworth, he was one of the founders of the test publishing concern The Psychological Corporation.

Based on his work with several twin studies, adoption studies and school dropout surveys, Thorndike was a committed hereditarian, with many of the social values that such a view entails. (For example, he believed in people rising through work to their own places in a meritocracy but suspected that much of that advancement was due to inherited gifts.) By all accounts, he was not a dogmatic and racist hereditarian, like many of his contemporaries. He merely believed in his own statistics:

> There can be little doubt that of a thousand ten-year-olds taken at random, some will be four times as energetic, industrious, quick, courageous or honest as others or will possess four times as much refinement, knowledge of arithmetic, power of self-control, sympathy or the like. It has been found amongst children of the same age and in essential respects, of the same home training and school advantages, some do in the same time six times as much or do the same amount with only a tenth as many errors.
>
> (Thorndike, 1911, pp. 7–8)

At the same time, he disagreed with those, such as Charles Spearman, who suggested that there was a strong role for general intelligence. His earlier evidence concerning identical elements in transfer of training suggested that instead, intelligence was a collection of many specific skills. Like Binet, he recognized that intelligence, at any rate, could not be measured as easily as heat is measured by a thermometer, as devoted as he was to a mathematical explanation of the psychological world. And he recognized the fallacy of assuming there was a gene for something just because we could name it: "Genetics is not written from the dictionary!" he would say.

Finally, speaking of the dictionary, Thorndike, in addition to all of his other tasks, compiled dictionaries for use in schools, but he did so in his usual scientific and methodical way. First, he and his colleague Irving Lorge compiled frequency norms of English words, by hiring a corps of people in the depths of the Great Depression to simply count the number of times a word appears in the pages of periodicals. (Thorndike would do this himself while waiting for trains, just as he would sometimes subject audiences of one of his public lectures to his latest psychological test.) Then he would include the most common words in his *Thorndike-Century Junior* and *Senior Dictionaries*. The definitions, some of them written by Thorndike himself, were always composed of words that were more common than the word being defined, a brilliant innovation, obvious today. You were likely brought up on one of the later editions (called the Thorndike-Barnhart)! Indeed, Thorndike's wordlists, updated, form the basis of many elementary school textbooks.[13]

Thorndike, then, was a strong advocate of the best possible science to be used in the service of the classroom. Indeed, his career is an object lesson on the illusion of the dividing line between basic and applied science. He recognized that one cannot focus on application at the expense of philosophical sophistication about how humans actually learn, and he certainly did not suggest that one could ignore technological or statistical sophistication. Theory, method, data and application cannot be separated in the best psychological work.

Functionalism Summarized: The American Psychology

Functionalism was a sprawling school, a perspective that became so diverse that instead of being overturned or refuted, was absorbed and assimilated into later views of psychology. It is only a slight exaggeration to suggest that all psychologists are functionalists today, whether they know it or not. It is so diverse that, to be helpful, I will end this chapter with a definition.

Look at Table 7.1, adapted from Owens and Wagner, 1992. First and foremost, functionalists believe that all psychological processes, whether physiological, behavioral or mental, are *adaptive*. An organism's evolutionary history has provided it with certain mechanisms to survive and prosper, and all of psychology is meant to examine how humans and animals use these mechanisms, together with what they have learned, to reach their goals. As an old distinction puts it, the structuralists, led by Titchener, studied what consciousness *is* and functionalists studied what consciousness is *for*.

Second, functionalists believe psychology should not be about analyzing all mental processes into tiny bits and putting them together, as Titchener's structuralists would have it, but to examine thought and behavior as continuous, ongoing and recurrent. Functionalism studies ongoing *processes* rather than mental contents.

Third, it makes no sense to a functionalist to study perception and action separately. Consider what happens when a baseball player catches a ball. The ballplayer begins with a set, a goal, a meaningful act defined by the game. The act of perception and the subsequent activities are defined by a purpose. Then, as he goes to catch the

Table 7.1 Functionalism Defined

1. All psychological processes (physiological, behavioral or mental) are *adaptive*.
2. Mental processes cannot be reduced to bits and then reconstructed. Thought and behavior are continuous, ongoing and recurrent.
3. Perception and action are not separate processes but are *coordinated* in their activity.
4. Functionalists are open to all kinds of methods: experimentation, mental testing, introspection, observation, etc.
5. Functionalists are not embarrassed to make practical contributions to society.
    a. G. Stanley Hall—developmental psychology
    b. John Dewey—education in a democracy, social activism
    c. James McKeen Cattell, Henry H. Goddard, Lewis Terman, Robert Yerkes—psychological testing
    d. Lightner Witmer—clinical psychology, school psychology
    e. E.L. Thorndike, Robert S. Woodworth—educational psychology

Source: Adapted from Owens & Wagner, 1992

ball, eyes, hands and legs are *coordinated* in their activity. The eyes direct the hand and the hand provides feedback to the eyes tracking the ball.

Fourth, functionalists are *open to all kinds of methods*, drawn from all kinds of disciplines—introspection where useful, experimentation where appropriate, observation when needed, behavior analysis where necessary (particularly with animals) and mental testing of individual differences in abilities, among other things.

Fifth and finally, unlike the structuralists, with whom they were competing in the early 20th century, the functionalists were not embarrassed to make *practical contributions to society*. A list of these practical contributions virtually defines the range of psychology today. One functionalist, G. Stanley Hall, was concerned with contributing to the practice of pedagogy and education. John Dewey was interested in education as well as social change. James McKeen Cattell, who studied with Galton as well as Wundt, invented mental testing, which was furthered and sometimes misused by Hall's students Lewis Terman and Henry H. Goddard. Robert Yerkes. E.L. Thorndike and Robert Woodworth contributed to the mental testing movement and educational psychology; Thorndike also provided the foundations in comparative psychology that, refined by Skinner, became the core of behavior modification (see the next chapter). Lightner Witmer, student and colleague of Cattell, opened the first psychological clinic in America at the University of Pennsylvania and started the movement for PhD psychologists to be enabled to practice as clinicians.

Notes

1. In each generation of the James family, there was a William and a Henry, making things confusing. Hence, William the psychologist, with brother Henry, the novelist, had a father named Henry (Sr.). William of Albany was the rich grandfather.
2. Indeed, the James family was plagued with mental disorders. William's father had suffered a serious anxiety attack in 1844; seven of his uncles were dead by 40 of various instabilities. Henry suffered from mysterious back ailments and depressions and his beloved little sister Alice from hysteria. Robertson James died of alcoholism and William's son, Billy, had spent time at McLean's. See Lewis (1991), Allen (1967) and Menand (1998).

3. James's real views on Wundt can be seen in a private letter to his esteemed friend, Carl Stumpf (see Chapter 6). He said: "since there must be professors in the world, Wundt is the most praiseworthy and never-too-much-to be respected type of the species. He isn't a genius, he is a *professor*—a being whose duty is to know everything and have is own opinion about everything in his [discipline].... He is the finished example of how much mere *education* can do for a man" (W. James, 1887, cited in H. James (1920).
4. The words translated here as "fixed ideas" were *idée fixe* in the original French; this term, meaning a central obsession or complex, is from the work of Pierre Janet. In making this allusion for his French correspondent, he is simultaneously showing that he knows that what Freud was saying was not all that new, implying that Freud might be crazy and possibly making the point that he believes Janet, not Freud, to be the more cautious scientist.
5. This, of course, is a Christian saying, and the *Varieties* is mostly a Christian book. But in these lectures, James also addresses Buddhism, Hinduism, Islam and Judaism, always in generous terms.
6. Recall also, from Chapter 1, that an anticipation is different than a foundation. I do not claim that James invented operationalism and that others who use the term necessarily got it from him. Operationalism as a philosophy of science is usually credited to the physicist Percy Bridgman (1882–1961).
7. This note scribbled by James was not original to him. It is found in multiple wordings back at least to 1856 (e.g. *The Essex Standard* [Newspaper] August 27, p. 2, col. 6, Colchester, England). See https://quoteinvestigator.com/2013/01/10/watch-your-thoughts/
8. Harvard had then the "Annex" for women; it became Radcliffe in 1894, but even then it did not offer graduate work.
9. And philosophy; she also served as president of the American Philosophical Society in 1916.
10. This was not uncommon among psychologists: Wundt's *Volkerpsychologie*, also influenced by Hegel and Haeckel, was based on the same idea (see Chapter 5).
11. Hall had even applied to the renowned African-American institution Howard University, for a post (in chemistry!) in 1872, after returning from his first trip to Germany, but before studying with James (Guthrie, 1998).
12. This example has a long history; it was used by Descartes to illustrate the operation of the nervous system. Dewey cites James here (1890/1983, p. 36).
13. Indeed, even works of art have been written from them. Dr. Seuss (Theodore Geisel) wrote *Green Eggs and Ham* with only the 50 most common words, all of them one syllable, except for, of course, "anywhere."

8 Behaviorism

Two Simultaneous Routes to the Psychology of Reflexes

Behaviorism seems, like functionalism, to be a quintessentially American school of psychology. A science based on the prediction and control of behavior is practical, seemingly anti-philosophical and nonintrospective in all senses of that word. Its focus on the environment suggested, for most of its practitioners, an optimism about change in human behavior and even human societies that was characteristic of America.

American functionalism was in fact one of its roots: Many of the discoveries of operant or instrumental conditioning can be traced to E.L. Thorndike's work with cats and his notion of the "survival of the fittest behavior." But the paradigm shift in psychology from the direct study of mind to the study of behavior also comes from another familiar source: that of the European revolution in physiology in the mid-19th century. In fact, the great Ivan Pavlov never considered himself a psychologist, but a physiologist; shortly after he began studying what would later be called classical conditioning, he had a Nobel Prize in the physiology of the digestive system to prove it. His goal was to anchor the conditioning processes in the brain. Another experimental physiologist influenced greatly both John B. Watson and B.F. Skinner: an immigrant from Germany by the name of Jacques Loeb (1859–1924). Loeb suggested that behavior was a property of a whole organism, not a particular brain center or the brain alone. This allowed the birth of the notion that a science of behavior alone could be constructed, without referring either to the underlying nerve physiology or to "mentalisms"—mental states (like "intelligence" or "will") that are said to cause behavior. The behavioral paradigm shift within psychology is linked not only to evolution through functionalism but also, paradoxically, to the same physiological movement that influenced Wundt. Psychology in general and behaviorism in particular took from these predecessors several assumptions that remain part of our paradigm today: belief in evolution, materialism, scientific determinism, reliance on controlled experimentation and reliance on only those data that can be empirically observed, or **positivism**.

Ivan Pavlov (1849–1936)

Ivan Petrovich Pavlov was the son of a Russian Orthodox priest in the small town of Ryazan, Russia. From his father, he acquired a love of learning, but also a spirit of self-denial and a love of hard physical work, for in 19th-century Russia, a priest's family was nearly as poor as the peasants in their parish and required to work the land for food like everyone else. Young Ivan was sent to the local ecclesiastical seminary at the age of 11, where his characteristic intensity and seriousness were first appreciated. He read voraciously and pestered the abbot of the monastery with commentaries on everything he read, and he was allowed to read nearly everything he could get his hands on. The young, idealistic monks allowed Pavlov to follow his passions for literature, science and even politics, even if that meant coming up short on theology and mathematics. For Pavlov was young in an extraordinary time for Russia. Tsar Alexander II had just freed the serfs from hereditary bondage to the land and was allowing new, Western ideas to be published in the periodicals. Tolstoy was writing *War and Peace* in the 1860s and had started a school for peasant children on his estate modeled on the latest American and European theories of education; Dostoyevsky had published *Notes From the Underground* and was embarking on the period of his most significant work. Even Darwin's theories were being taught in the seminary. Liberals in the cities were advocating Western science as a way for Russia to overcome its backwardness. Young Pavlov, shy in personal interactions but ferocious in intellectual debates, was caught up in the spirit of the times and converted to the medical materialism advocated by the physiologists of Germany: Helmholtz, Ludwig and du Bois-Reymond.

While studying natural science at the University of St. Petersburg, he began to advocate *nervism*, the notion that all organs of the body are controlled by the action of the nerves. Indeed, his thesis on the nerves of the pancreas allowed him to graduate with honors. He earned a medical degree (again with honors) across town at what would come to be called the Military Medical Academy of St. Petersburg.

Figure 8.1 Ivan Pavlov (1849–1936, with gray beard) with students at the St. Petersburg Military Academy and a German shepherd research dog.

Source: Photographer Karl Bulia, 1913

After his residency, his medical dissertation on the nerve action of the heart won him a fellowship to study with the heart pioneer in Berlin, Karl Ludwig. Thus, at the age of 37, in 1886, Ivan Petrovich Pavlov, MD, had already done significant work on the pancreas and heart, learned the latest methods in experimental physiology and surgery and had even studied blood pressure, using an early version of the pressure cuff that we use today. At the end of his fellowship in Germany, he embarked on a research program that he thought would be his life's work and would win him the Nobel Prize in 1904, the physiology of the digestive system. By 1891, he was professor of physiology at the St. Petersburg Military Medical Academy, where he would remain for the rest of his life, and he had been appointed the head of physiology for the new Imperial Institute for Experimental Medicine (Babkin, 1949).

Although it may seem that the digestive system has little to do with psychology, in Pavlov's case, nothing could be further from the truth. For it was his insights in this research area, in research technique as well as findings, that directly led to his famous work on conditioned reflexes. We will now consider this work in some detail.

Gastric Research

Before leaving Germany, Pavlov studied briefly in the laboratory of gastric researcher R.P.H. Heidenhain (1834–1897), himself a student of Emil du Bois-Reymond. From Heidenhain, Pavlov learned how to operate on the stomach of dogs to observe the formation of the gastric juice. Specifically, a pouch is separated from the stomach and left with a hole in the abdominal wall for collection of gastric juices. This idea was based on the observations of William Beaumont (1785–1853), a frontier U.S. Army doctor in Michigan, who reported the case of Alexis St. Martin, a Canadian trapper who was accidentally shot in the abdomen. Beaumont had given St. Martin 36 hours to live, but the tough Canadian trapper survived. When Beaumont sewed him up, however, there was not enough tissue left to completely close the wound, so it had healed leaving a hole in the abdominal wall that went straight through to the inside of the stomach. In gratitude, St. Martin had allowed Beaumont to insert bits of food into the stomach with a silk thread to determine how long it would take to digest various foods or to insert a small spoon to sample the gastric juices. (Unpleasant as this sounds, St. Martin allowed Beaumont to do this work periodically over several years; the trapper lived to be 86 years old!)

Replicating this work on dogs in the research lab was difficult. One could not puncture the stomach directly, as the hydrochloric acid would usually leak out and kill the dog. So Pavlov perfected a procedure of Heidenhain's in which the outer layer of the stomach was separated, leaving the stomach capsule intact; the layer could be attached to the abdominal wall and provide an enclosed tube of tissue that would continue to produce gastric juice for collection through an opening in the abdomen, a *gastric fistula*, carefully fitted with a noncorrosive tube. This procedure, still called "Pavlov's pouch" in the medical literature, preserved all of the nerves leading to the stomach, allowing the dogs to live relatively normally after healing from the surgery and to lead healthy lives while serving as research subjects (Babkin, 1949; Todes, 2002).

The care of his dogs was important to Pavlov for both humane and scientific reasons. Pavlov hated to kill dogs or cause them pain for research purposes and went to great lengths to minimize their suffering. He wrote,

> When I dissect and destroy a living animal, I hear within myself a bitter reproach that with rough and blundering hand I am crushing an incomparable artistic mechanism. But I endure this in the interest of truth, for the benefit of humanity.
> (Pavlov, 1904, quoted in Babkin, 1949, p. 162)

He constructed a state-of-the-art antiseptic operating theater for his dogs that was more sophisticated than most humans in Russia had access to at that time. He always used anesthesia, minimized the blood loss of the procedure and operated very carefully but quickly. It was said that he could finish an operation when others were just beginning. The dogs were always treated well post-operatively—on occasion during the hard years of the early Soviet Union, Pavlov would make sacrifices to keep them well fed. (He once complained bitterly to Lenin personally about lab funding at a time when complaints to the authorities could easily get someone killed or shipped to a gulag in Siberia; he got his funding.) Pavlov's lab assistants knew that the surest way to incur his wrath was to mistreat a dog.

It was also important that the trauma to the dogs be minimized to obtain good scientific data. Before Pavlov's work, what was known about the digestive system was obtained from animals under severe stress. But Pavlov knew that the body strove to maintain a balance in its functioning to preserve what the great French physiologist Claude Bernard (1813–1878) called the *milieu interior* or **internal environment**. Information gained from dogs in pain, under threat or distress, was useless in determining normal functioning, because the internal environment, when seriously out of balance, would produce data that would not be applicable to normal functioning.

Pavlov discovered from his work that it was not required that food reach the stomach before gastric juice is produced; therefore, he thought the signal to produce it should not come from the stomach but from the brain. Indeed, he perfected a surgery in which food would go in a dog's mouth and drop out the neck—a procedure called "sham feeding." (The gastric juice thus produced, strained, purified and boiled was sold to people as a medicine for stomach problems! The dogs did not starve but were fed meat powder directly into the stomach). But the signal might come instead from the saliva glands, so he developed an even more delicate surgical procedure to implant a salivary fistula into dogs' cheeks to collect salivary flow. But even in this case, Pavlov and his colleagues noted, food does not even have to enter the mouth to prompt saliva to flow. All one had to do was show the dog the food and he would salivate. Thus, Pavlov, a committed nervist, had conclusively proven that some signals for digestion come from the central nervous system. It is for this work, combined with his work on the nerve function of the pancreas, that he received the Nobel Prize in Medicine in 1904.

From Psychic Secretions to Conditioned Responses

Instead of discussing the physiology of the digestive system at his Nobel lecture, Pavlov decided to discuss his new work on psychic secretions or the stimulation of the flow of saliva by sight or sound. As was typical for him, he began right off with some data for the distinguished audience in Stockholm. Not only does the sight of food produce a salivary response, said Pavlov, but bread, being dry food, calls forth more saliva than meat. And the saliva called forth by food is rich in lubricating mucus to aid in digestion, but the saliva called forth by a threatening stimulus like sour acid or sand is a watery cleansing saliva. Thus, an automatic reflex from the brain, uncontrollable and nonconscious, shows considerable discrimination in its action (Pavlov, 1902/1928).

Pavlov was a very methodical and thorough researcher, and by 1902, he had switched the dozens of students and assistants in his well-equipped lab over from the gastric work to the study of what he at first called psychic secretions or psychical reflexes. At first, he and his colleagues simply verified the boundaries of the ability of the sight of food to cause salivation. They noted that the food presented at a distance over and over again, without ever allowing an animal to eat it, would provoke large amounts of saliva at first, but that the amount of saliva provoked would decrease to zero over successive presentations. This would come to be called **extinction**. The greater the number of presentations over a shorter time, the faster the extinction occurs. But all one would have to do to renew the association between sight and salivation would be to give the dog the food, and salivation would immediately increase and persist with sight of the food. Indeed, with a hungry dog not under threat, the placing of food in the mouth always, unconditionally, provokes a response. Food in the mouth is an **unconditional stimulus** for salivation, which is an **unconditional response** (or reflex), always given in reaction to food. Because the sight of food can, after successive presentations, fail to elicit salivation, the sight of food does not always have the power to elicit saliva; its power is *conditional*, dependent upon its pairing with edible food. The **conditional stimulus** thus must *acquire* its power to elicit the response of salivation and although the response is the same type of response as the unconditional response (e.g. salivation), it may often be different in magnitude (e.g. the amount of saliva elicited by the conditional stimulus might be less than the amount elicited by the unconditional stimulus). Thus, there is need for the fourth term: **conditional response** (or reflex). In describing these phenomena, Pavlov used the Russian word *ooslovny* for conditional; original English translations (e.g. Pavlov, 1902/1928) used the terms **conditioned** and **unconditioned** reflexes and the terminology stuck. (I will therefore use the expected English translations from here on, even though it's clear that the logic of the original terms is persuasive.)

Pavlov recognized that any object for which a conditioned association might be formed would have many stimulus properties: color, size, shape, sound, etc. Which properties, precisely, are crucial? He also knew, from observations in the lab, that many odd associations had been formed by his dogs. They began salivating upon hearing the footsteps of a lab assistant, on being placed into the experimental harness, on seeing common furniture, etc. Could such an association be formed to a wide variety of stimuli that were up to then completely neutral with respect to their ability to elicit salivation? Remember, the sight of food is always associated with food; it does not seem arbitrary. If arbitrary associations could be formed, then the process of conditioning would be a general property of learning in the brain, not just a logical pairing of those things that naturally occur together.

The classic experiment, replicated and varied many times over some 30 years in Pavlov's lab, was conducted in the following way: A hungry dog, well recovered from the surgery to implant a fistula leading directly from the salivary gland to the outside of the cheek, was brought into the lab (soundproofed, to avoid distractions) and put into a harness to which she had previously become accustomed. Many dogs would comply easily, allowing the assistant to connect tubing to the fistula that led to a container that collected and measured the flow of saliva. The first step would then be to determine that the stimulus to be used as a possible conditioned stimulus (CS) is free of any prior associations to the unconditioned stimulus (UCS). A stopwatch is started and the CS (a tone, a light, a metronome or yes, after about 1906, an electric bell [Thomas, 1997]) is presented for a specified amount of time—saliva production is measured. If the stimulus is presented briefly a few times and little or no saliva is produced, the experiment may begin. The CS (let's say, a tone) comes on for a specified time. The UCS is then presented, preferably overlapping slightly in time with the CS. In the classic experiment, the UCS was meat powder, presented mechanically, so that associations would be not made to the characteristics of the experimenter. This pairing of CS (tone) with UCS (meat powder) continued, typically on a schedule of several times, a few minutes apart. Pavlov called each pairing a **reinforcement** (which is not to be confused with the later concept of operant reinforcement, delivered after the response, not with the stimulus). With each reinforcement, the number of drops of saliva, the unconditioned response (UCR) increased to a maximum, usually quickly. At this point, if the experimenter presented the tone *alone*, without the meat powder, he would be likely to see a strong conditioned response of saliva (CR). Presenting the CS without the UCS would, over several trials, be associated with a decrease in the magnitude in the CR, unless one refreshed the association by presenting the UCS. The CR, in fact, may reduce to zero. But if one waits a couple of hours and produces the CS alone, one may see a **spontaneous recovery**—an increase in saliva response CR with no apparent reason.

From this basic experiment, varied in countless ways, came over 500 articles based on thousands of experiments over more than 30 years in Pavlov's lab. By 1916, Pavlov felt confident enough to state in a lecture, "It has been proved that *anything, whatever you will, from the external world, can be made a stimulus of the salivary glands*" (Pavlov, 1928/1916, p. 265, emphasis original). This included unlikely stimuli such as a cold touch or a scratch.

At this point, we can see the general definition taking shape of what would come to be called **classical conditioning**: Through the process of evolution, some events have come to act as stimuli (UCS) that always elicit certain adaptive responses (UCR) from an organism. Classical conditioning is the process by which neutral stimuli (CS) come to acquire the ability to elicit a similar form of that inborn reflex response (CR), through successive pairings close in time (reinforcements) of the CS with the UCS.

The basic phenomena of classical conditioning were commonly seen in several other labs as well as Pavlov's. Pavlov himself had written about the tendency of dogs to salivate to distal stimuli in reports of his digestive work in 1897 (Babkin, 1949). Only Pavlov took the step of turning these observations into an abstract law or definition, and only then do observations become a true scientific discovery with broad general implications. It may seem that this early history of classical conditioning is based on accidentally noticing a fact, but Pavlov was well aware that conferring the status of fact on an observation is a difficult task. He said, "Who doesn't think, cannot see facts. To notice a fact, one must know how to observe" (cited in Windholz, 1990, p. 69). One must then test the fact, by replicating the results of repeated experiments, so that one is capable of reproducing it at will. Only then, according to Pavlov, can that demonstrated fact be related to other facts through a theory. But, paradoxically, one must have a theory even to gather observations, because how can the experimenter know which facts are important for the theory? We will now turn to Pavlov's theory and methods.

Materialist Foundations of Conditioning: Ivan Mikhailovich Sechenov (1829–1905)

Perhaps Pavlov discovered classical conditioning because he had been prepared to see the world in terms of stimuli and responses by a remarkable article that he had read as a young man by the distinguished Russian physiologist Ivan Mikhailovich Sechenov. Sechenov had studied with Müller, Helmholtz, Ludwig and du Bois-Reymond in Berlin (see Chapter 5) and with Claude Bernard in Paris; while he was abroad, Darwin's *The Origin of Species* was published. Sechenov had returned from these journeys as a committed materialist, just at the time when such notions were beginning to be tentatively discussed in Russian society at large. In 1863, he attempted to publish his theoretical statement as "An Attempt to Establish the Physiological Basis of Psychical Processes" in a widely read intellectual journal. The imperial censors forbade his title as an obvious and radical attempt to do away with the soul and made Sechenov publish his work—in a purely medical journal—as "Reflexes of the Brain." (Presumably, one could speak of reflexes as being entirely of the body and thus circumvent theology.) Sechenov's readers surely got the point anyway (Kimble, 1996; Pavlov, 1955, introduction).

> "Reflexes of the Brain" contains a simple and radical argument: Every human activity, involuntary or voluntary, is triggered by an external stimulus and will end, inevitably, in a muscular movement unless inhibited. Every action is the result of a reflex and we know about reflexes in the brain of others only by observing their external results.
>
> (Sechenov, 1866/1952)

Stimulus always leads to response, and every thought or action must begin with a stimulus outside of the organism or from a physiological interior stimulus (e.g. hunger). Sechenov coined the term **psychical reflexes** to make his point clear. Sechenov knew of an extraordinary human case of a person deprived of all bodily sensations through a stroke; the man slept almost continuously, because no external stimulus could trigger the reflex to wake up. He had conducted similar experiments (that we would no doubt see as cruel) to deprive dogs of their senses. They, too, would rouse only to eat and drink. And of course, Sechenov had found evidence from numerous experiments involving electrical stimulation of frogs, done in the manner of Helmholtz, that supported his view (Kimble, 1996).

Sechenov also knew about **inhibition**, defined as the process by which nerve stimulation decreases rather than increases responding. Claude Bernard had discovered that salt crystals placed at the head of an animal's spinal column would inhibit reflexes that were artificially stimulated by electrical means. Sechenov also mentions that Ernst Weber had discovered that stimulating the vagus nerve slows down rather than speeds up the heart. Sechenov believed that much inhibition originated in the central nervous system, rather than in, say, the exhaustion of the nerves themselves. In a homespun example, Sechenov described the startle response of a young lady when he unexpectedly banged on a table. All of us would flinch involuntarily the first time this would happen, but our response would be inhibited by repeated experience. Inhibition was crucial to Sechenov's theory, because it explained why we could think a thing and not do it. He wrote, "The thought is the first two thirds of a psychical reflex" (Sechenov, 1952/1866, p. 116). The ability to think without movement simply is an inhibition of the final step of the reflex. Moreover, Sechenov suspected that the effect of the higher brain centers was to intensify a response. In this view, the stimulus was merely a spark and the bodily reflex the fuse.

> If an animal has had its higher brain centers disconnected, the reflex response is muted, but the higher centers amplify the response into an emotion, such as fright or love, which is a much more intense and unpredictable reaction, analogous to the fuse of the reflex igniting the gunpowder of emotion and conscious thought!
>
> (Sechenov, 1952/1866, pp. 93–94)

Pavlov and Sechenov knew of and respected each other's physiological work. Sechenov, for example, called Pavlov the best surgeon in Europe. Pavlov claimed that Sechenov's influence on his conditioning theory was unconscious, at least initially (Pavlov, 1928, p. 39), but in addition to the term psychic reflexes, the logic of conditioning was clearly foreshadowed in passages like the following, in which Sechenov explains a child's learning the word for "bell" by a continual pairing of its sight and sound with the word:

> If this process is repeated many times, the child begins to recognize the bell both by its appearance and by its sound. Subsequently, when, as a result of learning, the reflexes from ear to tongue take definite forms, the child begins to call the bell "ding-ding." The same occurs when it learns the real name of the bell, because this name, like "ding-ding" is a *conditional* sound. But what is the sequel: the successive reflexes acquired by learning lead to a perfect notion of the object, to knowledge in its elementary form.
>
> (Sechenov, 1952/1866, p. 82, emphasis added)

Sechenov's theory grounded Pavlov's classical conditioning in materialism and determinism, as well as positivism: If all actions or thoughts began as reactions to stimuli, there would be no need for psychic concepts like "will" or "intention" to start the action. Human reactions—reactions that are always physiochemical rather than spiritual, from the physiologist's point of view—can be traced to natural, physical, observable causes. That every stimulus must have a response is determinism, and that those stimuli and responses must be and would be observable externally is positivism.

Pavlov, already a positivist in his gastric research, became a positivist where the brain was concerned based on its usefulness. After consulting the psychological literature briefly, Pavlov and his colleagues had initially toyed with the notion that different salivation to different stimuli was a result of a dog's conscious choice, but the arguments led to confusion; Sechenov's theory, which avoided mind altogether, solved the problem.[1] As early as 1903, Pavlov had decided in favor of materialism even for mental processes—he began referring to "so-called psychical phenomena." By 1904, the terms unconditioned and conditioned reflexes were adopted, with the following statement:

> In conclusion, we must count it an uncontestable fact that the physiology of the highest parts of the central nervous system of the higher animals can not be successfully studied, unless one utterly renounces the indefinite pretensions of psychology and stands upon purely objective ground.
> (Pavlov, 1904/1928, p. 75)

Pavlov's Theory of Conditioning and the Brain

Being a physiologist, Pavlov became extremely interested in the location in the brain where conditioning happens. It would stand to reason that if there are so many functions of the cortex that were localized (e.g. the occipital lobe being related to vision, the temporal lobes to hearing, etc.), the ability to form conditioning bonds should also have a particular location. The trouble was, Pavlov could not find such a location, the removal of which would make it impossible to form conditioned associations. True, if a part of the cortex was removed that inhibited an animal's ability to feel touch on a body part, associations obviously could not be made to that part. And often after a surgery, an animal would appear to "forget" a previous learned association. But, unless the entire cortex was removed, a dog could still learn new associations taught after it had recovered from the surgery. Thus, Pavlov reasoned, conditioning was a general function of the brain not tied to a specific location (Pavlov, 1922/1928).

Pavlov, borrowing from his predecessors Bernard and Sechenov, postulated two opposing functions, excitation and inhibition. Every learned association of UCS with CS set up a center of excitation somewhere in the brain, but which might be a different place for each association. This excitation *irradiated* outward, accounting for the phenomenon of **generalization**, where similar stimuli to the CS would also provoke a CR. One may then condition a dog to make a **discrimination**: When food is presented to one stimulus, but never presented in association with a stimulus similar on a particular dimension, the dog will come to salivate only to the first one. In this way, inhibition acts against excitation to dampen generalization. (Pavlov believed that widespread, generalized inhibition resulted in sleep.) Dogs could make impressively fine discriminations in their salivation responses. In one case, for example, they could be made to salivate to ovals, but not circles. One could then change the ratio of length to width of the oval to come ever closer to a circle. Dogs could make the discrimination down to a ratio of 9:8. After this point, they would become agitated in their inability to discriminate. Pavlov called this agitation **experimental neurosis**. He argued that neuroses were essentially imbalances or conflicts between the mechanisms of excitation and inhibition and the generalized irradiation set up by these opposing forces.

Pavlov did not believe that all dogs were equally susceptible to these neuroses—he would never have agreed to John B. Watson's extreme environmentalism, for he had seen too many individual differences in how excitable his dogs were or how fast they learned, and he believed that these individual differences were largely innate. Even strong dogs, however, faced with an intolerable conflict, would become nervous or aggressive, or apathetic. Pavlov thus became interested, in his eighties, in psychiatric disorders, arguing that some of the characteristics of his dogs, partly innate and partly learned, could cautiously and provisionally be used to understand human disorders such as depression, obsession, paranoia, hysteria and hypnosis.

The Pavlov Laboratory

> What would I wish for the young people of my motherland who dedicated themselves to science? First of all—consistency. Of this very important condition for fruitful scientific work I cannot speak without emotion. Consistency, consistency and again consistency. Right from the very beginning inculcate in yourself the habit of strict consistency in acquiring knowledge.
>
> —Ivan Pavlov (1934/1955, p. 54)

Pavlov's lab was run like clockwork six days a week; Pavlov himself went to the lab every day, in at 9:00 out at 6:00, Sundays and holidays included, during the academic year (Babkin, 1949). New members of the lab would be asked first to familiarize themselves with the work of the laboratory by reading dissertations of other lab members, attending Pavlov's famous Wednesday morning seminars and observing experimental techniques. Soon the new lab member, usually a doctor working on his medical dissertation, would be assigned a few dogs who had had the necessary surgeries. In the years of Pavlov's research on conditioned reflexes, the dog was likely to simply have had a salivary fistula. If you were a member of Pavlov's lab, you would arrive early in the morning to bring the dogs to the lab from the animal house. You would put the dog into a loose harness and connect the salivary collection tubes. Experiments were nearly always designed by Pavlov and assigned to various investigators by him (Windholz, 1990; Todes, 2002).

As a new experimenter, you would most likely be assigned to repeat an experiment already done by someone else and write down every result in a book near the dog—the time and duration of stimulus presentation, the amount and rate of saliva production, etc. If your results replicated the results of the preceding experiment, all was well; you could then move on to a more complex experiment. If your results did not replicate the findings of the previous experiment, you would more than likely be raked over the coals by Pavlov, who had a serious temper and a tendency to curse like a sailor. But if you were man enough (or, after 1905, woman enough; Windholz, 1990) to stand up for your results and you could show that you had not deviated from Pavlov's precise instructions in conducting your experiment, then Pavlov might become intensely interested and troubled with the contradiction and would set about immediately to designing a third experiment to resolve the discrepancy.

Pavlov would say many times that he was most concerned with repeating the facts of an experiment reliably. Following a practice of Helmholtz, he would seldom believe a fact discovered in someone else's lab until it had been replicated in his own. Only when many facts had been collected and replicated could one begin to theorize, and only theories based on facts could accurately direct the hypotheses for the next experiments.

This method was enormously productive, leading to some 500 joint papers over 40 years. At any given time, there were dozens of workers, and this allowed Pavlov to systematically proceed logically with a program of research in his research "factory" (Todes, 2002). Table 8.1 shows the advantages of this methodical approach by briefly

Table 8.1 Pavlov's Discoveries Aided by Hume

Once Pavlov had settled on the basic aspects of the conditioning paradigm, he and his colleagues proceeded to solve the puzzles remaining in it systematically and methodically. As noted by Gray (1979), these discoveries can easily be arranged by the classic laws of association of Hume. In these examples, describe the conditions under which the CS can come to elicit the CR by pairing with the UCS.

Contiguity
- In order to form an associative bond between them, the CS must be close to the UCS in time and space.

Priority
- In order to form an associative bond, the CS should precede the UCS. It is best that they overlap slightly.
- However, a bond may be formed if the CS precedes the UCS by up to two minutes.
- Backward conditioning, with the UCS preceding the CS, rarely forms a bond and may be easily extinguished when it does.

Constant Conjunction
- The association reaches its maximum strength if the CS is paired with the UCS repeatedly and constantly.
- If a neutral stimulus is presented repeatedly before serving as a CS, it takes longer to form a bond between the CS and UCS. It is as if a constant conjunction with "NO UCS" inhibits later pairing of CS with UCS.
- Once an association has been established, if the CS is presented repeatedly without the UCS following, the ability of the CS to elicit the CR is diminished and eventually is *extinguished*.

Resemblance
- Although almost anything (bell, light, metronome, footsteps, buzzer, etc.) can serve as a CS, once the association has been made, the CR can come to be elicited by other stimuli that are similar to the CS on many stimulus dimensions.

summarizing some of these discoveries organized by Hume's empiricist criteria for causality: priority, contiguity, constant conjunction and resemblance (Gray, 1979; see also Chapter 3 for Hume's logic). Hume, of course, had spoken of ideas, but his logic of associations worked for stimuli and responses as well.

Pavlov's strong authority in the lab was not maintained despotically, but in the interest of efficiency. In Pavlov's lab, you did not work alone. It was a standard lab rule that you must aid other members of the laboratory in their work and freely exchange ideas (Babkin, 1949; Windholz, 1990; Todes, 2002). Most of Pavlov's working day was spent in the lab, walking around with a cup of tea, keeping track of the dozen or so experiments at one time and consulting with assistants. His occasional outbursts of anger were balanced by his concern for the welfare of his assistants or his dogs. He himself followed a rigorous schedule of work and rest, and even though he would himself come in to the lab every Sunday, he would chastise his assistants for doing so. Pavlov seemed to have developed a fine method of managing a large scientific enterprise: (1) Provide strong control by assigning experiments and issuing very clear instructions; (2) monitor progress frequently; (3) demand that all work together towards a common goal; (4) show great enthusiasm for successes and great displeasure for errors or superficial work; (5) discuss the implications of the work daily and (6) lead by example.

Pavlov the Man and Legend

Pavlov was revered by many of his colleagues to such an extent that in their reminiscences of him, he seems like a great character out of a Tolstoy novel. He was as earthy as a Russian peasant, as purely self-denying, incorruptible and devoted to his cause as an Orthodox hermetic monk, as devoted to modern progress as Levin from Tolstoy's *Anna Karenina* and as sentimental and bashful (outside the lab) as Pierre Bezuhov, the protagonist of *War and Peace*. Some of the stories may be exaggerated or apocryphal; as a dyed-in-the-wool materialist and famous Nobelist, he became a useful, if largely unwilling, figure in Soviet propaganda.[2] But there are enough such stories from so many sources that many of them must have been true.

Pavlov was without personal vanity. During his life, in the late Russian imperial era to the early Soviet Union, flattery was practically a way of life for those trying to get ahead. If Pavlov sensed that you were sincerely interested in his experimental work, he himself would be cordial and animated in discussing it. If he sensed, however, that you were responding merely to his fame or flattering him, he could be witheringly dismissive. And he made it clear that he was interested only in the true outcome of experiments. There are many stories of Pavlov, having exploded at an assistant, afterward being acutely embarrassed at his outburst. He would curtly but sincerely apologize when the facts were found to be in the assistant's favor or when others persuaded him that he had been unjust. The worst sin for a lab worker was scientific fakery, and Pavlov despised incompetent people promoted for political reasons, whether in the imperial or Soviet periods. More than once, in his poor days as a laboratory assistant, he refused a favorable career move, at great personal cost, when he did not respect the work of the man he would be working under, and his colleagues knew of this.

Indeed, his tenaciously loyal yet long-suffering wife Seraphima (another Russian stereotype!) was driven to distraction by his indifference to money. A famous story has it that Pavlov was conducting an experiment at home involving butterfly chrysalises, at the same time he was working in the physiology lab as an assistant and applying for professorial posts. He came home one day to announce to his wife that he had been denied a job that he had hoped to get, the second such job opportunity that year. Seraphima knew of her husband's tendency to be noble at her expense. Here they were, trying to raise a child in a miserable flat on about 50 rubles a month and Pavlov's renowned purity of motives had probably offended powerful people again! She went into Pavlov's study to upbraid him, wondering aloud how the family would keep body and soul together. Pavlov was looking at a dead chrysalis, dejected. He said, "Why do you bother me with such trivialities today, when all of my chrysalises have died!" (Babkin, 1949).

Even when they were poor, Pavlov would often arrive home without his paycheck, having loaned it to a colleague or used it to buy food for his dogs. After several such episodes, his wife put him on a strict allowance, putting a little money in his coat every morning. She would manage the house and their lives in such a way that Pavlov could think only of science.

Pavlov was sentimentally devoted to his wife as well. When they were courting, he bought her a pair of new shoes before she went on a trip. When she reached her destination, however, she found only one shoe in the box with a love note inside; he could not bear to be without her and had kept a shoe as a remembrance! He appeared to be aware that he could be impossible to live with. His friends report that, throughout his life, he could be overcome with gratitude that such an intelligent and patient woman would put up with him!

Finally, there are the stories of Pavlov, the peasant. He hated travel and foreign food, as much as he loved the intellectual stimulation that he would get by meeting with colleagues in Europe and America (where, as an old man in the 1920s, he was robbed of between $800 and $2000 by three rough men in Grand Central Station, in New York; the Rockefeller Institute, who was financing the trip, replaced the money; Thomas, 1997). During the academic year, his work discipline was legendary, but in the summers, at his *dacha* in Estonia, a perfect day for Pavlov would be a morning working in his garden, an afternoon playing a game of *gorodki* (a game like horseshoes), a simple bowl of *shti* (Russian cabbage soup) and an evening rereading a favorite Russian or English novel to his wife, who herself had a degree in literature. In spite of the tumultuous changes in government during his life, in spite of his personal losses (Pavlov lost the then stupendous sum of $73,000 from his Nobel Prize when the Soviet regime outlawed banks), he loved Russia.

He loved science, if anything, even more. He often called himself "an experimenter from head to toe." He took every opportunity in his public statements to preach for science, to convert others to its faith and practices, because he believed strongly in its benefits to humanity, as in this statement written in the depths of a bloody civil war in Russia:

> Let the mind rise from victory to victory over surrounding nature, let it conquer for human life and activity not only the surface of the earth but all that lies beneath the depth of the seas and the outer limits of the atmosphere, let it

command for its service prodigious energy to flow from one part of the universe to the other, let it annihilate space for the transference of its thoughts—yet the same human creature, led by dark powers to wars and revolutions and their horrors, produces for itself incalculable material losses and inexpressible pain and reverts to bestial conditions. Only science, exact science about human nature itself and the most sincere approach to it by the aid of the omnipotent scientific method, will deliver Man from his present gloom and will purge him from his contemporary shame in the sphere of inter-human relationships.

(Pavlov, 1928, p. 41)

American Behaviorism

Ivan Pavlov, as we have seen, was first and foremost a physiologist, not a psychologist. When he began the work that was to bring him lasting fame among psychologists, around 1902, he was completely unconcerned with the primary phenomenon that concerned most psychologists of that time in Germany and America, from Wundt to James: consciousness. As a materialist and monist, he believed that body—nerves and brain, gut and glands—were all that was worth studying; positivism as a method had produced highly replicable, mathematical results for the digestive system, as they would do for the nervous system. He did not so much rebel against psychology as consider it irrelevant. Although he would later come to know and agree with much that would become behaviorism, for Pavlov, behavior was simply a reliable measure that was both observable and replicable, nothing more.

It was Americans that would put the -ism in behaviorism. They did so as much for political reasons as for scientific ones, in a struggle for the purpose of psychology. They believed that it was high time for psychology to separate from philosophy and become a natural science. They believed it was time for psychology to address applied problems, rather than abstract problems in structuralist psychophysics. Optimistic in their outlook, they brashly made recommendations for change that went far beyond the data that they then had available and would often argue tenaciously for their point of view. Unlike Pavlov, in their hurry to fashion a science of behavior, they seldom had time to connect the behaviors to the brain; they simply assumed the connection and moved on.

Behaviorism as a school was founded by three men, none of whom had studied in Germany: E.L. Thorndike, John B. Watson and B.F. Skinner. Although Thorndike's doctoral dissertation, finished in 1898 (and graciously acknowledged as a predecessor by Pavlov [1928, p. 40]), deserves credit for being the first work to broach the subject, the substance of his work is much closer to that of Skinner and operant conditioning than to the classical conditioning discussed by Pavlov and Watson. Thus, we will begin here with the brashest of the group, the lightning rod who excited the enthusiasm and enmity of psychologists and the general public alike: John B. Watson.

John B. Watson (1878–1958)

In 1900, a young southerner named John Broadus Watson wrote to William Rainey Harper, the president of the then new University of Chicago. He had graduated from Furman University in Greenville, South Carolina, and was now stuck, at age 21,

Figure 8.2 John B. Watson (1878–1958)
Source: Getty Images

teaching at a local school. He was desperate to get away, believing that his only hope of advancement would be, as he said in the letter, to "study at a real university." There was, after all, no reason to stay. Watson's family had always been looked down upon in the town; his father, a no-account drifter and a drunk, left Watson's mother alone for months at a time to look after the farm and raise six children. John's mother had hoped that naming him John Broadus after the local Baptist preacher would save him for better things; she had even sold the farm to have money to move to Greenville and send her children to private school. But John was rebellious; he admitted later that, as a young man, he had gone out with a gun looking to fight black people for sport. He fought against authority even in college. He had had to stay an extra year at Furman, because his professor flunked him in a crucial course for "turning in his paper with the pages backward."[3] His mother had lived to see him graduate from Furman, but died less than four months later. There was nothing to keep him now (Buckley, 1989).

The University of Chicago was indeed a real university. Although then only 10 years old, it was founded on some of the fortune of John D. Rockefeller to be both a fine undergraduate institution and a graduate school to rival Johns Hopkins in the East. (The university's president, sparing no expense, had stolen more than half of the faculty away from G. Stanley Hall's Clark University—see Chapter 7). When Watson arrived there in 1900, Chicago's psychology department already boasted such faculty members as John Dewey and J. Rowland Angell, both founders of functionalism. Its department of biology had the distinguished Jacques Loeb (1859–1924) and Henry H. Donaldson (1857–1938). Watson was enrolled as a student in experimental psychology, which at the time, of course, meant introspection in the structuralist and functionalist modes. Some of his later animosity for consciousness comes from the simple fact that he found introspection stuffy and artificial. He simply was not good at it (Watson, 1936, p. 276). He added philosophy and neurology as two minors, but later in life, in his autobiography, he complained that philosophy "never took hold." He had to repeat the course on Kant; of Dewey, he said that he "never understood what he was talking about."

But Watson's minor in neurology offered a way out. He worked as a janitor and assistant in a laboratory with white rats[4] to earn his keep, and in this experience he found that he was comfortable with animals (he later said often that he liked animals as research subjects better than people: they were always on time and because they did not speak, they could be trusted [Watson, 1936; Burnham, 1994]). His dissertation, under the direction of Angell and Donaldson, was entitled *Animal Education: The Psychical Development of the White Rat* (Watson, 1903). In this work, he expanded on Donaldson's studies of the growth of nerve fibers in the rat's brain. Watson's hypothesis, in general, was whether rats' ability to learn was correlated with the degree of myelinization of the nerve fibers.[5] Watson found, by sacrificing rats after they had learned his mazes, that their ability to learn increased faster than their nerve growth did, giving the edge to learning. Watson's work was perhaps the first study to link brain growth to rat behavior (Buckley, 1989).

But, as Watson later acknowledged, the talented and iconoclastic German physiologist Jacques Loeb was perhaps an even greater influence than Donaldson. He had wanted to do his dissertation with Loeb, but Angell had warned him that Loeb was "not a safe man" for a new student to get involved with. Since Loeb influenced several other behaviorists, it is worth taking a moment to discuss why he was not safe and why he was nevertheless influential in psychology.

Jacques Loeb (1859–1924)

First, Loeb was seriously at odds with other physiologists. Although he was well acquainted with the Berlin physiology approach of du Bois-Reymond and Helmholtz, he disagreed strongly with their followers' tendency to reduce behavior to nerve action on specific spots in the brain (see Pauly, 1987). Like Pavlov, he had found that animals could overcome the effects of specific small lesions in the brain by learning ways around it. Unlike Pavlov, however, he did not even think that discovering the action of specific nerves was very important. Behavior, said Loeb, was a way for whole organisms to adapt to the environment. You might trace the tendency of animals to turn towards the sun to ganglion cells or the tendency of ants to follow chemical trails to chemical receptors, but how would you explain these same behaviors in plants and single-celled organisms, who do not have nervous systems at all? The answer was to simply look at the behavioral response of the organism (turn towards the sun; follow chemical trails) elicited or called forth by stimuli in the environment (direction of sunlight or brightness; increasing concentration of chemicals in the direction of the animal's movement). The tendency of an animal or plant to move in a direction by a physical or chemical stimulus in the environment is called a **tropism**, exemplified above by heliotropism and chemotropism. The concept of tropism explains why a moth goes toward a flame. Reducing such goal-directed behavior to physiochemical terms is the first step in getting rid of mentalistic concepts like "the will," and a step in the direction of behaviorism. Loeb called this the "mechanistic conception of life" (Loeb, 1912/1964). Focusing on the whole organism, rather than nerves alone, offered hope that a science of behavior itself—the study of the predictable relationships between stimuli and responses, even without reference to the brain—could be developed. This took behavior from physiologists and gave it to psychologists.

A second radical promise of Loeb's work was even more attractive to Watson: the promise of *control*, not only of behavior, but also of the shape of life itself. Just before Watson arrived at the University of Chicago, Loeb published accounts of two astounding lines of experimentation. First, by altering the condition of the development of embryos, Loeb had earlier caused a form of marine life called a tubularian to have heads at both ends of its body; Loeb said he could make as many of these as he pleased (Pauly, 1987)! Second and even more impressively, Loeb found that by changing the chemical concentrations in seawater in the lab, he could artificially fertilize sea urchin eggs *without the use of sperm*. He had, for the first time ever, successfully engineered life! An 1899 headline in the Boston Herald touted, "Creation of Life. Startling Discovery of Prof. Loeb. Lower Animals Created by Chemical Means. Process May Apply to Human Species. Immaculate Conception Explained" (cited in Pauly, 1987, p. 100).

Thus, at the time Watson knew him, Loeb was seen as a charismatic, energetic bad boy by physiologists and as a veritable Dr. Frankenstein by the popular press. To an ambitious, impressionable young man like Watson, who was more comfortable with animals than people, incapable of introspection, impatient with philosophizing and rebellious, Loeb was a powerful influence. Watson would soon introduce three of Loeb's notions into American psychology: the study of behavior as behavior of organisms, the mechanistic conception of life and the emphasis on prediction and control of behavior in the lab.

In these early years, John B. Watson was indefatigable, working long hours in the lab and the classroom, arguing impertinently with the university administration for money and making important friends in the profession. He continued his work with rats, studied seagulls one very hot summer in the Dry Tortugas in the Florida Keys, edited a volume of *Psychological Bulletin*, and organized meetings of the APA. All of this was played out on a very public stage, for Watson was receiving notice in the popular press, both positive and negative. *The Nation* had lauded his dissertation in 1903, but in 1906, Watson had attempted an experiment to prove that rats could learn mazes from bodily sensations alone. To do so, he successively removed from the rats sight, hearing and feeling from the soles of their feet and found that even with various sensory deficits they could still learn mazes. Even though Watson had not removed all of these senses from any one rat, animal rights activists (yes, there had been animal rights activists even since the time of Darwin) were outraged. Other psychologists came to Watson's aid, and from this episode, he learned the value of publicity. Both to earn extra money and to promote his views, Watson would frequently write controversial articles for the popular press, so he quickly became famous. He was hired by Johns Hopkins at three times his Chicago salary in 1909. His predecessor in the Hopkins job had been James Mark Baldwin, functionalist editor of *Psychological Review*. When Baldwin was fired for being caught in a Baltimore bordello with a black woman while running for the local school board (Robert Wozniak, personal communication, 1994; see Chapter 10), Watson got both his job and the editorship. By 1914, he was president of the American Psychological Association, one of the youngest to hold the post to this day (Buckley, 1989).

Psychology as the Behaviorist Views It

> Psychology as the behaviorist views it is a purely objective experimental branch of natural science. Its theoretical goal is the prediction and control of behavior. Introspection forms no essential part of its methods, nor is the scientific value of its data dependent upon the readiness with which they lend themselves to interpretation in terms of consciousness. The behaviorist, in his efforts to get a unitary scheme of animal response, recognizes no dividing line between man and brute. The behavior of man, with all of its refinement and complexity, forms only a part of the behaviorist's total scheme of investigation.
>
> (Watson, 1913, p. 158)

And then, in an address given in early 1913 at Columbia University and in its published version in *Psychological Review*, Watson took his stand. "Psychology as the Behaviorist Views It" is one of the most famous articles in psychology, but it is a political speech more than a scientific document. So it has been called the "behaviorist manifesto."

An English composition instructor might well appreciate the succinct strength of this first paragraph, quoted above. There is a lot in it, beginning with the term **behaviorist** itself. Although behavior had been studied as a part of psychology for more than 20 years by that point (see Danziger, 1997, Chapter 6; O'Donnell, 1985), this was the first time someone had publicly used the term behaviorist; Watson had been struggling for years with the conflict between philosophy and physiology in psychology. He would teach psychology from Titchener's textbooks and then go to the lab to do work on animals, only to have to retranslate his animal work into "animal psychology," relating it back to the evolution of consciousness. In 1909, he had written to Robert Yerkes, pioneer researcher of chimpanzee behavior,

> My interests are all . . . where an objective standard of determination is possible and interpretation takes the line of *the importance of the observed facts* . . . without

mentioning consciousness or deviating from a (wide) biological point of view. What is there left? Am I a physiologist? Or am I just a mongrel?

(Watson, letter to Yerkes, Oct. 29, 1909, cited in O'Donnell, 1985, p. 200; emphasis in original)

In another letter to Yerkes years later, he said that he had decided to create the behaviorist position by 1912 because "my stomach had had enough."

Then there is the phrase "objective experimental branch of natural science."

Later in the article, he takes issue with structuralist introspection. He begins by saying, "I do not wish to unduly criticize psychology." And then he goes on to unduly criticize psychology on the basis that introspection is not **replicable**.

> It has failed signally, I believe, during the fifty-odd years of its existence as an experimental discipline to make its place in the world as an undisputed natural science. Psychology, as it is generally thought of, has something esoteric in its methods. If you fail to reproduce my findings, it is not due to some fault in your apparatus or in the control of your stimulus, but it is due to the fact that your introspection is untrained. The attack is made upon the observer and not upon the experimental setting. In physics and in chemistry the attack is made upon the experimental conditions. The apparatus was not sensitive enough, impure chemicals were used, etc. In these sciences a better technique will give reproducible results. Psychology is otherwise. If you can't observe 3–9 states of clearness in attention, your introspection is poor. If, on the other hand a feeling seems reasonably clear to you, your introspection is again faulty. You are seeing too much. Feelings are never clear.
>
> (p. 163)

But Watson was not merely against structuralism. He was also against consciousness as studied by the functionalist, on two grounds. First, he noted that functionalists spend too much time on unresolvable mind-body issues. Most functionalists were calling themselves parallelists, following James's lead, which you recall is the position that mind events and body events were separate views of the same thing. They were most assuredly *not* **interactionists**, who believed that the mind (or soul) directly causes body events. To call a philosopher a Cartesian dualist was, by this time, an insult and that's what Watson does here.

> One of the difficulties in the way of a consistent functional psychology is the parallelistic hypothesis ... As a matter of fact I believe the functionalist actually thinks in terms of interaction and resorts to parallelism only when forced to give expression to his views. I feel that behaviorism is the only consistent and logical functionalism. In it one avoids both the Scylla of parallelism and the Charybdis of interaction. Those time-honored relics of philosophical speculation need trouble the student of behavior as little as they trouble the student of physics. The consideration of the mind-body problem affects neither the type of problem selected nor the formulation of the solution of that problem. I can state my position here no better than by saying that I should like to bring my students

up in the same ignorance of such hypotheses as one finds among the students of other branches of science.

(p. 166)

Second, he suggests that functionalists do not gain anything by talking about an "ongoing perceptual process" as opposed to a "percept" as the structuralist does. It is to him an argument over words. Neither one is observable, and it seemed to Watson silly to talk about an organism's adaptation to the environment without watching that organism in the environment.

Watson also notes in the first paragraph that prediction and control of behavior should be the *theoretical goal* and not merely the practical goal of psychology (Fancher, 1996). Our goal should not be to develop elaborate theories and then to find practical applications. It should be the other way around: To this view, application *is* science, in the sense that only when we know how to control something do we really know anything at all useful about how it works. Then we can make theories. This was a cardinal principle of the work of Watson's teacher, Loeb, and it goes all the way back to Francis Bacon (see Chapter 3).[6]

> If psychology would follow the plan I suggest, the educator, the physician, the jurist and the businessman could utilize our data in a practical way, as soon as we are able, experimentally, to obtain them. Those who have occasion to apply psychological principles practically would find no need to complain as they do at the present time. Ask any physician or jurist today whether scientific psychology plays a practical part in his daily routine and you will hear him deny that the psychology of the laboratories finds a place in his scheme of work. I think the criticism is extremely just. One of the earliest conditions which made me dissatisfied with psychology was the feeling that there was no realm of application for the principles which were being worked out in content terms.
>
> (pp. 168–169)

Finally, Watson "recognizes no dividing line between man and brute." He wrote,

> The psychology which I should attempt to build up would take as a starting point, first, the observable fact that organisms, man and animal alike, do adjust themselves to their environment by means of hereditary and habit equipments. These adjustments may be very adequate or they may be so inadequate that the organism barely maintains its existence; secondly, that certain stimuli lead the organisms to make the responses. In a system of psychology completely worked out, given the response the stimuli can be predicted; given the stimuli the response can be predicted. Such a set of statements is crass and raw in the extreme, as all such generalizations must be. Yet they are hardly more raw and less realizable than the ones which appear in the psychology texts of the day.
>
> (pp. 167)

To understand the relationship between stimuli and responses, one needs to exercise control over stimuli, of course, and Watson had attempted to hand-rear seagulls in the Dry Tortugas to determine the hereditary basis of their behavior and to determine the stimulus triggers in the environment. Although his studies there had been only moderately successful, he did not see why such a method could not be used with humans.

> My efforts in determining the stimuli which called forth such adjustments were crude indeed. Consequently, my attempts to control behavior and to produce responses at will did not meet with much success. Their food and water, sex and other social relations, light and temperature conditions were all beyond control in a field study. I did find it possible to control their reactions in a measure by using the nest and egg (or young) as stimuli. . . . Had I been called upon to examine the natives of some of the Australian tribes, I should have gone about my task in the same way. I should have found the problem more difficult: the types of responses called forth by physical stimuli would have been more varied and the number of effective stimuli larger. I should have had to determine the social setting of their lives in a far more careful way. These savages would be more influenced by the responses of each other than was the case with the birds. Furthermore, habits would have been more complex and the influences of past habits upon the present responses would have appeared more clearly. Finally, if I had been called upon to work out the psychology of the educated European, my problem would have required several lifetimes. But in the one I have at my disposal I should have followed the same general line of attack. In the main, my desire in all such work is to gain an accurate knowledge of adjustments and the stimuli calling them forth.
>
> (pp. 167–168)

"Psychology as the Behaviorist Views It" did not itself have much immediate impact (Samelson, 1981). Many of the criticisms against introspection were widely known already; indeed, even many Americans who had studied with Wundt were not terribly committed to his methods (see O'Donnell, 1985 and Chapters 5 and 7 of this book). And Watson's advisor J.R. Angell (1913) had even suggested that behavior was part of a limited solution to the problem at a conference in the previous year, though it was published in the *Psych Review* only after Watson's paper. There were only two responses in print immediately, from E.B. Titchener (1914) and Mary Calkins (1913), both largely negative, and Watson received only seven citations in *Psychological Review* between 1913 and 1920 (Coleman, 1988).

But Watson kept at it. First, in 1915, in his APA presidential address (published in 1916), he helped introduce the classical conditioning work of Pavlov to a wider audience with "The Place for Conditioned Reflexes in Psychology."[7] In 1919, he published his first text that attempted to make good on his promise of extending behaviorism to humans: *Psychology From the Standpoint of a Behaviorist* (1919). He immediately followed *that* with one of the most famous articles in the history of psychology: "Conditioned Emotional Reactions" (Watson & Rayner, 1920). This is the famed "Little Albert" experiment, cited in over 75% of introductory textbooks to this day.

The Little Albert Experiment

Little Albert B. was a calm and placid baby of normal health about nine months of age, the child of a nurse in a children's home. Watson and his assistant, Rosalie Rayner, were interested in whether fear reactions could be conditioned to formerly neutral objects. Although Pavlov's work was mentioned nowhere in the article, it is clear from the design that it is a simple experiment of his classical conditioning paradigm. Significantly, Watson did not choose a purely physiological response like salivation to food, but a response with psychological relevance: the innate tendency of humans to startle in response to a loud noise.

Before beginning the experiment proper, Watson and Rayner tested Little Albert to ensure that he was not in fact afraid of the stimuli that the researchers intended to use as conditioned stimuli. They report that Albert, confronted suddenly and for the first time successively with a white rat, a rabbit, a dog, a monkey, with masks with and without hair, cotton wool and even burning newspapers, was not afraid of any of them and usually reached out to touch them. They then tested whether a UCS-UCR reflex was present. While Rayner distracted the child, Watson snuck up behind Albert and struck a suspended steel bar with a mallet, producing a loud noise. Albert looked surprised, with s sharp intake of breath and raising of arms. After only two more noises, Albert was crying. Thus, the researchers established that the to-be-conditioned stimuli did not startle or frighten the child, whereas the loud noise did:

> Two months later, when Albert was 11 months old, the real experiment began. Albert was brought back into the lab and shown the white rat in a basket; he reached for it. As he touched it, the loud noise was produced and Albert fell forward on his face. He tried again, was again startled by the noise when he reached toward the rat and began to whimper.

- One week later, Albert seemed wary of the rat, but would still touch it if brought closer. After three pairings, Albert was cautious but still not crying and the rat presented alone produced noticeable but modest discomfort. After two more pairings of rat with sound, Albert finally cried when in the presence of the rat alone.
- Five days later, Albert still cried at the sight of the rat. Generalization of the response was then tried. He also cried when given a rabbit and less immediately, when given a dog. (He never cried when given blocks to play with several times in all phases of the experiments; thus, the reactions were not a part of a generalized crying fit). He also showed smaller negative reactions of withdrawal from a seal coat, cotton wool, a Santa Claus mask and Watson's hair, but not to the hair of his assistants.
- Five days later, Albert withdrew from the rat, but did not cry. The negative response was freshened by one pairing of the noise with the rat and Albert withdrew more strongly, but did not cry. The negative response to the rabbit was also freshened by a noise. Testing for generalization to the

setting, it was found that Albert did not react as strongly to the rat in a different room.
- One month later, he still showed tendencies to withdraw from the rat, the rabbit, the seal coat and even the Santa Claus mask.

Watson and Rayner end the article with the comment that they were prevented from deconditioning the fears because Albert moved away. They suggest that this could be done by pairing the conditioned object with soothing touch or candy or by simple extinction, the presentation of the conditioned object repeatedly without the UCS. They also say that they believe that the fears would persist over time unless deconditioned, in contrast to their own evidence (recall that the response did have to be freshened and that the response was milder in different contexts). They even take a potshot at Freud, suggesting that years hence an analyst would attribute Albert's fear of fur to being punished for reaching for his mother's pubic hair (p. 13)!

I have presented the original article in such detail here, because it seems that many textbooks over the years have presented the information wrong. They suggest variously that other stimuli were used or that Albert was deconditioned or they misreport the Freudian joke as fact! (Harris, 1979). They were even wrong about the unexpected nature of Albert's leaving the area; elsewhere, Watson reports that he knew Albert would be moving at least a month in advance and declined to attempt deconditioning. Another reason for reporting it is that this experiment, along with his textbook, was cited in nearly half of the psychology textbooks as early as the 1920s, when his manifesto was not being cited (it did not receive wide reporting until the 1950s—Todd, 1994). It was the combination of these two works that secured his lasting fame within psychology. His lasting fame outside of psychology was secured by even more outrageous popular works.

Scandal and Popularization

In 1920, John B. Watson was at the pinnacle of his profession, his reputation secure and growing within psychology, in spite of his brash style. With a successful textbook and his fame beginning even in the popular press, the president of Johns Hopkins had just increased his salary again to keep him from going elsewhere. Within three months, it all came crashing down. By 1921, Watson was fired from Johns Hopkins, never to hold a full-time job in psychology again. What had happened?

If Watson was a risk-taker within psychology, he was even more of one in his personal life. He had married his first wife, Mary Ickes, secretly, against the wishes of her powerful family in 1903; family lore has it that Mary had written a love note to the dashing and handsome Watson on her final exam in one of his classes at the University of Chicago. Soon after the marriage, Watson began seeing a woman from his past and he was being trailed by private detectives hired by his brother-in-law. Harold Ickes[8] had gone to the university president to demand that Watson be fired. Although the possible affair was hushed up, the marriage was never a strong one. When Watson began an affair with Rosalie Rayner shortly after she arrived with a degree from Vassar to be his graduate student in 1919, his wife had had enough and

Johns Hopkins was not nearly as tolerant as the University of Chicago. The Rayner family was powerful in Maryland; it had given money to Hopkins and one of the family members was a former senator. Watson's divorce was splashed all over the front pages. There were love letters, stolen by Mrs. Watson from Rosalie's bureau on a visit to the Rayners' home. One of them read, "Every cell I have is yours, individually and collectively. So likewise each and every heart reaction. I can't be more yours even if a surgical operation made us one" (*Watson vs. Watson*, 1920, cited in Buckley, 1989, p. 112). Watson was asked for his resignation, which he gave on the spot, and few of his colleagues defended him.

He moved to New York, married Rosalie a week after his divorce became final and was hired by the J. Walter Thompson Advertising Agency. Although he had to begin his assignment there selling Yuban coffee from store to store and working at a counter in Macy's, he was soon to rise to a vice presidency. There, he perfected the then already time-honored technique of the testimonial in advertising: If a pretty, handsome, rich or successful celebrity provokes a positive response in a customer, then associating that celebrity with a product in an advertisement would lead to the positive response being elicited by the product. Watson's 1928 campaigns for Pond's cold cream were classic: An ad with the title "Their glamorous beauty has captured the younger set in Chicago, Washington and New York" has a picture of a Miss Florence Noyes, "A Titian beauty, with delicate, apple-blossom skin. Miss Noyes, daughter of Mr. And Mrs. Ernest High Noyes of Chicago, a favorite of society, uses Pond's preparations to keep her skin always exquisite" (Coon, 1994). Likewise, the fear of a burned child could make a mother more likely to buy a tube of medicinal cream. Thus did Watson put conditioned emotional reactions to work.

Watson suggested that he was really at the agency as a showpiece, to suggest to clients that Thompson was new and scientific in its outlook. Anything he did to put psychology before the public would give credit to the agency, and he desperately still wanted to contribute to the field. So, he taught at night at the New School for Social Research, wrote articles for *Ladies' Home Journal* and even supervised Mary Cover Jones in her dissertation at Teachers College, Columbia University.

In her now-classic dissertation, Mary Cover Jones (1896–1987) deconditioned a boy named Peter of a set of fears that mimicked Albert's almost exactly, through what would later become known as **systematic desensitization**. Peter was exposed to a rabbit first in a cage across the room and then at successively closer distances, even out of the cage, until finally the fear was extinguished and he could touch the rabbit and let it nibble his fingers (Jones, 1924). Furthermore, extinguishing the fear of the rabbit simultaneously decreased his fear of a white rat and a coat, etc. Finally, as the treatments were interrupted for two months while Peter had scarlet fever, Jones's report notes spontaneous recovery of fear (without use of the term) to high levels after the absence, which was easily remedied. She also explored **counterconditioning**, by pairing a positive stimulus (food) with the rabbit. (Mary Cover Jones is rightly credited with this experiment in history of psychology textbooks, but it is less often reported that she is a pioneer in developmental psychology as well; she went on to do landmark work on the Berkeley Longitudinal Study of Development from the 1930s to the 1960s. See Chapter 10.)

Behaviorism

> Give me a dozen healthy infants, well-formed and my own specified world to bring them up in and I'll guarantee to take any one at random and train him to become any type of specialist I might select—doctor, lawyer, artist, merchant-chief, yes, even beggar-man and thief, regardless of his talents, penchants, tendencies, abilities, vocations and race of his ancestors. I am going beyond my facts and I admit it, but so have advocates of the contrary and they have been doing it for many thousands of years. Please note that when this experiment is made I am allowed to specify the way the children are to be brought up and the world they have to live in.
>
> —John B. Watson (1925, p. 82)

The lectures for the New School became Watson's most famous or infamous book, *Behaviorism* (1924), and above is his most famous quote. The first thing to remember about this book is that it is to some extent a lecture performance, and Watson was quite skilled at holding his audience. It is a book for a popular rather than a professional readership. In it, he is doing what many professors do in beginning courses: He is describing psychology but also telling what it is good for, how it should be used for one's benefit. He is looking for converts. (It is perhaps important to remember that New School students, then as now, were frequently adults in the working world taking night courses for practical benefit or personal enlightenment.) This is not to defend Watson, for here and in his other popular works he makes claims that have a strong flavor of racism, sexism (even misogyny) or unreasonable anger at society's conventions. But it is to put it in context.

Watson argues throughout that to control the circumstances of stimuli and responses is to be able to change customs for the better:

> The behaviorist is working under the mandates of society and consequently it does come within his province to say to society: "If you decide that the human organism should behave in this way, you must arrange situations of such and such kinds."
>
> (p. 7)

He mentions capital punishment, divorce, prohibition of liquor, war, fidelity in marriage and even the then recent Soviet Revolution as aspects of "experimental ethics" that could be studied by psychologists and could replace religion. If we could control behavior we could solve these problems, in a way that philosophy or religion has yet failed to do.

Behaviorism is an optimistic credo, and Watson's emphasis on environment as a determining factor would likely resonate to his class of striving, self-improving New Yorkers and Americans at large. He does not deny that physiological individual differences exist in individuals at birth, but he believes they are either relatively unimportant in the final outcome or *can be made to be* relatively unimportant by the efforts of parents, communities or striving individuals.

He claims that what we call instinct is either a consequence of simple physical makeup (Does a boomerang have an instinct to return to the thrower? he asks) or a basic reflex that has been modified by habit.

> Can it [psychology] not dispense with instincts? Can we not say that man is built of certain materials, put together in certain complex ways and as a corollary of the way he is put together and of the material out of which he is made—he must act (until learning has reshaped him) as he does act?
>
> (p. 86)

The book *Behaviorism* includes very little scientific data. Watson gives a good summary of Pavlov's work, a summary of the nervous system and a long discussion of the range of innate of infant reflexes and not much more. But the book certainly contains a lot of Watson. Again and again, he makes the point that even two individuals in the same family are given different treatment, undergo different experiences and thus turn out differently. Again and again, he advocates observation of one's own and others' behaviors and offers ways to change behavior for the better. Sometimes his recommendations are simplistic, and very often he goes far beyond his data. And his prejudices and minor obsessions are highly evident. In Watson's world, people, especially servants, cannot be trusted and the world is cold. The maid will stroke the genitals of a baby to calm it down. The chauffeur will turn a boy into a homosexual. Breaking the prohibition laws will lead to rampant crime through loss of respect of the law and so on.

The height of this bitterness is reached in a book that he wrote with his wife Rosalie, *Psychological Care of Infant and Child* (1928). In a chapter called "Too Much Mother Love" Watson begins by complaining how young children are kissed and hugged and coddled too much, which supposedly leads to infantile behavior and "invalidism" in adults. He recommends:

> Never hug and kiss them, never let them sit on your lap. If you must, kiss them once on the forehead when they say goodnight. Shake hands with them in the morning. Give them a pat on the head if they have made an extraordinarily good job of a difficult task. Try it out. In a week's time you will find how easy it is to be perfectly objective with your child and at the same time kindly. You will be utterly ashamed of the mawkish, sentimental way you have been handling it.
>
> (Watson & Watson, 1928, pp. 81–82)

Watson's views of women were also hostile:

> "a girl is foolish to spend the best years of her life in an office ... sharpening her brains when these things are of little importance to her in her emotional life as a woman." Modern women who stay home, however, have too much time on their hands and "They utilize this time in destroying the happiness of their children."
>
> (Watson, 1931, cited in Buckley, 1989)

After Rosalie died suddenly in 1935, Watson became even more moody and withdrawn. He became quite wealthy and famous. He had an expansive farm in Connecticut. But he would seldom be happy. Friends reported that after he retired from advertising in 1945, he would drink up to a quart of bourbon a day. He died in 1958 after having burned most of his personal papers. One of his sons, who had become a psychiatrist, committed suicide shortly after Watson's death.

Although John B. Watson's career in psychology proper was rather brief, his extraordinary public advocacy of behaviorism created a rallying point for like-minded psychologists and a bright bulls-eye target for his enemies. Under Watson, behavior the methodology became behaviorism the movement, a movement that became the dominant form of psychology taught in universities by the mid-1950s.

E.L. Thorndike

Pavlov came to behaviorism from the positivistic stance of physiology, and Watson came to behaviorism as a reaction against consciousness per se. But there was a third route to the study of behavior that has even older roots: that of the study of the animal mind. As we discussed in Chapter 4, Darwin and his protégé George John Romanes tended to ascribe to animals the ability to think almost like humans, for dogs to blithely deceive their owners or for ants to engage in athletic tournaments. In contrast, C. Lloyd Morgan had put forth what came to be known as Morgan's canon: "In no case may we interpret an action as the outcome of a higher psychical faculty if it can be interpreted as an outcome of the exercise of one which stands lower in the psychological scale" (Morgan, 1894/1903, p. 53). Morgan believed instead that most of animal learning could be explained by associative connections formed when an action leads to a desired consequence or trial-and-error learning. Morgan visited Harvard while E.L. Thorndike was a student there, and Thorndike's subsequent animal work was strongly influenced by Morgan's approach. In fact, his 1898 doctoral dissertation at Columbia, later published in expanded form as *Animal Intelligence* (Thorndike, 1898, 1911) has become a classic in the field, both for its clear rationale for avoiding mental explanations for animal behavior and for his pioneering work on the foundations of learning based on the consequences of behavior, later formalized by B.F. Skinner as operant conditioning.

Darwin and Romanes had relied on anecdotes and questionnaires sent in by correspondents to make their case for the linkage between human and animal minds. In *Animal Intelligence*, Thorndike criticizes this method:

> Human folk are as a matter of fact eager to find intelligence in animals. They like to. And when the animal observed is a pet belonging to them or their friends or when the story is one that has been told as a story to entertain, further complications are introduced. Nor is this all. Besides commonly misstating what facts they report, they report only such facts as show the animal at his best. Dogs get lost hundreds of times and no one ever notices it or sends an account of it to a scientific magazine. But let one find his way from Brooklyn to Yonkers and the fact immediately becomes a circulating anecdote. Thousands of cats on thousands of occasions sit helplessly yowling and no one takes thought of it or writes to his friend, the professor; but let one cat claw at the knob of a door supposedly as a signal to be let out and straightway this cat becomes the representative of the cat-mind in all the books.
>
> (Thorndike, 1911, p. 24)

Thorndike had indeed studied the "cat-mind" in a controlled fashion using many of what he called his "puzzle boxes." As shown in Figure 8.3, the boxes are constructed so that the cat cannot immediately escape, but must attempt to "think" to get out. Some of them could be opened by pulling wire loops or strings at the front or the back or top of the boxes, some could be opened by stepping on a pedal attached by pulleys to the door; some could be opened by pushing down on buttons or levers. In some of the boxes, the workings of the mechanisms were hidden from the cats.[9] The most difficult of the 14 such boxes required the cat to pull a loop and yank a string and turn a lever to get out.

Thorndike takes great pains to point out that what may look like complicated reasoning in animals may be far less than that. Although humans can easily select, out of the "gross total stimulus situation," what to focus on, it's much harder for cats:

> Thus the cat who climbed up the front of the cage whenever I said, "I must feed those cats," would climb up just as inevitably when I said, "My name is Thorndike," or "To-day is Tuesday." So cats would claw at the loop or button when the door was open. So cats would paw at where a loop had been, though none was there. The reaction is not to a well-discriminated object, but to a vague situation and any element of the situation may arouse the reaction. The whole situation in the case of man is speedily resolved into elements; the particular elements are held in focus and the non-essential is systematically kept out of mind. In the animal the whole situation sets loose the impulse; all of its elements,

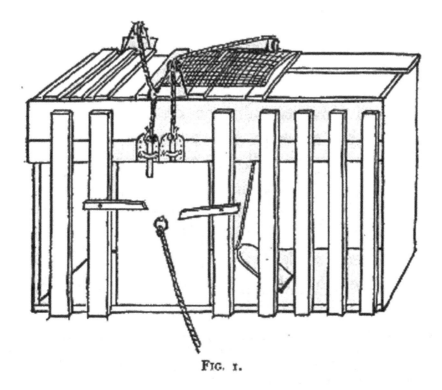

Figure 8.3 One of Thorndike's puzzle boxes for cats (Thorndike, 1911)

including the non-essentials, get yoked with the impulse and the situation may be added to or subtracted from without destroying the association, provided you leave something which will set off the impulse. The animal does not think one is like the other, nor does it, as is so often said, mistake one for the other. It does not think about it at all; it just thinks it and the it is the kind of "pure experience" we have been describing. In mental life we have accurate, discriminated sensations and perceptions, realized as such and general notions, also realized as such. Now, what the phenomena in animals we have been considering show is that they have neither.

(Thorndike, 1898, p. 119)

Figure 8.4 reproduces several of Thorndike's original graphs of time it took for cats to escape from various boxes. As you can see, there is some definite evidence to "trial-and-error learning": there is much error at the beginning, followed by a drop-off to correct behavior, but not before there are many ups and downs.

Thorndike noted that when a cat was placed in a closed box, it never took a step back, "sized up" a particular box and escaped. Instead, it first would claw and bite, and look for any opening to get out of the box directly. Thorndike assumed that the cat began from its native complement of responses inherited through evolution. He also recognized individual differences among cats. The feistier cats would strive to get out just to get out; they worked for "freedom." Others would be so lackadaisical (poor cat no. 11 was an "uncommonly sluggish cat," Thorndike, 1898, p. 13) that they needed to be let out by the experimenter a few times and rewarded with food.

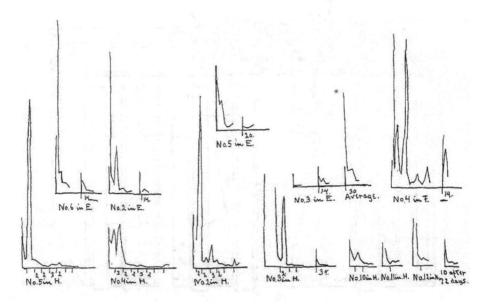

Figure 8.4 Thorndike's data from the puzzle box experiments. The dependent variable on the y-axis is time in seconds to escape from the box. "No. 3 in E" means "cat number 3 in box E"; each tick mark on the x-axis suggests a gap of a day; a tick mark with a number means a gap of that many days.

Note that the curves are not smooth; Thorndike argues forcefully that this suggests that learning is "trial and error" in nature (see text)

After they associate climbing out of the box with getting food, they will try to get out whenever put in.... A cat that is clawing all over the box in its impulsive struggle will probably claw the loop or string or button so as to open the door. And gradually all of the other non-successful impulses will be stamped out and the particular impulse leading to the successful act will be stamped in by the resulting pleasure, until, after many trials, the cat will, when put in the box, immediately claw the button or loop in a definite way.

(Thorndike, 1898, p. 13)

This tendency for the right response to be selected out by pleasant consequences and wrong responses to be filtered out by unpleasant or neutral consequences came to be called the **law of effect**, formally stated as follows:

The Law of Effect is that: Of several responses made to the same situation, those which are accompanied or closely followed by satisfaction to the animal will, other things being equal, be more firmly connected with the situation, so that, when it recurs, they will be more likely to recur; those which are accompanied or closely followed by discomfort to the animal will, other things being equal, have their connections with that situation weakened, so that, when it recurs, they will be less likely to occur. The greater the satisfaction or discomfort, the greater the strengthening or weakening of the bond.

(Thorndike, 1911, p. 244)

Experience in the easier boxes (after the time needed to get out had decreased from a couple of minutes to less than 10 seconds, for example) would aid in getting out of more difficult boxes, because a cat would first try the responses that had been successful in other boxes. Some of the cats could never get out of the more difficult boxes. Thus, in this elegant early study, much of the groundwork for learning by consequences, later called **operant conditioning**, was laid. For more examples of the behavioral concepts first described by Thorndike, see Table 8.2.

When Thorndike began his animal work, of course, neither Pavlov nor Watson had published the work for which they became famous (and B.F. Skinner was not yet born!). Therefore, he wasn't, at that time, a behaviorist. As we have seen in his work on educational psychology (Chapter 7), he never was squeamish about attributing cognition and selective attention to humans. In this he followed his mentor, William James. But he was, in essence, in favor of a **methodological behaviorism** for animals, simply because so much of their behavior could be explained without reference to their thought processes. If it were impossible in practice to tell the difference between concepts in the head of an animal and simple trial-and-error associations, it would be better, for simplicity's sake, to assume that that line did not exist.

If he was not a behaviorist, then what was Thorndike? He was an associationist, in that he assumed that stimuli and responses that are experienced often enough together would come to elicit one another.[10] But he was also a functionalist, in that what "stamps in" or "stamps out" a behavioral response was the adaptive consequence of behaving in that way. Indeed, you may have noticed that what Thorndike discovered is a kind of "natural selection of the fittest behavior": An animal in a puzzle box can emit a wide variation of behavior; the behaviors that are left after

Table 8.2 Thorndike's Principles of Animal Learning [Later Operant Behaviorism term for the same concept in brackets] (Adapted from Thorndike, 1911)

- *Multiple responses to situations*
  - Thorndike believed that to any "gross total stimulus situation" many varied, sometimes random responses are possible, and often seen in animal behavior.
  - Only those responses that receive the "law of effect" are saved. Useless responses decrease.

- *The Law of Effect*
  - Of several responses made to the same situation, those which are closely followed by satisfaction to the animal will be more firmly connected with the situation, so that, when it recurs, those responses will be more likely to recur. **Satisfiers "stamp in" a response**. [Positive reinforcement]
  - Those which are closely followed by discomfort to the animal will have their connections with that situation weakened, so that, when it recurs, those responses will be less likely to occur. **Annoyers "stamp out" a response**. [Positive punishment]

- *Learners have a "set" or an "attitude"*
  - What they have just been doing, or what was of use in a prior situation is what they will try first, and it is sometimes difficult to get them to change.

- *There are prepotent responses*
  - Animals have favorite responses; some are well-learned and tried first, and some are ingrained by evolution.
  - Prepotent responses are "powerful before" the experiment.

- *Law of analogy*
  - All other things being equal, stimuli that are similar to those which have evoked the response, will also evoke it [stimulus generalization].

- *Associative shifting*
  - One can gradually shift the association of one behavior by stamping in successive approximations to the goal. [shaping and fading] One can stamp in sequences of behaviors [chaining].

the environment administers pleasant or unpleasant results are *selected out* of that variability based on the adaptive consequences of engaging in that behavior for the animal. To use a bit more familiar evolutionary jargon, this is natural selection in ontogeny, rather than in phylogeny. This combination of associationism and evolutionary functionalism came to be called connectionism by historians to distinguish Thorndike's approach from that of later behaviorists, who preferred a more radical terminology.

In 1930, Pavlov was near the end of his life, Watson had been summarily booted out of psychology and Thorndike had moved on to educational psychology. But behaviorism was making good on its claim that psychology was a natural, biological science, rather than a kind of philosophy. It recognized no dividing line between human and other animals. It was rooted to traditional nervist physiology by Pavlov, through Sechenov; to experimental, holistic physiology, by Watson to Loeb; and to the evolutionary biology of Darwin and Morgan by Thorndike. Structuralism was dead: Wundt had died in 1920, after most of his American students had abandoned his methods, and Titchener had died in 1928. The battle was still underway with Gestalt psychology (see Edward C. Tolman and Clark L. Hull, later, and Chapter 6, earlier). And there was still one of Watson's criticisms to be dealt with: The messy language of adaptation bequeathed to behaviorism by functionalism needed to be reformed. It was left to B.F. Skinner to provide behaviorism with a language purified of much fuzzy meaning. As it happened, he would combine his gift of precise definition with skilled and provocative debating techniques and inspired mechanical tinkering to produce a technology of behavior.

B.F. Skinner

Life Before Psychology

Burrhus Frederic Skinner was born in 1904 in Susquehanna, a small railroad town in the hills of northeast Pennsylvania. His father was a hardworking lawyer with a small clientele, and his mother, Grace Burrhus Skinner, was a local beauty who had sung opera and recitals to local acclaim. Young Fred was subjected to both the joys and constraints of small-town life. In a town where everyone knew everyone else in those days, Fred and his younger brother could feel safe in roaming the town at will. There was a lot of unsupervised time, which Fred spent inventing games to play with his friends, learning about farm animals and local plants, writing stories and building things. He built scooters, rafts, wagons, slingshots and a cannon that shot vegetables over the roof (and occasionally through a neighbor's window). Once, he made a device to remind himself to hang up his pajamas: A sign that read, "hang up pajamas" was attached to a pulley system attached to a hanger. When Skinner hung up his pajamas, the sign would swing up out of the way.

Figure 8.5 B. F. Skinner (1904-1990) age 43 in his lab.

At school, classes were small enough for a bright boy to get individual attention, and Fred thrived on it. In eighth grade, when his father suggested that Shakespeare's plays were really written by Francis Bacon, Fred did his best to prove it to his bemused but encouraging teacher, reading biographies of Bacon and even attempting his masterwork, the *Novum Organum* (see Chapter 3). This was the beginning of a lifelong admiration of Bacon's inductive methods. Fred was considered a strong debater. In a letter written to recommend him for admission to Hamilton College (he had graduated high school second in a class of eight), a teacher wrote,

> It is only fair . . . to catalogue some of his bad traits as well as the qualities in his favor. Frederic is passionately fond of arguing with his teachers. He is quite a reader and although I don't think he actually supposes himself wiser than his teachers, I have found him [to give] that impression in extemporaneous debate. These debates are frequent for he requires a reason for everything and mere statements with no proof never find a ready believer in him. When he is engaged in a heated debate, Frederic is apt to resort to sharp and bitter retorts. This has lost several friends in the past, friends who failed to consider that the expression was stronger than the thought.
> (Skinner family scrapbook, cited in Bjork, 1993, p. 28)

The other side to this supportive small-town life was its provincialism and emphasis on conformity. Skinner's mother was very concerned with keeping up appearances: She would ridicule the petty failings of others and upbraid her sons and husband for minor infractions of decorum. Skinner said of her,

> She had *consented* to marry my father and there was an element of consent in her behavior with respect to him throughout his life. She had been the more prominent, the more successful and the more sought-after person in their group and my father barely made the grade in persuading her to marry him.
> (Skinner, 1976a, p. 25; emphasis in original)

As he became more successful, the father was always socially uncomfortable at higher reaches of society, berating himself at home and seeming boastful in public. After Fred's younger brother died suddenly as a teenager, the family went on a vacation to a resort to cheer themselves up, but stayed in their rooms the whole time for fear of making an error in etiquette. And Skinner's parents were not good at showing encouragement. As Skinner said, "They could not say that a person, friend, colleague or short story was good. They could not evaluate an experiment. And in giving them up as sources of praise, I never sought or found a replacement" (Skinner's personal papers, cited by Bjork, 1993, p. 25). Is it any wonder that one of young Fred's favorite books was Sinclair Lewis's *Main Street*, a sarcastic satire of small-town values? He finally described the reinforcement principles of this negative side of small-town life:

> People know each other and have done so over long periods of time . . . they are all a sort of common police force, censuring, commending, keeping in line . . . This general policing has its price . . . conformity is costly.
> (Skinner, 1968, cited by Bjork, p. 25)

At Hamilton College, in Clinton, NY, at first Skinner felt ill at ease with his classmates, who, on a fraternity-dominated campus, were just as status-conscious and uninterested in new ideas as people in his hometown were. But then, he discovered a more intellectual and urbane life through a friendship with his literature professor, Percy Saunders. Saunders regularly received writers, musicians and artists in his home; he was a friend of Ezra Pound and Robert Frost. He was far more tolerant of nonconformist ideas than were the citizens of Susquehanna. Skinner began to receive praise for his short stories and found an outlet for his acerbic wit in writing as "Sir Burrhus de Beerus" in a campus humor magazine. He resolved to become a writer after his junior year, when, at a writer's conference, Robert Frost agreed to evaluate some of his short stories and his future as a writer. Although Frost could not say whether Skinner had the fortitude to be a writer—whether he was "haunted with any impatience about what other people see or don't see"—he praised his "niceties of observation" and warned him not to be dry and academic. He finished, generously, with the statement: "You are worth twice anyone else I've seen in prose this year" (Bjork, 1993).

That was enough for Fred. When he graduated in the spring of 1926 with a degree in English, he got an agreement from his skeptical, practical father to support him for a year while he tried to write a novel. He built a study in the attic of his parents' home, now in Scranton, PA, and sat down to write. Skinner was later to describe this as his "Dark Year," for although he read James Joyce's *Ulysses*, Dostoyevsky's *The Brothers Karamazov* and Proust's *Remembrance of Things Past* and built a model sailing ship or two, he didn't write much for publication. He later said, "I had failed as a writer because I had nothing important to say," but that is not precisely true. He had little to say in fiction writing, but that was because he slowly came to realize that his real strength in writing was objective description, not describing his characters' thoughts or, like Dostoyevsky, arranging character and plot to make a specific moral point. He wrote to Professor Saunders that "the only kind of writing which fits my idea of pure literature is objective writing. I can't honestly or dishonestly do any other kind" (Bjork, 1993, p. 56). But Skinner couldn't see how to write literature with great themes using that method.

In retrospect, Skinner implied that this period of his life had not been wasted. He had then read a book by philosopher Bertrand Russell that began to provide an answer. Russell had called Watson's *Behaviorism* "massively impressive," and suggested that Hume's laws of association could be explained by conditioning principles. Russell defined knowing as a manner of reacting to the environment, not as involving a state of mind that only the person who has the knowledge can observe. Russell later moved on from behaviorism and Skinner never fully subscribed to Russell's point of view, but it stuck, especially after Skinner read Watson's work himself. Skinner said, "I came to behaviorism . . . because of its bearing on epistemology and I have not been disappointed" (Smith, 1986, pp. 262–263). After reading Russell, he contacted his college biology professor (who had assigned Jacques Loeb's work in his classes); Professor Morrill showed him the new (1928) English translation of Pavlov's *Conditioned Reflexes* and suggested that he apply to Harvard in psychology. Skinner was admitted without ever having taken a psychology course.

Before he went, Skinner did what any self-respecting writer of the 1920s would do: He lived a bohemian life in Greenwich Village in New York City for a few months (reading literature, going to parties, having an affair with a married woman;

Skinner, 1976a) and then went to Europe, where, among other things, he was flown in a biplane from Brussels to Paris and took another plane across the English Channel, only a year after Lindbergh's famous flight.

Skinner arrived at Harvard in 1928 with three books: Watson's *Behaviorism*, Pavlov's *Conditioned Reflexes* and Bertrand Russell's *Philosophy*. Looking forward toward the rest of his biography at this point, he would seem a committed behaviorist, and looking backward from this point, a "presentist" biographer (or autobiographer, in the case of Skinner's extended look back at his own life [Skinner, 1976a, 1979, 1983]) would of course find precedents. We can see already, for example, evidence of the playful tinkerer and inventor that would later invent the "Skinner box"; we can see a man strongly committed to clear and elegant verbal description and passionate and witty debate; and we can see a philosopher of science and social change. But though Skinner's science and philosophy was materialist, mechanist and nonintrospective in method, his *life* was none of these things. He was interested in the most modern literature; he played the saxophone and the piano well enough to work his way through Mozart sonatas; he suffered the joys of a happy childhood and the distress of an unhappy one and the pangs of love like the rest of us. As we will see, he was a doting father. And of course, he was introspective about his own motives in life and generally honest in describing them. In later life, Skinner would sometimes be vilified for describing humans as automatons, and he did give his critics ammunition. But, to explain himself, he would frequently recite a motto from the Roman orator Cicero: "*Homo sum: humani nihil a me alienum puto*" ("I am human: Nothing human is alien to me").

The psychology department at Harvard was then led by E.G. Boring, Titchener's devoted student of introspection. Skinner did not know much about this type of psychology and did not want to know much about it. One of its faculty members was Henry Murray, who taught a Freudian-based theory. Skinner told him dismissively that he taught "literary psychology"; he had given literature up for science. Instead, Skinner gravitated more towards the physiology laboratory of William J. Crozier (1892–1955). Crozier had been strongly influenced by Loeb's way of experimenting with whole organisms,[11] and Skinner's first attempt at research was to investigate geotropism in ants. But soon, at the urging of behaviorist Walter S. Hunter (1889–1954), he began studying the startle reflex in rats.

Behavior as a Function of Time; the Development of the Skinner Box

Skinner's early work with rats exemplified his common strategy of experimentation throughout his career (Coleman, 1987; Skinner, 1979).

First, Build an Apparatus

Skinner loved nothing better than tinkering in the well-stocked wood and metalworking shop. To study how startle reflexes affect running, he began with a box he called the Parthenon, a runway with a kind of silent starting gate, in which a rat could proceed a few steps toward food before being halted by a click (startle response). He traced the rat's movements manually with a pencil. He found too much variability in the tracing record.

Second, Try to Improve the Way a Record Is Made of the Behavior

He then made a runway suspended on wires: The rat starts down the runway, and each step vibrates the wires and sketches a pattern on a turning paper-covered kymograph. Too many messy oscillations in the wires. Tried running wheels, latency of response; they didn't work.

Third, Be Aware of Other Types of Behavior to Measure

When the rat is fed at the end of the run, it takes some time before it starts to run again. Maybe the pauses after feeding are themselves interesting. But who needs a runway to study feeding pauses? Maybe delay-to-eating could be a suitable variable. Maybe the physiologists, if not the psychologists, would like a way to measure ingestion, Skinner thought. All you would need is a cage that gives food and water.

Fourth, Automate the Procedure

What if the rat could feed itself? Skinner made up his own food pellets of a nutritious mash using a pill-roller machine. He fed them into the magazine. Now, how to get the rat to press the bar to feed itself? Maybe if you don't feed the rat and then let the pellets drop out of the pellet magazine (kerchunk!), it will come over to get the food and see the bar. Do that enough times and sure enough, they come running when they hear "kerchunk!" Make that happen only when they do something to the bar and soon enough, they're making their own little barpress-kerchunk-foodpellet sequences. And sure enough, they make more of them when they haven't eaten for a while and fewer after they have eaten.

Apply step 2: Connect bar pressing with the paper-covered rotating kymograph drum. Have a system by which every press advances the pen across the paper as it rolls if the paper cylinder rolls from left to right, that would be up a notch with each press. (In 1929, this was a windup system with strings, weights, gears and pulleys. Later, of course, electric motors were used; see Figure 8.6.)

Fifth, Examine the Curves Produced

This was Skinner's masterstroke, because all of the machines that he made were focused towards the goal of producing an accurate record of *behavior as a mathematical function of time*. It allowed him to examine **rates of responding**. The patterns in the curves were easy to see; fast rates of responding show as steep slopes; slow responding shows gradual slopes and no responding would be seen as a long straight line. One can also easily detect accelerations and decelerations. Pavlov had also looked at rates of saliva drops with the presentation of a conditioned or unconditioned stimulus, but he had not done so in such an elegant way. One of the other advantages of this method is that it records no irrelevant responses. It does not really matter how the rat makes the response; it could use its front paws, its back paws or its nose. Only those responses that are related to the dispensing of food or, to put it another way, to the adaptive function of feeding are recorded. Watson had suggested that behavior should

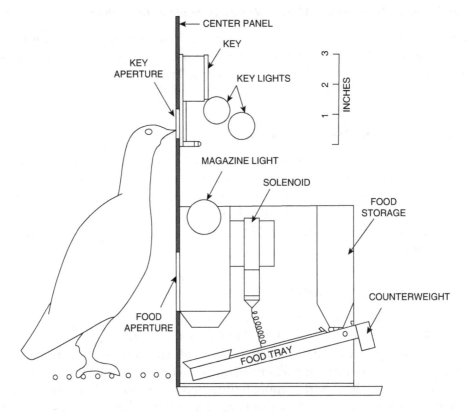

Figure 8.6 Schematic diagram of Skinner box (here depicted with a pigeon, which Skinner began using in the 1940s, from Ferster & Skinner, 1957)

be measured directly, by looking at the behavior, but it is not the form of the behavior that matters but its function, in this case, getting food. Thorndike had focused on time to escape but had described the varieties of behaviors generally. Skinner's method produced a stable way of measuring relevant behavior without unwanted variability, in a form that is easily read and virtually automatically produced.

The cages in which rats (and in Skinner's work from the mid-1940s on, pigeons) could feed themselves by pressing a bar and have the results automatically recorded in cumulative response curves were soon being called **Skinner boxes** (the name comes from Skinner's rival Clark L. Hull). In the improved standard version, the animal would stand on a wire mesh floor that could be electrified for a shock, and various lights could be used as discriminative stimuli (see later and Figure 8.7).

At the same time, the young Skinner was experimenting with a *language* and *philosophy* of behaviorism to go with his new methods of measurement. For a time, he would try to avoid using mental state words in his own conversations and, more obnoxiously, would correct others for doing so. This practice was tiresome for everybody, and he soon realized that it was no greater a sin for a behaviorist to use regular language in conversation than it was for an astronomer to talk about a beautiful sunset even though the sun doesn't technically set anywhere. But he did use the language in his doctoral dissertation (Skinner, 1931), "The Concept of the Reflex." After discussing the concept of the reflex going back to Descartes, he

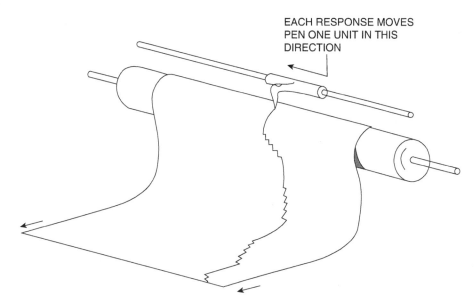

Figure 8.7 Paper kymograph (cumulative event recorder; from Ferster and Skinner, 1957)

stated that a reflex is merely a correlation between stimulus and response and other variables *outside the organism*. This was a rather bold statement for a graduate student to make, because he was expanding the concept: Reflex had meant unconscious, involuntary and unlearned behavior. He was expanding the construct to all behavior, which no one had yet done (but see the section on Sechenov, above; Skinner did not read Russian and Sechenov's work was not easy to come by in English). He thought the distinction between voluntary and involuntary behavior was unwarranted. Skinner was declaring himself to be a die-hard **determinist**. All behavior is determined by environmental circumstances, previous learning and inheritance. There is no free will. Therefore, no behavior is voluntary; everything we do is determined.

E.G. Boring, the department chair, was not pleased. In a critique of the dissertation, he wrote, "For this, you need more than a paper, you need propaganda and a school." Skinner, never one to shrink from debate, underlined that statement and wrote in the margin, "I accept the challenge." Boring removed himself from the dissertation committee and allowed Skinner to receive his doctorate in 1930 (Bjork, 1993, p. 97).

Skinner's Philosophy of Science

Like all the behaviorists, Skinner was at pains to distance the science of psychology from philosophy. But that does not mean that he did not think about the philosophy of science or have a philosophy of behaviorism. His philosophies in both of these areas were rather sophisticated. A detailed examination of his philosophy of science may be beyond the scope of this book, but a brief examination of his philosophical roots is in order, if only to reiterate that (1) most psychologists do have philosophical influences, (2) they often come from the philosophies of other sciences and (3) having a philosophy often produces fruitful ideas or methods for research.

As we have seen, Skinner was influenced by two philosophers before he even began his graduate education: empiricist Francis Bacon and the philosopher Bertrand Russell. As noted above, Skinner read Bacon's *Novum Organum* in high school. He shared with Bacon a strong preference for induction over deduction in science, a strong preference for proof by experimentation and the notion that any science worthy of the name should be one that leads to the betterment of human life (see Chapter 3). Bertrand Russell's review of *Behaviorism* in a literary magazine led Skinner to discover Watson and to read Russell's philosophy. At the time, Russell was investigating the possibility of a behaviorist analysis of philosophy. He wrote,

> In ordinary life, knowledge is something which can be tested by examinations, that is to say, it consists in a certain kind of response to a certain kind of stimulus. This objective way of viewing knowledge is, to my mind, much more fruitful than the way which has been customary in philosophy.
> (Russell, 1926, cited in Smith, 1986, p. 263)

In the same book, Russell discussed what is essentially a behaviorist explanation of language and even compared inductive logic to the result of classical conditioning. Skinner has said, "Russell took Watson seriously and so did I." Skinner was later to meet philosopher Alfred North Whitehead, who had coauthored a major work with Russell. Whitehead commented that young psychologists needed to keep abreast of developments in philosophy and Skinner, rather boldly, said that instead, what was needed was a "psychological epistemology."

In graduate school, Skinner first read *Science of Mechanics* (1942/1883), by physicist, psychologist and philosopher Ernst Mach, and Percy W. Bridgman's *The Logic of Modern Physics* (1927). Both philosophers were mentioned on the first page of the published version of his dissertation (Skinner, 1931). Mach, in particular, would turn out to be one of Skinner's greatest influences. Skinner took the following principles from Mach (Smith, 1986):

1. Science is the historical culmination of the development of craft and popular thought. In the same way that artisans learned to fashion tools and thus change the world, science has formulated some of those discoveries in an abstract way, with the same goal of controlling outcomes in the world in a more conscious, explicit and general way.
2. Science is a way for our species to adapt to the world. If human behavior, as the functionalists say, is adaptation, then science is merely an elegant form of behavior that aids survival. One might therefore study scientists to see what behaviors lead to the kind of science that increases advancement and survival of humanity. Only that form of science is worth doing.

"The biological task of science is to provide the fully developed human individual with as perfect a means of orienting himself as possible. No other scientific ideal can be realized and any other must be meaningless" (Mach, 1886/1959, p. 37).

3. Science should strive to provide a complete description of how the world works. Hypotheses may be useful, but hypotheses that are proven right are no longer needed; the results become part of the growing description. Bad hypotheses lead one astray, so description is more important.
4. Since the development of science is historical, it consists of unpredictable accidents. It is useless to try to formulate logical rules of science and expect them to always be true. Science is always changing and unfinished.
5. Science should be economical in its expressions, without excess concepts or fuzzy terms. If science is to really help us adapt, understanding it should be as little work as possible!
6. Cause and effect are simply correlations between two classes of phenomena. In Skinner's terms, one has discovered something if one has found that a stimulus predictably leads to a response and if following the response, some other thing increases or decreases the probability of that response. There is no "push or pull" in a cause; science is about simply observing that two or more things vary predictably together.

In the same class on the philosophy of science that introduced Mach's work, Skinner read physicist Percy W. Bridgman's *The Logic of Modern Physics* (1927). In this landmark work, Bridgman was attempting to deal with the problems caused in physics, and in science more generally, with the revolution caused by Einstein's theory of relativity. Essentially, Bridgman said that whereas under Newton, at least time and space were constant everywhere, under Einstein's theory, what one knows about time and space depend on where the observer is. If this is true, then, our only hope of clarity in science lies in using **operational definitions**. An operational definition is quite simply the notion that the definition of a scientific construct should be based on the operations used to measure it. Time depends on clocks and the movement of the observer relative to a frame of reference. For Skinner, the definition of "hunger" would become "time since an ordinary lab rat has been fed x grams of precisely formulated food" or "the state produced when a rat, having not been fed, loses a certain percentage of body weight."

Finally, consistent with his view of operational definition, Bridgman said that some questions in science were **meaningless questions**. A meaningless question is a hypothesis that cannot be resolved by any conceivable empirical test, once the fuzziness of natural language has been cleaned up by precise operational definitions.

This short summary of Skinner's philosophical positions shows why his arguments for behaviorism came to be more accepted by working psychologists than those of Watson, even if the psychologists were unaware of this background. Skinner's theory and method were highly consistent with one another and based in the most current scientific practices of his day. This consistency is obvious in the following list, which can be regarded as a virtual summary of Skinner's **radical behaviorism**:

1. Descriptions are more important than hypotheses. (Mach, Bacon)
2. Clarity in defining variables is paramount: They must be stated in unambiguous language, operationally defined and measurable. (Mach, Bridgman)
3. Causality is determined by constant conjunction between two observable events, carefully evaluated by controlled experimentation. (Mach, Bridgman, Hume, Russell, Pavlov)

4. Science and technology are allies; the purpose of science is the betterment of the human condition. (Bacon, Mach, Watson, Pavlov)

Skinner, of course, had other strong beliefs about science, as mentioned above. He was, for example, a thoroughgoing materialist, monist and determinist. And he even believed, with Mach, that science is itself an adaptive set of behaviors. He said many times that the laws of science themselves, such as the laws of physics or chemistry, are built by the reinforcement principles operating on scientists to produce them (e.g. Skinner, 1990)! But most of his well-known views can be traced to the above principles. His prohibition of mental language, for example, can be rationalized by Principle 2, above. His dislike of modern statistical reasoning (Skinner was extremely in favor of single-subject research designs over the use of means and standard deviations for groups of subjects) can be traced to Principle 1, as statistics require inferred conclusions rather than observation of behavior change.

One of the most interesting illustrations of Principle 3 is Skinner's view of **mentalisms**. Mentalisms are entities in the mind that are said to cause behavior, such as "will" or "the self" (or, for that matter, the "ego" or the "unconscious" or "I"). Mentalisms are not thoughts per se, but unobservable things that we attribute causal powers to. We eat too much because of "lack of self-control," for example, or because of "low self-esteem." According to Mach and Skinner, cause is only inferred by constant conjunction of external events, and there is no push or pull in causality. Thus, there is really no need for such mentalisms; they don't *do* anything on their own. They cannot be seen or used as observable data. What is worse, says Skinner, is that once we say that behavior is caused by something inside us, we give up looking for the events outside us that themselves might have caused both the thoughts or feelings and the behavior; we give up being able to control thoughts and actions by possibly manipulating the things we *can* see and control.

Does this mean that Skinner believed that thoughts do not exist? Perhaps surprisingly, Skinner believed that thoughts *do* exist; he called them **private events**. Skinner always considered the position that thoughts do not exist to be silly (although he was not a dualist; thoughts are simply what we call the results of certain events of our body). He knew that he had thoughts; he had no reason to think otherwise about other people. But the thoughts themselves do not enter into science as data.

The verbal *reports* of private events might be subject to science, though, in the following examples. Consider when you go to your doctor with a pain in your side. She may ask questions like "Where does it hurt?" or "Is it a sharp or a dull pain?"[12] She asks about these private events, because previous experience has suggested that people who answer a certain way will need a certain treatment and thus the answer will help them to get better. It's the correlation between the answer and the treatment that leads to successful outcomes, not the thought, but the thought might have been the interior stimulus for the verbal event. Similarly, Skinner always said that if you want to know what might serve as a reinforcer for someone, you could ask her. Her report could be used to narrow down the options, because people can observe their own behavior and report on it. They may be wrong, however, if a person says "I like chocolate" but will not change their behavior when given it; you know not to trust that statement. Perhaps the private events serve as a stimulus to behavior, but at least until we have ways of measuring the immediate biochemical correlates of thought (by the use of a functional magnetic image or a PET scan, perhaps), to make hypotheses about them is to ask a meaningless question.

Finally, that Skinner took Principle 4 to heart can be seen below; in the latter half of his career, after he arrived back at Harvard as a full professor in 1948 until his death in 1990, he concerned himself more and more with advocating behaviorist utopias, involving new forms of rewarding work and achievements, as well as new methods of childcare and education. We will address these achievements below.

The Behavior of Organisms

Over the next few years of postdoctoral fellowships, marriage and a new job at the University of Minnesota, Skinner did many experiments with rats and united his new philosophy to data into his now-classic book, *The Behavior of Organisms* (1938).

Skinner laid out in his first book the essential features of the theory that he followed for the rest of his life, and he did so in a style all his own. A work by B.F. Skinner is always an argument as well as a report of data, a debate about science, scientific concepts and constructs as well as a set of experiments. In this case, he begins right off the bat with philosophical positions. He says that behavior has been rarely studied in psychology because there are a number of unexplained concepts that are said to cause it. At one level, if we give humans free will, we ascribe the causes of our behavior to our "self" and then stop looking for other causes. At a scientific level, even behaviorists such as Watson, Pavlov and Thorndike ascribe causes to the nervous system. But neither of these things is directly observable; they are constructs inferred from our only source of information, behavior itself. Indeed, they are explaining behavior by referring to something that we know even less about, such as mentalisms like the self or constructs like the synapse. Skinner often said that C.N.S. should really stand for "conceptual nervous system."

Next, Skinner tackled the *language* that he would use in his "system of behavior." This language is purely *descriptive* and does not imply anything beyond the directly observable. For example, his definition of "behavior" is as follows:

> By behavior, then, I mean simply the movement of an organism or of its parts in a frame of reference provided by the organism itself or by various objects or fields of force. It is convenient to speak of this as the action of the organism on the outside world and it is often desirable to deal with an effect rather than with the movement itself, as in the case of production of sounds.
>
> (Skinner, 1938, p. 6)

He notes that common language is "clumsy and obese" and implies many concepts in its use:

> In English, for example, we say that an organism *sees* or *feels* objects, *hears* sounds, *tastes* substances, *smells* odors and *likes* or *dislikes* them; it *wants, seeks and finds*; it *has a purpose, tries* and *succeeds* or *fails*; it *learns* and *remembers* or *forgets*; it *is frightened, angry, happy* or *depressed; asleep* or *awake*; and so on. Most of these must be avoided in a scientific description of behavior.
>
> (p. 6, emphasis original)

The main problem here is that language implies motivations or past or future causes. "To try hard" implies a goal ahead of the behavior, and succeeding or failing requires a value judgment and, therefore, such terms must go. They needn't be replaced with jargon terms, however. If observable behavior can be explained in plain English, in such terms as "walking," then by all means use them.

Skinner was attempting to achieve for psychology what he could not for literature: explanation by pure description, without reference to motives or physiology, mentalisms or inferred constructs. This is the reasoning behind radical behaviorism.

Operant Conditioning

We have discussed the methods, philosophy and language of radical behaviorism that Skinner developed in a short period of time. Now it is time to discuss his major contribution to psychology: operant conditioning.

In *The Behavior of Organisms*, Skinner describes one of the difficulties with classical conditioning, which he describes as "Type S [for stimulus] conditioning." In Pavlov's scheme, to accomplish conditioning, one must first know the unconditioned stimulus that elicits the unconditioned response, because one gains control of the UCR by pairing a stimulus with the UCS. Each pairing of a CS with a UCS is called reinforcement. But often, the original eliciting stimulus cannot be found or brought under experimental control. If the stimulus is not known and controllable, one cannot do Type S conditioning. When the first thing one notices is a behavior but not the stimulus that elicited it, that behavior is technically called an **operant** and the process of modifying the rate of that response by the experimenter causing something to happen after the response is called operant conditioning.

Operant conditioning, or what Skinner originally called "Type R [for response] conditioning," is needed when the eliciting stimulus for a response is not known and therefore, in order to control behavior, one must do something after the response has occurred rather than at the time of the eliciting stimulus. In this case, reinforcement happens after a response has been given, rather than at the time of the stimulus, as in classical conditioning. If a reinforcement following a response strengthens it, in the sense of increasing its probability to be emitted again, then that action, whatever it is, is called a **positive reinforcement**. It is important to note that the definition of a reinforcement or reinforcer is based on its result rather than its characteristics. Often, positive reinforcements are synonymous with rewards; remember, Thorndike called them satisfiers. But not all positive reinforcers lead to a satisfying emotional event. For example, ink flowing from a pen reinforces the behavior of writing; without it, writing stops or extinguishes. When the ink flows, writing continues (O'Donohue & Ferguson, 2001). And different things act as rewards for different organisms and for the same organisms at different times (e.g. food serves as a reinforcer when the animal has not been fed for a while, but not at other times), so the reinforcement property is not intrinsic to the action or substance used as a reward. A reinforcer is a function, not at thing. All that matters is that after a response is emitted, an event follows. If or when that event occurs, the rate of that particular response increases, then and only then can the event in question be called a **reinforcer**.

This may sound like torturous reasoning, but it is not. The idea, remember, is to render the science of behavior as totally descriptive, to avoid explanations that rely on internal states or past or future actions.

In *The Behavior of Organisms*, Skinner focused largely on positive reinforcement, of different types, given at various rates and timings. He described the process of *extinction* of behavior when reinforcement is no longer given following a response. He described the process of *reconditioning* an extinguished response, finding that a previously reinforced response can be more easily relearned. (This is analogous to Pavlov's reconditioning of a CS-UCS pairing in classical conditioning.) He explored the notion of *drive* by addressing the variable of rate of responding as a function of time since feeding. Rats will of course respond at a higher rate when "hungry." And of course, he supplemented the text with graphs of the data of his experiments with rats.

Other aspects of operant conditioning that Skinner discusses in his first book, again following the work of Pavlov, are the notions of **stimulus generalization** and **stimulus discrimination**. If we go back to our original example of the rat in the prototypical Skinner box, we see that certain stimuli reliably occur with the delivery of food, like the "kerchunk" sound in the operation of the food pellet magazine. At the beginning of the learning process, even before the rat has learned to press the bar, when an experimenter is manually operating the feeder, the rat comes to "know" (i.e. reliably respond in such a way) that if that sound is present, food will be coming shortly. The experimenter can work with this possibility, say, by sounding a tone only when pressing a bar will provide food. When it is not sounded, pressing a bar is ineffective. When the stimulus *sets the occasion* for making a response, it is called a **discriminative stimulus**. The experimenter can then begin to *bring the behavior under more precise control*, in Skinner's terms. He or she does this by presenting other tones. At first, of course, the rat responds to many similar tones; the rat has spontaneously engaged in stimulus generalization. But only one tone actually works in providing the occasion for the rat to press the bar and get food; sooner or later, depending on how similar the tones are, the rat will respond only to the effective tone. When it does so, it has engaged in stimulus discrimination. One can vary this setup in a number of ways. For example, once discrimination has happened, an experimenter can foster stimulus generalization again by simply expanding the range of discriminative stimuli that signal the effectiveness of pressing the bar. However, if stimulus discrimination had been well learned, a rat might have to wait a long time before the responses are emitted to the new stimuli. Skinner notes in several places the logical point that in order for operant conditioning to happen, there have to be operants—that is, the rate of responding cannot be zero.

A further degree of fine-tuning of control can be developed if the experimenter only allows reinforcement to happen after certain *kinds* of responses, say pressing the bar and holding it down for a certain length of time or pressing it with a certain amount of force. This is the process of **response discrimination** or **response differentiation**, and it is produced by **differentially reinforcing** only some types of responses and not others. Similarly, if the experimenter then goes back to reinforcing all types of responses, the rat will eventually decrease the differential responding and respond to them all equally.

In this brief summary of Skinner's early work, one can see what gaining control over behavior really means. It involves *describing* behavior accurately and consistently, finding a way to *measure* behavior reliably, manipulating the constraints on a rat's behavior effectively to *increase or decrease rates* of behavior and finally, showing that the experimenter can *reverse* the process of behavior change.

In *The Behavior of Organisms*, Skinner alluded only briefly to the role of aversive stimuli in operant conditioning, what Thorndike would have called "annoyers." By 1953, in *Science and Human Behavior*, however, he attempted to expand on his brief comments on those stimuli, by creating the concepts negative reinforcement, punishment and withdrawal of reinforcers. Let's look at the paragraph where he introduces the concepts and interpret it.

> Events which are found to be reinforcing are of two sorts. Some reinforcements consist of *presenting* stimuli, of adding something—for example, food, water or sexual contact—to the situation. These we call *positive* reinforcers. Others consist of *removing* something—for example, a loud noise, a very bright light, extreme cold or heat or electric shock—from the situation. These we call *negative* reinforcers. In both cases, the effect of reinforcement is the same—the probability of response is increased. We cannot avoid this distinction by arguing that what is reinforcing in the negative case is the *absence* of the bright light, loud noise and so on; for it is absence after presence that is effective, and this is only another way of saying that the stimulus is removed. The difference between the two cases will be clearer when we consider the *presentation* of a *negative* reinforcer or the *removal* of a *positive*. These are consequences that we call punishment.
>
> (Skinner, 1953, p. 73, emphasis original).

There are thus four kinds of relationships between behavior and its consequences in operant conditioning, and they depend on what precedes or follows a given behavior.

Two of these situations cause behavior to *increase* in frequency:

1. A behavior is emitted by an organism; some consequence follows; the behavior is seen to increase in frequency. This is called the presentation of a **positive reinforcer** and the relationship between presenting a positive reinforcer and the increase in behavior is positive reinforcement.
2. A stimulus is presented to an organism. The organism emits a behavior and the stimulus ceases. The likelihood of that behavior occurring again increases. The absence or cessation of a **negative reinforcer** increases the probability of a behavior occurring again. If a behavior causes the removal of a negative reinforcer and the frequency of that behavior increases, then that behavior increase is called **negative reinforcement**.

Two of these situations cause behavior to *decrease* in frequency:

3. A behavior is emitted by an organism; some consequence follows; the behavior is seen to decrease in frequency. This is called the presentation of a negative reinforcer, and the relationship between presenting a negative reinforcer and the decrease in behavior is **punishment** (or sometimes, to be consistent, **positive punishment**).

4. The cessation of a usually present positive reinforcer decreases the probability of a behavior occurring again. If a behavior causes the removal of a positive reinforcer and the frequency of that behavior decreases, then that behavior decrease is called **withdrawal of positive reinforcement** (or sometimes, to be consistent, **negative punishment**).

Thus, in Skinner's terminology, *positive* means something *presented*; *negative* means something *taken away*. *Reinforcement* denotes a subsequent *increase in rate of a behavior* and *punishment* denotes a subsequent *decrease in rate of a behavior*, leading to the fourfold classification. It also has led to confusion among negative reinforcement and punishment among psychology students for half a century! Once again, not to beat a dead horse, *presenting* a negative reinforc*er* = positive punishment; *removing* a negative reinforc*er* = negative reinforcement. In the first situation, behavioral frequency goes down and in the second, it goes up. It is a paradox; a completely clear and logically consistent set of definitions has led to confusion!

Skinner wanted to extend the concepts of operant conditioning into a complete and useful science of behavior or, more precisely, a technology of behavioral engineering. In 1957, he published the fruits of dozens of single-subject experiments with pigeons, with his student, Charles Ferster, *Schedules of Reinforcement*. In this book, conceived as a kind of sequel to *The Behavior of Organisms*, Ferster and Skinner (1957) lay out not just the types of reinforcement, but also the effects of deploying reinforcement at different rates and intervals. Specifically, one could reinforce pigeons based on the number of suitable responses given following the last reinforcement. The simplest case of this is to reinforce every response, or **continuous reinforcement**. Alternately, one could reinforce, say, each fifth response. This type of schedule of reinforcement is called a **fixed ratio** schedule. It produces high levels of responding very quickly (see Figure 8.5). It is also not difficult to extinguish; the contingencies of reinforcement are so clear that if the reinforcement does not arrive on schedule, the bird rather quickly gives up. **Variable ratio** schedules present reinforcement on an average number of responses, such that, for example, a bird on a VR 5 schedule might randomly receive a reinforcement after 4, 5, 6 or 7 responses. Such a schedule, owing to its relative unpredictability, leads to high rates of behavior that is more resistant to extinguishing, when the reinforcements stop coming.

Similarly, one can deliver reinforcements on a stable schedule, triggered by the time on a clock, say, every 10 minutes, rather than by the number of responses the bird emits. Such a schedule is called a **fixed interval** schedule. In these situations, the animal is not really under control of the reinforcements; so, as a dog accustomed to a 5:00 feeding time will begin to whine at 4:00, animals tend to increase behaviors near the time of reinforcement, resulting in a flat rate of responding, but an increased responding near the time of reinforcement. This produces a "scalloped" effect near the reinforcement point on the rotating cumulative event recorder paper (see Figure 8.6). Finally, one may deliver reinforcements on a **variable interval** schedule, in which reinforcements are given at unpredictable times, for example, anytime between 8 and 12 minutes for a VI schedule of 10 minutes.

Such a schedule has interesting byproducts. First, because of its unpredictability, animals may continue to give responses long after reinforcements have ceased following behavior. Behaviors reinforced on this schedule are said to be *resistant to*

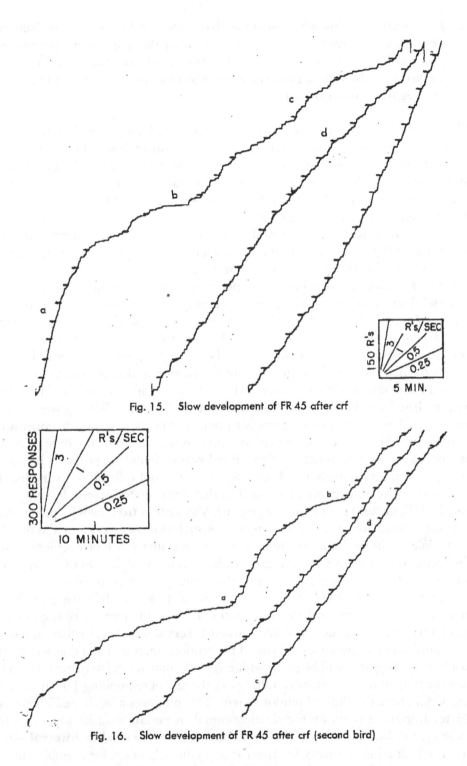

Figure 8.8 Fixed ratio patterns; this is fixed ratio of reinforcement after 45 responses
Source: Ferster & Skinner, 1957

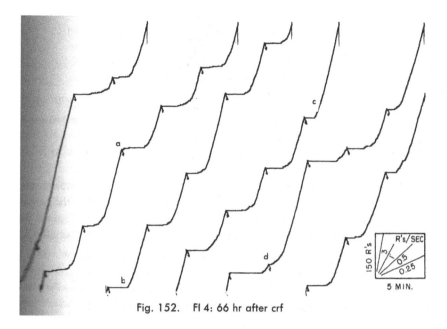

Figure 8.9 Fixed interval schedule of 4 (Note scalloped effect)

extinction. Second, whatever behavior the animal may be doing at the time of a reinforcement is strengthened, not just the behavior of interest. The random nature of a VR schedule tends therefore to lead a pigeon to perform *superstitious behavior*. The behavior the bird was performing actually has no effect on receiving reinforcement, but the pigeon acts as if it does.

Ferster and Skinner's book, weighing in at over 700 pages, became a veritable Bible for laboratory behaviorists, because it covered not only the four types of reinforcement and the four types of schedules, but many combinations: simultaneous schedules for two separate but coexisting behaviors; permutations of combinations of ratios and interval schedules; even an occasional experiment on a bird with part of the cortex removed or under the influence of drugs. Virtually all of the experiments reported here were single-subject designs, supported not by statistics, but graphs of the cumulative event recorder results of the particular birds.

Skinner was never satisfied with merely doing lab work to prove abstract principles, though this work did reinforce his tendency to tinker, as well as to experiment and observe. From his graduate school days, he wanted to contribute to the betterment of human society in some way. He was that rare combination of an abstract theorist and practical inventor. Skinner attempted to contribute to the world both as an engineer of things intended to change behavior and as a social reformer concerned with engineering a better social structure for the culture. We will deal with the inventor first.

Skinner the Inventor

In 1942, with money from the government, Skinner embarked on a research project for the war effort, which he and his colleagues dubbed "Project Pigeon." During

World War II, missile and bomb guidance was rudimentary at best. Bombs were not guided at all and rockets fell when they ran out of fuel. The purpose of the project was to evaluate the feasibility of pigeon-guided weapons. The pigeons would be trained before their mission to peck at a certain point on an aerial reconnaissance photo of the bombing site. Then, they would be placed inside the bomb hooked up to a guidance mechanism that would allow course correction as the pigeon, now looking at the actual bombing location through a sight, would peck at the view of the bombing site. The movements of the pigeon's head would correct the movement of the bomb towards its target. Problems were encountered not only with building the sensitive electronic feedback mechanisms, but also with getting a pigeon to be as accurate under battle conditions as it was in the Skinner box. The military eventually cut off funding for a project it considered unrealistic and quaintly old-fashioned in an age of gyroscopes and atomic energy (Bjork, 1993). Skinner, however, was convinced by the project to switch from rats to pigeons as research subjects; he also perfected the switches required for pigeons to press keys. This improvement was added to the standard Skinner box design.

At the end of the war, Skinner, like everyone else, was restlessly settling into domestic life and turned his attention to raising his children. He was disturbed that his first child, Julie, was so restrained by layers of clothing in cold weather (they were then living in Minnesota), and his wife was dismayed by the amount of cleaning and housework required. Skinner set out to build an enclosed self-contained environment that would essentially ease chores and provide freedom and stimulation for his second daughter, Debbie. The crib-sized enclosure, called a "baby-tender" or "air crib," was built into the side of the house, provided safety-glass windows both to the outside and inside. It was temperature and humidity controlled, with a stretched canvas floor that could be easily cleaned. The baby could be clothed in only a diaper even on cold days. Skinner's purpose for the device was purely practical, as with other, more traditional cribs. Debbie was quite often taken out of the device to play or eat and had toys to play with inside. She was never subjected to conditioning experiments.

The device was described in an article by Skinner (Skinner, 1945) in the *Ladies' Home Journal* in late 1945; much to Skinner's dismay, however, the editors changed the title to "Baby in a Box." This led those who did not read the article carefully to think that Skinner's daughter was reared entirely in the air crib or subjected to experimentation, which was not the case. The rumor persists to this day that Deborah Skinner committed suicide; she, in fact, grew up to be a successful artist, and her sister, Julie Skinner Vargas, followed her father's footsteps into behavioral psychology.[13] Skinner's daughters always defended him as a kind and loving man, and, in fact, he spent more time with them than was typical of many men of his generation, doing everything from changing diapers and dressing them for school to attending school plays (Vargas, 1972). His own personal philosophy of childrearing, particularly of young children, was rather benign. As we shall see, Skinner hated aversive conditioning of any kind. Typically, he would arrange his children's and grandchildren's living spaces so that they could not break or damage anything and thus avoid the necessity for punishment, at least in the home environment (Vargas, 1972). And, of course, Skinner and his wife Eve filled the home with music, literature and the arts, as well as science. Deborah Skinner claimed that the only lasting effects of having spent time in the air crib was having very flexible toes and preferring to sleep without a blanket!

In contrast to those who thought the device dehumanizing, several people were inspired by the article to build their own air cribs, and their letters to Skinner were generally complimentary. Skinner even tried to market the device, but he entered into contract with an unscrupulous businessman. The prototype his partner produced was cheap and unsafe, but a high-quality model was deemed prohibitively expensive due to postwar metal shortages. When the partner absconded with Skinner's investment money, he gave up (Bjork, 1993).

Another use of behavioral technology was also suggested by his daughters' education. While sitting in the back of Deborah's fourth grade class in 1955, he noticed what he saw as inefficiencies in education. Children finished their work at different times and required different levels of help. Furthermore, they needed to wait until the next day to receive feedback on their work. Skinner, ever the tinkerer, set about building what he called a *teaching machine* that could reinforce each individual student frequently (Skinner, 1958). The first machines were handmade cardboard contraptions in which the student would insert an answer on paper and then uncover the correct answer by sliding a door. Later, more sturdy plastic versions would light up when the right answers were given. The *programmed instruction* provided with the machines sequenced fill-in-the-blank questions so that there were many easy items at first. This insured frequent reinforcement, a minimum of punishment and opportunities to gain knowledge through practice. Skinner and his colleagues attempted to provide curricula for math and foreign languages and reading and memorization. After several years' work on the technology, however, he was again unable to get a company to produce a satisfactory model. Within psychology, however, the technology had modest success. *The Analysis of Behavior* (Holland & Skinner, 1961) was an even lower-tech version, producing the same effect with a book. On the first page was a question, e.g. "To avoid unwanted nuances of meaning in popular words, we do not say that a stimulus 'triggers,' 'stimulates,' or 'causes' a response but that it ____ a response." The student would then turn the page to find the answer: "elicits." The textbook was solely a collection of 48 sets of 30 questions each.

Lack of interest in his system at the time frustrated Skinner, who thought corporations and classroom teachers too averse to change. The arguments of his critics bore a striking resemblance to the Gestaltists' criticism of Thorndike (see Chapters 6 and 7), that his habit-based identical elements theory had focused too much on rote "piecemeal" learning. The cognitive revolution in psychology and education had begun. Leaders of the movement, such as Jerome Bruner, began touting "discovery learning" in the 1960s based loosely on the theories of Piaget and Vygotsky. It did not escape Skinner's notice, however, that when the desktop computer revolution began in the 1980s, self-reinforcing educational programs became commonplace, to say nothing of many computer-driven question-and-answer toys and games.

Skinner as Utopian Social Reformer

At about the same time as the venture of the air crib, Skinner was reading the literature of utopia and social reform and discussing the topic once a month with other interested academics and writers. He read Thomas More's *Utopia* itself, Francis

Bacon's *New Atlantis*, Samuel Butler's *Erehwon* (nowhere spelled backwards) and Thoreau's *Walden*. In spite of the controversy he sometimes encouraged, Skinner's personal motivations for creating and promoting his behavioral technology were always optimistic and altruistic. Remember that his heroes, Bacon and Mach, had both suggested that any science worthy of the name should be undertaken for the betterment of society. His explicit answer to this statement of principles was his first and only novel, *Walden Two* (1948).

Skinner wrote the novel in two months, beginning in the late spring of 1945. The Depression was over; the war had ensured, for a moment, full employment. Hitler was dead, and the tide had turned in the Allies' favor in the Pacific. Even the Russians were on our side. It was, he said, an optimistic time (Skinner, 1976b). He has stated that his reasons for attempting a novel about a better community were, first, to envision a society in which much of the drudgery was removed and the rest, shared equally. Second, he recognized the pleas of his wife and other women for new vocations and responsibilities other than housewife and mother. Third, he wanted to explore a society in which everyone could do what he or she liked in a supportive community that would not be wasteful of resources. And of course, he had always wanted to write a novel and conceded in his autobiography that the task was a fun way to indulge his ego. Finally, however, it was a way to promote his behaviorism beyond the lab, to explore what he called in the book an *experimental ethics*, the idea that human behavior could be manipulated and improved upon as with any other technology.

The novel begins as two young men just returned from the war visit Professor Burris, whose college psychology course they had taken before the war. They are looking for a fellow student, named Frazier, who claimed to have started an ideal community. Burris looks up his old student and the professor gathers up the young men, their girlfriends and a skeptical professor of moral philosophy and go off to visit his community, Walden Two. The rest of the novel is a tour of this revolutionary commune of 1000 people, interspersed with intense philosophical discussions led by Frazier (an obvious stand-in for Skinner himself) on the nature of work and leisure, human power relationships, marriage and children's education and the uses of technology in general for making human life better. Following are some of the principles of life in *Walden Two* on these topics.

Work

In pursuit of a life in which everyone does what he or she likes as much as possible, there are, no doubt, many difficult and undesirable tasks. Where they can be eliminated or improved through the use of technology (as in much of "housewifery"), they should be. Others should be evenly distributed to the community, for a *higher* wage per hour than that given for desirable tasks (pleasant tasks do not need as much external reinforcement). People should be encouraged to do a variety of jobs and to change as frequently as they like. Rates would be set and adjusted by demand by the board of planners and by labor managers. With the assumption that all women would work (a rather new assumption in 1945) and that full employment can be maintained in such a small community, the ideal would be four hours of paid work a day. Health care, day care and education would be provided by the commune and staffed by members. The rest of the day would be spent in self-reinforcing leisure pursuits, some of which (e.g. the performing arts) would be offered for the enjoyment of the community as a whole.

Family

Children would be largely reared in communal fashion, away from their parents for the most part, by childcare managers and educators, based on methods verified by practice, social agreement and experiment. One advantage of this practice, says Frazier, is that couples need not wait to get married or have children until they could afford it; the mature guidance of the day care managers would counteract their inexperience. Both would occur early, perhaps in one's teens. The assumption (a big one) is that marriages, freed of financial and child-rearing stress, would last longer (but they need not), and having children while young would allow people a more unencumbered future.

Government and Customs

Walden Two is run by a board of planners, begun by the founders; they are not elected and they select their replacements from managers. Managers are specialists who run the various functions, from the dairy to child rearing. Anyone may aspire to be a manager, but they get the job, presumably, on merit. The law is encoded in the Walden Code, which includes prohibitions against the usual crimes and infractions, but also social injunctions against gossip, speaking about community business to outsiders and surprisingly, perhaps, giving undue credit to people for their accomplishments or even saying "thank you" often. Failure to do a job well is not considered failure, but a sign that a person should do a different job. Failure at many jobs may suggest a disease which, presumably, can be cured by psychologists with behavioral techniques.

Acceptance by the Public

When published, the book did receive some positive reviews. But *Walden Two* depicts a kind of socialist utopia[14] and as such, the book drew fire from critics for whom a socialist utopia is no kind of utopia at all (see Krutch, 1953). Skinner was strongly criticized for suggesting that the community could be left in the hands of a non-democratic board of planners. Such a body would inevitably enforce conformity, said reviewers; even if the experimental society were successful in making people happy, it would be a kind of enforced happiness: "Once they are trained, the inhabitants of Walden Two have 'freedom.' But it is the freedom of those Pavlovian dogs which are free to foam at the mouth whenever the 'dinner' bell invites them to a nonforthcoming meal" (Jessup, 1948, cited in Bjork, 1993, p. 154). The reviewers often saw the mechanistic view of humanity to be dehumanizing, but Skinner took the lack of free will to be a given. It may be an open question as to whether such a society could succeed, but if it did, the fact that the community was designed would be an advantage, as we would then know how to do it again.

> What bothers [a reviewer] about *Walden Two* is simply that somebody planned it that way! Let the accidents of history work out a pattern and it's fine," said Skinner. "Let someone try it as an experimental plan and that's evil."
> (Skinner, 1955, cited by Bjork, 1993, p. 158)

To be fair, Skinner has at times seemed to pointedly ignore the darker aspects of his book. Although it was written before the full extent of the horrors of Hitler's and Stalin's regimes were known, by the time it was actually published, the knowledge of these regimes no doubt tainted many readers' perception of the book. George Orwell's dystopian critiques of Stalinism, *Animal Farm* (1945) and *1984* (1949), came out at about the same time and Aldous Huxley's *Brave New World*, published in 1932, had criticized a mechanized, planned view of society. And indeed, the book did not sell well at first, having sold only 9000 copies from 1948 to 1960. But it was soon caught up in the tidal wave of social change and youth culture of the baby boom, and by the early 1970s it had sold 100,000 copies. By the time of Skinner's death in 1990, it had sold over 2.5 million copies (Bjork, 1993).

Some of those who read the book in the 1960s were inspired to use *Walden Two* as a model for a new society and started communes based on its principles. The most famous and long-lasting of these are the Twin Oaks community in Virginia (Kincade, 1973, 1994) and a commune in Sonora, Mexico, called Los Horcones. Of the two, Los Horcones has more consciously integrated behavior analysis into its model, explicitly defending his methods on their website (www.loshorcones.org). Twin Oaks, perhaps because of its founding at the height of the counter-culture movements in 1968, promotes its feminist, eco-friendly, somewhat New Age practices, which deviate somewhat from Skinner's tastes (www.twinoaks.org). These two communities have not been quite as successful as Skinner's fictional counterpart; neither has ever grown beyond a hundred members and at times have had much fewer (Los Horcones currently is a community of about 40 inhabitants). But then, they had to start from scratch with fewer than 10 members each and with very little money. Fiction allowed Skinner to simply assume that the society was up and running!

Nevertheless, some Skinnerian ideas have succeeded. In both communities, Skinner's labor credit system, run by managers, works well, allowing tasks to get done reliably, people to change jobs frequently, if not daily, and a fair wage to be paid. Members own most things in common and turn over their individual wealth to the collective after a trial period. Boards of planners, however, are elected and rotated frequently. After some considerable early struggles, each community has become economically viable, if not entirely self-sufficient. Twin Oaks runs a factory that makes hammocks and Los Horcones subsists on farming. And each has raised children successfully. Los Horcones children use an individualized, behaviorist reinforcement system for their lessons (the commune was begun by psychologists who used behavioral techniques with developmentally delayed children). Some "Oakers" now have grandchildren in the community.

Both these real-life Walden Two experiments suggest that perhaps the greatest difficulty with starting and maintaining a new social structure is the amount of negotiation it takes. To live deliberately, as Thoreau suggested, but not to live alone, requires constant negotiation and compromise, which in itself creates occasional frustration, and some members leave the communes complaining that they feel little individuality and freedom. And in such a small community, there is ever-present social pressure to pull one's weight for the good of the commune. Those who do not get along do not escape negative social control or, in extreme cases, banishment. But balancing this, if the newsletters on the websites are any guide, is a strong positive sense of community, with no isolation. Such a lifestyle is clearly not reinforcing for everyone.

As *Walden Two* began selling well in the 1960s, Skinner was forced to face some of its critics repeatedly and as a result decided to provide another statement of his philosophical principles to the general public. The result, entitled *Beyond Freedom and Dignity* (1971) was, if anything, more radical than *Walden Two*.

In this extended philosophical essay, Skinner began by touting the progress of science over the 20th century. The advances in the science of physics led to advances in engineering, like space travel. Advances in biology led to advances in medicine. Both of these advances, implied Skinner, were linked to scientists' ability to dispose of internal causes like the "jubilation" that a falling rock was supposed to have felt in falling towards the earth in the time of Aristotle or the "life force" in biology. But no comparable technology of behavior had emerged from psychology because, unlike these sciences, psychology had preserved the "autonomous man"; we will not give up the fiction that an autonomous self, operating with free will, controls our own actions. In so doing, says Skinner, we do ourselves a disservice, because we abdicate the power and responsibility to change our own behavior for our own good and the good of humanity.

Just as we recognize that a rock falls to the earth because of mechanical laws or that the body operates on biochemical laws, we should realize, says Skinner, that there is no free will. Behavior is as lawful, as naturally determined, as astronomy and evolution. Whether we like it or not and we obviously don't, our behavior is solely the function of two things: innate genetic predispositions shaped phylogenetically by evolution and environmental control that shapes our behavior within our lifetimes, ontogenetically. This does not mean that feelings and thoughts do not exist, only that they depend on those two causes.

If freedom does not exist and feelings depend on external control, then we should study environmental contingencies to help increase those kinds of control—reinforcements and cultural practices—that make us *feel* free and to decrease those that do not. In other words, we should avoid physical force, punitive control by force of law and unpleasant social control and strive as much as possible to increase the rates of positive reinforcement in our lives. Only by relinquishing the myth of freedom can we take control of the problems of society. If we do not, says Skinner, we simply allow others to manipulate our feelings of freedom for their own purposes, because there are demagogues—politicians, tyrants, unscrupulous businessmen—who intuitively understand how to do this already. From Skinner's point of view, this belief in control is not in and of itself incompatible with liberal democracy. Where possible, people should be allowed to choose the reinforcers that motivate them, individually. Where this is not possible, cultural practices can be set up "freely" but deliberately, by negotiation. No one is really "choosing freely," of course, but as long as people feel that the aversive consequences of life have been spread around fairly, what difference would it make?

If we dispose of freedom, says Skinner, we must dispose of something even more cherished: the belief that we deserve credit for what we do that is good and blame for what we do that is bad. We must dispose of dignity and responsibility.

We give a person credit for situations when he or she appears to do things on his own, not under external control. Charity is more laudable when we do not know that it is given merely for a tax deduction. A president giving a speech or an anchor of the evening news seems more intelligent than us, until the camera pans back and we see that he or she is reading from a teleprompter! We give a person credit when he or she appears to do something that the rest of us might have trouble doing, like choosing duty over love, but that person is making the choice because of a reinforcement history that we cannot see from the outside. This credit is obviously itself reinforcing, because it is connected with receiving other good things: sex, food, love, etc. Thus, we hate giving up opportunities to receive credit and resist methods to ascribe the credit to external circumstances. (On the other hand it is easier to recommend harsh punishments for other people than for ourselves, because when we do something bad, we can see the "extenuating circumstances" that are harder to see when we look at others' behaviors.[15]) And we believe that if we took away the idea of the autonomous person we would thereby give up the notion of individual responsibility. We must ascribe responsibility somewhere, and it is easiest to do so to the individual. "Any move towards an environment in which men are automatically good threatens responsibility" (Skinner, 1971, p. 68). But, Skinner says, if we believe in personal responsibility, we bypass the possibility that by replacing aversive control with positive reinforcement we can change behavior.

Freedom and dignity work another way as well. If we ascribe stupidity or genetic inferiority or moral badness to a person, we exonerate the poor teacher or ineffective prison. Students do not get smarter and crime may not go down. Punishment teaches what not to do, while neglecting to teach the more acceptable behavior instead. Punishment and prisons may still be needed for serious infractions or violence, but if we do not use more positive methods of control for those who do behave well in prison, criminals essentially "go to school" in a culture of violence for their prison terms.

As one might imagine, this philosophy did not go over well with reviewers or the general public, but it certainly promoted vigorous debate. By this time, Skinner had been at the bully pulpit of a Harvard professorship for more than 20 years and was the recognized leader of a movement. Attention was paid to what he said, and he wound up on the cover of *Time* magazine and on television. And the attention was almost universally negative, from both the political left (e.g. Noam Chomsky, 1971) and the right (e.g. Ayn Rand, 1972/1982). Their criticisms were remarkably similar.

Both Chomsky (1971) and Rand (1972) claimed that, for a book on science or the philosophy of science, provides evidence in the way of scientific data, and no evidence, really, of success at modifying behavior at the cultural level. If individual achievement (as well as a belief in individual achievement) is indeed a product of social reinforcement, it is important for Skinner to specify exactly how that is done, rather than merely redefining the term individual achievement. We know very little about how a science of behavior might work on such a large scale, said Chomsky:

> Is Skinner saying that, as a matter of necessity, science will show that behavior is completely determined by the environment? If so, his claim can be dismissed as pure dogmatism, foreign to the "nature of scientific inquiry." It is quite conceivable that as scientific understanding advances, it will reveal that even with full details about genetic endowment and personal history, a Laplacean omniscience could predict very little about what an organism will do. It is even possible that science may some day provide principled reasons for this conclusion (if indeed it is true).
>
> But perhaps Skinner is suggesting merely that the term "scientific understanding" be restricted to the prediction of behavior from environmental conditions. If so, then science may reveal, as it progresses, that "scientific understanding of human behavior," in this sense, is inherently limited. At the moment, we have virtually no scientific evidence and not even the germs of an interesting hypothesis about how human behavior is determined. Consequently, we can only express our hopes and guesses about what some future science may demonstrate. In any event, the claims that Skinner puts forth in this category are either dogmatic or uninteresting, depending on which interpretation we give to them.
>
> (Chomsky, 1971, p. 184)

In such an uncertain situation, giving up the idea of "autonomous man" is dangerous. Faith is also required in the motives of behavioral scientists who would naturally gain power in such a world. How could one be sure that they serve the interest of the people? Skinner replies that the scientists are themselves controlled by reinforcement contingencies of those they control: "In a very real sense, then, the slave controls the slave driver, the child the parent, the patient the therapist, the citizen the government, the communicant the priest, the employee the employer and the student the teacher" (Skinner, 1971, p. 169). Ayn Rand countered in her review, "To this, I shall add just one more example: the victim controls the torturer, because if the victim screams very loudly at a particular method of torture, this is the method the torturer will select to use. (Rand, 1972/1982, p. 182).

She continued,

> The book's motive power is hatred of man's mind and virtue (with everything they entail: reason, achievement, independence, enjoyment, moral pride, self-esteem)—so intense and consuming a hatred that it consumes itself and what we read is only its gray ashes, with feeble, snickering obscenities (such as the title) as a few last, smoking, stinking coals. To destroy 'Autonomous Man'—to strike at him, to punch, to stab, to jab and if all else fails, to spit at him—is the book's apparent purpose and it is precisely the long range, cultural consequences that the author does not seem to give a damn about.
>
> (p. 182)

Despite such scathing criticism, Skinner did not give up philosophical pronouncements on our culture, although his tone modulated somewhat. He wrote articles in his later years with titles like: "Why We Are Not Acting to Save the World" and "What Is Wrong With Daily Life in the Western World?" (Skinner, 1987).

His productivity in later years continued unabated, owing to his system of writing: Three total hours a day, every day, no more and no less, controlled by a desk lamp that turned on and off at the appointed times. He reinforced himself by keeping track of the pages he had written and by including in the rest of his day such activities that rejuvenate him for writing the next day: listening to music, reading, social occasions, etc. Thus, his well-known dislike of free will did not prevent him from setting up systems to modify his own behavior. In fact, he was comforted by his belief in the effectiveness of operant conditioning in a way that perhaps only a man with a deep belief in determinism could be.

Skinner's Legacy Summarized

In one of his final statements on the philosophy of radical behaviorism, B.F. Skinner came full circle with an article entitled "Selection by Consequences" (Skinner, 1981). The title, of course, is a nod to Darwin. What Darwin's natural selection was to evolution, Skinner's operant conditioning would be to each of our lifetimes: The probability of learned adaptive behaviors occurring again was controlled by whether they truly had positive consequences for survival of an individual, not by their intrinsic worth, whatever that might mean. Cultures that survive are those that, tested by harsh reality, survive to protect their members. The style that an artist adopts is the style that leads to either profit or acclaim by peers or both, and the training of successful artists encourages a highly persistent pursuit of highly valued, but highly variably timed, reinforcers—a strategy that ensures resistance to extinction and even ultimately supports the *avant garde* (Skinner, 1974). Science that ultimately survives is the sort of science and technology that increases the well-being of the members of the culture that supports it. Scientists are reinforced by the results of their experiments to make their next hypothesis. It is in this sense that science explains reality, because if it didn't, the experiments themselves wouldn't work out (and if they didn't work out, scientists would stop doing them)!

As we have seen, few of these ideas were themselves new (if any ideas ever are). E.L. Thorndike had discovered the evolutionary metaphor for behavior, Ernst Mach adapted it for science and pragmatists like James and Dewey had developed evolutionary philosophies. And Watson had promoted an abiding faith in behaviorism; he, like Skinner, had made leaps in generalization far beyond the data available to him at the time. But Skinner was more than the rabble-rouser Watson was. His exacting language and laboratory work supported his skill in argument had begun to make the ideas practical in the professional therapeutic techniques of applied behavioral analysis and behavior modification (see later).

Other Behaviorists

In addition to the founders of the behaviorist school, there were a number of behaviorists who attempted to combine and extend the basic insights of Pavlov,

Watson, Thorndike and Skinner. Many more psychologists in this era were excited by the prospects of behaviorism than can be included here. We will focus here on two men who attempted to keep the emphasis on behavior, while allowing the "inside" of the organism to play a role in organizing behavior: Edward C. Tolman and Clark L. Hull.

Edward Chase Tolman (1886–1959)

Edward C. Tolman was born in Newton, Massachusetts, into a prosperous merchant family. He followed his brother, Richard (who became a renowned physicist) into the academic life, first earning a degree in chemical engineering at the Massachusetts Institute of Technology and then, in 1911, after reading William James, enrolling in Harvard's then combined department of philosophy and psychology. In the graduate program, he was exposed to both structuralism and Watsonian behaviorism and decided, typically, that neither suited him. Both were reductionistic, "molecular" theories: structuralism chopped consciousness up into bits and Watsonian behaviorism at the time focused on reducing the overall adaptive behavior of organisms to particular physical stimuli that elicit particular physiological responses. Tolman admired the precision of behaviorism; most of his laboratory work, like that of Watson, was related to the maze-running behavior of animals. But he followed students of James in emphasizing that behavior (as James had said of consciousness) should be studied as adaptive and goal-directed processes. Thus, Tolman's system began as a molar behaviorism, one that focuses on describing and explaining the purpose of behaviors for the animals and their relationships among each other, rather than individual reflexes.

Not surprisingly, given these preferences, Tolman found that he had an affinity for the ideas of Gestaltists, strengthened by a trip to Europe to see Koffka and Lewin in 1923. In particular, Tolman recognized that whereas a stimulus may be needed to elicit a response, stable long-term features of the stimulus environment—colors, shapes, terrains and gradients—maintain the response over longer periods. Tolman called these behavior supports **discriminanda**. Discriminanda are stimulus configurations that lead an animal to expect that certain behaviors can be carried out successfully. Similarly, there are features in the environment that, either through instinct or experience, have special meanings for the animal, that support the use of certain adaptive motor *responses*. These **manipulanda**, as Tolman called them, have properties like to-sit-upon or to-be-used-as-a-weapon. In essence, Tolman translated Lewin's *afforderungscharakter* or "valence" into animal behavior terms (Tolman, 1932, p. 37). In a very real sense, before behavior is learned, organization already exists in the world and in the animal's relationship to it. These concepts were described in Tolman's landmark book, *Purposive Behavior in Animals and Men* (1932), published while B.F. Skinner was just collecting the data that would result in the Skinner box and *The Behavior of Organisms*.

Tolman had many disagreements with Skinner's experiments demonstrating operant conditioning. In particular, we remember, Skinner suggested that a response is reinforced by the consequences after it, and without the consequences, no learning occurs. Tolman and his students at the University of California at Berkeley found that, to the contrary, well-fed rats that are put into mazes in which they are allowed to "explore," but are not rewarded, learn without error when a reward is offered. This is **latent learning**, in which the rats are learning a lot without reward.

For Tolman, what rats really need to learn is not particular stimulus-response connections, but the lay of the land—what class of stimuli are relevant in the problems they are given that will lead them to food goals. They engage in **vicarious trial and error**, which is a set of "looking around behaviors" before deciding on a difficult response. If rats are shocked from a metal food cup upon eating, they avoid it, but only if allowed to examine and "look around" *after* the shock. If the cage goes dark and the cup drops from sight, they do not learn to avoid the cup and the shock. Thus, the negative reinforcer itself is not enough for learning; some "thinking" is necessary. They engage in **hypothesis testing**: In an experiment in which the reward could be behind either black or white doors on the left or the right, they explore the stimulus dimensions *systematically* (all the black doors first, then all the white doors, then all the left doors and so on). In a word, they form **cognitive maps**: broad comprehensive maps of the stimuli coded by their usefulness that the rat uses to infer the best route to their goal. They attempt to use the best means to their ends, rather than being a slave to operant conditioning.

Tolman suggested that the reasons Skinner's rats (or later, pigeons) are tied to stimuli and responses is because the Skinner box has so tightly controlled both that the rat has no choice. In the real world, of course a rat needs to know the terrain, the territory, the whole complement of stimuli and what they are useful for to survive. This is consistent both with Tolman's training as a descendent of James and a fan of Gestalt.

Clark L. Hull (1889–1952)

Clark L. Hull, like Tolman, also began in behaviorism before Skinner and took a different path. At the height of his influence, from the late 1930s until his death in 1952, Hull provided an approach that rivaled and even exceeded Skinner's in popularity and complexity. But, in the same way that young Skinner was fascinated by Bacon's inductive logic, Hull was drawn as a sickly, introverted farmboy to the beautiful clarity of deductive logic in Euclid's geometry and Newton's physics. Like Skinner, he enjoyed tinkering with machines. He had attempted to earn a degree in engineering, but reluctantly decided on psychology when he realized that his frail health did not suit him for a profession that spent much time out in the field. And unlike engineering, psychology seemed a field that could allow his philosophical interests free rein. Seeing himself as a man in a hurry to make a contribution before his mental and physical powers failed, Hull methodically formulated a plan to conquer the field of psychology in diaries that he called "Idea Books." He would first and foremost avoid all Aristotelian internal motivation in his theories. Organisms were, in principle, machines, "self-maintaining robots," and should be treated as such. One way to rigorously avoid being led astray by tendencies to internal motives in theories, said Hull, is to set up rigorous logical structures for making those theories. Specifically, one should set up clearly mechanistic "postulates," as in geometry, which state what a theorist knows must be true. Hull stated these in logical-mathematical fashion, specifying variables, even if such variables had yet to be measured. He called his theory a **hypothetico-deductive system of psychology,** because he thought that the postulates were intended to precisely specify hypotheses that could later be verified, as experiments provided data to prove theorems and corollaries. Some of these could be quite complex. Consider the following postulate, from Hull's major work, *Principles of Behavior* (Hull, 1943):

POSTULATE 1

When a stimulus energy (S) impinges on a suitable receptor organ, an afferent neural impulse (s) is generated and propagated along connected fibrous branches of nerve cells in the general direction of the effector organs, via the brain. During the continued action of the stimulus energy (S), this afferent impulse (s), after a short latency, rises quickly to a maximum intensity, following which it falls to a relatively low value as a simple decay function of the maximum. After the termination of the action of stimulus energy (S) on the receptor, the afferent impulse (s) continues its activity in the central nervous tissue for some seconds, gradually diminishing to zero as a simple decay function of its value at the time the stimulus energy (S) ceases to act.

(Hull, 1943, p. 47)

We can see in this example that Hull is indeed trying to be both materialistic and physiological in his language. This type of statement serves to clarify exactly where effort should be applied to specify variables (e.g. exactly how short a latency? How high and in what units is maximum tendency and what represents "a relatively low value"?).

Hull's greatest contributions, in fact, relate to several constructs that he created to describe how goal-directed responses could be described in relation to habits in general terms. Some of the constructs he created in order to do this were **habit strength**, the **habit family hierarchy** and the **goal gradient**.

Habit strength (represented in Hull's distinctive system of notation as $_sH_R$) is a construct invented to unify several aspects of the way stimulus-response relationships operate. For example:

- Habit strength for some innate relationships (e.g. UCS-UCR in classical conditioning) may not be zero at birth or at the time a rat is studied in an experiment.
- Habit strength increases as the numbers of reinforcements (classical or operant) increase.
- As habit strength increases, the time it takes for an organism to respond to a given stimulus—*reaction latency*—decreases.
- As habit strength increases, number of errors decreases (or, more precisely, the percentage of responses that lead to a reinforcing consequence increases).

The construct of habit family hierarchy was created to deal with the fact that each stimulus typically evokes more than one response and that several stimuli may evoke the same response. If one considers that a complex sequence of behavior forms a stimulus-response chain from its beginning stimulus to ending response, with lots of

S-R connections in between (that is, a response often forms the stimulus for the next response), then on occasion, an S in the middle of the chain may provoke the final response, depending on the habit strengths of the S-R connections that make up the chain. There are thus families of habits connected by the hierarchy of their respective strengths. When an intermediate S-R connection fires off, even when the ultimate goal is not in sight, this is called a *fractional anticipatory goal reaction*, and since lots of stimuli are always evoking lots of responses, they eventually form habit structures that allow animals a lot of ways to reach their goals.

All of these connections, remember, are formed through operant conditioning, in which random responses are reinforced by consequences. Negative consequences tend to eliminate errors in movement towards a goal. The certainty of the response leading towards the goal is strongest just before you get there. You can see it, you can smell it, the cues are best remembered, etc. Errors are eliminated first at the final step. The farther away you get from the goal working backwards, the more possible ways there are to go wrong, more other pathways and more possibilities that distractions (other S-R connections that for the moment are stronger than the distant goal) will occur. If you turn it around and watch the progress of a rat through a maze towards a goal, you will therefore find that the rat moves slowly and tentatively first and then faster and faster as it nears the goal. (I also find that the last pages of a chapter are easier to write than the first.) The rat (and I and maybe you) is running down a goal gradient: Because errors get progressively less frequent the closer an organism gets to a goal, an organism proceeds faster the closer it gets to it.

The goal, of course, can't exert its power magically from the outside. Something a rat has yet to experience cannot influence its current behavior, at least to a materialistic behaviorist like Hull. That would be a teleological explanation, a bad thing in science. Therefore, the push must be from within, from a **drive** that needs to be satiated. It is the drive that keeps the animal going through a complex series of reinforced responses, making midcourse corrections, avoiding distractions, until it gets food or sex or freedom (all three are postulated innate drives).

In fact, "drive" is what was generally called an **intervening variable**. Intervening variables are hypothetical unobserved entities that are assumed or postulated as explanations for those things that we can observe. The hunger drive explains, for example, why rats will eat (and learn through reinforcement) at some times and not others. Indeed, given that several things may cause hunger and thirst and that several different kinds of responses may satiate them, sometimes such a variable is useful. "Habit strength" is another such intervening variable, because under it are grouped such things as described in the bullet list above. But when a theory depends upon several unobservable intervening variables, it causes serious difficulties.

What precision is actually gained in the following statement of the "law of primary reinforcement," for example?

> Whenever a reaction (R) takes place in temporal contiguity with an afferent receptor impulse (s) resulting from the impact upon a receptor of a stimulus energy (S) and this conjunction is followed closely by the diminution of a need (and the associated diminution of the drive, (D) and in the drive receptor

discharge s_D), there will result an increment, Δ ($s \rightarrow R$), in the tendency for that stimulus on subsequent occasions to evoke that reaction.

(Hull, 1943, p. 71)

The above law sounds reasonable in the abstract, until one tries to operationalize the variables (Estes et al., 1954). What sort of reaction? How is stimulus energy measured? Is there any way to measure the diminution of a drive independently of behavior itself? Ideally, if a theorist is going to make that general a statement, he or she should have hundreds of observations, probably from all of the senses and across a range of stimuli and so forth. It's fine to say that there is an increase in habit strength due to reinforcement, but when one tries to measure exactly how much of an increase there should be, there are a lot of complex questions about which experiments, under which conditions and how many experiments should be done to estimate the constant. Hull did not, in fact, use such a vast store of experiments to estimate his equations, so his system seems more precise than it actually was.

And yet Hull tried. $_sH_R = M(1-e^{-kw})e^{-it} e^{-ut'}(1-e^{-iN})$ is the mathematical formulation of a postulate that tries to describe habit strength in terms of things like delay of reinforcements, number or reinforcements, objective weight of food reinforcer and so on. It is not necessary that one actually understand the equation to realize that an equation with that many variables could fit almost any curve (Estes et al., 1954).

It is worth noting that Hull's excesses in the use of intervening variables was at least one reason why B.F. Skinner was so against them. Hull had published quite a few articles before the publication of Skinner's first major work on rat behavior, and their relations were cordial throughout the 1930s; it was Hull who named the Skinner box and brought Skinner to the wider notice of other behaviorists. Skinner reviewed *Principles of Behavior* respectfully, but privately wrote to the editor of the journal that the work was an "unbelievable muddle" that would lead to much "useless theorizing and experimentation."

That is, Pavlov and Watson had described how simple stimulus-response sequences could be built; Skinner, in his lab work with rats and pigeons, was describing at the same time as Hull how behaviors are selected by consequences, and Tolman was describing how, also in general, molar terms, rat behavior could be explained by their goal-directedness, but was expressing that behavior in Gestaltist terms. But Hull wanted to combine it all and wanted to describe behavior with the mathematical precision of a physicist, while linking behavior to the physiology of the sensory organs and the motor response system.

From the mid-1940s to the mid-1960s, behaviorism was the reigning scientific paradigm in most academic psychology departments throughout America. But there were many different theories within the paradigm: Hullians, Skinnerians and others engaged in many disputes, some of them philosophical and some of them resolvable through "puzzle-solving" experimentation. But there had developed a consensus that psychology was now the science of behavior. A premium was placed on clarity of description of stimuli and responses. In fact, the very terminology that we use today, including the definitions of independent and dependent variables, intervening constructs and operationalization of variables, began finally to be formalized in two influential articles by Tolman and Kenneth Spence, a student and close collaborator of Hull.

Any new approach to a subject taken by energetic young researchers also leads to fruitful broad extensions of the initial ideas. Some of these new extensions were very successful, in that they led to extended research programs and findings, often extending findings from the animal lab to real human problems. Some were less successful, and their failures indirectly led to the cognitive revolution in psychology. Below are a couple of examples.

Social Learning and the Analysis of Aggressive Behavior

Several students of Hull were interested in analyzing human aggressive behavior in Hullian behavioral terms. In their first attempt, *Frustration and Aggression* (Dollard, Miller, Doob, Mowrer, and Sears (1944/1998), John Dollard (1900–1980), Neal E. Miller (1909–2002), Leonard W. Doob (1909–2000), O. Hobart Mowrer (1907–1982) and Robert R. Sears (1908–1989) attempted to reinterpret standard Freudian terms in behavioral language. (All of the authors were students or colleagues of Hull at Yale.) For example, the authors agreed with Freud that aggression generally followed frustration (see Chapter 9), but that acts of aggression may be inhibited if past experience suggested that such responses would be punished. Sometimes, individuals would commit aggression towards individuals or objects less likely to punish instead of the powerful frustrating boss, for example; this is an explanation of the Freudian concept of displacement. In fact, if an individual anticipates particularly dire punishment for aggression, the inhibition would become so thorough that repression would result. If, however, the individual could commit aggression in some way, drive reduction (in Freudian terms, catharsis; see next chapter) should result, decreasing further aggression. Thus, in this example, Dollard et al. (1998/1944) described some of the conditions under which a response may be learned but not performed.

Dollard and Miller (1941/2000) had addressed the aspect of imitation of responses in an earlier book, *Social Learning and Imitation*. A child learns to imitate her older sister because such imitations tend to be rewarded, whereas imitating a younger child (behaving "immaturely") is not. It pays then, to observe the cues or discriminative stimuli that lead to rewardable behavior by the older child and copy him or her. For a younger child, it may pay to mimic the older sibling even if one cannot see or understand the cues leading to a behavior. As long as a model's behavior leads to positive results, people will follow that model; one may copy virtually everything that the model does through generalization. Hence, Dollard and Miller explained imitation of models, leadership and identification. Thus, Dollard, Miller and their colleagues had begun the approach called **social learning** or **observational learning**, in which children and adults can learn without performing behaviors but simply by observing the behaviors of others in context.

A talented Canadian undergraduate at the University of British Columbia, Albert Bandura (1925–present) asked his professors where the "stone tablets" of psychology—the 10 commandments or the Rosetta stones—were kept, and the answer was "University of Iowa." Hull's most famous student and collaborator Kenneth W. Spence (1907–1967) was the chair of the department there, and Robert Sears had taken over the Iowa Child Study Center from Gestaltist Kurt Lewin. Bandura arrived at Iowa in 1949 and was immediately interested in the problem of aggression, as described by Dollard and Miller and investigated in adolescent boys by Sears. Bandura followed Sears to Stanford in 1949. His work over the next decade, on the child-rearing patterns of parents of aggressive versus nonaggressive boys, was published as *Adolescent Aggression* (Bandura & Walters, 1959). In this work, they noticed that parents of aggressive boys encouraged them to be aggressive in school by encouraging their boys to solve their own peer disputes by fighting back. The parents were punitive towards the boys at home and aggressive towards school authorities and the boys were modeling that behavior.

This work was followed by a now-famous series of experimental studies on the effect of models on the rate of aggressive behavior in preschoolers (Bandura, Ross, & Ross, 1961, 1963). The studies typically allowed preschoolers to play with many toys, including a large, inflatable doll weighted at the bottom intended for punching. A baseline measure of aggressive play, such as punching, kicking or verbal aggression ("take that!"), was taken first. Then children observed either an adult aggressive model, who exhibited a high rate of novel physical and verbal aggressive behaviors, such as hitting the doll with a mallet, or an adult nonaggressive model, who ignored the doll and played with tinkertoys. Then, children were taken to another setting. In this setting, they were first frustrated in their wish to play with attractive toys; finally, their responses on the doll and other toys (e.g. shooting toy guns) were recorded. The series of studies showed the following outcomes:

- Children who were shown the aggressive model exhibited a tendency to higher levels of aggression than controls.
- The reverse was also true: Children who were shown the nonaggressive model showed less aggression than controls.
- Male models provoked more aggression than female models.
- Same-sex models promoted higher aggression than opposite-sex models; girls tended to imitate only the female's verbal aggression; boys would imitate males' physical aggression as well.
- Children shown an aggressive model who they saw being punished inhibited aggressive responses immediately thereafter, but showed that they had learned the responses later, when reinforced for aggression (Bandura et al., 1963).
- There was little difference in these effects owing to whether the model was live, on film or cartoon-like.
- There appeared to be little cathartic effect; that is, children given the opportunity to aggress, to "let out their frustrations," were more likely to increase rather than decrease their aggressive responses.

Thus, taken in the context of the previous social learning theory, Bandura and his colleagues supported the notion of imitation of novel responses suggested by Miller and Dollard (1941/2000) and the notion that learned responses can be inhibited in the context of anticipated punishment, suggested by Dollard et al. (1944/1998). But the catharsis hypothesis of Freud and the drive reduction approach of Dollard et al. (1944/1998) was called into question (Bandura & Walters, 1963). Moreover, the studies refuted the purely radical behaviorist notions of Skinner (and the selection by consequences mode of learning that went back to Thorndike and Morgan) that had implied that a behavior needed to be emitted by an organism before it is learned (e.g. Skinner, 1953); children could learn by observation alone; reinforcement dictated largely when and in what context the behavior was *performed* once learned.

To Bandura, aggression was a perfect kind of behavior to test Skinner's notion. If aggression truly had to be learned only by trial and error, many people would be maimed or killed learning it correctly.[16] Imitation was key to such vital adaptive learning. But imitation also opened the door to cognitive factors in learning: One must attend to the model, perceive its similarity to you, evaluate the cues and the likelihood of the consequences and so on. Without assuming symbolic representation of the model inside the head and even identification with it, some of the results of social learning experiments could not be explained (imitation depended on the social prestige of the model, for example). By 1986, Bandura was rejecting the terms social learning and observational learning in favor of a social cognitive theory, which went far beyond behaviorism and aggression to include such cognitive notions as *self-regulation*, *self-reinforcement* and the effects of beliefs about one's competence in situations, dubbed *self-efficacy* (Bandura, 1986).

Behavior Therapy

There were three independent sources for the term **behavior therapy**. One comes directly from Skinner; the two others come directly from reactions against the traditional Freudian model of therapy then in use for treatment. In 1953, B.F. Skinner and his students Ogden Lindsley and H.C. Solomon undertook a very basic study to determine whether psychotics in Metropolitan State Hospital, Waltham, MA, could be conditioned to pull a plunger for food or other reinforcement (Lindsley, Skinner, & Solomon, 1953). The term behavior therapy was first used then to outline the mere possibility of treatment of severe schizophrenia.

In 1957, a psychologist in London, Hans Eysenck (1915–1997), published one of the first articles that evaluated the success of therapy for neurosis in comparison to a control group. He reported that while only 44% of those treated with psychoanalysis improved in their condition, 64% of those given "eclectic" treatments improved. But the rate of improvement for those given only medication and reassurance by their family doctors was about 72%. Eysenck's dissatisfaction with analysis-based treatment led him to promote therapy based on behavioral methods in 1958, with a textbook to follow in 1960. The book helped popularize the term behavior therapy in England and America. Finally, perhaps the most significant early adopters of the term were two South African psychiatrists Joseph Wolpe (1915–1997) and Arnold Lazarus. Wolpe had studied with a student of Kenneth Spence after becoming disenchanted with psychodynamic medical treatments he used as a psychiatrist during the Second World War. Wolpe and Lazarus (1966) treated patients by pairing successively stronger anxiety-provoking stimuli with muscle relaxation responses. Since relaxation inhibits anxiety, the stimulus comes to lose its power to upset the patient. This Pavlovian-influenced behavior therapy[17] came to be called **systematic desensitization**.

In part to differentiate the Skinnerian operant approach from Wolpe and Lazarus's classical conditioning behavior therapy, the term **behavior modification** (Ullmann & Krasner, 1965) came into use, along with **applied behavior analysis** soon thereafter (Baer, Wolf, & Risley, 1968). Finally, although the term **cognitive behavior therapy** was first explicitly used by Lazarus in 1971, it came to be used in broad ways by many different researchers and therapists. In general, cognitive behavior therapists try to get clients to change or evaluate their thought processes as well as their behaviors in therapy. They are asked to repeat certain statements, praise or dialogues to themselves (e.g. Meichenbaum, 1977), to evaluate "irrational cognitions" (e.g. Ellis, 1955) or to try to get clients to avoid making unwarranted generalizations from limited experiences (e.g. Beck, 1976). When such cognitive training is combined with direct behavioral practice in the world, such treatment can be quite effective in relatively few sessions. Although these approaches do not satisfy purists in either behaviorism or cognitive psychology, they collectively comprise perhaps the largest contingent of therapists in the American Psychological Association today. See Table 8.3 for other pioneers in the explosion of behavioral therapy in the 1960s and 1970s.

Table 8.3 Behavior Therapy Pioneers (a limited list)

Pioneer	Mentors	Year of first	Contribution or Development
Mary Cover Jones	J. B. Watson	(1928)	Counterconditioning to remove fears
O. Hobart Mowrer	C. L. Hull	(1938)	Treatment of bedwetting through classical conditioning
Ogden R. Lindsley	B. F. Skinner	(1953)	Use of operant behavior therapy with psychotic patients
Joseph Wolpe & Arnold Lazarus	L. Reyna via K. W. Spence	(1958)	Counterconditioning of relaxation response to remove phobias, anxiety (systematic desensitization by reciprocal inhibition)
Hans Eysenck	Cyril Burt	(1960)	British popularizer of behavior therapy
Sidney W. Bijou	K.W. Spence	(1961)	Child behavior therapy.
Donald M. Baer	S. W. Bijou	(1968)	Child behavior therapy
Todd R. Risley	S. W. Bijou	(1968)	Child behavior therapy
Montrose M. Wolf	J. Michael, S. W. Bijou	(1968) (1964)	Founded *J. of Applied Behavior Analysis* First attempt at behavioral treatment for autism Coined "time out"
Ivar Lovaas	S. W. Bijou	(1974)	Systematic, rigorous ABA treatment for autism
Teodoro Ayllon Nathan Azrin		(1965)	Token economies in mental institutions
Albert Ellis		(1955–1993)	Rational emotive behavior therapy
Aaron T. Beck		(1977)	Cognitive behavior therapy for depression, anxiety disorders, etc.
Donald Meichenbaum		(1977)	Cognitive behavior therapy for posttraumatic stress disorders

Conclusion: Why We Are All Behaviorists Now and Why We Don't All Call Ourselves Behaviorists

Behaviorism began as a reaction to structuralism and functionalism. Introspection was not replicable, behaviorists said, and the terms used to describe concepts were fuzzy and unhelpful. And by the time behaviorism as a theoretical approach fell out of favor, by approximately 1980, cognitive approaches came back into vogue in subfields ranging from therapy to social and developmental psychology. It has even become respectable to study consciousness again! Does that mean we are back where we started? Skinner certainly thought so (Skinner, 1987). But most of the rest of us don't agree.

For one thing, the language of stimulus and response and independent and dependent variables was solidified during these years. Defining psychology as behavior made it easier for us to talk to one another (Danziger, 1997). By clarifying our language for us, behaviorists made it possible to hope for replication. Even experiments in cognitive psychology stand or fall on what a participant *does in response to stimuli*. How the results are interpreted is a different matter. Particularly from a presentist viewpoint, it is easy to see how behaviorism alters how those of us within the paradigm talk, even today, about what are acceptable experiments and data.

But we don't all call ourselves behaviorists today in part because behaviorism could not explain certain behaviors efficiently. If a person is behaving in a certain way and the stimuli controlling that behavior cannot be found, sometimes it is necessary (or at least easier) to suggest that the stimulus is in the head. If people learn behavior and no reinforcements are visible, it is sometimes necessary (or at least easier) to suggest that modeling is the cause. To cite one example, Skinner wrote a complex and interesting argument about how language might be learned through reinforcement (*Verbal Behavior*, 1957). And it's true that if children learn the language of their parents, this had to be part of the answer. But the vast number of sentences that a child utters not only have not been reinforced by others, they also have probably never been said by anyone before! Moreover, words have many different meanings in context, and it's hard to explain how these meanings operate without resorting to an invisible world inside the head and innate structures that deal with language (Chomsky, 1959, 1966).

So it became fashionable once again to consider humans as thinkers, who represent the world inside our heads in order to adapt to it. But that doesn't mean we could become full-fledged Cartesian dualists again. There could be no spooky stuff in there. Enter the computer, an inanimate machine that right from the beginning could show aspects similar to human verbal behavior and calculation, in surprising ways. It could appear to receive, store and analyze coded, language-like inputs and give sometimes surprising answers, like the magic of consciousness, but we know it's not magic. Its limitations could even be matched up to human ones. A computer with limited baud rate, processing speed or bandwidth could be likened to a human who could attend to only a few things at once. William James had described this in the good old introspectionist days, but now we have a cold hard object that we can program to mimic us and, by analogy, help us to understand how we work.

Finally, there was nothing really wrong with behaviorism. Where it is practical to have high control over behavior, in schools, in institutions, in homes where parents rule, many aspects of behaviorism are still being profitably used therapeutically today to effect behavioral change. Likewise, as Skinner himself proved, it is possible to engineer changes in one's own behavior. Beyond individuals, however, there are problems. Yes, it's probably true, in some sense, that a culture is a reinforcement system, that scientists do their work because of the reinforcements they receive, that artists keep producing art that either sells or receives social respect. But explaining *how* these things work would take a long time by the behaviorist method and we just couldn't wait, any more than we could wait for Titchener's methods to become practical. It's probably true that if we had total control of external circumstances, a lot of behavior could be predicted and controlled. But to whom do we give that control, and would it be ethical to turn the world into a giant token economy if we could? And the point is moot, because we can't. This takes nothing away from the impressive accomplishments of highly ethical behavior modification specialists to say that there are limitations to their methods. Psychology took the methodological rigor that behaviorism left us with and moved on, as history does, whether we want it to or not.

Notes

1. In Pavlov's standard account of this disagreement (e.g. Pavlov, 1928, p. 38), his student Dr. Snarskii took the subjective side and Pavlov the materialist side; Todes (1997) argues that it was, for a time, the other way around. He claims that Snarskii even suggested Sechenov as the solution. Given the collaborative nature of Pavlov's lab, however, the truth will remain unclear.
2. This, in spite of the fact that he is reported to have said, "If that which the Bolsheviks are doing in Russia is an experiment, for such an experiment I should regret giving even a frog" (Babkin, 1949, p. 161).
3. Or so Watson said, repeatedly. Biographer Kerry Buckley (1989) could find no evidence in Watson's transcripts that he had failed the course. Watson's statements about himself should be taken with a grain of salt, as he loved a good story more than the literal truth. Unfortunately for history, he burned most of his personal papers. When asked why, he said, "When you're dead, you're dead."
4. Buckley (1989) reports that Chicago was the first American psychology department to use the white rat systematically as research subjects. But see Small (1901) for a preceding exception at Clark.
5. Myelin acts as an insulator to nerve axons, making the electrical action of neurons faster. Axons begin at birth largely unmyelinated, and myelinization increases with age to maturity.
6. Some have seen aspects of James's pragmatism and Dewey's instrumentalism in Watson's work, but Watson himself never spoke of them. Perhaps the background of these philosophies provided the soil, but not the seed, for behaviorism.
7. Watson must have known a little about Pavlov's work before he published his manifesto. His friend, Robert Yerkes, had published a short summary translation of Pavlov in 1909: Yerkes and Morgulis (1909). But as we have seen, Watson had taken the route to behaviorism starting from other beginnings. Pavlov merely provided support (or ammunition) for defending Watson's views (Watson, 1936).
8. Harold Ickes was used to getting what he wanted. He was later a powerful advisor and secretary of the interior for the administration of Franklin Delano Roosevelt.

9. Thorndike was criticized on this point by Wolfgang Köhler, who believed that animal reasoning should only be studied if all of the relevant factors for solving a problem were available to the animal (see Chapter 6).
10. In fact, in his early work, he thought that association might be all that was necessary to learn, described as the law of exercise: "The Law of Exercise is that: Any response to a situation will, other things being equal, be more strongly connected with the situation in proportion to the number of times it has been connected with that situation and to the average vigor and duration of the connections"(Thorndike, 1911, p. 244). By the 1930s, he had changed his mind; he then believed that all learning was the result of classical conditioning or the law of effect.
11. Crozier also followed Loeb's work on the processes of creating life; another of his students was Gregory Pincus, inventor of the birth control pill.
12. In fact, Skinner suggested that the term sharp or dull pain were merely analogies to concrete events—sharp pains are generally caused by sharp objects and dull pains by dull objects. The same language is then metaphorically transferred to describing internal pains (Skinner, 1974).
13. The rumor may have originated by mixing up Skinner's and Watson's children. John B. Watson's son, a psychiatrist, committed suicide in midlife, after his father had passed away (Buckley, 1989).
14. Skinner's socialism is strictly nongovernmental, entered into consciously by the founding inhabitants. He was largely against agitating for change within existing governmental structures, believing that the current reinforcement contingencies corrupting current politicians would corrupt future ones as well. It's better to start societies from scratch.
15. Social psychologists call this "the fundamental attribution error."
16. Bandura once drolly remarked to an interviewer that if one had to learn throwing grenades by trial and error, it would give a new meaning to the phrase "A Farewell to Arms" (Evans, 1989, p. 8).
17. For a while it was called "reciprocal inhibition."

9 Psychoanalysis
A Theory for Its Time and Place

> Biographers are fixated on their hero in a quite particular way.
> —Sigmund Freud (1910)

> Whoever turns biographer commits himself to lies, to concealment, to hypocrisy, to embellishments and even to dissembling his own lack of understanding, for biographical truth is not to be had and even if one had it, one could not use it.
> —Freud (1936; both quotes cited by biographer, historian and psychoanalyst Peter Gay, 1988, pp. xv–xvi)

No other branch of psychology owes more to a sustained act of creative will of one man than does psychoanalysis to Sigmund Freud. When one examines a picture of Freud, the most arresting feature is the intense gaze with which he regards the photographer. One might expect this in the 50-year-old experienced therapist, former hypnotist and leader of a movement. But take a look at the eyes in the second photo of Freud, shown here at the age of 8 with his father. The same gaze is present even here, demonstrating the beginnings of an intensity shown in the boy as a hunger for knowledge, in the young man as a tendency to idolize great men and ideas and to openly desire fame and in the older man to jealously guard his discoveries and to disown those who disagreed with him. One can also see the great intelligence of one who knew five languages and was steeped in classical learning, a medical doctor who wrote respected neurology textbooks and did close work with a microscope and dissecting scalpel, all before he took up his work by the famous couch.

To say that the development of psychoanalysis is closely tied to the life of Freud is not to say that he was the heroic originator of all of the ideas contained in it, as his legend might suggest. Recent Freud scholarship has stressed just how much he was a man of his time, a brilliant synthesizer of ideas common in the medical and scientific worlds of Europe, rather than a rebel in the vanguard. Our historicist task, then, is to place him in this context. But since we have the advantage of presentist hindsight, we must also recognize that there are also places where Freud may have gone seriously wrong in his assumptions or diagnoses. Some of these errors, to be sure, are errors that anyone in his day might have made; others are more suspect and continue to have ramifications in the present.

Finally, there is the thorny question of how Freud might have managed and controlled his own legend. Freud hated biographers and was extraordinarily concerned with how his life and his science would be remembered. He started burning his correspondence, notes and drafts of manuscripts while still in his twenties, before he was famous, and did so periodically, until his fame was assured. He attempted to acquire letters he had sent to others, but he was fortunately unsuccessful. Much of what records and papers that remained were kept under seal in the Freud Archives, hidden from view or available only to trusted loyalists, for as long as 50 years after his death in 1939. (There are even a few mysterious letters still sealed into the 22nd century [Roazen, 1982]!) Thus, new "Freuds" are always emerging, colored by the hero worship, transference love or Oedipal rebellion of the writers. Freud himself would probably be appalled, but he would also have reason to be secretly pleased at having originated the psychoanalytic method of biography to which he is now being subjected.

Freud's Early Life and Times

Sigmund Schlomo Freud[1] was born above a blacksmith's shop in what was then Freiberg, Moravia (now Pribor, Czech Republic), on May 6, 1856. His father was then a wool merchant who could never really seem to make his business prosper. In his forties, with two grown sons, Jacob Freud had married his third wife, Amelia, a 19-year-old beauty, in 1855; Sigmund was her first child. When Sigmund was 4, the family moved from bucolic Freiberg to Vienna, the cosmopolitan capital of the Austro-Hungarian Empire. There, the family grew; in no time, Freud had five sisters and a younger brother, in addition to his half-brothers, who soon emigrated to England. The remaining large family lived in an apartment in the Jewish quarter, but only Sigmund had his own room. From the beginning, his mother considered him destined for greatness and gave him special privileges. Her personality was described by contemporaries as "autocratic" and "domineering," but she was completely devoted to her eldest son, whom she called her *Goldener Sigi*. When Sigmund complained that his sister's piano playing was disturbing his studies, the piano was removed. Freud later said, "a man who has been the indisputable favorite of his mother keeps for life the feeling of being a conqueror, that confidence of success that often induces real success" (Freud, 1919/1978, SE[2] 17, p. 156).

Young Sigmund was, by all accounts, a brilliant student from the start. At his *Gymnasium*, a college preparatory high school, he was first in his class for six of eight years. He became fluent in English, Spanish and French, as well as in the usual Latin and Greek. His letters to friends, always passionate, were also erudite beyond his years. At age 16, he remarked to a friend, prophetically, "It gives me pleasure to apprehend the thick texture of connecting threads that accident and fate have woven around us all" (letter to Emil Fluss, cited in Gay, 1988, p. 26).

According to Freud biographer Peter Gay (1988), the 1860s up until about 1890 were relatively good years to be Jewish in Catholic Vienna. Jews attained complete legal rights in 1859 after having suffered generations of restrictions on where they could live or travel and prohibitions on purchasing land. They were already well represented in several professions, from banking to journalism and medicine. There were even Jews in local government posts. It was a time when, as Freud later said, every ambitious Jewish boy had a government minister's portfolio in his school satchel. Freud's father was fluent in reading Hebrew, but he was intent on bringing his children up in the new assimilated ways. They spoke German, not Yiddish, at home and celebrated Passover and Purim as nonreligious family holidays. Nevertheless, anti-Semitism was always just below the surface: Freud's Catholic nursemaid would take Sigmund to Mass, trying to convert the little boy. He would always remember a story his father told him of the time when he was walking along the road and a soldier rode by and knocked his hat off into the gutter, laughing and calling out epithets. Sigmund asked his father what he did in response, hoping to hear that his father fought back. Instead, he had only picked up his hat and walked on, something the son vowed never to do. As Freud was entering the University of Vienna in 1873, a stock market crash, a depression and a cholera epidemic began to increase anti-Semitic scapegoating until by the 1890s it became an ever-present factor in Freud's life in Vienna. In spite of these pressures and his atheism, Freud never renounced his culture and in fact grew more combative against anti-Semitism and more supportive of liberal Jewish social causes as the situation got worse.

So even early on, Freud was brilliant, proud and ambitious, brought up to expect greatness in a world where he would certainly have to strive hard for it. There were opportunities, but also obstacles, real prejudices and perceived prejudices that led to resentments and redoubled efforts. Because the foundations of psychoanalysis were built in the actual personal apprenticeships, relationships and experiences of Freud, we will approach the history of psychoanalysis, then, as a biography. It will be a biography that would not please Freud himself or his more loyal followers, for recently much of Freud's ideas and personal behavior have been called into question. But he also brought about an unparalleled change in worldview in the early 20th century, and that achievement must be credited to him as well. As the poet W.H. Auden once wrote in "In Memory of Sigmund Freud,"

> If often he was wrong and at times absurd,
> to us he is no more a person now
> but a whole climate of opinion

The Austro-German Zeitgeist: High School and the University of Vienna

If we look at Freud's biography with a presentist eye for where elements of his theory may have come from, the first place to look, surprisingly, is in his high school psychology textbook. The text used in Freud's high school in the early 1870s was written by a follower of Johann Friederick Herbart (1776–1841), a German associationist and idealist. Unlike the British associationists, who tended to follow Locke's notion of the mind as a "storehouse of ideas," Herbart, following Locke's contemporary, Leibnitz (1646–1716), believed that ideas were active rather than passive. We can each hold opposite ideas in mind, but at any given time, one predominates and the other is inhibited below the threshold or *limen of consciousness*. Herbart said that ideas thus submerged were *unbewüsst* or "unconscious'd." Ideas also strove for self-preservation and even though they were temporarily inhibited, they were never destroyed. Since the number of things that could be consciously perceived at any one time is small, this meant effectively that a massive number of ideas is being "unconscious'd" at any given time. The Freudian idea of **repression** (*verdrängen*) is much more complex than Herbart's notion, but with hindsight, it is easy to see the similarities. Freud himself never mentioned this particular influence, but it is nearly certain that he encountered it.

Another route from which he may have learned of Herbart's ideas is from Gustav Fechner (see Chapter 5), who obviously owes the notion of sensory thresholds to Herbart. Fechner also may have borrowed his basic notion of the mathematical nature of the relationship between the soul and the body from Herbart. Freud repeatedly referred to him as "the great Fechner"; after all, Fechner's psychophysics gave the hope that the mind would finally be explicable by science. Freud never met Fechner, who died while he was still in medical school, but he was admired by many of Freud's later teachers and mentors, among them Brücke, Meynert and Breuer (see later).

When Freud entered the University of Vienna, in 1873, like many modern freshmen, he was undecided on his career. Almost immediately, he enrolled in the courses of the great psychologist Franz Brentano, the only courses that he was to take in college that did not involve biology or medicine. As was noted in Chapter 6, Brentano had been a priest and Aristotelian scholar within the Catholic Church until he left in a dispute over the then new doctrine of papal infallibility. He had switched to philosophy, but still considered himself devout; he even carried himself like a monk, with an intense gaze, long beard and apparent indifference to worldly matters. Freud was captivated by his magnetic lectures. He took five courses with Brentano and followed him after class to debate religion with him (Gay, 1988). Freud wrote of him often to his friends, calling him "a damned clever fellow." Freud would ultimately not be convinced by his religious arguments and strengthened his own atheism, but he briefly considered philosophy as a career. Brentano thought well enough of Freud to later arrange for him a job translating John Stuart Mill into German and may have introduced him to his medical friends Josef Breuer and Theodor Meynert, who would be pivotal for Freud.

What ideas did Freud borrow from Brentano for what later became his theory? We may never know for sure, as he burned his early notes, and his autobiography and his more or less approved biography (Jones, 1953) do not give Brentano much credit, but scholars have noted several similarities in their thought (see Fancher, 1977; Barclay, 1964). First, for Brentano, all thought is motivated and goal driven; desires, wishes and judgments are fully real actions of the mind. Centuries of philosophy have made us uncertain of what objects are really out there, but our wishes and desires are immediately present to us and color everything else we think about. Second, these wishes and desires must normally be subjected to a kind of reality testing by a strong consciousness or ego. Third, Brentano recognizes that in order to truly understand adult thought, one must try to understand how it is built up from the simpler forms of childhood. Doing this retrospectively from adulthood is difficult and fraught with potential error. Finally, in Brentano's work, he addresses in detail the question of whether unconscious thought might exist, a topic of considerable interest among philosophers even in 1874. But, here he parts company with his famous student: "The question 'Is there unconscious consciousness?' in the sense in which we have formulated it, is, therefore, to be answered with a firm 'No'" (Brentano, 1874/1973, p. 137).

Along with this dalliance in philosophy, Freud settled down into hard work, in biology and medicine and at first was more enamored of the former than the latter. He was attracted to science by a famous long poem erroneously attributed to Johann Wolfgang von Goethe (1749–1932), "On Nature." Goethe, the grandfather of the German *Naturphilosophie* movement that influenced Hegel (see Chapter 5), promoted a noble, almost religious view of natural science; his famous play, *Faust*, suggests that the pursuit of knowledge is worthy of selling one's soul. "Natural objects," he wrote, "should be sought and investigated as they are and not to suit observers, but respectfully as if they were divine beings." Fortunately, by Freud's time, the emotional impulses of the movement were beginning to be tamed by hard scientific investigation, so that poetic statements on the nobility of science were tempered with methodological rigor.

Freud's teachers followed this calling. Freud's next mentor was the physiologist Ernst von Brücke, a formidable Prussian who had studied in Berlin with Müller and who had taken the materialist pledge of the 1847 group with Helmholtz, du Bois-Reymond and Ludwig. He advocated a physiology based purely on physiochemical processes, a deterministic science based on exacting observation and dissection. And he immediately put Freud to work on the anatomy of lower animals, both to elucidate their structures and to establish evolutionary links. For example, Freud did close work on dissecting eels to discover their sexual organs, dissecting fish spines to investigate neurons and ganglion cells.

Brücke, 40 years Freud's senior, was clearly a father figure for him: Freud later called him "the greatest authority he had known" and named a son Ernst after him. The six years he spent in Brücke's institute were some of the happiest in his life; he made fast friends with Brücke's assistants, whom he also emulated. He wanted most of all to be a physiologist. But it was not to be. Brücke's assistants were relatively young men and were unlikely to give up their posts. And Freud was quite poor. It is unrecorded where he got the money for tuition, but he at times seemed to be subsisting on about the equivalent of a dollar a day while a student and that often obtained from tutoring. In the company of scientists, such frugality was not so remarkable; graduate students, then as now, were a rather scruffy lot. But Freud had fallen in love and his poverty really began to chafe. In what was apparently a whirlwind romance of a few months in 1882, he became secretly betrothed to Martha Bernays. He was so penniless and without prospects, he was sure her solidly middle-class Jewish family would not accept him. After a fatherly talk with Brücke, he decided, regretfully, to redouble his efforts to become a doctor, specializing in neurology.

So, Freud entered into his residency rotations through the various medical specialties at Vienna General Hospital. But he still tried to do research, this time under brain anatomist and psychiatrist Theodor Meynert (1833–1898). While there, he traced the route of nerves in the medulla oblongata, creating his own methods to do so. Later, he wrote insightful works on aphasia and a text on the cerebral paralyses of

Figure 9.1 Ernst Wilhelm Ritter von Brücke, physiologist (1819–1892)

children, which was so extensive that the bibliography alone ran to 14 pages; some have indicated that this work alone might have secured his professional reputation.

By the end of Freud's medical training, he had been thoroughly steeped in the principles of Austro-German philosophy and practice of science and medicine:

- He believed in the nobility of the scientific enterprise and was ambitious to make his name in it.
- He had been shown, by Herbart and Fechner, that ideas were kept in the unconscious by dynamic forces, rather than stored peacefully in Locke's storehouse.
- From Brentano, he learned that desires and wishes were an intrinsic and necessary component of thought. Thought is always directed towards a goal; it is never static.
- Brücke had trained him in crucial elements of the Helmholtzian scientific approach: materialism, determinism, close observation, meticulous laboratory work.
- His own work in the lab taught him the importance of evolution; his work on the wards in aphasia and neurology taught him the relationship between brain and body and the importance of accurate diagnosis.

The Cocaine Episode

In 1883, Freud read a paper about the effects of a new drug, which had been shown to increase the endurance of German troops on maneuvers. Freud had been working very hard and was prone to occasional mental strain and exhaustion, so he decided to try some. The therapeutic prospects of cocaine were largely unknown, so it seemed a good research opportunity as well, one that might make him famous and able to marry his fiancée sooner rather than later. So, he procured an expensive gram of the substance, dissolved a 20th of a gram in water and drank it. Soon he was calling it a "miracle drug" and taking it regularly for depression and indigestion. He wrote to his fiancée, Martha Bernays,

> Woe to you, my Princess, when I come. I will kiss you quite red and feed you until you are plump. And if you are froward you shall see who is the stronger, a gentle little girl who doesn't eat enough or a big wild man *who has cocaine in his body*. In my last severe depression I took coca again and a small dose lifted me to the heights in a wonderful fashion. I am just now busy collecting the literature for a song of praise to this magical substance.
> (Freud to Martha Bernays, June 2, 1884, cited in Jones, 1953, vol. I, p. 84, emphasis original)

He did some brief research and published a rapturous essay on its potential: "On Coca." In the essay (which some have suggested Freud wrote while literally on cocaine; Webster, 1995, p. 46), he describes it as producing "the most gorgeous excitement" in laboratory animals and describes a dose as "an offering." He also claimed that it had no side effects and no addictive properties. Moreover, he claimed that cocaine was effective in overcoming addiction to morphine. He had offered some to an old friend who worked for Brücke. Because of an injury to the nerves in his hand, his friend was in constant pain and had become addicted to morphine, so Freud suggested that he take cocaine to wean himself off of what Freud assumed was the more dangerous drug.

Freud was wrong. Yes, his friend had temporarily given up morphine, but he was soon in the grip of a voracious cocaine habit of a gram a day, which was costing him the then large sum of 600 marks a month (Jones, 1953). After a while, he was taking both cocaine and morphine. At first, Freud thought that his friend was simply an exceptional case. Moreover, he claimed he had warned his friend against injecting rather than swallowing it. But he had rushed his euphoric article into print less than six weeks after he himself had tried the drug and about a month after his friend had begun his "treatment," so he had made a promise of its effectiveness before he knew the outcome. A year later, moreover, he was recommending injection of cocaine enthusiastically in another paper, when he knew his friend was in desperate straits. He died six years later, still in the grip of the addiction (Jones, 1953; Webster, 1995). By 1886, it was quite clear that there were problems with cocaine addiction in many people. Another writer was severely critical of Freud, calling cocaine "the third scourge of humanity" (after alcohol and morphine).

It was perhaps ironic that Freud had come very close to making a discovery of cocaine's major medical use. In the final paragraph of his first article, he hinted at cocaine's possible use as a local anesthetic (he had noticed that it made one's mouth numb when swallowing). But an ophthalmologist friend, Carl Koller, had also noticed this, as he helped Freud with some tests. After Freud left on vacation, Koller tested cocaine on animal eyes and his own and sent a quick paper to a journal (Jones, 1953).

Freud had missed his first chance for fame and nearly damaged his own reputation. When he was up for promotion to *Privatdozent* (essentially adjunct lecturer), he did not mention his cocaine publications in his resume. He had also shown a troubling tendency to ignore complicated and ambiguous findings in favor of writing a clear story with himself as a hero. It would not be the last time he would do this.

Jean-Martin Charcot: Napoleon of the Neuroses

In 1885, through the influence of Brücke and Meynert, Freud won a postdoctoral fellowship to study with Jean-Martin Charcot in Paris. Charcot (1825–1893) was probably the most famous neurologist and neuroanatomist in Europe. He was the head of La Salpêtrière, a vast charity hospital and insane asylum for women. Shrewdly, Charcot had recognized early in his career that while doing work at such a place was not glamorous, it provided a gold mine of patients with exotic disorders, and he had made the most of it. He was known for having first diagnosed amyotrophic lateral sclerosis (what we call Lou Gehrig's disease was then called Charcot's disease), multiple sclerosis and other degenerative neurological disorders, among other diseases. Some 15 syndromes and diseases were named after him. He had done fine work in aphasia and localizing the effects of particular brain diseases. Virtually every French neurologist had studied with him. Some of his students included Joseph Babinski (of the Babinski reflex), Giles de la Tourette (of Tourette's syndrome), Pierre Janet (see below) and later, even Alfred Binet, creator of the Binet-Simon intelligence test (see Chapters 4 and 10). By the time Freud arrived in October 1885, Charcot had built the asylum up from a backwater into a virtual medical city of 45 buildings and 4,000 patients. He had built anatomy and pathology labs, photographic darkrooms and other state-of-the-art facilities (Ellenberger, 1970).

Hysteria

Once his success had been assured in neurology, Charcot began to deal with the controversial subjects of hysteria and hypnotism. The diagnosis of **hysteria** had had a long and confusing history. The term comes from the Greek word *hysterus*, meaning womb, and in ancient times up to the 17th century it was thought to be purely a disease of women, due to wandering of the womb, which was thought to be allowed to roam freely with a kind of spirit of its own within the body. Veith (1965) has found that the origin of this idea goes all the way back to Ancient Egypt, whose physicians would hold noxious smoke to the nose of the patient (to move the womb down) or below the vagina (to move the womb up). Centuries later, the distinctive symptom of the wandering womb was preserved in the so-called "hysterical fit," the first part of Charcot's diagnosis of hysteria. *La grande hysterie* would begin in a woman by a sensation of a womb traveling upward in her body until it reached the throat, leaving her gasping for air, as if there were a ball in the throat—the so-called *globus hystericus* symptom. Then there would be an arching of the back, to the point of being up on the head and toes, sometimes with pelvic thrusting. This would be followed by a period of unconsciousness and foaming at the mouth. The disorder would sometimes involve rigid poses or trancelike states. At this point, you may suspect that what Charcot was studying was an exotic form of epileptic grand mal seizure and, indeed, he recognized the similarity. He had put these patients in a ward of "hystero-epileptics"; his initial interest in this disorder was based on a desire to separate the diagnoses. But the diagnosis of hysteria could mean almost anything at the time, and Charcot stretched his own diagnosis to fit the accepted notion. Hysteria essentially came to mean any apparently organic disease (paralysis, deafness, blindness, convulsions, etc.) for which the patient's symptoms do not match the typical presentation of symptoms for that disease and for which no organic cause could be found. Persons with hysterical deafness might consider themselves to be deaf, but be able to hear some things and not others, for example. Similarly, people with hysterical paralysis, typically of one side or the other (hysterical hemiplegia), would have a pattern of sensation on the affected limb or limbs that would be different from that of a true paralysis patient (Webster, 1995).

From ancient times to the mid-19th century, a cause of the disorder was supposed to be a lack of female sexual satisfaction. Cases of male hysteria had been reported since the 1600s, but even in 1859, when the French physician Briquet wrote a detailed report of 430 cases, he estimated a 20:1 ratio of women to men with the disease (Ellenberger, 1970). Briquet discounted the sexual theory, pointing out that the disorder was much higher among prostitutes than nuns in France. But in Freud's day, belief in the sexual etiology of the disorder was still quite prevalent. He once overheard someone at a party at Charcot's say emphatically that the source of such complaints was "always, always in the marriage bed." At the same time, a joke was going around in the all-male medical profession that the prescription for hysteria was, in Latin, *penis normalis, dosim repetatur* (repeated doses of a normal penis—Jones, 1953, p. 249). Gynecologists held to this interpretation longer than many other specialists, even into the 20th century (and in America as well as Europe), because it may have affected their livelihood. Many women who came to their practices with a large range of psychosomatic complaints were diagnosed as having hysteria. Maines (1999) reports that, in a day in which masturbation was considered (a) a grievous sin, (b) medically debilitating and dangerous and (c) not usually done by women anyway, a woman could go to her doctor for "vulvular massage" to "relieve tension" by achieving a "hysterical paroxysm." Such treatments no doubt assured a steady flow of patients!

Hypnotism

One peculiar feature of hysteria and hysterical fits caused Charcot to experiment with hypnosis, beginning in the late 1870s. These fits could be brought on by external cues from the environment, like posthypnotic suggestion. One visitor to the Salpêtrière reported that, during a patients' ball, when a gong was struck accidentally, several hysterical patients reverted to frozen statues (Ellenberger, 1970). He reported to the *Academie des Sciences* in 1882 that he was able to reproduce these states in five hysterical patients through hypnotism, essentially bringing them through "lethargy" (drowsiness), "catalepsy" (a trancelike state, waking but without consciousness or sensation) and "somnambulism" (in which the patient can perform actions of which they are not conscious). The paper caused a sensation, for Charcot claimed a physiological link between hysteria and hypnotism: Only "degenerate" hysterics with an innate predisposition could be hypnotized. Hypnotism was thus claimed by the science of medicine, lifting it out of its long disrepute.

The *Academie* had twice rejected hypnotism as dangerous charlatanism. In English- and German-speaking countries, hypnotism (*hypnotisme* in French) was actually referred to as "mesmerism" after its promoter Franz Anton Mesmer (1734–1815). Dr. Mesmer received his medical degree from the University of Vienna based on his thesis that the forces of the planets have an effect on human diseases. In this thesis, he propounded that all living things have an electromagnetic force within them called *animal magnetism* that can be influenced by movement of the planets or by the ministrations of people such as himself, who knew how to harness and focus its effects for healing purposes. After marrying an heiress, Mesmer treated patients in Vienna, but then moved to Paris in 1778 and opened an exclusive salon where he charged large fees for women of the aristocracy to be "magnetized." His treatment involved sitting close to the patient, knees touching, pressing his thumbs into her hands and peering deeply into her eyes. He would pass his hands over the affected body part, all the time talking softly, with the smell of orange blossoms in the dim light, soft eerie glass harmonica[3] music playing in the background. His aim was to provoke a "crisis" similar to the hysterical fit that Charcot later noted. Several such sessions were to lead to a cure. As he became successful, he would hold mass sessions with 200 patients at a time (Ellenberger, 1970), conducted with Mesmer in a magnificent lavender robe and iron wand. Sometimes the sessions were held outdoors under a "magnetized" oak tree (Veith, 1965).

But Mesmer's success was not to last. Embittered assistants, doctors and physicists denounced him as a quack, and the French government became concerned about the erotic nature of the sessions. They demanded proof that he had discovered a magnetic fluid and set up a commission that included chemist Lavoisier and the American ambassador Benjamin Franklin. They devised a test, in which Mesmer agreed to magnetize one of two trees. If a series of patients chose the magnetized tree as having therapeutic effects, the hypothesis would be proven. Mesmer failed. He left Paris under cloudy circumstances in 1785, having been driven out by angry ridicule. Mesmerism remained a favorite risqué party entertainment in Europe and America through the 19th century, but French scientists would have nothing to do with it until Charcot's paper almost 100 years later. Had anyone else claimed its efficacy, he would have been criticized severely, but at the time Charcot's fame in Paris was at its peak. His reputation carried the day.

Charcot's reputation after his discovery was, if anything, even more illustrious than before it, for he became known for his near-miraculous cures. The following is reported by one of his admiring students, Dr. Lyubimov:

> Many patients were brought to Dr. Charcot from all over the world, paralytics on stretchers or wearing complicated apparatuses. Charcot ordered the removal

of those appliances and told the patients to walk. There was, for instance, a young lady who had been paralyzed for years. Charcot bade her stand up and walk, which she did under the astounded eyes of her parents and of the Mother Superior of the convent where she had been staying. Another young lady was brought to Charcot with a paralysis of both legs. Charcot found no organic lesion; his consultation was not yet over when the patient stood up and walked back to the door where the cabman, who was waiting for her, took off his hat in amazement and crossed himself.

(Lyubimov, 1894, cited in Ellenberger, 1970, p. 95)

Charcot, a stern, magnetic figure, whose wizardry, along with his Gallic facial features and dignified hauteur, earned him the title "The Napoleon of the Neuroses," was famous for his meticulously prepared Friday lectures. With princes and notables in attendance, he would bring in patients from the hospital wards. Charcot could bring on a hysterical crisis in a patient by hypnotizing her and applying a suggestion that, after awaking, the patient would become paralyzed with a slap on the back. He

Figure 9.2 Engraving based on a painting by André Broulliet: "A Clinical Lesson at La Salpêtrière" (1887), painted at the height of hysteria's popularity in the popular culture in Paris and months after Freud's postdoctoral fellowship with Charcot. This composite, based on placing studies of individuals into a tableau, includes many notables who worked with him, including Joseph Babinski (of the Babinski reflex) and Georges Gilles de la Tourette (of Tourette's syndrome). The woman swooning next to Charcot is Blanche Wittman, known as "Queen of the Hysterics" and a favorite patient of Charcot's, is probably acting out, consciously or unconsciously, the three stages of "*la grande hysterie.*" A full list of the "participants" in the original color painting can be found on Wikipedia, with copious notes.

could similarly remove a hysterical paralysis through hypnosis, right in front of the eyes of astonished members of the audience. Hysterics were susceptible to hypnosis because of a degenerate hereditary weakness, he explained. Hypnotism and hysteria had the same root, so if a subject were hypnotizable, that in itself was a sign of hysteric susceptibility. Women were much more likely to be hysterics than men were, but if a man were subjected to a fright, as was not uncommon in construction or railroad accidents, he too could develop phantom paralyses. These puzzling paralyses (sometimes called, in men, "railway spine" or "railway brain"), which others had ascribed to organic causes such as a blow to the head, might come and go and be manipulated by hypnotism (Webster, 1995; Ellenberger, 1970; Sulloway, 1979). Moreover, Charcot suggested that men, unlike women, did not need to be susceptible by heredity to acquire hysteria; the trauma would be sufficient.

Barely a week after arriving in Paris in 1885, 29-year-old Sigmund Freud saw one of Charcot's dazzling performances and was transformed by it. He wrote to his fiancée the next month,

> I think I am changing a great deal. Charcot, who is one of the greatest physicians and a man whose common sense borders on genius, is simply wrecking all my aims and opinions. I sometimes come out of his lectures as from out of Notre Dame, with an entirely new idea about perfection. . . . Whether the seed will bear fruit, I don't know, but what I do know is that no other human being has ever affected me in the same way.
> (Letters, pp. 184–185; cited in Sulloway, 1979, pp. 30–31)

Eager to get close to the great man, Freud volunteered to translate a volume of Charcot's lectures into German and was rewarded by an invitation to a party at his palatial home. All of Paris was there: writers, artists, musicians, scientists, doctors. His home included expensive artworks and a library of rare books; he quoted Shakespeare in English and Dante in Italian. Freud, perhaps mourning his move from physiology to neurology, may have decided at this point to take Charcot as a model for his life: High ambition, intellect, worldly power and nobility of purpose seemed united in one person.

Freud returned home after only four months in Paris a changed man. He began lecturing at the university, married after a four-year engagement and started accepting patients as a neurologist. Before we leave the Charcot period, however, we must address a final consequence of the trip for Freud; the presentation of what he had learned in Paris to the Society of Viennese Physicians later that year. As Freud presents the episode in his autobiography, he received an astonished and hostile reception when he reported to them that, yes, hysteria was found in males as well as females and at a higher rate than had been supposed. The minutes of the meeting indeed suggest that the audience was disappointed in Freud, not for his radical statements, but for his lack of originality and subtlety. The society knew very well that male hysteria was possible; what they disagreed on was whether Charcot was justified in expanding the classic definition of hysteria to railway spine in particular. Some suggested that when a man falls from a scaffold or narrowly misses being hit by a train, one can't immediately rule out organic lesions. Others were well aware of

Charcot's disturbing tendency to overgeneralize: He was claiming that hysteria took many forms, had many symptoms and was, in effect, everywhere. They did not deny hysteria in men, only that these particular cases were hysteria in men. It was to the society a competent, non-earthshaking ordinary paper, and they criticized it like they did anyone else's paper: courteously, but stringently (Jones, 1953; Ellenberger, 1970; Sulloway, 1979). Freud was stung and bitterly attributed the response, remembering it years later, to the conservatism of the Viennese medical society. He went to the meetings less often after his rebuke. He also withdrew from lab work, having been banished by Meynert from the neuroanatomy lab for dabbling in hypnotism. Freud's teachers in Vienna believed that hypnotism removed inhibitions, allowing patients to improperly release erotic impulses; Meynert suggested that hypnotism might permanently undermine hysterics' fragile self-control and leave them worse off. He thereafter wanted nothing more to do with hypnotism or Freud (Sulloway, 1979).

Freud's colleagues were right to be skeptical. A few of Charcot's French colleagues, such as Hippolyte Bernheim, bluntly stated that they had hardly ever seen patients in their practices that displayed the three stages of *la grande hypnotisme* or *la grande hysterie*. Bernheim and his followers strongly doubted that ability to be hypnotized indicated anything about susceptibility of hysteria or any other mental disorder. They suspected that Charcot's patients had consciously or unconsciously fit their symptoms to what the great man wanted, for either attention or reward. Indeed, when Charcot died in 1893, many disgruntled former interns or residents who had worked under him confessed that they had often prepared the patient either by hypnotizing her before the demonstration and testing the effects or simply, when pressed for time, by describing the symptoms that were required to the patient and giving her money. They did this to avoid the terrible wrath of Charcot, who might well have fired them if the demonstration did not come off well. Charcot, by this time, virtually never went on hospital rounds, so the secret was easy to keep. Charcot was autocratic, arrogant and vindictive. A bad recommendation from him could wreck one's career. He was also sloppy in his methods. Speaking to his audience, he would first describe the symptoms to be demonstrated—in front of the patient—and then demonstrate them. This would invariably lead to getting the response he wanted. Bernheim suggested that hypnotism did not cure anything real; it removed a non-existing set of symptoms connected to a disease caused by suggestion. It did this by simply providing another layer of suggestion. Bernheim suggested the physiological link between hysteria and hypnotism was false. It certainly was not necessary to have an innate susceptibility to hysteria to be hypnotized; he believed anyone could be hypnotized under the right conditions. Bernheim's view won the day; within 10 years of his death, all of Charcot's students had disowned him and even the diagnosis of hysteria itself was being seriously questioned (see The Problem of Hysteria section). Had it not been for his pivotal role in Freud's story, Charcot would be more obscure today, for hysteria as a diagnosis has virtually disappeared (see The Problem of Hysteria section).

But after Paris, Freud's fascination with Charcot provided him with a new direction, a way to continue doing science in the neurologist's consulting room. Freud had already been primed to believe in Charcot's linkages between hypnosis, hysteria and sex by his knowledge of a strange case study, related to him by his friend and benefactor, Josef Breuer. Breuer's patient, immortalized in the psychoanalytic literature as the case of Anna O., would be the first patient to be treated by the new "talking cure," psychoanalysis.

Josef Breuer and the Case of Anna O.

> Hysterics suffer mainly from reminiscences.
> —Breuer & Freud (1893–1895, p. 7)

Freud met Josef Breuer (1842–1925) in 1879, while still in medical school. Breuer, 14 years Freud's senior and also Jewish, represented what Freud might become. By the time Freud met him, Breuer had already published significant work in physiology relating to the discovery of the balance function in the semicircular canals of the ear and the breathing reflex. He had declined a professorial post to practice neurology and was a respected family doctor to Meynert and Brentano. The generous, warm-hearted Breuer was quite taken with the intelligent and intense young medical student; once again, Freud had a father figure to depend on. Freud visited the Breuers frequently for dinners and at their summer home. At one point, Breuer was "lending" Freud money virtually every month, money that he refused to allow him to pay back. Freud, in gratitude, dedicated his book on aphasia to Breuer and named his first daughter Mathilde, after Mrs. Breuer. In the fall of 1882, Breuer confided to Freud the details of a most puzzling case, a young woman who was requiring daily visits for a most peculiar treatment.

Anna O. was a young woman from a good bourgeois Jewish family, intelligent, literate and kind, but naïve. Breuer said, "the element of sexuality was astonishingly undeveloped in her" (Breuer & Freud, 1893–1895, p. 21). She had fallen ill in 1880 while nursing her beloved father in what turned out to be his fatal illness. Her symptoms began as a severe nervous cough, followed by a convergent squint around the eyes, followed progressively by alarming paralyses of her right side, then most of her left side, her neck muscles and her back. Later, after Breuer was called in, she would only speak English or bits she knew of other languages, though her first language was German and though she could understand those who spoke German around her. At one point, she had stopped drinking water and would eat only oranges. She could not recognize people she knew and appeared not even to see strangers.

Although plagued by hallucinations of snakes and the room closing in on her in the day, she was in a state of somnambulism in the afternoon and deep periods of auto-hypnosis, which she called *absences* or "clouds" around sundown. This offered a road to treatment, for Breuer noted that if she talked about her hallucinations to Breuer every evening during the absences, her mind would be much clearer afterwards at night, when she would imagine poems and stories, even into the next day. Though the benefit would last only a couple of days, she recognized that it was helping, calling the treatment the "talking cure" or "chimney sweeping" (Breuer & Freud, 1893–1895, p. 30).

Breuer was astonished at her excellent memory in this trance. She could remember things that had happened on the same day one year earlier, as confirmed by her mother's diary. Breuer began taking advantage of this memory by suggesting that she talk about the episode where a particular symptom had first appeared. When they had laboriously traced back to the first occurrence and talked it out, the symptom would subside. This process took months, but it also gave clues as to how the symptoms came about. It seems that one night in 1880, when she was exhausted from nursing her father, she fell into a waking nightmare about black snakes; terrified, she tried to drive away the snake, but found that her arm had gone to sleep over the back of the chair, numb and temporarily paralyzed. She tried to pray, but could remember only children's verses in English. Then, she was awakened by a train whistle. The next day, the paralysis reoccurred, when something in the garden reminded her of the snake. Thereafter, any reminder would have the same effect. That day, she was so tired, anxious and distracted, that she didn't hear the surgeon come in. In her extreme anxiety and guilt, she could not eat and went into a trance, which began recurring. So the poor woman would have her symptoms triggered by anything that reminded her of her guilt for having failed her father that night.

Reliving that night, at first bit by bit and then all at once in a dramatic final session, supposedly cured her. The case ends:

> After this, she left Vienna and traveled for a while; but it was a considerable time before she regained her mental balance entirely. Since then she has enjoyed complete health.
>
> (Breuer and Freud, 1893–1895, pp. 40–41)

That "considerable time," as it turned out, was an understatement, for it has long been known that Anna O. was not cured by Breuer's therapy. Carl Jung had suggested in 1925 that she was "far from cured." Ernest Jones (1953) reported that Freud told him a different story of the case, which Freud himself confirmed in a footnote in a later edition, after Breuer's death. According to this account, Breuer and Anna had become rather close in their daily visits, to the extent that Breuers' wife was becoming suspicious of her husband who after all was visiting an attractive young woman at her bedside day after day. When they were nearing the close of treatment, Breuer arrived one day to find Anna in the throes of hysterical childbirth, and she claimed that the nonexistent child was his own. He calmed her with hypnosis and left "in a cold sweat (Jones, 1953, 225)." Breuer supposedly took his wife on a second honeymoon, on which a daughter was conceived. Freud's story is convenient because it (1) suggests that the case was of sexual origin, (2) implies the attachment of patient for therapist, *transference* and the similar feelings that develop in a therapist for his patient, *countertransference* and (3) it allows Freud to imply that much sexual material in *Studies on Hysteria* was downplayed by Breuer, who was squeamish about sex and afraid of scandal.

Even this story cannot be literally true, however, because the daughter supposedly conceived on the vacation was born before Breuer had finished treating Anna (Ellenberger, 1970). Breuer was not squeamish about sex; he had frequently and publicly supported Freud, writing in the *Studies in Hysteria*, "I do not think I am exaggerating when I assert that *the great majority of severe neuroses in women have their origin in the marriage bed*" (Breuer & Freud, 1895/1955, p. 246, emphasis original). Around the same time, in a speech to physicians, he said,

> We simply know nothing about the sexuality of girls and women. No physician has any idea of what sorts of symptoms an erection evokes in women, because the young women do not want to talk about it and the old ones have already forgotten.
> (Breuer, 1895, cited in Freud and Fliess, 1985, p. 151, note 1.)

He had dealt with several other cases of hysteria before and after Anna O., in which he diagnosed a sexual cause. He acknowledged that such cases were emotionally difficult for him but did not deny their sexual basis and cautioned younger practitioners not to avoid discussing it with their patients (Sulloway, 1979).

More critically, though, Henri Ellenberger discovered in 1972 that Anna O., whose real name was revealed by Jones to be Bertha Pappenheim, was committed to an asylum on July 12, 1882, barely a month after her treatment with Breuer was reportedly concluded. The records show she had a severe case of morphine addiction (which Breuer had prescribed for pain of facial neuralgia), and she had almost the full range of symptoms that Breuer reported, from her difficulties with German, to a squint, to trances, hallucinations and convulsions. Breuer himself was evidently involved in the commitment, for a copy of his original case notes, with the same wording as found in the published version, were found in the file (Ellenberger, 1972). She was to be committed three more times between 1883 and 1887 (Sulloway, 1979).

There is even a school of thought that suggests that Ms. Pappenheim was not suffering from hysteria at all, but from a real physical disease (see Webster, 1995, for a provocative review of this hypothesis). The possible diagnoses range from a paralysis of an eye muscle, which led to double vision and other visual symptoms (Thornton, 1976), to brain effects of tuberculosis, contracted from nursing her father, to encephalitis, to multiple sclerosis. Along these lines, the most persuasive diagnosis is temporal lobe epilepsy, brought on by a possible lesion on the cortex where the motor area meets Broca's area. Broca's area is involved in expressive speech (sometimes affecting only one language, as with Anna O.), and it is so close to the motor area that paralyses are often found to co-occur (Orr-Andrewes, 1987). Epilepsy itself is often a symptom of brain lesions, and several of the symptoms of Anna O. are also symptoms of a temporal lobe seizure: blurred vision, double vision, restriction of visual field, misidentification of objects and faces and a feeling of slanted walls and even the trance states and out-of-body feelings themselves. Such states may have been exaggerated by morphine and chloral hydrate that were prescribed by Breuer. If on top of all this we add that the patient was being reinforced for certain symptoms and for removing them, it is possible that some of the symptoms would wax and wane.

The problem with the exclusively medical approach, aside from the difficulties of diagnosis a century after the disorder, is that Bertha Pappenheim got better—later than described by Breuer, perhaps, but eventually. She became an influential social worker in Frankfurt am-Main, Germany. She founded a journal, directed several institutes, rescued Jews from persecution all over Europe and became almost legendary in her selfless commitment to social causes by her death in 1936 (Jones, 1953).

Figure 9.3 Anna O., the case name for Bertha Pappenheim (1859–1936). Pappenheim was not cured by Breuer, but more than recovered later, devoting her life to helping poor, homeless and trafficked Jewish women within an Orthodox Jewish context. This photo of her was taken in 1882 (age 22), soon after she finished therapy with Breuer. It was found in Bellevue Sanatorium outside Vienna, where she was almost immediately committed, with the same symptoms and case notes by Breuer himself.

West Germany issued a stamp with her likeness in 1954 (Ellenberger, 1970). Reports from her later years noted her vigorous mental health. Thus her transformation is a mystery. For the record, Pappenheim was herself dismissive of Breuer's treatment of her, calling him in later life "a Nervous specialist she had seen once." Whether this is because she truly believed she had cured herself after his intervention or merely because she wished to avoid talking about personal matters cannot be determined.

Because of the case of Anna O., Freud for several years called Breuer the discoverer of psychoanalysis. However, *Studies in Hysteria* contained four other case studies of treatments by Freud, all described by pseudonyms that have now become famous: Frau Emmy von N., Miss Lucy R., Katharina and Fräulein Elisabeth von R. The lengthy nature of the case studies (which, it is always good to remember, are themselves highly condensed and somewhat disguised summaries of a long analytic process) requires that they be summarized briefly.

Frau Emmy was the first case in which Freud tried Breuer's method. She came to him with a tendency to make an odd clacking noise when frightened. She would compulsively say, "Keep still—Don't say anything!" In addition, she was afraid to eat or drink much and afraid of animals. Like Anna, her life had been marred by the death and illness of her loved ones. She had found her mother dead when she was 15. Her brother had died of tuberculosis when she was 19; her husband had died very suddenly and one of her daughters was often sick enough to require constant nursing for extended times. Finding she was easily hypnotized, Freud first relieved her of her fear of animals by having her talk under hypnosis about times when her brother threw dead animals at her. He found that her fear of eating was related to disgust when her sick brother would spit blood at mealtimes. Her clacking noise was due to a compulsion to make a noise when she needed to remain quiet for her daughter's sake and so on. Although Freud continued to use baths, electricity and massages—the tools of neurologists in the 1880s—he considered wiping away the mental pictures of the original events in hypnosis to be the operative treatments. Although she left Freud in good health, a footnote in a later edition in 1924 implied that Frau Emmy had gone to several other practitioners with the same stories to be cured again. In the original version, no sexual causes were mentioned, but the footnote attributed some of her maladies to the fact that she wished to remarry, but was prohibited by the terms of her husband's will.

The other cases had several similarities:

- Each involved apparently physiological symptoms: pains, sensitivity to touch or smell or anxiety attacks with palpitations and hyperventilation.
- Each suggested a sexual cause for hysterical symptoms (a repressed love of a governess for her employer, desire of an unmarried sister for her brother-in-law and of experiencing and witnessing—in the case of Katharina—cases of incest).
- Each involved a so-called cathartic cure: By reliving past events, the symptoms were relieved. Paradoxically, even reliving painful memories, such as incest, caused a lightening of mood.

In addition, basic aspects of the theory of repression and the conduct of therapy are already present in this early work, as succinctly pointed out by Sulloway (1979) and as summarized in Table 9.1

Pierre Janet (1859–1947)

This view of mental energy as a kind of electrical water, flowing around circuits within the brain, being dammed up and released, was common among psychiatrists

Table 9.1: Breuer-Freud View of Hysteria

Economic aspect	The amount of nerve energy ("sum of excitation") must remain level; the question is how the surplus is "spent"		Nerve energy must go somewhere
Dynamic aspect	Nerve energies may be dammed up or blocked		
Topological aspect	There are levels	Conscious, preconscious, unconscious	
Dualistic aspect	Can be explained in a psychological, rather than physiological, manner		

of the late 19th century. Treatments for neurosis, sometimes called neurasthenia, included the "rest cure" advocated by American physician S. Weir Mitchell (1829–1914) involving complete rest and separation from stimulation such as social interaction or reading and writing. In addition, he advocated overfeeding with rich foods such as milk. Such a cure was aimed at replenishing a neurotic's store of mental energy by bolstering their physical health. This notion was also advocated by another pioneer of dynamic psychology, Pierre Janet (1859–1947), who eventually rose to the top of the French psychological and psychiatric establishment after Charcot. Janet proposed that mental energy flowed according to its *psychological force* or total amount and according to its *psychological tension* or the constriction on its movement. Too little force meant depression. A certain amount of tension is good, so that the force can be harnessed and expended on adaptive tasks. But if a person has experienced a severe trauma, a great amount of energy may be expended to deal with its emotional consequences, sometimes leading to obsessive behavior. A person who wastes a lot of his or her mental energy on maladaptive obsessive thoughts and compulsive behavior is said to be in the grip of an *idée fixe* or "fixed idea." These fixed ideas, often subconscious, were to Janet the source and cause of hysteria. Following his teacher Charcot, Janet believed they could be relieved through hypnotism, automatic writing (writing under hypnosis) and discussion with the patient. This treatment could only be conducted after a careful *psychological analysis*, in which the therapist estimates the depth of unconsciousness of each idea. Then, the therapist attempts *psychological synthesis*, in which he attempts to construct a timeline of acquisition of the ideas. Like Breuer, he began with the most superficial problems and worked backwards to the deep-seated ones.

In 1886, Janet first became famous for his study of the first of several of his cases of what would become known as multiple personality disorder (in the *Diagnostic and Statistical Manual*, 3rd ed., of the American Psychiatric Association, 1980) or dissociative identity disorder (in *DSM-IV*, 1994). The first case, a hysteric named Leonie, showed, under hypnosis, three personalities, one of which was herself as a little girl. Through hypnosis and automatic writing, he would provoke hysterical crises, but after such crises, the patient would be better. It is significant that Janet's work with several such cases was published as *L'Automatisme Psychologique* (1889) (*Psychological*

Automatisms) before Breuer and Freud published their first communication on their work in 1893, and Janet's work on these cases began seven years before in 1882, at almost the exact time that Breuer was finishing treatment of Anna O. Indeed, William James describes the case of Leonie in *Principles of Psychology* (1890/1983, p. 365 ff) and was a regular correspondent with Janet; James's description of psychopathological states of consciousness draws heavily on Janet's insights.

Thus, many of the ideas that we credit to Freud today were anticipated by Janet. Breuer and Freud acknowledged his work in the preliminary communication of 1893 and in *Studies in Hysteria* (1895). Janet arrived at La Salpêtrière shortly after Freud had left, so they did not meet then. But Ellenberger (1970) finds that there was a conference that both Janet and Freud had attended as early as 1889 and even goes so far to suggest that the intention to publish *Studies* may have been formed after Freud read *Psychological Automisms*. Freud believed all his life, however, that Janet was allowing rumors to spread that Freud had copied his ideas; Freud refused to see him on a number of occasions (Jones, 1957, p. 214). There were a number of differences, however, between their theories:

- In Janet's early theory, he shared the notion with Charcot that there was an innate, possibly hereditary "psychological insufficiency." Breuer and Freud did not agree.
- Janet's theory did not place sex at the center of his view of hysterical traumas. The centrality of sex was of such importance to Freud that he ostracized psychoanalysts, among them Carl Jung and Alfred Adler, for denying it.
- As a therapist, Janet was far more directive than Freud claimed to be. Free association was not a part of his method, nor did he believe that merely bringing an idea to consciousness would result, by itself, in relief. Instead, he focused on psychological economics. One needed to (1) increase the income, through ample rest, (2) diminish expenditure, by, for example, removing social acquaintances who are "energy-eaters" and (3) liquidate debts, by removing, wherever possible, fixed ideas (Ellenberger, 1970, p. 380[4]). In order to do this, Janet suggested reorganizing one's life as much as his or her subconscious.

Wilhelm Fliess (1858–1928)

Shortly after publication of *Studies in Hysteria*, Freud broke with Breuer over the role of sex in the development of hysteria. Specifically, Freud came to believe that *every case* of hysteria was due to the premature shock of childhood sexual abuse. The so-called **seduction theory** made a very strong claim that sexual abuse in childhood causes hysteria, almost in the direct causal way that a virus causes a cold. This was the hypothesis that Breuer could not accept, even though he accepted the possibility that some cases might be sexual in nature. This caused an irreparable break in their friendship, as Breuer wrote to a colleague some years later:

> Freud is a man given to absolute and exclusive formulations: this is a psychical need which, in my opinion, leads to excessive generalization. There may, in addition be a desire *d'epater le bourgeois* [to shock the old fogies].
> (From a letter to Swiss psychiatrist August Forel, 1907, cited in Sulloway, 1979, p. 85)

After the break with Breuer, Freud needed a new sounding board during what would turn out to be the most crucial years of development of the theory. He would find him in a nose and throat doctor from Berlin, Wilhelm Fliess (1858–1928). Fliess and Freud had been corresponding since 1887, but by 1892, they had become close personal friends. They exchanged drafts of their papers, comments about patients and updates on their increasingly radical theories.

Freud sent drafts of his theories of the causes of neurosis to Fliess. Reading them, one can see what Breuer might have been skeptical about, for at this early stage of theorizing, Freud was thinking like a rather literal-minded MD. Every psychiatric neurosis had a specific sexual cause: nervous exhaustion, or neurasthenia, was caused by excessive masturbation (lesser bouts of masturbation led to predisposition for the disease). Incomplete intercourse, through prolonged virginity, abstinence or early withdrawal to avoid pregnancy (coitus interruptus), led to anxiety disorders. Anxiety in women was caused by impotence or premature ejaculation of their partners. Melancholia (depression) is mourning the loss of sexual drive or frigidity and so on. And of course, hysteria was thought to be due to a sexual shock before puberty and obsession to attempting to repress the memory of sexual pleasure before puberty (see Freud letters to Fliess in 1894–1895, drafts D through I, Freud and Fliess, 1985).

Fliess's theories were even more radical: Fliess believed that the conditions of the nose were indicative of the condition of the sexual organs. Spontaneous swelling of the nose during women's menstruation and occasional nosebleeds in pregnancy and menstruation were cited as support for the so-called *nasogenital reflex*. The fact that the erectile tissue in the nose becomes filled with blood during sexual arousal, as do the genitals and nipples, was also cited as proof of the link. There was even a *primal smell* theory, developed by evolutionist Ernst Haeckel (see Chapter 4). In this theory, the connection between nose and genitals is linked to the idea that in mammals, the sense of smell is critical to sexual arousal, for example, in allowing a male dog to determine whether a bitch is in heat. We humans may have repressed this tendency, but we still respond to smell stimuli in sex.

Fliess believed that one might develop *nasogenital reflex neurosis*, with wide-ranging symptoms, if one does not lead a healthy sex life. Thus, Fliess believed, incredibly, that masturbation caused nasal congestion and that an unhealthy sex life was also associated with the incidence of migraine. Thus, surgery on the nose or more interestingly, application of cocaine to certain *genital spots* within the nose would alleviate hysterical or neurotic symptoms (along with much else, one might imagine)!

Fliess also believed in the existence of two periodic physiological cycles: a female cycle, based on the monthly menstruation average of 28-day cycles, and a male one, being a cycle of 23 days. Both sexes have both cycles, which dominate at certain time of the month; when both are at a low ebb, critical days occur on which death or illness might occur. Often, Fliess's theories seem to be almost like occult numerology: Not only are bad things *likely* to occur on critical days because of a low ebb in physical strength, but they *must* occur at this time.

Today, these theories seem like ludicrous fantasy. But Sulloway (1979) has found that both the nasogenital reflex and periodicity were believed by more than a few medical men in the 1890s. The nasogenital theory was favorably noted by the pioneering sex researchers Richard von Krafft-Ebing, also at University of Vienna (1840–1902), and the English physician Havelock Ellis (1859–1939). Periodicity in the natural world is of course commonplace, having been noted by Darwin himself. But Fliess used his 23- and 28-day cycles differently; his flexible formula $x \cdot 23 \pm y \cdot 28$ could be used to predict or in this case postdict after the fact any number whatsoever, so if one knows the number of days between events, one can always find values of x and y that fit.

For a time, Freud believed it all and virtually hailed Fliess as an unrecognized genius. The relationship intensified and Freud developed a kind of emotional dependence on Fliess (because we no longer have Fleiss's letters to him, it is difficult to know whether Fliess reciprocated with the same intensity). Freud said, "Your praise is nectar and ambrosia to me" (Freud and Fliess, 1985, p. 87). He would berate Fliess for not writing if as much as a week had passed without a letter and avidly looked forward to their meetings "as to the slaking of hunger and thirst" (Freud and Fliess, p. 193) when they met in Vienna, Berlin or various vacation spots.

Freud allowed Fliess to operate on his nose, ostensibly to alleviate neurotic symptoms of his own and migraines; he also believed that he would die at age 51 ($51 = 28 + 23$). In fact, he referred a patient to Fliess for nasal surgery to alleviate simple "hysterical" stomach pains. After the surgery, the patient, Emma Eckstein, went rapidly downhill, ran a fever and had profuse nosebleeds. Later, when she did not get well, Freud engaged another doctor to examine Emma and found that Fliess had left a half-meter length of gauze in her sinus! When it was removed, in Freud's presence, Freud nearly fainted and Eckstein turned white, passed out and nearly died. In his letters, Freud still could not admit Fliess's incompetence, consoling him by describing the mistake as one that anyone might make. The patient took some time to recover. Freud consoled Fliess that he had not lost faith in him: "For me, you remain the physician, the type of man into whose hands one confidently puts ones life and the life of his family" (p. 186). Freud even suggested that "she had always been a bleeder" and that "she bled out of *longing*" for attention from Fliess and Freud (Freud and Fliess, 1985, p. 186, Freud to Fliess Letter of May 17, 1896, emphasis original)!

Fliess was Freud's confidante in the process of creation of the most crucial parts of the theory of psychoanalysis. Throughout 1896 and 1897, Freud came to believe Fliess's ideas on the inherent **bisexuality** of all forms of life. Freud was predisposed to believe this by his early anatomical dissection work on certain bisexual fishes in Brücke's lab (Sulloway, 1979). In all vertebrates, both sets of sexual organs are visible in the developing fetus, and in humans, sex is not determined until the seventh week of pregnancy. One-half of this bisexuality must be repressed, thought Freud, for normal sexual development.[5] In later versions of the theory, he suggested that strong repression of the admission of homosexuality might even lead to paranoia.

Even more significantly, Freud explores in the Fliess correspondence the beginnings of his **psychosexual stage theory**. Perhaps one should say that Freud and Fliess explored together *their* psychosexual stage theory, for on this point it is hard to know from the letters and writings of both men where Fliess leaves off and Freud begins. Both were believers in Ernst Haeckel's recapitulation theory that proposed that evolution is repeated in the life of each individual child (see Chapter 4) and in 1895, both men had a baby in the house, Fliess his first boy and Freud his last child, the future analyst Anna. Fliess noted that his boy had little erections while sucking on the breast or on his thumb and confirms Freud's theory of infantile sexuality. Fliess published his theory on what would later be called **erotogenic zones** even before Freud, describing the quasi-sexual way the infant uses its mouth to gain gratification: "I would just like to point out that the sucking movements that small children make with their lips and tongue on periodic days . . ., the so-called *Ludeln*, as well as thumb-sucking, must be considered the equivalent of masturbation" (Fliess, 1897, cited in Sulloway, 1979, p. 173). This interpretation, of course, is the one that Freud would make of the **oral stage** of development later in "Three Essays on Sexuality" (1905).

In the same book, Fliess expresses interest in the **anal stage** by careful attention to his child's frequency and character of bowel movements. He connected the feelings of shame to a "frustrated excitation" of the libido, using much the same terms that Freud would use in describing the development of the superego in the anal stage. The **superego**, in later Freudian theory (Freud, 1920), is developed through the induction of shame about bodily functions during toilet training in the anal stage of development in toddlerhood. The superego thereby becomes the largely unconscious guard of morality. For Fliess, the preoccupation with feces at this time is a vestige of the time in evolution when bodily odors played a crucial part in mating (note the importance of the nose!); although we deemphasize this preoccupation now that we walk upright, Fliess considered this evidence of recapitulation. This very suggestion became part of Freud's psychosexual theory:

> "Now, the zones which no longer produce a release of sexuality in normal and mature human beings must be the regions of the anus and of the mouth and throat. . . . In animals these sexual zones retain their power: where they do so in humans the result is perversion."
> (Freud & Fliess, 1985, Letter from Freud to Fliess, Nov 14, 1897)

Finally, Freud explicitly credits Fliess in his first complete description of the psychosexual stages theory (Freud, 1905) with the discovery of the **latency stage**, that long period after the repression of the Oedipal conflict between age 5 and puberty, in which sexuality is normally largely repressed.

Much was happening to Freud in the years 1895–1900. In his consulting room, he was aggressively leading his patients to believe in their own supposedly unconscious memories of seduction or rape by family members and then, more specifically, by fathers, but some of his patients would have none of it and terminated therapy. In *The Aetiology of Hysteria* (Freud, 1896/1962), he had again rushed to print before he had the evidence, as in the cocaine episode. He claimed he had dealt with 18 cases that confirmed the childhood seduction hypothesis. In his letters to Fliess—in 1897—he suggested that *none* of these cases were actually complete (Webster, 1995).

Freud was feeling frustrated over his lack of success, inadequate as a clinician and possibly guilty for having led his patients so strongly towards the literal seduction hypothesis. In one case, he at first convinced a patient that a cracked mouth and speech impediment were the result of unremembered forced oral sex with her father, when she was 12. When she confronted her father with the supposition, he vehemently denied it. Freud wrote,

> She is now in the throes of the most vehement resistance, claims to believe him, but attests to her identification with him by having become dishonest and

swearing false oaths. I have threatened to send her away and in the process convinced myself that she has already gained a good deal of certainty that she is reluctant to acknowledge.
(Letter to Fliess, January 3, 1897, pp. 220–221, Freud and Fliess, 1985)

To Freud, then, vehement denial was essentially evidence that something had happened, rather than evidence of his own error. Threatening a dependent patient with withdrawal of services for disagreeing was a form of coercion, whether he was aware of it or not.

In 1896, Freud's father died. Freud praised his father's wisdom and lightheartedness in a letter to Fliess, but said, "By the time he died, his life had long been over, but in my inner self the whole past has been reawakened by this event. I now feel quite uprooted" (Letter to Fliess of Nov. 1, 1896, in Freud and Fliess, 1985, p. 202)." The death of Freud's father precipitated a flood of dreams and memories that would not subside. Freud realized that these materials would have to be analyzed and, of course, he was the only one who could do it. He began a daily regimen in early 1897 of unearthing his earliest memories, transcribing his dreams and practicing free association in interpreting the results. **Free association**, though used earlier by Francis Galton and around the same time by Carl Jung, as yet an unknown psychiatrist in Zurich, became the cornerstone of Freud's method of analysis. The patient was first asked to describe a dream. If no interpretations suggested themselves immediately, the patient was to allow himself to freely state *everything* that came to mind for each dream element, one at a time, *no matter how absurd, trivial, irrelevant or embarrassing it might seem*. Then one could look at the collection of associations to separate dream elements and try to knit them together into a complete interpretation.

So, Freud began with his earliest memories, particularly those fraught with strong emotions or sexual themes. For example, he recalled seeing his nursemaid nude and being bathed in red water that she had bathed in before. He recalled stealing for her. He recalled a memory what he feared might have been sexual intimations between his young, beautiful mother and his half-brother, who was almost her age. When the nursemaid was arrested for her theft, he recalled missing her terribly—fearing that his mother had gone as well, asked his half-brother whether she was also locked up like the nursemaid. He unlocked a cabinet and when she wasn't there, little Sigi cried all the louder until his mother returned. And of course, there was a strong memory of seeing his mother naked in a train compartment on a journey at about the age of 2. He wanted to possess his mother in a vague but powerful sexual way. These memories brought up such strong emotions of fear, rage and jealousy, towards his brothers and his father, that Freud felt he had come up with a truth not only about his family and himself, but also for everyone. This set of emotions was, he thought, a universal stage, recapitulated in development in all of us. These emotions explain why the scene in the Greek drama *Oedipus Rex* in which Oedipus realizes that he has mistakenly married his mother and killed his father cause such revulsion. We repress these feelings, for to do otherwise would be to destroy the fabric of civilized life. He thought that just such an Oedipal drama is played out in *Hamlet*.

In such a way, Freud discovered (some would say concocted) the **Oedipal conflict** from his own family drama, revealed in self-analysis. Specifically, each boy in the preschool years wants to possess his mother and sees his father as a rival, but even his prelogical mind knows that he is powerless in the face of his strong father to win her. To resolve the problem successfully, the boy must identify with the father and repress the longings for the mother. Unresolved longings for the mother come to be invested in an **Oedipus complex**. Freud himself was the favored son of a dominant mother and a kind but ineffectual father. To understand his feelings for them is a large step towards real, non-neurotic maturity, because, as we have seen, Freud as a boy and young man was both playing out the role of a mother's favorite and looking for strong father figures, even, in his idolization of Fliess, creating them.

One thing he did *not* find in his memories was sexual abuse by his father, and yet he realized, from his own psychological symptoms, that he *should* find such an episode, to be consistent with the literal interpretation of the seduction theory. And yet, there appeared to be an epidemic of incest in the small confines of Freud's circle of patients in Vienna. In a landmark letter to Fliess of September 21, 1897, Freud renounces his literal seduction theory. The improbabilities had finally become too much to sustain the theory. But then, why did his patients keep coming up with stories of incest? One possibility, of course, was that Freud was all but asking for them in therapy, but this is not the hypothesis that he considers. Instead, he begins to think that those stories are *fantasies* of incest. And what would be the motivation for fantasies? Recapitulation of the history of the species:

> Biologically, dream life seems to me to derive entirely from the residues of the prehistoric period of life [between the ages of one and three]—the same period which is the source of the unconscious and alone contains the etiology of all the psychoneuroses, the period normally characterized by an amnesia analogous to hysterical amnesia. The formula suggests itself to me: what is *seen* in the prehistoric period produces dreams, what is *heard* in it produces fantasies; what is *experienced* in it produces the psychoneuroses. The repetition of what is experienced in that period is in itself the fulfillment of a wish; a recent wish only leads to a dream if it can put itself in touch with material from this prehistoric period, if the recent wish is a derivative of one or can get itself adopted by one.
> (Letter to Fliess, March 10, 1898, p. 302, Freud and Fliess, 1985; emphasis in original)

In this way, Freud snatches victory from the jaws of defeat. His seduction theory is wrong, but not the insights gained from it (or so he thinks). Prehistory determines the kind of fantasies and dreams that we have. Because at the unconscious level we have the same prehistory, the dreams of our current lives all begin to seem somewhat the same, no matter what life experiences we have had or what immediate stimulus in our daily lives has prompted it. Recapitulation theory has, of course, been disproven today (see Chapter 4), but it was an acceptable theory of evolution, perhaps the dominant one, in Vienna at this time.

Interpretation of Dreams

From 1897 to 1899, Freud worked on what he considered his most original work, *Die Traumdeutung* or *The Interpretation of Dreams* (Freud, 1900/1913). As he stated in the first chapter, Freud believed that he had discovered a new scientific way to determine the psychological meaning of dreams. Prior to his work, there had been two main approaches to explaining dreams. The ancient way saw dreams as portents of the future or guides to actions in difficult times. Typically, such approaches had relied on predicting the future or interpreting messages from God, by decoding set symbols. Popular "dream books" provided the set supernatural meanings of dream symbols for such interpretations.

In contrast, the scientific community had shown very little interest in dreams. Prior discussions of them had suggested that dreams were nothing more than reactions to external stimuli prior to waking (e.g. a fire alarm being incorporated into a frightening dream) or to internal bodily sensations (inability to run in a dream due to normal nighttime paralysis in sleep). Scientists had recognized that the material for dreams was generally taken from the concerns of the day, but they did not examine dreams for hidden meanings.

Although Freud obviously disagreed with the supernatural interpretation of the ancient approach, he decided that it was nearer the truth: Dreams had a purely *psychological* purpose rather than a physiological one. They were not messages from the great beyond, but they were unquestionably trying to tell the dreamer something, in disguised form. The interpreter's job was to seek the meaning of the dream in the dreamer's own life. By encouraging the dreamer to free associate to elements in the **manifest content**—the actual text of the dream given by the dreamer—the interpreter could discover the **latent content** of the dream—what forbidden and hidden message the dream conveys to the dreamer. The interpreter can decode the symbols in the dreams of a particular patient only if he or she knows the patient intimately.

Freud's interest in dreams can be traced to a particular point in time, and indeed, a particular dream of his own on the night of July 23–24, 1895. We will use this dream, analyzed in Chapter 2 of *Interpretation*, to explain Freud's method and terminology.

First, let us describe the material and circumstances surrounding the occasion of the dream: Freud notes that the dream is caused by the comments of an acquaintance, who had just seen Freud's former patient, here called Irma. He remarked that Irma was better after having seen Freud, but not entirely well. In addition, Freud had recently written up case notes to transfer his patient to another doctor, here referred to as Dr. M. These facts provided the raw material for the manifest content of the dream, otherwise known as **day residue**—recent events on the dreamer's mind that the dream seems to be about. The dream is given verbatim, below (Freud, 1900/1913, 3rd ed., p. 89):

> A great hall—a number of guests, whom we are receiving—among them Irma, whom I immediately take aside, as though to answer her letter and to reproach her for not yet accepting the "solution." I say to her: "If you still have pains, it is really only your own fault."—She answers: "If you only knew what pains I have now in the throat, stomach and abdomen—I am choked by them." I am startled and look at her. She looks pale and puffy. I think that after all I must be overlooking some organic affection. I take her to the window and look into her throat. She offers some resistance to this, like a woman who has a set of false teeth. I think, surely, she doesn't need them.—The mouth then opens wide and

I find a large white spot on the right and elsewhere I see extensive grayish-white scabs adhering to curiously curled formations, which are evidently shaped like the turbinal bones of the nose.—I quickly call Dr. M, who repeats the examination and confirms it. . . . Dr. M looks quite unlike his usual self; he is very pale, he limps and his chin is clean-shaven. . . . Now my friend Otto, too, is standing beside her and my friend Leopold percusses her covered chest and says "She has a dullness below, on the left," and also calls attention to an infiltrated portion of skin on the left shoulder (which I can feel, in spite of the dress). . . . M says: "There's no doubt that it's an infection, but it doesn't matter; dysentery will follow and the poison will be eliminated." . . . We know, too, precisely how the infection originated. My friend Otto, not long ago, gave her, when she was feeling unwell, an injection of a preparation of propyl . . . propyls . . . propionic acid . . . trimethylamin (the formula of which I see before me, printed in heavy type). . . . One doesn't give such injections so rashly. . . . Probably, too, the syringe was not clean.

Freud makes several associations:

- Otto is the friend who suggested that Freud had not cured Irma; with the dirty injection and infection, Freud takes revenge on Otto for this by suggesting that he is careless. Otto had also given Freud a terrible bottle of liquor that smelled like propyl; trimethylamin is a chemical implicated in sexual functioning.
- Dr. M. was in life a noted expert who didn't think much of Freud's theories (perhaps Meynert?); here, he makes a ridiculous diagnosis that dysentery does not matter.
- Irma is not a cooperative patient, like many of Freud's patients at the time: In his dream, he has substituted Irma's symptoms with those of her friend, who is a more docile hysteria patient. If Irma has a real rather than a hysterical disorder, Freud is not responsible for curing her, for that is not his specialty.
- Also implicated in the dream are at least three other patients: one, Freud accidentally poisoned by too much medicine; he had turned to Dr. M for assistance in the case. A second had been prescribed cocaine for a nose ailment; Freud had used the treatment himself, both times with bad results, for which he was reprimanded. The cocaine also reminded him of the recent death of the friend in the cocaine episode. It was Freud who rashly prescribed cocaine and made him an addict.
- References to the bones in the nose, of course, implicate Fliess and his disastrous treatment of Emma Eckstein.
- Although Freud does not say so, the gray patches remind one of the patient who had such patches around her mouth; he had forced a sexual interpretation of the symptom on the patient, as he does on Irma in the dream.

Thus, Irma's injection dream is a revenge dream on Otto and Dr. M. It also reflects Freud's anxiety as to his medical competence and guilt for his errors. It may even signal subconscious doubts about the seduction theory that he was to present prematurely the next year and reject the year after that. The dream shows rich

condensation: each event has many overlapping and buried symbolisms. Finally, the dream has two **wish fulfillments**: first, the revenge upon colleagues he does not like and second, the wish that Irma no longer be his patient, because she is far from cooperative.[6] Freud claimed that *all* dreams were wish fulfillments. The message of dreams is what we would do if we were not prohibited by propriety and practicality.

Although a few of the interpretations above are my own (the last two bullet points), the interpretations that Freud does admit to are quite frank and embarrassing, astonishing for the time. That the admissions are embarrassing is part of the point. Not only may the dreamer not be aware of the implications in his or her conscious life, but also their insights may be so dangerous that they cannot be directly admitted even in dreams and must be covered over by symbols. Not coincidentally, Freud's reports of dreams and case studies may themselves be disguised, for many of his patients lived in his own neighborhood in his circle of friends. Thus, a Freudian dream report is twice or three times removed from the data that make it up!

Just as Freud earlier ran into trouble by assuming that every case of hysteria was due to sexual abuse in childhood, so did his assumption that every dream is a wish fulfillment become hard to sustain. In fact, as Webster (1995) notes, several of the dreams he reports appear at first glance to conclusively disprove his theory. For example, a woman who disliked vacationing with her mother-in-law so much that she made reservations to vacation far away from her, nevertheless dreamed of taking a vacation with her. The patient complained that surely this is not her wish. The patient who dreamed this was frequently resistant to Freud's interpretations in analysis. Thus, he notes, she had dreamed this dream *solely to prove him wrong*! Nor is this an isolated case of inverted interpretation in the several editions of his dream book. In another case, one of Freud's school acquaintances who had become a lawyer dreamed that he had lost all of his cases. Since he dreamed it after he had attended Freud's lecture on the subject, Freud interpreted the dream as an act of envy toward him: The man had always been ranked lower in class standing than Freud and so dreamed the dream to invalidate his theory! This kind of dream proved so troublesome that Freud added a category of *counter-wish dreams* to the 1909 revision of the book. Such people were emotional masochists and thus dreams that seemed to be painful or that led to undesirable consequences actually were wish fulfillments (Webster, 1995)! Such ingenious additions to the theory of dreams make it impossible to disprove.

The *Interpretation of Dreams* sold only a few hundred copies total in the first few years. People did not seem to take notice of Freud until he was finally promoted to professor at the University of Vienna, after 1902. But its publication signifies a clear shift in Freud's interests. He begins to pay attention only to the psychological interpretations of psychoanalysis and not the physiological or evolutionary bases for his theory. The following year, when he introduced **parapraxes** or "Freudian slips" through his book *Psychopathology in Everyday Life* (Freud, 1901), the cornerstones of the theory are in place: the method of free association and the use of dreams and slips for interpretation; the psychosexual stage theory and its implications that childhood sexual fantasies are common and the tripartite mind: **consciousness** and the **unconscious** separated by a censor to negotiate between them, in the "anteroom" of the unconscious—the **preconscious**.

Three Essays on the Theory of Sexuality

> By demonstrating the part played by perverse impulses in the formation of symptoms in the psychoneuroses, we have quite remarkably increased the number of people who might be regarded as perverts. It is not only that neurotics in themselves constitute a very numerous class, but it must also be considered that an unbroken chain bridges the gap between the neuroses in all their manifestations and normality. After all, Moebius could say with justice that we are all to some extent hysterics. Thus the extraordinarily wide dissemination of the perversions forces us to suppose that the disposition to perversions is itself of no great rarity but must form a part of what passes as the normal constitution.
>
> ... The postulated constitution, containing the germs of all the perversions, will only be demonstrable *in children*, even though in them it is only with modest degrees of intensity that any of the instincts can emerge. A formula begins to take shape which lays it down that the sexuality of neurotics has remained in or been brought back to, an infantile state. Thus our interest turns to the sexual life of children and we will now proceed to trace the play of influences which govern the evolution of infantile sexuality till its outcome in perversion, neurosis or normal sexual life.
>
> —Freud (1905/1989, p. 258; emphasis in original)

At this point in time, around 1902, the basic method of psychoanalysis in the consulting room through the use of dream analysis, free association and parapraxes was well established. But the theory of what Freud considered the science of psychoanalysis, as opposed to the therapy, had a gaping hole: How then do inappropriate sexual fantasies that he had seen in analysis come about and what possible function do they serve? In "Three Essays on the Theory of Sexuality" (first published in 1905, but revised and added to until 1924), Freud consolidated his observations in the correspondence with Fliess into a complete theory, by welding the psychosexual stages to the theory of neuroses.

The "Three Essays" suggest that the cause of sexual fantasies lies in a predetermined unfolding of psychosexual stages coming into conflict with the demands of society. To Freud, these stages are universal in all of us, arising as they do from recapitulationist evolution and the constraints of society nearly so. He said,

> I believe that these primal phantasies, as I should like to call them and no doubt a few others as well, are a phylogenetic endowment. In them the individual reaches beyond his own experience into primeval experience at points where his own experience has been too rudimentary. It seems to me quite plausible that all the things that are told to us today in analysis as phantasy—the seduction of children, the inflaming of sexual excitement by observing parental intercourse, the threat of castration (or rather castration itself)—were once real occurrences in the primeval times of the human family and that children are simply filling in the gap in individual truth with prehistorical truth. I have repeatedly been led to suspect that the psychology of the neuroses has stored up in it more of the antiquities of human development than any other source.
>
> (Freud, 1916, SE 16, p. 371)

In the first 1905 essay, he surveys the literature on sexual perversion, already fairly extensive even in his day. His rhetorical strategy is to suggest that a wide range of aberrations is more common than realized, not necessarily the result of "degenerate" genetic or physical constitutions. He describes oral and anal sex, fetishism and sadism or masochism in this vein. By slight contrast, he claims that homosexuals, known then by the term *sexual inverts*, are technically abnormal due to an error in development. But they are not in fact necessarily psychologically unusual or unhealthy in other ways. In fact, Freud argues in the paragraphs quoted above that we all are potentially some kind of sexual deviants, should we not negotiate the sequence of stages successfully.[7] Then he describes the sexual stages: associating them with a particular deviance if one were to become fixated in the stage or on that particular erotogenic zone: oral-cannibalistic, anal-sadistic, phallic-Oedipal, latency and the final normal stage, of genital organization. At each stage, children are interested in stimulation of their own bodies and their own curiosities. Their sexual satisfaction normally comes from thumb sucking in the oral phase, for example, or curiosity about feces in the anal stage or their theories about anal birth, etc. as a preschooler. In the phallic stage, children develop the first stage of proper object choice through resolving the Oedipal conflict, then sexual energies are submerged or **sublimated** through acceptable pleasures of learning in the latency stage of childhood. The sexual instinct is kept alive through stimulation of muscular play or riding of horses or trains. Then at puberty, masturbation returns and each adolescent seeks an appropriate sexual object, but in most the character of the desired individual bears some resemblance to the opposite-sex parent.

This condensed summary shows Freud's solution to the problem of why sexuality is so present in his consulting room. We are all biologically driven, sexual beings from birth and we seek to satisfy these urges in both physical, autoerotic ways and through fantasies and dreams, since we cannot do so normally until after puberty. This process is both normal and universal and fraught with peril at every point. There are many ways for it to go wrong, only some of which now involve exposure to sex at a young age. By incorporating Fliess's suggestions, Freud escapes his earlier diagnostic rigidity, but it also makes the theory extremely flexible, by interpreting virtually every activity of childhood as sexual.

When the stage theory is combined here with the **libido theory**, the classical theory is nearly complete. He says,

> We have defined the concept of libido as a quantitatively variable force which could serve as a measure of the processes and transformations occurring in the field of sexual excitation.... The analyses of the perversions and psychoneuroses has shown us that this sexual excitation is derived not from the so-called sexual parts alone, but from all the bodily organs.
> (Freud, 1905/1989, pp. 285–286, 1915 revision)

This libido becomes represented as "ego libido" in the mind and can be affixed to any object: the mother, the therapist (as in transference) or any appropriate or inappropriate sexual objects. It can be submerged in proper ways, through **sublimation** unconsciously in socially appropriate ways, such as the quest for knowledge or the production of art. It can be dammed up, fixated or **cathected** (attached in the mind to a love object) in maladaptive attempts to gain gratification or to control others or to fill a need.[8] It can be channeled into habitual characters, as when an individual, severely punished during toilet training, comes to fear his own desires in an anally retentive personality (Freud, 1908).

In his long journey from biological scientist, through medical training, through clinical experience, Freud came to replace biological-materialistic explanations with biological *metaphors*, which he then speaks of as if they are real mechanisms. These metaphorical mechanisms are not themselves visible to us in daily life, of course. They are rationally and imaginatively *inferred* from the operation of the dualistic mind world. They are inferred from *interpretation* of meanings and *symbols* in our daily lives, themselves idiosyncratic to every individual. The mature theory is thus far from being based on empirical data, let alone at risk of being disproved by it. True, we would do well to remember that the criterion of falsifiability, of operational definitions or the codification of independent and dependent variables, were still to be developed when Freud constructed his theory, but even at the time, it was considered dangerously unscientific by some.

Final Revisions to the Theory: Id, Ego, Superego and the Death Instinct

In Freud's final statement of the mature theory, in *Beyond the Pleasure Principle* (1920) and finally, *The Ego and the Id* (1923/1989), he almost completely discards recognizable reference to either neurophysiology or specific evidence from patients to build a functional psychological model of the mind and not the brain. Freud recognizes that his description is an extensive metaphor, a description of the mind as if it had layers and depths. The metaphor is functional in that at its base is an attempt to explain how the organism reproduces and survives, and thus sexual impulses remain at its core.

Specifically, the sexual energy or libido is the source of goal-directed mental action. This sexual energy flows like spring water from a deep internal source outside of our awareness. This source is the **id**; our conscious mind is completely unaware of it, but it provides us with energy to survive, reproduce and contend with the outside world. Unpleasant experiences and frustration dam up libido in the id and thus heighten internal pressure and tension. Thus, the id operates on the **pleasure principle**. It is always striving for the pleasant release. Erotic impulses are felt as needs by the id, and at the beginning of life, the infant mind is nothing but a mass of libido looking for a love object on which to attach this energy in *object cathexis*. This is most likely the mother or specifically, at first, the mother's breast. If the mother gratifies the infant's wants, healthy release is granted every time the infant meets its beloved object and is fed. If not, the need is invested in an unconscious representation of the mother, never fully gratified, and is always seeking release, even though the conscious personality may be unaware of its early source.

The **ego** is the part of the mind that directly processes perceptual information and attempts to help the body survive and the id to gratify its needs. Most of it, as noted above, is conscious, and it includes the verbal voice of the mind. It rides and steers the id forces like the rider of a horse, within the dictates of the **reality principle**, attempting to choose the line of greatest advantage instead of yielding in direction of least resistance. The ego is aware of some of the things and people it loves, of course, and rationalizes why the person ends up doing the things he or she does, but the *source* of its reasons and its loves are deeper in the unconscious, in the id.

The source of why we don't do what we would like to do is also deep in the unconscious, in the superego. As we grow, beginning in the anal stage and proceeding through the phallic stage and the Oedipal conflict, we are constantly frustrated by the demands of others. The child does something to gratify an urge and is often punished by the beloved mother or other loved ones, who follow the strictures and morality of their culture. Thus comes fear of disobedience and the feeling that we may be abandoned by the love object if we do not yield to the punishment. This build-up of fear, shame and guilt, indeed our entire moral sense, is partially irrational, a gut-level feeling. If punishment in early childhood, before the child is able to think rationally (i.e. while his or her ego is weak) is particularly severe, it may lead to obsessiveness or to irrational timidity.

The moral heavy-handedness of the superego is not necessarily evil; it is necessary for civilization. Most of what we create in culture, from arts and artifacts to fame and fortune, come from trying to gratify our wants within the constraints of society. We desexualize or sublimate our libidinal urges into useful pursuits: A man or woman ultimately becomes powerful, successful and admired to achieve the love of the mother or mate. The ultimate cause of all of this industriousness has been repressed, of course, and we offer other rationalizations for our actions. The rationalizations are necessary because we need to bring reality and pleasure into alignment in ways that our culture will accept. This is how sublimation leads to civilization. The summary of the actions of the id, the ego and the superego can be left to Freud himself:

> From the other point of view, however, we see this same ego as a poor creature owing service to three masters and consequently menaced by three dangers: from the external world, from the libido of the id and from the severity of the super-ego. Three kinds of anxiety correspond to these three dangers, since anxiety is the expression of a retreat from danger. As a frontier-creature, the ego tries to mediate between the world of the id, to make the id pliable to the world and by means of its muscular activity, to make the world fall in with the wishes of the id. In point of fact it behaves like the physician during analytic treatment: it offers itself, with the attention it pays to the real world, as a libidinal object to the id and aims at attaching the id's libido to itself. It is not only a helper to the id; it is also a submissive slave who courts his master's love. Whenever possible, it tries to remain on good terms with the id; it clothes the id's Unconscious Commands with its Preconscious rationalizations; it pretends that the id is showing obedience to the demands of reality, even when in fact it is remaining obstinate and unyielding; it disguises the id's conflicts with reality and if possible, its conflicts with the superego too, in its position midway between the id and reality, it only too often yields to the temptation to become sycophantic, opportunist and lying, like a politician who sees the truth but wants to keep his place in popular favor.
>
> (Freud, 1923/1989, pp. 656–657)

Thus, there are three voices of the self: "I want to do that," says the id; "You can't do that," says the superego; "I can do that," says the ego, "but only if I'm sneaky." The battle is all about adapting inner stresses to outer demands, as an aid to survival. But what about those times when humans are destructive, when they seem driven to cause pain to others? Freud's view of humanity was often darkly pessimistic and not merely because he had developed a view of people driven by urges of which they are unaware. He witnessed the increasing crescendo of violence in the 20th century, from anti-Semitism in the daily aggravations of life in Vienna to the senseless carnage of the First World War to the rise of the Nazi Party. There seemed to be great reservoirs of hate spilling out all over the world.

On the smaller stage of his analytic couch, he began to realize that even acts of love and sex had violent elements in them: Certainly, there was rape and sadism to explain, but also aggression in normal sexual acts, a wish to possess, become one with or annihilate the other or even the self, for a moment in orgasm. Furthermore, why, if the pleasure principle were operating, would many of his patients wish to enter into self-destructive relationships again and again or even repeat, over and over again in analysis, accounts of painful moments of life? After having spent many years describing the ways of the life-instinct or libido or Eros, he now became interested in a death instinct or Thanatos, which worked in opposition to Eros. Thanatos was supposed to be a drive to return to the state of non-life, no tensions, back to the earth. Freud himself realized that he had little direct evidence for it; it contradicted theories of life from Aristotle to Darwin for an organism to actually *want* to die (rather than to kill for mere reproductive advantage or die for altruistic reasons). Freud attempted to solve both the problem of why we return to hurts and why we might regress to earlier states by saying that all of the deaths experienced by the species and all the ways we can hurt ourselves or one another are encoded, through Lamarckism, in our genes and we are destined to recapitulate them. Thus, a trauma in this life activates those in our evolutionary history (see Sulloway, 1979, p. 393 ff).

The death instinct was perhaps the least accepted part of the theory, even to Freud's loyal followers, because it seemed almost mystical. By this time, the reader may be beginning to tire of the increasingly torturous logic in Freud's arguments as well. But, he has, finally, a larger purpose for introducing the death instinct: to give a warning about the future of civilization itself. If the death instinct overcomes the constructive powers of the id, as harnessed by the beneficial constraints of the superego, and if we band together en masse to celebrate the perverse excitement of nihilism, as was happening all over the world in the last decade of Freud's life, then we are doomed. In his famous 1930 essay "Civilization and Its Discontents," he writes,

> And now, I think, the meaning of the evolution of civilization is no longer obscure to us. It must present the struggle between Eros and Death, between the instinct for life and the instinct of destruction, as it works itself out in the human species. This struggle is what all life essentially consists of and the evolution of civilization may therefore be simply described as the struggle for life of the human species. And it is this battle of giants that our nursemaids try to appease with their lullaby about [the existence of] Heaven.
>
> (Freud, 1930 in Gay, 1988, p. 756)

The Psychoanalytic Movement

Freud and his friendly biographer Ernest Jones (1954) have implied that between the years 1886, when he received what he perceived to be a rejection by the Viennese physicians of his theories, and 1902, he was isolated from the broader scientific community while he formulated the tenets of his theory in correspondence with Breuer and Fliess. He had, it is true, received considerable criticism for his seduction theory in 1896, which he abandoned in 1897, but did not renounce in print until 1905. But in the 1890s, he had published two well-regarded neurology textbooks, several well-praised translations of others' work and, in 1895, *Studies in Hysteria* with Breuer. William James cited Breuer and Freud in his lectures *Varieties of Religious Experience* in 1901. In 1900, The *Interpretation of Dreams* was published, to wide notice, garnering about 40 reviews totaling over 17,000 words (Sulloway, 1979). Some of the attention was very positive, calling the book "epoch-making" and "*psychologically the most profound that dream psychology has produced thus far.*" This attention did not satisfy Freud, who wanted the particular attention of the scientific journals, rather than the general press. Some of this professional attention was negative and similar to current criticisms of psychoanalysis. His use of dream analysis in psychiatry was seen as a throwback to "old wives psychiatry" after half a century of attempts to biologize the field. The symbolic method was viewed with some suspicion. Applied psychologist William Stern commented,

> The inadmissibility of this game of dream interpretation as a scientific method had to be emphasized with all trenchancy; because the danger is great that uncritical minds might like this interesting play of ideas and that we would thereby pass into a complete mysticism and chronic arbitrariness. One can then prove everything with anything.
> (Stern, 1901, cited in Sulloway, 1979, p. 456; emphasis in original)

It is perhaps understandable that Freud might deemphasize praise, as one always remembers the negative reviews.

In 1902, however, after years, on and off, of teaching courses as an untenured lecturer, he finally received a professorial post at the University of Vienna. To finally be called "Herr Professor Dr. Freud" was a great boost and a title of great stature in Austro-German society (see Chapter 5). In the same month, he inaugurated the "Psychological Wednesday Society" with four other members, including, most notably, Alfred Adler. At first, they simply met in the waiting room of Freud's apartment and practice at Berggasse 19 in Vienna, reading and discussing papers on psychoanalysis.[9]

From the very beginning, some of the participants seemed to think that psychoanalysis was more than simply a new therapy for hysteria. Wilhelm Stekel, a physician and author, remembered of those first meetings of the Wednesday Society:

> There was complete harmony among the five, no dissonances; we were like pioneers in a newly discovered land and Freud was the leader. A spark seemed to jump from one mind to the other and every evening was like another revelation.
> (Stekel, cited in Gay, 1988, p. 174)

Each meeting consisted of a paper read to the assembled group, followed by coffee, cakes and cigars. Then there was discussion, sometimes heated, especially in later years. Freud, however, was always allowed the last word, as one of the early participants remembered:

> The last and decisive word was always spoken by Freud himself. There was an atmosphere of the foundation of a religion in that room. Freud himself was its new prophet who made the heretofore prevailing methods of psychological investigation appear superficial.
>
> (Graf, 1942, cited in Gay, 1988, p. 174)

Sometimes, the topics discussed turned quite personal, as the members shared their past sexual histories with one another. This was necessary since, from the beginning, the group were experimenting with analyzing their dreams in front of the others. In time, many of them would undergo analysis with Freud as well. These activities led to a dangerous amount of personal material held in common by the members that could be used later as ammunition in debates.

Break With Fliess

Freud was exceptionally eager to gain control over the priority of the ideas in psychoanalysis. In 1904, two books came out almost simultaneously on the supposed inherent bisexuality of all humans. They mentioned Freud in connection with the idea, but totally ignored Fliess's contribution. Fliess found out that one of the two authors had been Freud's patient and that the other author had provided a draft of his book to Freud. When Fliess confronted Freud, he at first lied about knowing the second author. Then he sent Fliess the typeset galley proofs of his "Three Essays," asking how Fliess wanted to be cited in the corrected work. There was the whole psychosexual stages theory that Fliess and Freud had worked on closely together! A couple of places of mentioning Fliess's name would not be sufficient credit; in Fliess's eyes, he had been robbed and Freud was in league with the robbers! He broke off contact with Freud (Freud & Fliess, 1985; Kerr, 1993).

Alfred Adler (1870–1937)

Perhaps the most accomplished of the little band in Freud's waiting room was Alfred Adler. Adler had begun life in similar circumstances to Freud, as a poor Jewish boy, the second child of a proud, optimistic but struggling wheat merchant. Alfred's mother was often gloomy and ill, but unlike Freud, Alfred was not her favorite of her six surviving children. Alfred was always striving to match the achievements of his elder brother, Sigmund, who had done well in real estate. (This struggle within families for love and recognition was later incorporated into Adler's theories of family constellation and birth order.) The Adlers briefly lived in the same quarter and went to the same gymnasium as Freud (years after him), and Adler studied medicine at the University of Vienna as well. But Adler had merely passed his exams with the lowest passing grade, rather than aspiring to the heights of an academic or scientific career.

He set up shop as a general practitioner in 1899 in a poorer quarter of Vienna than had Freud, in part out of commitment to public health. His first book had been on improving the sanitary conditions of the working life of tailors, who were generally even worse off than Adler had been. Whereas Freud had expended much energy to rise to the level of a proper bourgeois gentleman, Adler was active in socialist politics in his youth and continued to live rather modestly, even as his fame grew all his life. He was even less committed to Judaism than Freud: He converted to Protestantism in 1904.

Adler is said to have come to Freud's attention when he wrote a letter in Freud's defense to a newspaper that had published a bad review of the *Interpretation of Dreams*, although the review or letter cannot be found (Jones, 1954). From the start of the Wednesday Society, in 1902, it is helpful to remember that the theory and practice of psychoanalysis were hardly set in stone. The only case studies yet published were those in Breuer and Freud (1895). Of course, some of the techniques were referred to in *The Interpretation of Dreams* and *The Psychopathology of Everyday Life*, but mostly as little examples, rather than complete case histories. The method of therapy was not systematically described in print anywhere. Freud was clearly the leader of the little group, but it was reasonable for the little band of Viennese to believe that they could contribute to the developing theory at the time. Alfred Adler was among the first to do so.

Adler was publishing summaries and defenses of Freud's ideas by 1905, but then struck out somewhat on his own with *Studies in Organ Inferiority* (1907). Adler's view was that illness was often due to particularly ill-functioning organs; overcompensation for the defect might physically strengthen the organ and give a feeling of mastery. Psychologically, for example, someone with eye diseases may feel inferior in relation to others and overcompensate by becoming a painter. But the so-called **inferiority complex**[10] might lead to neurosis if compensation failed. Even if overcompensation is successful, the cost of committing so much psychological resources to it might lead to neurosis. Adler said that if the insufficiency were with sexual organs or performance, it might lead to hysteria or sexual perversions that were mentioned by Freud. Not all neuroses are sexual, but if any organ inferiority were great enough to impede a person's competition for mates, it could lead to sexual difficulty. Indeed, one difficulty Adler noted was that in a masculine society, feminine traits are seen as negative and therefore the perceived "weakness" of feminine traits may be compensated for by **masculine protest** of either men or women dissatisfied with the label.

At first, Freud was pleased with Adler's innovation, but as time went on, tensions would develop, as Adler was perceived by Freud as deviating from the cause. Organ inferiority is based on a biological substrate and leads to personality and social consequences, which pleased Freud. And the processes of compensation begin in childhood, which is also consistent with his views. But Adler from the start suggested that not all neurosis is due to sexual causes. Worse, he later suggested that the Oedipal complex did not make sense and deemphasized not only its importance, but the importance of past memories in general, downplaying the importance of the unconscious and giving more emphasis to the ego. Finally, and perhaps most damningly, Adler stressed humans' need to dominate others, based on Friedrich Nietzsche's notion of a human "will to power." The basic driving force of why people feel inferior and want to overcome it is due not to the dives of libido, but to an aggressive drive to dominate. These disagreements would eventually lead to a break between them over the primacy of repressed sexuality in psychoanalysis.

The Zurich School and Rising International Recognition

In the very same 1904 letter in which he informed Wilhelm Fliess of the first bisexuality book, Freud also bragged about a glowing review of some of his work by none other than Eugen Bleuler (1857–1939), full professor of psychiatry at the University of Zurich, Switzerland, and director of the progressive and modern public insane asylum there, the Burghölzli. Under Bleuler, the Burghölzli had become the most humane institution in Europe for the treatment of schizophrenia, a term he had coined himself.

The previous diagnosis of *dementia praecox* or premature, progressive mental deterioration was first defined by Emil Kraepelin (1856–1926). Kraepelin, an asylum psychiatrist and professor of psychiatry at Munich, had supervised the first systematic set of diagnoses based on rigorous observation of the course of mental illness over time, as well as on mere presenting symptoms. Having also studied with Wilhelm Wundt in the 1870s, he brought the emphasis on psychological functioning to experimentation to psychiatry and attempted to base his diagnoses on large numbers of cases. In this massive task, he systematized the diagnoses of the psychoses, including manic-depressive disorder and paranoia. His was a strongly biological model of psychosis, and he pioneered the rudimentary study of psychopharmacology in these disorders (for example, he forbade his patients or staff the use of alcohol; abstinence was also the rule at the Burghölzli). Throughout his late career, Kraepelin was an implacable foe of Freud. To Kraepelin, Freud's theories attributed mental illness to unobservable internal mechanisms. After a time experimenting with the use of psychoanalysis with schizophrenics, analysts, including Freud himself, conceded that their treatments were ineffective with most psychoses and concentrated only on what were later considered "functional neuroses" (see Freud, 1923).

Bleuler was distinctive in this era for his guardedly hopeful, pragmatic approach to mental illness. He ran the asylum solely for the benefit of the patients, at a time when most psychiatrists assumed that such patients were doomed by hereditary degeneration. Bleuler had noticed two simple things: first, that patients responded well to simple conversation about their problems, in spite of their delusions; so he made sure that the psychiatry residents talked at length to each patient at least every other day. Second, he had observed that getting the patients to perform whatever work they could do would keep their delusions at bay. As soon as they stopped working, their delusions usually came back, but some cases appeared to even be cured by the treatments, at least to the point that they were functioning well enough to be released back to the community. Bleuler's selfless and tireless work was matched only by his open-minded acceptance of new developments in the field, including the work of Charcot, Janet and the new work of Freud. From Bleuler's perspective, the cures for bizarre forms of hysteria touted in the case studies of Breuer and Freud (1895), if true, would be both astonishing and in line with Bleuler's hopeful view. In turn, the recognition of Bleuler meant much to Freud, for the most dedicated young psychiatrists would now know of his work.

Bleuler had been conducting studies on a word association test that involved comparing the associations typically given by normal adults under conditions of rest and fatigue with the associations given by his patients under those conditions. He noticed, first of all, that the associations given by the patients were more varied and unstable than those given by normals. This looseness of associations meant that the patients were more susceptible to passing ideas and less certain about the boundaries of their sense of self. The term schizophrenia was meant to more precisely describe the broken self and to remove the assumption of irreversible biologically based mental decline from the dementia praecox diagnosis.

Carl Gustav Jung

One of the brilliant young assistants given the task of collecting the data for this experiment was Carl Gustav Jung (1875–1961). His intimate knowledge of the content of the delusions of the asylum patients allowed him to note that the associations

Figure 9.4 Carl Gustav Jung (1875–1961), approximately 35 years old

that they made to words on the test would invariably relate to their delusions, some of them with sexual content. This was consistent with Janet's notion of thought as directed by subconscious complexes, as well as with the new work of Freud. Jung also had experience in Bleuler's version of talk therapy. For example, one of his patients had caused the death of one of her children by inadvertently giving him unclean water. When the boy died of typhoid fever, the mother was tormented by obsessive ruminations that her secret dislike of the boy might have caused his death. Simply confessing the secret to Jung allowed her to get well enough for discharge.

Thus, both the association experiments and Jung's clinical experiences at the Burghölzli seemed to confirm some of what Freud had written. But he had already been predisposed to consider the unconscious as a mysterious and potent force by his own early life and temperament. Jung was born in Basel, Switzerland, as the only son of parents from two distinguished Protestant families. His paternal grandfather was a distinguished professor of medicine, rumored to have been the illegitimate son of the German cultural giant Johann Wolfgang von Goethe. If his grandfather's profession were not imposing enough, this rumor, never actually confirmed, gave Jung a sense of destiny all his life. Jung's father was a conventional clergyman, but because he was ineffectual and somewhat henpecked by his wife, Carl had less respect for him than for his exalted grandfather. Jung's mother herself came from a family of Protestant ministers, the Preiswerks, but she was also strongly influenced by the spiritualism fad then sweeping the world and held numerous séances at home, without her husband's knowledge.[11] Jung was already an introverted, dreamy boy, with a tendency to be tormented at school by peers for his fainting spells. But Grandfather Preiswerk had written his sermons with his wife sitting behind him "to keep the devil out," and much to the chagrin of his second wife had had weekly audiences with the ghost of his first wife. The combination of introversion and a strongly spiritual home life had a deep effect on Jung.

Indeed, Jung's mother and cousin were reputed to have psychic powers. The powers (or delusions) of his cousin Helene Preiswerk became the basis of Jung's medical dissertation. For a time, Jung had a crush on Helene, as she did on him; when his college friends unmasked some of her trickery at a séance, Jung began to realize that some of her "powers" were exaggerated to please him. In such an environment, it is hardly surprising that Jung was also prone to have lucid dreams. At about 12 years of age, Jung had a dream in which God, on his throne, defecated. The enormous turd crushed a Catholic Cathedral, leaving Jung with an odd feeling of exhilaration. Dreams like this were common to Jung throughout his life and provided him, he said, with spiritual guidance.

By the time he had risen to be Bleuler's second in command at the Burghölzli, Jung had grown to be a physically strong, imposing young psychiatrist, with a seemingly boundless energy and a capacity for speaking passionately for hours on the subjects that interested him, which even early on included the occult as well as psychiatry. This seeming contrast between outward vitality and inward mysticism is something that often captivated people, especially women, in his presence, but often tormented Jung in secret, for he worried about the hereditary taint of mental disease in himself.

So, Jung wrote to Freud in early 1906, sending along copies of the papers on the association experiments and Freud wrote back, subtly asking for more contact

("I am confident that you will often be in a position to back me up, but I shall also gladly accept correction," he wrote [Freud to Jung, April 11, 1906/1974, p. 3]). Jung obliged, writing back that he had already been defending Freud against his enemies in debate, although he had his doubts about whether the cause of hysteria was "exclusively" sexual. Furthermore, Jung said that "Bleuler is now completely converted" to his views (Jung to Freud October 5, 1906/1974, p. 5). In the very next letter, Freud makes a confession that is very emotional for such formal times: "I venture to hope that in the course of years you will come much closer to me than you now think possible" (Freud to Jung, October 7, 1906/1974, p. 5). In March 1907, after having sent 19 letters between them, Jung visited Freud in Vienna. Jung and Freud talked non-stop for 13 hours! From afar, Jung had admired Freud, but after meeting him, Jung admitted to having a "religious crush" on Freud.

Freud also got much out of the link with Zurich, for his young evangelist had been making influential converts there. Burghölzli-trained psychiatrists eventually beat paths to Freud's door and became part of his inner circle. In addition to Jung and Bleuler, Max Eitingon, Karl Abraham, Ernest Jones, Sándor Ferenczi and A.A. Brill had all trained, at least for some time, at the Burghölzli and ended up all over the world—Abraham was from Berlin, Jones was from England, Eitingon from Russia, Ferenczi from Hungary and Brill from America. Freud's little Viennese Wednesday Society had only about 20 members in 1906, all Jews and virtually none with the kind of either academic or medical credentials that Jung had. There were MDs there, but mostly undistinguished general practitioners. Jung, by contrast, was already an established published researcher in psychiatry, with the second highest job in the asylum and from a distinguished family. And of course, he was clearly not Jewish, a considerable advantage in a time and place in which anti-Semitism was high. Already, almost 30 years before the rise of the Nazi Party, many physicians considered Jews to be a "degenerate race" which, according to the hereditability of degeneracy, would only become more "degenerate" over time (Kerr, 1993).

Of course, Freud did not believe in degeneracy of races or cultures; in spite of his respect for Darwinian biology, one of the essentially hopeful aspects of psychoanalysis was its promise to heal what to then had largely been considered a hereditary weakness and taint. But there was the public relations aspect of the prospect of being labeled a Jewish science to deal with.

Jung's institutional connections, combined with his Christian background, made him ideal, in Freud's eyes, to lead an international movement. For a time, Freud saw Jung as his "son and heir": To the dismay of the Vienna contingent, at the First International Congress for Psychoanalysis, in 1908, Freud gave Jung the editorship of the new journal, the *Yearbook for Psychoanalytic and Psychopathological Research*. Diplomatically, Freud listed Bleuler as a cofounder of the journal. But the relationship between Freud and Jung was never entirely smooth, for Freud, as the father, demanded loyalty and Jung, the son, desired some measure of independence.

America's Introduction to Psychoanalysis: The 1909 Clark Conference

As was noted in chapter 7, in 1909, Clark University was celebrating its 20th anniversary and President Hall wanted to celebrate with a grand international conference.

He invited 29 lecturers from all the sciences, among them Sigmund Freud. He had also invited Wundt, but he cordially declined due to ill health and other engagements. So Hall filled the hole in his roster with Carl Jung. Freud's faithful acolyte, the Hungarian analyst Sándor Ferenczi, joined them for the trip. At the conference, they met up with British psychoanalyst (and Freud's authorized biographer) Ernest Jones and American psychoanalyst A.A. Brill. All in all, quite a coup for the new psychoanalytic movement and a feather in Freud's cap, who generally loathed America and Americans,[12] but who was willing to overlook this for an expense-paid trip and the promise of an honorary doctorate.

Freud was not yet as well known in America as he would become after the First World War and was hungry for the recognition it would bring. Hall, for his part, found that he had much in common with Freud. Both, of course, had a deep appreciation of German culture. In addition, Hall had thought that American prudery regarding sex was unhealthy. His own sexual awakening had taken place in the then more liberal climate of Germany many years before and he had studied and taught the psychology of sex as an academic subject frequently (Rosenzweig, 1994). He had come to agree with Freud that sex was a basic instinctual drive. Yet, Freud and Hall were still Victorian men; they both considered the sexual drive so strong that it must be controlled by cultural prohibitions and sublimation, defined as the redirection of sexual energy into culturally valued pursuits. Sublimation was in fact a major preoccupation voiced in the pages of Hall's *Adolescence* (1904). The strength of the sex drive explained the sublime emotional experience of religious ecstasy in the theories of both men, but Hall considered this a good thing, while Freud abhorred religion in all its forms (Hall, 1904, particularly volume 2; see Freud, 1933, for his thoughts on atheism). Finally, both Freud and Hall had constructed stage theories of development based on the evolutionary notion of recapitulation.

Freud gave five lectures at the Clark Conference, in German (which the great majority of his sophisticated audience understood).[13] He described the case of Anna O., giving due credit to Breuer; he discussed the concepts of resistance and repression, manifest and latent dream content, the method of free association as contrasted with hypnosis and infantile psychology; he briefly hinted at the dynamic functional properties of his view of the mind, that he would not publish for another 11 years, in the final theory (Freud, 1920). His lectures, later translated in the local newspapers, were clear enough for laymen to follow and included Freud's trademark use of evocative metaphors. Jung lectured on the free association method as used with dementia praecox patients (Bleuler had only coined schizophrenia the year before, so this term was not used) and ended his lectures with some observations on child sexuality, including the "little Hans" case of Freud and some disguised observations of his preschool-aged daughter's supposed sexualized behavior (Rosenzweig, 1994).

The trip was a great success. On the night of September 10, Hall had a dinner at his home for William James to meet Freud and Jung. Freud even had a private talk with James as he carried the frail old man's bag to the train station (James was to die within the year from a heart condition).[14] Hall published translations of the talks in his *American Journal of Psychology*; there was a symposium on Freud's ideas at the American Psychological Association in December 1909. Freud impressed the

Boston neurologist, Dr. James Jackson Putnam, who became the first president of the American Psychoanalytic Association in 1911 (Hall served as president in 1916) (Rosenzweig, 1994). Freud was even pleased at how much the general public were interested; on the ship over to America, he had seen his cabin steward reading *The Interpretation of Dreams* (Jones, 1955)!

But it was on the American trip that the tensions between Freud and Jung began. The two men already knew (or suspected) an extraordinary amount about each other's private lives. Freud was aware of Jung's dealings with Otto Gross, who had been a perennial patient at the Burghölzli for drug addiction. Gross became interested in Freud's work and thereupon began practicing a kind of "wild analysis" to all comers at café tables throughout Germany and Switzerland. Rather than practicing the sober clinical science that Freud was expounding, Gross was a social revolutionary, and psychoanalysis was his weapon to overturn patriarchal social structures. He wanted society to go back to what he considered an earlier time in the social evolution, a time of paganism, in which all humans were polygamous. "Repress nothing!" he would exhort to his clients and friends and anyone else who would listen. Any strong sexual impulse suppressed would lead to disease! Free love and free sexual expression were necessary to human health and deep enlightenment! Such lectures were accompanied by many sexual affairs and liberal quantities of cocaine, opium and morphine. By 1907, Gross had written a book lauding Freud's theories and sent it to Freud. In 1908, Otto's wife finally had him committed again to the Burghölzli and Freud directed Jung to supervise his case. After weaning Gross carefully from all of his drugs, Jung began an epic analysis with Gross. One session lasted 30 hours! More astonishingly, Gross would periodically turn the tables on Jung and analyze *him*. Hospital case notes show that Jung's letters presented a far too rosy picture to Freud of how the case was going, right up to the day Gross escaped from the hospital (Noll, 1994). After bouncing around Europe erratically for the next few years, Gross was found dead of pneumonia in an abandoned warehouse.

Freud knew at the time of the Clark Conference that Jung's first analysis patient, Sabina Spielrein, a young Russian Jewish medical student, had fallen in love with Jung and fantasized about having his child, much to the chagrin of her mother. Spielrein and her mother had taken it on themselves to each write to Freud directly. Jung's letters to Spielrein suggest very strongly that he had fallen in love with her; during the time Gross was preaching polygamy and pagan sexual abandonment in conversations with Jung, the affair with Spielrein may have become sexual. Jung, by then a married man, was arranging meetings with Spielrein out of his office (Kerr, 1993). Note the delicate (and tantalizingly ambiguous) romantic code in the following from a draft of a letter that she may have sent to Freud in 1909: Freud's copy, if it was sent, cannot be found.

> To suffer this disdain at the hands of a person [Jung] whom one loved more than anything in the world for four, five years, to whom one gave the most beautiful part of one's soul, to whom one sacrificed her maidenly pride, allowing oneself to be kissed, etc., for the first and perhaps last time in my life, because when he began my treatment, I was nothing more than a naïve child.
>
> (cited in Kerr, 1993, p. 223)

To us, of course, this implies scandal; Jung himself seems to have worried about scandal for years. To Freud, it would be scandal only if the outside world knew about it; among the closed circle of analysts, it could simply be interpreted as transference and countertransference due to the instability of a woman at a crucial state in analysis with an inexperienced therapist. In other words, he believed Jung—who described the relationship as a transference/countertransference difficulty—and not Spielrein.

But Jung also knew some things about Freud: He had described his unconscious bisexual attraction to Fliess and he probably mentioned the failure of the Anna O. case. Most explosively, Jung long claimed that on his first visit to Vienna, Freud's sister-in-law Minna Bernays confessed that he was in love with her. Jung took this to mean that they were having an affair right under the nose of his wife, as Minna lived in their back bedroom! Most historians consider this story to be wildly improbable and there is as yet no solid evidence for it beyond Jung's assertion (although implacable Freud foe Frederic Crews [2017], in his recent deconstruction of the entire Freud legend, believes it occurred). Freud was an exceedingly proper man outside of the consulting room and, unlike Jung and Gross, would be unlikely to risk his reputation and his wife's support on such a dangerous liaison. But Jung claimed that the triangle precipitated the break between himself and Freud. On the ships over and back from visiting America, the two men analyzed each other's dreams. Jung told an interviewer in 1957,

> On the [American] trip Freud had some dreams that bothered him very much. The dreams were about the triangle—Freud, his wife and his wife's sister. Freud did not know that I knew about the triangle. And so, when Freud told me about the dream in which his wife and her sister played important parts, I asked him to tell me some of his personal associations with the dream. He looked at me and said, "I could tell you more, but I can't risk my authority."
>
> (Billinsky, 1969, p. 42)

In his autobiography, Jung relates the story slightly differently, saying, "That sentence burned itself into my memory; and in it, the end of our relationship was already foreshadowed. Freud was placing personal authority above truth" (Kerr, 1993, pp. 266–267).

But there was more to come. In March 1910, the Viennese Psychoanalytic Association was expanded into the International Psychoanalytic Association at a conference in Nuremberg, Germany. Here, Freud attempted to install Jung as president of the association *for life*. The model for the society, worked out secretly among Freud and his friends Ferenczi and Jones, was to be that of a family, with Freud as the father-king and Jung, almost literally, the prince. The Viennese members, including pioneers Adler and Stekel, were so outraged that they forced Freud to back down and appoint Jung as president for two years. Freud showed up uninvited at a hostile meeting of the Austrians after the debacle and said, reportedly, from the recollection of a participant, Fritz Wittels:

> "Most of you are Jews and therefore incompetent to win new friends for the new teaching. Jews must be content with the modest role of preparing the

ground. It is absolutely essential that I should form ties in the world of general science. I am getting on in years and am weary of being perpetually attacked." Seizing his coat by the lapels, he [Freud] said: "They won't even leave me a coat to my back. The Swiss will save us—will save me and all of you as well."

(Wittels, 1924, cited in Kerr, 1993, p. 287)

In answer, two of the Viennese, Alfred Adler and Wilhelm Stekel, formed a new journal, still with Freud as "Director," but without Jung. Moreover, word had gotten out that Freud and Jung had denied the opportunity for psychiatrists who disagreed with them to attend, and this angered many people, for it was not consistent with normal scientific practice. Bleuler, in particular, refused to join the new society, taking many of those other Swiss who were not already convinced with him. A year later, he would withdraw as journal editor. (Jung later attributed Bleuler's failure to join to "homosexual resistance" and accused him of becoming a passive-aggressive woman (letter of Jung to Freud, November 13, 1910; Letters, 1974, p. 220).

Freud thus felt besieged, with the whole enterprise threatening to come down around him before it had even begun. Freud admitted to Jung that Adler was a repeat of the Fliess rebellion. He decided to force Adler out, first of the editorship of the journal and then of the society. Freud thought that Adler's focus on aggression would create a "psychoanalysis without love," and he could not abide his neglect of the unconscious and the Oedipal complex. By 1911, the letters between Freud and Jung became rather nasty concerning Adler. Freud often claimed that people who disagreed with him had resistances—blocks against him, based on their unconscious complexes. But when he was really angry with them, he would diagnose them with a mental illness. In a letter of June 15, 1911, after informing Jung of Adler's resignation from the society, he wrote, "Paranoid intelligences are not rare and are more dangerous than useful. As a paranoiac, he is right about many things, but wrong about everything. A few rather useless members will probably follow his example" (Freud, 1911/1974a, p. 428).

Several members did follow Adler's example and resigned. Adler immediately formed the Society for Free Psychoanalysis, and Freud forbade the remaining members of his society to join. But now, Freud began having serious problems with Jung. One of his patients, a Frau C., had left Vienna and gone to Jung to complain that Freud was cold and unfeeling. Jung, irritated at Freud's inability to allow him independence, agreed with her and the story got back to Freud, who said, "If you really feel resentment towards me, there is no need to use Frau C. to vent it ... The trouble with you younger men seems to be a lack of understanding in dealing with your father-complexes" (Freud/Jung letters, 1911/1974b, p. 476).

Freud had known of Jung's interest in mythology and approved of it, as long as the sexual nature of the libido was acknowledged. From the very beginning, Freud and his followers published essays analyzing not people but fictional stories and cultural practices. Anyone who walked into Freud's office could immediately see that it was stuffed with statues and art with primitive and classical Greek and Roman themes.

Freud himself was working on analyzing the evolution of the cultural taboo of incest in his work "Totem and Taboo (1913)." In this work, Freud claims, largely on the basis of books that he had read in mythology, anthropology and evolutionary theory, that in the remote past, we all lived in primate hordes with a single alpha male, who could mate with all of the females and drove off all of the adolescent males in the troop. In the deep primordial past, the younger males killed the father to have access to females. In their horror, they realized that they would now have to kill each other and so they dealt with the death of their father by deifying him into a totemic God. All of this is passed down in Lamarckian fashion to us in the Oedipal complex: Each of us wishes to kill our fathers and possess our mothers, sexually. This concept is literally encoded in our genes. With this article, in one fell swoop, Freud solidified the sexual/biological nature of libido, explained the Oedipal complex and explained why sons like Jung are so rebellious.

Jung had been invited on his own to speak at Fordham University in New York. For the first time, publicly, he radically deviated from Freud (Kerr, 1993, p. 420). The libido, says Jung, is not entirely sexual; it is merely psychic energy of any kind. The unconscious is a mythopoetic realm, and its use of poetic imagery is how it conveys to us in cryptic form what it wants us to do, as seen in innumerable religions, cultural myths and stories. According to evolution, our individual wish is to survive at all costs. Hence, sexual drive is important, and since it cannot be expressed directly in society or else civilization will fall, the desires of the libido are in the **personal unconscious**. But culture itself is a survival mechanism; indeed, some cultural traditions suggest that some must be sacrificed so that all will survive. These cultural species survival mechanisms are encoded, again in a Lamarckian fashion, into a wordless, instinctual memory that expresses itself in common symbolisms across cultures, over and over again. These are said to be in the **collective unconscious**.

The separation between the two men was by now inevitable. The problem had become that each man was now interpreting every action of the other as repressed neurotic conflict. Jung was slighted by not being invited to a meeting with Freud until it was too late to attend. This was repressed hostility, said Jung. The postmark shows I mailed it in time, said Freud; you have not resolved your conflict over me. Later, at a conference in Munich, Jung had interpreted a paper by Jones about Amenhotep, the ancient pharaoh who expunged his father's name from monuments in a move to found monotheism. Freud saw this as a wish to kill the father; Jung interpreted it as an understandable urge for the son to make a name for himself. Jones caught the deeper meaning. Freud fainted! Jung carried him to the couch and wrote later, "As I was carrying him, he half came to and I shall never forget the look he cast at me. In his weakness he looked at me as if I were his father" (cited in Kerr, 1993, p. 429). As Jones recalled it, Freud looked at Jung and said, "How sweet it must be to die!"

When they returned, Freud noted that the mysticism expressed in Jung's paper was itself a neurosis. My neurosis, said Jung, what about yours? I've been damaged trying to cope with your neurosis. Let each of us deal with our own neuroses; if you weren't neurotic, mine wouldn't bother you, said Freud. Jung exploded,

> You go around sniffing around all of the symptomatic actions in your vicinity, thus reducing everyone to the level of sons and daughters who blushingly admit the existence of their faults. Meanwhile, you remain on top as the father, sitting pretty. (Kerr, 1993, pp. 435–436. See, for a less condensed version of the fight, Chapter 16, Kerr, 1993; Freud/Jung letters, 1974.)

As John Kerr (1993) points out in his account of the Freud/Jung relationship, *A Most Dangerous Method*—the title is William James's assessment of psychoanalysis—there is a second sense in which the method is dangerous other than its use of symbolism: The opportunity for emotional blackmail between analyst and analysand is very high. With the invention of psychoanalysis, one can no longer automatically accept someone's word on his or her assessment of their own motivations. No one ever has, of course, but in Victorian society, elaborate codes of social behavior kept such behavior in check while fostering large amounts of genteel hypocrisy. If psychoanalysis elevates getting at what one *really* means as a measure of success in therapy, who gets to say what *real* is, given that both parties presumably have unresolved conflicts?

Consider the situation of psychoanalysis in the years 1912–1914 from Freud's point of view. Adler, Stekel and Jung had all deserted him, taking adherents with them. He had alienated Bleuler and had never had Kraepelin and his students in his camp. Meanwhile, psychoanalysis had begun to take off, starting new branches in several countries in Europe and the Americas. But Freud had never published a "manual for psychoanalysis" to train those interested in the therapy, so people were making things up in his name. There was no way to assure quality control. Even people he thought were sober and responsible had endangered the enterprise by having affairs with patients, and there were crazy converts like Otto Gross preaching free love at café tables to artists and bohemians. He was in grave danger of losing control of the movement. Thus, in 1912, after Adler's defection and hearing that relations were severely strained with Jung, Ernest Jones proposed setting up an "Old Guard" of still-loyal members. This group, called The Committee, would swear never to deviate from tenets of the theory—such as the Oedipal complex, sexual basis of the libido, childhood sexual stages and repression—without dispensation from Freud and the committee. They were to operate in *total secrecy*. Freud agreed to this measure, confessing a secret delight in belonging to a secret fraternity by giving all of the members special rings to wear. Henceforth, all publication would come through them and committee members would write articles in his defense when Freud was attacked. The Committee included Ernest Jones, Otto Rank, Sándor Ferenczi, Hanns Sachs, Karl Abraham, Max Eitingon and Freud.

In 1914, Freud published "A History of the Psychoanalytic Movement" in the *Yearbook*, in which, in scholarly style that belied the venom in his personal correspondence with Jung (which would remain hidden for over 50 years), he spelled out why Adler and Jung were "regressions" from psychoanalysis in no uncertain terms (Freud, 1914/1917). He wished them well but declared them beyond the fold. When it was published, the entire Zurich Psychoanalytic Society, including Jung, resigned membership in the International Association.

Finally, there was the problem of training of new analysts. My long recitation of the squabbles of the founders of psychoanalysis should make it clear that analysts, being human, are quite fallible. Hearing the troubles of many patients, discussing intimate sexually charged matters day after day and confronting their own internal turmoil is a difficult task. Moreover, intelligent men and women also had a distressing ability after a while to rebel and leave Freud's community. Freud had continually avoided publishing a manual for analysts, for some good reasons. Every analysis is different. Symbols are idiosyncratic to each patient's individual life. A great amount

Figure 9.5 Members of "The Committee," 1922: (left to right seated) Freud, Sàndor Ferenczi and Hanns Sachs; (standing) Otto Rank, Karl Abraham, Max Eitingon and Ernest Jones.

of tact is necessary in deciding to offer interpretations to the patient, and perhaps most delicately, the patient must form an emotional bond with the therapist in transference. Though it is unnatural, the therapist must avoid countertransference, while remaining sympathetic and supportive. All of these factors are art rather than science and difficult to convey in a manual. But in these years, Freud finally began publishing brief papers on technique. Some of his suggestions set the procedure for classical orthodox psychoanalysis for decades:

- Carefully select the patient. Not all patients are suitable for the soul-searching rigor of analysis. Intelligent, articulate, introspective patients are best. It is best not to know the patient in other personal or professional settings. Analysts should not provide therapy for family members.
- Warn the patient that the process will be difficult. Explain to the patient that he or she is required to say everything, without exception, in free association of their dreams or life events. Freud typically conducted 50-minute sessions six days a week per patient. The patient must pay even for sessions missed. Patients who frequently missed sessions or delay payment may be resistant. The topic should be taken up in analysis.
- It is best to say as little as possible to the patient during early sessions. The analyst is positioned so as not to look at the patient, and the analyst must not reveal any personal information about him- or herself. Analysis should not follow the common reciprocal rules of normal social interaction and courtesies. This protects

both the patient and therapist from possible entanglements and indiscretions. Early on, Freud even suggested that notes not be taken during the session itself, but from memory afterwards. The analyst listens intently, using his own intuitions to aid interpretations, which are to be revealed at opportune moments later in therapy.
- The lack of information given about the therapist encourages the patient to project the feelings and patterns of past relationships onto the therapist. This is **transference**, which is essential to treatment, and there may be several phases, from hostile transference, to erotic transference to, finally, transference to trusting, open relationship with the analyst as a benevolent helper in healing.

Learning how to do analysis is a subtle, artful task requiring both self-knowledge and intuitions about the motives of others. After the First World War, it thus became a requirement for all analysts to themselves undergo analysis and to periodically see an analyst for their whole careers, as a check against countertransference or allowing their own complexes to drive the analyses of their patients.

In effect, by setting up The Committee, rewriting the history of psychoanalysis and taking steps to formalize the training of analysts, he was shoring up the position of psychoanalysis in the world and protecting himself from attack. For good measure, during the hard years of the First World War, he gave two beautifully written, self-consistent and comprehensive sets of lectures at the University of Vienna, published in 1920. Most of his psychoanalytic colleagues had been drafted into the war, and three of his sons volunteered to fight. Since his private practice also dried up temporarily, he had time to embark upon the final phase of speculative theory building, which would result in the notions of id, superego and ego and the death and life instincts.

These protective actions, however, had the negative effect of isolating psychoanalysis from the scientific world for the remainder of Freud's life and to a great extent thereafter. Freud was diagnosed in 1923 with cancer of the jaw, probably a result of his severe smoking habit, which he was never able to finally give up. Over the last 16 years of his life, Freud would have over 30 operations on his jaw; he would have to wear a painful prosthesis on the jaw that affected his ability to speak publicly (Gay, 1988). He would still accept patients, but more and more, they would be students in training analyses. Patients would naturally come to Freud first; they would often be referred to Freud's colleagues, when possible. Getting those referrals often meant remaining in Freud's good graces. More than once, a theoretical disagreement caused Freud to cut off the supply of patients. From his point of view, this was only natural, given his early followers' tendency to tarnish the luster of psychoanalysis with odd personal and professional behavior. But the effect, of course, was to stifle disagreement. At a more intimate level, analysts who themselves remained in analysis might have disagreements with Freud analyzed away as unconscious resistance to authority. Training in psychoanalysis would be conducted mostly in privately funded psychoanalytic institutes rather than universities. Between 1910 and 1933, in addition to Vienna, psychoanalytic institutes were founded in Berlin, Budapest, London, Paris, Rome, Amsterdam, Jerusalem and New York (Gay, 1988).

Freud's last years were difficult. In 1933, the Nazis in Germany ceremoniously burned his books. "What progress we are making," he told Ernest Jones. "In the

Middle Ages, they would have burnt me; nowadays they are content with burning my books" (Gay, 1988, pp. 592–593). In 1938, when the Nazis took over Austria, he had reason to believe that they would not be content with burning only his books. Nazi brownshirts entered his home while Freud was out, whereupon Mrs. Freud politely asked them to sit down; she handed over the household money and said, "Won't the gentlemen help themselves?" Freud's youngest daughter Anna, by now Freud's chief caretaker and a child analyst herself, opened the safe, which they emptied of approximately the equivalent of $840 and left. When Freud heard about it later, he remarked with dark irony that not even he charged that much for an hour's work (he usually charged the then hefty sum of $25 a session, however) (Jones, 1957). The Freuds would have to leave Vienna. The Gestapo occupied the apartment across the street and were keeping close tabs on them. Freud's oldest son Martin, a lawyer, was held for a day and Anna was later interrogated at length at Gestapo headquarters. It was better to be interrogated than not: Anna requested to be interviewed, because she knew that when closing time came, they dealt with the backlog by rounding up those who were still waiting to be seen—they were then summarily shot. Anna survived without incident, but her father was very badly shaken.

Fortunately, Freud was famous and had many friends in high places. He had coauthored a book with the American ambassador to France, who brought his plight to the attention of President Roosevelt himself. Jones worked connections in the British government and Princess Marie Bonaparte, a patient and benefactor, worked on France. The Freud family left on June 4, 1938, for London. Freud was 82 years old; he had lived 78 of them in Vienna and more than 40 at Berggasse 19. As his last act, he had to sign a statement that the Gestapo had treated him well and he added, with a bitter gallows humor, "I can heartily recommend the Gestapo to anyone" (Jones, 1957, p. 226). Freud died in London, September 23, 1939, as the world exploded again in war. Four of Freud's sisters died in the Holocaust that followed.

Evaluating Freud's Legacy

Evaluating Freud's historical legacy is difficult, because as with perhaps no other figure in the history of psychology, people tend to take sides. Supporters have tended to see him as a Promethean genius of great personal integrity, intuitive insight and compassion. He single-handedly discovered The Unconscious and courageously fought Victorian prudishness about sexuality, while admitting his mistakes. As he neared the end of his life, he became world-weary but undaunted, hiding his disappointment in his fellow man under a mordant wit. Psychoanalysis, for Freud's supporters, was not merely a medical therapy but a philosophy and worldview. To undergo analysis is to attempt the hard road from unconscious darkness and compulsion to self-enlightenment and mature rationality in a Godless world.

His detractors see him as a man of overweening ambition obsessed with his own legacy to the point of distorting case study narratives, denying credit to other colleagues and keeping his own failures as secret as possible. He was petty, vindictive, authoritarian and even vengeful, tolerating no dissent. The whole edifice of psychoanalysis, say his detractors, was built on very little data, mostly from his own life and the smallest fraction of even his own set of patients. To add insult to injury, he may have been a pretty poor therapist to boot, rarely having cured a patient, even though he came close at times to bullying them, in spite of his directions to other analysts to avoid directiveness. And yet, the elaborate theory was constructed in such a way that it can never be proved wrong. Whatever else he was engaged in, it cannot be called science.

Although there is no overlap between these views, there is a third position: that Freud, whatever his personal characteristics, may today simply be considered old-fashioned. This historicist position suggests that he was behaving in accordance with the standards of his day. The late 19th century was the time of scientist as hero and the medical doctor as the new scientist practitioner in the white coat. Statistics was in its infancy, experimentation in medical settings new, rare and unformed. Freud was no more autocratic and sexist (and probably less racist) than those of his day. His struggle to build a deterministic science with sexual-biological causes was what scientists did in the age of Darwin and Haeckel. Freud's view of evolution was wrong, but so was that of many distinguished, thoughtful people of his time. His tendency to believe his patients and to downplay his own role in suggesting their stories was no more unusual for its day than Wundt or Fechner's faith in the reality of their own introspective data. When for much of his life even the definitions of independent and dependent variables or operational definitions did not exist and Karl Popper was not even born, Freud can hardly be held to scientific standards higher than that of his colleagues. At the same time, trenchant criticisms of his methods were made even by Freud's peers. Failure to deal with at least some of them is a flaw that can be laid on the doorstep of psychoanalysis even today.

The Problem of Hysteria

Despite its very long history (Veith, 1965), the diagnosis of hysteria began to fall out of favor after Charcot's death in 1893; as early as 1911, there were strong criticisms that the diagnosis was useless:

> Nowadays, the cry is ever louder: away with the name and concept of hysteria: there is no such thing and what we call hysteria is either an artificial, iatrogenic product or a mélange of symptoms which can occur in all sorts of illnesses and are not pathognomic of anything.
>
> (Gaup, 1911, cited by Webster, 1995)

By 1925, the diagnosis was rare, and in 1952, when the first edition of the *DSM* was published, it was not included. Part of the problem was that hysteria was a negative diagnosis, a diagnosis given when other physiological diagnoses were not appropriate, and therefore, it became a garbage bin where all sorts of problematic diagnoses were thrown. This leads to high rates of misdiagnosis. In 1955, a study of 85 diagnoses of hysteria of older inhabitants of asylums in Britain found that as many as 32, or 37% of the cases, *did* have a physiological cause after all, with some misdiagnoses leading to death (Slater, 1965). Thus, the very disease that psychoanalysis was created to cure had disappeared, and it had largely disappeared even while the first generation of psychoanalysts were alive. Some of its disappearance is understandable: Most of the major diagnostic techniques, from lumbar puncture to X-rays and EEGs, were not available to Freud as his theory was formulated. As diagnostic procedures improved, major categories, from epilepsy to tumors, were carved away from hysteria into their own diagnostic categories. The rest have been placed into diagnostic categories like "dissociative disorders," a diagnosis that is itself in dispute today (Crews, 1995; McNally, 2003). At any rate, by the 1920s, Freud was well on the way to redefining hysteria and repression as universal aspects of the human condition, having long disposed of the literal seduction theory. This made diagnosis per se of less importance to analysis, but also removed it from the possibility of disproof.

As noted in the quote above, some of the cases of hysteria were undoubtedly *iatrogenic* or produced by the highly suggestive treatment itself. The waxing and waning of symptoms in the Anna O. case may be one example of this. Three other factors may be briefly stated here as possible contributors to the rate of hysteria:

1. In a time when few effective treatments existed, physicians had an incentive to develop an excellent bedside manner. When little could be cured, comfort could at least be offered. Patients who needed the comfort may have exaggerated their symptoms consciously or unconsciously to justify the attentions of the doctor and receive the comfort. Such so-called *secondary gain* was endemic in 19th-century relationships between patients and doctors. It is less common today, when psychiatric disorders can be ameliorated by anti-depressant drugs, rather than only by extended sympathy.
2. In cultures and times when authority is respected, doctors might have strong powers over their patients. Uncritical patients might engage in self-fulfilling prophesies and behave like a hysteric. In more recent years, it has become fashionable for therapists to conceive of their patients as clients, lessening the authority of the doctor and lessening the likelihood of hysterical symptoms. Some feminist historical critiques of Freud take this line of argument, as many analytic patients were and are female and their doctors, male. (see e.g. Bernheimer & Kahane, 1985; Micale, 1995, pp. 66–87).
3. Laypersons usually are aware of the basic diagnostic categories of their time. Thus, they may themselves interpret their own symptoms as hysteria and present to the physician precisely those symptoms when they arrive for treatment. As Freud and his theories became more famous, many patients and analysts in training would interpret their symptoms within the psychoanalytic worldview and seek him out. Thus, the more famous he became, the less likely Freud would be to see patients that disconfirm his theory. This might have been true even if hysteria diagnoses were declining elsewhere.

Freud as Therapist

Critics of Freud have pointed out an even more disturbing problem with his work: He may not have been a very good therapist and may even have engaged in coercive and dishonorable or at least self-deceptive practices in therapy. Freud published only a half-dozen actual case studies after Breuer and Freud (1895); all but one of these may have been failures, just as the case of Anna O. now appears to be. All of the identities of these famous patients are now known. Moreover, some of Freud's therapy process notes have been unearthed; these notes were written at the time and presumably used to prepare the articles. Combined with the surviving, and now unexpurgated, letters to Fliess, Jung and others, a fuller picture of Freud's competence and honesty as a scientist practitioner can now be given.

For example, the first published case after the book with Breuer, done in 1900 but published in 1905 (Freud, 1905a), is known as "Dora." Her father had brought her, at age 18, to Freud depressed and suicidal, withdrawn and strongly disobedient to her parents. It soon became clear that she had good reason to be depressed. Her father was carrying on an affair with a friend's wife. The friend had forced a sexual kiss on Dora when she was only 14 and was now making advances on her again. She told her father; the friend denied it. Given the circumstances, it would be convenient if Dora would herself have an affair with the older man, for then her father's affair could continue. Freud tried to convince the girl that she actually had repressed sexual longings for the older man (and his wife!) and she was inappropriately and defensively overreacting to the man's "attentions." (In the published version, Freud made Dora two years older at the time of the first kiss.) Letters to Fliess at the time suggest that Freud had to be quite forceful in putting forth his views, in contrary to the later rules for analysts to be nondirective. He interpreted virtually every dream in a sexual way and considered Dora's nervous habit of fingering her locket as a masturbatory fantasy. But the patient would not budge and finally, after four months, she ended therapy, "uncured" of a hysterical repression she perhaps did not have (Sulloway, 1991; Crews, 1995). Intentionally or not, Freud appears to have become implicated in this dysfunctional family and dismissed Dora's concerns.

Of his two most extensive case studies, only "The Rat Man" case appears to have been a qualified success. Freud first presented his case at the First International Congress of Psychoanalysis in 1908, in a mesmerizing five-hour case study lecture. In this richly bizarre case of obsessive-compulsive behavior and phobia, a young lawyer-soldier had become obsessed with the thought that his fiancée and his father would be eaten by rats, of which he had inordinate fears. During annual military service obligation, a captain had told him of a gruesome Chinese torture in which a naked prisoner has a clay pot affixed to his buttocks. A large rat has been imprisoned in the pot and it scrambles in panic to escape. Then the torturer places a hot poker into a hole in the pot, terrorizing the rat, who bites and scratches the prisoner's buttocks and burrows into them; the prisoner dies of hemorrhage and the rat of suffocation. Freud ingeniously, by a typically circuitous route, connect's the Rat Man's father to rats (a gambler is a *Spielratten* in German) and his fiancée to rats through *heiraten* (to marry). All of this was linked to the patient's repression of anal sex fantasies and certain childhood events. When these fantasies were brought to consciousness, apparently, the Rat Man was no longer afraid of rats or of attack. Freud's posthumously released therapy process notes show that the chronology and the length of therapy were subtly changed to better support his conclusions in the published versions. Some have been suspicious not only of the torturous reasoning but also of the completeness of the cure, but the patient was killed in the First World War, so the long-term final result could not be verified (Mahony, 1986; Sulloway, 1991).

Finally, there is the infamous case of the seriously hysterical "Wolf Man" (Freud 1918/1955). A wealthy Russian aristocrat had become almost incapable of taking care of himself without his servants, passively apathetic, nervous, intermittently phobic. This patient had told Freud a dream early in therapy and again and again thereafter. He had had the dream when he was four, in which he saw some wolf-like dogs in the tree outside his house. Afraid he would be eaten, he woke up. Free associations led to a child's story about an old wolf being pulled by the tail, to other associations to the tail and climbing or mounting upon the wolf and so on. Freud concluded that the patient had seen rear intercourse by his parents when he was under the age of 2. The vision of the primal scene had prematurely awakened his libido and induced a passive homosexual tendency towards men and ability only to be excited by women seen from the rear. In essence, Wolf Man's problem was early fixation of the sexual instinct on the improper object due to a sexual shock.

This was Freud's most detailed case history, based on a four-year analysis and a reanalysis on a short relapse. It was supposed to be crucial proof of childhood sexuality and fixation at a time when Freud was under attack by apostates and defectors. But the success in relieving the especially early and deep-rooted neurosis, if it did occur, was never lasting. The Wolf Man, subsequently identified as Sergei Pankejeff, was passed around the Viennese analytic community for more than 60 years, going in and out of analysis and was for a time being financially supported by the society. When he was an old man, in the early 1970s, still riven with self-doubt and neurosis, a journalist tracked Pankejeff down and interviewed him and the perennial patient said of his supposed "cure": "It's all false . . . In reality, the whole thing looks like a catastrophe. I am in the same state I was when I first came to Freud and Freud is no more" (Obholzer & Pankejeff, 1982, p. 36.).

This most complete case study has itself come under serious criticism by Freud's most implacable modern doubters. Patrick Mahony (1984, p. 52) has remarked that the infant Pankejeff was remarkably observant of his parents' sexual act, seeing it, from his crib, from several angles simultaneously, a feat that "would exceed the ingenious staging of any pornographic film producer." Pankejeff himself, in his journalistic interview, suggested it was improbable, as Russian children of his class slept in their nanny's room, rather than their parents'. Frederick Crews, one of Freud's fiercest modern critics, pointedly summarizes the torturous arguments in the case study:

> The wolves. Freud explains, were the parents; their whiteness meant bedclothes; their stillness meant the opposite, coital motion; their big tails signified, by the same indulgent logic, castration; daylight meant night; and all this could be traced most assuredly to a memory *from age one* of Pankejeff's mother and father copulating, doggy style, no fewer than three times in succession while he watched from the crib and soiled himself in protest.
> (Crews, 1995, p. 46; emphasis in original)

A close reading of the case study shows that Freud sometimes suggests that the primal scene happened and at other points calls the memories "products of construction" rather than recollection. As a prosecuting attorney might say, "you can't have it both ways."

Two of the remaining cases were not even analyses, per se. In the "Little Hans" case, he met the five-year-old boy only once. The boy had understandably developed a fear of horses after witnessing a carriage accident. Freud and the boy's father, an analyst, constructed an interpretation that fit with Oedipal love of mother and opposition to the father. (The father was represented by the horse—fear of the horses outside conveniently kept the boy close to his beloved mother, in the house, as well.) Another published case of paranoia was based on a published autobiography; Freud never met the patient himself.

All of Freud's cases—now with historical context added—share some similarities:

1. They are necessarily selective in their presentation of information.
2. Freud is revealed to be more active than his myth suggests, both in coming up with interpretations based on what the theory requires and in pushing patients to accept his interpretations.
3. The published case studies are very artfully presented to lead the reader to the expected conclusions. Often Freud disarmingly hints that he is uncertain at various points and then asserts that what he was uncertain of is true. He hints, "this and other information, led me to believe," asserting reassuringly that there is other information, without showing it. Sometimes, he points out that he still needs other information and then presents it in the case at an opportune moment. Meticulous scholarship has shown that he often rearranges chronology to produce the effect (Mahony, 1982, 1986, 1989).
4. The method of (a) using dream material, (b) asking the dreamer to free associate, sometimes several times, to the dream material, followed by (c) offering interpretation that itself does not even stick close to the literal meanings of the associations, much less the dreams or assertions of the patients, as in the Wolf Man case, can lead to any conclusion.

To be sure, Freud had many more patients than the ones that ended up as case studies. They populated his lectures and articles, provided dreams for the successive editions of *The Interpretation of Dreams* and thus gave the impression that the theory rests on a vast store of clinical knowledge. But these persons are never presented in enough detail for scientific or historical criticism.

Freud was criticized even in his own day, for the "heads I win, tails you lose" form of logic in his conclusions and addressed it specifically. On the one hand he stated unequivocally, "There is no stronger evidence that we have been successful in our effort to uncover the unconscious than when the patient reacts to it with the words 'I didn't think that' or 'I didn't (ever) think of that'" (Freud, 1989, p. 669). On the other hand, he also said of constructions in analysis, "We do not pretend that an individual construction is anything more than a conjecture which awaits examination, confirmation or rejection. We claim no authority for it" (Freud, 1937, SE 13, p. 265).

Taken all together, the course of Freud's life and work progressively came to undercut the scientific basis for his beliefs as time went on. Some of the shift from materialist neurology to a symbolic therapy was intentional—he realized, around 1905, that a complete model of the nerve side of a dualistic psychology was not probable in the near future. But he continued until the end of his life to maintain that the sexual instinct and the vestiges of its evolutionary history were the bases for his science and his therapeutic cures. Otherwise, one of the central notions of scientific determinism would not hold: Not only is every action and reaction in the mind supposed to be based on a natural, physical cause, but that cause is supposed to be *discoverable*. If psychoanalysis were *only* about symbolic substitutions, then there would be little ability to determine just what was a symbol of what. If every neurosis were, at some level, reducible to sexual development, then an anchor remained in the natural world. Converting libido into a nonspecific life force, as Jung recommended, would remove this lynchpin to reality and psychoanalysis would descend into mysticism. To contemplate such an end to his life's work would have been abhorrent to Freud.

Developments in Psychoanalysis After Freud

The final statement of the theory, which Freud admitted was speculative and a purely functional description of human motivation, effectively fixed the id, ego and super-ego in the minds of analysts as real entities. In the early years of analysis, Freud's

Figure 9.6 Anna Freud, Berlin, 1928
Source: Photo by Imagno/Getty Images

libido drive theory was dominant, but surprisingly quickly, the ego became as dominant in psychoanalytic theory as it was supposed to be in a healthy psyche. Although she never renounced her father's theory, Anna Freud (1936/1946) began this trend by emphasizing and expanding her father's construct (Freud, 1895, 1926/1936) of **ego defense mechanisms**: Some of these defense mechanisms were said to be healthy in certain situations, such as the defense of *intellectualization*, in which a surgeon envisions a bloody surgery as an intellectual problem to be solved, rather than as a life-and-death matter. Other defense mechanisms were less laudatory, such as *projection*, in which one attributes faults to another person that were actually in one's self, or *displacement*, as when one acts out hostility on a wife that was meant for a boss. Although Anna Freud enumerated nine of these defenses, some theorists (e.g. Bibring, 1961, in Fine, 1979, p. 296) have postulated as many as 39.

This strong focus on how the ego promotes adaptation to unpleasant reality through the use of defense mechanisms in both the childhood and the adulthood of the patient is called **ego psychology**. There are perhaps as many varieties of ego psychology as there are psychoanalytic theorists, which makes it difficult to summarize the post-Freud period, but a common way of explaining this point of view is to contrast it with Freud's drive psychology. For Freud, the major conflicts were *intrapsychic* battles between the id and the superego, both partly or wholly unconscious. These battles are expressed by fantasies, wishes and dreams in the psychoanalytic session. Bringing the real meaning of these intrapsychic unconscious conflicts to light is the goal of therapy. For ego psychologists, by contrast, the ego is an "organ of adaptation" that looks outside the self in *extrapsychic* clashes with other people and obstacles in the world (Hartmann, 1939). A person is said to have weak **ego strength** if he or she deals with stressful conflicts in their lives by the use of repetitive, stereotyped, self-destructive or in a word, maladaptive behaviors. This preference of ego psychologists for external behavior over fantasy is a relative one. Ego psychologists do not consider themselves to be behaviorists, because many of the maladaptive behaviors may result from how a patient sees the world, which they believe would not be adequately reflected by external stimuli and behavior. Most ego psychologists believe that the inner conflicts described by Freud still exist, but they are stabilized by habitual ways in which a person tries to meet the demands of the physical and social environment.

For an ego psychologist, the answer to the question "Why am I still so concerned with what my mother thinks of me that I cannot contradict her?" does not begin necessarily with an unresolved Oedipal conflict. Rather, the question would be answered by examining what a set of behaviors and beliefs in the present are doing for the patient. What does the patient gain and what does the mother gain by perpetuating a maladaptive feedback loop of behavior and belief?

When the patient realizes an acceptable answer to this question, she has, in a sense, achieved conscious insight into possible motivations of her behavior, but the "unconscious" is a much less literal place in the view of ego psychologists and the mere insight does not itself relieve the pain that the maladaptive behavior has caused. By using this now purely functional and metaphorical view of how the mind works (or to be less dualistic, "how the person adapts"), ego psychologists can eliminate reliance on Freud's outdated biological or evolutionary beliefs. They can also more quickly attack the problems that led a patient to therapy in the first place.

Another important variant on the traditional drive theory is called **object relations theory** (Greenberg & Mitchell, 1983). Object-relations theory flourished after the Second World War mostly in Great Britain, where Anna Freud lived after escape from the Nazis. These analysts keenly recognized that much of the time in therapy is spent talking about important people in a client's life. The first of these are, of course, the patient's parents and family, but the concept extends to anyone that a client loves or hates. Each of us invests much psychic energy in these others or, more precisely, in *mental representations* of others. As noted above, this emotional investment in others is called *cathexis*. In Freud's drive theory, a developing child simply uses others (in a primitive unconscious way) to gratify the pleasure principle.

Object theorists differ greatly among each other, but in general, they differ from Freud in conceptualizing loved ones as ends in themselves, rather than as means to pleasure. The predisposition to seek out the mother is inborn, adaptive for survival but prone to misdirection in development. Melanie Klein (1882–1960), a Viennese play therapist analyzed and trained by Freud's friend Sándor Ferenczi, was a transitional figure from Freud to object relations: She believed that most of a child's fantasies in play were actually directed towards winning the love of her parents or punishing them for doing things that separates a child from them. Having also immigrated to London to escape the Nazi threat, she engaged in a bitter lifelong dispute with Anna Freud (1895–1982), who did not believe in Klein's broad psychoanalytic interpretations of very young children. W.R.D. Fairburn (1889–1964) suggested that the impulses of the id were not based on gratifying pleasure, but towards purely engineering and maintaining the connection with others. The libido is not pleasure-seeking, but object-seeking, and will seek that object even to the extent of experiencing pain. D.W. Winnicott (1896–1971) emphasized that the *good-enough mother* would provide in early life a protected space for the child to develop an early feeling of power. In order for this feeling of power to develop, mother and baby must be in exquisite synchronization in the first months of the child's life. Later, when the harsh realities of life impinge upon this idyllic relationship, the baby can rely on *transitional objects* like teddy bears or blankets to aid the separation and individuation from the maternal object. A mother who does not devote herself to the infant in this way may wind up producing a child with a *false self*—one who sees him- or herself as primarily a reflection of what the mother wants, rather than a *true self* of his or her own. John Bowlby (1907–1990), a British student of Klein, created attachment theory by merging psychoanalysis with *ethology*, the study of animal behavior in evolutionary context. A secure attachment to a responsive mother is said to result in a child who engages in exploratory behavior; insecure attachments are said to lead to either extensive attachment disorders or merely anxious or distant personalities (see Chapter 10).

This is just a sampling of object-relations perspectives. Some, like Heinz Kohut (1913–1981), focus on **self psychology** or how one differentiates healthy self-love from healthy love of others, as opposed to needier narcissistic controlling relationships with others. Others, like the American Harry Stack Sullivan, emphasize that the personality is instead a sum of relations with others and practice a kind of **interpersonal psychoanalysis**. There were psychoanalysts like Erich Fromm (1900–1980), who focused on how larger *cultural structures* affect the psyche and relationships with others. In this case, Fromm believed that capitalist society deforms and distorts relationships between people, by fostering love relationships that center on ownership. A couple may engage in a selfish relationship known as *egoism a deux*, in which they speak of *having* a wife rather than *being* a husband or lover. And finally, there is Erik Erikson (1902–1994), a protégée of Anna Freud, who reconceptualized Freud's psychosexual stage theory as, instead, a **psychosocial stage theory**. Erikson was concerned with how identities are chosen through passing through several social challenges, from separating oneself from parents, to learning accomplishment in elementary school, to finding a career or a life partner or a meaningful, fulfilling life in old age. How these stages are resolved differ from culture to culture, but if the challenges are not met, they affect emotional development and creative productivity. Erikson had his own issues with orthodox Freudian drive theory. In particular, he thought Freudians were much too concerned with finding the origins of traumas, an approach that he called "originology" (Friedman, 1999). Second, he thought that Freudians were too concerned with uniformity of belief on certain articles of faith, an approach he called "creedalism."

A Final Word

There are two questions that still need to be answered about Freud's project. First, regardless of the personal ethics of its founders, is psychoanalysis a science? Second, if the answer is no, does it matter?

It seems clear that psychoanalysis is not a science in the traditional sense. There are no studies of orthodox psychoanalysis that involve public hypotheses before an analysis begins to prove or disprove the existence of entities such as an id or superego. Analytic studies do not operationalize variables or use independent and dependent variables and control conditions, and replication is not their goal, per se, as every client is different. Case studies are rarely quantitative and are typically selective both in presentation of data and in the characterization of that data (as confidentiality sometimes requires changing particulars of the case). Analysis uses a common-sense confirmatory strategy rather than a disconfirmatory one. All information given by the client is used to seek out patterns in thoughts, emotion and behavior. Patients' personal relationships, past and present, and the individual's perceptions of those relationships are key, but so are symbolic interpretations of those relationships, as well as present adaptive conflicts. The psychoanalyst trusts that his or her vantage point outside the patient's system of conflicts offers a certain objectivity, allowing the analyst to see patterns of which the client is literally not aware. Furthermore, truly important conflicts or maladaptive neurotic behaviors or personality structures are assumed to be *overdetermined*: that is, they have more than one cause, and those causes may be longstanding, historical or self-maintaining. Thus, the analyst has faith that true conflicts will have more than one manifestation, that the same problems will recur across a patient's history and in many different contexts.

Critics who condemn analysis on its lack of scientific basis often seem to be talking past adherents, requiring analysis to pass criteria that Freudians do not accept. Adherents to the analytic position sometimes protest that analysis cannot and should not be scientific, owing to this richness and highly contextual nature of their data;

an analytic process is more of a craft and art than a science. Moreover, it is an applied art, concerned more with helping people than collecting data.

In this view, psychoanalysis becomes more a search for meaning rather than a search for causes, more of an aid to philosophical self-enlightenment than an attempt to heal an injury. The patient and his or her analyst are attempting to construct together an explanation that the patient can accept about what brought him or her to this point. Neither one of them can know what is really the truth about the past or even the present, but their job is to construct a theory of life that the patient can subscribe to. This life philosophy should be one that leads to self-aware success rather than to bewildered failure.

Fine, say critics, but clients should know in advance what they are signing up for. Is it reasonable to expect such vaunted goals from one's therapist? Freud himself didn't think so, saying several times that the purpose of analysis was to convert misery into common unhappiness. Many therapists, in spite of their elevated philosophical positions, would be uncomfortable becoming a guru. And perhaps one should be suspicious of those who are *not* uncomfortable with such a philosophical advisor position.

Critics have also accused analysis of being *scientistic* rather than scientific. Its authority rests, inappropriately, on its association with experimental scientific medicine. Its practitioners, particularly in the United States, tended to be psychiatrists or other medical practitioners and use the nomenclature of diagnosis and even the social structure of the office visit. Enterprises that use the trappings of science, but not its methods, are scientistic rather than scientific and are unintentionally misleading. Paradoxically, a patient's belief in this authority may make therapy more effective, but it can also make the patient more suggestible to the biases of the therapist. If one of the therapist's and patient's unexamined shared beliefs is that the unconscious life is *more true or real than one's conscious life*, then the search for unconscious causes may overwhelm the therapeutic purpose of analysis. In a recent trend in depth psychology known as the recovered memory movement, women who have no memory of parental sexual abuse in childhood and no witnesses or other evidence have been convinced in therapy that they have been abused in childhood (Loftus, 1994; Crews, 1995; McNally, 2003).

If therapists insist on believing that abuse memories recovered in therapy, with no corroborating evidence, are nearly always true, then it really does matter if psychoanalysis is or is not a science, because the therapists' claims have enormous consequences in the real world—parents who did not abuse their children could be and have been convicted at trial only to have verdicts overturned (and the therapists sued for malpractice). In this regard, it has proven surprisingly easy to experimentally inculcate false memories of, say, being abducted by aliens, particularly if the client has been hypnotized. The only way to answer the second question above negatively—that it does *not* matter that psychoanalysis is a science—would be for the therapist and client to agree at the outset that the full truth about one's past can never be known. Therapy thereby becomes a task of *consensually validated social construction*. The client has certain beliefs about how she came to be in therapy, a narrative of her life that includes triumphs, traumas, mistakes and injustices, as he or she remembers them. The therapist's task is to aid in reconstructing the narrative, validating some parts, evaluating and questioning others, in such a way that the story arrived at and agreed upon helps the client thrive in the world beyond the therapy session. Because there is often enough rich material in anyone's life to support many hypotheses of how we ended up, all of us edit and emphasize certain events to produce our own biased "case study." If we can never know for sure what the *right* story is, we can at least construct a helpful story. (See Rivera & Sarbin, 1998, for examples of the advantages and dangers of social construction.)

The good part of this approach is that it makes us aware that all of us, including Freudians, are subject to cultural stories. Depth therapy in this mode questions, rather than taking at face value, what it means to call someone or oneself a "victim" or "survivor" in our culture, for example, or what it means to be a "good daughter." Some constructionist critics have looked at the assumptions of therapy itself (e.g. Spence, 1982; Gergen, 1999). The bad part is that it undermines the progressive modern character of science, which relies on deterministic, operationalized and verifiable constructs. It is perhaps ironic that in the space of barely a century, psychoanalysis has gone from the promise of anchoring our emotional lives in science to largely giving up the project. Freud would not be pleased, but as we have seen, analysis has merely continued down the road he started it on.

Notes

1. Freud's first name was actually *Sigismund*. He began using Sigmund as an adolescent, but he never explained the change. Schlomo was the Hebrew name under which he was registered at his synagogue; he never used that either.
2. "SE" denotes *The Standard Edition*, the 24-volume compilation and translation of Freud's work by James Strachey.
3. The glass harmonica, which is nothing more than a series of glasses on a table filled with graduated amounts of water, was invented by Benjamin Franklin. Played with wet fingers, the instrument gives off an eerie tone that some described as emotionally "shattering" (Ellenberger, 1970). Mozart, who knew Mesmer socially in Vienna, wrote some pretty pieces for it.
4. Most of Janet's work is not translated into English. For a thorough English summary of his life and work, see Ellenberger (1970, pp. 331–417). My summary here is based largely on this source.
5. Incidentally, Freud faced his own supposed bisexual tendency by admitting to friends later that there was probably an unconscious and unconsummated attraction to Fliess that he later overcame (see notes on pp. 2–3 in Freud and Fliess, 1985).
6. Freud also notes that Irma's friend, whom he prefers to Irma, reminds him of his shy and docile wife! Elsewhere in his work, he frankly notes that he prefers women he can protect.
7. In these essays, he discusses sexuality with a distinctively Freudian balance of judgmental conservatism with a modern open-mindedness: "I know these things exist," he seems to be saying, "Let's not get carried away," but also "There is a great danger, if sex is not performed in the traditional way, of becoming a serious neurotic."
8. Note how Pierre Janet's "*idée fixe*" is here smoothly integrated into psychoanalysis.
9. The first topic discussed was, appropriately enough, the psychology of cigar smoking; Freud smoked up to 20 cigars a day! Later, when questioned about the phallic and oral symbolisms of his habit, Freud is reported to have protested, "Sometimes a cigar is only a cigar!" (Kerr, 1993).
10. The term inferiority complex originally comes from Pierre Janet, but its origins in organ inferiority is mostly Adler's contribution.
11. This was the same fad that influenced William James to take up the presidency of the American Society for Psychical Research. Jung's mother was also fond of the theology of the Swedish mystic Swedenborg, a favorite of James's father, as well as of Carl Jung himself.

12. He often made resentful remarks about Americans' obsession with money, even while he envied the fact that they had a lot of it (see Gay, 1988, pp. 562–570). This was a common, even clichéd, view of many Europeans at that time. After the First World War, with the Austrian economy in ruins, he needed American patients' and students' dollars to stay afloat.
13. Remember that German fluency was virtually required for psychologists in 1909; his audience included James, Titchener and about a dozen other students of Wundt, as well as German émigré professors such as the anthropologist Franz Boaz and German invitees William Stern.
14. See Chapter 7 for James's private views on Freud's "most dangerous method."

10 The Developmental Approach

Modern developmental psychology is a child of evolution. As the scientific study of children began in the 19th century, rigorous Victorian self-improvement was mixed with the spiritual upward evolution of Hegel and the new theories of Darwin and Haeckel to lend a new urgency to the need for child-rearing data and advice. In Victorian households, children began to be regarded with more pity and sentimentality than had been customary before, especially among the middle classes (note, for example, the waiflike children in Dickens's novels); this likely increased parents' sense of responsibility for their care. In this new era, the "right" way to raise children, previously discussed only in terms of religious instruction, now became an issue for scientists (Shuttleworth, 2010). Then and now, when psychological theories are applied to children, they come with implied moral prescriptions and warnings that invade, appropriately or not, the supposedly value-free precincts of science. To say that one has a good child means that one has a child that has turned out well and who is on his or her way to a competent adulthood.

The increasing importance of children also finally made them an appealing object of study for scientists, a veritable laboratory of evolution and epistemology. Darwin himself kept a diary of the growth and behavior of his firstborn son, in hopes that his development would shed light on the evolution of instincts and emotion (Darwin, 1877). G. Stanley Hall began to make his mark in the 1880s by uniting psychology and education into a movement for scientifically based childcare known as the child study movement. His erstwhile students H. Herbert Goddard, Lewis Terman and Arnold Gesell applied Hall's evolutionary biological bias to the practical world of intelligence testing and child growth and development, for a time deemphasizing environmental factors. As we shall see, Goddard and Terman used the new intelligence test of French functional psychologist Alfred Binet to prove their eugenicist ideas, in direct contradiction of his wishes and his more sophisticated developmental theory.

James Mark Baldwin, founder of the American functionalist journal *The Psychological Review*, combined the new theories of evolution and physiology with an interest in children's development of knowledge in his theory of genetic epistemology, which the great Swiss biologist, philosopher and psychologist Jean Piaget took as the formal name for his theory of children's development of physical and mathematical knowledge, uniting Baldwin's difficult philosophy with Binet's simple but effective ways of gently questioning children.

Piaget's genetic epistemology was focused, as its name implies, on how children construct for themselves a useful model of the world of object knowledge for themselves. But Piaget's discussion of the social world of the child was less successful and did not catch the imagination of psychologists and philosophers as much as did his description of knowing the world of objects. L.S. Vygotsky had read and was excited by Piaget's and Baldwin's early work, the work of the Gestaltists (Chapter 6), James and Thorndike (Chapter 7) and Pavlov (Chapter 8), as well as Karl Marx and Friedrich Engels. He saw a larger role for cultural, historical and social influences on cognitive development than these theorists did and created, in his brief career, a theory that is still casting a shadow more than 70 years after his death.

Others would focus more on children's emotional development. In Vienna, a darker view of child development would emerge from psychoanalysis. Each of the stages in Freud and Fliess's psychosexual theory essentially exemplifies the notion of a critical period hypothesis for personality development: If certain challenges are not met at the appropriate time, the growth of a child's personality will be fixated or stunted, leaving a child with conscious or unconscious unresolved conflicts and emotional frustrations. The first generation of child analysts, Freud's daughter Anna and Melanie Klein (both of whom were living in London by the time of the Second World War) fought bitterly, but produced through the reactions of their students, Erik Homberger Erikson (1902–1994) and John Bowlby (1907–1990), a more sophisticated approach to child-caregiver attachment and subsequent development of children's personalities. Finally, in this chapter, we will discuss how developmentalists have dealt with the issue of *socialization* or how children's caretakers encourage them to internalize the social roles and expectation of their cultures. In the 20th century, explanations of the socialization process have moved from learning theories to psychoanalytic approaches, to social learning to social cognitive explanations. Fortunately, these small paradigm shifts can be most easily illustrated in the lives and work of researchers who eventually formed a single group at Stanford University: Robert Sears, Albert Bandura and especially Eleanor Maccoby.

Evolution and Child Development: Wilhelm Preyer

> Speaking generally, the child presents in a passing state the mental characteristics that are found in a fixed state in primitive civilizations, very much as the human embryo presents in a passing state the physical characteristics that are found in a passing state in the classes of inferior animals.
> —Hippolyte Taine (1877, p. 259)

> Heredity is just as important as individual activity in the genesis of mind. No man is in this matter a mere upstart, who is to achieve the development of his mind (Psyche) in his individual experience alone; rather must each one, by means of his experience, fill out and animate anew his inherited endowments, the remains of the experiences and activities of his ancestors.
> —Wilhelm Preyer (1881/1898, pp. xiv–xv)

Developmental psychology began as a separate area of study at the moment when children began to be seen as living laboratories of evolution. As discussed in Chapter 4, there were at least two forms of evolution: Darwinian natural selection and the recapitulation theory of Haeckel. As early as 1839, when Darwin's firstborn William Erasmus was an infant, Darwin made careful observations of his child's movements and emotions, in the hopes of using this material to argue that a basic set of emotions were innate and therefore inherited and evolved. In 1872, when Darwin finally published *The Expression of Emotions in Man and Animals*, he compared the facial expressions of children with those of other animals, establishing an evolutionary link. In 1877, he published the 37-year-old observations of his son in response to some similar observations of innate cognitive development by French writer Hippolyte Taine (1828–1893), quoted at the start of this section. As you can see, however, Taine's comment implies much more: that a child can be seen as a veritable roadmap to evolution. This, of course, is the basic underlying idea of Ernst Haeckel's biogenetic law: Ontogeny recapitulates phylogeny. If every child repeats the history of our species in the course of his or her development, as Haeckel suggested, then understanding child development scientifically is a crucial task for evolutionists.

When a German colleague of Haeckel's, Wilhelm Preyer (1841–1897) wrote *Das Seeles des Kindes* (1881) (*The Mind of a Child*, 1898), an extensive and methodical record of the first three years of his firstborn son, he certainly had both Darwin's and Haeckel's theories in mind (Preyer cites Darwin several times). His aim was to chart the course of "mental genesis," the universal sequence of the emergence of sensory abilities that leads to the development of conscious intentionality or, as his old-fashioned term would have it, the will. He believed that these skills are not merely present at birth, nor are they imprinted on the child's blank slate of a mind. Rather, the beginnings of these abilities are given by evolution and modified by experience.

Carefully, every day, more than three times a day, he would observe his child and thereby discover many things that remain in child development textbooks to this day (Preyer, 1881/1898):

- that infants are born with reflexes such as blinking to light, sucking and palmar grasp.
- that infants are near-sighted and see black, white, red and yellow before blue and green, and depth perception must be learned.
- that it is often difficult to catch their attention or keep it.
- that the child responds to loud noises with a grimace very early and responds to the pitches in language tones in the first months.
- that the social smile begins at about two months.
- that pointing begins around the tenth month.

Preyer also gives surprisingly accurate accounts of motor development in walking and feeding and of language development. Finally, he discovers some benchmark behaviors that become central to Piaget's later accounts of infant behavior. He states that *"willing cannot take place until after the forming of ideas"* (Preyer, 1898, p. 331, emphasis original), suggesting that mental representation is necessary to the formation of a sense of self.

In spite of Preyer's association with Haeckel, he does not explicitly mention his theory of recapitulation in *The Mind of the Child*, focusing instead on a descriptive account of development. The same restraint was not practiced by G. Stanley Hall, the man who wrote the introduction for the American edition of Preyer's book (Preyer, 1898).

By 1895, G. Stanley Hall had been the first president of the American Psychological Association (in 1892) and was rapidly becoming the leading expert in child development in this country. In fact, as was more fully discussed in Chapter 7, Hall was a functionalist, a Haeckelian recapitulationist, a Lamarckian and a supporter of psychoanalysis in America. On the strength of his founding the child study movement in America, his massive work *Adolescence* (1904) and his early parent questionnaires on child behavior, Hall is considered the father of developmental psychology in America. This title would please Hall, never one to refuse an accolade, but his belief in the evolutionary biological determinism of development led his students Lewis Terman, H.H. Goddard and Arnold Gesell to promote an innatist, eugenist agenda for the first half of the 20th century (see Chapter 4). Terman and Goddard promoted these views through the using a then new test of intelligence by French psychologist Alfred Binet in ways that he would never have approved of; under the label of "child hygiene," Gesell's reassuring tables of maturation implicitly defined what was normal in child development and what was *not* normal for a generation of psychologists and pediatricians.

Alfred Binet (1857–1911)

Alfred Binet is most famous for the development, with Theodore Simon, of the first practical intelligence test for children with difficulties in school. The test, published by Binet and Simon in 1905 has been in use so long that its innovations seem obvious to us today. A child takes a test consisting of many heterogeneous tasks requiring relatively complex thought, arranged from easy to hard: vocabulary, mathematics, detecting patterns, recognizing logical absurdity, etc. It requires less than an hour and a half to administer and has relatively definitive right or wrong answers. The child's answers are interpretable because they can be compared with how other children his own chronological age—the standardization group—have done on the test. It is assumed that if the child is given the same test a few weeks later, he will do about the same, that his test results are reliable. We also assume, almost without question, almost unconsciously, that the test measures an attribute that the child carries around inside him or her and that the amount of that attribute is relatively stable over time, at least relative to the child's peers. Some of us even have suspicions that that quantity is somewhat heritable and can and will be passed down to our children.

Yet Binet was not a eugenicist and made no claims concerning the heritability of intelligence. He did not consider intelligence to be unchangeable and his greatest wish was to raise the mental level of low-scoring children. The technical aspects of the tests were of less concern to him than how their results would be used. He was a broad-based, scientific Functionalist psychologist with a specific positive social goal of helping children diagnosed with mental deficiency.

Before Binet was assigned the task to develop a test to determine which children would need extra help to succeed in school, he struggled to find his profession and then his place in psychology. But his rigorous honesty about his mistakes allowed

Figure 10.1 Alfred Binet (1857–1911).

him to develop a sophisticated view of intelligence and its measurement, ahead of the American eugenicists and mental testers (Wolf, 1973; Cairns & Cairns, 2006).

He turns out to have been correct in his modesty and because of it, he seems modern today, which might be small compensation for his trouble.

Essentially, Binet had to learn four lessons to come up with the test we know today:

1. That patients, doctors, teachers, researchers and children are all subject to social suggestion—self-fulfilling prophesies based on preconceptions or a willingness to please the examiner.
2. That intelligence testing should focus on individual differences in complex, higher-level thought rather than in simple judgments.
3. That the various abilities that make up intelligence develop across childhood, such that children generally become more competent with age. Every step

of test construction should be empirically validated and test scores cautiously interpreted.
4. Exactly how many abilities there are, how they develop and how changeable they are by intervention are unknown. To assume that what is measured is genetic and unchangeable is a grave error.

"Suggestibility Is the Cholera of Psychology." Early Studies on Hysteria and Cephalometry

Alfred Binet was born in 1857 to a physician father and a mother of modest artistic talent in Nice, France. Alfred and his mother moved to Paris after his parents' divorce to pursue his education at a distinguished high school. He was not the best student there. In fact, he later remembered with anger that a teacher had once said to him that he would "never have a 'true' philosophic spirit. (Cited in Gould, 1996, p. 183)" He then received his license to practice law, but never completed the graduate work. He tried medicine but did not complete that either. In his early twenties, his distress in finding a vocation apparently led to a breakdown and a six-month rest cure at approximately the age of 20.

Then, Binet finally set out on his own. He began his interest in psychology by reading the works of associationist J.S. Mill (see Chapter 3), publishing his first paper on his work in 1880 and his first book on an extension of his views in 1886. But he also read widely in the psychology of his day, on topics such as evolution, free will and determinism and the nature of consciousness. Although he would later do numerous psychophysical and experimental self-observation laboratory experiments and review dozens of them in his capacity as the editor of the journal *L'Anée Psychologique*, he was never fully convinced of their value. Unlike many psychologists of his day, he never learned enough German to be converted by Wundt. Instead, he was fluent in English; when he finally discarded the notion that all thought could be explained by the association of ideas, he eventually became a Functionalist in effect if not in name.

Another reason for his rejection of the associationist approach was his developing interest in the unconscious, not discussed by Mill. In 1883, his former classmate Joseph Babinski introduced Binet to Jean Charcot (see Chapter 9) and he would spend the next 7 years at the Salpêtrière. There, he would study the phenomenon that Mesmer had called Animal Magnetism. But Binet and his colleague Féré took the term literally. When hypnotized, the women at the Salpêtrière could easily be positioned at will, like dolls and the pose would remain. A patient in the trance would be placed with both arms straight on a table. Then, for example, Binet would position the patient's left arm up with the left finger and thumb extended. The magnet would be placed near the right hand. After two minutes, the left arm would slowly come down and the right arm would go up. (Binet & Féré, 1888, p. 125). One could similarly close the right eyelid and open the left, simply by moving the magnet across the patient's head from one side to the other. Binet and Féré even claimed that the magnet reversed "complementary emotions" like complementary colors: The magnet could turn love to hate or happiness to sadness!

In their book on the subject, Binet and Féré (1888) followed Charcot's views to the letter (see Chapter 9): only hysterics, because of their hereditary degeneration, could by hypnotized; the patients would exhibit the three stages of "le grand hysterie" and so on. But other researchers, particularly the Belgian J.L.R. Delboeuf (1831–1898), were skeptical. He visited Salpêtrière to see for himself and indeed saw some patients that seemed to have the symptoms described. But he also saw some of the magnetism experiments repeated:

> ... there, finally, I was present at the experiments on transfer. But when I saw how they did these last experiments; when I saw that they neglected elementary precautions, for example, not to talk in front of the subjects, announcing in fact aloud what was going to happen; that, instead of working with an electromagnet activated without the knowledge of either the subject or the experimenter, that latter was satisfied to draw from his pocket a heavy horseshoe; when I saw that there was not even a *machine-électrique* in the laboratory, I was assailed with doubts which, insensibly, undermined my faith in all the rest.
> (Delboeuf, 1889, translated and cited by Wolf, 1973, p. 49)

In the late 1880s, a debate raged between Charcot's advocates and followers of Hippolyte Bernheim (1840–1919) of Nancy, France. Not only could Delboeuf and Bernheim not replicate the results once the proper controls were added, they *could* replicate the experiments *without* the proper controls—or without the magnet! They could get the effects by suggesting to the patient that a bottle or piece of paper was magnetized or they could announce that they were magnetizing an arm while really magnetizing a leg and the patient would follow only the instructions! (Bernheim, 1897, cited by Wolf, 1973). Burned by these results, Binet broke with Charcot in 1890 and finally retracted his claims in an 1892 article.

Binet recognized that his patients had been under the influence of suggestibility, but he was not done learning the lesson of its dangers. In the late 1890's, he and his colleague Theodore Simon measured the "cephalic volume" of hundreds of children's heads using a fabric tape measure to assess circumference. This measure was then correlated with a child's class rank, as assessed by the children's teachers. The mean difference between the groups of smart vs. dull children was very small, about a milliliter, in spite of having measured over 250 subjects. Binet regretfully but manfully admitted his error in print: He and Simon had not been blind to the children's class status when doing the measurements and even the small differences in the expected direction could be due to wishful thinking on the researchers' part: "I feared that in making measurements on heads with the intention of finding a difference, I would be led to increase, unconsciously and in good faith, the cephalic volume of intelligent heads and to decrease that of unintelligent heads (Binet, 1900, p. 323, cited in Gould, 1996)." Because the bias is unconscious, even well-meaning interpreters can be biased.

Characteristically, Binet took this sad failure to heart. He would later bitterly call suggestibility "the cholera of psychology," and after his test was developed he would warn against overinterpretation of the scores almost every chance he got. He would even publish a book on the subject (*La Suggestibilité*, Binet, 1900) that would anticipate insights on children's vulnerability to coercive interviewing in courtroom trials over 90 years later (see e.g. Ceci & Bruck, 1995).

The Importance of Individual Differences in Complex Tasks

But here we must come to an understanding of what meaning to give to that word so vague and so comprehensive, "the intelligence." Nearly all the phenomena with which psychology concerns itself are phenomena of intelligence: sensation, perception, are intellectual manifestations as much as reasoning. Should we therefore bring into our examination the measure of sensation after the manner of the psychophysicists? Should we put to the test all of his psychological processes? A slight reflection has shown us that this would indeed be a waste of time.

It seems to us that in intelligence, there is a fundamental faculty, the alteration or the lack of which, is of the utmost importance for practical life. This faculty is judgment, otherwise called good sense, practical sense, initiative, the faculty of adapting oneself to circumstances. To judge well, to comprehend well, to reason well, these are the essential activities of intelligence. A person may be a moron or an imbecile if he is lacking in judgment; but with good judgment, he can never be either.

(Binet & Simon, 1973/1916 [English], pp. 42–43; original date in French, 1905)

After he left the Salpêtrière, Binet was somewhat at loose ends. He studied embryology with his father-in-law, a recognized expert in the field. He wrote a curious book titled The *Psychic Life of Micro-Organisms*, claiming to have seen adaptive behavior in them. He began work that would culminate in a doctorate in 1894. His dissertation in natural science was entitled "A Contribution to the Study of the Subintestinal Nervous System of Insects."

So it would seem that Binet would be headed almost anywhere except towards what he became known for. *We* know what he is known for, however, and because of that we can see the beginnings of his interests in the development of intelligence in this period of floundering. With extra time on his hands, he began to devise little intelligence tests for his daughters, three and five years old in 1890. He realized, as most parents do, that his two daughters had very different personalities. He asked his girls to describe a house. Madeline, the older daughter, focused on the concrete details of the scene and described them succinctly and accurately. Little Alice, by contrast, saw the task as an opportunity to tell a story about the people who lived in that house and precociously used the house as symbol of the people who lived in it. Binet was therefore convinced of great individual differences in intellectual tasks. Furthermore, he began to realize that intelligence was a global function, not something that can be explained by diligently explaining every cognitive step in every little isolated process of perception and thought (as Wundt would have preferred to do). In a study on sensitivity of touch, he said, "in external perception, the exterior force does not dominate us; rather it is we—our intelligence—who dominate it" (Binet, 1903, in Pollack & Brenner, 1969, p. 28).

In one of the little tasks he gave his children, for example, he would place two groups of small white counters on the table and ask the child to choose which group has more. His four-year-old daughter could usually guess (or count) which group was bigger. When he replaced the small white counters in one group with larger green ones, however, the larger one was seen to have more, even when there were fewer green counters than white ones (Binet, 1968/1890a).[1] Thus, perception is not a stable or static process, but one influenced by higher-level thought.

Other inklings of the famous intelligence test come from another 1890 study of children's perceptions. He finds that his daughters could recognize drawings of animals as such by 19 months, but no pictures of body parts until after age 4. In a brief vocabulary test that is very like the one given in the latest version of the Stanford-Binet, he noted that the young children's definitions were usually based on functions rather than categories or descriptions. For example, to be thirsty is "to drink and drink and drink."

From these very basic beginnings, Binet realized the great importance of individual differences in thought processes. Even more importantly, he recognized that the more complex the thought process, the more these differences matter:

> The higher and more complex a process is, the more it varies in individuals: sensations vary from one individual to another, but less so than memory; memory of sensations varies less than memory of ideas and so on. The result is that if one wishes to study the differences between two individuals, it is necessary to begin with the most intellectual and complex processes and it is only secondarily necessary to consider the simple and elementary processes.
> (Binet & Henri, 1895, cited in Cairns & Cairns, 2006, p. 103)

So, around 1895, Binet knew that intelligence should not be seen as a simple set of perceptual abilities, but a complex process of adaptive judgment. He knew that there were many individual differences in these processes. He and his colleagues investigated everything from body measurements to handwriting analysis. He had begun to come up with a set of cognitive tasks for testing. But he still treated the problem of subnormal intelligence as a diagnosis. He conducted several detailed case studies of lower-than-normal and higher-than-normal intelligence, feeling that only in-depth, time-consuming portraits of individuals could be valid (Cairns & Cairns, 2006). As late as 1904, Binet was still holding this view, when necessity intervened.

The late 1800s was a time of gradual reform in the French educational system. In 1899, the Free Society for the Psychological Study of the Child was founded, in part to force the French Ministry of Public Instruction to deal with the problem of how to determine which children needed more help than the average student. The society contained teachers, principals, government inspectors, professors, lawyers and others with interests in education and was intended to be France's counterpart to American G. Stanley Hall's child study movement. Binet, who then ran the experimental psychology laboratories at the Sorbonne, was president of the society by 1903. By early 1904, the society had submitted a petition to the government demanding that poorly performing children be given special classes (Wolf, 1973). Binet threw himself passionately into the problem of how to test these children, and now, the society would provide the resources to do so.

Binet's biographer, Theta Wolf (1973), argues that Binet's insight of age-normed tests came at a specific moment in 1904. The society's commission on memory conducted a simple study of memorization of long strings of numbers (later called digit span) and lines of Latin prose by 10- to 14-year-olds. In the public schools of the day, children of wide ranges of ages were often placed in grades according to ability, so that a 10-year-old might be placed in grades from 5 to 8, for example. Binet noticed that 10-year-old children in the fifth grade remembered less than half the number of lines as 10-year-olds in the seventh grade! This finding was mostly replicated in a study of 250 children in six schools. "*We are here at the very heart of psychology,*" he wrote (Wolf, 1973, p. 166, emphasis in original).

In the same crucial year, other teacher members of the society were devising achievement tests of mathematics or general knowledge and giving them to children of varying ages. Most significantly, physicians Blin and Damaye (see Damaye (1903) and Wolf (1973) for discussion in English; also Nicolas, Andrieu, Croizet, Sanitioso, & Burman, 2013) conducted a study of 250 subjects incarcerated for moral degeneracy for crimes such as kleptomania or sexual abuse—they argued, improbably, that these subjects' intellects were untouched—from the ages 7–26 with 20 questions and a total score of 100 (Binet & Simon, 1905/1916, p. 28). The test tapped such general knowledge as names for objects, body parts and definitions of trades or professions. They argued that the test examined "observable behaviors" defined practically by "popular and varied notions" (Wolf, 1973, p. 175) rather than by psychological notions of attention or memory per se. Binet removed the questions answerable by simple yes or no answers as being too susceptible to suggestion and decreased the number of items requiring very specific knowledge. Then Binet and Simon went out and gathered data from dozens of normal and mentally retarded adults and children on their item performance. Blin and Damaye had tested only those in hospitals or other institutions: The use of a normal sample was new. Binet and Simon added items based on their own hunches or from suggestions by teachers. Those tests that showed no differences among ages were thrown out. Interestingly, they preferred items that showed noticeable differences between two different ages, clear recognizable breakpoints in success.

The tests, to be orally given by a trained and sensitive examiner, were then arranged by difficulty, with some overweighting at the lower levels, so as to provide the ability to diagnose differences among the more or less affected retarded children. Tests that had been passed by 80% of children at a given age during the process of normative data gathering were placed at that *mental level*, and test items were given from easiest to hardest. A child was said to be at the mental level where he had passed all of the items of that level. Partial credit was given for occasional items passed above that level, until all the items at a given level were failed.

The resulting test (Binet & Simon, 1905/1916) contained just 30 items, shown in Table 10.1. Compared to the current intelligence tests, the test is quite easy. Note that the first item, "*le regard,*" is simply tested by the examiner lighting a match and watching the child follow the match. The child passes the 16th item by determining the difference between "paper and cardboard" or "a fly and a butterfly"—these items distinguish between the five- and seven-year levels. When the test is given to an adult, one must get all the way to item 27 to test the upper limit of retardation, approximately age 12, with comprehension questions (e.g. "When a person has offended you and has come to offer his apologies, what should you do?"). The

Table 10.1 The Tests on Binet and Simon's (1905) First Intelligence Test

1. "*Le Regard*"
2. Prehension Provoked by a Tactile Stimulus
3. Prehension Provoked by a Visual Perception
4. Recognition of Food
5. Quest of Food Complicated by a Slight Mechanical Difficulty
6. Execution of Simple Commands and Imitation of Simple Gesture
7. Verbal Knowledge of Objects
8. Verbal Knowledge of Pictures
9. Naming of Designated Objects
10. Immediate Comparison of Two Lines of Unequal Lengths
11. Repetition of Three Figures
12. Comparison of Two Weights
13. Suggestibility
14. Verbal Definition of Known Objects
15. Repetition of Sentences of Fifteen Words
16. Comparison of Known Objects from Memory
17. Exercise of Memory on Pictures
18. Drawing a Design from Memory
19. Immediate Repetition of Figures
20. Resemblances of Several Known Objects Given From Memory
21. Comparison of Lengths
22. Five Weights to Be Placed in Order
23. Gap in Weights
24. Exercise Upon Rhymes
25. Verbal Gaps to Be Filled
26. Synthesis of Three Words in One Sentence
27. Reply to an Abstract Question
28. Reversal of the Hands of a Clock
29. Paper Cutting
30. Definitions of Abstract Terms

first intelligence test does not actually offer medical diagnoses; Binet and Simon found that doctors were notoriously inconsistent in applying the accepted labels idiot, imbecile or weak. Neither does the test imply a disease process or prognosis. It does not include the notions of mental age, intelligence quotient or superior levels of intelligence, all of which were added by later researchers. It did not even test the minimum that a child needs to know to enter a school grade. Rather the tests are properly *psychological* rather than pedagogical. They are *holistic tests of relatively complex judgment*, rather than laboratory memory or attention tasks: Although they do not require schooling, they do require knowledge about the world. And they had been *empirically validated*—given to a large number of both normal and abnormal adults and children from places like the Salpêtrière as well as normal children from public schools. The only tests that were kept were those that *showed reliable age differences in children*. Binet was well aware that most children who *have* been to school would do better on the test and that children kept out of school would do worse. That they do not *require* school does *not* mean that the scores were *unaffected by schooling*.

Binet's Cautious Views on the Development of Intelligence

> · Our purpose is to be able to measure the intellectual capacity of a child who is brought to us in order to know whether he is normal or retarded. We should therefore study his condition at the time and that only. We have nothing to do with either his past history or with his future; consequently, we shall neglect his etiology and shall make no attempt to distinguish between acquired and congenital idiocy.... As to that which concerns his future, we shall exercise the same abstinence; we do not attempt to prepare or establish a prognosis and we leave unanswered the question of whether his retardation is curable or even improvable. We shall limit ourselves to ascertaining the truth with regard to his present mental state
>
> —Alfred Binet (1916/1905, p. 37)

In part because Binet is known for creating such an eminently practical test and its design was pragmatic, it is sometimes said that he had no theory of intelligence. Nothing could be further from the truth. His theoretical sophistication about intelligence was probably more advanced than most of his peers, in part because he had struggled for so long with the question. The easy answer would have been to follow the eugenicists and mental testers who took over his test after his death in 1911 (see Chapter 4 and later) and to state that intelligence was innate and stable (Galton), heritable by a single recessive gene and resistant to environmental influences (H.H. Goddard), observable in the simplest tasks (James McKeen Catell) and differed by race and criminality, so that lower intelligence was a threat to the moral order of society (Laughlin, Davenport). As far as we can tell, Binet agreed with absolutely *none* of these assumptions.

In part he didn't, because he recognized that they were only assumptions:

> A few modern philosophers ... assert that an individual's intelligence is a fixed quantity, a quantity which cannot be increased. We must protest and react against this brutal pessimism. We shall attempt to prove that it is without foundation.
>
> (Binet, 1909/1984, pp. 105–106)

On the contrary, he believed that children who scored poorly on the test should be put in classes of "mental orthopedics" (p. 111) to raise their intelligence, not infinitely, but substantially. He noted that eventually, in education, one may reach the limit of their intellectual capability, but it may take years of growth and training to get there. As we noted above, Binet believed that the most functionally important aspect of intelligence is judgment, but that did not mean that he believed that intelligence consisted only of judgment. On the contrary, he was aware that in order to exercise judgment, many other skills were necessary, each of which could perhaps be improved, leading to increases in function:

> Now if we consider that intelligence is not a single function, indivisible and of a particular essence, but rather that it is formed by the chorus of all the little functions of discrimination, observation, retention, etc., the plasticity and extensibility of which have been determined, it will appear that the same law governs the

whole as its parts and that consequently anyone's intelligence can be developed. With practice, training and above all, method, we manage to increase our attention, our memory, our judgment and literally to become more intelligent than we were before.

(Binet, 1909/1984, p. 107)

Another reason Binet was cautious in theorizing was that he knew what he did not know. He knew he did not know how many skills there were in intelligence. He did not know how fast each skill normally developed and how much of the development was due to learning. Some skills might develop quickly and others slowly. Some skills might be necessary for other skills to develop but not necessarily sufficient. For all these reasons, he declined to offer prognoses with his tests or even to claim that they measured a linear quantity: "The scale, properly speaking, does not permit the measure of the intelligence, because intellectual quantities are not superposable and cannot be measured as linear surfaces are measured" Binet, 1905/1973, p. 40.

Most importantly, although he suggested that a rule of thumb for noting retardation would be three years behind in school, he was careful not to take the term retarded literally as a developmental delay. He did not use the term mental age but preferred the term mental level instead. (The classic ratio intelligence quotient of mental age divided by chronological age times 100 was proposed by the German psychologist William Stern in 1912). A mental age suggests a permanent condition, as no environmental condition can change one's age. Mental level is a much more neutral term, something that denotes merely a test score that could be raised and lowered by many factors.

The test underwent two more revisions under his direction, in 1908 and 1911 (before his death later that year). But then, the translation and updating of the test passed into the hands of the American and British eugenicist movements, led by H.H. Goddard in the U.S. and Cyril Burt in the U.K. These researchers had no such reservations. They believed, without foundation, that the test measured reliably a stable, internal, global and heritable mental quantity, all things that Binet would have disapproved of and of which Simon later said was a "betrayal of the scale's objectives." This sordid story is told in Chapter 4, both because the foundation of these eugenicist beliefs is rooted in misinterpretations of Darwin and because Binet does not deserve to be tarred with the same brush as these researchers. In his last years, Binet was clearly a developmental experimental psychologist tasked with helping children in school. That is what his test is still best used for, and it deserves to escape its historical taint at last.

Hall's Students and the Binet Test

Henry Herbert Goddard (1866–1957)

Hall's commitment to biology and simplistic genetic determinism was passed down to his graduate students, all of whom began their careers as eugenicists—and touted Binet's test as a method to prove the inheritance of intelligence—though each moderated his views later in life. Henry Herbert Goddard began life as a bright ambitious

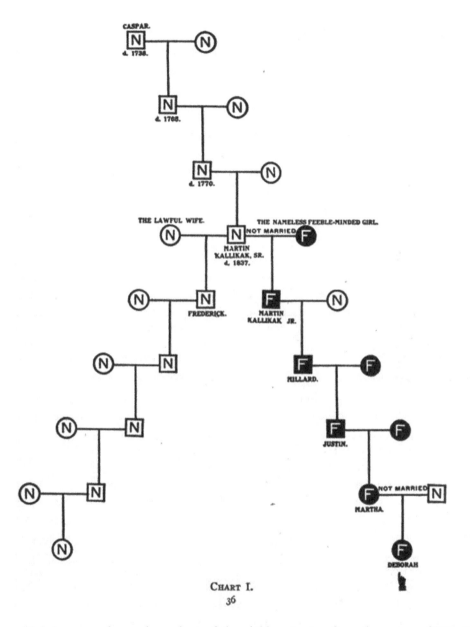

Figure 10.2 A supposed genealogy chart of the children issuing from the union of "Martin Kallikak" and an unnamed, presumably feeble-minded "tavern girl." N = Normal. F = Feeble-minded. Sx = Sexually immoral. A = Alcoholic. I = Insane. Sy = Syphilitic. C = Criminalistic. D = Deaf. d. inf. = died in infancy. T = Tuberculous. Hand points to child in Vineland Institution. The offspring chart of Martin and his lawful wife, Susan (not shown), are all said to be normal. The data are based on reputation only, based on highly informal interviews by Elisabeth Kite.

Source: Goddard, H.H. (1912). *The Kallikak Family: A Study in the Heredity of Feeblemindedness*. New York: Macmillan. Online: Gutenberg.

boy of a solid Maine Quaker upbringing during a time of great revival of religious faith in general. His father died when he was nine and his mother Sarah was a famous traveling Quaker evangelist. Herbert spent his young life in boarding schools, where he chafed at the constraints of his decidedly nonscientific classical education. After attending Haverford College, outside of Philadelphia, he took a series of teaching jobs. He was once again teaching back in Maine when he heard one of Hall's famous quasi-religious speeches exhorting the optimistic secular gospel of the child study movement. Goddard was then accepted to study with Hall himself at Clark University in 1896. He completed his dissertation under Hall on the scientific explanation of the many "mind-cure" movements then in America, including everything from garden-variety quacks to Mary Baker Eddy's Christian Scientist movement. His answer was that suggestion, whether it be from hypnotism or a simple placebo effect, was the source of success of these movements and that we are susceptible to such supposed powers thanks to our highly evolved flexible brains. Soon, Goddard was himself writing circulars claiming that child study was "a great educational revival, in which the hearts of teachers and parents are being purified though the holy fires of a regenerated love and newly consecrated devotion to the rights of childhood" (Goddard, 1900, cited in Zenderland, 1998, p. 49).

This kind of zeal was needed, as schools were seeing overwhelming growth; although in 1890, only 1% had attended high schools (Joncich, 1968), the number of children in high schools increased by 250% in the succeeding decade alone. Primary school attendance, by now state-supported in the United States, had increased 54% (Zenderland, 1998, p. 57). This kind of marriage of science and religion, social reform and medicine and "mental hygiene" was common in the progressive era in America. In this spirit of a calling to better the world through science, Goddard accepted a post as director of the Training School for Feeble-Minded Girls and Boys in Vineland, New Jersey, in 1906. Immediately, as he first threw himself into the work, he recognized that he had a problem. Observing closely the 300 children in his care, he noticed a wide variety of mental disabilities in them. Some could memorize scripture at great length but could not tie their shoes. Some were aggressive and some submissive. Medical authorities were woefully contradictory on the subject. He struggled to find useful psychological tests, consulting Lightner Witmer at the University of Pennsylvania and inviting experts to meet with members of the "Feeble-Minded Club," a group of influential benefactors and professionals who had an interest in special education. Nothing he found worked better than the intuitive judgments of his staff in predicting children's success. Finally, on a trip to Europe in 1908, while assiduously visiting some 90 special schools, he came across a flier by an obscure Belgian psychologist praising Binet's methods. Goddard, having not met with Binet while in France, met with one of Binet's Belgian colleagues and saw the test in action. When he returned home, he found a report of Binet and Simon's 1908 revision, translated it and gave it to 400 children. By 1910, the data from this study persuaded members of the American Association for the Study of the Feeble-Minded to endorse its use, unanimously.

The use of the Binet test took off in American schools in the ways one might expect. On the one hand, Goddard and his colleagues lobbied school systems urgently; his first coup was in New Jersey in 1910; New York followed soon after, when extrapolating from a small sample, Goddard calculated that 15,000 children in New York City needed special services. Vineland held summer schools for dozens of special education teachers from as far away as Salt Lake City. When these teachers went home, they started using the Binet tests without permission of their schools, but their use inevitably spread. By the time Lewis Terman would make the classic Stanford-Binet revision of 1916, Goddard had obligingly mailed out 22,000 copies to anyone who had asked, everywhere in the country, trained test administrators or not (Zenderland, 1998)!

Goddard was so convinced of the worth of the new scientific test that at first he had the view that mental retardation was a recessive single-gene defective trait: Following the new science of "Mendelism," he believed a child born to two parents who were morons would of necessity be a moron himself. What would follow from such a union would be a child who would almost inevitably descend to poverty, immorality and alcoholism. With feeblemindedness would come a lack of moral self-control. Thus, care should be taken to prevent such a child from breeding.

Goddard supported his work by sending out assistants to the field to interview relatives and neighbors of residents of Vineland. An investigation of the heredity of one of his charges, pseudonymously named Deborah Kallikak (from the Greek *kalos*, "good," and *kakos*, "bad") became *The Kallikak Family: A Study in the Heredity of Feeblemindedness* (1912). The ancestor of the "Kallikak" line was Martin, who had fathered children from both an upstanding Quaker wife and a feebleminded tavern girl around the time of the American Revolution. Of the 480 descendants of the tavern girl, the intelligence of more than half could not be determined, but among the rest, 143 were "conclusively" determined to be feebleminded and only 46 normal. Of the 496 on the "good" side, however, all but two were normal, and the good half of the family was so proud of its lineage that it had kept convenient records.

The Kallikak study was followed soon by Goddard's most extensive work, *Feeblemindedness: Its Causes and Consequences* (1914), which, using the same retrospective methods on a larger scale, was replete with genealogy charts and judgments that combined sketchy impressions with confident and definitive claims.

The data for both works was, however, all retrospective and composed of anecdotes told over kitchen tables to Goddard's chief researcher, Elisabeth Kite. In many cases, neither the questions that elicited the neighbors' stories nor their verbatim answers were recorded. Thus, when later challenged to come up with the name of the tavern girl that founded the bad line of the Kallikaks, Kite could not do so (Zenderland, 1998).

One of the ironies of Goddard's work, especially as seen from our current perspective, is that Goddard did not consider himself a reactionary protecting white upper-class privilege. He thought of himself as a progressive, trying to better the lives of those who were mentally challenged by improving methods of detection of those who needed help and touting eugenics as a preventative measure. Unlike those at Charles Davenport's and Harry Laughlin's Cold Spring Harbor Institute, he did not use his data for arguing that welfare payments should be discontinued but suggested they should be increased. Later in life, he recanted his earlier belief in eugenics.

Lewis M. Terman (1877–1956)

Hall's student Lewis M. Terman (1877–1956), at Stanford, converted the instrument from Binet's screening device for mental retardation to a test of the whole range of intelligence up to "superior adult" that became the Stanford-Binet test. Like his intellectual hero, Francis Galton, Terman began his career as a committed eugenicist (see Chapter 4): He was most concerned with finding and researching the lives of the "gifted" (a label Terman invented) individuals at the top of the range. His longitudinal study of the lives of about 1500 of these children with IQs above 135, the Genetic Study of Genius (later renamed the Terman Study of Gifted Children) is the first and longest-running major longitudinal study in developmental psychology; it began in the 1920s and will continue until the last participant dies. Indeed, many of the children in Terman's study were successful, but as the study contained no control group children of average intelligence, it is difficult to say whether the study participants were more successful than other children. Terman frequently intervened in the lives of his subjects in a fatherly fashion to insure their success, writing letters of recommendation for jobs and, in one case, saving the family of a Japanese-American child from the U.S. internment camps during the Second World War. In some cases, being picked as a "Termite" was itself encouraging enough to a child to inspire him or her to achieve; this effect and Terman's well-intentioned interventions probably lessened the value of the study's results (Leslie, 2000). But the study at least proved that smart children were normal in other ways, rather than sickly or neurotic, and the research served as a wonderful advertisement for the spread of the use of intelligence tests in American life. Finally, that almost every school in the United States has a "gifted and talented" class is surely, at least in part, due to Terman's pioneering efforts.

Arnold L. Gesell (1880–1961)

Hall's most successful graduate student from the period of his developmental work was probably Arnold L. Gesell (1880–1961). Gesell's time with G. Stanley Hall was brief, but formative. He was a self-assured, calm young man from a solid Wisconsin German-American background. Like Goddard and Terman, he was also interested in the problems of exceptional children, having done stints as a teacher and principal before and after receiving his degree in psychology from Wisconsin under Hall's student Joseph Jastrow. He spent a scant two years at Clark getting his doctorate under Hall, absorbing his mentor's respect for stages of growth. He accepted a post at Yale in 1911 as a professor of "child hygiene" and was quickly made director of Yale's new Psycho-Clinic, even before he had finished an additional MD degree. Although Gesell began his career as a socialist, intending to reform the schools along the democratic lines of John Dewey, by 1913, he had become a eugenicist. Citing an estimate of 26% of feebleminded and insane inhabitants in his hometown of Alma, Wisconsin, population 1000, he stated,

> We need not wait for the perfection of the infant science of eugenics before proceeding upon a course of supervision and segregation which will prevent the

Figure 10.3 Arnold Gesell (1880–1961) examining a baby in his observation dome while research associates and camera operators observe through the scrim

Source: Getty Images

horrible renewal of this defective protoplasm that is contaminating the stream of village life.

(Gesell, 1913, p. 15, cited by Harris, 2011, p. 311)

Perhaps because he had training in both psychology and medicine, Gesell recognized in a way that Goddard and Terman did not, that before one could define exceptional or abnormal at the bottom or top of the distribution, one needed to define what normal meant. In particular, he needed to understand not only the individual difference approach at each age, but also how intelligence *developed* from infancy onward. His method was simple: He would use the high technology of his age and make silent films of many children at each age (Gesell's father had owned a photography business). He constructed a dome, covered with muslin on the inside, so that when lighted from within, the walls appeared solid to a baby and hid the noisy, scary equipment. But Gesell would sit in the dark on the other side, calmly filming through the scrim. He would then review the films for common behaviors and growth in physical coordination. He and his long-time colleagues, Frances Ilg (1902–1981), a pediatrician, and Louise Bates Ames (1908–1996), would then fashion a portrait of each age and disseminate the information in nontechnical language (Ames wrote books with titles like *Your Two Year Old: Terrible or Tender?* or *Your Four Year Old: Wild and Wonderful*). Ames and Ilg would found the Gesell Institute of Human Development in 1950. Gesell, Ilg and Ames quickly became identified with the maturational point of view in child development. In the 1930s through the 1950s, Gesell's gentle manner and Ames's friendly books of milestones were highly reassuring to parents. A biologically timed childhood is preferable to a Victorian one, in which parents are always on the watch for spoiling their children or otherwise leading them into sin. Even John B. and Rosalie Raynor Watson wrote in 1928 about the dangers of "Too Much Mother Love," as one of their chapter titles would have it. In Gesell's approach, the child knows what he or she is doing; the parent is an educated, informed, protective observer of an unfolding self. This approach was later followed implicitly by such child-rearing pediatrician experts such as Dr. Benjamin Spock (1903–1998) and Dr. T. Berry Brazelton (1918–2018).

James Mark Baldwin (1861–1934)

American functionalist psychologist, James Mark Baldwin, is little known by today's undergraduate psychology students, but he was once highly regarded among his peers, who ranked him as the fifth most important psychologist in the world in 1897. Baldwin traveled a road familiar to psychologists of his generation, from philosophy of mind to Wundtian experimentalism and neural materialism to a strongly evolutionary functionalism. And then he went beyond it, to a highly original view of the development and evolution of mind and social interaction. Baldwin, like Freud, wanted a complete system of human activity; his theory integrated evolution not only with development of children but also with social psychology and the development of logical thought and even aesthetic judgments (Wozniak, 2001). This was a tall order and even to the extent that he incompletely achieved his goal, his dense writing style sometimes prevented him from communicating his theory clearly to others.

Baldwin created the first psychological laboratory in Canada at the University of Toronto in 1893; he co-founded the functionalist journal *Psychological Review* in 1894—to this day one of the most influential journals in psychology—and he occupied the first endowed chair in the United States for scientific psychology at Johns Hopkins. By 1897, he was the president of the APA (Wozniak, 2001). Like Sigmund Freud, William James and John Dewey, Baldwin was a systematizer rather than a reductionist: Whatever he learned went into his theory as he tried to account for new developments in physiology, psychology and evolutionary theory. What follows is a brief summary of these strands of his thought.

Philosophical Foundations for a Linkage Between Thought and Things

Baldwin's psychology was always, first and foremost, informed by epistemology. How do our minds come to know about the world, or as Baldwin would put it, what is the relationship between thought and things? As an undergraduate, he was aware of three strands of thought that suggested that the way we see the world is in some way constrained by the natural construction of the mind. First, the Scottish philosopher Thomas Reid's (1710–1796) "common sense" philosophy was taught to Baldwin by the Scots Presbyterians who ran Princeton in those days. Simply put, the common sense philosophy, serving as an antidote to Hume's skepticism, claims that there are constraints on how our mind may see the world. We all have the same constraints; therefore, there should be some statements to which we all must agree (Reid, 1764). Rightly considered, these statements map onto the world and cannot contradict one another. The totality of such statements constitute reality. Baldwin also dabbled briefly with the pantheistic monism of the Renaissance rationalist philosopher Baruch Spinoza (1632–1677) (Baldwin, 1926). In Spinoza's view, thought and things are two attributes of the same substance, which themselves are only attributes of God himself. God is Nature and Nature is God, containing everything that is. For every thought there is a thing, which is but two sides of the same coin. Finally, Baldwin was keenly aware of Kant's view that there are certain *a priori* structures of mind that must exist in order for us to process the sensations that become our internal view of the world.

These three early philosophical influences set Baldwin as a rationalist instead of an empiricist. Logic constitutes the structure of mind and the ways by which we interpret experience. Experience alone does not add up to thought. But Baldwin recognized that to continue in this path of pure philosophy would doom him to irrelevancy in the late 19th century. Like many of his contemporaries, he took a trip to Germany to learn "the New Psychology" of Fechner and Wundt in 1884 and 1885. On this trip, Baldwin came to believe that the processes of attention, sensation and perception behaved according to natural laws that could be mathematically measured. That the mind behaved according to laws need not be solely proven by the logical methods of philosophers, but also by empirical investigation. By 1890, Baldwin had left religion and metaphysics behind, but not his obsession with thought and things (Wozniak, 2001).

Also in 1889, an ordinary but earth-shattering thing occurred to James Mark Baldwin: He had a daughter and then another soon after (Wozniak, 2001). Children have a disconcerting way of blowing philosophical systems out of the water. At birth, they know very little, cannot introspect and are not capable of rational thought and yet they learn sophisticated things quickly as a matter of course. Parents cannot load them with knowledge and then wind them up and let them go; they must learn on their own, resiliently correcting errors through their own actions while never breaking down. Logical thought is built by the experience of growing children, not inherited by them as a genetic birthright. Over the next few years, like Alfred Binet, Charles Darwin and Wilhelm Preyer, Baldwin observed his daughters closely and carefully. He began to realize that the relationship of our thoughts to things in the world cannot be a predetermined given, as Spinoza or Kant would have it, but must be revised on the fly (Wozniak, 2001). Even though children do not think like adults, they appear to acquire, through their own actions on the world, through physical reaching as infants, through symbolic actions as children and through approximations to logic as an adolescent, successive stages of partially adequate modes of thought.

Mental Development of the Child and the Race (1895)

At this point, Baldwin began thinking seriously about the three roots of functionalism: first, that all behavior is adaptive; second, that it is acquired and refined by continuous, self-correcting loops of sensation and action; and third and most importantly, that it is both a product of evolution and sometimes a force directing it. His first description of his thoughts on the matter was in *Mental Development of Child and the Race* (1895/2001).[2]

All Thought and Behavior Is Functionally Adaptive

As Baldwin explained in this groundbreaking though difficult book, young organisms are not blank slates. Because they are evolved organisms, there are certain things that they need to acquire, such as food, oxygen, territory, shelter from elements or predators and so forth. Thus, any organism is in some kind of mismatch or disequilibrium with its environment and is motivated to resolve the discrepancy, to seek out the kind of stimulation that will satiate its hunger, allay its fear or simply satisfy its curiosity.

Thus, all behavior and thought is functionally adaptive. *Every evolved organism, especially humans, must have goals that need to be satisfied.* These actions can be as simple as reaching for an object (for an infant) or, for an older child, connecting with a baseball while swinging a bat or solving a math problem. Once an action brings this satisfaction, the child is motivated to repeat the action, not merely for reinforcement (which in any event is a concept invented after Baldwin) but also to keep the good stimulation happening. Baldwin called this tendency to repeat motor actions over and over again to maintain the state of pleasant consequences a **circular reaction**.

All Learning Happens in Self-Corrective Feedback Loops of Sensation and Action

Circular reactions are essentially behavioral feedback loops. Every attempt to grasp an object (e.g. when an infant reaches toward a mobile above her crib) is slightly different, leading to slightly different results; errors decrease over time, the action becomes faster and more efficient and a series of actions can fire off all at once to get good stimulations. This is our old friend habit, what James called the "great flywheel of society" (James, 1890/1983, p. 125). Once an infant gets a habit, of course, she can deploy it in other similar situations; when she gets good stimulation back, that is called an act of **assimilation**: using a similar action in a new place. But sometimes, habits do not work in a new situation. If an infant could not break, replace and revise habits, he could not grow. When old habits do not work, children create novel behaviors. Baldwin called the process of creating new adaptive patterns of behavior **accommodation**. Like the other functionalists (see e.g. Dewey's explanation of the reflex arc in Chapter 7), Baldwin believed that there was no place where a sensation was converted to an idea and then back into a response, but that behavior was a continual feedback loop of action, successive approximations to a goal, maintained in an effort to adapt to the environment. "The environment" as a singular noun is perhaps a misleading term because it too is always changing, keeping an organism always off balance, always acting, always learning.

Baldwin then developed a stage theory of cognitive development. We have seen stage theories before, first in Freud's theory of psychosexual development and then in G. Stanley Hall's Lamarckian and Haeckelian recapitulation theory of child development. Stage theories postulate that development happens not by simply building up copies of knowledge from the world, as John Locke's empiricist theory would suggest, or habits, as Thorndike and Skinner would have it. Rather, stage shifts imply that as a child reaches certain milestones in what they know or can do, shifts also occur in *how* they learn and act on the world.

According to Baldwin's theory, children who learn by the sensorimotor method of circular reaction feedback loops are prelogical. When preschool children begin to use symbols and language to reason deductively but make significant errors, they are in the quasi-logical stage of Baldwin's theory. In this stage, the child deals with the problem of the inner imagination vs. the outer world, the private self and the stubborn reliable outer world, between thoughts and things. The sense of self mediates between his inner life and the outer world. By imitating, the child takes the outside world in; by imagining, he plays with representations, memories and fancies of the outside world, and by play, he acts those fantasies out in the world, with the full belief that they are not real. It is through this feedback system that the child realizes that he has control of his inner world, the world of symbols, simply by thinking things into existence or imagining. He can also have control of at least some of the outer world through physical activity. *He learns about the separate realities of the inner and outer worlds by what he can do with them or to them.* In the logical period, children develop a non-egocentric view of themselves and the world: They recognize that objects have an independent reality and there is such a thing as a fact. Facts can be corroborated by gathering information on one's own and seeing if the new information corresponds with the old; they can also be affirmed by asking other people. They look for evidence and contradictions and thus can deal with gathering up information inductively and making conclusions or can deductively try to rectify contradictions (Baldwin, 1895/2001).

The concern of Baldwin's final stage, the hyperlogical period of adulthood, is not merely the stability of the physical world or what can be verified through logic or even our knowledge of the social world but the meaning that we assign to objects or beliefs. It involves artistic or aesthetic judgments. A good work of art is a "fitting" depiction of its idea. The pieces of plot and characterization, thrilling and poetic speeches and dialogue, all fit together to bring us to reflect on something important (Baldwin, 1906–1911). It is in this sense that Othello is about jealousy, but it is also about the inevitable fate that Othello's pride and weakness for jealousy places upon his character. We should at the end not only pity Desdemona, his murdered wife, but also Othello, who loves "not wisely, but too well." As we shall see, significant aspects of the first three stages of Baldwin's theory made it into to Jean Piaget's famous stage theory.

Baldwin's Evolutionary Theory: The Baldwin Effect

As I mentioned above, Baldwin's theory was extraordinarily ambitious: Like others of his generation, he was thunderstruck by the implications of evolutionary theory and wanted to make a self-consistent, non-contradictory theory unifying epistemology, development, evolution and social psychology. But he had a problem also common to intellectuals of his day: Should he bet on Darwin's directionless natural selection approach to evolution or Lamarck's and Haeckel's theories of acquired characteristics and recapitulation? Although the tide began turning towards natural selection starting with the experiments of August Weismann in the 1890s (see Chapter 4), the modern synthesis of genes and evolution was not finalized until the 1940s. Although he began his career leaning heavily towards recapitulation, as did Hall and Freud, he soon realized, along with C. Lloyd Morgan and Henry F. Osborne, that the neo-Darwinists were most likely right: Behaviors are not directly passed down from parent to child biologically; things learned by the body and brain can't be passed to the sex cells for reproduction.

What can be passed down is the capability for learning new behaviors. According to this theory, which Baldwin called organic selection but which modern biology calls the **Baldwin Effect**, primates who can learn behaviors quickly have an enormous advantage over those who cannot, and so the offspring of those primates should survive in greater numbers than those of the slow learners. This means that there is a higher likelihood of those in the smart lineage to rediscover at each generation useful behaviors. The behaviors most likely to survive would, in turn, be those that help survival of the offspring of that lineage, boosting their already considerable survival advantage. If the selection pressure were great enough, perhaps most of the survivors would be acquiring the behaviors almost automatically and an instinct would develop in the population. It might be even more likely, however, for evolution to favor those who had more flexible brains, with fewer instincts but greater behavioral plasticity, as was suggested by William James (see Chapter 7 and Baldwin, 1902). Such superflexible primates would (and did) populate the earth, whatever the ecological niche! One other consequence of such an evolutionary push towards plasticity and flexibility is the tendency, across evolutionary generations, to delay maturity of offspring. Across phylogeny, essentially, primate babies get younger and younger (more immature at birth) until they reach the situation of humans, whose offspring need a very long time of learning before reaching adulthood. The theory implies that youth equals flexibility of learning; modern neurophysiology supports Baldwin's intuition in that the brain is relatively malleable until puberty and relatively unchangeable after it.

Baldwin's Evolutionary Social Psychology

There is another way to pass down useful lessons without resorting to Lamarck, of course. Once a species has memory, consciousness and an ability to communicate, its members could teach one another adaptive behaviors, passing down knowledge non-genetically through culture. This, Baldwin said, was **social heredity**. In his award-winning book *Social and Ethical Interpretations in Mental Development* (Baldwin, 1899/1973), Baldwin suggests that the social world is not merely a new layer on top of the biological organism but truly critical to the development of our sense of self and our ideas. Recall that Baldwin's genetic epistemology suggests that we do not learn by merely copying things directly from the world. It is by imitating others that we come to learn something. We must *do* to understand. If this is the case, then the behaviors of others become part of ourselves. Moreover, when we assume that others have minds like us, we project onto others characteristics we know about ourselves. If the other is in us and our view of others is colored by our intuitions about ourselves, then it seems wrong to separate artificially the social world from the cognitive one.

Since we all imitate each other, culture serves as a generalizing force that makes us more like each other in our society, so that we can understand one another. But there is always the chance that someone will produce a new and adaptive variation, a new behavior (like literacy or women voting), a new commercial product or process (like email, cell phones or the internet in our day) or an original work of art. A new fashion may catch on or even a new religion, as when our ideas of a forgiving God replace those of a punishing one. If an idea is too weird, too far ahead of its time, it might not survive and might even create fear and skepticism in society or a backlash. But if it is built on common knowledge and extends it, and if it really helps us understand and adapt to our world, the innovation may spread throughout society.

Thus, James Mark Baldwin constructed a complete theory of psychology based on the tenets of functionalism. Humans are evolved organisms, who must adapt to fulfill their biological goals of reproduction, nutrition and safety. They learn by acting on the world and constructing feedback loops of experience. Experience is filtered through the structure and character of thought prevailing in developing in human ontogeny at any given stage of development. And this development of knowledge, about things, about self and about the social world, proceeds by survival of adaptive ideas. Finally, all of this learning in individual lives is contained within the grand sweep of evolution itself.

Why didn't Baldwin's theory catch on? What he probably considered his masterpiece, a three-volume work called *Thought and Things: A Study of the Development and Meaning of Thought or Genetic Logic* (Baldwin, 1906–1911), a dense philosophical treatise that essentially attempts to do nothing less than explain how slippery consciousness stabilizes across growth into the ability to think at the highest levels of abstraction, is little read today. Although Baldwin had done observations and the occasional experiment, by the late 1890s his theoretical ideas had far outstripped his or others' ability to verify them. He left behind no new methods with which to conduct experiments. But finally, we should not underestimate the power of historical bad luck. By 1908, Baldwin had left America for France, fired and disgraced for a personal indiscretion among black prostitutes in segregated Baltimore while running for the local school board (Wozniak, 2009). (The French, with a collective Gallic shrug, welcomed him with open arms.) These historical facts may explain why he may be one of the most important theorists in psychology you (or your professors) may never have heard of.

Bad luck for Baldwin was good luck for others. When Baldwin left, Johns Hopkins hired the energetic young firebrand John B. Watson (see Chapter 8). He received in the bargain the editorship of *Psychological Review*. It was here that Watson published his behaviorist manifesto "Psychology as the Behaviorist Views It," and thus the behaviorist movement began to eclipse Baldwin's philosophical functionalism in America. But behaviorism never caught on in France. Instead, Baldwin got to know such French luminaries as Pierre Janet (see Chapter 9). Janet had lunch frequently with Baldwin in Paris and then recommended his ideas to his brilliant young student from Geneva, Jean Piaget. Baldwin had also impressed Piaget's future boss at the

Institut Jean-Jacques Rousseau in Geneva, the insightful and levelheaded Edouard Claparéde (1873–1940).

Jean Piaget (1896–1980)

Early Life: Consecrating His Life to a Biological Explanation of Knowledge

Jean Piaget was born in the quiet university town of Neuchâtel, Switzerland, about 60 miles from Geneva, in a French-speaking canton (province) bordering France. His father was a well-respected and careful history professor at the nearby college. His son later said he was "a man of painstaking and critical mind, who dislike[d] hastily improvised generalizations" (Piaget, 1952, p. 237). Jean's mother, Rebecca, was a religious, socially conscious Christian socialist and kindhearted proto-feminist with a nervous temperament. Piaget suggested that she could be difficult to live with, so he admitted retreating into his own "private, but non-fictitious" world (p. 238).

Young Jean joined the university-supported club for kids "Friends of Science" and published his first small paper on the sighting of an albino sparrow when he was only nine years old in the club journal. There he learned about evolution and how to present his research to other scientists. As the protégée of the director of the local natural history museum, he collected and classified species of local freshwater mollusks, particularly snails, after school. He was even offered a position at age 16 as an assistant curator of the mollusk collection at the museum but turned it down to finish high school (Vidal, 1994)!

But the young Piaget was even more idealistic than most scientists were. He was struggling with a contradiction between the mechanistic universe of science and the wish to live a compassionate and immediate moral life, even as he recognized that the intellectual proofs of God's existence were weak. His philosophically minded godfather introduced him to the work of Henri Bergson (1859–1941), perhaps the most popular French philosopher of his day. Bergson's (1911) *Creative Evolution* offered the young man a way out of his conflict.

Bergson was a dualist, who made a distinction between an objective scientific view of time and each person's subjective view of time as it is lived. Physical scientific time (at least before Einstein) was regular, composed of an infinity of equal packets of experience. Once physical laws are understood, they are mathematically predictable and can be run backwards or forwards. Bergson called subjective, lived time (like the direct experience of William James's stream of consciousness) duration (*durée*). Duration is intuitive and elastic, depending as it does on memory. Unlike physical events, truly creative mental acts are unpredictable and therefore irreversible. Bergson equated life with duration and believed that the evolution of life displayed creative properties, like the mind (Vidal, 1994). Unlike his materialist contemporaries, Bergson still believed in the *élan vital*, a directional life force. Evolution, to Bergson, had an internal impulse upwards towards greater mentality. Sometimes he writes as if the purpose of bodily life is to support the mind. Later, Piaget commented about the influence of Bergson on his thought:

First of all, it was an emotional shock. I recall one evening of profound revelation. The identification of God with life itself was an idea that stirred me almost to ecstasy because it now enabled me to see in biology the explanation of all things and the mind itself. In the second place, it was an intellectual shock. The problem of knowing (properly called the epistemological problem) suddenly appeared to me in an entirely new perspective and as an absorbing topic of study. It made me decide to consecrate my life to the biological explanation of knowledge.

(Piaget, 1952, p. 240)

Another aspect that Piaget took from Bergson was the belief in holism vs. reductionism. Thought, said Bergson, cannot be explained by examining only its parts:

That life is a kind of mechanism I cordially agree. But is it the mechanism of parts artificially isolated within the whole of the universe or is it the mechanism of the real whole? The real whole might well be, we conceive, an indivisible continuity. The systems we cut out within it would, properly speaking, not be parts at all; they would be partial views of the whole. And with these partial views put end to end, you will not make even a beginning of the reconstruction of the whole, any more than, by multiplying photographs of an object in a thousand different aspects, you will reproduce the object itself.

So of life and the physio-chemical phenomena to which you endeavor to reduce it. Analysis will undoubtedly resolve the process of organic creation into an ever-growing number of physio-chemical phenomena and chemists and physicists will have to do, of course, with nothing but these. But it does not follow that chemistry and physics will ever give us the key to life.

(Bergson, 1911/1998 translation, p. 31)

These insights came to Piaget when he was only 15, at the same time he was exploring biology in the lab and lakes near his home. But he still had some work to do to unify science and religion in his own mind. His conflicts were intensified as World War I erupted in 1914. Even though he was relatively safe in neutral Switzerland, his faith, both in science and in God, were tested, and he may have suffered a bout of respiratory illness as a result of his intense studies. From the fall of 1915 to the summer of 1917, he spent much of the time at a health resort in the splendid Swiss Alps (Vidal, 1994), but the effect of this idyllic setting was probably dampened by the presence of 6000 wounded soldiers. At this time he wrote two works, which he later disparaged as "juvenile" efforts at philosophy, but that hold seeds of his later theory: a prose poem called "The Mission of the Idea" and a philosophical novel called *Recherche* (Search [or Research]). Piaget may have had reason to be embarrassed by them, as a lot of us would be embarrassed if our teenage diaries were published. They are filled with anguished purple prose on lofty ideas. But, looking back from the present, we can see the foundation of his theory in these intense writings.

The young hero of his philosophical novel *Search*,[3] a stand-in for Piaget himself, is Sébastien, who is hurt and retires to a small cabin on a mountain to heal. While there, in intense prayer, he discovers his mission in life: "And replete with a sacred emotion, he received with happiness but also with dread the divine mission of using his life for reconciling science and religion" (Piaget, 1918, p. 96; translated in Chapman, 1988, p.20). There are many crises in the young man's life as he veers from false elation to depression. Along the way, he rejects both religious dogma and introspective philosophy and settles on science, whose findings he believes to be capable of being true, even though each set of facts is incomplete and each theory idealized. Like Bergson, he rejects the reductionist, elementarist view of science (see the beginning of Chapter 6), which to him overemphasizes the parts at the expense of the whole.

This notion of parts in equilibrium with a whole is seen at all levels in science (Chapman, 1988). In a developing organism, the parts, the organs, form a self-maintaining whole: The parts do not make sense without the whole and vice versa. The cell composes the organism and the organism sustains the cell. In evolution, the giraffe with a long neck can reach the leaves; the plant with thorns is less likely to be eaten; the giraffe with a thick tongue can eat them. In psychology, general concepts and individual instances remain in balance (see Kant, Chapter 5). In sociology, the individual composes the society that forms the individual. The young Sébastien-Piaget even postulated a circle of sciences: Biology underlies psychology and the theory of knowledge, which leads to logic, which leads to mechanics, which underlie the principles of physics, which govern the theories of chemistry and biochemistry, which lead back to biology! Nothing exists in isolation.

Thus, when not yet 20, Piaget was developing the single Big Idea that would inform his work for the rest of his life: *Thought naturally forms structures; these thought structures tend toward organic wholes, not collections of ideas.*

Finally, what status did the young Sébastien-Piaget give to faith and religion to resolve the crisis? Sébastien believes that science gives the laws of the world; faith—which is human action, not knowledge—is the engine in us to discover these laws. Social salvation is the realization of the ideal equilibrium in ourselves, in others and in society (Piaget, 1918, in Gruber & Vonèche, 1977, p. 50). Science can help with the discovery of these ideals. Piaget finally came to the position that God is not a cause of physical events but a source of meaning and value; God works through humanity, not on it. "God is not a Being who imposes Himself on us from without; His reality consists only in the intimate effort of the seeking mind" (Piaget, 1930, p. 37; cited in Chapman, 1988, p. 72). Studying the development of the evolved rational mind was therefore not inconsistent with a religious viewpoint for Piaget.

This was his last public statement on religion per se, but he never lost interest in the moral realm. His first attempt to explain it was in *The Moral Judgment of the Child* (1932), and he revisited the issue of a moral society in 1965, as he was nearing 70 (Piaget, 1966/1995). And his ideas on the stage-dependent nature of moral reasoning strongly influenced the work of researchers such as Lawrence Kohlberg (1927–1987) and Eliot Turiel (1938–present) and in critical reaction to the implied sexism in Kohlberg's moral stage theory, Carol Gilligan (1936–present). Both the young and the old Piaget believed that the highest form of human relationships were reciprocal cooperative ones entered into by autonomous individuals.

In reading this section, some of you will be concerned that we are dealing with some kind of mystical nut as well as a genius, similar to Piaget's fellow Swiss, Carl Jung! (Is it the low oxygen at that altitude or the sublime views in the Alps? Freud vacationed in them, too, on the Austrian side!) You will not see these religious epiphanies in any child development textbook. As a man, Piaget became a relatively sober scientist, searching for evidence, describing children's behavior and slowly building his theory over more than 50 years and 57 books and 483 papers, alone and in collaboration with others, first at the Institut Jean-Jacques Rousseau and then, after 1955, at his own Center for Genetic Epistemology. As we will discuss below, Piaget was after nothing less than a theory of knowledge that tries to explain everything from why a baby bangs her rattle to how evolution happens to why the history of science happened just as it did. As a final reminder in this section, let's take one final look at the brilliant teenager in the throes of discovery, with this ecstatic passage from *Recherche*, that summarizes the plan:

> From the conception of the species from which he [Sébastien] had started, he had in fact come to see an organization, that is, an equilibrium between the qualities of the whole and the qualities of the parts, in every living unity and every individual. Every real organization is in an unstable equilibrium, but by the very fact of its existence, it tends toward a total equilibrium which is an ideal organization, just as a crystal misshaped by the rock which encloses it tends to perfect form or again as the irregular trajectory of a star has a regular figure for a law.
>
> ... The ideal organization is the good, the beautiful, the religious equilibrium and it is toward this organization that morality, art and mysticism tend. ... No more need of philosophy. ... science shows that these organizations, real or ideal, are also the laws of psychology and sociology and the circle of the knowledge of life is thus closed, resulting in the last analysis in a positive theory of knowledge, which concludes with the incapacity of reason for breaking the circle and descending to the bottom of things.
>
> (Piaget, 1918, pp. 96–99, in Chapman, 1988, p. 20)

Starting His Career

Piaget received his PhD in biology from the University of Neuchâtel in 1918, at age 21, on species classification in the *Limnaea* genus of snails, a research area he had been working in for a decade by that point. He spent the spring semester 1919 learning about psychoanalysis from Bleuler and Jung at the Burghölzli Asylum in Zurich. By fall, he was in Paris at the Sorbonne to study philosophy with rationalist neo-Kantian philosopher Leon Brunschvicg (1869–1944) and psychology with Pierre Janet (Charcot's student, the discoverer of multiple personalities—see Chapter 9) and also carrying a letter of introduction from one of his professors to Theodore Simon (1873–1961), Binet's collaborator on their early intelligence test, who was given his post in the psychological laboratory after Binet's untimely death in 1911. But Simon left town, leaving the psychology laboratories to Piaget with the suggestion that he standardize a new version of Cyril Burt's variation on the intelligence test.

This Piaget proceeded to do, at first half-heartedly and then with increasing interest. But he found that he was ill-suited to ask different children the same standardized questions over and over, because he could not resist asking the children who gave "wrong" answers why they thought that! What Piaget really discovered in his work on intelligence testing, however, was a method. He had a gift for posing simple questions that would help children demonstrate their thought processes and then to gently challenge them on their statements, as in the following example: "And how many brothers have you got?—*One, Paul.*—And has Paul got a brother?—*No.*—But you are his brother, aren't you?—*Yes*—Then he has a brother?—*No*" (Piaget, 1924/1977, p. 98).

Piaget explained the importance of this discovery in a later autobiographical statement:

> Now from the very first questionings I noticed that though Burt's tests certainly had their diagnostic merits, based on the number of successes and failures, it was much more interesting to try to find the reasons for the failures. Thus I engaged my subjects in conversations patterned after psychiatric questioning, with the aim of discovering something about the reasoning process underlying their right, but especially their wrong answers.
>
> (Piaget, 1952, p. 245)

Because the method was based on the psychiatric questioning he had learned at the Burghölzli, Piaget called this questioning technique his clinical method, but it was never about diagnosis. It might also be called a critical method or critical exploration, because part of every interview involves challenging and contradicting children's perceptions. The criticism thus is intended to highlight what a child really knows or how a child really thinks, as opposed to his or her snap judgments (Leslie Smith, 2007, personal communication). It was about an attempt to discover how the children acquired knowledge and constructed reality in their minds from their own action. It was an attempt to study epistemology through using children as informants. Before Piaget, philosophers had attempted to study epistemology through introspection of their own adult minds, and psychologists had largely studied adults introspecting. But adults generally do not remember accurately how they learned to think in the first place! It is the primary job of children to figure out the world, so Piaget considered it appropriate to study the genesis of thought in the life of the child. Therefore, borrowing the term from Baldwin, he called his theory genetic epistemology.

Piaget borrowed a lot from James Mark Baldwin: Like Baldwin, he was an evolutionary rationalist, who focused on the development of children's adaptive rational cognition. Baldwin's terms circular reaction, assimilation and accommodation play significant roles in his theory. Piaget accepted Baldwin's core belief that children learn through acting in order to understand rather than passively copying the external world; and as we will see, Piaget's theory of evolution is strongly similar to Baldwin's organic selection. But Piaget always downplayed Baldwin's influence. He claimed to have discovered Baldwin's theory from Janet well after he had started on his own, and though they were in Paris at the same time, they seem never to have met (Piaget, 1982). At any rate, Baldwin should surely not get the credit for the lifetime that Piaget spent supervising systematic tests of his own theory with children that make Baldwin look good in retrospect. It was this work that made Piaget more famous than Baldwin today. And there were differences as well: Very little of Baldwin's theory of social heredity made it into Piaget's theory.

Piaget's Genetic Epistemology

> Thus my observations that logic is not inborn, but develops little by little, appeared to be consistent with my ideas on the formation of the equilibrium toward which the evolution of mental structures tends; moreover, the possibility of directly studying the problem of logic was in accord with all my former philosophical interests. Finally, my aim of discovering a sort of embryology of intelligence fit in with my biological training; from the start of my theoretical thinking I was certain that the problem of the relation between the organism and environment extended into the realm of knowledge, appearing here as the problem of the relation between the acting or thinking subject and the objects of his experience. Now I had the chance of studying this problem in terms of psychogenetic development.
>
> —Jean Piaget (1952, p. 245)

Before describing and evaluating the stage system of development that made Piaget so famous, we should perhaps define, as much as possible on his own terms, what Piaget was and was not.

First, Piaget was an epistemologist, not a psychologist. He was less interested in the study of child development than in using the way children think to illuminate how humans construct a system of thinking about and adapting to the world. Piaget was uninterested in abnormal behavior, in differentiating average children from geniuses or imbeciles or in correlational studies of heredity vs. environment. Modern-day psychologists have been frustrated by the lack of precision in Piaget's choice of research subjects, his lack of attention to experimental control and statistical analysis or even his indifference about describing his methods fully in his writings. He was often satisfied with giving examples of qualitatively different types of behavior that children pass through on their way to attaining the ability to reason logically, abstractly and scientifically, which Piaget considered the pinnacle of Western thought.

The methods of philosophers are different from those of psychologists: They start from first principles or axioms and build on them. What then, are the bare minimum abilities that a child must have for building knowledge? Piaget assumed that all children begin with certain reflexes obtained through evolution: sucking, grasping and so on. They are innately curious, in that they reach out, literally and figuratively, to have sensory experiences in the world. This curiosity is a constant in Piaget's theory: To use the language of the behaviorists, with whom he profoundly disagreed, the drive for knowledge is self-reinforcing; if it were not, we would soon die out, because we need to know about the reality of the world to survive in it. The child is an active participant in constructing his knowledge and this is done not by merely copying the world (as, for example, Locke suggested when he suggested that ideas in the head correspond to the primary and secondary qualities in the world).

Instead, when a one month old reaches out towards his mother's blouse, the memory of reaching and getting a squishy sensation back becomes a **scheme** or a memory of a sensorimotor act. When the child reaches out to grasp another piece of cloth—say, a blanket, he recognizes the sensation he gets back from the action as the same as that of the blouse and assimilates it to the scheme of squishy objects. Essentially, assimilation happens when a child recognizes that an experience is similar to one he had before (the recognition that blanket = blouse = assimilation to the schema of squishiness). Eventually, the child will attempt to use the same action to pull to him the bars on his crib or to grasp a hard ball and fail at first. When the child then attacks the problem with another action and gets back success, but with different sensations, he has created a memory of a different useful type of action, a different scheme. This corrective action when the world fails to yield, resulting in a different scheme, is called accommodation (Piaget, 1967). Assimilation, recognizing the old, is balanced with accommodation, adapting to the need for new behaviors. As the child matures physiologically, he becomes capable of more actions, which he refines through acting upon the world and so on. Knowledge is not copied; it is constructed. New knowledge is differentiated out of old in a fashion analogous to the process by which a zygote differentiates into new organ systems in embryology.

By way of summary, read the quote from Piaget's autobiography that began this section. It should now be clear how the near-mystical philosophical epiphanies of Piaget's youth—all that business about the unity of the parts with the whole in a balanced structure—were merged with his biological, psychological and philosophical training to result in an embryology of knowledge and an epistemology that truly relies upon the study of children's active engagement with the world.

Constructing the Stage Theory

Piaget's true genius may be in tying this complicated philosophy to the actions of individual children and thus systematically collecting the kind of data that would support his theory. Piaget's complete theory is vast and was not constructed neatly in order, starting with infancy and working his way up. But from the historian's point of view, Piaget's life's work can be divided up into three basic periods: In the 1920s and 1930s, Piaget collected, classified and developmentally ordered children's behaviors. In the 40s and 50s, Piaget turned his attention to the famous stage theory, considering how children's thought formed a sequence of developmental structures, focusing on what he called *structures d'ensemble* (structures of the whole) or operational structures. Finally, towards the end of his life, from the mid-60s to his death in 1980, Piaget returned to biology to discuss the evolution of intelligence and began refocusing his efforts away from *stages* of thought to the *processes* that underlie the construction of the structures. This reevaluation was still incomplete at the time of his death.[4] The four main stages, arguably Piaget's most famous contribution to psychology, are plotted out here to fit within Piaget's own development. It is best to think of the stages of cognitive development as moving from solipsism or no point of view in the **sensorimotor stage** of infancy, to egocentrism in the **preoperational stage** of preschool, to logical thought in the concrete world, in the **concrete operational stage** of the elementary school years, to finally, abstract, hypothetical, scientific thought of adolescence, in the **formal operational stage**.

Piaget's Early Phase: Sensorimotor and Preoperational Thought

> At the outset of mental evolution, there is no definite differentiation between the self and the external world, i.e., impressions that are experienced and perceived are not attached

to a personal consciousness sensed as a "self," nor to objects conceived as external to the self. They simply exist in a dissociated block or are spread out on the same plane, which is neither internal nor external but between these two poles. These opposing poles will only gradually become differentiated. It follows that, because of this primitive lack of dissociation, everything that is perceived is centered on the subject's own activity.
—Piaget (1943/68, in Kitchener, 1986, pp. 12–13)

In 1921, at age 25, Piaget was invited by Edouard Claparéde (1873–1940) to become the research director at the Institut Jean-Jacques Rousseau, a research center and school that was founded by Claparéde in 1912 to promote child-centered education as a science. Piaget first spent a good deal of time observing children at the school and after his marriage to Valentine Chatenay in 1923, he observed his own children, Laurent, Lucienne and Jacqueline, as well. Starting with *The Language and Thought of the Child* (1923/1926), Piaget wrote five books concerned mostly with children's thought from birth to around age 11.[5] These books are some of Piaget's most engaging works. They are filled with transcriptions of children's own conversations, play and responses to the questions that the "funny gentleman" would ask them! In this early period, Piaget approached the classification of children's thinking using a method that he had used with snails: First, he classified the different kinds (or genera) of behaviors that a group of children exhibit—that is, he developed a classification system. Then he rank-ordered these types by their complexity with the assumption that more complex types come later in development. Finally, he collected data to determine whether the more primitive forms of thought are indeed found in younger children and more complex, less egocentric, more abstract forms of thinking are found most often in older children.

The Sensorimotor Stage

According to Piaget (1927), the newborn baby is entirely *solipsistic*. Solipsism is different from egocentricity, because the egocentric child of the preschool years is simply evaluating all knowledge from his own point of view; he may not know that others have different points of view, but at least the child has a point of view and therefore a rudimentary sense of self. The solipsistic baby does not have a point of view; she is not a self who is experiencing an outside world, she *is* merely a continuous stream of experience. She loses interest when an object goes behind a screen. She lives in the moment, at the mercy of fleeting sensory experiences. She also clearly does not yet have object permanence, defined as the knowledge that solid objects continue to exist when one does not perceive them. This knowledge must be constructed through acting on the world over and over again, through use of the circular reaction. At first, a child engages in what Piaget called a **primary circular reaction**, engaging in repeated pleasurable movements with one's own body, such a baby kicking her feet repeatedly or a baby sucking his thumb. Piaget's daughter, Jacqueline, was, at seven months, kicking her feet when she accidentally hit a doll hanging from a mobile (Piaget, 1927). She immediately began kicking the doll over and over again. When Piaget removed the doll, the kicking stopped and resumed when the doll was brought back. The child is now repeating actions with objects to maintain interesting stimulations, as when a child bangs a rattle over and over to hear the sound and feel the sensory feedback from the strike of the rattle. Circular reactions with objects are called **secondary circular reactions**; at some point in the first year, the child begins to coordinate actions with two or more objects; by early in the second year, the child appears to be deliberately varying his actions to get an intended result (**tertiary circular reactions**) and so on.

The child in this period is performing motor actions in order to get a sensory result, setting up a feedback loop of learning. What the child is learning is: *through my actions, I can predictably have an effect on the world.* It is the predictability of this feedback that gradually "convinces" the child that objects are fully real, that they exist beyond his immediate perceptions. The child does not yet have the ability to think in symbols and words, only in these sensorimotor feedback loops. Piaget later called this first stage in his system the **sensorimotor period or stage** (Piaget, 1936). Thus, as can be seen in Table 10.2, each advance in the complexity of circular reactions is associated with a gradual increase in the ability to deal with objects until the child passes what is called the *object permanence test.* Piaget describes this test in *The Construction of Reality in the Child* (Piaget, 1937/1954).

Piaget's daughter Jacqueline is 18 months old. He lays out a handkerchief, a jacket and a felt beret on the table. Then, he puts a small pencil in his hand, closing his hand to hide it only when Jacqueline sees in there. Then, he puts his hand under the handkerchief and shows her his closed fist, saying "Coucou [his pet name for his daughter], the pencil!" (Piaget, 1937/1999, p. 80). He then does the same with the jacket and finally puts his hand under the beret, where he leaves the pencil. When he asks his daughter to find the pencil, she turns over each of the covers until she finds it under the beret, laughing triumphantly.

That she keeps searching for the pencil tells us that Jacqueline knows that "That pencil must be somewhere!" If she can do this, she must be reminding herself to keep looking by referring to a memory or an image of the pencil in her mind. She is referring to a *representation* of the object, by representing it to herself in her mind until she finds the actual pencil. At this point, Jacqueline has achieved **object permanence**: She knows that objects continue to exist outside of her perception of them.

Piaget recognized that the ability to represent the world in a child's own mind is a major step. It is not merely a quantitative change in amount of knowledge, but a qualitative shift in how the child acts towards the world. A child need not be tied to his momentary sense experiences anymore but instead can remember things that happened in the past. He is no longer surprised when his mother's face reappears from behind her hands in a game of peek-a-boo. Using **deferred imitation**, he can

Table 10.2 Object Permanence in the Sensorimotor Stage of Piaget's Genetic Epistemology

- 0–6 wks: infant does not search for covered objects
- 6 wks–4 mos: infant stares at spot where object is hidden
- 4–8 mos: infant will reach only for partially hidden object
- 8–12 mos: infant will search for hidden object but keeps looking where she found it first (A not-B error)
- 12–18 mos: infant will search in a second place if he saw it moved, but not if moved in secret

imitate an action that he saw yesterday or last week, rather than just the action of moments ago. And around the time of object permanence, he can recognize himself in a mirror. As the quote at the beginning of this section shows, the child has now developed a stable sense of what is in himself and what are objects outside of him. He has developed a self, a point of view.

Piaget believed that object permanence and deferred imitation could not happen without the ability for representation. Moreover, he believed that once a child was capable of representation, his way of processing the world has radically changed, so that he can be said to be in an entirely new stage of thought: the preoperational period or stage.

If certain relatively rapid permanent changes in thought and behavior have wide consequences in the way that children deal with the world, beyond just learning new facts or skills, this is a good reason for a stage theory. Unlike the behaviorists, who believed that essentially the same laws were used in learning, from pigeons and rats to humans of any age, the genetic epistemologist believes that the way a child learns is determined by the way he can learn at a particular point in development. The laws of learning in the butterfly differ from those in the caterpillar and so do the laws of the infant, preschooler, child and adolescent. We have met stage theories before: Freud (and other psychoanalysts, like Erik Erikson) and G. Stanley Hall have stage theories. Their theories, however, are based explicitly on Haeckel's recapitulation theories. Although fixation can stop their progress, recapitulation theories are preordained by evolution. Piaget, by contrast, believed that knowledge structures are not innate, simply triggered by maturation,[6] genes or an evolutionary predetermination, nor are they almost completely learned, as the behaviorists would have it. Structures of knowledge self-organize to be in balance of parts and whole and are *constructed* by children's actions on the world. Thus, as opposed to innatism or empiricism, the educational philosophy built on Piaget's ideas is called, by some, **constructivism**.

The Preoperational Stage

When a child achieves object permanence in the latter half of the second year, it makes sense that a child's ability to label things with words increases. When things have an independent existence apart from one's self and no longer are felt to disappear when not in front of a child, it makes sense that the objects should have names. These words, in turn, should take on the quality of symbols, in that they stand for the objects themselves. Whereas in the sensorimotor period, the schemes were literally memories of wordless action sequences and assimilation was the process of using the same action sequence on the world, children are said to be acting in a preoperational fashion when they act on the world using language and symbols and assimilate and accommodate in this realm as well as the physical one. When they overgeneralize the concept of bird by saying "big white bird!" while pointing at an airplane, they are assimilating the plane to their symbolic scheme for bird. When they learn that a new word is needed to differentiate the concepts of bird and plane, they have accommodated their mental schemata to include a new concept. In this way, the processes of assimilation and accommodation, which were sensory and motor in character, now become symbolic. Instead of merely reaching for objects, a child can act upon the world by saying the word with a questioning or demanding intonation and a pointing finger, so that someone can get the object for her ("Juice?!").

Children make symbols out of actions and pictures as well as words. A child applies the semiotic (or symbolic) function to play when she unites feeding a doll with a spoon to other actions, like rocking the doll and changing its diaper. All of these actions fit into the scheme, a symbolic role of mother. The child knows she is pretending—that the doll is a symbol of a child, that she is playing the actions of mother. The activity is no less involving because of that. A preschool child's drawing is not realistic; in spite of adults' beliefs that children are concrete, their drawings show a symbol for a dog next to a symbol of a doghouse, next to symbols of a flower and grass in the yard of a symbolic house. The objects are drawn flat, without perspective or later, with several sides visible at once. Cartoons are beloved by children because of their unambiguous symbolic nature. Stories include characters like the "princess." Heated discussions can occur on the playground concerning whether a child is playing the "right" way, of whether a princess would act this way or that. Stories themselves are schemes and children like to hear the same ones over and over. Their play is **symbolic play**, their art is symbolic art, their stories are symbolic narratives. In each of these activities, there are variations upon themes, a gradual extension of their knowledge out from a central story. Play *is* assimilation; imitation of novel actions is accommodation. Children take information from the world and make it their own. They seldom copy directly what an adult is doing but filter the world through their own knowledge.

Piaget's earliest topic of interest, however, and arguably what made him famous, was in explaining the logical errors of children of this age. Most of these errors arise from two basic problems. First, children by the age of 2 or so have a sense of self as distinct from the objects around them; with this sense of self, they have begun to have, literally, a point of view. But they cannot yet imagine that other people might have different points of view. This tendency in children below the age of 6 or so to reason purely from their own perspectives is called **egocentrism**.

Egocentrism occurs because the child's ability to represent the world in memory comes with a temporary disadvantage: Two-dimensional pictures of objects cannot fully be integrated into a three-dimensional representation of objects. Thus, in Piaget's famous *three-mountains task*, a child is placed on one side of a table with three large papier-mâché mountains of differing sizes, with different visual features, and asked to draw what he or she sees. Then, a doll is placed on a different side of the table and the child is asked to draw what the doll sees. Four-year-old children typically draw what they and not the doll sees. They have difficulty making mental transformations on their internal picture, integrating multiple views into one three-dimensional, rotating representation.

Egocentrism has consequences for the social interaction in the preschool years as well. Until about the age of 5, children's play is not truly social, around a given theme, with considerable give and take. Rather, even though Jimmy says he is playing with Johnny, the two children may be acting out entirely different scenarios while sitting side by side, in *parallel play*. Similarly, children of this age who have been shown what is in a closed box have difficulty understanding that others, who haven't looked in the box, will not also know what is in it.

Interestingly, children's egocentrism does not prevent them from making hypotheses about how the world works. Most things happen in a child's world because someone caused them to happen. Therefore, the child believes that inanimate objects, especially if they move, are alive (*animism*), just like her; the child believes that someone (possibly God) has created natural objects (*artificialism*) and that they must have been created for a purpose or reason (*moral cause*). They believe by being good, they can cause good things to happen or that being bad causes bad things to happen (magical causality + moral cause). Each of these beliefs—sometimes encouraged by cultures through religious training—is evidence that preschool children argue by grafting their active characteristics onto the world (Piaget, 1927).

Sometimes, children reason poorly simply because they cannot hold several, sometimes contradictory, premises in their heads at the same time. Magical thinking essentially involves focusing only on the wish and the goal, while ignoring whatever intermediate steps and contradictions must arise. This is *syncretism*, and it results in a peculiar run-on surreal logic. When asked to explain "When the cat's away, the mice will play," Kauf (age 8) says, "Some people get excited and never do anything, because they are too tired, just as cats get tired chasing chicks and hens." As Piaget (1923/1955) said, "The mind leaps from premise to conclusion without stopping on the way" (Piaget in Gruber and Voneche, 1977, p. 87).

After his initial works from the 1920s established the general characteristics of young children's thought through simple questions, and after he spent much of the early 1930s investigating the object concept in infants (Piaget, 1936, 1937/1954), Piaget and his colleagues Alina Szeminska (a Polish former student of Kurt Lewin in Berlin who began working with Piaget in 1928) and Bärbel Inhelder (1913–1997) (who arrived in 1932 and collaborated closely with Piaget until his death) began studying children's understanding of the physical world and mathematics from early to middle childhood (Piaget & Szeminska, 1941/1964; Piaget & Inhelder, 1941/1974).

In these works, Piaget first mentions his most famous construct: the notion of **conservation**. Essentially, conservation is the idea that quantities do not change even when their perceptual qualities do: Six candies are six candies, whether arranged close together, far apart or in a circle (*conservation of number*); a quantity of clay does not change even though it can sometimes be made to look like a ball or a snake (*conservation of mass*); a string is the same length folded or stretched out (*conservation of length*) and so on.

The first type of conservation discussed by Piaget and Szeminska (1941/1964) was *conservation of liquid volume*, and it will be used as an example here. The test begins by pouring out two quantities of water into beakers of the same height, width, depth and shape; the water is usually in different colors for ease of reference. At this point, the experimenter tries to get the child to agree that the quantities are the same. Having done so, the experimenter pours the water from one of the identical beakers into a tall thin beaker right in front of the child. Then, the examiner asks the child, "Now are they still the same or does one of them have more?" Under the standard conditions of presentation, children in the preoperational period would usually answer that the tall, thin beaker now holds more water. Then the examiner pours the water back into the original container to show the child that the quantity has not changed. Children on the younger end of the age range typically not only say that there is now the same amount, but continue to assert that when the examiner pours the water back into a tall thin (or shorter, fatter) beaker that the quantity of water has changed again, that there is more because it is taller (or fatter).

Piaget's explanation for this behavior is that children are misled by the obvious change in one dimension, while ignoring the less obvious change in the other direction, that is: even though the column of water is now taller, it is also thinner. To use Piagetian technical jargon, the child exhibits *centration* in perception, "centering" on a change in one dimension while ignoring the change in the other. In the early part of the preoperational stage, the dimension that gets more (an *affirmation*) is focused on; only with time can the dimension that is simultaneously decreased (a *negation*) be noticed and integrated with the affirmation.

Thus, in the same way that a child in the preoperational period cannot deal with two different literal viewpoints simultaneously, the child has difficulty dealing with two perceptual changes simultaneously. In later refinements, Piaget required that the actual pouring be done behind a screen first, because he wanted to evaluate whether children are making *internalized mental transformations* of perceptions and logically *deducing* that the water must have been poured, rather than merely watching it. Although nine-year-olds have little trouble with this, it is usually beyond preschoolers. And preoperational children may also have difficulty with *classification tasks* that require them to know that items can be sorted simultaneously by several different rules (small, red triangles vs. large blue rectangles and all other combinations besides).

The core lesson that must be learned by children in the preoperational stage, then, is how to use mental representations. Without them, children could neither use past experience nor have a sense of self as separate from the world. They could not use symbols or language, learn social roles or use the valuable forward-looking function of fantasizing the future through play. But they struggle with thinking about two things at once, with getting beyond their own perspective towards a more objective view. They can make empirical abstractions (these pebbles are light and those are heavy), but rather than using deductive logic (applying a rule to a particular instance) or inductive logic (generalizing a rule from many instances), they use a kind of transductive logic, linking particular instances to particular instances (Piaget, 1924/1928, p. 184). They seem to be making up rules as they go along, because the rules change from instance to instance (e.g. metal things float, but pie plates float because they're big; sometimes even the same object floats at different times).

Transductive logic is also what Piaget would later call pseudoempirical abstraction (Piaget, 1977/2001). Pseudoempirical abstraction differs from mere empirical abstraction in that a child attempts to form a conscious rule of how objects are related to each other; it's pseudoempirical because the rule is based not so much on the characteristics of the objects themselves as on how a child decides to organize them. She can decide on tall vs. short, big vs. small; heavy vs. light and then try to explain actions by the grouping: "it fell because it is heavy." But to the preschooler, these actions are momentary and they may shift their explanations in an instant. They cannot follow arguments with several steps. No wonder preschoolers seem—to adults—flighty, tied to what's going on at the moment, kids with "short attention spans!" But by applying rules, acting with objects repeatedly—grouping, stacking, classifying, weighing, comparing—the child is paradoxically moving away from the objects themselves and focusing instead on the relations among them. Pseudoempirical abstraction, then, is the first small step to constructing mathematical rules that will apply to all objects.

The building blocks of children's later structure of thought are not merely millions of associations, as the empiricist/behaviorist school from Locke to Skinner would have it, but conscious *reflections* on the empirical abstractions. As Kant had noted much earlier, empirical knowledge is merely the content of thought, not thought itself. But Immanuel Kant (see Chapter 5) had considered this thought to be innate: For Piaget, thought is built step by step through action on the world. As we will discuss below, with each reflecting abstraction, a child's consciousness literally grows. But for now, the preoperational child's consciousness is narrow, focused through a keyhole at one rule, one view at a time. But this is certainly an improvement over the end of the sensorimotor stage, when true consciousness and a sense of self had barely begun. In the next stage, what Piaget called "the grasp of consciousness" widens yet again.

Piaget's Middle Phase: Building the Theory of Operational "Structures of the Whole"

The Concrete Operational Stage

Beginning in the 1940s, Piaget and his colleagues finally were ready to investigate the development of logical thought as a complete structure. This had, of course, been Piaget's goal from his epiphany of the relationship of parts to wholes in the Swiss mountains of his childhood. Piaget's key insight had always been that knowledge never exists in isolation. Every bit of real conscious knowledge[7] implies its negation and much of it is nested in hierarchies of meaning. The average three-year-old knows about "dogs"; the nine-year-old knows about "collies" and "animals." In school he learns that there are animals and nonanimals (plants, rocks and buildings, say), mammals and nonmammals, vertebrates and invertebrates and of course, raptor and vegetarian dinosaurs! One grandmother is his father's mother and another is his mother's mother and one grandmother is also his cousin's grandmother, but not the other. A six-year-old has difficulty understanding that she can be an African-American, a Catholic and a New Yorker, all at once; a 12-year-old does not. Baseball cards and Pokémon characters (or even, for the young Piaget, snails!) can be organized and reorganized.

In the preoperational stage, the general quality of children's logical thought is fragmented, egocentric and tied to the immediate context. But the child in elementary school at first slowly and then ever more quickly learns that there is order in the world that does not depend on viewpoints, that is stable and unchanging. This order in the world is conveyed by the mathematics we can use to describe it. For example, $1 + 0 = 1$ or $1 \times 1 = 1$ are identity operations in that the number is not changed by the operations given. This is true always and everywhere, regardless of what objects are being counted and whether the objects are arranged in a line or a circle. There are other properties of numbers, in that addition is the reverse of subtraction: $3 + 2 = 5 - 2 = 3$. There is commutativity ($3 + 2 = 2 + 3$) and associativity $3 + (2 + 4) = (3 + 2) + 4$ and so on. These things are not just empirically so, in that whatever numbers you try, the operations are *necessarily* true: They must be that way.

Thus, if you give a conservation test to a typical nine-year-old child, his responses are very different from those of the preoperational preschooler mentioned in the preceding section. First, as in the earlier example, the examiner gets the child to agree that two liquid quantities in the same size and shaped beakers are the same, and then she pour the contents of one beaker into a tall, thin beaker as before (the examiner does this behind a screen, so that she can be assured that the child is using simultaneous internal mental transformations to reason out the problem). The conversation between child and examiner then might go as seen in Figure 10.4.

It was always crucial to Piaget that the child not only get the right answer, but that he be able to explain his reasoning (in the same way that he thought it crucial to push children to explain their wrong answers). In the example in Figure 10.4, the child says that there is the same amount of water as before because it is the same water—he asserts that before equals after and therefore proves that he knows the principle of *identity*. He notes that it must be the case and therefore asserts a *logically necessary* truth. In this example, he makes his use of logic explicit by stating it conditionally: *If* you poured all the water from one beaker into the other, *then* it *must* be the same.

Examiner: "Now is there the same amount of water in this glass as in that one or does one glass have more [pointing to the two beakers with water still in them]?"

Child: "Did you pour all the water in the short glass into the tall one?"

E: "Yes."

C: "Then there is the same amount."

E: "How do you know?"

C: "Well [pointing to the empty glass], it's the same water as before {identity}. If you poured all the water in the short glass into the tall one, then it has to be the same amount {necessity}!"

E: "Is there some way you can prove it to me? It looks like there might be more in the tall glass."

C: "The tall glass is taller, but it is also thinner {compensation}. I can prove it's the same by just pouring the water from the tall glass back into the empty short one." [He carefully pours it back, moves the two short beakers next to each other to measure.] "See? They're the same!" {reversibility}

Figure 10.4 Use of Piaget's clinical method to test conservation of liquid volume. See the text for explanation of terms.

Then he shows the ability to do two different mental transformations simultaneously by using the operation of *compensation*: It is taller, but it is also thinner. Finally, he proves it by showing that he knows *reversibility*: He can reverse the operation by pouring it back. In Piaget's theory, an operation is a *reversible* internalized mental transformation, and an operational structure or *structure d'ensemble* is a set of logical mental transformations coordinated among themselves. The child discussed here has internalized the coordinated mental actions of identity, compensation, necessity and reversibility. Preschool children, as we have discussed, typically do not have complete operational structures, so they are called preoperational. Elementary schoolchildren, on average, can conserve, showing that they can deduce the logical answers when given concrete objects to reflect upon; thus, their behavior is said to be in the concrete operational stage. Concrete, in Piagetian theory, means that children can think logically about objects that exist and actions that are possible, not hypothetical. As the structures of their minds in this stage are internalized, children do not have to have the objects in front of them to answer questions about them correctly (Sinclair, 1971, cited in Gallagher & Reid, 1981, p. 86).

The change from the typical response of the preoperational child to the dialogue seen in Figure 10.4 doesn't simply happen overnight. In a typical critical exploration of the problem, an examiner would give a preoperational child more than one example and ask the same general questions about water poured from the starting beaker to a shorter, flatter container, say, or from one beaker to many smaller cups and perhaps the same tasks would be done behind a screen and then directly before the child's eyes. One reason for this is simply for accuracy's sake: Piaget was conservative about claiming whether a child was solidly "in" a stage. Behavior, like snails, comes in pure types and in evolutionary transitional forms!

But perhaps even more crucially, Piaget often wished to gently force a child to see the contradictions in her own reasoning, so that he could watch a child try to resolve them. He was mindful of a principle named "Claparéde's Law" after his old colleague:

> As long as one is successfully meeting one's needs and adapting to the environment, consciousness of self or internal mechanisms does not arise. Only when there is some frustration (environmental obstacle or hindrance) do we even become aware of ourselves and our internal mental lives.
> (Kitchener, 1986, p. 23)

Thus, making a child aware of contradictions is helping her to become more widely conscious of her thought.

Early on, at perhaps four years old, a child may, disconcertingly, simply deny the evidence of his own eyes and not even see the contradictions in nonconserving liquid volume, essentially defending the structure of thought he has built, giving the same answer each time or switching due to the social pressure of the examiner, only to revert to the same wrong answers the next week. Like a thermostat, each attempt to throw a child into disequilibrium makes the child expend energy to bring him back to where he started. Every new bit of information is assimilated into his current mental structure and no contradiction is seen. The inconvenient bits are thrown away.

But as a child has more and more experience with objects, attempting to master the water bucket in the sandbox, looking at the soda in his glass and the soda bottle simultaneously, fighting with his brother to make sure he doesn't get less juice—and as he simultaneously grows older—he will inevitably notice and try to resolve contradictions, so that the next time that our friendly Piagetian examiner comes around, he will be seen to struggle more, change his mind more, try harder to resolve the discrepancies. A child might, for example, first discover that by pouring water back, he can get back to the beginning, but deny that this *must* be the case and that the reason is that when the water gets shorter, it *simultaneously* get fatter. When the logical structure is incomplete, the child's reasoning is unstable. This child is not just in disequilibrium, reverting like a thermostat to his previous structure, but disequilibrating. The very structure of his thought is changing. He is accommodating, changing the structure more now and assimilating less. He is seeking a stable state in which everything fits again, but he must do it at a higher level. He is using his own activity to self-regulate his knowledge, to equilibrate. A thermostat never changes its settings; it is a mere machine. But a child is an organism. He or she self-regulates, adapts, grows and learns, all at the same time, and these changes happen, says Piaget, through his or her own actions. *Growth in knowledge is sparked by a feedback process of questioning, contradictions and consequences.* Self-correction happens when a child can anticipate what will happen and compare the result to her predictions. Then she can raise her expectations in a self-feedback loop (Gallagher & Reid, 1981). Recalling the terminology of the last section, **equilibration** happens when affirmations (obvious, positive changes) and negations (less obvious, negative changes) are in balance.

Piaget often gave children of this age tasks that they had never done before, hoping that the child would use the internal structure to solve the problems. If the child has the complete structure implied by conservation of liquid volume, he might, with only a small amount of difficulty, deduce the principle that objects of the same volume displace the same amount of water, even if the child has never been taught the principle, because the new complete structure dictates that if two bodies are the same wide, tall and deep, they *must* displace the same water. This is the power of deductive logic and a strong proof that such an internal structure exists. Similarly, Piaget and his colleagues have tested many types of conservation, in two dimensions (conservation of number, length and area) and three dimensions (conservation of liquid volume, solid volume and mass). Typically, children pass the tests of conservation for two-dimensional problems before the three-dimensional ones, and the speed with which they move through the sequence is determined partly by experience with reasoning about objects.

One aspect of cognitive development in the concrete operational stage is that children become increasingly conscious of their own thought: They not only know how to solve problems, they come to know what they know. The philosopher Immanuel Kant would have called this "apperception," and modern cognitive science would call it metacognition, but Piaget, more appealingly, calls it "the grasp of consciousness" (Piaget, 1976). Throughout middle childhood and, indeed, all the way to adulthood, the grasp of consciousness widens, so that a child who at first needs to work step by step through problems, without seeing how that problem relates to others, can now see classes or types of problems.

Consider children trying to learn multiplication and division. Piaget and his colleagues have investigated this problem with tasks involving common multiples (Piaget, 1977/2001). This starts with a set of blue and red poker chips and a simple set of instructions:

> Can you make a stack of chips out of the red ones by taking three at a time? Can you make a stack of blue ones taking two at a time? Now, I want you to make a stack of blue chips just as high as the stack of red chips. Remember to take the blue chips two at a time and the red chips three at a time.

Piaget started with four-year-olds, but they did not stop to plan. For one thing, they were intensely occupied with counting individual chips, counting and adding one, two, three and then counting the stacks. If they reached the correct answer of two stacks of six, they were completely surprised, could not explain it and could not do it again. They were concerned with pseudoempirical abstraction on individual chips, taking things one at a time and grouping them. Eight-year-olds, by contrast, treated a group of three as a single object and had little difficulty coming to the right answer. In fact, they knew it was the right answer and why, when they got to it.

Relating to groups of three and skipping the action of counting is obviously "grasping" a larger mental object and widening consciousness. Understanding that these actions fit with in a larger structure of multiplication is larger still. Once a child realizes this, everything she knew about numbers needs to be reconfigured: Counting leads to adding and subtracting; adding over and over is multiplication and so on. By reflecting on this in a top-down fashion, the child integrates not just new bits of knowledge, but also new structures with old ones. Simultaneously, of course, a child may be learning in math class from the bottom up. At first, simple memorization of "times tables" might be involved, coupled with an explanation in math class of how multiplication is simply repeated addition. The child needs to perform the operations for herself to note the relationships: $(3 + 3 + 3) = (3 \times 3) = 9$ and thus larger and larger structures are built and the child moves farther and farther from physical poker chips and more into the conscious use of operations inside her own head. She is no longer reflecting about objects, but reflecting on the operations on the objects.

Once the properties of the stages had been constructed, Piaget, in his own final phase of theorizing, began to focus more on the processes of holistic learning than on the structures. The process discussed above of projecting up from knowledge the child already knows and projecting down of more abstract principles is called *reflecting abstraction*. In this example, reflecting abstraction happens as children link their developing knowledge about actions with objects (classifying ordering from smallest to largest, counting forwards and backwards) with their knowledge about numbers. One can learn times tables by memorization (followed by reinforcements, perhaps), but that by itself is not reflecting abstraction. One can learn procedures (akin to software subroutines) for multiplying three digit numbers, but that by itself is not reflecting abstraction either. One reason that children struggle with word problems in spite of knowing their times tables or procedures, Piaget would say, is that such methods of teaching math rely on remembering and not on knowing. Indeed, Western children who learn in such a manner make often meaningless mistakes (forgetting to carry a one or making a mistake by an order of magnitude because columns are not lined up), that eight-year-olds selling candy in the streets of Brazil, who deal with problems like "one box is 35 cents, how much are 4 boxes?" never do. However, we teach abstract systems in school because we want our children to integrate mathematical knowledge all the way up to calculus or statistics. We want them to be able to operate outside the realm of objects or even of cardinal numbers, entirely within an abstract system of formal logic and math, to deal with hypotheses and possible (or necessarily impossible) consequences, to move from the concrete uses of logic and numbers to contemplation of its formal structure. A child who can operate at this level is adept at formal operations, the fourth and final stage of Piaget's system.

The Formal Operational Stage

Now that we have reached the final stage of Piaget's system, it is time to reveal the end point of cognitive development, in his view. To Piaget, the highest form of thought is abstract logico-mathematical knowledge. The rules of logic and mathematics are the same everywhere, no matter what content they are applied to. In most industrialized societies with formal schooling, children begin to be introduced to the rigors of algebra, negative, rational and irrational numbers and the construct of infinity as an essential idea roughly at the beginning of adolescence. These mathematical entities have meaning only in a wholly abstract structure of reasoning. Similarly, at adolescence, children begin to learn about experiments that contain control conditions and that vary more than one variable. Consider a classic task from Inhelder and Piaget (1958). In the pendulum problem, children are shown a pendulum, a weight on a string attached to a support, so that the weight is allowed to swing freely: Soon after the weight on the string is let go, the weight will go the same distance with each swing. The examiner explains that there are three possible variables that might affect the period (length) of the swing: (1) the height of the support, (2) the length of the string and (3) the weight on the end of the swing. The task is to determine which variables matter in affecting the period of the pendulum.

In such an experiment, the child must first understand the notion of variable (e.g. that a range of values are possible, from short to long, tall to short or light to heavy). As you might guess, most nine-year-olds can easily understand this notion. Indeed, they are often taught this idea in elementary school science classes. The problem comes, however, when children are asked to deal with several variables at once. The concrete operational child will often proceed to vary two or even three variables at the same time in trying to discover the principle that governs the period. For example, he might try the heavier weight with the short string and the tall support, followed by the lighter weight with the longer string and short support. A moment's reflection should tell you that he is unlikely to reach a solution with this method, especially if he does not systematically record the results as he tests options. A far more effective method would be to decide at the outset to vary the levels of weight, say, while keeping string length and height constant and then to move through the possible combinations in a systematic way, varying string length while holding weight and support height constant and so on.

But in order to do this, a child must know to determine this plan of attack in advance, recording the results, checking that she has tested the entire problem space of all possible combinations and recorded all possible results. Then, she can examine the results knowing that the answer, if there is one, *must* be in her data somewhere. If it is not, the answer would be found in a variable not anticipated to be operating (material of string, etc.). As it happens, the only variable to make a difference in period length is the length of the string, but at the outset of the experiments, it could have been otherwise.

Experiments, by their very nature, deal in the world of the possible, with the "what could have been." (Laypeople sometimes forget that if a scientist knew what she would find in an experiment, there would be no reason to do it in the first place!) They are essentially condensed hypothetical logical arguments: *If* string length is the only important variable in the pendulum problem, *then* as the string gets longer, the period will get longer, *but* there should be no change in period when weight or pendulum height is varied. If the period *never* changes as the pendulum height goes from short to tall and *never* changes as the weight goes from light to heavy, but *always* changes with a noticeable change in string length, then the child knows (at least for the variables tested in the ranges given) that this *must* be the answer, because all of the combinations were checked out.

Inhelder and Piaget (1958) often made the point that for the concrete operational child, reality dominates possibility, but for a formal operational child, possibility dominates reality. In a similar way that preschoolers are misled by perceptual transformations, the elementary school child is confused by having to evaluate several hypotheses simultaneously. A hypothesis is a statement about a possible state of affairs in the future; that which is hypothetical might be true in the future or it might not. A multiple variable hypothesis contains as many possible futures as there are possible combinations of outcomes from the variables under study. It is no wonder that science is hard!

Dealing with the hypothetical requires imagination first and then limiting imagination to the plausible, the possible and finally, of the possible, the true (Piaget, 1955). Young children, around 7, asked to draw what they would do if they had a third eye, often simply place the third eye between the other two, saying simply that it would help them "see better." Older children, around 11 or 12, might instead put the eye where it would do something that they cannot already do, such as on the back of the head, to see who's sneaking up on them, or in the hand to help them see around corners! Adolescents, given the proper science training, might then be able to apply the abstract principles of evolution to make educated guesses of which of the many possible positions might have evolved and under what circumstances and which are likely never to evolve and even to guess at possible ways in which we might have ended up with two and only two eyes.

So children in the formal operational stage can use their internal structures-of-the-whole to help them plan, deal with hypothetical outcomes and exclude inoperative variables. But, finally, they have one skill that makes it possible for them to do all of these things, and that is the skill to separate principle from content. A 10th grader can appreciate the abstractions of geometry or algebra without calculating anything. An adolescent can unite conservation of liquid volume with conservation of solid mass, with conservation of length, number, area or any other substance under a principle such as "matter cannot be created nor destroyed" and "changes in appearance do not affect changes in amount." By uniting all of these structures, a formal operational child is essentially performing operations on operations! Her consciousness has widened to the point where she can compare artistic styles, efficiencies of engines and the oppression or fairness of dictatorships or economic systems. As she moves to grasp more and more abstract "objects" with her thought, she uses not only reflective abstraction, but also reflects on those abstractions (reflected abstraction) and on the larger structures of thought themselves (metareflection; see Piaget 1977/2001)! Finally, the adolescent comes to know not only what she's doing or even why she does it or that it must be so, but also what rules of deductive logic she is using.

Remember also that Piaget is not a maturationist; these changes do not happen to everyone automatically, but only with relevant experience. Claparéde's Law applies even more forcefully here than in the other stages. It is probably not absolutely necessary to survival for most people to understand Western science or logic, even if knowing it would give them certain useful powers over the world. If they never encounter the kinds of conflicts to need to learn these lessons, they may not learn them. Most of us in industrialized societies learn them in school or even in universities or graduate schools. Many in other societies learn abstract skills such as sea navigation or pyramid building through apprenticeship. And even the most educated of us make logical errors frequently, sometimes to our detriment and sometimes with harmless consequences. But we expect our lawyers, doctors and engineers to consider many ways in which arguments, medicines and airplanes or bridges may fail before they actually do! We even expect our novelists to create plausible characters that act believably in the possible worlds of their imagination.

Piaget's Evolutionary Theory

In the last 15 years of his life, Piaget resumed publishing in an area that he began researching almost 60 years before: the evolutionary biology of snails, as an example and metaphor for the evolution of intelligence. He did this essentially to answer a big question: How are the experiences (behaviors, body modifications, etc.) acquired by members of a species passed down to future generations? In other words, how does ontogeny affect phylogeny? Lamarck's inheritance of acquired characteristics had been disproved, and Piaget did not believe that his stages were simply a recapitulation of evolutionary stages in the life of each child. But Piaget also felt that there was something more than simple natural selection going on. Piaget did not disagree with this basic Darwinian process, which he called *variational evolution*, but he thought that more was needed. Classic neo-Darwinism only allows for random mutations in the genes leading to phenotypes that survive or die depending on the environment; it deemphasizes *organic evolution*: the possibility that gene mutations must be accepted not only by the environment, but also by the existing structure of a self-regulating, developing organism.

Selection, Piaget said, was not an "automatic lottery based on the simple probabilities of encounter or nonencounter with elements of the natural environment, but rather as an active choice which is the outcome of teleonomic, that is, regulatory activities" (Piaget, 1977, p. 5). In basic genetic theory, each *genotype* (DNA code) can result in different *phenotypes* (sets of characteristics actually seen in bodies and behaviors) depending on the environments in which an organism finds itself. The theoretical range of possible phenotypes allowed by a genotype is called a *range (or norm) of reaction*. Some genotypes allow a wide range of reaction, whereas others are fairly *canalized* and allow only a few outcomes: The environment cannot change one's blood type for example, but many things in the environment might affect how a person's intelligence is expressed even if its range is defined in part by inherited genes.

Piaget had also read what was then cutting-edge research on the genetic regulation of growth. He knew both that certain environments can turn genes on or off (Jacob & Monod, 1961) and that certain regulatory genes can be switched on or off at various times in the life of a child from conception to maturity to make an organism more or less susceptible to environmental influences (in other words, certain genes can make a reaction range shrink or grow—development is more or less canalized—at different times of development; Waddington, 1957).

With this in mind, Piaget did experiments on the growth, inheritance and evolution of 65,000 snails. The genome for snail shells allows for different phenotypes expressed in different conditions. Snails that grow in still ponds have elongated shells; those that grow in choppy ponds have round shells. These shell types activate other genes, so that for example, snails in choppy waters have stronger foot muscles to grab on to rocks better. In Piagetian terms, the environmental conditions lead to disequilibrium, calling forth certain genetic responses. Changing of shell shapes, for example, can be regulated by speeding up or slowing down the rate of growth of certain stages of shell development. This would be solving a mismatch with the environment by "growing into it." This ability to resolve the mismatch by growth is truly equilibration in Piaget's sense. If the change in an environment is too severe, a genotype might not have enough flexibility to allow an organism to survive. In this case, it is possible that a mutation may save the day (as in normal neo-Darwinian processes), but the mutation might come in a characteristic, in a regulatory gene or in the ability to react to environmental change. Whether the mutation actually helps is dependent, however, not just on environmental conditions, but also on the structure of the organism at the time the mutation arrives, whether the organism can *assimilate* the change! In some cases, only a mutation that mimics a useful phenotype will be assimilated into the genotype, and it will look like a phenotype has "stuck." A phenotype that becomes part of the genotype and that can therefore be passed down to offspring is called a phenocopy (Piaget, 1974/1980).

Piaget's interest in epistemology and behavior led him to consider the possibility of behavioral phenotypes: Essentially, behaviors can help an organism survive, and a truly advantageous behavior would help an organism survive in several environments. In fact, animals that can move, do move to better environments. Piaget's theory of evolution, like his theory of knowledge, depends on organisms acting on the world.

Thus, we can see how Piaget's notion of part to whole equilibration, assimilation and structural wholes were applied by him to his evolutionary theory. His theory is by no means proven. In particular, biologists are highly skeptical of Piaget's phenocopy notion, and few examples have yet been found to verify it. But even though Lamarck's and Haeckel's theories were long ago properly discarded, there have been arguments among evolutionary biologists about the role of development for more than 30 years (see e.g. Gould, 1977, 2002). In particular, a new area of biology known as evo-devo explores the powerful effects of genes being turned off or turned on at various times in embryological development that determine body structure: The same gene that determines bilateral symmetry in leg development in insects, for example, is also implicated in development of vertebrate legs (Carroll, 2005, 2006). The sequencing of the human, mouse and nematode genomes, among others, proves that the number of genes that code for characteristics between other species and ourselves differs much less than we used to think. This makes the role of regulatory genes comparatively more important, as it becomes apparent that it is less the genes we have that differentiate us from other organisms, but when they are turned on and off in development.

Evaluation and Summary of Piaget's Genetic Epistemology

Piaget noted in the autobiographical essay he wrote at midlife that he had "consecrate[d] his life to the biological explanation of knowledge" as a young man. It is odd to hear the religious word "consecrate" from a scientist, but as it turned out, Jean Piaget kept his solemn promise. His epistemology is an epistemology of organisms—children, not machines. They adapt to the world by acting on it, satisfying their ever-growing curiosity about it, rather than passively being molded by it, as the behaviorists emphasized. Children make hypotheses about the world, test them, meet contradictions and try again. They are not blank slates, as Locke stated, nor are they genetically or evolutionarily determined by a maturational plan, as Hall and Gesell claimed. Their knowledge is not a collection of elementary atomistic bits, but a coherent structure that allows them eventually to deduce answers to questions, and that is a self-organizing, largely self-regulating system. Addition implies subtraction; superordinates imply subordinates; children keep trying until everything fits, until they gradually become self-aware explorers, correlating the data they are gathering to the developing structures in their minds.

A List of Misconceptions About Piaget

Piaget's accomplishments in psychology place him on a historical plane with other major figures like William James, Sigmund Freud and B.F. Skinner. Like these scientist-philosophers, he extended his theory as far as he was able and created his own language to do so. As with these others, it is imperative to try to find out what he actually said than what others have said he said, but his prolific flood of writings makes this difficult. I have tried to present his work as whole as possible and not reduce his work to the written equivalent of memorizable sound bites, but I also have sympathy for those who have oversimplified his work out of desperation! In closing, here are a few criticisms and misunderstandings, forthrightly answered.

Misconception 1. The theory is all about the stages. Describe them and you know Piagetian theory.

No. In fact, Piaget began to speak of coherent stages only around 1945 (Chapman, 1988). Before that, he described the development of separate behaviors that he had observed. His focus on stage structure began in his middle period. He had only begun to describe the processes that children used to move from stage to stage (reflective abstraction, self-regulation, equilibration) late in life, and some of his late works dealing with these processes were not translated into English until more than 10 years after his death. They are often given short shrift in textbooks, in part because of this. Piaget's theory is more popular in Europe than in the U.S. Some empirical work supporting the theory has not been and is unlikely to be translated into English.

Misconception 2. Children move through the stages as a result of maturation; they will not understand anything about things learned in later stages.

Piaget virtually never explained the growth of knowledge by maturation. Children must act on the world to know and construct their own understanding. Challenging them with complex concepts sometimes provokes contradiction that furthers growth of understanding. But asking whether a child can be pushed through the stages by a super-enriched program was dismissed as "The American Question" by Piaget.[8]

Misconception 3. If a child is not capable of all types of reasoning typical of a stage, this is necessarily a disproof of Piaget's theory.

No. Because children learn about the world actively, they will pass tests with which they have had the most experience first within a stage. A child may pass conservation of mass before conservation of liquid or vice versa. If a child were capable of solving the pendulum problem, but not conservation of mass tasks, this would be a problem for the theory. Training a child on a task rarely allows him or her to progress ahead rapidly, but the experience may improve performance slightly (see Inhelder, Sinclair, & Bovet, 1974, for training studies).

Misconception 4. Teachers are unnecessary or harmful to learning.

Piaget was always against memorization and in favor of understanding gained by discovery. He believed a child must invent knowledge to understand, but that does not mean he needs to understand to invent. A skillful teacher challenges the child, aids the right discoveries and dissuades the wrong ones. Piaget was for many years the head of the Montessori Society in Switzerland and held other posts in education.

The following criticisms, however, have some merit:

1. Piaget ignored emotional development.

    This is true. He did speak occasionally of the role of "affect" but mostly in explaining simple motivation.

2. Piaget explored insufficiently how much and what kind of experience led to what kind of outcomes.

    Although education and experience are givens to Piaget, he seldom studied how different kinds of experience would lead to different outcomes. Some research, particularly that of Pierre Dasen, explored cross-cultural implications of Piaget's work, but cultures usually are seen as agents to speed up or delay development, rather than to promote different kinds of outcomes.

3. Piaget and his colleagues did explore occasionally how peers affected one another's reasoning—through contradictory points of view, for example (Doise & Mugny, 1984). But he viewed cognitive development as moving from solipsism to egocentrism to sociality and neglected the fact that the sociocultural world is always attempting to influence the child from birth and the child is interacting socially at the same time. This criticism was leveled by the Russian-Soviet psychologist Lev Semenovich Vygotsky (1896–1934). We will turn to his theory next.

Lev Semenovich Vygotsky (1896–1934)

So far in this book, whenever child development is mentioned, theorists have focused on one aspect of development at the expense of another. Hall, Freud and Gesell focused on the unfolding of Lamarckian stages or maturation, but they deemphasized the role of experience. Thorndike, Watson and Skinner, heirs to the empiricist tradition, focused on experience at the expense of developmental growth. Baldwin's and Piaget's theories were more sophisticated: Children do come equipped with biological drives and predispositions to act on the world and construct their own thought through their own actions. In these theories, new information is assimilated into a current structure of thought, but the demands of reality, disrupting the equilibrium of the structure, forces the child to accommodate his or her actions to new experiences.

But something is left out even of these sophisticated models of development. To Piaget, the child begins separate from the social world and seemingly remains so (except for charmingly answering a psychologist's questions) for much of childhood. Caregivers are rarely discussed as active forces in shaping the child's activity, promoting some culturally approved actions at the expense of others. Far from being left on his or her own, a child is being guided by others from the beginning towards the expectations of their culture by teachers, parents, peers and others. On the other side of the relationship, the child still grows, enlarging physical and cognitive competence. Moreover, it is clear that from a very early age—even in a nine-month-old pointing to a glass of juice—that children *want* to communicate to others, regardless of whether they can do so with perfect logic. How can such conversations fail to contribute to a child's cognitive development? A child is always with a caretaker, who guides her through her culture, which is situated in an entire history of how that culture came to be the way it is at that moment. That history has left books, tools, social structure and, most importantly, language and logic, which themselves structure what language is used, what the mother and child talk about and the rules of how and when a child negotiates with mother greater and greater independent competence and independence.

These intersections of culture, caretakers and cognitive competence are the intersections that most interested L.S. Vygotsky, who was born in the same year as Jean Piaget, but in a world away from Switzerland in the far more tumultuous Russia before the Soviet Revolution. And just as peaceful Switzerland shaped an introverted but industrious Piaget, the combination of intellectual ferment and social upheaval, war and poverty, idealism and ideology in Russia shaped Lev Vygotsky and gave him opportunities that, as a Jew, he could never have aspired to in calmer times.

He grew up in Gomel, Byelorussia, the son of a middle-class bank manager and a schoolteacher. As in much of Europe, Jews were a persecuted minority in the Russian empire, subject to discrimination, harassment and pogroms—episodes of outright mob violence, condoned by the authorities; when Vygotsky was only 7, his father, respected in the community, organized the Jewish defense against such a pogrom (Valsiner & van der Veer, 2000). From a young age, his incisive critical mind was molded in daily conversation with a tutor, in the fashion of Socratic dialogues (or Yeshiva training); the limited biographical material we have on Vygotsky suggests that his tutor was enough of a freethinking dissident to have been exiled to Siberia (Kozulin, 1990).

When he started formal schooling in his teens, Vygotsky's brilliance was readily recognized; he became an admirer of the difficult historical theories of Hegel, who had postulated that the zeitgeist, the spirit of the times, evolved ever upward through the dialectical clash of one idea (a **thesis**) opposing its opposite (**antithesis**) and resulting in a **synthesis**, an entirely new phenomenon contained in neither opposing idea (see Chapter 5). Moreover, Vygotsky was fascinated by Hegel's view that thought is determined by one's culture; he was remembered by former schoolmates as having had many discussions on the meaning of Jewish cultural history. His reading was broad, deep and voracious.

Vygotsky graduated first in his class with a gold medal. He wanted to study literature at Moscow University (in spite of his parents' wishes that he study medicine or law), and as a medal winner it was virtually certain that he would be accepted, in spite of the limited quotas for Jews allowed at the university. But the authorities were dismayed that too many Jews were gaining entrance in this way and changed the quota system at the last minute to admit Jews only by lottery. Either through the sympathetic intervention of an examiner or by sheer luck, Vygotsky was admitted (Kozulin, 1986)! But the same crackdown that affected Jewish admission also put constraints on the freedom of speech of professors and expelled many students from Moscow University; many of the more freethinking or even revolutionary professors resigned and began teaching at Shanyavsky, a private university, where they could say what they wanted. Soon, Vygotsky followed them. Finally enrolled as a student in history and philosophy, Vygotsky read everyone from Spinoza and Descartes to William James, phenomenologist Edmund Husserl (a student of Carl Stumpf—see Chapter 6) and Sigmund Freud. He also took some courses at the Moscow Institute of Psychology, opened only in 1912 under the direction of G.I. Chelpanov, who promoted an eclectic mix of Wundtianism, functionalism and phenomenology. Later, in psychology, Vygotsky would be just as widely read: One can find references in his writings to Thorndike's and Köhler's animal work, Wilhelm Wundt, Max Wertheimer, Kurt Lewin,[9] James Mark Baldwin, John B. Watson, Pierre Janet, Eugen Bleuler and Jean Piaget! Vygotsky added this sophisticated international intellectual background to a complete knowledge of the work of his Russian compatriots Pavlov, Bekhterev and Sechenov and, of course, Hegel, Marx and Engels.

Vygotsky received a degree in literature in 1916 from Shayanavsky University, submitting a thoughtful thesis on Hamlet that was influenced by new literary theories and by the new psychological realism of the famous Moscow Art Theater. In fact, he rarely missed a major theater performance in Moscow and wrote many reviews (Valsiner & Van der Veer, 2000). He was then forced by circumstances to return home to Gomel to teach in a teachers' training school and to try to keep afloat during the German occupation after the First World War, the beginnings of the Russian Revolution and the terrible civil war that followed it. In 1920, while living in these times of violence and poverty, he contracted tuberculosis while caring for his dying brother. The disease would eventually kill Vygotsky himself in 1934.

Thus, when Vygotsky returned in late 1923 to Moscow to a new Soviet world, he was a man in a hurry. Chelpanov had been deposed that year, for studies of consciousness in the Wundtian or functionalist traditions were considered subjective and bourgeois, incompatible with Marxist theory. Chelpanov had been replaced by K.N. Kornilov, a rather undistinguished psychologist before the war, who had the political advantage of being a Communist. But the "reflexologists" Bekhterev and Pavlov were still in favor. They were at least materialists who avoided consciousness (Communism had converted Hegel's insights on the dialectic of ideas into the materialistic worldview of social evolution emerging from class struggle—hence, Communism's formal name: dialectical materialism). However, in this brief period, the new Soviet psychologists were coming up with a reflex for everything, similar to John B. Watson in America at the time (who hated the Russian Revolution, but nevertheless lectured to his students that he was searching for the simple stimulus to that rather complex revolutionary reaction; Watson, 1925). Vygotsky's staunch friend and colleague, the neuropsychologist Alexander Romanov (A.R.) Luria (1902–1977) said later that much of this preference for reflexes was simple word games:

> Perception, as far as I remember, we started calling the reception of a signal for reaction, attention [became] the limitation of reaction, memory—the preservation with production of reaction, emotions—emotional reactions. Wherever possible (and impossible) we added the term "reaction" honestly believing that we were doing something serious and important.
>
> (Luria, 1978, cited and translated in Kozulin, 1990, p. 80)

Vygotsky reintroduced himself to the Moscow psychological community with a bold presentation at the Second All-Russian Congress on Psychoneurology in Leningrad, January 6, 1924. Instead of reducing all behavior to reflexes or reactions and ignoring consciousness, as Sechenov, Pavlov and Bekhterev had done, Vygotsky attempted to define how consciousness arose from reflexes and then surpassed them to create higher mental activities such as language, culture, deliberate memorization and social interaction. In other words, he began with Pavlov and ended with Marx, but passed Western psychological luminaries such as James and the Gestaltists on the way.

Vygotsky (1926) began by saying that reflexology is at a turning point: Its practitioners wish to explain all human behavior, but reducing everything to conditional reflexes cannot do that. In the first place, once a conditional reflex has been learned, it is increasingly easy to condition similar reflexes throughout the body, suggesting to Vygotsky the existence of a central place where the learning passes through. He thought this central place was consciousness, in which a response to a stimulus can itself be a stimulus to the next response. Finally, as Sechenov (see Chapter 8) had said that thought was merely the first two-thirds of a reflex response that, if not inhibited, would become speech or action, thought can simply be seen as self-stimuli. In fact, language and words thus serve as *reversible stimuli*, in that language can serve as a thought stimulus to oneself or a social stimulus to others. The next step in the argument was Vygotsky's big leap—the social origins of consciousness and of the self:

> These reversible reflexes, that create the basis for consciousness (the interlacing of the reflexes), also serve as the basis of social interaction and the collective co-ordination of behavior, which, by the way, points to the social origin of consciousness. From the whole mass of stimuli one group clearly stands out for me, the group of social stimuli, coming from people; it stands out because I myself can reconstruct these stimuli, because they very soon become reversible for me and thus determine my behavior in another way from all others. They make me comparable, identical with myself. The source of social behavior and consciousness also lies in speech in the broad sense of the word. Speech is on the one hand a system of reflexes of social contact and on the other hand primarily a system of reflexes of consciousness, that is, for the reflection of the influence of other systems.
>
> (Vygotsky, 1926/1997, p. 42)

No doubt, the young upstart (he was only 27) couldn't have convinced everybody in the audience. But what he did in his talk was to start from materialism and reflexes to reintroduce many of the subject areas of psychology that were about to be thrown out by the politics of the moment. Twenty-one-year-old A.R. Luria, who was in the audience that day, was electrified by the talk and suggested later that he knew that Vygotsky was "a man to be reckoned with" (Luria, 1979, p. 39). He was hired virtually on the spot to be a faculty member of the newly reorganized Moscow Institute of Psychology. By April, without even having found an apartment, Vygotsky had moved to Moscow to live in the basement of the institute, meeting frequently with his young colleagues Luria and A.N. Leontiev, the three of whom later became known as "the troika" of Soviet psychology in Moscow.[10] Whether Vygotsky was aware that he was giving a job interview is not exactly clear, but he certainly said all the right things without compromising his central vision, a political knife-edge he would walk on for the rest of his life.

As this early speech shows, language is thus very powerful in Vygotsky's theory. Its most important function is as a cognitive mediator: The usual definition of mediator is something that acts as a go-between, an aide or a tool. In Vygotsky's theory, *language is a tool to aid thought.* Vygotsky was fond of the following example: Suppose that a woman has been asked by two men to go out and let us also suppose, for the sake of argument, that she considers the two men exactly equal in merit. How is she to choose? She could tell herself that she will go out with the first one who calls or the one who asks her most earnestly and so on. These criteria are entirely arbitrary; they were made up by her on the spot. They require self-awareness in consciousness, defined by Vygotsky as the "experience of experiences," and they bear no real connection to the stimulus and cannot be predicted by it. She could also use an accepted cultural practice to help her decide, such a flipping a coin or drawing for straws. One of the most interesting aspects of this example is that once she has made up her mind how to decide, she has also made up her mind to be a "slave" to the result! In this way, language can be used as a tool for promoting higher-level thinking (Valsiner & Van der Veer, 2000, p. 365).

In Vygotsky's work, *language and culture are essential to higher-level thought.* The insight comes from many sources, but chief among them are the theories of Marx and Engels, whose philosophy covered not merely Communism, but the evolution of humanity itself. Vygotsky seems to have been a committed reader of Marx: His writing is not marred by the tendency to spout dogma to avoid running afoul of authorities. He stated that he wished to integrate Marx into his work organically, rather than by citation, and to avoid excluding Western writers just because of their bourgeois origins (Vygotsky, 1978). Ironically, perhaps the best proof that Vygotsky was an independent thinker may be that his work was banned within a year of his death; those who worked with him were forbidden to discuss his work for more than 20 years thereafter.

Essential to Marxist theory is Engels's assertion that the evolution of labor—with its cognitive requirements for social cooperation, division of labor, specialization and hierarchical structure—has literally transformed human thought. Occasionally, Engels writes as if the evolution of our species itself may have been shifted by the requirements of labor: "It [labor] is the prime basic condition for all human existence and this to such an extent that, in a sense, we have to say that labor created man himself" (Engels, 1876/1987, p. 453). Specifically, Engels argued that the turning point in human evolution is when apes began to walk upright, thus enabling tool use. Those who discovered how to use tools were conferred an advantage in economic subsistence, reproduction and survival. Thus, according to Engels, changes in the hand muscles of early hominids were driven by the effects of labor on evolution!

Vygotsky starts from this point in his discussion of the evolution of thought, using the comparative psychology of Wolfgang Köhler to make the case that the evolution of tool use with objects and the evolution of language begin separately and unite later to allow the use of language as a tool. Vygotsky was very interested in Köhler's work with the apes on Tenerife (Köhler, 1925/1948; see Chapter 6). Köhler's work that shows that chimpanzees can use sticks to get a banana seems to support the notion that tool use can and did develop without language; Vygotsky was also aware of Piaget's early work describing the sensorimotor character of infant thought, which is qualitatively radically different from thought with words. Thus, the infant can, for example, perform repetitive actions with objects, such as a baby rattle or, a little later, bat away an object that is partially covering a toy, all before the first easily recognizable word.

But Vygotsky, unlike Piaget, notes that even in these situations, there is a social dimension. For example, by nine months of age, most babies are showing what psychologists call intentionality (see Brentano section, Chapter 6). It is pretty easy for an observer to tell that a child of this age wants something from a caregiver. Typically, since the child has no words, this is seen when he raises his arms up and grunts to be picked up or points imperiously at a piece of candy or a toy on a high shelf and says "Ga!" A child's caregiver helps him out and by handing him the wanted object, while saying "I'll get it!" at the same time, she makes the interaction a social and linguistic one. To Vygotsky, all human activity is social, even interactions with children who are not yet fully capable of social interaction themselves.

When Vygotsky tried a simple demonstration experiment with children about the age of 3 or 4 (which I will reconstruct and paraphrase here; Vygotsky, 1978), he discovered something interesting. A four-year-old girl was put in a room and shown there was a piece of candy high up in a cupboard. The room also contained a stepstool and a long wooden stick. Vygotsky reports that the girl tries to solve the problem using the tools available: First, she tries to reach the candy and says "Can't get it! I'll get the stool!" Then, she brings over the stool and stands on it, reaching as high as she can, saying again, "Still can't get to it!" She's stumped for a moment and looks around. She sees the stick, says, "The stick!" and takes it over to the stool and cupboard. Standing on the stool, she uses the stick to reach up to the back of the cupboard and pulls the candy towards her with the stick until it falls out, whereupon she triumphantly cries, "Got it!"

This task resembles the problem solving of Köhler's apes, with an added feature: The girl *talks herself through* the problem, using language as a tool every bit as much as she uses the stool and the stick. If we recall Köhler's experiments, the apes could not solve problems with several steps immediately without prior experience, and they certainly never cooperated with other apes. The four-year-old, by contrast, has shown that when the line of evolution of tool use is recapitulated in her own development, the ability to think in words is added to it. This tendency for children to solve a problem by talking to themselves out loud, often in the presence of others but not talking directly to them, Vygotsky calls **private speech**. As children get older, of course, they continue to use language as a tool, but they do not need to say the words out loud to accomplish the task. They are almost certainly talking to themselves "inside their heads," even though others can't hear them. This is **inner speech**, and it is the final step of the process of internalization of cognitive processes (or simply **internalization**). Thus, for Vygotsky, all cognition begins as external social interaction between child and a more experienced, usually older member of the culture (parent, teacher, older sibling, babysitter) and then slowly becomes completely internal and silent. Interestingly, even adults sometimes revert to private speech, speaking out loud to themselves if the task is really difficult, like finding their way to a new destination or putting together inexpensive Swedish furniture!

How is Vygotsky's notion of the social genesis of intelligence seen in everyday life? For small children, parents act often as an external memory device. They remind a child to pick up his clothes or to not forget his bag lunch. Parents hold in their minds the steps of very complex tasks, like baking cookies, and dole out the steps in the process to the child who is helping them. They remind a child to avoid danger and error (Careful! It's hot! Let me do that! Measure the flour over the sink or you'll make a mess!). Every parent helps the process of internalization of thought by guessing what a child is capable of, restricting the child's movement for safety's sake and then watching while the child tries it out. In essence, the parent stands one or two steps ahead of what a child can do alone and helps him or her not only to complete the task, but also to develop the internal thinking strategies to structure his or her own actions. Over time, the parent backs away, giving fewer instructions or reminders, because the child gains the skill to remind him- or herself. Thus, intelligence is not just what one carries in one's head. For every child, at each moment in the course of development, there is a set or **zone of independent competence**: things she can do independently, without help; there are also, of course, things she cannot yet do under any circumstances. But in between things they can do alone and things they can't do, there is a much wider group of tasks that a child can accomplish with the help of a more experienced other. These tasks—the tasks that children can do with help—are in what Vygotsky (1978) called the **zone of proximal development** (**ZPD** or **zoped**), and the process by which caregivers give the help by standing one step ahead of a child and "leading them through" the ZPD has been called **scaffolding** (Wood, Bruner, & Ross, 1976). As the child learns more, the set of tasks in the zone of independent competence grows, and the zone of proximal development is always one step ahead, moving ahead of a child's skill like the wake around the bow of a moving ship!

Being a brilliant young man with the accepted general views for the time helped Vygotsky to rocket to the top of his profession. He held positions at the Moscow Institute of Psychology and founded the Institute for Defectology (abnormal psychology and special education) and was a member of a movement to try to reform education known as "pedology" (see Vygotsky 1931/1993a; Vygotsky 1924/1993b; Vygotsky 1929/1993c). Central to this reform was a radical belief that intelligence is social, not carried entirely in one's head. Binet's standardized intelligence tests, which Vygotsky knew about but disliked, test only actions in the zone of independent competence. Vygotsky thought that the test scores only sorted children into levels or worse, that the eugenic users of such tests thought that intelligence was unchangeable. The tests said nothing about how to teach children to overcome their deficits. In fact, the test score sorted children together who, although they may have been given the same poor score, were very different in their strengths and weaknesses. It is as if a person sorting colored blocks placed all red, blue and yellow blocks in a category called "not black." Simply calling very different children "abnormal" or "subnormal" because of the similarity of their IQ scores has the same uninformative effect (Vygotsky, 1931/1993a). One child might be able to benefit from help more than another might. And knowing which suggestions they take and how many hints they need tells a teacher more about what skills are just at that point coming into being and therefore more easy to influence and strengthen. As Vygotsky said,

> From the point of view of their independent activity they are equivalent, but from the point of view of their immediate potential development they are sharply different. That which the child turns out to be able to do with the help of an adult points us toward the zone of the child's proximal development. This means that with the help of this method, we can take stock not only of today's completed process of development, not only the cycles that are already concluded and done, not only the processes of maturation that are completed; we can also take stock of processes that are only now in the state of coming into being, that are only ripening or only developing.
> (Vygotsky, 1956, pp. 447–448, cited in Wertsch, 1985, p. 68)

Vygotsky had a pressing need to help children with mental and physical handicaps, and he recognized (as Binet himself did) that a literal diagnosis of "developmentally retarded or delayed" was too simple. Drawing on Alfred Adler's idea that people with a defect often become high achievers to compensate for it, Vygotsky claimed that education had neglected the positive forces created by a defect. Handicapped children use their strengths to compensate for their deficits in ways that other children don't have to do and therefore follow many different developmental courses. Indeed, Vygotsky said, by way of example, "The psychology of blindness is essentially the psychology of victory over blindness" (Vygotsky, 1924/1993b, p. 57). Vygotsky's individualized method of testing, though neglected in the West to this day, was an insightful way to promote this idea (see Campione, Brown, & Ferrara, 1982, for modern attempts to use Vygotsky's theory of intelligence with the mentally disabled).

Thus, several great themes run throughout Vygotsky's work: Language is a tool for thinking, cognition begins as social interaction and becomes internalized, intelligence itself is social and develops in social interactions. But Vygotsky was also a great theorist of the effect of culture and history on child development, and as such is considered the father of the **cultural-historical school of psychology**. The deep insight of this school of thought is that culture is in every process of development. Culture is everywhere and nowhere in human life. It is everywhere in the sense that every relationship between people, every identity that one chooses to take up (such as masculinity or femininity or cultural role like "father" or "doctor") and every child development belief is to some degree cultural. It is nowhere in the sense that culture is often invisible to those wholly within it, and culture dictates what we would never do (such as asking an elderly person to give up her seat on an uncrowded subway train) as much as what we would do, but cultural proscriptions that are never challenged do not seem like culture at all.

Since Lamarck was proved wrong, culture is the only way that we have to pass on change. Every culture in turn is a product of history and thus all child development, beliefs about children and ways of bringing them up are also historically situated. But Vygotsky was most interested in the kind of cultural practices that directly change the ways we think as well as what we think. Anthropologists tell us, for example, that the first writing was usually used to keep track of trade, counting number and types of items traded. Artifacts, such as inscribed animal bones or knotted strings, were probably used for this purpose and allowed humans to contemplate more sophisticated exchanges. These items, as well as writing itself and conscious methods of rehearsal organization of materials and the like, constitute artificial memory and as such change the ways we are able to think from when we were relying only on natural memory. Furthermore, the uses to which memory was put have changed over time. In medieval times, religious texts, expensive and rare, were secreted in monasteries. The purpose of reading and writing was not to extract information or to evaluate arguments for debate, but to change the heart. To learn something "by heart" was therefore to have your heart and actions changed by having read and remembered the words. New techniques for using written words are always being developed. For example, there is no recorded use of words having been used to organize other words—that is, use of an index—in ancient Rome (Danziger, 2008).

Think, then, about how many ways writing allows us to organize, assimilate, criticize, revise and create our thoughts. But education consists of more than reading and writing. Consider also how different learning is in a formal classroom—with a teacher and chalkboard in front of many students—from apprenticing to a weaver or a musician. In formal classrooms, lists of items can be put up to be memorized, from various categories. The abstract categories of clothing, tools, foods and so on seem like natural ways to organize the world to Westerners. However, as the Vygotskian researcher Michael Cole and his colleagues discovered (replicating an earlier study by Luria, 1976), only students who have been trained in formal schools structure the world in this way; among the Kpelle culture in Liberia, items are organized by use: the knife that cuts the orange is grouped with a cup to put the juice in. Kpellans sent to the mission school organize items like school-taught children in the West; others do not (Cole, Gay, Glick, & Sharp, 1971). The chalkboard, the arbitrary tests and the teacher who teaches a body of literature are all cultural artifacts that teach the children many ways to think, and some of those ways are not explicitly in the curriculum itself, but rediscovered over and over by generations of schoolchildren being taught to live in a world of symbols in which sophisticated thought must be done decontextualized from where it was taught. For example, all children taught in the industrialized nations must learn arbitrary but potentially powerful memorization techniques like elaborative rehearsal, even though they are rarely explicitly taught in classrooms (Moely et al. 1992).

By contrast, the traditional Kpellan rice farmer learned to farm on the farm and continues to farm there. He might categorize types of rice or local leaves like Westerners do dogs and cats, because doing so has a psychological usefulness in his world. Westerners, on the other hand, categorize African leaves very poorly and derive no memory benefit from categorizing the leaves in this way (Cole et al., 1971).

Vygotsky never meant to imply that those from pre-industrialized societies were incapable of the kind of "higher level thought" that formal schooling inculcates in students. On the contrary, Marxist theory suggests that human thought can be and is changed by the economic changes that new technology brings. In an attempt to document such changes, Vygotsky and Luria undertook a challenging study of thought patterns of Uzbek farmers in the 1930s during forced collectivization of their land. They found, essentially, that traditional farmers were empiricists rather than rationalists! Luria gave them syllogisms like

> Sarvar and Aziz always drink vodka together; when one is drinking vodka, the other one is always drinking vodka. Now, Sarvar is drinking vodka. Is Aziz also drinking vodka?
>
> (Luria, 1976, p. 110)

The traditional farmers often declined to make the deduction, saying something like "How do I know? I wasn't there!" They based their conclusions almost entirely on practical experience, rather than on abstract logic. Luria's work suggested that after modern practices were instituted, including widespread literacy, the farmers' thinking processes might change, but not quickly enough to satisfy the commissars back in Moscow. The work was also banned for 30 years.

What is it then about schooling that makes the difference? Vygotsky called the type of cognitive development described in the early stages of Piaget's genetic epistemology **natural or spontaneous development** (Vygotsky, 1934/1984). According to Vygotsky's analysis, in infancy—Piaget's sensorimotor stage—natural development is largely biological; in the preschool (preoperational) years, children's nascent language skills focus on the use of words and ideas in an everyday way in social interaction and pretend play. They do not yet consciously see words as abstractions in interrelated conceptual structures (for example, as organized in hierarchical classifications like animal, mammal, domestic animals, dog and collie). As children grow, however, they begin to become more conscious and logical in their use of concepts, and as their consciousness expands, they become more aware of the ever-present demands of culture, through the action of caretakers, teachers, schools and the media. At this age, the differences between the minds of children taught in traditional apprenticeships versus formal schooling become apparent. Schooling takes everyday thought and everyday concepts and makes children aware of their interrelationships and teaches children to consciously navigate, analyze and add to whatever interrelationships their culture finds important. Once concepts are seen as being part of these structures of meaning, everyday concepts become, in Vygotsky's terms, scientific concepts, and their conscious elaboration in school is called **scientific development**.

Consider, as an example, a Vygotskian explanation of learning math. Preschoolers and young children can learn basic math, such as conservation of number, counting and basic addition and subtraction by manipulating objects and counting on their fingers outside of school. Indeed, unschooled eight-year-old children who sell fruit and candy in the streets of Brazil can make change, without error, for any number of pieces of candy or fruit; they do so, in fact, with fewer errors than children taught math in school (Saxe, 1997). In part, the candy sellers are more accurate because they add the total amounts together rather than using the schooled place-value system, in which children add and subtract ones and tens separately and make mistakes carrying over the ones. But the unschooled children have great difficulty generalizing their knowledge to other, similar problems, whereas children who have been to school have much less difficulty using math in many different contexts. Scientific concepts like the scientific math taught in school are transferrable; everyday concepts, like everyday math, are not. In fact, the hallmark of "scientific learning" is that things learned in school become *decontextualized*: useable everywhere and infinitely expandable. Schoolchildren often have a problem, though, recontextualizing their knowledge when needed. This is why many of us grew up hating word problems! Finally, every time a new math system is learned in school, the old math must be redefined and subordinated to it. When we begin to learn algebra and calculus as teenagers, what we thought we knew about numbers needs to change and this change is hard for many of us, but we gain vast generality of application when we make the shift. The advantage of such math is that we can use it for exalted purposes like engineering a space shuttle and figuring out how to shoot it into space and get it back, but the equations deal with ranges of numbers systematically analyzed in countless simulations and hypothetical situations.

Vygotsky's theory does not emphasize cultural-historical context at the expense of biological and cognitive development and neither does he keep individual and cultural development separate from one another. Rather, he sees child development as a dialectical process, a fruitful struggle between individual/biological development (thesis) on the one hand and cultural-historical processes (antithesis) on the other. The individual is not merely enveloped in culture but penetrated by it in a thousand different ways, producing a Hegelian synthesis called development. The process is an upward spiral across history, assuring that the child of tomorrow cannot be the child of today. To sound a slightly revolutionary note, we might say that the conditions of Labor (capital [or capitalist?] L) are being changed by new technologies and means of production (computers, Blackberries, Twitter, Facebook, Google, Skype, Wi-Fi, Spark Notes, Wikipedia, 24/7 working conditions of the new consultant/entrepreneurs, etc.) to produce the New Child of the Future!

Emotional Development

Deborah Blum (2002) begins her excellent biography of primate researcher Harry Harlow with some startling statistics about foundling homes and orphanages in 19th- and early 20th-century America. In 1915, a study of 10 such institutions by New York physician Henry Chapin showed that the mortality rate for babies committed to nine of these institutions was 100%, two years after being admitted. As appalling as this was, some orphanages succeeded in killing their charges even faster, with mortality rates in some institutions exceeding 90% at the end of only one year.

Physicians of the time understandably blamed this death rate on infectious diseases. The orphanages were often dirty and overcrowded, so that when one child got streptococcus or typhoid, the disease would rage like wildfire through the institution, killing many children (Spitz, 1945). And doctors, who were beginning to understand bacterial transmission, thought they had the remedy and so they put up signs reading, "Don't touch the children."

Quarantine and antisepsis were rigorously practiced in children's wards of hospitals and orphanages, to some effect: By midcentury, psychiatrist Rene Spitz (1945, 1946) reported rough death rates of "only" 37%! Many of these deaths were no longer due to infectious diseases, but from failure to thrive, severe weight loss or developmental stunting. Spitz used the term "hospitalism" as a diagnostic syndrome to bring attention to the plight of children in orphanages and long-term hospital care, especially infants (Spitz, 1945). Infants at risk for death cried inconsolably (the fear of touching infants having removed the consolations of a loving embrace) and engaged in such bizarre behaviors as self-clasping, rocking, self-biting and self-stimulating through flicking their fingers in front of their eyes. This was followed by near-complete apathy, sickness and often death.

Harry Harlow (1905–1981)

Meanwhile, at the University of Wisconsin, a primate researcher named Harry Harlow was finding some of the same symptoms in young rhesus monkeys. In those days, rhesus monkeys were imported from India, and they would often arrive very ill. In part because of this, Harlow had set up the first primate breeding colony in the

Figure 10.5 Harry Harlow (1905–1981) with baby rhesus macaque monkey and a "wire mother"
Source: Getty Images

United States in the 1930s, and after his monkeys suffered a tuberculosis outbreak, he began keeping the monkeys in clean, well-lighted, separate cages; but his baby monkeys, even those who were well fed round the clock by dedicated grad students, still were not doing well. They would sit in their cages, rocking back and forth, sucking their thumbs. The baby rhesus monkeys looked quite forlorn, with their big eyes and expressive faces. "We had created a brooding colony, not a breeding colony," Harlow would say (Blum, 2002, p. 146). It was all the more striking to Harlow, who knew very well from his work on monkey intelligence that normally reared monkeys were intensely curious and smart problem-solvers. Often, they would set to work on problems without external reward, and when given the choice between whether to press a button to have either tasty fruit or a look at a changing interesting scene outside their cage, would choose the scene, repeatedly, for hours at a time (Harlow, 1950; Harlow, Harlow, & Meyer, 1950; Butler & Harlow, 1954). But in contrast, the isolated monkeys separated early from their mothers would show very low exploration of their surroundings and would be socially inept. When it came time for breeding, the isolated monkeys were confused and frightened by the other monkeys and would retreat to a corner of the enclosure (Harlow, Dodsworth, & Harlow, 1965). There was one thing that seemed to comfort the baby monkeys: The students had insulated the cold floor of the cages with soft cloth diapers, and the monkeys would snuggle with them obsessively and shriek if they were removed for cleaning (Harlow, 1958). Bill Mason, then a graduate student in the lab, suggested that the monkeys be given a choice between a block of wood with soft covering and a metal feeding rack to cling to. It was quickly determined that the monkeys preferred the fuzzy object (no author [APA Lifetime Achievement Award], 1996; Blum, 2002). What happened next is a classic example of scientific creativity. Harry Harlow, on a plane back from a scientific committee meeting, looked out the window at the soft clouds and envisioned an experiment with the proper comparison, using two surrogate mothers—inanimate lab substitute mothers for the young monkeys. Both "mothers" would have wireframe bodies and heads of croquet balls, with black wooden noses, bicycle reflectors for eyes and plastic mouths and ears. One mother would have no bottle for feeding, but would be covered with padded terrycloth and warmed with an interior light bulb. The other mother would have a body made of wire mesh, not covered, but with a warmed bottle of formula, as a single "breast" in the middle of its body (Harlow, 1958).

This little variation on Mason's initial design was crucial for two reasons. First, both psychoanalytic and learning theories strongly suggested that the bond between mother and child was based on feeding. For behaviorists, it was simple reinforcement; for psychoanalysts, longing for the breast carries a strong unconscious motivation from the oral phase throughout life, but feeding on demand from a stable caregiver was considered crucial for normal development and avoiding "oral fixation." If the monkeys chose the cloth mother, from whom they could get comfort but no food, over the feeding wire mother, this would disprove both theories. Second, giving symbolic heads to the wireframe objects is what made them "mothers" and would allow Harlow to not-so-subtly suggest that the experiments might be relevant to human mother-baby attachment as well. Harlow actually wanted the faces to be ugly so that critics could not say that monkeys preferred a cute face. In fact, the monkeys didn't care which face the mothers had. One little monkey arrived early and was placed with a mother that had no face yet. Later, when the face was added, the monkey repeatedly turned the head to the blank side! No matter how ugly your mother may be, she is still *your* mother and you love her. Harlow, with his acerbic sense of humor, said, "A mother's face that would stop a clock will not stop a baby". (Harlow & Suomi, 1970, p. 164).

Harlow's lab began throwing its considerable resources towards the surrogate mother studies around 1956, four years after the death of Clark L. Hull and around the time that Ferster and Skinner's (1957) bible of reinforcement schedules was published (see Chapter 8). Midwestern American university psychology departments, including Harry Harlow's department at University of Wisconsin-Madison, were said to practice "dustbowl empiricism," a kind of "just the facts, ma'am" behavioristic paradigm-driven emphasis on data above all else. Pediatricians thought that human newborns were largely a collection of hardwired reflexes until two to three months of age or even the end of the first year; until that time, the infant was thought to be "functionally decorticated" or purely a "reflex organism" (Stone, Smith, & Murphy, 1973, pp. 3–4), and the maturationism of Gesell and Ilg still held sway. No one but psychoanalysts was talking about mother-child emotional relationships, and they were using unreliable retrospective accounts told in therapy. And behaviorists did *not* talk to psychoanalysts!

Even the new emphasis on animal behavior interpreted in natural context, the science of ethology, had not begun to penetrate animal labs in the U.S. from Europe. Harlow put his new graduate student Bob Zimmerman in charge of the surrogate mother studies (Harlow & Zimmerman, 1959), and Zimmerman was worried about doing a dissertation on monkey mother love that deviated from the learning paradigm, fearing that the other professors on a doctoral orals committee would roast him alive (Blum, 2002)!

All this would begin to change in 1958, when Harry Harlow, then the newly elected president of the APA, revealed the first report of the surrogate mother studies in his presidential address, titled, simply but provocatively, "The Nature of Love" (Harlow, 1958). The data presented were startlingly clear: Every baby monkey reared away from their real mothers in the lab preferred the contact comfort of the cloth mothers, even those who were fed on the wire mothers. They would hop over to the wire mother to feed and then hop right back to the warm fuzzy cloth mother, clinging almost exclusively to her day and night. An experiment was set up in which a baby monkey was placed in a cage with both wire and a cloth mother, and the baby was frightened by a noisy windup toy. The babies, even those raised on wire mothers, ran to the cloth mother for comfort and a few were even comforted to the point that they would "threaten" the clangy noisy toy monster. In another study, the "open field" test, the researchers took advantage of rhesus monkeys' fear of an open field. When infant monkeys were placed in a large open room with several toys and objects that monkeys reared by their real mothers generally approached with curiosity, the lone baby would scream and huddle in a corner. Placing a wire mother in with the baby was no help, even if the monkey was raised with it. But place a baby with a cloth mother and the baby would run to her for comfort. After some clinging, the baby would venture out to explore the toys, like a normally raised monkey.

And these studies were only the beginning. As in any thriving lab with a good idea, more studies extended the findings further:

- If the cloth mothers are encased in clear plexiglas, the babies will try to cling and then adapt (Harlow, 1958).
- Babies preferred rocking cloth mothers to stationary ones (Mason, 1978).
- They preferred a swinging mother to a rocking one and had better physical coordination if they were raised on one (Mason & Berkson, 1975).
- As surrogate mothers cannot hug back, some experiments were done in which baby monkeys were reared with dogs; these monkeys were more curious than other surrogate raised monkeys and after a time could be reintegrated into a social monkey colony and be indistinguishable from their peers (Harlow & Suomi, 1970).

Harlow's "Nature of Love" talk caused a sensation when the popular press got hold of the published version, and Harlow was suddenly famous and in demand by newspapers, women's magazines and television. Mothers were often pleased to be valued by the scientific community at last (although their opinions of Harlow's work would change after the women's movement took off in the 1970s). The data were obvious even to the nonspecialist, but the talk and article also included some of Harlow's charming if nonscientific bits of doggerel poetry, accompanied by photos of mother-baby pairs from the animal kingdom:

> The Hippopotamus
> This is the skin some babies feel
> Replete with hippo love appeal.
> Each contact, cuddle, push and shove
> Elicits tons of baby love.
> (Harlow, 1958, p. 677)

(Harlow was infamous for his puns and at this point in his career, he would leave little silly lines of poetry on his students' desks at night in the lab for the students to find in the morning: Blum, 2002.) For the moment, all was triumph for Harry Harlow. Later, as we will see below, his research would produce more unsettling results. But one more significant event also occurred for him during the period of experimentation that would result in the 1958 address. Even before the publication of "The Nature of Love," British ethologist and Cambridge University professor Robert Hinde (1923–2016) met Harlow at a pioneering early California meeting between ethologists and American comparative psychologists and told his friend, London psychoanalyst John Bowlby, about Harlow's early results. Bowlby sent Harlow a note dated August 8, 1957, asking for more information and enclosing a draft of his own article, titled "The Nature of the Child's Tie to His Mother" (Bowlby 1958; van der Horst, LeRoy, & van der Veer, 2008). Harlow was so impressed by the article that, in a later letter, he called it his "reference Bible" for future research (van der Horst et al., 2008, p. 376) and indeed, Bowlby's article included, nestled amongst elegant Freudian explanations, a roadmap of both men's research careers. Both Bowlby and

Harlow cite each other for the first time in their papers of 1958 and continued thereafter. They sent dozens of letters between them over the next decade and met at several conferences. A close examination of Harlow's work shows that he did indeed plan his research program to support Bowlby's theories; later, in a review of the animal literature, Mineka and Suomi (1978), students of Harlow, explicitly suggested that the protest and despair phases of Bowlby's work applied to monkeys. The paper Bowlby gave Harlow had caused a firestorm of protest in Britain as well: Discussions of love were just as revolutionary on the other side of the Atlantic. But Bowlby later recalled that his work was only taken seriously by his analytic colleagues as a result of Harlow's incontrovertible surrogate mother studies (van der Horst et al., 2008). To understand why these two men, the blunt empiricist born in an Iowa farm town and an upper-class British psychoanalyst, son of the king's surgeon, were so drawn to each other, we need to examine the life and times of John Bowlby, the great theorist of infant attachment, and Mary D. Salter Ainsworth, his student who turned into his distinguished equal collaborator.

John Bowlby (1907–1990)

Edward John Mostyn Bowlby was born into a world of upper-class British privilege. His father, Sir Anthony Alfred Bowlby, was a distinguished surgeon and professor at St. Bartholomew's Hospital, an expert in war wounds from his service in the Boer Wars and later, a high-level medical officer at the General Headquarters of the British Expeditionary Forces in the First World War. He was honorary personal surgeon to King George V, who awarded him the hereditary title of baronet (obituary, Sir Alfred Bowlby, 1929). John later evaluated his father in retrospect to have been an "inflated bully" towards his sons (Karen, 1994).

The young John did not see much of his important father or of his mother either. Typical of her time and class, she did not believe in spoiling her children with undue affection: She saw her children every day after tea for an hour in the afternoons, except for summer holidays in Scotland. In fact, the Bowlby children were not allowed to eat with their parents until age 12 and then only for dessert. John was raised by nannies and was left particularly bereft when one beloved nanny left John at the age of 4. John remembered being very lonely when he was sent off to boarding school at age 11; although he later told his wife that he wouldn't send a dog away at that age, publicly he was more circumspect. It was, after all, a common experience for children of his generation and class and would likely be perceived as normal, he said, by less sensitive children (van Dyken, 1998).

He spent his high school years in naval training at the Royal Naval College, with further work at University College, London, and received his MD with honors from Cambridge in 1933. Simultaneously, he became interested in psychology and took the final exams in the "moral sciences" (philosophy and psychology) in 1928. While at Cambridge, he became interested in psychoanalysis based on the book *Instinct and the Unconscious* by Bartlett's mentor, the distinguished anthropologist and psychiatrist and founder of the Cambridge psychology lab, W.H.R. Rivers (1864–1922).

From the start of medical training to be a psychiatrist and psychoanalyst and almost daily for seven years thereafter, Bowlby was in analysis with Joan Riviere

(1883–1962), a follower of Melanie Klein (1882–1960). Klein was a child analyst who focused not on a young child's daily life but on his or her fantasies, and in her theory those fantasies are elaborate indeed for an infant. In the first year, the infant has a love/hate relationship with the breast, without a conception of the mother as a whole being: The breast can be all-giving or, when the child's needs are not met by a neglectful mother, the breast can be devastatingly cruel. In Kleinian theory, these fantasies, developed in the irrational oral phase, could become the basis for an internal cognitive representation of the mother for the child and are seen as plaintive cries for love or revenge fantasies that the preschooler enacts against his or her parents during play.

If a young child's fantasy life is this rich, Klein reasoned, it hardly matters what the mother actually does in later years. Thus, she felt justified in ignoring much of the mother and child's real day-to-day existence, focusing on elaborate symbolic interpretations of a child's play instead, leaving the mother in the waiting room.

Bowlby was highly critical of this position for the rest of his life, as he was of the views of some that bottle-feeding could result in disturbed attachment of the child to the mother. From our vantage point today, we might find Klein's position ludicrous. A mother is far more than a breast, even if we were to grant that the infant could have such elaborate thought processes (which current research on infant memory clearly does not support). Bowlby even apparently argued against Klein's theory in his analysis with Riviere. Orthodox Freudians would of course have seen such stubbornness as unconscious resistance arising from Bowlby's childhood; Bowlby had some difficulty getting Riviere to approve his membership to the British Psychoanalytic Society in 1937 and he rarely spoke of her thereafter (Karen, 1998).

Bowlby did not deny the insights of psychoanalysis. But he wanted to validate those insights with something approaching scientific rigor, something verifiable outside of the retrospective accounts and highly subjective interpretations created in a therapist's office. He found the first such variable in his first major study at the Child Guidance Center in London. From 1936 to 1939, he collected data on 44 child thieves between the ages of 6 and 16 (Bowlby, 1946). As he wrote up these case studies, he noted that many of these children had disturbed, neglectful or manipulative parents, but that their abuse was often hard to systematically categorize or quantify. Fourteen of these young thieves were what he called "affectless": they seemed to care for nothing and no one. They had bonded with neither their parents, their caregivers at the center, nor the children who lived there. Twelve of these 14 children had had long separations from their mothers at an early age. Such separations had been easily documented and were not in dispute, and they seemed to be clearly associated with oddly detached behavior.

Bowlby's concern with parental separation was astute and timely. The Second World War and the Great Depression that preceded it caused many children in Europe to be separated from their parents: The Kindertransport program in Germany and Austria helped many Jewish children to escape the Hitler regime to London without their parents. Many British children were sent to live in the countryside to avoid the London bombings, and many children were left orphaned by the war or by the Holocaust. Anna Freud, who had escaped from Vienna at great peril just in the nick of time with her father, ran a London nursery during the war with

American Dorothy Burlingham for such children and noted their sometimes desperate attempts to maintain closeness with their new caregivers and to repress the awareness of the danger around them. One child refused to let other children touch her substitute caregiver, trying to keep her for herself, but was conflicted. "My very own Mary Ann," she would say plaintively, "but I don't like her" (Burlingham & Freud, 1944).

By 1948, the newly established World Health Organization of the United Nations commissioned Bowlby to put together a report on the situation of homeless children in Europe (Bowlby, 1951). He traveled for weeks in Europe and the U.S., consulting with experts on the effects of maternal separations and, especially, the life of young children in group settings, such as hospitals, nurseries and orphanages. What he was told was alarmingly consistent. Several observational studies (e.g. Spitz, 1945; Spitz & Wolf, 1946; Goldfarb, 1947) suggested that very young infants separated from their mothers (below three months) may adapt well to an institution if they receive substitute care; if they do not, said Bowlby, three periods follow: After a short angry *protest period*, a period of inconsolable crying that lasts for months may ensue. During this *despair period*, the child has a tragically sad expression on his or her face. This would be followed by *detachment*, a period of apathy towards the caregivers and slowed reaction to stimuli, followed by stupor, drops in developmental progress, loss of weight, illness or even death (Spitz & Wolf, 1946). Marked behavioral abnormalities were also seen in the babies, involving *stereotopies*—obsessively repetitive behaviors like rocking back and forth, waving fingers repeatedly in front of their eyes or obsessive sucking, genital touching or other kinds of self-stimulation. Over time, even these would stop. Reuniting a baby with a mother, provided they had developed a good relationship with her before institutionalization, led to almost complete cessation of these behaviors and a marked increase in functioning. No control children, not separated from their mothers, showed these problems. René Spitz (1887–1974), a Jewish Vienna-born psychoanalyst who had immigrated to the United States, said that this behavior resembled depression in adults, so he called it anaclitic depression—a depression caused by a broken or inadequate attachment to a maternal "love object," according to the Freudian terminology of the day (Spitz & Wolf, 1946). Anyone who has seen Spitz's moving silent film *Psychogenic Disease in Infancy* (1952; see the film at www.archive.org/details/PsychogenicD) would notice the depressive aspects of these children's behaviors.

Bowlby's report was more influential than he expected. He had passionately recommended that children not be removed from their mothers just because the mother was unwed or their houses were unkempt, but only in cases of serious abuse or neglect. Children should be placed with relatives if possible and foster parents if not, as soon as possible. Retitled *Child Care and the Growth of Love* (1952), it sold more than half a million copies in paperback internationally (Karen, 1994) and instigated the removal of young children from orphanages and the placement of them in foster care in many countries, including the U.S.

This movement was resisted in many cases by the medical establishment of the day. It had long been the custom in Britain and in the U.S. for children who were admitted to hospitals for serious illnesses not to be allowed to see their parents. A survey in 1951 found that of the 1500 hospitals in Britain, only 300 allowed children to be visited daily by their parents and then only for half an hour and 150 prohibited visiting altogether. The typical hospital allowed two–four hours a week, on one or two days (Robertson & Robertson, 1989). The hospital staff had noticed that when parents visited, the reunions were tearful affairs and when the parents left, young children would cling desperately to them and beg to be taken home. The longer the child was in the hospital without the parent, the more "settled" (read: detached) they became and so naturally, for the smooth functioning of the hospital, the staff limited visiting hours to an absolute minimum. James Robertson, a colleague of Bowlby's convinced of the possible long-term effects of such separation on children's emotional development, decided to expose this policy by a simple method. He edited 40 methodical hours of filmed observation of a well-behaved two-year-old girl named Laura into a 30-minute film, entitled *A Two-Year-Old Goes to Hospital* (1952). Robertson had gotten a special dispensation to allow Laura's parents to visit every other day, but even so, she pleaded piteously to her parents to take her home in their earlier visits. As time went on over the weeks, Laura appeared to disengage with her parents, to steel herself against the time when they would leave again. She became less and less responsive. After returning home, she had a brief period of regressing in her sleeping and toileting behaviors, but then, Robertson said, she recovered, "lit up by a light bulb from within" (Robertson film, 1952; Karen, 1994).

When the film was screened at a Royal Society for Medicine conference, Robertson was attacked:

> I was immediately assailed for lack of integrity", Robertson said. "I had produced an untrue record. I had slandered the professions. I had tricked the hospital; I had chosen an atypical child of atypical parents. I had ... filmed selectively and edited it dishonestly. People stood up and said that their children's wards were not like that, two-year-olds were not like that, no parents ever complained, etc., etc.
> (Interview with Robertson, 1977, quoted in Karen, 1994, p. 78)

The reception was no better in the rest of the United Kingdom or in the U.S. Some wanted it banned. Robertson even withdrew the film from general release for a time. Hospital personnel shunned him (Karen, 1994). Eventually, however, Robertson convinced a hospital administrator to allow him to film the effects on children allowed unlimited visiting hours for their parents. This was supposed to be an experiment for six weeks on one ward only. But Robertson said that the hospital was so pleased with the results that they eventually extended the privileges to all the children's wards and Robertson made a happier, companion film to his first work called *Going to Hospital With Mother* (1955). Unlimited visiting rights for parents did not become standard until the 1970s.

Bowlby's Theory of Attachment: The Attachment and Loss Trilogy

Over the next 20 years, from roughly the early 1960s to the early 1980s at the Tavistock Clinic in London, Bowlby applied his wealth of clinical and research knowledge on the bonds of infants to their caretakers to the development of a general **theory of infant attachment** and the effects on mental health and personality development when such attachments go awry. This resulted in an erudite and compassionate masterpiece that both accepted the clinical insights of psychoanalysis while attempting to replace its quasi-mystical theoretical excesses with updated evolutionary mechanisms. In the first of these volumes, *Attachment* (1969, revised in an updated second edition in 1982), Bowlby sets out the plan for the entire series. He notes that troubled adults looking backwards to their childhood in analysis can always find a plausible reason why they turned out the way they did, but that plausible reason, constructed after the fact by a patient desperately looking for a cause among his store of memories, may not be the actual reason for their adult misery. For example, an adult who believes that his parents' divorce was the cause of his painful adolescence may not actually have been more miserable than adolescents from intact families, but those children would choose a different memory as a cause. On the other hand, looking forward is difficult, because there are so many possible routes to adulthood from childhood. Retrospective accounts are always fiction, to some extent, because like all writers of good fiction, if we look back at our own lives, we want the ending to be plausible, to make the most satisfying sense possible, even if in actual fact, it may not. Scientists, unlike fiction writers, cannot imagine all the details of a single story to make it come out right. They must determine the likelihood of many possible outcomes in a real world from a childhood trauma, looking forward.

Second, psychoanalysis focuses almost entirely on a hydraulic mental energy metaphor. Libidinal energy must be released, through the gratification of drives or neurosis, and pathological personalities will develop. But where does all this energy come from? How do we measure the drives? Do children begin as pathological psychotics or neurotics with irrational fears, to be repressed in the functioning adult?

Bowlby tried in his trilogy to reform these aspects of psychoanalysis through research on the effects of the psychologically toxic "pathogen" of maternal separation on children's emotional development (Bowlby, 1969/1982, p. 5). He would use primary observational data of children's behavior, since given the trauma of maternal loss, human experiments could not be ethically done. But as such systematic observations had been rarely done at the time, despite the wealth of medical anecdotes discussed above, he would also rely on animal data.

He would ultimately use the animal data to replace the Freudian drive theory with a thoroughgoing analysis of infant attachment and maternal bonding in the animal world. Heretofore, when psychologists and psychiatrists had talked about an instinct, it was merely a placeholder for drives, in the sense, for example, that a sex drive is "explained" circularly as an instinct for procreation. In contrast, using the then new science of **ethology**, Bowlby made his case that the attachment of an infant to its caretaker is a species-specific instinctual adaptation to the fact that human children have a long period of vulnerability before maturity, necessitating a strong child-caregiver bond. Bowlby, like ethologists, was more interested in the how and why of attachment behavior than in claiming a simple "instinct for attachment."

Ethology is the area of biology that concerns itself with analysis of animal behavior in natural settings. The goal of ethologists is to examine how animals' instinctual behaviors aid in survival and reproduction in their habitats. Bowlby drew upon the work of the 20th-century pioneers of this science, Konrad Lorenz (1903–1989), Niko Tinbergen (1907–1988) and Karl von Frisch (1886–1982), who won the 1973

Nobel Prize in Physiology for their joint accomplishments. Unlike the pioneering American animal behaviorists, who focused largely on associationist learning principles that are the same across most species, the European ethologists assumed that every animal has evolved a set of instinctual responses that may be modified but cannot be eradicated. These instincts are specific to each species, though they do have a phylogeny: Each set of behaviors is passed down through evolutionary history, if adaptive, to species that share common descent. They also have an ontogenetic course: The instinctual behaviors can be modified somewhat, but not infinitely, by interaction with the environment of the individual growing animal, and the behavior may fade as the animal matures and can fend for itself.

For example, Lorenz's work on precocial birds (birds that walk soon after hatching), like geese, chickens and ducks, showed that they would attach or imprint on the first moving object of a certain size that they see in the first 24 hours after hatching. Usually, of course, this would be a mother hen, but it could be anything from a green triangle on a string (Einsiedel, 1975) to Lorenz himself (Lorenz, 1981). Lorenz imprinted graylag goslings on himself to allow him to study them more closely; a famous photo shows the tall, bearded, pipe-smoking Austrian ethologist being followed by a line of goslings across his estate in the Vienna Woods! Subsequent research on similar bird species shows that imprinting is considerably more difficult after the initial *sensitive period* of behavioral plasticity. In birds, other attachments can be formed, but the new attachments extend rather than erase the earlier one.

The tenacity of these early attachments, Lorenz argued, has an evolutionary survival function: Any chick or gosling that did not bond strongly to its mother was liable to wander off and be eaten! Moreover, this process of infant attachment is seen throughout the vertebrate and mammalian species: Lambs, who imprint by sight on the mother ewe, can imprint on many odd things during the early sensitive period, if the ewe or another sheep is not available. In one case, a lamb was imprinted by experimenters on the test pattern of an old black and white TV: When the pattern was on, the lamb stuck closely to it and behaved normally; when it was off, the lamb would become very distressed, bleating loudly to bring the mother back and running around the cage. Lambs have been known to wound themselves in this process (Cairns, 1955, cited in Cairns, 1979). Similar behavioral systems—following, crying to bring the mother, etc.—are seen in some primates, including rhesus monkeys (but not all monkeys; Bonnet monkeys are distressed only for a short period to the loss of a caregiver and adapt rather quickly [Cairns, 1979]). This distress is called separation anxiety in the ethological literature and serves the adaptive protective purpose of keeping the young of highly mobile species near their mothers. Of course, if an animal continued to have separation anxiety for its mother through adulthood, that would no longer be adaptive and so it fades after a few months, like the human babies' palmar grasp. And for some species, perhaps, separation anxiety or exclusive attachment to one mother would be maladaptive even in infancy.

Freud, who had studied embryological sensitive periods, also believed in emotional sensitive periods that have consequences for personality development. According to the theory, an infant who is not given reliable emotional and dietary nurturance on demand runs a great risk of becoming fixated in the oral stage and in consequence may grow up to be narcissistic or psychopathic. But classical psychoanalysis is a hydraulic drive theory. It emphasizes a lack or an overabundance of psychic energy. If there is too little libidinal energy (to use Freud's terms), a child is compelled to seek it out; if there is too much, its flow must be blocked (repressed) or usefully channeled (sublimated). If one has a good, responsive mother, who provides the breast on demand, the child becomes attached (cathected) to the mother, largely because she is a source of nutrition. In one of the few things that behaviorists agreed with Freudians on, behaviorists also believed that the cause of attachment is simple reinforcement through feeding; the Freudians proposed a complex, active cognitive model that follows from this that the behaviorists did not, but the cause of infant-mother attachment was the same for both theories.

Bowlby recognized that the hydraulic drive model was only a metaphor, as Freud himself seemed to accept later in his career (see Freud, 1920). No physiological ways to measure the flows of energy were ever found. By the mid-1950s, when Bowlby began studying the ethological literature in earnest, psychoanalysts had proposed all sorts of drives that could not be disproven; some of them were contradictory, like Klein's love/hate relationship of an infant for a breast. In addition to the physiological implausibility of drives, there was the problem of evolutionary and developmental implausibility: If a baby is merely recapitulating what he has inherited in Lamarckian fashion, it might be barely plausible that he could have highly complex fantasies and reasoning abilities at a very young age. In the neo-Darwinian paradigm, which allows no transfer of memories across generations, such cognitive sophistication is virtually impossible in an 18-month old.

Bowlby believed that if he could recast quasi-mystical and circular Freudian drives as ethological imprinting instincts, he could make human attachment scientifically testable. But instincts themselves are more than stimulus-response reactions for ethologists: They are full-fledged adaptive mechanisms for survival. Thus, despite their presence in every member of a species, sometimes without the need for learning, they must be flexible to aid survival. How is this resilient flexibility achieved?

Here, Bowlby relies on a theory of the computer age, new at the time of his early theorizing: that of the engineering science of control or **cybernetics**. Cybernetics originated around the time of the Second World War as radar-controlled targeting systems and missiles were first envisioned. A cybernetic anti-aircraft gun relies on detection, recognition and continuous feedback from radar to automatically lock onto and follow its target until it fires. In an analogous fashion, a baby relies on a continuous feedback loop of caring to form a bond with a caregiver and will strive to maintain that contact by any means necessary within her small repertoire of behaviors: by crying, smiling, seeking eye contact, reaching and, later, walking. If a caregiver is similarly motivated and is sensitively responsive to the child's bids for closeness, all will be well. If the mother is depressed, unresponsive, angry or awkward, the baby will still try her best, but the resulting relationship may be filled with anxiety, clinginess, dependence or, in the worst cases, protest, despair, desperate self-stimulation and detachment. In a final updating for the information processing age, Bowlby suggested that such adaptive or maladaptive feedback loops coalesce and consolidate into partly unconscious cognitive representations of caregivers in the minds of children.

464 *The Developmental Approach*

Thus, Bowlby's work united the insights of psychoanalysis with the new evolutionary science of animal behavior and then cutting-edge work on cybernetic information processing. But the theory was intended to help explain and solve a pressing practical problem: how to help infants who were removed abruptly from their caregivers avoid the possibly permanent damage to their future emotional lives. Bowlby feared that children housed in orphanages would be permanently damaged by their early lack of emotional nurturance, and the permanence of attachment of other animals to their caregivers did not give him reason to hope for the recovery of human infants.

Mary D. Salter Ainsworth (1913–1999)

Bowlby's own training in psychoanalysis left him ill-equipped to conduct empirical studies to support his theory. For that he had an excellent collaborator: Mary

Figure 10.6 Mary Dinsmore Salter Ainsworth (1913–1999), age 60, 1973
Source: Getty Images

D. Salter Ainsworth. Mary Salter (1940) was an American-born psychologist who spent her formative years in Canada. Her 1939 Toronto dissertation in developmental psychology, *An Evaluation of Adjustment Based on the Concept of Security*, was based on W.E. Blatz's security theory, which emphasized that unless an infant has a dependable source of comfort in the family in the early years, he or she may end up in either dependent relationships in adulthood or possessing an exaggerated, self-isolating sense of independence. Blatz called this feeling of familial security a "jumping off point," and Mary Salter called it "a **secure base** from which to work" (van der Horst, 2011). After a stint in World War II working in personnel selection and women's rehabilitation in the Canadian Women's Army Corps, she married Leonard Ainsworth and followed him to London for his graduate work in 1950. Her psychological research training and interests would seem tailor-made to complement Bowlby's desire for a data-based examination of attachment at the Tavistock Institute. Although she worked with Bowlby for only three years, her path was set.

The Ainsworths next moved to Uganda, where Mary almost singlehandedly conducted a detailed examination of infant attachment among the Ganda people. The richly detailed set of case studies was later published as *Infancy in Uganda* (Ainsworth, 1967). This study of 26 mothers and 28 babies under two years of age in their own homes combined the participant-observer method of anthropology, which studies behavior in cultural context, with the ethological emphasis of studying mother-child bonds in evolutionary context. As often happens when one immerses oneself in a new culture, Ainsworth began seeing old behaviors with new eyes, but with the fresh eyes of a *psychologist*. She noticed immediately that babies after about nine months differentiated their behavior between their mother and other mothers: The baby would cry when the mother left but not when others did; their welcomes were qualitatively stronger when their mothers returned compared to others. The babies flew to their mothers and buried their faces in their mothers' laps when frightened; alternatively, she noted that babies comfortable in their mothers' presence would crawl away to explore the world, always keeping the mother in sight: "The mother seems to provide a secure base from which these excursions can be made without anxiety" (Ainsworth, 1967, p. 345; Karen, 1994).

Additionally, she noticed when things were different: Overburdened mothers, with other children, unsupportive husbands or extensive work obligations, seemed to have a more tumultuous relationship with their babies, who would cling to their mothers anxiously or, in the worst circumstances, not seem attached at all.

Although Ainsworth knew that this was exploratory, correlational research, she was not able to begin to confirm her hypotheses for more than a decade, until after her relocation to Johns Hopkins in Baltimore and recovery from the stress of her divorce from Leonard Ainsworth. But finally, as she was devising a study to replicate her findings cross-culturally, she thought how to reproduce in her Baltimore lab the kinds of separations and reunions she had seen in Ganda homes. If a baby was attached to his or her mother by 12 months of age, she reasoned, the child in the presence of the mother would feel comfortable exploring a strange but safe and interesting environment, like a nice carpeted lab playroom (with, to be sure, cameras behind a one-way mirror!) using the mother as a secure base. If the mother were to leave, though, most babies would show distress, like the separation anxiety seen when lambs are separated from their mother ewes. **Securely attached** babies would presumably run to the mother with arms up when she returned, showing joy or being easily comforted in her embrace. **Insecurely attached** babies would either be anxious and hard to calm down (**anxious-resistant attachment**) or would show anger and rejection to the mother (**avoidant attachment**). This procedure, aptly known as the **strange situation procedure**, is used to this day in many studies to research the health of the caregiver-baby interaction (which is not to say that all agree on what the strange situation shows; see below). Ainsworth succinctly described how this 20- to 30-minute assessment was invented:

> I thought, Well, let's work it all out: We'll have the mother and baby in a strange environment with a lot of toys to invite exploration. Then we'll introduce a stranger when the mother's still there and see how the baby responds. Then we'll have a separation situation where the mother leaves the baby with the stranger. How does the baby respond to her departure? And when the mother returns, how does the baby respond to the reunion? But since the stranger was in the room during the first departure, we'd better have an episode in which the mother leaves the baby entirely alone. Then we could see whether the return of the stranger would lessen whatever distress has occurred. Finally, we'll have another reunion with the mother. We devised this thing in half an hour.
> (Interview with Ainsworth cited in Karen, 1994, p. 147)

The strange situation measure is not without its problems. Ainsworth preferred small, richly observed studies, done by those who had been intensively trained in her observational methods by her or her followers. Even Ainsworth's Baltimore replication of her work in Uganda used a sample size of less than 30 mother-infant pairs (Ainsworth, Blehar, Waters, & Wall, 1978). A child who seems avoidant may instead have an innate temperament that pushes her to be phenomenally independent and self-possessed; indeed, parents living in cultures where self-reliance is prized and physical contact discouraged (Germany, for example) show more avoidant babies. Does that mean German babies are damaged? If mother and baby are undergoing a difficult period, say after they have just moved house or are enduring a father's military deployment, the behaviors seen in the strange situation may not indicate anything permanent about their relationship. Finally, if the results of attachment studies are taken too rigidly, they might be interpreted to mean that children without a single caregiver—an especially solicitous stay-at-home mother in the kind of nuclear family that used to be the norm in America—may be in danger of future unhappiness. As a final analysis, though, it now seems that in the wide range of rearing styles in "good enough families," whether women work or not, in the hustle and bustle of imperfect middle-class or working-class lives, children are quite resilient and adaptable. It is perhaps at the extreme, in the kinds of situations of terrible neglect, that initially worried Bowlby, where attachment theory and research has had most effect.

At last, with Ainsworth's work, John Bowlby had one kind of evidence that was needed to support his theory and to contribute to its future development, and Ainsworth herself became a full partner in contributing to that theory. In dividing up historical credit, women very often do not receive their due (Bärbel Inhelder's work with Jean Piaget is a case in point: see earlier, this chapter). In this case, however, it can be said that her work was essential to solving the problems that Bowlby's elegant theory raised in the postwar era.

Therapy for Monkeys?

Meanwhile, back in Wisconsin, Harry Harlow, taking his cues from Bowlby's work, continued his work on early deprivation of maternal contact on rhesus monkeys, and the picture he painted of the effects of such deprivation was growing darker. He had already discovered that feeding was not enough. But when these motherless monkeys grew up, they could not handle sexual contact; the behaviors of motherless males were also inadequate (Mason, 1960). If they had babies by artificial insemination, the babies were actually lucky if their mothers just apathetically ignored them, which was usually the case. Other motherless monkeys were horribly violent and killed their babies by beating them, smashing their head against the floor or biting them, if the staff did not rescue them in time. They did not cradle the infants, no matter how often the infants desperately tried to cling to them, and they tragically kept coming back for more. But the mothers "raised" on the cloth mothers were not better (Seay, Alexander and Harlow, 1964). A cloth mother may be warm and fuzzy, but she is not responsive and cannot teach any skills to her offspring. Clearly, there were learning effects: All of the three motherless mothers who had second babies were adequate mothers to their second-borns; a later, larger study of motherless mothers substantiated this view (Ruppenthal, Arling, Harlow, Sackett, & Suomi, 1976). But there were glimmers of hope. Monkeys raised with dogs were largely rehabilitated, showing the same level of curiosity as normal monkeys (Mason & Kenney, 1974). Even a small amount of social interaction with other age mates per day lowered the aberrant behaviors of the baby motherless monkeys (Mason, 1960).

The next set of studies from Harlow's lab extended the work on isolating monkeys. Earlier work had simply taken the monkeys away from their mother at a few days or weeks of age and kept them in single cages. Harlow next isolated baby monkeys in small lighted soundproof chambers for either six months or a year. As expected, six months' isolation produced monkeys in whom all of the worst behaviors of isolation were intensified: The babies rocked back and forth autistically, engaged in self-biting and thumb sucking. Placing these monkeys in cages with normal age-mates backfired: The isolated monkeys would show extreme fear and confusion, sometimes attacking their companions, leading to counter-attacks and ending with the isolate monkeys cowering and rocking in the corner (Harlow et al., 1965). But if the six-month-old isolates were gradually placed with three-month-old normal monkeys, at first a few hours a week and then under free interaction conditions, the younger monkeys would do what all normal baby monkeys do: They tried to cling to the backs of the isolate monkeys. If rebuffed, the younger monkeys would retreat for a while, which had the effect of allowing the isolated monkeys to become accustomed to them and let them cling. Thus, the younger "therapist" monkeys would bring the isolated monkeys out of their shells and an attachment would form. After six months of therapy with the younger monkeys, despite having been severely abnormal after isolation, the isolates' overall behavior could not be distinguished from the therapists' behavior. After a further year in the company of others, human observers could not pick out the monkeys who had been isolated from those who had not. The monkeys had been effectively rehabilitated (Suomi & Harlow, 1972).

The monkeys who were isolated for a year were, at first, thought to be unredeemable. Even a short time with younger monkeys proved to be too much for them. One such monkey fainted when a scientist tried to cradle it in his hands. Harlow's last graduate student Melinda Novak suggested that a very slow desensitization procedure, similar to Mary Cover Jones's "Peter" study, might work (see Chapter 8). First, one would start off the isolated monkeys in open cages where they could just see other monkeys and self-pace their exposure, and thus acclimate to their company. Only after slow stages of familiarization could the formerly isolated monkeys be allowed to cohabit with a younger monkey. In this way, even horribly damaged monkeys could be brought some way back to normalcy, to the social level of their therapist monkeys (Novak & Harlow, 1975).

Thus rehabilitated, the year-isolated monkeys could be carefully reintroduced to age mates and further improve their social skills almost to the level of normalcy (Novak, 1979).

The final set of studies that Harlow coauthored with his students, most notably, Stephen Suomi, were inspired by Harlow's own personal pain, as his biographer has noted (Blum, 2002). Harlow was seen by many as a driven man. Even after his triumphs, like the APA presidential speech, he was always fearful that he could not come up with the next success. His intense work schedules—directing studies, serving on scientific committees, funding the lab, writing articles, up to 20-hour days—had ruined his first marriage and estranged him from his children. When his second wife died after a protracted battle with breast cancer, he fell into a deep depression, compounded by alcohol dependency, that required hospitalization. He emerged from that crisis with an interest in the causes and cures of depression, and he thought that his lab could construct a monkey model of human depression, as he had for maternal separation, and then attempt to cure the monkeys (Blum, 2002). A new, even more cruel, apparatus was created, in which monkeys, first reared normally for 45 days, would be placed for up to six weeks (McKinney, Suomi, & Harlow, 1971; Young, Suomi, Harlow, & McKinney, 1973). The cage was a V-shaped funnel of a box that Harlow, with unflinching but frightening honesty, called "the pit of despair," and it was extremely effective in creating the hopelessness that is depression. Monkeys would at first try to cling to the top of the cage but would inevitably slide down and be unable to climb out. After a couple of days of struggle, all of the monkeys would give up and sink apathetically to the bottom of the cage and stay there. If a monkey were kept in this situation for up to a month, he would be rendered catatonic and almost could not recover. Two monkeys emerged and starved themselves to death. One monkey, having been normally raised for the first month and a half, was cheerfully normal; after being in the pit for six weeks, he was reintegrated to the monkey colony and was never the same. The researchers put fewer than a dozen monkeys in the chambers and could stand it no more. They took the cages apart and never used them again. Although the articles based on the studies mention no ethical qualms, Harlow's colleagues were appalled (Blum, 2002).

Times were changing on many fronts. Harlow could conduct studies involving what we would doubtless consider animal abuse today. Harlow had a standing rule that animals should not suffer negative consequences unless some attempt would be made to rehabilitate them; in addition, of course, he was following the then standard use of animals in studies deemed unethical for human experiments: "Remember, for every mistreated monkey, there exist ten million children," he said. "If my work will point this out and save only one million human children, I really can't get overly concerned about ten monkeys" (Blum, 2002, p. 292). But that is now not considered enough. The psychological field as a whole was slow to accept outside ethical regulation of its experiments. The first Federal Animal Welfare Act was enacted in 1966, but it covered mainly dogs and cats and stopped at the laboratory door. Legislation covering experiments on monkeys passed only in 1970 and Animal Use Ethics Committees were established as a part of a 1985 extension of the act (from the U.S. Department of Agriculture website; Adams & Larson, 2012). As comparison, the Belmont Report "Ethical Principles and Guidelines for the Protection of Human Subjects of Research" (governing respect for human autonomy, informed consent, minimization of harm and lack of coercion in all federally funded research) was published as late as 1978 (United States National Commission for the Protection of Human Subjects in Biomedical and Behavioral Research, 1978).

Perhaps ironically, by the mid-1970s, Harlow, Bowlby and Ainsworth, who had begun their careers advocating for the worth of mothers and children when discussing emotion in psychology was strongly discouraged, when the insights and contributions of women were devalued and newborn behavior was considered to consist only of reflexes, began to run afoul of the women's movement. Women began to feel like researchers' focus on their role only in child rearing was insulting. Both of the men were fighters and they weren't about to modify their expression to meet the current fashion, so they seemed by current standards to be reactionary sexists, especially when their comments were assessed out of the context of their careers. In 1989, the year before his death, John Bowlby said this during the then raging day care debate, in an interview with Robert Karen:

> This whole business about mothers going to work . . . it's so bitterly controversial, but I do not think it's a good idea. I mean women go out to work and make some fiddly little bit of gadgetry, which has no particular social value and children are looked after in indifferent day nurseries. . . . Looking after other people's children is very hard work and you don't get many rewards for it. I think that the role of parents has been grossly undervalued, crassly undervalued. All the emphasis has been put on so-called economic prosperity.
>
> (Karen, 1994, p. 319)

These views were echoed by Ainsworth around the same time (Karen, 1990).

Harry Harlow's comments on "women's lib" were even worse. His sharp wit could be sweet or stinging; in the 1970s, he would say outrageous things intentionally to get a rise out of the women in the audience:

> A woman's libber's not a saint
> She's just a girl with a complaint
> The sexes aren't created equal
> A tragic story with no equal.
> (Blum, 2002, p. 242)[11]

The social changes of the 1960s and 70s for women in wealthy Western countries led to a heightened sense of concern for children's welfare. As middle-class women entered the workplace in larger numbers in the generation after the postwar homemaker generation of the baby boom, they worried how children would fare in day care, if Harlow, Bowlby and Ainsworth were right. The answer is complex, but decades of research have concluded that although quality of day care does matter, the size of effects on children's emotional well-being are small and day care experiences do not override an otherwise positive home life (see e.g. Belsky et al., 2007). In fact, Head Start and other early quality day cares can have both intellectual and emotional benefits for the school readiness of disadvantaged children compared to full-time home rearing in poor or troubled families and communities (Love, Chazan-Cohen, Raikes, & Brooks-Gunn, 2013). Within the wide normal range of "good enough" parenting, rather than perfect parenting (a term originating with British object-relations psychoanalytic practitioner and theorist D.W. Winnicott [1896–1971]), children seem to be remarkably resilient rather than fragile. The most important contribution of attachment theory, however, concerns the effect of early caregiving that is far below the norm, which was, after all, Bowlby and Spitz's original concern.

The Importance of Attachment in Current Research

One episode in recent history shows the developmental consequences of terrible early rearing conditions. In 1967 in the country of Romania, during the reign of Communist dictator Nicolae Ceausescu, it was ordained that all women must have five children, a policy insured by monthly government pregnancy tests and severe punishments for abortion or contraception. As his grip on power in his Stalinist police state grew, he also decreed that virtually all of the gross national product would go to foreign debt, impoverishing and starving his people (Blumenthal, *New York Times*, Dec. 26, 1989). Romanians, faced with more mouths to feed but nothing to feed them, consigned their children to horrible state orphanages, where they were left in squalid conditions, unattended for days at a time, with several children per crib. When Ceausescu was executed in the Christmas Day Coup of 1989, authorities were faced with a huge number of orphans who had lived in such conditions, sometimes for years, and nowhere to put them. As there was no functioning foster care system, some children were randomly assigned to Romanian foster families as they came available and others were left in the orphanage until more foster parents were trained or they were adopted or reunited with family members. A team of American researchers started the Bucharest Early Intervention Project to study the differences over time between those children who remained in the institution, children in normal Romanian families and children raised in foster families (e.g. Zeanah, Smyke, Koga, Carlson, & The BEIP Core Group, 2005).[12] Other children were adopted by middle-class Canadian (Chisholm, Carter, Ames, & Morison, 1995; Chisholm, 1998) or English (Rutter, Sonuga-Barke, Beckett, & Castle, 2010) families, compared to other groups and kept track of for years.

Typically, the children, when discovered, were less than half of the normal mental age on many scales. But the good news from these studies is that for those who had spent less than two years in the orphanages, the children bounced back well physically and mentally. By the age of 11, those in the English study were within normal weight limits and were above 90 on average IQ. For most children raised normally, IQ stabilizes by this age, but the Romanian orphans continued to improve intellectually into their teens. This is consistent with what the other studies found, to varying degrees. However, a high proportion of these orphans show what is known as disorganized attachment. Children with disorganized attachment do not seem to have preferred attachment figures. They might be extremely cautious or wary of forming attachments to caregivers or, alternatively, be as over-eagerly friendly to total strangers as to family members or sometimes alternate between the two states. If it persists, such children may be diagnosed as having reactive attachment disorder (RAD), which includes both fear and withdrawal (like Harlow's monkeys) or overfriendliness in the list of symptoms. These children are sometimes described as desperate for a caring connection, but terrified of being punished if they seek it. More than 40% of the Romanian English adoptees, who have been followed by researchers longest and most rigorously, show these traits into adulthood, as well as a "quasi-autistic" inability to read subtle social cues, along with attention deficits and cognitive deficiencies in complex planning and reasoning. Rutter et al. (2010) call this constellation of traits deprivation-specific psychological patterns, and they are rarely seen in children who have not been severely abused. And some children, even among those raised some time in very poor conditions, do not show these patterns at all and do fairly well over time.

Orphanages have not been eradicated everywhere. In Russian "baby homes," for example, caregivers in 24-hour shifts, with 48 hours off, are expected to feed 16 infants in a single hour, with an average child-to-caregiver ratio of 14 to 1. This is not a plum job, except for those whose second job on their off days claims much of their attention, so turnover in caregiving is so great that a child could have been cared for by as many as 100 different caregivers by the age of 4. Once again, a consortium of American researchers attempted to improve conditions. In a control home, working conditions were kept the same, but the home was spruced up and medical attention improved. In a second home, caregivers—many who had been raised in conservative, punishment-filled provincial Russian poverty—were given 60 hours of paid training, including 19 written modules, in responding sensitively and immediately to children's bids for affection, but kept to their regular shift schedule. A third home received the same training, but fewer children to care for, "family time" of two hours daily with their charges and a more rational work schedule of seven hours a day for four days and one 12-hour shift a week—no more one day on and two days off. Children always had at least one of their two familiar caregivers present for consecutive days. Those who had been given special sensitivity training did use it, but only those who had sensitivity training *and* better working conditions kept it up over time and, when they did, their children excelled on nearly every measure: from weight and height gain to muscle coordination, to social responsiveness, to self-care and language skills, to cognitive ability and healthy, creative, interactive play. And the caregivers were much happier with their jobs and likely to continue in them (St. Petersburg-USA Orphanage Research Team, 2008). It is clear that neither children nor caregivers benefit from being warehoused! The researchers hope that the positive results will lead to an eventual reform of the baby home system, especially as virtually all severely disabled children in Russia are cared for in this system; they often benefit the most from the improvements.

In conclusion, contemporary critics could find many faults with the early research on emotional development. Even if one agrees that Harlow's research on monkeys has something to say about human children, he or she might be appalled at the ethics of the work. Bowlby's work is more heavily laden with Freudian jargon than one might like these days. Ainsworth's expectation that her 30-minute strange situation would say something about the effect of early mother-child interaction on later personality traits is probably overoptimistic, the measure is a complex qualitative one and her sample sizes were too small. Children across a wide range of cultures in normal circumstances or even poor circumstances with one loving person to cling to are pretty resilient. And yet, these researchers were tapping into something real: Every human child needs at least one consistent, loving caregiver who is sensitive to the child's needs and responsive to his or her bids for affection. More than one such caregiver is fine and no such caregiver need be perfect. If that caregiver is lost, find another quickly, for the longer the child is without one, the harder it will be to ameliorate the damage, but never assume that the damage does not occur or that it cannot be lessened by a dedicated application of love.

Social Development: The 20th-Century History of Socialization

The study of the social development of children is notoriously broad and diffuse. It includes areas as diverse as the effect of parental rearing styles on children's identification or other later behavior with parents, children, teachers and others, to gender role identification, to aggression or friendship with peers or siblings, to morality or acceptance of societal conventions and much else. Adding to the difficulty is the fact that all social development must be interpreted with reference to societal norms of behavior—the permissible range of social behavior allowed within a culture to which a child is expected to conform. In other words, the study of what children *do* in social situations is intimately and unavoidably linked with what children *should do* to be a good child and what parents *should do* to produce an adult who internalizes and follows these societal norms. In developmental psychology, this is called the process of socialization, or how children are brought up by their parents, teachers and social structures to conform to the cultural standards of that time and place. The study of socialization is therefore the science of a value-laden process.

The history of socialization research, like the work on early emotional development, was influenced strongly by the cross-fertilization of the two grand theories of the mid-20th century of psychoanalysis and behaviorism, and the framework of socialization research was first built on a bold attempt to unite these two disparate theories by a group of students or colleagues of Clark L. Hull at the Institute for Human Relations at Yale University. In *Frustration and Aggression* (1939), the authors John Dollard, Neal Miller, Leonard Doob, O.H. Mowrer and Robert R. Sears were concerned with translating Freudian drive-related behaviors into testable behavioristic propositions (see also Chapter 8). They forthrightly state that aggression is always a consequence of frustration: "[T]he proposition is that the occurrence of aggressive behavior always presupposes the existence of frustration and contrariwise, that the existence of frustration always leads to some form of aggression" (Dollard, Miller, Doob, Mowrer, & Sears, 1939, p. 1). They point out that living in social groups requires suppressing aggression, but in so doing, the aggressive impulse has not been dissipated, but is often redirected and expressed by verbal or physical aggression later towards the object of frustration or a substitute, as when a husband berates his wife after losing an argument with his boss or that a child might play roughly with her toys after her mother denies her an ice cream cone. When the *goal response* is emitted in this way, the behaviors leading up to it are reinforced.

Before B.F. Skinner argued that drives should be removed from behaviorist theory entirely,[13] both psychoanalysis and behaviorism were drive theories that suggested that reaching a goal satiated a hunger, sex, freedom or social affiliative drive. Not reaching that goal led to frustration, and frustration led inevitably to aggression in some form. Other Freudian concepts that the Hullians were concerned with (Dollard et al., 1939; Sears, 1943; see also Borstelmann & Maccoby, 1992, September 15) were *anaclitic identification*, in which children were motivated to imitate their same-sex parent, and *defensive identification*, in which children were driven not to imitate the opposite-sex parent. Of course, the difficulties involved in these identifications are dealt with in the resolution of the Oedipal conflict, and a failure to resolve it might lead to *dependency*, a serious difficulty for children raised in independence-obsessed America.

Robert R. Sears (1908–1989), Eleanor Maccoby (1917–2018) and Albert Bandura (1925–present): Socialization and Social Learning at Yale, Harvard and Stanford

Robert R. Sears began and ended his career as a loyal son of Stanford University. His father taught at the School of Education, and he earned his undergraduate degree at Stanford where he met Pauline (Pat) Snedden (1909–1994), also the daughter of a Stanford professor and psychology student. After he completed his PhD on goldfish conditioning at Yale under Hull and she completed her master's degree at Teachers College, Columbia University, they were married. A short stint at Illinois convinced Robert Sears to shift his focus from the conditioning lab to the development of personality, which at that time was dominated by psychoanalytic ideas. The Searses returned to Yale, with Robert as professor and Pat as a doctoral student in clinical psychology. His work on *Frustration and Aggression* (Dollard et al., 1939) and her PhD were completed there. From 1942 to 1949, Robert was the director of the Iowa Child Welfare Research Station, the oldest child development institute in the country, briefly overlapping with Kurt Lewin (see Chapter 6) and while Albert Bandura was a graduate student at Iowa. Then it was on briefly to Harvard to start the Laboratory of Human Development at the Harvard Graduate School of Education and to start the massive interview study of 379 mothers that became *Patterns of Child Rearing* (discussed later; Sears, Maccoby, & Levin, 1957). When he left in 1953 to chair the Stanford Psychology Department, he turned over direction of the project to Washington State native Eleanor Maccoby, who had followed her husband Nathan to Boston and was finishing her PhD from the University of Michigan in

B. F. Skinner's lab, while simultaneously working on surveys at the Institute of Social Relations with Jerome Bruner and Sears.

Soon, Sears had hired Bandura and Maccoby for Stanford, and finally, Pat Sears was given a tenure-track position at the Department of Education, 17 years after receiving her PhD, having had to work on the fringes of the academic system because of essentially sexist anti-nepotism rules, although she had a career as a psychotherapist of children. The Searses founded a child development institute at Stanford that continues to this day and stayed there for the rest of their lives (biographical information from Sears, 1980, and Chronbach, Hastorf, Hilgard, & Maccoby, 1990).

The Searses and their coauthors of *Patterns of Child Rearing* (Sears et al., 1957[14]) had great ambitions. After a small pilot study showed some promise (Sears, Whiting, Nowlis, & Sears, 1953), the Sears group (at Harvard, then Stanford) conducted what they hoped would be a definitive study. Recasting the frustration-aggression hypothesis and other Freudian ideas into testable forms was meant to explain how 379 New England mothers, broadly middle class and presumably white—no race is mentioned, although there is some diversity in national origin—choose to rear their children, what effect their practices have on their kindergarten child's development and why they choose their methods. A meticulous two-hour open-ended but structured interview asked mothers, in nonjudgmental commonsense terms, about some behaviors that are important to Freudian theory, such as breast-feeding and weaning, toilet training, sexual behavior (masturbation and sex play), sex typing, identification and development of conscience. The interviewers also asked about some behaviors thought to relate to developmental consequences, such as parental warmth and discipline techniques such as praise and punishment, including spanking. Of most interest were behaviors that might be considered *changeworthy* or likely to need intervention by the parents to avoid. For example, *dependency* was seen as necessary in any good mother-child bond in infancy, but a bad thing later on from the point of view of both Freudian theory and also the dominant American cultural value of no-nonsense independence.

> The ultimate aim of the socialization process, as it relates to dependency, is for the child to be fond of the mother rather than passionately attached to her, to be pleased by her attention, but not incessantly to demand it.
> (Sears et al., 1957, p. 140)

But Sears and his team were not like John Watson—a pat on the head is not enough:

> In a normal young child, the dependency motive appears to be a powerful one. It cannot be eliminated and it cannot be ignored. In fact, the more the child's efforts to satisfy it are frustrated, the more insistent and all-absorbing are his supplications.
> (Sears et al., 1957, p. 140)

The problem was that the study failed to find much evidence for these assumptions. Although the long interviews were laboriously transcribed and coded so that parental practices could be correlated with mothers' reports of behaviors, such correlations were small. If psychoanalysts were right, there should be some correlation between warmth of mother, feeding on demand, breast-feeding vs. bottle-feeding or age at weaning, and mothers' reports of dependency behaviors, and there were none. Frustrating a child's bids for feeding did not have inappropriately high dependency, disconfirming the researchers' predictions. The relationship between mothers' current warmth and current dependency was slightly stronger, but even significant correlations were under $r = .20$.

Concerning parental aggression, Sears et al., 1957, postulated that there seemed to be a dichotomy between *love-oriented techniques* like praise as a means of reward, isolation as punishment and withdrawal of love as punishment on the one hand and *object-oriented techniques*, such as tangible rewards, deprivation of privileges or spanking as punishment on the other. And the one finding that the authors unequivocally support is that *punishment does not work:*

> The evidence for this conclusion is overwhelming. The unhappy effects of punishment have run like a dismal thread through our findings. Mothers who punished toilet accidents severely ended up with bedwetting children. Mothers who punished dependency to get rid of it had more dependent children than mothers who did not punish. Mothers who punished aggressive behavior severely had more aggressive children than mothers who punished lightly. They also had more dependent children. Harsh physical punishment was associated with high childhood aggressiveness and with the development of feeding problems.
>
> Our evaluation of punishment it that *it is ineffectual over the long term as a technique for eliminating the kind of behavior toward which it is directed.*
>
> (Sears et al., 1957, p. 484, emphasis original)

Two further large studies were done to substantiate Freudian developmental ideas. Sears, Rau, and Alpert (1965) added two episodes where they watched how four-year-old children made bids for attention of their mother in completing a task and interviews conducted with mothers, fathers and preschool teachers. Here, too, there was little support for the hypothesis that dependency was a singular personality trait related to rearing practices. There were six independent measures of dependency in the study and six of maternal warmth. Of the 36 correlations done, three were significant for boys and none for girls (Sears et al., 1965, p. 246; Yarrow, Campbell, & Burton, 1968, p. 40; with so many correlations, two such significances would be expected by chance alone even if there were really no relationship between the variables in the real world). A final study using the same interview items as Sears et al. (1957), but examining 252 correlations, found only 18 significances at the $p < .05$ level (Yarrow et al., 1968) and most of those implicated a connection between parental aggression and dependency.

This is not to say that the studies found nothing, but most of what they found was consistency in answers on the questionnaire, in that, for example, strict parents favored controlling discipline methods whenever questions involving discipline came up. What they were actually doing or how consistent they were in applying their principles, as opposed to what they believed they were doing, could not be answered in an interview study or in brief observations.

Marian Radke-Yarrow (1918–2007), a pioneering woman in psychology, known for her work on prejudice and altruism in children (Weerakkody, 2011), wrote a well-timed "relentlessly critical" critique of the flaws of interview socialization studies, especially those that rely heavily or exclusively on mothers' reports of their children's behavior (Yarrow, 1963). When it came time to publish the results of some of her own work, she was even more critical (Yarrow et al., 1968). Some of her points (Yarrow, 1963) were:

1. The data are self-reports from "extremely ego-involved reporters." Mothers have a vested interest, consciously or unconsciously, in being seen as good mothers.
2. The mothers in these studies read baby advice books such as those by Dr. Benjamin Spock[15] or Arnold Gesell or advice in women's magazines and were therefore likely, consciously or unconsciously, to report the norms rather than their actual behaviors.
3. The questions asked for modal behavior (e.g. "What do you usually do when your child asks for help?") which requires a mother to *remember* many instances and to implicitly make very complex judgments and averages of her practices.
4. Mothers are required to rate their own and their child's behaviors relative to other mothers and children.
5. When a mother knows that the child and father will be asked similar questions individually, she tends to be less critical than when she believes that only she is being interviewed.

The construct of dependency had promised to unite the drive theories of behaviorism and psychoanalysis in the 1940s, when both were riding high. It was also consistent with trait theories of personality, which hoped at the time to reduce personalities to a set of stable, internal global traits that help people persist and adapt across contexts. Age-inappropriate dependency was seen in the mid-20th century as a negative in psychological theories, American cultural norms and, in some cases, called regressive behavior in psychiatric diagnosis. And that was not all. Sears et al. (1965) attempted to substantiate the Freudian notion of identification, that children must identify with the same-sex parent and reject as a model the opposite-sex parent. Whether a child does this was supposed to be related to the warmth of the parents, the use of love-oriented discipline, the high demands of parents and use of the parents as models of good behavior. Although both boys and girls sought out positive attention from the appropriate parents, none of the above factors was significant.

So who was wrong, Freud or the researchers and their methods? It is very hard to interpret why studies fail, but the failure of these studies caused a waning of interest in Freudian explanations of social development. The third major "changeworthy" behavior of interest to the Sears group was aggression, based on the frustration-aggression hypothesis, which was used by Dollard et al. (1939) to explain everything from a child's anger at not getting ice cream to racism and Nazi Germany. Sears et al., 1957, had concluded punishment to be counterproductive and Sears et al., 1965, had interpreted the fact that aggression was higher in stricter families as the notion that aggression for boys is related to a strong punitive father who demands aggression in his son, but who frustrates him by brooking no aggression towards himself—in other words, aggressive modeling with suppression of aggressive expression.

This left the way open for Albert Bandura and Richard Walters's (1963) **social learning theory**, which in turn led to the boost in **social cognition**. As the reader will recall from Chapter 8, operant conditioning requires that a response be emitted and then reinforced for learning to occur. Bandura and Walters's social learning theory (Bandura & Walters, 1963), by contrast, suggests that many novel behaviors are learned first by observing a model, similar to oneself, perform the behavior correctly and be reinforced for it. The child thus learns the behavior without being reinforced for it at the time and then only emits the behavior in situations where he or she can expect reinforcement. This process, sometimes called *observational learning*, was confirmed by Bandura's famous "bobo doll" aggression studies (Bandura, Ross, & Ross, 1961, 1963): Children shown an aggressive model being reinforced for performing novel aggressive acts in play played aggressively; children shown a model not being reinforced for aggressive acts could still perform the novel aggressive acts when given the opportunity to be rewarded for them. But what is often not mentioned is that children who were merely frustrated (by not being allowed to play with some attractive toys) did not play aggressively later; moreover, children who did play aggressively would be predicted by the frustration-aggression hypothesis to decrease their aggression later having "satisfied the aggressive drive and achieved catharsis," as the Freudian jargon would put it. This did not happen. Children reinforced for aggression became more aggressive, not less so, later (see Chapter 8). Thus, Bandura and his colleagues called the frustration-aggressive hypothesis into question, along with psychoanalytic explanations for social behavior. Drive theories in general became more and more in disrepute, and the reign of social learning theory began in the field of social development.

The last, but by no means least, Stanford professor to be discussed in this section is Eleanor Maccoby (1917–2018), who in her lifetime has been a significant contributor to or supporter of almost every major subfield of social development up to the present day. This includes socialization (e.g. Sears et al., 1957; Maccoby, 2007), development of sex roles (e.g. Maccoby & Jacklin, 1974; Maccoby, 1998), aggression (e.g. Maccoby, 2004), divorce and custody arrangements (e.g. Maccoby, 1999, 2005), parent-child interactions (Martin, Maccoby, & Jacklin, 1981), and much, much more; a stroll through the PsycINFO database finds her contributing to everything from selective attention to birthweight to neonatal hormones. And of course, she is one of the pioneering women of psychology, who would frequently be the only faculty woman on committees in her early career, suffering subtle and blatant discrimination from some, along with receiving considerable and deserved help from others (Maccoby, 1989).

As she relates in her autobiography (Maccoby, 1989), Eleanor Emmons was born in Tacoma, Washington, in 1917. Her mother had been a professional musician before she married Eleanor's father, who owned a wood milling factory. As they had no sons, Eleanor was allowed to be a tomboy, who would rather climb trees than do girl things. She began reading at four and never stopped, four to six books a week as a child and, later, the English and Russian novelists. In high school, a girl was walking down the hall with a copy of *The Origin of Species* under her arm; she was so excited

Figure 10.7 Eleanor Emmons Maccoby (1917–2018)

about reading it that Eleanor read and discussed it and much else, together with her new friend. This was not a radical thing to do in her family, as they had become relatively freethinking Theosophists, a quasi-religious pantheistic group that also draws on Eastern and Western philosophy and science. In high school after conducting and failing to replicate some experiments on ESP, Eleanor became skeptical of the Theosophists' more mystical ideas and gave them up (along with their vegetarianism!). She was growing up during the Great Depression in a part of the country where radical political movements were occurring and became interested in liberal and even socialist social causes, something she continued with, on and off, with varying degrees of enthusiasm and disillusionment throughout her life.

If this gives the impression that her work was colored by political beliefs, it should not. Throughout her life, when any system of thought threatened to become a faith resistant to empirical challenge—and that includes faiths like behaviorism and feminism, she would take from them what was valuable and move on. Following this period of youthful searching, she became a curious, appropriately skeptical intellectual scientist. In an interview for the Society for Research in Child Development, for which she served as president (1981–1983), she stated,

> I have felt and still feel that the important thing about having a career in psychology is first of all to decide whether you are a scientist. Now I'm talking about having a career as a research psychologist and not a therapist, which I think takes quite different skills. But if you're going to be an academic person who does research and teaching, you have to be an intellectual. Not everyone is and not everyone values it, even. So you have to be a pretty intense and committed reader, I think, for one thing, as well as a consumer of research, other people's

research. You have to care about how experiments come out and be guided by their results.

(Maccoby, 1992, p. 1)

After two years at Reed College in Oregon, separated by a year when she learned shorthand to make tuition money as a secretary, she was inspired by a professor to study at the University of Washington-Seattle with Edwin Guthrie (1886–1959), a behaviorist who believed, contrary to Thorndike and Skinner, that learning (in cats) could happen without reinforcement, simply by associating stimuli and responses. This was called *contiguity theory*. Eleanor became a behaviorist. She said Guthrie made her study the classic textbook by Earnest Hilgard and Donald Marquis's *Conditioning and Learning* (1940; Hilgard and Marquis were at Yale with Hull, and Sears and Hilgard moved to Stanford before Sears was invited back; Sears, 1980) from cover to cover. She was at Washington when Skinner's *Behavior of Organisms* (Skinner, 1938) came out, and they read and discussed it avidly, especially because it directly contradicted Guthrie!

At Washington, Eleanor Emmons met, courted (on a tennis court, actually) and married, at the start of her senior year, another bright young psychology student from Reed College named Nathan (Mac) Maccoby (1912–1992), and they began their tricky path together as the prototypical two-professor family. After he finished his master's degree at Washington, Eleanor followed her husband for the next eight years, when both of them started graduate school at the University of Michigan; Eleanor Maccoby would not be offered a full-time, tenure-track faculty position until 1958.

At this point, I hear my readers groan, "Not another talented woman subordinating herself to her husband's career!" Fortunately, that is *not* what happened. I will now detail in full what did happen as a case example of the best-case scenario for the career of a highly competent woman in her day. She followed Mac to Oregon without finishing her BA degree—they were both bored; she came back and finished. She followed him to Washington, DC. He got a job doing opinion research for the War Department before being drafted into another research unit in the War Department in 1942. She got a job doing opinion research working under Rensis Likert, the inventor of the Likert scale, and creating, giving and analyzing opinion research—a new study every 10 weeks—for the war effort. She met folks like Earnest Hilgard (by then at Stanford), who was no doubt impressed that she knew his book cover to cover, and Jerome Bruner (Harvard), among others. After the war, Likert wanted to move his crack opinion research team wholesale to the University of Michigan, where Donald Marquis, who was no doubt also impressed that Eleanor knew his book from cover to cover, allowed her and Mac into the graduate program. Mac finished first and got a faculty job in Boston; Eleanor followed, without finishing her dissertation. That was OK. By 1949, Skinner, who undoubtedly knew Hilgard and Marquis, was at Harvard and no doubt impressed that she knew *his* book cover to cover, even if she had been a Guthrie-ite (and a woman—throughout her time at Harvard, she had to have men check out books from the library for her, as women were not allowed to do such things at Harvard, of course). He gave Eleanor Maccoby space in his lab to finish her dissertation. She finished her Michigan PhD over the summer. Jerome Bruner (1915–2016) wasn't in the psychology department, but he was at the Institute for Social Relations on the Harvard campus, where they were allowed to do more fun things than the behaviorists were. That was fine for Eleanor, who was, after all, well read in social sciences and a little burned out with all behaviorism all the time—and Bruner had surveys that needed tending. Robert Sears, who knew Marquis (remember Sears's dissertation on conditioning goldfish?) and probably Bruner, was stolen from Harvard to be chair at Stanford, and *he* had surveys that needed tending that he was leaving behind, so he left Eleanor Maccoby in charge. That became Sears et al., 1957. Congratulations, said Sears, the book is done. It's 1958. Why don't you and Mac come take a sabbatical at Stanford? Intellectually stimulating work, gorgeous views in the not-yet-Silicon Valley of Palo Alto. Eleanor could not take a sabbatical, of course, because she was not technically a professor—couldn't be, you see, because this was Harvard and she wasn't a man (as late as 1972, of the 752 professors at Harvard, only 14 were women, seven of them in one department). Technically, she lost her job. Fortunately, Bob Sears was a stand-up guy and surprised them both with tenure-track job offers. Only Eleanor was in the Psych Department; Mac could do survey research in the Department of Communications, which he would be setting up. Besides, the nepotism rules prevented both halves of a married couple being in the same department. By the 1960s, Eleanor was a full professor. When the student radicals took over the administration building in the protests, they got hold of the personnel files and read the professors' salaries out loud. Eleanor Maccoby found out that she was the lowest paid tenured full professor on campus. That was rectified immediately. By the end of her career, she had published over 100 books and articles, even though for much of that time she was part-time raising their kids. The earliest article listed in PsycINFO is in 1947 and the latest is 2007 at the age of 90.[16]

Maccoby graciously downplays the role of sexism in her career, saying that at every point she needed one, an opportunity presented itself and she took it. She assumed that her worth would be rewarded and it was. She even is grateful for Stanford allowing her to go part time when childrearing obligations that traditionally fall to women fell on her. But it's clear that she felt she needed to be encyclopedically well read, she had male colleagues willing to buck the system for her and a supportive spouse and she was still underpaid. Such were the complications of the lives of women professionals in the mid-20th century.

The life of Eleanor Maccoby is a useful case study for another reason: She was present and involved in every major shift in the study of social aspects in development in the 20th century. As discussed above, she began her career as a strict behaviorist, cut her teeth in applied work and was influential in the waning days of psychoanalytic explanations of socialization. The remainder of this section will address her contributions to the social learning period of the 1960s and 70s, the rise of social cognition starting in the 80s and the present emphasis on biobehavioral explanations. Although she contributed to every area of social development, one of the areas to which she has been truly indispensable is children's development of gender roles and gender-typed behavior, to which we now turn.

Eleanor Maccoby's contribution to the literature on the development of sex differences is exemplified by (but not exhausted by) three books, spread over more than

30 years. Maccoby's gender work began solidly in the social learning paradigm—psychoanalytic explanations were no longer used, and it was clear that cognition and biology would need to be added to behavioristic explanations. Maccoby and her colleagues postulated three mechanisms for children to acquire cultural norms of gender roles (see Maccoby & Jacklin, 1974):

1. *Direct socialization*: Family, teachers and peers would reinforce appropriate behavior and punish inappropriate behavior directly.
2. *Imitation and modeling*: Children imitate and model the actions of their same-sex parent and same-sex peers.
3. *Self-socialization*: A child first grasps which gender he or she is and seeks out and matches his or her behavior to activities appropriate to that self-definition.

Later (Maccoby, 1998), she would add a fourth determinant:

4. *Gender group context*: It is inaccurate to consider masculinity or femininity as a stable, internal personality trait. For example, boys are not more or less social overall than girls are, and there are few noticeable differences between genders when alone. The differences emerge in gendered groups and are expressed mainly in those contexts.

The first two books, Maccoby (1966) and Maccoby and Jacklin (1974), were published at the beginning and at the height of the feminist movement, respectively, but they were not feminist works. Instead, they were comprehensive surveys of all of the work in gender difference studies in psychology of the preceding 20 years, "sourcebooks" for researchers to use as a starting point for their own work—a little dry, but solidly scientific. Maccoby's scientific principles would not allow for any other approach, of course, but such a plan was also shrewd. She said later that there were some who objected to such an evenhanded treatment in a time of social change, but impartial scientific analysis could not be dismissed easily by critics as partisan rhetoric (Maccoby, 1989).

The books were difficult to write for two reasons: First, although most psychological studies strove for gender balance in their samples, the studies were often not *about* finding gender differences. In fact, researchers to this day often pray that there will *not* be sex differences in their results, because if the study had been set up for some other purpose (e.g. to study general human of memory or perceptual abilities), the sex differences could not easily be explained. Second, even when a study *was* about finding sex differences, when such differences were not found, the study was less likely to be published. This is known as the "file-drawer problem." If there are 10 studies on any topic and only one of them finds significant differences in the dependent variables between groups, that one is likely to be published, leaving the other nine in the scientists' file drawers, overestimating how easy it might be to get a certain effect. But when people believe that gender differences are real and natural, it is all the more important to know when such differences are not replicated, as long as the studies are well designed and controlled, because there may be many areas of behavior where the received opinion—that boys and girls differ—is wrong.

So, Maccoby and her colleagues scoured the literature, sent out letters to find the studies in the file drawers, threw out the bad studies, ordered the rest according to possible theoretical explanations, provided many tables of whether boys, girls or neither were found to engage in a given behavior more often or whether their parents and others encourage sex-typed behaviors differentially between their sons and their daughters (in Maccoby & Jacklin, 1974, there were 101 such tables, often with 20 studies each!) and included references and abstracts of every study in the appendices. Oh, and when interesting studies were found in other species or other cultures bearing on the problem, they included these for good measure. The two books were similar in structure: Maccoby and Jackin (1974) was merely an update to Maccoby (1966), necessary to take into account the vast increase in research over that time.

What did they find? First, there were very few cognitive gender differences in perception, memory or language. Girls show earlier verbal facility, remain equal to boys in general verbal ability until around age 11, at which time girls begin and continue to outdistance boys. Boys excelled in math or visual-spatial tasks, but not generally until adolescence and, of course, such differences were silent on whether the differences were biological or social in origin.

Socially, Maccoby and Jacklin (1974) found that males are more aggressive and more likely to subordinate their own beliefs to that of the male peer group, where dominance ranking is important. Girls are more compliant to adults in childhood, but not usually among other girls. Their behavior cannot be described as passive.

Maccoby and Jacklin also believed that their meticulous review had dispelled some myths about gender differences: Girls are not more social or suggestible than boys; they do not have lower self-esteem or achievement motivation; girls are just as able to be analytic or to deal with academic abstraction as boys, and so on. The fact that few would put forth such hypotheses today, when women have reached parity or superiority in college, law and medical school attendance and success, among other things, can be seen as signs of how far society has come in the last 40 years.

Almost 25 years later, in *The Two Sexes: Growing Up Apart, Coming Together* (Maccoby, 1998), Maccoby believed that the search for differences between the sexes had just about run its course. Far more interesting, she said, is to study how the genders maintain their social separation in childhood within genders and how they come together in adolescence. Yes, young boys engage more in rough and tumble play, but laughingly in good humor most of the time. But girls can be just as boisterous as boys when boys aren't hogging the toys or equipment; in free play, they tend to take turns being boisterous, rather than directly tussling. Most boys, in the company of other boys, would consider it a serious breach of the rules to wrestle a girl. In fact, the unstated but extremely clear rules—that rival the specificity of a State Department communique—about when it is permissible to touch the opposite sex cannot be violated in middle childhood without risking teasing (Sroufe, Bennett, Englund, Urban, & Shulman, 1993). Girls will stay close to an adult, but only because they need someone to intercede for them with boys; when boys aren't around, they ignore the adult.

This new approach to analysis of social interactions is *more cognitive rather than behavioral and more contextual than trait-based.* Maccoby concludes that much of what we used to think of as macho or feminine personality traits are actually properties of dyads or groups and sometimes based on seemingly complicated calculations: For example, children who have seen a film with four same-sex models who agree on how to behave will follow those models, but there is little uniformity in their behavior if the models disagree (Perry & Bussey, 1979).

Thus, the cognitive revolution begat social cognition in the 1980s, and those who examined social development followed the trend. Finally, today there is an even newer trend that incorporates biology into social behavior; we have already discussed the evolutionary psychology movement at the end of Chapter 4, but a particularly extreme form of this came from entomologist E.O. Wilson's (1975) book *Sociobiology*, which attempted to suggest that we are altruistic in direct proportion to the amount of genes we share with one another, using examples from ants to wolves; the last chapter on humans set off a firestorm of protest, because all of the social learning theory and much else was discarded in an attempt to reduce social behavior to genes.

Developmentalists, who after all, deal with growing organisms, rarely make that mistake. A case in point would be the career of the late Robert B. Cairns (1933–1999), who studied with Robert Sears and received his PhD from Stanford in 1960. His career began with studies of attachment in lambs (e.g. Cairns, 1966a) and included the biological and hereditary underpinnings of aggression in rats (see Cairns, Gariépy, & Hood, 1990, for a review). He began, with his wife Beverly Cairns and generations of graduate students, a 25-year longitudinal study of aggressive vs. nonaggressive children that included the reinforcing and punishing consequences of these children's behavior in the classroom, the social structure of the peers around them and their self-concepts and beliefs about the social cognitions of other children. They also studied the developmental rise of aggression after puberty and decrease in early adulthood, gender differences in aggression between boys and girls, the physiological reasons and correlations for aggression and the socialization practices when it came time for the participants in the study to rear their own children (see Cairns & Cairns, 1994; Cairns, Cairns, Xie, Leung, & Hearne, 1998).

Children have bodies, brains, minds and social behaviors, all of them interacting all of the time and changing, in tandem and in sync with maturation, socialization and growths in reasoning, memory and intelligence. We developmental scientists, as the new, more interdisciplinary practitioners are called, therefore pretty much take all of psychology and much else as our field of study. I attended a conference not long ago in "Developmental Social Cognitive Neuroscience" (Zelazo, Chandler, & Crone, 2010). Finally, beliefs about children and the theories and methods to study them inevitably change over time, so we can claim history of childhood and history of psychology as our areas, too. Robert and Beverly Cairns also wrote the chapters on the history of developmental psychology for the *Handbook of Child Psychology* (Cairns, 1983; Cairns & Cairns, 2006). Robert was also founding director of the Center for Developmental Science at the University of North Carolina—Chapel Hill from 1993 until his death in 1999.[17]

Notes

1. If this seems like the Piagetian task of conservation of numbers, it is no accident. Piaget studied in the early 1920s with Binet's colleague in constructing the intelligence test, Theodore Simon, and Piaget was, of course, familiar with much of the French psychological literature of the day (see later, this chapter).

2. The term "race" is not used here to differentiate the different human racial groups; rather, Baldwin used race to mean "the human race" or "the human species."
3. The philosophical novel/memoir form can be seen in the *Confessions* of St. Augustine or a book by the same title written by Piaget's fellow Genevan and author of the philosophical educational work *Emile*, Jean-Jacques Rousseau (1712–1778).
4. For the sake of clarity, my exposition of his theory will not always follow the order of his discoveries, and I will treat the theory itself as a completed object. For example, I will discuss Piaget's stage of infancy, the sensorimotor period, before the preoperational (preschool) period, even though his earliest book (Piaget, 1923) deals largely with the second period and he moved on to infancy later (Piaget, 1927, 1936). Moreover, the processes of circular reaction, reflective abstraction and equilibration, refined late in his career (Piaget 1978/2001), fit naturally in explaining how one stage becomes another. Finally, Piaget often circled back again to ages and stages to help integrate them into his ever more sophisticated theory, making a strict historical account difficult and beyond the scope of this book (but see Chapman, 1988, for an attempt at a biographical approach).
5. These are *The Language and Thought of the Child* (Piaget, 1923); *Judgment and Reasoning of the Child* (Piaget, 1924); *The Child's Conception of the World* (1926/1972b); *The Child's Conception of Physical Causality* (1927/1972a); and *The Moral Judgment of the Child* (1932/1968). His discussion of infancy begins in the paper "The First Year of Life of the Child" (Piaget, 1927).
6. This is, of course, contrary to Arnold Gesell's maturational theory, which was popular in America until after his death in 1961 opposing learning theories, which were also popular (see earlier and Note 7, below).
7. Conscious knowledge is the kind of knowledge that you "know that you know." Kant had called this "apperception"—see Chapter 5.
8. Piaget's notions were brought to the attention of the Americans by Stanford professor John Flavell in the early 1960s (Flavell, 1963). Behaviorism was the reigning paradigm at the time, so Piaget's dismissive attitude should be considered in this context of strong bias for learning principles.
9. Vygotsky was apparently a close friend of Gestaltist Kurt Lewin, whom he visited in Berlin in 1925. Lewin was on his way back from visiting Vygotsky in 1933 when he learned that all Jewish professors, including himself, had lost their jobs in Hitler's Germany. In 1920s' Berlin, Lewin's first seven graduate students were young women from Moscow (Ash, 1995).
10. A troika is a three-bladed, horse-drawn sled carriage used for fast movement through snowy Russian streets.
11. This is all the more perplexing when one realizes that Harry Harlow's wives were both extremely smart and competent. His first wife Clara Mears Harlow—whom he remarried after the death of his second wife—was a subject in Lewis Terman's longitudinal study of genius-IQ children and a graduate student in psychology at UW-Madison when they met. His second wife, Margaret Kuenne Harlow, earned a PhD from the University of Iowa under Kenneth Spence (see Chapter 8). She became Harlow's lab manager but was not listed as faculty until the year of her death. Discriminatory anti-nepotism rules of the day often meant that faculty wives could not themselves be faculty. Clara Mears's faculty mentor advised her to drop out of the grad program when she married Harry, which she did (Blum, 2002).
12. Most studies of previously institutionalized vs. adopted children are severely flawed by the fact that the better-off children are usually adopted first. The shortage of foster parents allowed for random assignment to conditions (which would be unethical if there were enough parents for all) and thus increased the validity of the study, but if someone wanted to adopt or care for a child in the institutionalized group, the child was allowed to exit the study to a better life; no child who had left the institution was returned there.
13. In his first major publication, *The Behavior of Organisms* (Skinner, 1938), which was written before his rise to prominence, Skinner still endorsed drives; he played no role in the debate discussed here.
14. The title page also notes the assistance of Edgar L. Lowell, Pauline Snedden Sears and anthropologist of child rearing John W.M. Whiting.

15. Benjamin Spock (1903–1998), one of the first pediatricians with training in psychoanalytic concepts, published *The Common Sense Book of Baby and Child Care* first in 1946, sold 50 million copies through six editions and became the authority on child rearing for the babies of the baby boom. His relaxed advice for their parents to "trust yourselves" replaced the harsher Victorian advice common in earlier times, such as that of Watson and Watson (1928) (see Chapter 8). Irascible conservatives blamed him for the youth upheavals of the 1960s, because it was said that baby boom kids had been "Spocked when they should have been spanked."
16. And now, I will stop referring to her by her first name, which I did only to distinguish her from her husband in this paragraph. I didn't, after all, write about Fred when talking about Skinner, at least in adulthood. The first-name trick is a demeaning sexist tactic.
17. As a personal note and full disclosure: I am a developmental psychologist. I attended Cairns's History of Developmental Psychology course as a graduate student at UNC and learned about Sears, Maccoby, Bandura, James Mark Baldwin and others. I took a History of Childhood course with Jaan Valsiner there, who also taught me about Vygotsky and sociocultural underpinnings of child development. From Meredith West I learned ethology and last, but certainly not least, my mentor and dissertation advisor, Peter A. Ornstein, who earned his PhD at the University of Wisconsin while Harlow was there, taught me verbal learning, information processing and how to be a mensch. All of them encouraged my initial forays into the history of psychology. I am greatly indebted to them all.

Bibliography

Adams, B., & Larson, J. (2012). *Legislative history of the animal welfare act.* Retrieved from www.nal.usda.gov/awic/pubs/AWA2007/intro.shtml.

Adler, A. (1907/1917). *Studies in organ inferiority and its psychical compensation.* New York, NY: The Nervous and Mental Disease Publishing Company.

Agassi, J. (1963). *Towards an historiography of science.* The Hague, Netherlands: Mouton & Co.

Ainsworth, M. D. S. (1967). *Infancy in Uganda: Infant care and the growth of love.* Baltimore, MD: Johns Hopkins University Press.

Ainsworth, M. D. S., Blehar, M. C., Waters, E., & Wall, S. (1978). *Patterns of attachment. A psychological study of the strange situation.* Hillsdale, NJ: Lawrence Erlbaum Associates.

Alexander, P. (1985). *Ideas, qualities and corpuscles: Locke and Boyle on the external world.* Cambridge, England: Cambridge University Press.

Allen, G. W. (1967). *William James: A biography.* New York, NY: Viking Press.

American Psychiatric Association. (1980). *Diagnostic and statistical manual of mental disorders* (3rd ed.). Washington, DC: American Psychiatric Association.

American Psychiatric Association. (2000). *Diagnostic and statistical manual of mental disorders* (4th ed., text revised). Washington, DC: American Psychiatric Association.

Amsel, A. (1989). *Behaviorism, neobehaviorism and cognitivism in learning theory: Historical and contemporary perspectives.* Hillsdale, NJ: Lawrence Erlbaum Associates.

Amsel, A., & Rashotte, M. E. (1984). Introduction. In A. Amsel & M. E. Rashotte (Eds.), *Mechanisms of adaptive behavior: Clark L. Hull's theoretical papers, with commentary* (pp. 1–11). New York, NY: Columbia University Press.

Anderson, J. W. (1980). *William James's depressive period (1867–1872) and the origins of his creativity: A psychobiographical study* (Doctoral Dissertation), University of Chicago Press.

Angell, J. R. (1907). The province of functional psychology. *Psychological Review, 14*, 61–91.

Angell, J. R. (1913). Behavior as a category of psychology. *Psychological Review, 20*, 255–270.

Angell, J. R. (1961). James Rowland Angell. In C. Murchinson (Ed.), *A history of psychology in autobiography* (vol. 3). New York, NY: Russell & Russell.

Aquinas, T. (n.d./1964). *Summa theologiae: Latin text and English translation, introductions, notes, appendices and glossaries.* Cambridge, England: Blackfriars.

Ariew, R. (1992). Descartes and scholasticism: The intellectual background to Descartes' thought. In J. Cottingham (Ed.), *The Cambridge companion to Descartes.* New York, NY: Cambridge University Press.

Aristotle. (n.d./1965). *De Anima* (R. D. Hicks, Trans.). Amsterdam: Adolf M. Hakkert.

Aristotle. (n.d./1990). *Generation of animals* (A. L. Peck, Trans.). Cambridge, MA: Harvard University Press.

Asch, S. E. (1955). Opinions and social pressure. *Scientific American, 193*(5), 31–35.

Ash, M. G. (1995). *Gestalt psychology in German culture, 1890–1967: Holism and the quest for objectivity*. Cambridge, England: Cambridge University Press.

Atkinson, R. C., & Shiffrin, R. M. (1968). Chapter: Human memory: A proposed system and its control processes. In K. W. Spence & J. T. Spence (Eds.), *The psychology of learning and motivation* (Vol. 2, pp. 89–195). New York, NY: Academic Press.

Auden, W. H., & Mendelson, E. (1991). *The collected poems*. London: Vintage Books.

Augustine. (n.d./1942). *The confessions of St. Augustine* (J. G. Pilkington, Trans.). New York, NY: Liveright Publishing Corp.

Axtell, J. L. (1968). *The educational writings of John Locke*. Cambridge, England: Cambridge University Press.

Babkin, B. P. (1949). *Pavlov: A biography*. Chicago: University of Chicago Press.

Backe, A. (2001). John Dewey and early Chicago functionalism. *History of Psychology*, 4(4), 323–340.

Bacon, F. (1620/1854). Novum Organum. In B. Montague (Ed. & Trans.), *The works of Francis Bacon*. Philadelphia, PA: Parry & Macmillan (original work published in 1620).

Baer, D. M., Wolf, M. M., & Risley, T. (1968). Current dimensions of applied behavior analysis. *Journal of Applied Behavior Analysis*, 1, 91–97.

Baird, J. C., & Noma, E. (1978). *Fundamentals of scaling and psychophysics*. New York, NY: John Wiley & Sons.

Baldwin, J. M. (1899/1973). *Social and ethical interpretations in mental development*. New York, NY: Arno Press.

Baldwin, J. M. (1902). *Development and evolution, including psychophysical evolution, evolution by orthoplasy, and the theory of genetic modes*. New York, NY: MacMillan Co.

Baldwin, J. M. (1906–1911). *Thought and things: A study of the development and meaning of thought or genetic logic* (vol. I–IV). London: S. Sonnenschein.

Baldwin, J. M. (1926). *Between two wars, 1861–1921: Being memories, opinions and letters received by James Mark Baldwin*. Boston, MA: Stratford Co.

Baldwin, J. M. (2001). Mental development of child and the race. In R. H. Wozniak (Ed.), *Selected works of James Mark Baldwin: Developmental psychology and evolutionary Epistemology* (vol. 1). Bristol, England: Thoemmes Press (original work published in 1895).

Bandura, A. (1986). *Social foundations of thought and action: A social cognitive theory*. Englewood Cliffs, NJ: Prentice Hall.

Bandura, A., & Walters, R. H. (1959). *Adolescent aggression: A study of the influence of child-training practices and family interrelationships*. New York, NY: Ronald Press Co.

Bandura, A., & Walters, R. H. (1963). *Social learning and personality development*. New York, NY: Holt, Rinehart and Winston.

Bandura, A., Ross, D., & Ross, S. A. (1961). Transmission of aggression through imitation of aggressive models. *The Journal of Abnormal and Social Psychology*, 63(3), 575–582.

Bandura, A., Ross, D., & Ross, S. A. (1963). Imitation of film-mediated aggressive models. *Journal of Abnormal and Social Psychology*, 66(1), 3–11.

Barclay, J. R. (1964). Franz Brentano and Sigmund Freud. *Journal of Existentialism*, 5, 1–35.

Barnes, T. C., & Skinner, B. F. (1930). The progressive increase in the geotropic response of the ant aphaenogaster. *Journal of General Psychology*, 4, 102–112.

Barone, D. F. (1996). John Dewey: Psychologist, philosopher, and reformer. In G. A. Kimble, C. A. Boneau, & M. Wertheimer (Eds.), *Portraits of pioneers in psychology* (vol. 2, pp. 61–74). Washington, DC: American Psychiatric Association.

Barone, D. F., Maddux, J. E., & Snyder, C. R. (1997). *Social cognitive psychology: History and current domains*. New York, NY: Plenum Press.

Bartlett, F. C. (1997). *Remembering: A study in experimental and social psychology.* Cambridge, England: Cambridge University Press.
Barzun, J. (1983). *A stroll with William James.* New York, NY: Harper & Row.
Beck, A. T. (1976). *Cognitive therapy and the emotional disorders.* New York, NY: International Universities Press.
Bekhterev, V. M. (1933). *General principles of reflexology: An introduction to the objective study of personality.* London: Jarrolds Publishers.
Belsky, J., Vandell, D. L., Burchinal, M., Clarke-Stewart, K. A., McCartney, K., & Owen, M. T. (2007). Are there long-term effects of early child care? *Child Development, 78*(2), 681–701.
Bergson, H. (1998). *Creative evolution* (A. Mitchell, Trans.). Mineola, NY: Dover Publications (original work published 1911).
Berlin, I. (1960). The concept of scientific history. *History and Theory, 1,* 1–31.
Bernfeld, S. (1949). Freud's scientific beginnings. *American Imago, 6,* 163–196.
Bernheim, H. (1886/1897). *Suggestive therapeutics: A treatise on the nature and uses of hypnotism* (C. A. Herter, Trans.). New York, NY: Putnam's Sons (original work published 1886; English edition published 1897).
Bernheimer, C., & Kahane, C. (1985). *In Dora's case: Freud—hysteria—feminism.* New York, NY: Columbia University Press.
Billinsky, J. M. (1969). Jung and Freud: The end of a romance. *Andover Newton Quarterly, 10,* 39–43.
Binet, A. (1890a). *On double consciousness: Experimental psychological studies.* Chicago: Open Press.
Binet, A. (1890b). The perception of lengths and numbers by some small children (pp. 77–92). [La perception des longuees et des nombres chez quelquez petits enfants]. *Revue Philosophique, 30,* 68–81.
Binet, A. (1890c). Children's perceptions (pp. 93–126). [Perceptions d'enfants]. *Revue Philosophique, 30,* 582–611.
Binet, A. (1895). The measurement of visual illusions in children (pp. 130–144). [Le measure des illusions visuelles chez les enfants]. *Revue Philosophique, 40,* 11–25.
Binet, A. (1896). *Alterations of personality.* New York, NY: D. Appleton & Company.
Binet, A. (1900). *La Suggestibilité.* Paris: Sleicher Frères.
Binet, A. (1902). The influence of exercise and suggestion on touch threshold (pp. 13–27). [Influence de l'exercise et de la suggestion sur le position du seul]. *Anèe Psychologique, 9,* 235–248.
Binet, A. (1903). From sensation to intelligence (pp. 28–76). [De la sensation a l'intelligence]. *Revue Philosophique, 55,* 449–467, 592–618.
Binet, A. (1905/1916). New methods for the diagnosis of the intellectual level of subnormals. In E. S. Kite (Ed. & Trans.), *The development of intelligence in children.* Vineland, NJ: Publications of the Training School at Vineland.
Binet, A. (1973). New methods for the diagnosis of the intellectual level of subnormals. In E. S. Kite (Ed. & Trans.), *The development of intelligence in children* (pp. 274–329). New York, NY: Arno Press (original work published in 1911).
Binet, A. (1984). *Modern ideas about children* (S. Hessler, Trans.). Albi, France: Presses de l'Atelier Graphique Saint-Jean (original work published in 1910).
Binet, A., & Féré, C. (1888). *Animal magnetism.* New York, NY: D. Appleton & Company.
Binet, A., & Henri, V. (1894). Investigations on the development of visual memory in children (pp. 127–129). [Recherches sur le développment de la mémoire visuelle des enfants]. *Revue Philosophique, 37,* 348–350.
Binet, A., & Simon, T. (1905/1916). Upon the necessity of establishing a scientific diagnosis of inferior states of intelligence. In E. S. Kite (Ed. & Trans.), *The development of intelligence in children* (pp. 9–36). Baltimore, MD: Williams & Wilkins Company.
Binet, A., & Simon, T. (1973a). New methods for the diagnosis of the intellectual level of subnormals. In E. S. Kite (Ed. & Trans.), *The development of intelligence in children* (pp. 34–181). New York, NY: Arno Press (original work published in 1905).

Binet, A., & Simon, T. (1973b). New methods for the diagnosis of the intellectual level of subnormals. In E. S. Kite (Ed. & Trans.), *The development of intelligence in children* (pp. 182–273). New York, NY: Arno Press (original work published in 1908).

Binet, A., & Simon, T. (1973c). *The development of intelligence in children* (E. S. Kite, Trans.). New York, NY: Arno Press (original work published in 1916).

Bjork, D. W. (1993). *B. F. Skinner: A life*. New York, NY: Harper-Collins.

Blatz, W. E. (1944). *Understanding the young child*. Toronto, Canada: Clarke, Irwin University Press.

Block, N. J., & Dworkin, G. (Eds.). (1976). *The IQ controversy: Critical readings*. New York, NY: Pantheon Books.

Blom, J. J. (1978). *Descartes: His moral philosophy and psychology*. New York, NY: New York University Press.

Blum, D. (2002). *Love at GOON park: Harry Harlow and the science of affection*. New York, NY: Berkley Books.

Blumenthal, A. L. (1975). A reappraisal of Wilhelm Wundt. *American Psychologist, 30*, 1081–1088.

Blumenthal, R. (1989). Upheaval in the East: Obituary; The Ceausescus: 24 years of fierce repression, isolation and independence. *New York Times*. Online. Retrieved from www.nytimes.com/1989/12/26/obituaries/upheaval-east-obituary-ceausescus-24-years-fierce-repression-isolation.html.

Boring, E. G. (1950). *A history of experimental psychology* (2nd ed.). New York, NY: Appleton Century-Crofts.

Borstelmann, L. J. (1983). Children before psychology: Ideas about children from antiquity to the late 1800s. In P. H. Mussen & W. Kessen (Eds.), *Handbook of child psychology* (4th ed., vol. 1, pp. 1–40). New York, NY: Wiley-Blackwell.

Borstelmann, L. J., & Maccoby, E. (1992). *Interview of Eleanor Maccoby by Lloyd Borstelmann at Stanford University*. Retrieved from www.srcd.org/sites/default/files/documents/maccoby_eleanor_interview.pdf.

Bowlby, J. (1946). *Forty-four juvenile thieves; their characters and home-life*. Oxford, England: Bailliere, Tindall & Cox.

Bowlby, J. (1951). Maternal care and mental health. *Bulletin of the World Health Organization, 3*, 355–534.

Bowlby, J. (1952). *Maternal care and mental health*. Geneva: World Health Organization.

Bowlby, J. (1958). The nature of the child's tie to his mother. *International Journal of Psycho-Analysis, 39*, 350–373.

Bowlby, J. (1969/1982). *Attachment*. New York, NY: Basic Books.

Bowlby, J. (1991). *Charles Darwin: A new life*. New York, NY: W. W. Norton & Company, Inc.

Bredo, E. (1998). Evolution, psychology and John Dewey's critique of the reflex arc concept. *Elementary School Journal, 98*(5), 447–466.

Brentano, F. (1874/1973). *Psychology from an empirical standpoint* (A. C. Rancurello, D. B. Terrell, & L. McAlister, Trans.). London: Routledge.

Breuer, J., & Freud, S. (1893–1895/1978). Studies on hysteria. In J. Strachey (Ed. & Trans.), *The standard edition of the complete psychological works of Sigmund Freud* (vol. 2, pp. 1–18). London: The Holgarth Press.

Bridgman, P. W. (1927). *The logic of modern physics*. New York, NY: Macmillan.

Bringmann, W. G. (1975). Wundt in Heidelberg: 1845–1874. *Canadian Psychological Review/Psychologie Canadienne, 16*(2), 124–129.

Bringmann, W. G., Bringmann, N. J., & Ungerer, G. A. (1980). The establishment of Wundt's laboratory: An archival and documentary study. In W. G. Bringmann & R. D. Tweeney, (Eds.), *Wundt studies: A centennial collection* (pp. 123–159). Toronto, Canada: C. J. Hogrefe.

Brock, W. H. (1992). *The Norton history of chemistry*. New York, NY: W. W. Norton & Company, Inc.

Brook, A. (1994). *Kant and the mind*. Cambridge, England: Cambridge University Press.

Broughton, J. M., & Freeman-Moir, D. J. (1982). *The cognitive-developmental psychology of James Mark Baldwin: Current theory and research in genetic epistemology*. Norwood, NJ: Ablex.

Brown v. Board of Education., 347 U.S. 483. (1954).

Buckley, K. W. (1989). *Mechanical man: John Broadus Watson and the beginnings of behaviorism*. New York, NY: Guilford Press.

Buckley, K. W. (1994). Misbehaviorism: The case of John B. Watson's dismissal from Johns Hopkins university. In J. T. Todd & E. K. Morris (Eds.), *Modern perspectives on John B. Watson and classical behaviorism* (pp. 19–36). Westport, CT: Greenwood Press.

Burkhardt, R. W. Jr. (1977). *The spirit of system: Lamarck and evolutionary biology*. Cambridge, England: Cambridge University Press.

Burlingham, D., & Freud, A. (1944). *Infants without families*. London: George Allen & Unwin.

Burnham, J. C. (1994). John B. Watson: Interviewee, professional figure, symbol. In J. T. Todd & E. K. Morris (Eds.), *Modern perspectives on John B. Watson and classical behaviorism* (pp. 65–74). Westport, CT: Greenwood Press.

Buss, D. (1992). Mate preference mechanisms: Consequences for partner choice and intrasexual competition. In J. H. Barkow, L. Cosmides, & J. Tooby (Eds.), *The adapted mind: Evolutionary psychology and the generation of culture* (pp. 249–266). New York, NY: Oxford University Press.

Buss, D. M., Abbott, M., Angleitner, A., Asherian, A., Biaggio, A., Blanco-Villasenor, A., . . . Yang, K.-S. (1990). International preferences in selecting mates: A study of 37 cultures. *Journal of Cross-Cultural Psychology, 21*(1), 5–47.

Butler, R. A., & Harlow, H. F. (1954). Persistence of visual exploration in monkeys. *Journal of Comparative and Physiological Psychology, 47*(3), 258–263. doi:10.1037/h0054977.

Butterfield, H. (1931). *The Whig interpretation of history*. London: Ball.

Cahan, E. D. (1992). John Dewey and human development. *Developmental Psychology, 28*, 205–214.

Cahan, E. D. (1993). *Hermann von Helmholtz and the foundations of nineteenth-century science*. Berkeley, CA: University of California Press.

Cahan, E. D., & White, S. H. (1992). Proposal for a second psychology. *American Psychologist, 47*, 224–235.

Cairns, R. B. (1966a). Development, maintenance and extinction of social attachment behavior in sheep. *Journal of Comparative and Physiological Psychology, 62*(2), 298–306. doi:10.1037/h0023692.

Cairns, R. B. (1966b). Attachment behavior of mammals. *Psychological Review, 73*(5), 409–426. doi:10.1037/h0023691.

Cairns, R. B. (1979). *Social development: The origins and plasticity of interchanges*. San Francisco: W. H. Freeman & Co.

Cairns, R. B. (1983). The emergence of developmental psychology. In P. H. Mussen (Ed.), *Handbook of child psychology* (Vol. 1, 4th ed.). New York, NY: John Wiley & Sons.

Cairns, R. B. (1992). The making of a developmental science: The contributions and intellectual heritage of James Mark Baldwin. *Developmental Psychology, 28*(1), 17–24.

Cairns, R. B., & Cairns, B. D. (1994). *Lifelines and risks: Pathways of youth in our time*. New York, NY: Cambridge University Press.

Cairns, R. B., & Cairns, B. D. (2006). The making of developmental psychology. In R. M. Lerner (Ed.), *Theoretical models of human development. Volume 1 of handbook of child psychology* (6th ed., W. Damon & R. M. Lerner, Editors-in-chief). Hoboken, NJ: Wiley-Blackwell.

Cairns, R. B., Cairns, B. D., Xie, H., Leung, M., & Hearne, S. (1998). Paths across generations: Academic competence and aggressive behaviors in young mothers and their children. *Developmental Psychology, 34*(6), 1162–1174. doi:10.1037/0012-1649.34.6.1162.

Cairns, R. B., Gariépy, J-L., & Hood, K. E. (1990). Development, microevolution and social behavior. *Psychological Review, 97*, 49–65.

Calkins, M. W. (1906). A reconciliation between structural and functional psychology. *Psychological Review, 13*, 61–81.

Calkins, M. W. (1908a). Psychology as science of self: I. Is the self body or has it body? *Journal of Philosophy, Psychology and Scientific Methods, 5*, 12–20.

Calkins, M. W. (1908b). Psychology as science of self: II. The nature of the self. *Journal of Philosophy, Psychology and Scientific Methods, 5,* 64–68.

Calkins, M. W. (1908c). Psychology as science of self: The description of consciousness. *Journal of Philosophy, Psychology and Scientific Methods, 5,* 113–122.

Calkins, M. W. (1913). Psychology and the behaviorist. *Psychological Bulletin, 10,* 288–291.

Calkins, M. W. (1915). The self in scientific psychology. *American Journal of Psychology, 26,* 495–524.

Calkins, M. W. (1961). Autobiography of Mary Whiton Calkins. In Murchison, Carl. (Ed.) *History of Psychology in Autobiography* (Vol. 1, pp. 31–61). New York: Russell and Russell. (Original work published in 1930).

Campione, J. C., Brown, A. L., & Ferrara, R. A. (1982). Mental retardation and intelligence. In Sternberg, R. J. (Ed.), *Handbook of human intelligence.* New York, NY: Cambridge University Press.

Carroll, S. B. (2005). *Endless forms most beautiful: The new science of evo devo and the making of the animal kingdom.* New York, NY: W. W. Norton & Company, Inc.

Carroll, S. B. (2006). *The making of the fittest: DNA and the ultimate forensic record of evolution.* New York, NY: W. W. Norton & Company, Inc.

Cassirer, E. (1981). *Kant's life and thought* (J. Haden, Trans.). New Haven, CT: Yale University Press (original work published in 1918).

Cattell, J. McK. (1906). Conceptions and methods of psychology. In H. J. Rogers (Ed.), *Congress of arts and science, universal exposition, St. Louis, 1904. Volume V. Biology, anthropology, psychology, sociology.* Boston: Houghton, Mifflin Co.

Ceci, S. J., & Bruck, M. (1995). *Jeopardy in the courtroom: A scientific analysis of children's testimony.* Washington, DC: American Psychological Association.

Chapman, M. (1988). *Constructive evolution: Origins and development of Piaget's thought.* New York, NY: Cambridge University Press.

Chesterton, G. K. (1901, Feb.). Review of Pearson, K. National life from the standpoint of science. *The Speaker,* February 2, p. 488.

Chisholm, K. (1998). A three-year follow-up of attachment and indiscriminate friendliness in children adopted from Romanian orphanages. *Child Development, 69,* 1092–1106.

Chisholm, K., Carter, M. C., Ames, E. W., & Morison, S. J. (1995). Attachment security and indiscriminately friendly behavior in children adopted from Romanian orphanages. *Development and Psychopathology, 7,* 283–294.

Chomsky, N. (1959). A review of B. F. Skinner's verbal behavior. *Language, 35,* 26–58.

Chomsky, N. (1966). *Cartesian linguistics: A chapter in the history of rationalist thought.* New York, NY: Harper & Row.

Chomsky, N. (1971, December 30). The case against B.F. Skinner. *The New York Review of Books.*

Chronbach, L. J., Hastorf, A. H., Hilgard, E. J., & Maccoby, E. E. (1990). Robert R. Sears (1908–1989). *American Psychologist, 45,* 663–664.

Cohen, I. B. (1985). *Revolution in science.* Cambridge, MA: Belknap Press of Harvard University Press.

Cole, M., Gay, J., Glick, J. A., & Sharp, D. W. (1971). *The cultural context of learning and thinking.* New York, NY: Basic Books.

Coleman, S. R. (1984). Background and change in Skinner's metatheory from 1930 to 1938. *The Journal of Mind and Behavior, 5,* 471–500.

Coleman, S. R. (1987). Quantitative order in B.F. Skinner's early research program, 1928–1931. *The Behavior Analyst, 1,* 47–65.

Coleman, S. R. (1988). Assessing Pavlov's impact on the American conditioning enterprise. *Pavlovian Journal of Biological Science, 23,* 102–106.

Coleman, W. R. (1964). *Georges Cuvier, zoologist: A study in the history of evolution theory.* Cambridge, MA: Harvard University Press.

Collins, A. M., & Quillian, M. R. (1969). Retrieval time from semantic memory. *Journal of Verbal Learning and Verbal Behavior, 8*(2), 240–247.

Coon, D. J. (1982). Eponymy, obscurity, Twitmeyer and Pavlov. *Journal of the History of the Behavioral Sciences, 18*, 255–262.

Coon, D. J. (1994). "Not a creature of reason": The alleged impact of Watsonian behaviorism on advertising in the 1920's. In J. T. Todd & E. K. Morris (Eds.), *Modern perspectives on John B. Watson and classical behaviorism* (pp. 37–64). Westport, CT: Greenwood Press.

Copelston, F. C. (1972). *A history of medieval philosophy*. New York, NY: Harper & Row.

Cosmides, L., Tooby, J., & Barkow, J. H. (1992). Introduction: Evolutionary Psychology and conceptual integration. In J. H. Barkow, L. Cosmides, & J. Tooby, (Eds.).: The adapted mind: Evolutionary psychology and the generation of culture (pp. 3–18). New York, NY: Oxford University Press.

Cottingham, J. (1992). *The Cambridge companion to Descartes*. Cambridge, England: Cambridge University Press.

Cox, B. D. (1997). The rediscovery of the active learner in adaptive contexts: A developmental-historical analysis. *Educational Psychologist, 32*(1), 41–55.

Craik, F. I., & Lockhart, R. S. (1972). Levels of processing: A framework for memory research. *Journal of Verbal Learning & Verbal Behavior, 11*(6), 671–684.

Cranston, M. (1957). *John Locke: A biography*. London: Longmans Green.

Crews, F. C. (1995). *The memory wars: Freud's legacy in dispute*. New York, NY: New York Review of Books.

Crews, F. C. (2017). *Freud: The making of an illusion*. New York: Metropolitan Books, Henry Holt & Company.

Daly, M., & Wilson, M. (1988). *Homicide*. New York, NY: Aldine.

Damaye, H. (1903). *Essai de diagnostic entre les états de débilités mentales*. Paris: Steinheil.

Damasio, A. R. (1994). *Descartes' error: Emotion, reason and the human brain*. New York, NY: Putnam's Sons.

Danziger, K. (1980). Wundt and two traditions of psychology. In R. W. Rieber (Ed.), *Wilhelm Wundt and the making of a scientific psychology* (pp. 73–87). New York, NY: Plenum Press.

Danziger, K. (1983). Origins and basic principles of Wundt's völkerpsychologie. *British Journal of Social Psychology, 22*(4), 303–313.

Danziger, K. (1990). *Constructing the subject: Historical origins of psychological research*. Cambridge, England: Cambridge University Press.

Danziger, K. (1997). *Naming the mind: How psychology found its language*. London: Sage.

Danziger, K. (2008). *Marking the mind: A history of memory*. New York, NY: Cambridge University Press.

Darwin, C. (1839). *The narrative of the voyages of H.M. Ships Adventure and Beagle* (1st ed.). London: Colburn.

Darwin, C. (1859). *On the origin of species by means of natural selection, or the preservation of favoured races in the struggle for life*. London: John Murray.

Darwin, C. (1871). *The descent of man and selection in relation to sex*. London: Murray.

Darwin, C. (1872). *The expression of emotions in man and animals*. London: Murray.

Darwin, C. (1877). A biographical sketch of an infant. *Mind, 2*, 285–294.

Darwin, C. (1974). *The descent of man, and selection in relation to sex* (revised ed.). Detroit: Gale (original work published in 1874).

Darwin, C. (1998). *The origin of species by means of natural selection or the preservation of favored races in the struggle for life* (6th ed.). New York, NY: Modern Library (original work published in 1872).

Darwin, E. (1796). *Zoonomia: or, the laws of organic life*. London: J. Johnson.

Darwin, F. (Ed.). (1958). *The autobiography of Charles Darwin and selected letters*. New York, NY: Dover Publications (original work published 1892).

Dawkins, R. (1976). *The selfish gene*. Oxford: Oxford University Press.

Deese, J. (1960). The open and closed mind. *The Journal of Nervous and Mental Disease, 131*(6), 556–557.

Dennett, D. C. (1981). *Brainstorms: Philosophical essays on mind and psychology*. Cambridge, MA: MIT Press.

Dennett, D. C. (1991). *Consciousness explained*. Boston, MA: Little, Brown & Co.

Dennett, D. C., & Haugeland, J. (1987). Intentionality. In R. L. Gregory (Ed.), *The Oxford companion to the mind*. Oxford: Oxford University Press.

Descartes, R. (1960). *Discourse on method and meditations* (L. J. LaFleur, Ed. & Trans.). Indianapolis, IN: Bobbs-Merrill (original work published 1637).

Descartes, R. (1978/2007). A letter to Princess Elisabeth of Palatine. In L. Shapiro (Ed.), *The correspondence between Princess Elisabeth of Bohemia and René Descartes*. Chicago: University of Chicago Press (original work published in 1645).

Descartes, R. (1988). The passions of the soul. In J. Cottingham (Ed.), R. Stoothoff, & D. Murdoch (Trans.), *Descartes: Selected philosophical writings*. Cambridge, UK: Cambridge University Press (original work published in 1649).

Desmond, A. (1994). *Huxley: From devil's disciple to evolution's high priest*. Reading, MA: Perseus.

Desmond, A., & Moore, J. (1991). *Darwin: The life of a tormented evolutionist*. New York, NY: W. W. Norton & Company, Inc.

Dewey, J. (1896). The reflex arc concept in psychology. *Psychological Review, 3*(4), 357–370.

Dewey, J. (1899a). Psychology and social practice. In J. A. Boydston (Ed.), *Middle works* (vol. 1). Carbondale, IL: Southern Illinois University Press.

Dewey, J. (1899b). Psychology and social practice. Lecture to the APA. In Sokal, M. M. (1992). Origins and early years of the APA: 1890–1906. *American Psychologist, 47*, 111–122.

Dewey, J. (1903). *Studies in logical theory*. Chicago: University of Chicago Press.

Dewey, J. (1905). Instrumentalism. In J. A. Boydston (Ed.), *Middle works* (vol. 3, pp. 153–157). Carbondale, IL: Southern Illinois University Press.

Dewey, J. (1917). The need for social psychology. In J. A. Boydston (Ed.), *Middle works* (vol. 10, pp. 53–63). Carbondale, IL: Southern Illinois University Press.

Dewey, J. (1939). Biography of John Dewey. In P. A. Schilpp (Ed.), *The philosophy of John Dewey* (pp. 3–45). New York, NY: Tudor Publishing Co.

Dewey, J. (2008). From absolutism to experimentalism. In:. Jo A. Boydston (Ed.), *The later works of John Dewey: 1929-1930: Essays, the sources of a science of education, individualism, old and new, and construction of a criticism*. Carbondale, IL: Southern Illinois University Press.

Dewsbury, D. A. (1990). Early interactions between animal psychologists and animal activists and the founding of the APA committee on precautions in animal experimentation. *American Psychologist, 45*, 315–327.

Diamond, S. C. (1980). Wundt before Leibzig. In R. W. Rieber (Ed.), *Wilhelm Wundt and the making of a scientific psychology* (pp. 3–70). New York, NY: Plenum Press.

Diehl, L. A. (1986). The paradox of G. Stanley Hall: Foe of coeducation and educator of women. *American Psychologist, 41*, 868–878.

Doise, W., & Mugny, G. (1984). *The social development of the intellect*. Oxford: Pergamon Press.

Dollard, J., Doob, L., Miller, N., Mowrer, O., & Sears, R. (1939). *Frustration and aggression*. New Haven, CT: Yale University Press.

Dollard, J., Miller, N. E., Doob, L. W., Mowrer, O. H., & Sears, R. R. (1944). *Frustration and aggression*. London: Kegan Paul.

Donders, F. C. (1869). On the speed of mental processes. In W. G. Koster (Ed.), *Attention and Performance II. Acta Psychologica, 30*, 412–431.

Duncker, K. (1945). On problem-solving. *Psychological Monographs, 58*(5), i–113 (original work published 1935).

Eastman, R. F., & Mason, W. A. (1975). Looking behavior in monkeys raised with mobile and stationary artificial mothers. *Developmental Psychobiology, 8*(3), 213–221. doi:10.1002/dev.420080306.

Ebbinghaus, H. (1908). *Psychology: An elementary text-book.* New York, NY: Arno Press (original work published as Abriss der Psychologie, First English edition 1908).

Ebbinghaus, H. (1964). *Memory: A contribution to experimental psychology.* New York, NY: Dover Publications (original work published 1885 as Über das Gedchtnis. Untersuchungen zur experimentellen Psychologie.).

Ehrenfels, C. V. (1890/1988). On Gestalt qualities. In B. Smith (Ed.), *Foundations of Gestalt theory.* Munich: Philosophia Verlag.

Einsiedel, A. A. (1975). The development and modification of object preferences in domestic White Leghorn chicks. *Developmental Psychobiology, 8,* 533–540.

Eldredge, N. (2000). *The triumph of evolution and the failure of creationism.* New York, NY: W. H. Freeman.

Ellenberger, H. F. (1970). *The discovery of the unconscious: The history and evolution of dynamic psychiatry.* New York, NY: Basic Books.

Ellenberger, H. F. (1972). The story of "Anna O": A critical review with new data. *Journal of the History of the Behavioral Sciences, 8,* 267–279.

Ellis, A. (1955). New approaches to psychotherapy techniques. *Journal of Clinical Psychology, 11*(3), 207–260.

Ellis, B. J. (1992). The evolution of sexual attraction: Evaluative mechanisms in women. In J. H. Barkow, L. Cosmides, & J. Tooby (Eds.), *The adapted mind: Evolutionary psychology and the generation of culture* (pp. 267–288). New York, NY: Oxford University Press.

Engels, F. (1987). The part played by labor in the transition from ape to man. In *Marx/Engels collected works* (vol. 25). New York, NY: Progress Publishers (original work published 1876).

Erik Erikson, 91, Psychoanalyst who reshaped views of human growth, dies. (1994, May 13). *The New York Times.*

Estes, W. K., Koch, S., MacCorquodale, K., Meehl, P., Mueller, C. G. Jr., Scoenfeld, W. N., & Verplanck, W. S. (1954). *Modern learning theory: A critical analysis of five examples.* New York, NY: Appleton-Century-Crofts.

Evans, R. I. (1989). *Albert Bandura: The man and his ideas: A dialogue.* New York, NY: Praeger.

Fagan, T. K. (1996). Witmer's contributions to school psychological services. *American Psychologist, 51*(3), 241–243.

Fancher, R. E. (1977). Brentano's psychology from an empirical standpoint and Freud's early metapsychology. *Journal of the History of the Behavioral Sciences, 13*(3), 207–227.

Fancher, R. E. (1996). *Pioneers of psychology.* New York, NY: W. W. Norton & Company, Inc.

Fechner, G. T. (1946). The three motives and grounds of faith. In W. Lowrie (Ed. & Trans.), *The religion of a scientist.* New York, NY: Pantheon Books (original work published 1863).

Feinstein, H. H. (1981). The "crisis" of William James: A revisionist view. *The Psychohistory Review, 10,* 71–80.

Fernald, A. (1992). Human maternal vocalizations to infants as biologically relevant signals: An evolutionary perspective. In J. H. Barkow, L. Cosmides, & J. Tooby (Eds.), *The adapted mind: Evolutionary psychology and the generation of culture* (pp. 391–428). New York, NY: Oxford University Press.

Ferster, C. B., & Skinner, B. F. (1957). *Schedules of reinforcement.* New York, NY: Appleton-Century-Crofts.

Festinger, L., & Carlsmith, J. M. (1959). Cognitive consequences of forced compliance. *The Journal of Abnormal and Social Psychology, 58*(2), 203–210.

Festinger, L., Riecken, H. W., & Schacter, S. (1956). *When prophecy fails: A social and psychological study of a modern group that predicted the destruction of the world.* Minneapolis, MN: University of Minnesota Press.

Fine, R. (1979). *A history of psychoanalysis.* New York, NY: Columbia University Press.

Fisher, H. (1992). *Anatomy of love: A natural history of mating, marriage and why we stray*. New York, NY: W. W. Norton & Company, Inc.

Flavell, J. H. (1963). *The developmental psychology of Jean Piaget*. Princeton, NJ: D Van Nostrand.

Flavell, J. H. (1970). Developmental studies of mediated memory. *Advances in Child Development and Behavior, 5*, 181–211.

Forrest, D. W. (1974). *Francis Galton: The life and work of a Victorian genius*. London: Paul Elek.

Freeman-Moir, D. J. (1982). Chapter 6: The origin of intelligence epistemology. In J. M. Broughton & D. J. Freeman-Moir (Eds.), *The cognitive-developmental psychology of James Mark Baldwin: Current theory and research in genetic epistemology* (pp. 127–168). Norwood, NJ: Ablex.

Freud, A. (1946). *The ego and the mechanisms of defence*. New York: Intrnational Univeristy Press (original work published in 1936).

Freud, S. (1895/1978). Studies on hysteria. In J. Strachey (Trans.), *The standard edition of the complete psychological works of Sigmund Freud* (Vol. 2). London: The Hogarth Press (original work published 1895).

Freud, S. (1901/1978). Psychopathology in everyday life. In J. Strachey (Trans.), *The standard edition of the complete psychological works of Sigmund Freud* (Vol. 2). London: The Hogarth Press (original work published 1901).

Freud, S. (1905/1978). Three essays on the theory of sexuality. In J. Strachey (Trans.), *The standard edition of the complete psychological works of Sigmund Freud* (Vol. 7). London: The Hogarth Press (original work published in 1905).

Freud, S. (1905/1989). Three essays on the theory of sexuality. In P. Gay. (Ed.), *The Freud Reader*. New York, NY: W. W. Norton & Company, Inc.

Freud, S. (1905a/1978). Dora, fragments of an analysis of a case of hysteria. In J. Strachey (Trans.), *The standard edition of the complete psychological works of Sigmund Freud* (Vol. 7). London: The Hogarth Press.

Freud, S. (1906/1974). Letter from Freud to Jung, October 7, 1906. In C. G. Jung, S. Freud, & W. McGuire (Eds.), *The Freud/Jung letters: The correspondence between Sigmund Freud and C.G. Jung*. Princeton, NJ: Princeton University Press.

Freud, S. (1906/1974). Letter from Freud to Jung, October 7, 1906. In C. G. Jung, S. Freud, & W. McGuire (Eds.), *The Freud/Jung letters: The correspondence between Sigmund Freud and C.G. Jung*. Princeton, NJ: Princeton University Press.

Freud, S. (1908/1978). Character and anal erotism. In J. Strachey (Ed.), *The standard edition of the complete psychological works of Sigmund Freud* (Vol. 9). London: The Hogarth Press.

Freud, S. (1913). *The interpretation of dreams* (3rd ed., A.A. Brill, Trans.). New York, NY: Macmillan Company (original work published 1900).

Freud, S. (1911/1974a). Letter from Freud to Jung, June 15, 1911. In C. G. Jung, S. Freud, & W. McGuire (Eds.), *The Freud/Jung letters: The correspondence between Sigmund Freud and C.G. Jung*. Princeton, NJ: Princeton University Press.

Freud, S. (1911/1974b). Letter from Freud to Jung, December 31, 1911. In C. G. Jung, S. Freud, S., & W. McGuire (Eds.), *The Freud/Jung letters: The correspondence between Sigmund Freud and C.G. Jung*. Princeton, NJ: Princeton University Press.

Freud, S. (1913/1978). Totem and Taboo. In J. Strachey (Ed.), *The standard edition of the complete psychological works of Sigmund Freud* (Vol. 13). London: The Hogarth Press.

Freud, S. (1914). Zur Geschichte der psychoanalytischen Bewegung. *Jahrbuch Der Psychoanalyse, 6*.

Freud, S. (1916/1978). Introductory lectures on psycho-analysis. In J. Strachey (Ed.), *The standard edition of the complete psychological works of Sigmund Freud* (Vol. 16). London: The Hogarth Press.

Freud, S. (1917). The history of the psychoanalytic movement. In A.A. Brill (Trans.), *Nervous and mental disease monograph series 25* (pp. 1–58). New York: Nervous and Mental Disease Pub. Co. (original work published in 1914).

Freud, S. (1918/1955). *From the history of an infantile neurosis. The standard edition of the complete psychological works of Sigmund Freud, Volume 17 (1917-1919): An infantile neurosis and other works* (pp. 1–124). London: The Hogarth Press (original work published in 1918).
Freud, S. (1919). A childhood recollection from Duchtung and Wahrheit. In J. Strachey (Trans.), *The standard edition of the complete psychological works of Sigmund Freud* (vol. 17). London: The Hogarth Press.
Freud, S. (1920/1978). Beyond the pleasure principle. In J. Strachey (Trans.), *The standard edition of the complete psychological works of Sigmund Freud* (Vol. 18). London: The Hogarth Press.
Freud, S. (1923/1989). The ego and the id. In P. Gay (Ed.), *The Freud reader*. New York, NY: W. W. Norton & Company, Inc.
Freud, S. (1930/1978). Civilization and its discontents. In J. Strachey (Trans.), *The standard edition of the complete psychological works of Sigmund Freud* (Vol. 21). London: The Hogarth Press.
Freud, S. (1933/1978). New introductory lectures in psychoanalysis. In J. Strachey (Trans.), *The standard edition of the complete psychological works of Sigmund Freud* (Vol. 22). London: The Hogarth Press.
Freud, S. (1936). Inhibitions, symptoms and anxiety. *The Psychoanalytic Quarterly, 5*(1), 1–28 (original work published in 1926).
Freud, S. (1937/1964). Constructions in analysis I. In J. Strachey (Trans.), *The standard edition of the complete psychological works of Sigmund Freud* (Vol. 23: 1937–1939, pp. 258–269). London: The Hogarth Press (original work published in 1937).
Freud, S. (1962). The aetiology of hysteria. In J. Strachey (trans.) *The standard edition of the complete psychological works of Sigmund Freud*, volume 3 (187–221). London: Hogarth Press. (Original work published in 1896).
Freud, S., & Fliess, W. (1985). *The complete letters of Sigmund Freud to Wilhelm Fliess, 1877–1904* (J. M. Masson, Ed.). Cambridge, MA: Belknap Press of Harvard University Press.
Friedman, L. J. (1999). *Identity's architect: A biography of Erik H. Erikson*. New York, NY: Scribner.
Frolov, Y. P. (1938). *Pavlov and his school: The theory of conditioned reflexes*. London: Kegan Paul Trunch & Trubner.
Fuller, J. O. (1981). *Francis Bacon: A biography*. London: East-West Publications.
Furumoto, L. (1991). From "Paired Associates" to a psychology of self: The intellectual odyssey of Mary Whiton Calkins. In A. Kimble, M. Wertheimer, & C. White (Eds.), *Portraits of pioneers in psychology* (pp. 57–72). Washington, DC: American Psychological Association.
Gallagher, J. M., & Reid, D. K. (1981). *The learning theory of Piaget and Inhelder*. Monterey, CA: Brooks, Cole Publishing Co.
Galton, F. (1869/1892). *Hereditary genius*. London: Macmillan. First edition in 1869.
Galton, F. (1908/1909). *Memories of my life*. New York, NY: E. P. Dutton & Co.
Galton, F. (1965). *Natural inheritance*. London: Macmillan (original work published 1889).
Gasman, D. (1971). *The scientific origins of national socialism*. New York, NY: American Elsevier.
Gaukroger, S. (1995). *Descartes: An intellectual biography*. New York, NY: Oxford University Press.
Gay, P. (1988). *Freud: A life for our time*. New York, NY: W. W. Norton & Company, Inc.
Gergen, K. J. (1999). *An invitation to social construction*. London: Sage.
Gick, M. L., & Holyoak, K. J. (1980). Analogical problem solving. *Cognitive Psychology, 12*, 306–355. Reprinted in Aitkenhead, A. M., & Slack, J. M. (Eds.). (1986). *Issues in cognitive modeling*. Hillsdale, NJ: Lawrence Erlbaum Associates.
Goddard, H. H. (1914). *Feeble-mindedness: Its causes and consequences*. New York, NY: Macmillan.
Goethe, J. W. (1941). *Faust: Parts one and two* (George Madison Priest, Trans.). New York, NY: Alfred A. Knopf.
Goldfarb, W. (1947). Variations in adolescent adjustment of institutionally reared children. *American Journal of Orthopsychiatry, 17*, 499–557.
Gould, S. J. (1977). *Ontogeny and phylogeny*. Cambridge, MA: Belknap Press of Harvard University Press.

Gould, S. J. (1980). *The panda's thumb: More reflections in natural history.* New York, NY: W. W. Norton & Company, Inc.

Gould, S. J. (1996). *The mismeasure of man* (revised and expanded ed.). New York, NY: W. W. Norton & Company, Inc.

Gould, S. J. (2002). *The structure of evolutionary theory.* Cambridge, MA: Belknap Press of Harvard University Press.

Gray, J. A. (1979). *Ivan Pavlov.* New York, NY: Viking Press.

Greenberg, J., & Mitchell, S. (1983). *Object relations in psychoanalytic theory.* Cambridge, MA: Harvard University Press.

Gruber, H. E. (1981). *Darwin on man. A psychological study of creativity* (2nd ed.). Chicago: University of Chicago Press.

Gruber, H. E., & Vonéche, J. J. (1977). *The essential Piaget.* Northvale, NJ: Jason Aronson Inc.

Guthrie, R. V. (1998). *Even the rat was white: A historical view of psychology* (2nd ed.). Boston: Allyn and Bacon.

Haeckel, E. (1874). *Anthropogenie; oder, Entwickelungsgeschichte des menschen. Keimes- und stammesgeschichte* [Anthropogenie:or the evolutionary history of man]. Leipzig, Germany: Verlag von Wilhelm Engelmann.

Haeckel, E. (1904). *Kunstformen der Natur [Art Forms in Nature].* Leipzig und Wien: Verlag des Bibliographlischhen Instituts.

Hahn, R. (1988). *Kant's Newtonian revolution in philosophy.* Carbondale, IL: Southern Illinois University Press.

Hall, G. S. (1891). The principles of psychology by William James. *The American Journal of Psychology, 3*(4), 578–591.

Hall, G. S. (1904). *Adolescence: Its psychology and its relations to physiology, anthropology, sociology, sex, crime, religion and education* (vol. I and II). New York, NY: D. Appleton & Company.

Hall, G. S. (1911). *Educational problems.* New York, NY: D. Appleton & Company.

Hall, M. B. (1966). *Robert Boyle on natural philosophy.* Bloomington, IN: Indiana University Press.

Hargreaves-Maudsley, W. N. (1973). *Oxford in the age of Locke.* Norman, OK: University of Oklahoma Press.

Harlow, H. F. (1950). The formation of learning sets: Learning and satiation of response in intrinsically motivated puzzle performance by monkeys. *Journal of Comparative and Physiological Psychology, 43,* 289–294.

Harlow, H. F. (1958). The nature of love. *American Psychologist, 13*(12), 673–685. doi:10.1037/h0047884.

Harlow, H. F., Dodsworth, D. O., & Harlow, M. K. (1965). Total social isolation in monkeys. *Proceedings of the National Academy of Sciences, 54,* 90–96.

Harlow, H. F., Harlow, M. K., & Meyer, D. (1950). Learning motivated by a manipulation drive. *Journal of Experimental Psychology, 40,* 228–234.

Harlow, H. F., & Suomi, S. J. (1970). Nature of love: Simplified. *American Psychologist, 25*(2), 161–168. doi:10.1037/h0029383.

Harlow, H. F., & Zimmermann, R. R. (1959). Affectional responses in the infant monkey. *Science, 130,* 421–432. doi:10.1126/science.130.3373.421.

Harris, B. (1979). Whatever happened to Little Albert? *American Psychologist, 34,* 151–160.

Harris, B. (2011). Arnold Gesell's progressive vision: Child hygiene, socialism and eugenics. *History of Psychology, 14*(3), 311–334.

Hartley, D. (1966). *Observations on man: His frame, his duty and his expectations.* Gainesville, FL: Scholars' Facsimiles and Reprints (original work published in 1749).

Hartmann, H. (1939). *Ego psychology and the problem of adaptation.* New York, NY: International Universities Press.

Hawkins, M. (1997). *Social Darwinism in European and American thought: 1860–1945.* Oxford, England: Cambridge University Press.

Hegel, G.W.F. (2009). *The phenomenology of spirit: The phenomenology of mind* (J. B. Baillie, Trans.). Lawrence, KS: Digireads.com Publishing (original work published 1807).

Heider, F. (1958). *The psychology of interpersonal relations*. New York, NY: John Wiley & Sons.

Heider, F., & Simmel, M. (1944). An experimental study of apparent behavior. *The American Journal of Psychology, 57*(2), 243–259.

Heider, F. (1983). *The life of a psychologist*. Lawrence, KS: University Press of Kansas.

Henle, M. (1978). One man against the Nazis—Wolfgang Köhler. *American Psychologist, 33,* 939–944.

Hicks, R. D. (1965). *Aristotle: De anima*. Amsterdam: Adolf M. Hakkert.

Hilgard, E. R., & Marquis, D. G. (1940). *Conditioning and learning*. New York: Appleton-Century.

Himmelfarb, G. (1962). *Darwin and the Darwinian revolution*. New York, NY: W. W. Norton & Company, Inc.

Holland, J. G., & Skinner, B.F. (1961). *The analysis of behavior: A program for self-instruction*. New York, NY: McGraw-Hill.

Holton, G., & Roller, D. (1958). *Foundations of modern physical science*. Reading, MA: Addison Wesley.

Hooke, R. (1665). *Micrographia: Or some physiological descriptions of minute bodies made by magnifying glasses with observations and inquiries thereupon*. London: The Royal Society.

Horgan, J. (1996). *The end of science: Facing the limits of knowledge in the twilight of the scientific age*. Reading, MA: Helix Books.

Huizinga, J. (1996). *The autumn of the middle ages* (R. J. Payton & U. Mammitzsch, Trans.). Chicago: University of Chicago Press (original work published in 1921).

Hull, C. L. (1932). The goal-gradient hypothesis and maze learning. *Psychological Review, 39,* 25–43.

Hull, C. L. (1934). The concept of habit family hierarchy and maze learning. *Psychological Review, 41,* 33–52.

Hull, C. L. (1943). *Principles of behavior*. New York, NY: Appleton-Century-Crofts.

Hume, D. (1777). *Essays and treatises on several subjects*. London: Cadell (original work published 1748).

Hume, D. (1777). *My own life*. London: Strahan.

Hume, D. (1777). *An Enquiry concerning human understanding*. In Essays and treatises on several subjects (pp. 283–296). London: Cadell (Original work published 1748).

Hume, D. (1882). Dialogues concerning natural religion. In T. H. Green and T. H. Grose (Eds.) The philosophical works of David Hume, volume 2. London: Longmans Green (Original work published in 1779).

Hume, D. (2000). *A treatise of human nature* (D. F. Norton & M. J. Norton, Eds.). New York, NY: Oxford University Press (original work published 1739).

Humphreys, K. (1996). Clinical psychologists as psychotherapists: History, future and alternatives. *American Psychologist, 51,* 190–197.

Inhelder, B., & Piaget, J. (1958). *The growth of logical thinking from childhood to adolescence*. New York, NY: Basic Books.

Inhelder, B., Sinclair, H., & Bovet, M. (1974). *Learning and the development of cognition*. Cambridge, MA: Harvard University Press.

Jacob, F., & Monod, J. (1961). Genetic regulatory mechanisms in the synthesis of proteins. *Journal of Molecular Biology, 3*(3), 318–356.

James, H. (1920). *The letters of William James. In two volumes*. Boston, MA: The Atlantic Monthly Press.

James, W. (1865/1987a). "The Origins of the Human Races," By Alfred R. Wallace. In F. Burkhardt (Ed.), *The works of William James: Essays, comments and reviews*. Cambridge, MA: Harvard University Press.

James, W. (1865/1987b). Lectures on the elements of comparative anatomy. By Thomas Henry Huxley. In F. Burkhardt (Ed.), *The works of William James: Essays, comments and reviews*. Cambridge, MA: Harvard University Press.

James, W. (1868/1987). Two reviews of the variation of animals and plants under domestication. In F. Burkhardt (Ed.), *The works of William James: Essays, comments and reviews*. Cambridge, MA: Harvard University Press.

James, W. (1875/1987). Grundzüge der physiologischen Psychologie. By Wilhelm Wundt. In F. Burkhardt (Ed.), *The works of William James: Essays, comments and reviews*. Cambridge, MA: Harvard University Press.

James, W. (1882/1912). On some Hegelisms. In W. James (Ed.), *The will to believe and other essays in popular philosophy*. New York, NY: Longmans, Green and Co.

James, W. (1890/1983). *Principles of psychology*. Cambridge, MA: Harvard University Press.

James, W. (1892). *Psychology: Briefer course*. London: Macmillan.

James, W. (1896). *The will to believe: And other essays in popular philosophy*. New York, NY: Longmans, Green and Co.

James, W. (1902/1982). *The varieties of religious experience: A study in human nature*. New York, NY: Penguin Books.

James, W. (1907/1974). *Pragmatism, a new name for some old ways of thinking: Popular lectures on philosophy*. New York, NY: Meridian Books.

James, W. (1912). *Essays in radical empiricism*. New York, NY: Longmans, Green.

Janet, P. (1889). *L Automatisme psychologique [Psychological automatisms]*. Paris: Félix Alcan.

Joncich, G. (1968). *The sane positivist: A biography of Edward L. Thorndike*. Middletown, CT: Wesleyan University Press.

Jones, E. (1953–1957). *The life and work of Sigmund Freud* (vol. I–III). New York, NY: Basic Books.

Jones, E. E., & Harris, V. A. (1967). The attribution of attitudes. *Journal of Experimental Social Psychology*, *3*(1), 1–24.

Jones, M. C. (1924). A laboratory study of fear: The case of Peter. *Pedagogical Seminary*, *31*, 308–315.

Jones, W. T. (1969). *The medieval mind* (2nd ed.). New York, NY: Harcourt, Brace & World.

Jordanova, L. J. (1984). *Lamarck*. Oxford: Oxford University Press.

Jung, C. (1906/1974). Letter from Jung to Freud, October 5, 1906. In C. G. Jung, S. Freud, & W. McGuire (Eds.), *The Freud/Jung letters: The correspondence between Sigmund Freud and C.G. Jung*. Princeton, NJ: Princeton University Press.

Jung, C. (1910/1974). Letter from Jung to Freud, November 13, 1910. In C. G. Jung, S. Freud, & W. McGuire (Eds.), *The Freud/Jung letters: The correspondence between Sigmund Freud and C.G. Jung*. Princeton, NJ: Princeton University Press.

Kant, I. (1978). *Anthropology from a pragmatic point of view*. Carbondale, IL: Southern Illinois University Press (original work published in 1798).

Kant. I. (1990). *Critique of pure reason* (J. M. D. Meikeljohn, Trans.). Amherst, NY: Prometheus (original work published 1781).

Karen, R. (1990). Becoming attached. *The Atlantic*, pp. 35–70.

Karen, R. (1994). *Becoming attached: Unfolding the mystery of the infant-mother bond and its impact on later life*. New York, NY: Warner Books.

Karen, R. (1998). *Becoming attached: First relationships and how they shape our capacity to love*. New York, NY: Oxford University Press.

Kerr, J. (1993). *A most dangerous method: The story of Jung, Freud and Sabina Spielrein*. New York, NY: Alfred A. Knopf.

Kevles, D. J. (1995). *In the name of eugenics*. Cambridge, MA: Harvard University Press.

Kimble, G. A. (1996). Ivan Mikhailovich Sechenov: Pioneer in Russian reflexology. In G. A. Kimble, C. A. Boneau, & M. Wertheimer (Eds.). *Portraits of pioneers in psychology* (vol. 2, pp. 33–45). Washington, DC: American Psychological Association.

Kinkade, K. (1973). *A Walden two experiment*. New York, NY: Morrow Quill.

Kinkade, K. (1994). *Is it Utopia yet?* Louisa, VA: Twin Oaks.

Kitchener, R. F. (1986). *Piaget's theory of knowledge: Genetic epistemology & scientific reason*. New Haven, CT: Yale University Press.

Kloppenber, J. T. (1986). *Uncertain victory: Social democracy and progressivism in European and American thought–1870–1920*. New York, NY: Oxford University Press.

Koffka, K. (1935). *Principles of Gestalt psychology*. New York, NY: Harcourt, Brace & World.

Köhler, W. (1947). *Gestalt psychology*. New York, NY: Liveright Publishing Corp.

Köhler, W. (1948). *The mentality of apes* (E. Winter, Trans.). London: Routledge & Kegan Paul (original English edition published 1925).

Köhler, W. (1971). *The selected papers of Wolfgang Köhler* (M. Henle, Ed.). New York, NY: Liveright Publishing Corp.

Kozulin, A. (1986/1934). Vygotsky in context by Alex Kozulin. In L. Vygotsky (Ed.), *Thought and language*. Cambridge, MA: MIT Press.

Kozulin, A. (1990). *Vygotsky's psychology: A biography of ideas*. Cambridge, MA: Harvard University Press.

Krutch, J. W. (1953). *The measure of man*. Indianapolis, IN: Bobbs-Merrill.

Kuhn, T. S. (1962). *The structure of scientific revolutions*. Chicago: University of Chicago Press.

Lachman, R., Lachman, J. L., & Butterfield, E. C. (1979). *Cognitive psychology and information processing: An introduction*. Hillsdale, NJ: Lawrence Erlbaum Associates.

Leslie, M. (2000, July–August). The vexing legacy of Lewis Terman. *Stanford Magazine*. Retrieved from https://alumni.stanford.edu/get/page/magazine/article/?article_id=40678.

Levine, T. Z. (1985). *From Socrates to Sartre: The philosophic quest*. New York: Bantam Books.

Lewin, K. (1920/1999). Socializing the Taylor system (pp. 297–320). In M. Gold (Ed.), *The complete social scientist: A Kurt Lewin reader* (pp. 37–66). Washington, DC: American Psychological Association.

Lewin, K. (1936). *Principles of topological psychology* (F. Heider & G. M. Heider, Trans). New York, NY: McGraw Hill.

Lewin, K. (1997). Some social-psychological differences between the United States and Germany. In G. W. Lewin (Ed.), *Resolving social conflicts*. Washington, DC: American Psychological Association (original work published in 1948).

Lewin, K. (1999). The conflict between Aristotelian and Galilean modes of thought in contemporary psychology. In M. Gold (Ed.), *The complete social scientist: A Kurt Lewin reader* (pp. 37–66). Washington, DC: American Psychological Association (original work published in 1931).

Lewin, K. (1948). *Resolving social conflicts: Selected papers on group dynamics*. Oxford: Harper.

Lewin, K., Lippitt, R., & White, R. K. (1939). Patterns of aggressive behavior in experimentally created social climates. *Journal of Social Psychology, 10*, 271–279.

Lewis, R. W. B. (1991). *The Jameses: A family narrative*. New York, NY: Farrar, Straus and Giroux.

Lewontin, R. (1994). *Inside and outside: Gene, environment and organism* (Heinz Werner Lecture Series, 20), Worcester, MA: Clark University Press.

Ley, R. (1990). *A whisper of espionage: Wolfgang Köhler and the apes of Tenerife*. Garden City, NY: Avery.

Lindsley, O., Skinner, B. F., & Solomon, H. C. (1953). *Studies in behavior therapy (Status Report I)*. Waltham, MA: Metropolitan State Hospital.

Locke, J. (1959). *An essay concerning human understanding* (A. C. Fraser, Ed., in two volumes). New York, NY: Dover Publications (original work published in 1690).

Locke, J. (1968). Some thoughts concerning education. In J. L. Axtell (Ed.), *The educational writings of John Locke*. Cambridge, England: Cambridge University Pressv work published in 1693).

Loeb, J. (1964). *The mechanistic conception of life*. Cambridge, MA: Belknap Press of Harvard University Press (original work published 1912).

Loftus, E. F., & Ketcham, K. (1994). *The myth of repressed memory*. New York, NY: St. Martin's Press.

Lorenz, K. Z. (1981). *The foundations of ethology*. New York, NY: Springer-Verlag.

Love, J. M., Chazan-Cohen, R., Raikes, H., & Brooks-Gunn, J. (2013). What makes a difference: Early head start evaluation findings in a developmental context. *Monographs of the Society for Research in Child Development*, 78(1), Serial no. 306.

Lovejoy, A. O. (2001). *The Great Chain of Being: The study of the history of an idea*. Cambridge, MA: Harvard University Press (original work published in 1936).

Lowrie, W. (1946). *Religion of a scientist*. G. Th. Fechner (Ed.) and W. Lowrie (Trans). New York: Pantheon.

Luria, A. R. (1976). *Cognitive development: Its social and cultural foundations*. Cambridge, MA: Harvard University Press.

Luria, A. R. (1979). *The making of mind: A personal account of Soviet psychology*. Cambridge, MA: Harvard University Press.

Maccoby, E. E. (1966). *The development of sex differences*. Stanford, CA: Stanford University Press.

Maccoby, E. E. (1989). Eleanor E. Maccoby. In G. Lindzey (Ed.), *A history of psychology in autobiography* (vol. VIII, pp. 290–335). Stanford, CA: Stanford University Press. doi:10.1037/11347-009.

Maccoby, E. E. (1992). Trends in the study of socialization: Is there a Lewinian heritage? *Journal of Social Issues*, 48(2), 171–185.

Maccoby, E. E. (1994). The role of parents in the socialization of children: An historical overview. In R. D. Parke, P. A. Ornstein, J. J. Reiser, & C. Zahn-Waxler (Eds.), *A century of developmental psychology* (pp. 589–616). Washington, DC: American Psychological Association.

Maccoby, E. E. (1998). *The two sexes: Growing up apart, coming together*. Cambridge, MA: Belknap Press of Harvard University Press.

Maccoby, E. E. (1999). The custody of children in divorcing families: Weighing the alternatives. In R. Thompson & P. Amato (Eds.), *The postdivorce family: Research and policy issues* (pp. 51–70). Sage Publications.

Maccoby, E. E. (2004). Aggression in the context of gender development. In M. Putallaz & K. L. Bierman (Eds.), *Aggression, antisocial behavior and violence among girls: A developmental perspective* (pp. 3–22). New York, NY: Guilford Press.

Maccoby, E. E. (2005). A cogent case for a new child custody standard. *Psychological Science in the Public Interest*, 6(1), i–ii. doi:10.1111/j.1529-1006.2005.00019.x.

Maccoby, E. E. (2007). Historical overview of socialization research and theory. In J. E. Grusec & P. D. Hastings (Eds.), *Handbook of socialization: Theory and research* (pp. 13–41). New York, NY: Guilford Press.

Maccoby, E. E., & Jacklin, C. N. (1974). *The psychology of sex differences*. Stanford, CA: Stanford University Press.

Mach, E. (1942). *The science of mechanics* (5th ed., T. J. McCormack, Trans.). La Salle, IL: Open Court (original work published in 1883).

Mach, E. (1959). *The analysis of sensations and the relation of the physical to the psychical*. New York, NY: Dover Publications (original work published in 1886).

Mahony, P. (1986). *Freud and the rat man*. New Haven: Yale University Press.

Mahony, P. (1989). *On defining Freud's discourse*. New Haven: Yale University Press.

Mahony, P. J. (1982). *Freud as a writer*. New York, NY: International Universities Press.

Mahony, P. J. (1984). *Cries of the wolf man*. New York, NY: International Universities Press.

Maines, R. P. (1999). *The technology of orgasm: "hysteria," the vibrator and women's sexual satisfaction*. Baltimore, MD: Johns Hopkins University Press.

Mandler, J. M., & Mandler, G. (1964). *Thinking: From association to Gestalt*. New York, NY: Wiley-Blackwell.

Mann, J. (1992). Nurturance or negligence: Maternal psychology and behavioral preference among preterm twins. In J. H. Barkow, L. Cosmides, & J. Tooby (Eds.), *The adapted mind: Evolutionary psychology and the generation of culture* (pp. 367–390). New York, NY: Oxford University Press.

Marrow, A. J. (1969). *The practical theorist: The life of Kurt Lewin*. New York, NY: Basic Books.

Martin, J. A., Maccoby, E. E., & Jacklin, C. N. (1981). Consequences of mothers' responsiveness to interactive bidding and nonbidding in boys and girls. *Child Development, 52*, 1064–1067.

Mason, W. A. (1960). Socially mediated reduction in emotional responses of young rhesus monkeys. *The Journal of Abnormal and Social Psychology, 60*(1), 100–104.

Mason, W. A. (1978). Social experience and primate cognitive development. In G. Burghardt & M. Beckhoff (Eds.), *The development of behavior: Comparative and evolutionary aspects.* New York, NY: Garland STPM Press.

Mason, W. A., & Berkson, G. (1975). Effects of maternal mobility on the development of rocking and other behaviors in rhesus monkeys: A study with artificial mothers. *Developmental Psychobiology, 8*(3), 197–211. doi:10.1002/dev.420080305.

Mason, W. A., & Kenney, M. D. (1974). Redirection of filial attachments in rhesus monkeys: Dogs as mother surrogates. *Science, 183*(4130), 1209–1211. doi:10.1126/science.183.4130.1209.

Masson, J. M. (Ed.). (1985). *The complete letters of Sigmund Freud to Wilhelm Fliess, 1887-1904.* Cambridge, MA: Belknap Press of Harvard University Press.

Mayr, E. (1982). *The growth of biological thought: Diversity, evolution and inheritance.* Cambridge, MA: Belknap Press of Harvard University Press.

Mayr, E. (1991). *One long argument: Charles Darwin and the genesis of modern evolutionary thought.* Cambridge, MA: Harvard University Press.

McKinney, W. T., Suomi, S. J., & Harlow, H. F. (1971). Depression in primates. *American Journal of Psychiatry, 127*, 1313–1320.

McNally, R. J. (2003). *Remembering trauma.* Cambridge, MA: Belknap Press of Harvard University Press.

McPherson, J. (1988). *Battle cry of freedom.* New York, NY: Oxford University Press.

McReynolds, P. (1996). Lightner Witmer: A centennial tribute. *American Psychologist, 51*(1), 237–240.

McReynolds, P. (1997). *Lightner Witmer: His life and times.* Washington, DC: American Psychological Association.

Meichenbaum, D. (1977). *Cognitive-behavior modification: An integrative approach.* New York, NY: Plenum Press.

Menand, L. (1998). William James & the case of the epileptic patient. *The New York Review of Books, 45*(20), 81–93.

Menand, L. (2001). *The metaphysical club.* New York, NY: Farrar, Straus and Giroux.

Mendel, G. (1866/1930). *Experiments in plant-hybridisation.* Cambridge, MA: Harvard University Press.

Messerly, J. G. (1996). *Piaget's conception of evolution: Beyond Darwin and Lamarck.* Lanham, MD: Rowman & Littlefield.

Meyer, D. E., & Schvaneveldt, R. W. (1971). Facilitation in recognizing pairs of words: Evidence of a dependence between retrieval operations. *Journal of Experimental Psychology, 90*(2), 227–234.

Micale, M. S. (1995). *Approaching hysteria: Disease and its interpretations.* Princeton, NJ: Princeton University Press.

Mill, J. (1829). *Analysis of the phenomena of the human mind.* London: Baldwin and Cradock.

Mill, J. (1967). *Analysis of the phenomena of the human mind* (2nd ed., J. S. Mill, Ed.). New York, NY: Augustus M. Kelley (original work published 1869).

Mill, J. S. (1859). *On liberty* (2nd ed.). London: J.W. Parker.

Mill, J. S. (1863). *Utilitarianism.* London: Parker, Son and Bourn.

Mill, J. S. (1873). *Autobiography.* Longmans, Green, Reader & Dyer.

Mill, J. S. (1974). A system of logic ratiocinative and inductive. In *Collective works volume 8. Book 7: On the logic of the moral sciences.* Toronto, Canada: University of Toronto Press; London: Routledge and Kegan Paulv work published in 1843).

Miller, G. A. (1956). The magical number seven plus or minus two: Some limits on our capacity for processing information. *Psychological Review, 63*(2), 81–97.

Miller, N. E., & Dollard, J. (1941). *Social learning and imitation*. New Haven: Yale University Press.

Mills, J. A. (1998). *Control: A history of behavioral psychology*. New York, NY: New York University Press.

Mineka, S., & Suomi, S. J. (1978). Social separation in monkeys. *Psychological Bulletin, 85*(6), 1376–1400. doi:10.1037/0033-2909.85.6.1376.

Moely, B. E., Hart, S. S., Leal, L., Santulli, K. A., Rao, N., Johnson, T., & Hamilton, L. B. (1992). The teacher's role in facilitating memory and study strategy development in the elementary school classroom. *Child Development, 63*(3), 653–672.

Monod, J. (1971). *Chance and necessity*. New York, NY: Alfred A. Knopf (A. Wainhouse, Trans.) Paris: Editions du Seuilv work published 1970 as *Le Hasard et la necessite*).

Morgan, C. L. (1900/1970). *Animal behaviour*. London: Edward Arnold (Johnson Reprint).

Morgan, C. L. (1903). *An introduction to comparative psychology* (New ed., revised). London: Walter Scott (original work published in 1894).

Morgan, C. L. (1912). *Instinct and experience*. London: Methuen & Co.

Morgan, C. L. (1930). *The animal mind*. New York, NY: Longmans, Green & Co.

Morgan, C. L. (1973). *Habit and instinct*. London: Edward Arnold (New York, NY: Arno Press Reprint)v work published in 1896).

Moxley, R. A. (1999). The two skinners, modern and postmodern. *Behavior and Philosophy, 27*, 97–125.

Miller, G. A. (1956). The magical number seven, plus or minus two: Some limits on our capacity for processing information. *Psychological Review, 63*, 81–97.

Müller, J. (1840/1843). *Elements of physiology* (W. M. Baly, Trans.). Philadelphia, PA: Lea and Blanchard.

Murdock, B. B. J. (1962). The serial position effect of free recall. *Journal of Experimental Psychology, 64*(5), 482–488.

Murray, D. J. (1988). *A history of Western psychology* (2nd ed.). Englewood Cliffs, NJ: Prentice Hall.

Muschinske, D. (1977). The nonwhite as child: G. Stanley Hall on the education of nonwhite peoples. *Journal of the History of the Behavioral Sciences, 13*(4), 328–336.

Newton, I. (1721). *Opticks: Or, a treatise of the reflections, refractions, inflections and colors of light (Third, corrected edition)*. London: William and John Innys. (First edition published 1704).

Nicolas, S., Andrieu, B., Croizet, J.-C., Sanitioso, R. B., & Burman, J. T. (2013). Sick? Or slow? On the origins of intelligence as a psychological object. *Intelligence, 41*(5), 699–711.

Noll, R. (1994). *The Jung cult: Origins of a charismatic movement*. Princeton, NJ: Princeton University Press.

Noll, R. (1997). *The Aryan Christ: The secret life of Carl Jung*. New York, NY: Random House.

Novak, M. A. (1979). Social recovery of monkeys isolated for the first year of life: II. Long-term assessment. *Developmental Psychology, 15*(1), 50–61.

Novak, M. A., & Harlow, H. F. (1975). Social recovery of monkeys isolated for the first year of life: I. Rehabilitation and therapy. *Developmental Psychology, 11*(4), 453–465.

Obholzer, K., & Pankejeff, S. (1982). *The wolf-man: Conversations with Freud's patient—Sixty years later*. New York: Continuum.

O'Donnell, J. M. (1985). *The origins of behaviorism: American psychology, 1870–1920*. New York, NY: New York University Press.

O'Donohue, W., & Ferguson, K. E. (2001). *The psychology of B. F. Skinner*. Thousand Oaks, CA: Sage.

Olesko, K., & Holmes, F. (1993). Experiment, quantification and discovery. Helmholtz's early physiological researches, 1843–50. In D. Cahan (Ed.), *Hermann von Helmholtz and the foundations of nineteenth-century science*. Berkeley, CA: University of California Press.

Ornstein, P. A., Baker-Ward, L., & Naus, M. J. (1988). The development of mnemonic skill. In F. R. Weinert & M. Permutter (Eds.), *Memory development: Universal changes and individual differences* (pp. 31–49). Hillsdale, NJ: Erlbaum.

Orr-Andrewes, A. (1987). The case of Anna O.: A neuropsychiatric perspective. *Journal of the American Psychoanalytic Association, 35*, 387–419.

Owens, D. A., & Wagner, M. (1992). *Progress in modern psychology: The legacy of American functionalism*. London: Praeger.

Pace, E. (1998). Benjamin Spock, world's pediatrician, dies at 94. *Monographs of the Society for Research in Child Development, 35*(5). doi:10.2307/1165649.

Paley, W. (1802/1850). *The works of William Paley* (p. 471). Philadelphia, PA: Crissy & Markley.

Partridge, G. E., & Hall, G. S. (1912). *Genetic philosophy of education: An epitome of the published educational writings of President G. Stanley Hall*. New York, NY: Sturgis & Walton Company.

Pauly, P. J. (1987). *Controlling life: Jacques Loeb and the engineering ideal in biology*. New York, NY: Oxford University Press.

Pavlov, I. P. (1928). *Lectures on conditioned reflexes, vol. 1: Twenty-five years of objective study of the higher nervous activity (behaviour) of animals* (H. Gantt, Ed. & Trans). New York, NY: International Publishers (original work published in 1902).

Pavlov, I. P. (1941). *Lectures on conditioned reflexes, vol. 2: Conditioned reflexes and psychiatry* (H. Gantt, Ed. & Trans). New York, NY: International Publishers.

Pavlov, I. P. (1955). *I. P. Pavlov: Selected works* (J. Gibbons, Ed. & S. Belsky, Trans.). Moscow: Foreign Languages Publishing House.

Peirce, C. S. (1878/1997). How to make our ideas clear. In L. Menand (Ed.), *Pragmatism: A reader*. New York, NY: Vintage Books.

Perry, D. G., & Bussey, K. (1979). The social learning theory of sex differences: Imitation is alive and well. *Journal of Personality and Social Psychology, 37*(10), 1699–1712.

Peterson, L., & Peterson, M. J. (1959). Short-term retention of individual verbal items. *Journal of Experimental Psychology, 58*(3), 193–198.

Piaget, J. (1918). *Recherche*. Lausanne: La Concorde.

Piaget, J. (1924/1977). Judgment and reasoning in the child. In H. E. Gruber & J. J. Vonéche (Eds.), *The essential Piaget*. Northvale, NJ: Jason Aronson Inc.

Piaget, J. (1926). *The language and thought of the child* (M. Warden, Trans.). London: Kegan Paul & Cov work published in 1923).

Piaget, J. (1927/1977). The first year of life of the child. In H. E. Gruber & J. J. Vonéche (Eds.), *The essential Piaget*. Northvale, NJ: Jason Aronson Inc.

Piaget, J. (1930). *Immanentisme et foi religieuse* [Immanentism and religious faith]. Groupe romand des anciens membres de l'Association chrétienne d'étudiants {Romand group of former members of the Christian Student Association}. Typescript.

Piaget, J. (1936/1977). The origins of intelligence in children. In H. E. Gruber & J. J. Vonéche (Eds.), *The essential Piaget*. Northvale, NJ: Jason Aronson Inc.

Piaget, J. (1952). Autobiography. In E. Boring (Ed.), *History of psychology in autobiography* (vol. 4). Worcester, MA: Clark University Press.

Piaget, J. (1952). Jean Piaget. In E.G. Boring, H. S. Langeld, H. Werner, & R. M. Yerkes (Eds.), *History of psychology in autobiography* (vol. 4). Worcester, MA: Clark University Press.

Piaget, J. (1954). *The construction of reality in the child*. New York, NY: Basic Books (original work published in 1937).

Piaget, J. (1955/1958). Formal thought from the equilibrium standpoint. In B. Inhelder & J. Piaget (Eds.), *The growth of logical thinking*. New York, NY: Basic Books, Inc.

Piaget, J. (1957). *Logic and psychology* (W. Mays, Trans.). New York, NY: Basic Books.

Piaget, J. (1965). *The moral judgment of the child* (M. Gabain, Trans.). New York, NY: First Free Press (original work published in 1932).

Piaget, J. (1966/1995). Moral feelings and judgments. In H. E. Gruber & J. J. Vonéche (Eds.), *The essential Piaget*. New York, NY: Basic Books.

Piaget, J. (1967). *Six psychological studies*. New York, NY: Random House.

Piaget, J. (1968). *The moral judgement of the child*. London: Kegan Paul (original work published in 1932).

Piaget, J. (1969). Genetic epistemology. *Columbia Forum*, *12*(1), 4–11.

Piaget, J. (1972a). *The child's conception of physical causality*. Totowa, NJ: Littlefield Adams (original work published in 1927).

Piaget, J. (1972b). *The child's conception of the world*. Totowa, NJ: Littlefield Adams (original work published in 1926).

Piaget, J. (1974). *Experiments in contradiction* (Derek Coltman, Trans.). Chicago: University of Chicago Press (original work published in 1974 as *Recherches sur la contradiction*. Paris: Presses Universitaires de France).

Piaget, J. (1974). *Recherches sur la contradiction. 2. Les relations entre affirmations et negations. Etudes d'épistémologie génétique* (vol. 32). Paris: Universitaires de France.

Piaget, J. (1976). *The grasp of consciousness: Action and concept in the young child*. Cambridge, MA: Harvard University Press.

Piaget, J. (1977). *The development of thought: Equilibration of cognitive structures*. New York, NY: Viking Press.

Piaget, J. (1978). *Behavior and evolution* (D. Nicholson-Smith, Trans.). New York, NY: Pantheon Books (original work published in 1976 as *Le comportement moteur d'evolution*. Paris: Editions Gallimard).

Piaget, J. (1980). *Adaptation and intelligence: Organic selection and phenocopy*. Chicago: University of Chicago Press (original work published in French in 1974).

Piaget, J. (1980). *Adaptation and intelligence: Organic selection and phenocopy*. Chicago: University of Chicago Press (original work published in 1974 as *Adaptation vitale et psychologie de l'intelligence: Selection organique et phenocopy*. Paris: Hermann).

Piaget, J. (1982). Reflections on Baldwin, an interview conducted and presented by J. Jacques Vonéche. In J. M. Broughton & D. J. Freeman-Moir (Eds.), *The cognitive-developmental psychology of James Mark Baldwin: Current theory and research in genetic epistemology* (pp. 80–86). Englewood Cliffs, NJ: Ablex.

Piaget, J. (1985). *The equilibration of cognitive structures: The central problem of intellectual development* (T. Brown & K. J. Thampy, Trans.). Chicago: University of Chicago Press (original work published in 1975 as *L'equilibration des structures cognitives: Probleme central du developpement* by Presses Universitaire de France).

Piaget, J. (1987a). *Possibility and necessity: Volume 1: The role of possibility in cognitive development* (H. Feider, Trans.). Minneapolis, MN: University of Minnesota Press (original work published in 1981 as *Le possible et le nécessaire, 1: l'evolution des possibles chez l'enfant*. Paris: Presses Universitaires de France).

Piaget, J. (1987b). *Possibility and necessity: Volume 2: The role of necessity in cognitive development* (H. Feider, Trans.). Minneapolis, MN: University of Minnesota Press (original work published in 1983 as *Le possible et le nécessaire, 2: l'evolution des nécessaire chez l'enfant*. Paris: Presses Universitaires de France).

Piaget, J. (1999). *The construction of reality in the child*. London: Routledge (original work published in 1937).

Piaget, J. (2001). *Studies in reflecting abstraction* (R. L. Campbell, Ed. & Trans.). Philadelphia, PA: Taylor & Francis Group, LLC (original work published as: Recherches sur l'abstraction réfléchissante. Paris: Presses Universitaires de France. Original work published in 1977).

Piaget, J., & Garcia, R. (1974). *Understanding causality* (D. Miles & M. Miles, Trans.). New York, NY: W. W. Norton & Company, Inc. (original work published in 1971 as *Les explications causales*. Paris: Presses Universitaires de France).

Piaget, J., & Inhelder, B. (1974). *The child's construction of quantities: Conservation and atomism*. London: Routledge and Kegan Paul. Print (original work published in 1941).

Piaget, J., & Szeminska, A. (1964). *The child's conception of the number* (C. Gattegno & F. M. Hodgson, Trans.) London: Routledge & Kegan Paul (original work published in 1941).

Piaget, J., & Warden, M. (1928). *Judgment and reasoning in the child*. London: K. Paul, Trench, Trubner & Co. Ltd (original work published in 1924).

Pillsbury, W. B. (1897). A study in apperception. *The American Journal of Psychology*, 8(3), 315–393.

Pinker, S. (1994). *The language instinct*. New York, NY: Harper Collins.

Pinker, S. (1997). *How the mind works*. New York, NY: W. W. Norton & Company, Inc.

Plaas, R. (1994). *Kant's theory of natural science*. Dordrecht, Netherlands: Kluwer Academic Publishers.

Pollack, R. H., & Brenner, M. W. (1969). *The experimental psychology of Alfred Binet: Selected papers* (F. K. Zetland & C. Ellis, Trans.). New York, NY: Springer.

Pope, A. (1891). *An essay on man. Moral essays and satires*. London: Cassell & Company Ltd.

Popper, K. R. (1962). *Conjectures and refutations: The growth of scientific knowledge*. New York, NY: Basic Books.

Popper, K. R. (1983). *Realism and the aim of science*. London: Routledge.

Popper, K. R. (2002). *The logic of scientific discovery*. London: Routledge (original ly published in 1934 as *Logik der Forschung*).

Preyer, W. T. (1898). *The mind of the child: Part 1: The senses and the will* (H. W. Brown Trans.). New York, NY: D. Appleton & Company (original work published in 1881).

Priestly, J. (1790). *Hartley's theory of the human mind, on the principle of the association of ideas, with essays relating to the subject of it*. London: J. Johnson.

Profet, M. (1992). Pregnancy sickness as adaptation: A deterrent to maternal ingestion of teratogens. In J. H. Barkow, L. Cosmides, & J. Tooby (Eds.), *The adapted mind: Evolutionary psychology and the generation of culture* (pp. 327–366). New York, NY: Oxford University Press.

Quammen, D. (2010). Being Jane Goodall: Her 50 years of work have made us rethink chimps. *National Geographic*, 218(4), 110.

Rand, A. (1982). The stimulus and the response. In *A. Rand philosophy: Who needs it* (pp. 167–197). Indianapolis, IN: Bobbs-Merrill (original work published 1972).

Rashotte, M. E., & Amsel, A. (1999). Clark L. Hull's behaviorism. In W. O'Donohue & R. Kitchener (Eds.), *Handbook of behaviorism* (Chapter 5, pp. 119–158). San Diego, CA: Academic Press.

Reid, T. (1764). *An inquiry into the human mind: On the principles of common sense*. Dublin: Alexander Ewing, in Dame-Street.

Rhine, J. B. (1934). *Extra-sensory perception*. Boston, MA: Bruce Humphries.

Richards, R. J. (1987). *Darwin and the emergence of evolutionary theories of mind and behavior*. Chicago: University of Chicago Press.

Richards, R. J. (2008). *The tragic sense of life: Ernst Haeckel and the struggle over evolutionary thought*. Chicago: University of Chicago Press.

Rips, L. J., Shoben, E. J., & Smith, E. E. (1973). Semantic distance and the verification of semantic relations. *Journal of Verbal Learning and Verbal Behavior*, 12(1), 1–20.

Rivera, J. H., & Sarbin, T. R. (1998). *Believed-in imaginings: The narrative construction of reality*. Washington, DC: American Psychological Associations Press.

Roazen, P. (1982). Paul Roazen on errors regarding Freud. *The International Journal of Psycho-Analysis*, 63, 260–261.

Robertson, J. (1952). *A two-year-old goes to hospital* [Film]. London: Tavistock Child Development Research Institute.

Robertson, J. (1958). *Going to hospital with mother* [Film]. London: Tavistock Child Development Research Institute.

Robertson, J., & Robertson, J. (1989). *Separation and the very young*. London: Free Association Books.

Robinson, D. N. (1982). Johann William Friedrich Hegel. In *Toward a science of human nature: Essays on the psychologies of Mill, Hegel, Wundt, & James* (pp. 84–125). New York, NY: Columbia University Press.

Robinson, D. N. (1982). *Toward a science of human nature: Essays on the psychologies of Mill, Hegel, Wundt, & James*. New York, NY: Columbia University Press.

Robinson, D. N. (1982). Wilhelm Wundt. In *Toward a science of human nature: Essays on the psychologies of Mill, Hegel, Wundt, & James* (pp. 127–172). New York, NY: Columbia University Press.

Roche, A. F. (1992). *Growth, maturation and body composition: The felts longitudinal study 1929–1991*. New York, NY: Cambridge University Press.

Rodis-Lewis, G. (1998). *Descartes: His life and thought* (J. M. Todd, Trans.). Ithaca, NY: Cornell University Press.

Rokas, R. (1992). Achieving the just society in the 21st century: What can Skinner contribute? *American Psychologist, 47*, 1499–1506.

Romanes, J. (1883/1906). *Animal intelligence*. New York, NY: D. Appleton & Company.

Rosenberg, R. (1982). *Beyond separate spheres: Intellectual roots of modern feminism*. New Haven, CT: Yale University Press.

Rosenzweig, S. (1994). *Freud, Jung and Hall the king-maker: The historic expedition to America (1909)*. St. Louis, MO: Rana House Press.

Ross, D. (1972). *G. Stanley Hall: The psychologist as prophet*. Chicago: University of Chicago Press.

Rundus, D. (1971). Analysis of rehearsal processes in free recall. *Journal of Experimental Psychology, 89*, 63–77.

Ruppenthal, G. C., Arling, G. L., Harlow, H. F., Sackett, G. P., & Suomi, S. J. (1976). A 10-year perspective of motherless-mother monkey behavior. *Journal of Abnormal Psychology, 85*, 341–349.

Russell, B. (1945). *A history of western philosophy*. New York, NY: Simon & Schuster.

Rutter, M., Sonuga Barke, E. J., & Castle, J. (2010). I. Investigating the impact of early institutional deprivation on development: Background and research strategy of the English and Romanian adoptees (era) study. *Monographs of the Society for Research in Child Development, 75*(1), 1–20.

Sacks, O. (2001). *Uncle Tungsten: Memoirs of a chemical boyhood*. New York, NY: Alfred A. Knopf.

Sacks, O. (2003). Scotoma: Forgetting and neglect in science In R. B. Silvers (Ed.), *Hidden histories of science*. New York, NY: New York Review Books.

Salter, M. D. (1940). An evaluation of adjustment based upon the concept of security. *University of Toronto Studies, Child Development Series, 18*, 72.

Samelson, F. (1981). Struggle for scientific authority: The reception of Watson's behaviorism, 1913–1920. *Journal of the History of the Behavioral Sciences, 17*(3), 399–425.

Samelson, F. (1987). Was early mental testing: (a) Racist inspired, (b) Objective science, (c) A technology for democracy, (d) the origin of multiple choice exams, (e) None of the above? (Mark the right answer). In M. Sokal (Ed.), *Psychological testing and American society, 1890–1930*. New Brunswick: Rutgers University Press.

Sarup, G. (1978/1988). Historical antecedents of psychology: The recurrent issue of old wine in new bottles. In L. T. Benjamin (Ed.), *A history of psychology: Original sources and contemporary research* (pp. 11–20). New York, NY: McGraw-Hill.

Saxe, G. B. (1997). Selling candy: A study of cognition in context. In M. Cole, Y. Engeström, & O. A. Vasquez (Eds.), *Mind, culture and activity: Seminal papers from the laboratory of comparative human cognition* (pp. 330–337). New York, NY: Cambridge University Press.

Scarborough, E., & Furumoto, L. (1987). *Untold lives: The first generation of American women psychologists*. New York, NY: Columbia University Press.

Scarre, G. (1998). Mill on induction and the scientific method. In J. Skorupski (Ed.), *The Cambridge companion to Mill* (pp. 112–138). Cambridge, England: Cambridge University Press.

Schneider, W., & Pressley, M. (1989). *Memory development between 2 and 20*. New York, NY: Springer-Verlag.

Sears, R. R. (1943). *Survey of objective studies of psychoanalytic concepts.* New York, NY: Social Science Research Council.

Sears, R. R. (1980). Robert Sears. In C. Murchison (Ed.), *A history of psychology in autobiography* (Vol. 8, pp. 395–433). Washington, DC: American Psychological Association.

Sears, R. R., Maccoby, E. E., & Levin, R. V. (1957). *Patterns of child rearing.* Stanford, CA: Stanford University Press.

Sears, R. R., Whiting, J. W. M., Nowlis, V., & Sears, P. S. (1953). Some child-rearing antecedents of aggression and dependency in young children. *Genetic Psychology Monographs, 47,* 135–236.

Sears, R. R., Rau, L., & Alpert, R. (1965). *Identification and child rearing.* Stanford, CA: Stanford University Press.

Seay, B., Alexander, B. K., & Harlow, H. F. (1964). Maternal behavior of socially deprived Rhesus monkeys. *The Journal of Abnormal and Social Psychology, 69*(4), 345–354.

Sechenov, I. (1952). Reflexes of the brain. In K. Koshtoyants & G. Gibbons (Eds.), S. Belsky (Trans.), *I. Sechenov: Selected physiological and psychological works.* Cambridge, MA: MIT Press (pp. 31–139) (original work published in 1866).

Sedley, D. N. (2003). *The Cambridge companion to Greek and Roman philosophy.* Cambridge, England: Cambridge University Press.

Shepard, R. N., & Metzler, J. (1971). Mental rotation of three-dimensional objects. *Science, 171*(3972), 701–703.

Shute, C. (1964). *The psychology of Aristotle.* New York, NY: Russell & Russell.

Shuttleworth, S. (2010). *The mind of a child: Child development in literature, science and medicine.* Oxford, England: Oxford University Press.

Simon, L. (1998). *Genuine reality: A life of William James.* New York, NY: Harcourt, Brace & Co.

Sir Alfred Bowlby, A. Obituary (1929). *The British Medical Journal, 1*(3563), 747–749.

Siraisi, N. G. (1990). *Medieval and early Renaissance medicine: An introduction to knowledge and practice.* Chicago: University of Chicago Press.

Skinner, B. F. (1931). The concept of the reflex in the description of behavior. *Journal of General Psychology, 5,* 427–458.

Skinner, B. F. (1938). *The behavior of organisms: An experimental analysis.* New York, NY: Appleton-Century-Crofts.

Skinner, B. F. (1945, October). Baby in a box. *Ladies' Home Journal,* 30–31, 135–136, 138.

Skinner, B. F. (1948). "Superstition" in the pigeon. *Journal of Experimental Psychology, 38,* 168–172.

Skinner, B. F. (1948). *Walden two.* New York, NY: Macmillan.

Skinner, B. F. (1950). Are theories of learning necessary? *Psychological Review, 57,* 193–216.

Skinner, B. F. (1953). *Science and human behavior.* New York, NY: Macmillan.

Skinner, B. F. (1958). Teaching machines. *Science, 128,* 969–977.

Skinner, B. F. (1971). *Beyond freedom and dignity.* New York, NY: Vintage Books.

Skinner, B. F. (1974). *About behaviorism.* New York, NY: Alfred A. Knopf.

Skinner, B. F. (1976a). *Particulars of my life.* New York, NY: Alfred A. Knopf.

Skinner, B. F. (1976b). *Walden two revisited* [Introduction]. New York, NY: Macmillan.

Skinner, B. F. (1979). *The shaping of a behaviorist.* New York, NY: Alfred A. Knopf.

Skinner, B. F. (1981). Selection by consequences. *Science, 213,* 501–504.

Skinner, B. F. (1983). *A matter of consequences.* New York, NY: Alfred A. Knopf.

Skinner, B. F. (1986). What is wrong with daily life in the Western world? *American Psychologist, 41,* 568–574.

Skinner, B. F. (1987). Why we are not acting to save the world. In B. F. Skinner (Ed.), *Upon further reflection* (pp. 1–14). Englewood Cliffs, NJ: Prentice Hall.

Skinner, B. F. (1990). Can psychology be the science of mind? *American Psychologist, 45,* 1206–1210.

Skinner, B. F., & Vaughn, M. E. (1983). *Enjoy old age: A program of self-management.* New York, NY: W. W. Norton & Company, Inc.

Slamecka, N. J. (1985). On comparing rates of forgetting. *Journal of Experimental Psychology: Learning, Memo~ and Cognition, 11*, 812–816.

Slater, E. (1965). Diagnosis of "Hysteria". *The British Medical Journal, 1*(5447), 1395–1399.

Small, W. S. (1901). An experimental study of the mental processes of the rat. *The American Journal of Psychology, 11*, 133–165.

Smith, L. D. (1986). *Behaviorism and logical positivism: A reassessment of the alliance.* Stanford, CA: Stanford University Press.

Sobel, D. (1999). *Galileo's daughter: A historical memoir of science, faith and love.* New York, NY: Walker & Co.

Sokal, M. M. (1984). The Gestalt psychologists in behaviorist America. *American Historical Review, 89*(4–5), 1240–1263.

Sokal, M. M. (1987). *Psychological testing and American society, 1890–1930.* New Brunswick: Rutgers University Press.

Sokal, M. M. (1990). G. Stanley Hall and the institutional character of psychology at Clark 1889–1920. *Journal of the History of the Behavioral Sciences, 26*(2), 114–124.

Spence, D. P. (1982). *Narrative truth and historical truth: Meaning and interpretation in psychoanalysis.* New York, NY: W. W. Norton & Company, Inc.

Spencer, H. (1851/1865). *Social statics: Or the conditions essential to happiness specified and the first of them developed.* New York, NY: D. Appleton & Company.

Spencer, H. (1870). *The principles of psychology* (2nd ed., vol. 1). London: Williams & Norgate.

Spencer, H. (1904). *An autobiography* (vol. 1). New York, NY: D. Appleton & Company.

Spitz, R. A. (1945). Hospitalism: An inquiry into the genesis of psychiatric conditions in early childhood. *Psychoanalytic Study of the Child, 1*, 53–74.

Spitz, R. A. (1946). Hospitalism: A follow-up report. *Psychoanalytic Study of the Child, 2*, 113–117.

Spitz, R. A., & Wolf, K. M. (1946). Anaclitic depression: An inquiry into the genesis of psychiatric conditions in early childhood. *Psychoanalytic Study of the Child, 2*, 313–342.

Sroufe, L. A., Bennett, C., Englund, M., Urban, J., & Shulman, S. (1993). The significance of gender boundaries in preadolescence: Contemporary correlates and antecedents of boundary violation and maintenance. *Child Development, 64*(2), 455–466.

Stack, G. J. (1970). *Berkeley's analysis of perception.* Paris: Mouton & Co.

Stephen, L. (1900/1968). *The English utilitarians.* New York, NY: Augustus M. Kelley.

Stevens, S. S. (1957). On the psychophysical law. *Psychological Review, 64*(3), 153–181. doi:10.1037/h0046162.

Stevens, S. S. (1960). On the new psychophysics. *Scandinavian Journal of Psychology,* 127–135. doi:10.1111/j.1467-9450.1960.tb01278.x.

Stevens, S. S. (1971). Issues in psychophysical measurement. *Psychological Review, 78*(5), 426–450. doi:10.1037/h0031324.

Stocking, G. W., Jr. (1965). On the limits of "presentism" and historicism in the historiography of the behavioral sciences. *Journal of the History of the Behavioral Sciences, 1*, 211–218.

Stone, L. J., Smith, H. T., & Murphy, L. B. (1973). *The competent infant: Research and commentary.* New York, NY: Basic Books.

Street, W. R. (1994). *A chronology of noteworthy events in American psychology.* Washington, DC: APA.

Sulloway, F. J. (1979). *Freud, biologist of the mind: Beyond the psychoanalytic legend.* New York, NY: Basic Books.

Sulloway, F. J. (1991). Reassessing Freud's case histories: The social construction of psychoanalysis. *Isis, 82*(2), 245–275.

Suomi, S. J., & Harlow, H. F. (1972). Social rehabilitation of isolate- reared monkeys. *Developmental Psychology, 6*, 467–496.

Symons, D. (1979). *The evolution of human sexuality.* New York, NY: Oxford University Press.

Symons, D. (1992). On the use and misuse of Darwin in the study of human behavior. In J. H. Barkow, L. Cosmides, & J. Tooby (Eds.), *The adapted mind: Evolutionary psychology and the generation of culture* (pp. 137–159). New York, NY: Oxford University Press.

Taine, H. (1877). M. Taine on the acquisition of language by children. *Mind, 2*, 252–259 (original work published in French in *Revue Philosophique*, January 1876, *1*, 3–23).

Taylor, E. (1996). *William James on consciousness beyond the margin.* Princeton, NJ: Princeton University Press.

Taylor, E. I. (1990). New light on the origin of William James's experimental psychology. In M. G. Johnson & T. B. Henley (Eds.), *Reflections on the principles of psychology & William James after a century* (pp. 33–61). Hillsdale, NJ: Lawrence Erlbaum Associates.

Taylor, F. W. (1911/2006). *The principles of scientific management.* New York, NY: Cosimo.

Thiel, T., & Kreppner, K. (2002). Uses of the film-technique for a thorough study of growth and development. *From Past to Future, 3*(2), 32–44.

Thomas, R. K. (1997). Concerning some Pavloviana regarding "Pavlov's bell" and "Pavlov's mugging". *The American Journal of Psychology, 110*, 115–125.

Thorndike, E.L. (1898). Animal intelligence: An experimental study of the associative processes in animals. *Psychological Review, Monograph Supplements, 2*, 1–109.

Thorndike, E.L. (1903). *Educational psychology.* New York, NY: Science Press.

Thorndike, E.L. (1906). *The principles of teaching.* New York, NY: A. G. Seiler.

Thorndike, E.L. (1911). *Animal intelligence.* New York, NY: Macmillan (Reprinted Bristol, England: Thoemmes Press, 1999).

Thorndike, E.L. (1913). *Educational psychology. Vol. 2. The psychology of learning.* New York, NY: Teachers College, Columbia University Press.

Thorndike, E. L. (1922). *Eductional psychology: Briefer course.* New York: Teachers College Press.

Thorndike, E. L., & Murchison, C. (1936). Edward Lee Thorndike. In C. Murchison (Ed.), *A history of psychology in autobiography volume III* (pp. 263–270). Worcester, MA: Clark University Press.

Thorndike, E., & Woodworth, R. (1901a). The influence of improvement in one mental function upon the efficiency of other functions. *Psychological Review, 8*, 247–261, 384–395, 553–564.

Thorndike, E., & Woodworth, R. (1901b). The influence of improvement in one mental function upon the efficiency of other functions. The estimation of magnitudes. *Psychological Review, 8*, 384–395.

Thorndike, E., & Woodworth, R. (1901c). The influence of improvement in one mental function upon the efficiency of other functions. Functions involving attention, observation and discrimination. *Psychological Review, 8*, 553–564.

Thornhill, R., & Palmer, C. T. (2000). *A natural history of rape: Biological bases of sexual coercion.* Cambridge, MA: MIT Press.

Thornhill, R., & Thornhill, N. W. (1983). Human rape: An evolutionary analysis. *Ethology and Sociobiology, 4*, 137–173.

Thornton, E. M. (1976). *Hypnosis, hysteria and epilepsy: An historical synthesis.* London: Heinemann Medical.

Tipton, I. C. (1974). *Berkeley: The philosophy of immaterialism.* London: Methuen.

Titchener, E. B. (1899). *A primer of psychology.* New York, NY: Macmillan.

Titchener, E. B. (1914). On "Psychology as the Behaviorist Views It". *Proceedings of the American Philosophical Society, 53*, 1–17.

Titchener, E. B. (1926). *A beginner's psychology.* New York, NY: Macmillan.

Todd, J. T. (1994). What psychology has to say about John B. Watson: Classical behaviorism in psychology textbooks, 1920–1989. In J. T. Todd & E. K. Morris (Eds.), *Modern perspectives on John B. Watson and classical behaviorism* (pp. 75–108). Westport, CT: Greenwood Press.

Todes, D. P. (1997). From the machine to the ghost within: Pavlov's transition from digestive physiology to conditional reflexes. *American Psychologist, 52*(9), 947–955.

Todes, D. P. (2002). *Pavlov's physiology factory: Experiment, interpretation, laboratory enterprise.* Baltimore, MD: Johns Hopkins University Press.

Tolman, E. C. (1932). *Purposive behavior in animals and men.* New York, NY: Century.

Tooby, J., & Cosmides, L. (1992). The psychological foundations of culture. In J. H. Barkow, L. Cosmides, & J. Tooby (Eds.), *The adapted mind: Evolutionary psychology and the generation of culture* (pp. 19–136). New York, NY: Oxford University Press.

Trivers, R. L. (1985). *Social evolution.* Menlo Park, CA: Benjamin, Cummings.

Ullmann, L. P., & Krasner, L. (Eds.). (1965). *Case studies in behavior modification.* New York, NY: Holt, Rinehart and Winston.

United States. National Commission for the Protection of Human Subjects of Biomedical and Behavioral Research. (1978). *The Belmont report: Ethical principles and guidelines for the protection of human subjects of research.* Washington, DC: Department of Health, Education, and Welfare, National Commission for the Protection of Human Subjects of Biomedical and Behavioral Research.

Valsiner, J., & van der Veer, R. (2000). *The social mind: Construction of the idea.* Cambridge, England: Cambridge University Press.

van der Horst, F. C. P. (2011). *John Bowlby: From psychoanalysis to ethology.* West Sussex, England: Wiley-Blackwell.

Van der Horst, F. C. P., LeRoy, H. A., & van der Veer, R. (2008). "When strangers meet": John Bowlby and Harry Harlow on attachment behavior. *Integrative Psychological and Behavioral Science, 42*, 370–388. doi:10.1007/s12124-008-9079-2.

Van Dyken, S. (1998). *John Bowlby: A biographical journey into the roots of attachment theory.* London: Free Association Press.

Vargas, J. (1972). B.F. Skinner: Father grandfather, behavior modifier. *Human Behavior, I*, 19–23.

Veith, I. (1965). *Hysteria: The history of a disease.* Chicago: University of Chicago Press.

Vidal, F. (1994). *Piaget before Piaget.* Cambridge, MA: Harvard University Press.

Vrooman, J. R. (1970). *René Descartes: A biography.* New York, NY: Putnam's Sons.

Vygotsky, L. S. (1926/1987). The methods of reflexological and psychological investigation. In R. W. Rieber (Ed.), *The collected works of L.S. Vygotsky. Volume 3. Problems of the theory and history of psychology.* New York: Springer U.S.

Vygotsky, L. S. (1978). *Mind in society. The development of higher psychological processes.* Cambridge, MA: Harvard University Press.

Vygotsky, L. S. (1986). *Thought and language.* Cambridge, MA: The MIT Press (original work published in 1934).

Vygosky, L. S. (1993a). Defects and compensation. In R. Rieber & A. Carton (Eds.), *The collected works of L. S. Vygotsky* (vol. 2, pp. 52–64). New York, NY: Plenum Press.

Vygotsky, L. S. (1993b). Fundamental problems in defectology. In R. W. Rieber & A. S. Carton (Eds.), J. E. Knox & C. B. Stevens (Trans.), *The collected words of L. S. Vygotsky. Volume 2. The fundamentals of defectology (Abnormal psychology and learning disabilities)* (pp. 29–51). New York, NY and London: Plenum Press (original work published in 1929).

Vygotsky, L. S. (1993c). Fundamental problems in defectology. In R. W. Rieber & A. S. Carton (Eds.), J. E. Knox & C. B. Stevens (Trans.), *The collected words of L.S. Vygotsky. Volume 2. The fundamentals of defectology (Abnormal psychology and learning disabilities)* (pp. 29–51). New York, NY and London: Plenum Press (Original work published in 1929).

Waddington, C. H. (1957). *The strategy of the genes.* London: George Allen & Unwin.

Walle, A. H. (1992). William James' legacy to alcoholics anonymous: An analysis and a critique. *Journal of Addictive Diseases, 11*(3), 91–99.

Watson, J. B. (1903). *Animal education*. Chicago: University of Chicago Press.
Watson, J. B. (1913). Psychology as the behaviorist views it. *Psychological Review, 20*, 158–177.
Watson, J. B. (1916). The place of the conditioned-reflex in psychology. *Psychological Review, 23*, 89–116.
Watson, J. B. (1919). *Psychology from the standpoint of a behaviorist*. Philadelphia, PA: Lippincott.
Watson, J. B. (1925). *Behaviorism*. New York, NY: People's Institute Publishing (originally published in 1924).
Watson, J. B. (1936). John Broadus Watson. In C. Murchison (Ed.), *A history of psychology in autobiography* (pp. 271–281). Worcester, MA: Clark University Press.
Watson, J. B. (1967). *Behavior: An introduction to comparative psychology*. New York, NY: Henry Holt & Company (original work published in 1914).
Watson, J. B., & Rayner, R. (1920). Conditioned emotional reactions. *Journal of Experimental Psychology, 3*, 1–14.
Watson, J. B., & Watson, R. R. (1928). *Psychological care of infant and child*. New York, NY: W. W. Norton & Company, Inc.
Webster, R. (1995). *Why Freud was wrong: Sin, science and psychoanalysis*. New York, NY: Basic Books.
Weerakkody, I. (2011). Profile of Marian Radke-Yarrow. In A. Rutherford (Ed.), *Psychology's feminist voices multimedia internet archive*. Retrieved from www.feministvoices.com/marian-radke-yarrow/.
Weinberg, S. (1998). The revolution that didn't happen. *The New York Review of Books, 45*(15), 48–52.
Weiner, J. (1994). *The beak of the finch*. New York, NY: Vintage.
Weiner, J. (1999). *Time, love, memory: A great biologist and his quest for the origins of behavior*. New York, NY: Alfred A. Knopf.
Weismann, A. (1893). *The germ-plasm: A theory of heredity*. New York: Charles Scribner & Sons (N. Parker & H. Rönnfeldt, Translators).
Wertheimer, M. (1938). Gestalt theory. In W. D. Ellis (Ed.), *A source book of Gestalt psychology* (pp. 1–11). London: Kegan Paul, Trench, Trubner & Company (original work published in German as Über Gestalttheorie in 1925).
Wertheimer, M. (1959). *Productive thinking* (Enlarged ed., M. Werthemer, Ed.). New York, NY: Harper & Row (original work published in 1945).
Wertheimer, M., & Riezler, K. (1944). Gestalt theory. *Social Research, 11*(1), 78–99.
Wertsch, J. V. (1985). *Vygotsky and the social formation of mind*. Cambridge, MA: Harvard University Press.
Westfall, R. S. (1980). *Never at rest: A biography of Isaac Newton*. Cambridge, England: Cambridge University Press.
White, S. H. (1992). G. Stanley Hall: From philosophy to developmental psychology. *Developmental Psychology, 28*(1), 25–34.
White, R. K., & Lippitt, R. O. (1960). *Autocracy and democracy: An experimental inquiry*. Oxford: Harper.
Wills, G. (1992). *Lincoln at Gettysburg: The words that remade America*. New York, NY: Simon & Schuster.
Wilson, E. O. (1975). *Sociobiology: The new synthesis*. Cambridge, MA: Belknap Press of Harvard University Press.
Wilson, E. O. (1978). *On human nature*. Cambridge, MA: Harvard University Press.
Wilson, M., & Daly, M. (1992). The man who mistook his wife for a chattel. In J. H. Barkow, L. Cosmides, & J. Tooby (Eds.), *The adapted mind: Evolutionary psychology and the generation of culture* (pp. 289–322). New York, NY: Oxford University Press.

Windholz, G. (1986). A comparative analysis of the conditional reflex discoveries of Pavlov and Twitmyer and the birth of a paradigm. *The Pavlovian Journal of Biological Science*, 141–147.

Windholz, G. (1988). Pavlov and the Rockefeller foundation. *The Pavlovian Journal of Biological Science*, *23*, 107–110.

Windholz, G. (1990). Pavlov and the Pavlovians in the laboratory. *Journal of the History of the Behavioral Sciences*, *26*(1), 64–74.

Witmer, L. (1996). Clinical psychology: Reprint of Witmer's 1907 article. *American Psychologist*, *51*(3), 248–251.

Wolf, T. (1973). *Alfred Binet*. Chicago: University of Chicago Press.

Wolpe, J., & Lazarus, A. A. (1966). *Behavior therapy techniques: A guide to the treatment of neuroses*. Oxford: Pergamon Press.

Wood, D. J., Bruner, J. S., & Ross, G. (1976). The role of tutoring in problem solving. *Journal of Child Psychiatry and Psychology*, *17*(2), 89–100.

Wozniak, R. H. (1982). Chapter 1: Metaphysics and science, reason and reality: The intellectual origins of genetic epistemology In J. M. Broughton & D. J. Freeman-Moir (Eds.), *The cognitive-developmental psychology of James Mark Baldwin: Current theory and research in genetic epistemology* (pp. 9–46). Norwood, NJ: Ablex.

Wozniak, R. H. (2001). Development and synthesis: An introduction to the life and work of James Mark Baldwin. In J. M. Baldwin & R. H. Wozniak (Eds.), *The selected works of James Mark Baldwin*. Bristol, England: Thoemmes Press.

Wozniak, R. H. (2009). James Mark Baldwin, professional disaster and the European connection. *Rassegna Di Psicologia*, *26*(2), 111–128.

Wundt, W. M. (1897). *Outlines of psychology* (C. W. Judd, Trans.) Leipzig, Germany: Wilhelm Engelmann.

Wundt, W. M. (1904). *Principles of physiological psychology* (5th German ed., E. B. Titchener, Trans.). New York, NY: Macmillan.

Wundt, W. M. (1916). *Elements of folk psychology* (E.L. Schaub, Trans.) London: George Allen & Unwin (original work published in 1912).

Wundt, W. M. (1973). *An introduction to psychology* (R. Pinter, Trans.). New York, NY: Arno Press (original work published in 1911).

Yarrow, M. R. (1963). Problems of methods in parent-child research. *Child Development*, *34*(1), 215–226. doi:10.2307/1126842. Retrieved from www.feministvoices.com/marian-radke-yarrow/.

Yarrow, M. R., Campbell, J. D., & Burton, R. V. (1968). *Child rearing: An inquiry into research and methods*. San Francisco: Jossey-Bass.

Yarrow, M. R., Campbell, J. D., & Burton, R. V. (1970). Recollections of childhood: A study of the retrospective method. *Monographs of the Society for Research in Child Development*, *35*(5), doi:10.2307/1165649.

Yerkes, R. M., & Morgulis, S. (1909). The method of Pawlow [sic] in animal psychology. *Psychological Bulletin*, *6*, 257–273.

Yolton, J. W. (1969). *John Locke: Problems and perspectives*. Cambridge, England: Cambridge University Press.

Young, L. D., Suomi, S. J., Harlow, H. F., & McKinney, W. T. (1973). Early stress and later response to separation. *American Journal of Psychiatry*, *130*, 400–405.

Zeanah, C. H., Smyke, A. T., Koga, S. F. M., Carlson, E., & The BEIP Core Group. (2005). Attachment in institutionalized and non-institutionalized Romanian children. *Child Development*, *76*, 1015–1028.

Zeigarnik, B. (1927/1938/1990). On finished and unfinished tasks. In W. D. Ellis (Ed.), *A source book of Gestalt psychology* (pp. 300–314). Highland, NY: Gestalt Legacy Press (original work published 1938).

Zelazo, P. D., Chandler, M., & Crone, E. (2010). *Developmental social cognitive neuroscience.* New York, NY: Taylor & Francis Group, LLC.

Zenderland, L. (1998). *Measuring minds: Henry Herbert Goddard and the origins of American intelligence testing.* Cambridge, England: Cambridge University Press.

Zuriff, G. E. (1985). *Behaviorism: A conceptual reconstruction.* New York, NY: Columbia University Press.

Index

Note: Page numbers in *italic* indicated figures. Page numbers in **bold** indicate tables.

Abraham, Karl 372
Absolute, the 143–144
absolute threshold 154
accommodation 414, 424
acquired characteristics 92, 122; *see also* Lamarck, Jean-Baptiste Pierre Antoine de Monet de
action research 203
act psychology 180
adaptive traits 128
Adler, Alfred 6–7, 367–369, 376
Adolescence 240, 243, 397
Adolescent Aggression 327
Aetiology of Hysteria, The 355
African Americans 245–246
Agassiz, Louis 213
aggressive behavior 326–328, 475
agnosticism 114
Ainsworth, Mary D. Salter 464–467
air cribs 312
alchemy 50; and chemistry 52
Alexander II 265
Alexander the Great 28
altruism 106
ambiguous figures 187
American Journal of Psychology, The 173, 250
anal stage 355
Analysis of Behavior, The 313
Analysis of the Phenomena of the Human Mind 77
Angell, Frank **166**
Angell, James Rowland 247, 249–250, 279, 284
Animal Education: The Psychical Development of the White Rat 279
Animal Intelligence 290
animal magnetism 399
animal psychology 188–192, 281, 283, 290

animals 39, 85–86, 92, 114–115, 218, 254–255; *see also* apes; birds; chickens; comparative anatomy; comparative psychology; dogs; monkeys; rats
Animal Use Ethics Committees 469
anomalies 10, **12**, 14
Anthropology From a Pragmatic Point of View 140
antitheses 143, 443
ants 115
anxious-resistant attachments 466
apes 190–192
apperception 138, 162, 484n7
applied behavior analysis 329
a priori concepts 137–138
Aquinas, Thomas, Saint 26–27, 31–32
argument from design 70, 88, 93; *see also* natural theology
Aristotle 26–27, 28–31; and animal classification **85**; and Bacon, Francis 49; *De Anima* 30; and nature 84–86; and perceptions 37
arts 3–4
Asch, Solomon 4
assimilation 414
associationism 81–83
associations 71–72, 77–78
associative priming 177
assortive mating 120
astrology 6
astronomy 11, 146–148
atomistic theories 82
attachment 460–465, 470–472
Attachment 461
attributions 206
attribution theory 207
Augustine, Saint 26–28
autocracy 201
avoidant attachments 466

516 Index

axons 331n5
Ayllon, Teodoro **329**
Azrin, Nathan **329**

Babinski, Joseph *343*
Bacon, Francis 47–51, 49, 295
Baer, Donald M. **329**
balance theory 205–207
Baldwin, James Mark **166**, 247, 249, 281, 394, 412–418; *Psychological Review* 250; *Social and Ethical Interpretations in Mental Development* 416
Baldwin Effect 416
Bandura, Albert 326–328, 477
Beaumont, William 266
Beck, Aaron T. **329**
Beekman, Isaac 34
bees 86
Beethoven, Ludwig van 141–142
behaviorism 20, 204, 277, 281–284, 293, 330–331
Behaviorism 288–289
behavior modification 329
Behavior of Organisms, The 19, 305–306, 484n13
behavior therapy 328–329
bells 271
Bentham, Jeremy 78
Bergson, Henri 418
Berkeley, George 64–67
Bernard, Claude 267, 271
Bernays, Martha 337
Bernays, Minna 375
Bernheim, Hippolyte 345, 400
Beyond Freedom and Dignity 317–319
Beyond the Pleasure Principle 363
bias 5
Bijou, Sidney W. **329**
Binet, Alfred 124, 132n2, 397–406
Binet-Simon intelligence tests 123, 132n2, 397–399, 403–404
biographical histories 18–19
birds 462; *see also* finches
bisexuality 354, 392n5
Blanchard, Phyllis 244
Blatz, W.E. 465
Bleuler, Eugen 369
Boas, Franz *243*
bodies 41
Bois-Reymond, Emil du 151
Bonaparte, Napoleon 141
Boring, E.G. 78, **166**, 178n4, 301
botany 88
Bowlby, John 457–464

Boyle, Robert 52–54
brainstorming 193
breasts 458
Bretano, Franz 180–181, 336–337
Breuer, Josef 346–350
Bridgman, Percy W. 263, 302, 303
Brill, A.A. 242, 372
Broca's area 348
Brown vs. [Kansas] Board of Education 245–246
Brücke, Ernst von 151, *152*, 337, *338*
Bruner, Jerome 313
Bruno, Giordano 24, 26
Buck, Vivian 123
Buck vs. Bell 123
Buffon, George Louis 89
Burgerstein, Leo *243*
Burlingham, Dorothy 459
Burt, Cyril **329**
Butterfield, Herbert 20

Cairns, Beverly 483
Cairns, Robert B. 483
Calkins, Mary Whiton 235–238
capitalism 82
Carnegie, Andrew 121
Cartesian coordinate system 35
Cartesian dualism 39–40
Cartesian Linguistics 44
Cartesian theatre 45–46
catastrophism 90
cathexis 389
Catholic Church 24–26
cats 290–293
Cattell, James McKeen **166**, 229, 250, 251, 262
causes 29
Ceausescu, Nicolae 470
cephalometry 399–400
Charcot, Jean Martin 22, 340–346
Chelpanov, G.I. 444
chemistry 52
chickens 255
Child Care and the Growth of Love 459
children 198–201, 289, 413–416; and aggression 327–328; and cribs 312; and recapitulation theory 110, 111, 113, 240–241; and women 244; *see also* developmental psychology; education; girls; stage theory
child study movement 256
chimpanzees 8
Chomsky, Noam 44
Christmas Carol 100
chronological histories 18

cigars 392n9
circuits 248
circular reactions 414
"Civilization and Its Discontents" 365
Civil War 21
Claparéde's Law 433, 438
Clark, Kenneth Bancroft 245
Clark, Mamie Phipps 245
Clark Conference 242–244, 372–381
classical conditioning 269–270
clinical psychology 252
cocaine 339–340
cognition 162
cognitive behavior therapy 329
cognitive dissonance 207–208
cognitive maps 322
Cold Spring Harbor Laboratory 121, 126
collective unconscious 377
colonization 242
Committee, The 378–380
common sense 30, 38, 206
Common Sense Book of Baby and Child Care, The 485n15
Communism 446
comparative anatomy 90
Comparative Anatomy of Angels, The 153
comparative psychology 114–116
complex ideas 57
concrete experienced order 185
condensation 360
conditioned responses 267–270
Confessions 27
conflicts 197–198
conformity 4
conformity experiments 207
connectionism 258
consciousness 158–159, 217–218, 227, 360, 445; *see also* stream of consciousness
conservation 429, 432
Construction of Reality in the Child 426
constructivism 427
continuity 186
continuous reinforcement 309
contradictions 234
control conditions 150
Copernicus, Nicolaus 11, *12*, 24; *De Revolutionibus Orbium Coelestium* *12*, 25–26; and Galileo Galilei 32
corporal punishment 60–61
corpuscles 52–54
counter-conditioning 287
creativity 4
Crews, Frederick 385
Crick, Francis 126

criminals 114
critical period hypothesis 241
Critique of Pure Reason 136
Crozier, William J. 298
cultural determinism 144
cultural-historical school 449
cultural structures 389–390
cultures 449
Cuvier, Georges 89–91, 92
cybernetics 463

Damasio, Antonio 45
Darwin, Charles 3, 19; and children 394, 396; *Descent of Man, and Selection in Relation to Sex, The* 104, 106; and Ernst Haeckel 109–110; *Expression of the Emotions in Man and Animals, The* 396; and human evolution 102–107; life of 93–99; and natural selection 99–102; *Origin of Species, The* 102; and paradigm shift 114; *see also* materialist-evolutionary shift
Darwin, Erasmus 94–95
Das Kapital 106
Dawkins, Richard 128
day residue 358
De Anima 30
deductive logic 29–30, 49–50
defense mechanisms 388
deferred imitation 426–427
degeneracy 372, 403
De Humani Corporis Fabrica 25
Delboeuf, J.L.R. 400
democracy 200–201
Dennett, Daniel 38–39, 45–46
dependency 475
De Revolutionibus Orbium Coelestium 25
Descartes, Rene 15, 24; *Discourse on Method* 34; and dualism 38–41; historical context of 21; life of 32–34; and mathematics 34–35; and natural world 26; and paradigm shift 43–44; *Passions of the Soul* 41–43; and psychology 44–46; and reason 35–38; *Summa Theologica* 31; *see also* philosophical shift
Descent of Man, and Selection in Relation to Sex, The 104, 106
detachment 459
determinism 151, 301
detour problems 190
development: emotional 452–453, 472; maturational 241; natural 451; proximal 448; scientific 451–452
developmental psychology 196–201, 394–395; and evolution 395–397; *see also* children

Dewey, John 246–251, 262, 279
dialectic 143
dialectical materialism 145
Dickens, Charles 100
dictionaries 261
differential reinforcement 307
discriminanda 321
Discourse on Method 34
discrimination 272
discriminative stimulus 307
displacement 388
dogs 104–105, 115–116; and behaviorism 266–267, 269, 272–273
Dollard, John 326, 472
Donaldson, Henry H. 279
Doob, Leonard W. 326, 472
dreams 357–360
drives 324
dualism 134, 217, 282
DuBois, W.E.B. 246
Dubois-Reymond, Emil *152*
Duffy, Elisabeth 18

Ebbinghaus, Hermann *152*, 164–166, 174, 175–176
Eddington, Arthur 6, 64
Eddy, Mary Baker 408
education 194–195; and child study movement 256; and John Locke 59–64; *see also* children; mastery learning; teaching
educational psychology 259
efficient causes 29
ego 226, 363–364, 388
Ego and the Id, The 363
egocentrism 428
Ehrenfels, Christian von 181
Einstein, Albert 6, 192, 303
Eitingon, Max 372
élan vital 145, 418
elegance 182
elementarism *see* reductionism
elementaristic theories 82
elements 29
Eliot, George 108
Ellis, Albert **329**
Ellis, Havelock 353
embryos 110–111
Emerson, Ralph Waldo 211
Emmons, Eleanor *see* Maccoby, Eleanor
emotions 43, 45
empiricism 47, 81–83
Engels, Friedrich 446
Enquiry Concerning Human Understanding, An 67–68

environments 131
epilepsy 348
epistemological empiricism 47
epistemology 35
equilibration 434
Erikson, Erik 390
erotogenic zones 354–355
ESP *see* extrasensory perception (ESP)
essences 29
ethology 462
Euclid of Alexandria 34
eugenics 120–126, 406
evolution 84, 144, 416; and children 395–396; and consciousness 217–218, 223; and humans 102–107; and James, William 213–214; and psychology 131–132; *see also* natural selection
evolutionary psychology 126, 127–131
exemplars 183
experience errors 67, 168
experimental ethics 314
experimental neurosis 273
experimentation 81, 167–172, 436–437; and pragmatism 235; and structuralism 167–172; *see also* little Albert experiment; priming experiments
Expression of the Emotions in Man and Animals, The 396
extinction 268
extrasensory perception (ESP) 13–14, 234; *see also* spiritualism
Eysenck, Hans 328, **329**

faculty psychology 140
Fairburn, W.R.D. 389
falsificationists 5, 6–8, **9**
families 315
fathers 63
Faust 133, 337
Fechner, Gustav 134, *152*, 153–156, 164, 174–175
Federal Animal Welfare Act 469
feeblemindedness 408–409
Feeblemindedness: Its Causes and Consequences 409
feeding 454
Ferenczi, Sándor 242, 372
Ferster, Charles 309
Festinger, Leon 207–208
fields 193, 197
file-drawer problems 481
final causes 29
finches *98*, 101–102
First Cause 70

Fisher, Ronald A. 1, **127**
FitzRoy, Robert 97
fixed ideas 263n4
flattery 275
Flavell, John 484
Fleming, Alexander 5
Fliess, Wilhelm 352–357
formal causes 29
formal discipline 256
forms 27, 29
fossils 90
Franklin, Benjamin 392n3
free association 356
Free Society for the Psychological Study of the Child 402–403
Freud, Amelia 334
Freud, Anna *387*, 388, 458–459
Freud, Jacob 334, 335
Freud, Sigmund 19, *152*, *243*; *Aetiology of Hysteria, The* 355; *Beyond the Pleasure Principle* 363; and bisexuality 354, 392n5; and Charcot, Jean Martin 344–345; "Civilization and Its Discontents" 365; and cocaine 339–340, 359; and consciousness 227–228; *Ego and the Id, The* 363; and fixed ideas 264; and Fliess, Wilhelm 352–357, 367; foundations of 22; "History of the Psychoanalytic Movement, A" 378; *Interpretation of Dreams* 357–360, 366; and Jung, Carl G. 373–378; legacy of 381–382, 387–392; life of 333–338; and memories 93; and money 337, 393n12; name of 392n1; and Nazis 380–381; and psychoanalytic movement 366–367; and recapitulation theory 113; and sexuality 361–363; *Studies in Hysteria* 350; theory of 363–365; as therapist 383–387
Freudian slips 360
Freudian therapy 19
Frisch, Karl von 461–462
Fromm, Erich 389
Frost, Robert 296
Frustration and Aggression 326, 472
Fuegians 105
functionalism 172–174, 246; in America 261–262; and Hall, G. Stanley 238–242; tenets of 250
fundamental attribution errors 206–207

Galapagos Islands 98, 101
Gale, Harlow **166**
Galen of Pergamon 25–26
Galilei, Galileo 32
Gall, Franz Joseph 256
Galton, Sir Francis 116–121, **127**
Ganda people 465
gastric research 266–267
gemmules 119
gender roles 481–482; *see also* sexual differences
generalization 272
genetic epistemology 423–424, 440
genotypes 439
Gesell, Arnold 241, 476, 484n6
Gesell, Arnold L. 410–412
Gestalt 5, 179–180
Gestalt laws of perception 185
Gestalt psychology 179–180, 195–196; and developmental psychology 196–201; founding of 182–184; historical context of 204–205; and industrial psychology 201–203; principles of 184–188; and problem solving 192–195
Gettysburg address 21
"gifted and talented" classes 410
girls 241–242; *see also* children
glass harmonicas 392
goal gradients 323
God 3; and Aquinas, Thomas 31; and Augustine, Saint 28; and Berkeley, George 66–67; and Descartes, Rene 36, 38; and Great Chain of Being 86–87; and Hartley, David 76; and Hume, David 68–70; and reason 238–239; as watchmaker 97; *see also* religions; religious experiences
Goddard, Henry H. 123, 244, 262, 406–409
Goethe, Johann Wolfgang von 133, 337
Going to Hospital With Mother 460
Goodall, Jane 8
Gossett, William S. **127**
Gould, Stephen Jay 19, 100
Great Chain of Being 86–88
"great man" theory 18
Gross, Otto 374
Guthrie, Edwin 479

habits 323
Haeckel, Ernst 109–111, 396; *Kuntsformen der Natur 112*; *Riddle of the Universe, The* 123
Hale, Edward Everett 231
Hall, G. Stanley 18, *152*, **166**, *243*; *Adolescence* 240, 243, 397; *American Journal of Psychology, The* 173, 250; and children 394, 397; and functionalism 238–242, 262; and James, William 229; *Psychological Review* 240; and sexuality 373; and women 244–245; and Wundt, Wilhelm 172
Harlow, Clara Mears 484n11

Harlow, Harry 453–457, 467–470, 484n11
Harlow, Margaret Kuenne 484n11
Harper, William Rainey 277
Hartley, David 75–77
Harvey, William 38, 42
hearts 42–43
Hegel, George Wilhelm Friedrich 141–145
Heidenhain 266
Heider, Fritz 205–207
Helmholtz, Hermann von 134, 148–152, *152*
Henry VIII 24–25
Herbart, Johann Friedrick 335–336
Hereditary Genius 119–121
Hipp chronoscope *160*
historicism 21, 144
histories of ideas 18, 19–20
history 16–18
"History of the Psychoanalytic Movement, A" 378
holism 179
Holmes, Oliver Wendell 123
Hooke, Robert 52; *Micrographia* 53
hospitals 460
Hull, Clark L. 322–326, **329**
human evolution 102–107
humanities 3
Hume, David 67–75; *An Enquiry Concerning Human Understanding* 67–68; and conditioning **274**; *A Treatise on Human Nature* 67
Huxley, Thomas Henry 44, 103–104, 108–109, 114
hybrid vigor 124
hypnotism 341–346, 399–400
hypothesis testing 322
hysteria 340–341, 344–345, 347–351, 352, 355, 382–383, 399–400

Ickes, Harold 331n8
Ickes, Mary 286
id 363
idealism 134
ideas 56–59
idée fixe 263n4, 351, 392n8
identical elements 257–258
identification 473
idols 50
immaterialism 65
immigrants 123
inclusive fitness 128
independent competence 448
Index of Prohibited Books 26
inductive logic 5, 49–50
inductivists 5–6

industrial psychology 201–203
Infancy in Uganda 465
inferiority complexes 368, 392n10
information processing 176–178
Inhelder, Bärbel 429
inhibition 271
innate ideas 38, 55
inner speech 447
insights 191
instincts 115
instrumentalism 249
intellective souls 30, 38
intellectualization 388
intelligence 122, 124–125, 132n2; development of 405–406; and individuality 401–404; *see also* Binet-Simon intelligence tests
intelligence tests 448
intentionality 180
interactionists 282
interference effects 166, 175
internal environments 267
internalization 447
interpersonal psychoanalysis 389
Interpretation of Dreams 19, 357–360, 366
intervening variables 324
introspection 67, 158, 168, 171–172, 173, 174, 219, 237; *see also* self-observation
isolation 467

James, Alice 262n2
James, Henry, Jr. 211, 262n1, 262n2
James, Henry, Sr. 211
James, Robertson 262n2
James, William 1, 15, 178n2, *243*, 262n1; and altered mental states 226–229; contributions of 235; and David Hume 75; and depression 214–215; and evolution 213–214; family of 210–213; and Leonie 352; and pragmatism 233–235; *Principles of Psychology, The* 209, 215–220, 246; and psychologist's fallacy 67; and religious experiences 229–233; and the self 224–226; and stream of consciousness 220–224; *Varieties of Religious Experience, The* 155–156, 210; and Wundt, Wilhelm 263n3
James, William (of Albany) 210–211, 262n1
Janet, Pierre 221, 226–227, 263n4, 350–352, 351–352
jealousy 130–131
Jennings, Herbert *243*
Jesuits 33
Jews 334–335, 372, 443
Johnson, Samuel 66
Jones, Ernest 242, 372, 378

Jones, Mary Cover 287, **329**
Judd, Charles H. **166**, 172–173
Jung, Carl G. 18, 242, *243*, 370–372; and Freud, Sigmund 373–378
just noticeable difference 154, 155

Kallikak, Martin **407**, 409
Kanizsa triangles 187–188
Kant, Immanuel 134–141; *Anthropology From a Pragmatic Point of View* 140; *Critique of Pure Reason* 136; on dining 178n1; *Metaphysical Foundations of a Natural Science* 139
Karchevskaya, Seraphima 276
Karen, Robert 469
Kepler, Johannes 11
Kinnebrook, David 146–147
Klein, Melanie 389, 458
knowledge 2–3
Knox, Ronald 66
Koffka, Kurt 183–185, 192
Köhler, Wolfgang 183–184, 188, 190–192, 446–447
Kohut, Heinz 389
Koller, Carl 340
Kornilov, K.N. 444
Kpellans 450
Kraepelin, Emil 369
Krafft-Ebing, Richard von 353
Kuhn, Thomas S. 9–13
kymographs *161, 300*

laboratory rooms *169*
Lamarck, Jean-Baptiste Pierre Antoine de Monet de 91–92, 93, 100; *see also* acquired characteristics
lambs 462
language 45, 104, 305, 446–447
Language and Thought of the Child, The 425
latency stage 355
latent content 358
latent learning 321–322
L'Automatisme Psychologique 351
law of effect 293
law of error 118
law of specific nerve energies 149
law of use and disuse *see* acquired characteristics
laws of association 71–73
Lazarus, Arnold 328, **329**
Leakey, Richard 8
Lewin, Kurt 192, 208n1, 484n9; and developmental psychology 196–201; and industrial psychology 201–203; and social psychology 203

Ley, Ronald 192
libido theory 362
life spaces 196–201
light 75
Lincoln, Abraham 21
Lindsley, Ogden 328, **329**
lines of force 193
Linnaean classification 88–89
Linnaeus, Carolus 88
Lippitt, Ronald 200
Lippmann, Walter 125
Little Albert experiment 284–286
Little Hans 386
Locke, John 15, 51–55; educational philosophy of 59–64; historical context of 21; and ideas 55–59; and reflection 67; *Some Thoughts Concerning Education* 59; *see also* philosophical shift
Loeb, Jacques 264, 279–281
Logic of Modern Physics, The 302, 303
Lorenz, Konrad 461–462
Lorge, Irving 261
Los Horcones 316
Lovaas, Ivar **329**
love 455–456
Ludwig, Karl 151, *152*, 266
Luria, Alexander Romanov 44
Luther, Martin 24

Maccoby, Eleanor 477–482
Mach, Ernst 302
Malthus, Thomas 100–101, 107
manifest content 358
manipulanda 321
Marian Evans *see* Eliot, George
marriages 105
Marx, Karl 106, 446
masculine protest 368
Maskelyne, Nevil 146–147
mastery learning 258–259
masturbation 341, 353
material causes 29
materialism 67, 96, 134; and evolutionary psychology 128; and mechanism 145–146
materialist-evolutionary shift 23
mate selection *see* sexual selection
mathematics 434–435
Mead, George Herbert 164
meaningless questions 303
Meichenbaum, Donald **329**
melancholia 353
melodies 181–182
memories 164–165
memory drums 175

memory strategies 176
Mendel, Gregor 28, 122
Mendeleev, Dimitri 173
mental chemistry 80
mental compounding 76, 77
Mental Development of Child and the Race 414
mental discipline 256
mental illness 369
mentalisms 304
mental rotation experiments 177
mental tests 251
Mesmer, Franz Anton 342
mesmerism 342, 399
Metaphysical Foundations of a Natural Science 139
method of radical doubt 36
methodological empiricism 47
Meyer, Adolf 243
Meynert, Theodor 337, 345
Michael, Jack **329**
Micrographia 53
Milgram, Stanley 208
Mill, James 77–78; *Analysis of the Phenomena of the Human Mind* 77
Mill, John Stuart 78–81; *Autobiography* 79; *On Liberty* 82–83
Miller, Neal E. 326, 472
mind-cure movement 231, 408
Mind of the Child, The 396
minds 145, 146; and Cartesian dualism 39–41; and consciousness 158–159; and souls 153
miracles 69–70
Mitchell, David 252
Mitchell, S. Weir 351
modes of perception 58
monism 67, 134
monkeys 103, 453–456, 467–470
Moore, Addison 247
Moral Judgment of the Child, The 420
Morgan, C. Lloyd 116, 190, 254, 290
Morgan's canon 116
morning sickness 129
morphine 339
mothers 453–456, 458, 467
Moulton, Bess 255
Mowrer, O. Hobart 326, **329**, 472
Mozart, Wolfgang Amadeus 392n3
Müller, Johannes 148–152, *152*
multiple personality disorder 351
Münsterberg, Hugo **166**, 229
Murray, Henry 298
myelin 331n5

nasogenital reflex 353
naturalism 131–132

naturalistic hypothesis 4
natural proof *see* argument from design
natural selection 99–103; *see also* evolution
natural theology 84, 88–91; *see also* argument from design
"Nature of Love, The" 455
Nazis 200, 204, 380–381
negative reinforcement 308
neo-Darwinism 122
nervism 265
neurosis 353
"New Psychology" 145, 164, 166, 250
Newton, Isaac 54; *Opticks* 75
nonsense syllables 165, 175–176
normal science 10, 13
nothingness 138
Novak, Melinda 468
Novum Organum 49

O., Anna 346–350
obedience studies 208
objectivity 3–4, 8
object permanence 426–427
object relations theory 389
observational learning 326
observations 4, 169
Oedipal complex 356–357
On Liberty 82–83
ontogeny 110
operant conditioning 293, 320
operants 306
operational definitions 170
operationalism 234, 263n6
Opticks 75
oral stage 355
organicism 144
originality 4
Origin of Species, The 102
orphanages 471, 484n12
Othello 415

Pace, Edward Aloysius **166**
paired-associate method 237
Paley, William 97
pandas 102
Pankejeff, Sergei 385
Pappenheim, Bertha *see* O., Anna
paradigms 10–12
paradigm shifts 10–15
parallelism 217
parapraxes 360
parenting 394, 412, 442–443, 470; *see also* children; mothers
passions 41–43
Patrick, George **166**

Patterns of Child Rearing 473
Pavlov, Ivan P. 18, 151, *152*, 264–266; and brain 272–273; and gastric research 266–267; laboratory of 273–275; life of 275–277; and Watson, John B. 23
Pavlov's pouch 266
Pearson, Karl **127**
Peirce, Charles Sanders 233
penicillin 5
personal equations 147–148
personal unconscious 377
phenomena 136; *see also* sensations
phenotypes 439
philosophical shift 23
Philosophical Studies 159, 162
philosophy of science 3–5, 302–303; and falsification 6–9; and paradigms 9–16; traditional 5–6
phi phenomenon 5, 182–184
phrenology 256
phylogeny 110
Piaget, Jean 113, 132n1, 418–424; and children 394–395; and concrete operational stage 431–436; *Construction of Reality in the Child* 426; and evolutionary theory 438–440; and formal operational stage 436–438; *Language and Thought of the Child, The* 425; misconceptions of 440–442; and preoperational stage 427–431; and sensorimotor stage 425–427; and stage theory 424–425, 484n4
pigeons 311–312
Pillsbury, Walter A. 170, **171**
Planck, Max 192
Plato 27, 28, 85
play 428
pleasure principle 363
poems 165
Popper, Karl Raimund 6–8, **9**
positive reinforcement 306
positivism 264
power functions 175
pragmatism 233–235
preconscious 360
Preiswick, Helene 371
preparadigmatic science 15
presentism 20–21
Present State of Knowledge Concerning Muscular Action, The 157
Preyer, Wilhelm 395–397
Priestley, Joseph 76–77
primacy effect 176
primal smell theory 353
primary circular reactions 425
primary qualities 37, 38

Prime Mover 70
priming experiments 177; *see also* experimentation
principle of correlation of parts 89
Principles of Behavior 323
Principles of Physiology 148–149
Principles of Psychology, The 108, 209, 215–220, 239, 246
private events 304
private speech 447–448
problem solving 192–195, 257
Profet, Margie 129
projections 388
Project Pigeon 311–312
proximity 186
psychical reflexes 270
psychic secretions 267–268
psychoanalysis 368, 381, 390–392, 395
psychoanalytic movement 366–367
Psychological Care of Infant and Child, The 289
Psychological Corporation, The 251
Psychological Review 240, 250
psychological stage theory 390
psychologist's fallacy 67, 219
psychology: and evolution 131–132; interdisciplinarity of 22; origin of 1–2; paradigm of 13–16
Psychology from an Empirical Standpoint 180
psychophysical isomorphism 185
psychophysical parallelism 75
psychophysics 154, 174–175
psychosexual stage theory 354
Ptolemy 11
punishments 308, 318, 326, 475–476
Purposive Behavior in Animals and Men 321
Putnam, James Jackson 374
puzzle solving 13

qualitative relationships 184
qualities 37, 56
quantitative variables 184
questionnaires 240

races 106, 484n2
racism 114, 242
Radke-Yarrow, Marian 476
rates of responding 300
rationalism 37–38
Rat Man 384
rats 279, 298–300, 322, 331n4
Rayner, Rosalie 285–287, 289
reaction times 159, 162, 176–178, 247
reality principle 363–364
recapitulation theory 110–113, 111–114, 240–241

recency effect 176
Recherche 419–421
reductionism 179
reductionistic theories 82
reflecting abstraction 435
reflection 56
reflexes 115, 268
regression towards the mean 120
Reid, Thomas 412–413
reinforcement 269, 306–311
relativism 144
religions 3–4
religious experiences 229–233, 243–244
replication 4–5, 282
repression 336
resemblances 72
responses 268, 307
rest cure 351
reversible figures 187
Reyna, L. **329**
Riddle of the Universe, The 123
Risley, Todd R. **329**
Rivers, W.H.R. 457
Riviere, Joan 457–458
Robertson, James 460
Romanes, George John 114–116
Roman Inquisition 24
Roosevelt, Theodore 246
roundabout-way experiments 190
Royal Observatory 146
Russell, Bertrand 297

salivation 267–268, 272
Sanford, Edward 237
Saunders, Percy 296
scaffolding 448
scala naturae see Great Chain of Being
Sceptical Chymist, The 52
schedules 309
Schedules of Reinforcement 309
schemas 138
schemes 423
scholasticism 31–32
Schopenhauer, Arthur 22–23
Science of Mechanics 302
sciences 3, 17, 302–303, 390–392
scientific management 202
scientific revolutions 11, **12**
Scripture, Edward Wheeler **166**
Sears, Robert R. 326, 472, 473–483
Sechenov, Ivan *152*, 157, 270–272
secondary circular reactions 426
secondary qualities 37
secure bases 465

security theory 465
seduction theory 352, 355, 357
self 73–75, 224–225
self-esteem 226
self-healing 230
Selfish Gene, The 128
self-observation 158, 167–168, 173; *see also* introspection
self psychology 237, 389
sensations 36–38, 56, 81; *see also* phenomena
sensitive souls 30, 38
separation anxiety 462
sexual abuse 352, 355, 357
sexual differences 107, 480–482; *see also* gender roles
sexuality 232–233, 243–244, 352–353, 361–363, 373, 384, 392n7
sexual selection 106, 129–130
Shakespeare, William 49
"shell shock" 19
Sherrington, Sir Charles 44
similarity 186
Simon, Theophile 132n2, 483n1
simple ideas 57
simplicity 187
skepticism 64
Skinner, B.F. 19, 264, 294–298, **329**, 473; *Analysis of Behavior, The* 313; *Behavior of Organisms, The* 305–306, 484n13; *Beyond Freedom and Dignity* 317–319; and inventions 311–313; legacy of 320–321; and operant conditioning 306–311; philosophy of 301–305; *Schedules of Reinforcement* 309; and social reform 313–320; *Walden Two* 314–317
Skinner, Deborah 312
Skinner, Grace Burrhus 294, 296
Skinner box 298–301
Smith, Adam 82
snails 439
Snedden, Pauline (Pat) 473
Social and Ethical Interpretations in Mental Development 416
social cognition 477
Social Darwinism 105, 108
social heredity 416
socialization 395, 472, 473–483
social learning 326–328
Social Learning and Imitation 326
social learning theory 477
social psychology 203
social reform 313–320
social revolutionists 5, 9–13
Sociobiology 483

sociohistorical histories 18, 19
solipsism 67, 425
Solomon, H.C. 328
Some Thoughts Concerning Education 59
sons 63
souls 30, 33, 39–41, 114, 153, 230–232
Soviet Union 275
space 137
Spanish Inquisition 24
Spartans 123
Spearman, Charles **127**, 260
special creation 90
Spence, Kenneth W. 326, **329**
Spencer, Herbert 107–109, 213
Spielrein, Sabina 374
Spinoza, Baruch 413
spiritualism 228–229; *see also* extrasensory perception (ESP)
Spitz, René 459
Spock, Benjamin 476, 485n15
spontaneous recovery 269
St. Martin, Alexis 266
stage theory 241, 424–425; and concrete operational stage 431–436; and formal operational stage 436–438; and preoperational stage 427–431; and sensorimotor stage 425–427
Stanford-Binet test 123, 244
statistics 116–119, 126, **127**
Steckel, Wilhelm 366
Stein, Gertrude 246
Stekel, Wilhelm 376
stereotopies 459
sterilizations 123, 124
Stern, William *243*
Stevens' Power Law 175
stimuli 248, 268, 307, 445
strange situation procedure 466
Stratton, George Malcolm **166**
stream of consciousness 220–224; *see also* consciousness
structuralism 166–172
Structure of Scientific Revolutions, The 9–10
Stuart, John 80
Studies in Hysteria 350
Studies in Organ Inferiority 368
Stumpf, Carl 181–182
subjective idealism 65–66
sublimation 243, 362, 373
substance dualism *see* Cartesian dualism
suggestibility 400
sulfur 52
Summa Theologica 31
Sumner, Francis Cecil 245–246

Suomi, Stephen 468
superego 355
Sydenham, Thomas 51, 54
syllogisms 29–30
symbolic play 428
Symons, Donald 131
synthesis 443
systematic desensitization 287, 328
Szeminska, Alina 429

taboos 376–377
tabula rasa 55
Taine, Hippolyte 396
talk therapy 371
Tanner, Amy 244
Taylor, Fredrick W. 202
Taylorism 202
teaching 255–256; *see also* education
teaching machines 313
teleology 94
tendencies 62
Terman, Lewis M. 123, 126, 244, 262, 410
tertiary circular reactions 426
theses 143, 443
Thing and Medium 205
Thorndike, E.L. 190, 253–261, 262, 264, 290–294
Thought and Things: A Study of the Development of Thought or Genetic Logic 417
thoughts 181
time 137, 145
Tinbergen, Niko 461–462
Titchener, Edward B. 18, 67, **166**, 167–172, 178n4, 229, *243*
Tolman, Edward Chase 321–322
Tonpsychologie 182
tools 104
topological psychology 198
Tourette, Georges Gilles de la *343*
transcendent ideality 138
transductive logic 430
transfer 257
transference 380
Treatise on Human Nature, A 67
trial-and-error learning 116, 190–191, 254, 292; *see also* vicarious trial and error
troika 484n10
tropism 280
Twin Oaks 316
Twitmeyer, Edwin 23
Two Sexes: Growing Up Apart, Coming Together, The 482
Two-Year-Old Goes to Hospital, A 460

unconscious 83n1, 360, 377
unconscious inference 157
uniformitarianism 91
universal law of causation 81
utilitarianism 78–79

valences 197–198
Varieties of Religious Experience, The 155–156, 210
vector psychology 198
vegetative souls 30
verbal learning 175–176
verbal mediators 176
Vesalius, Andreas 25–26
vibratiuncles 75
vicarious trial and error 322; *see also* trial-and-error learning
volition 162–163
Völkerpsychologie: An Investigation of the Laws of Development of Language, Myth and Custom 163
Vygotsky, Lev S. 395, 442–452, 484n9
Vygotsky, L.S. 164

Walden Two 314–317
Wallace, Alfred Russel 19, 99
Warren, Earl 246
Washburn, Margaret **166**
Watson, James 126
Watson, John B. 1, 15–16, 20, 23, 264, 277–279, 280, **329**, 331n3, 331n7; *Animal Education: The Psychical Development of the White Rat* 279; and Baldwin, James Mark 417; *Behaviorism* 288–289; historical context of 21–22; life of 286–287; *Psychological Care of Infant and Child, The* 289
Weber, Ernst Heinrich *152*, 154, 174–175
Weber constant 154, 155
Wedgewood, Josiah, II 96
Wednesday Society 368

Weissmann, August 122
Wertheimer, Max 5, 182–183, 184, 192, 195
Whig Interpretation of History 20
White, Ralph K. 200
Wilberforce, Samuel 103
will 43, 74–75
Wilson, E.O. 483
Wilson, Woodrow 256
Winnicott, D.W. 389
wish fulfillments 360
Wissenschaft 133
Witmer, Lightner **166**, 171, 251–253, 262
Wittman, Blanche *343*
Wolf, Montrose M. **329**
Wolfe, Harry Kirke **166**
Wolf Man 385
Wolpe, Joseph 328, **329**
women 244–245, 263n8, 469–470, 477, 479–480; *see also* Calkins, Mary Whiton; hysteria
Woodworth, Robert S. 257, 262
work 314–315
World War I 19
Wundt, Wilhelm 1, *152*, 156–159; and experimental methods 159–163; and James, William 263n3; *Philosophical Studies* 159, 162; *Present State of Knowledge Concerning Muscular Action, The* 157; and structuralism 166–167; *Völkerpsychologie: An Investigation of the Laws of Development of Language, Myth and Custom* 163–164
Wyman, Jeffries 213

Yerkes, Robert 123, 260, 262, 331n7

zeitgeist 19
Zimmerman, Bob 455
zones 448
zones of permitted action 198
Zoonomia 95
Zurich school 369–370